RELIGION IN
SOCIOLOGICAL PERSPECTIVE

Sixth Edition

SAGE was founded in 1965 by Sara Miller McCune to support the dissemination of usable knowledge by publishing innovative and high-quality research and teaching content. Today, we publish more than 850 journals, including those of more than 300 learned societies, more than 800 new books per year, and a growing range of library products including archives, data, case studies, reports, and video. SAGE remains majority-owned by our founder, and after Sara's lifetime will become owned by a charitable trust that secures our continued independence.

Los Angeles | London | New Delhi | Singapore | Washington DC

RELIGION IN SOCIOLOGICAL PERSPECTIVE

Sixth Edition

KEITH A. ROBERTS
Hanover College

DAVID YAMANE
Wake Forest University

Los Angeles | London | New Delhi
Singapore | Washington DC

Los Angeles | London | New Delhi
Singapore | Washington DC

FOR INFORMATION:

SAGE Publications, Inc.

2455 Teller Road

Thousand Oaks, California 91320

E-mail: order@sagepub.com

SAGE Publications Ltd.

1 Oliver's Yard

55 City Road

London EC1Y 1SP

United Kingdom

SAGE Publications India Pvt. Ltd.

B 1/I 1 Mohan Cooperative Industrial Area

Mathura Road, New Delhi 110 044

India

SAGE Publications Asia-Pacific Pte. Ltd.

3 Church Street

#10-04 Samsung Hub

Singapore 049483

ISBN 978-1-4522-7582-6

Acquisitions Editor: Jeff Lasser

Editorial Assistant: Alexandra Croell

eLearning Editor: Gabrielle Piccininni

Production Editor: Laura Barrett

Copy Editor: Melinda Masson

Typesetter: C&M Digitals (P) Ltd.

Proofreader: Jeff Bryant

Indexer: Judy Hunt

Cover Designer: Candice Harman

Marketing Manager: Erica DeLuca

15 16 17 18 19 10 9 8 7 6 5 4 3 2 1

CONTENTS

PREFACE

Religion is a complex phenomenon. It involves a meaning system with an interrelated set of beliefs, rituals, symbols, values, moods, and motivations. Each of these interacts in diverse and complex ways with one another, sometimes being mutually supportive and sometimes conflicting. Religion is also a structural system with established statuses, organizational patterns, and even bureaucratic dilemmas. This structural system is itself diverse and multifaceted, characterized by both conflicts over self-interests and strains toward coherence and integration. Finally, religion is composed of a belonging system, with friendship networks, group boundaries, and informal norms that may be quite independent of the formal structure or official meaning systems. These three subsystems of religion are themselves *interdependent*, forming a larger system that is in some ways coherent and in some ways in tension and discord. Further, religion is part of a larger social system, and as such it both affects and is affected by this larger system. It is precisely this complexity of religion, including the complexity of its relationship to the larger society and to the world system, that we explore in the following pages.

This book is designed as an introduction to the sociology of religion. Our intent has been to present and illustrate the basic theories sociologists use to understand the social dimensions of religion. First and foremost, we seek to help students understand the *perspective* from which sociologists view religion. By the time students have finished this book, they should understand the central theories and methods of research in the sociology of religion, and they should have an idea of how to apply these analytical tools to new groups they encounter. The goal of this text is to be *illustrative* rather than all-encompassing. Insofar as it is adopted as a text in a university or seminary course, we have assumed that it will be complemented with monographs or anthologies that explore the specific groups or specific processes the instructor chooses to emphasize.

Theoretically, the 6th edition continues to draw on a wide range of perspectives. We seek to help students recognize the contributions of various theoretical perspectives and the blind spots of each theory. Conflict, functional, social constructionist, and rational choice paradigms are used throughout the text, and various middle-range theories are utilized to explore specific processes. Despite the effort to introduce many perspectives, however, we have made an effort to enhance integration of the text by using one framework throughout the book. That perspective, which stresses both structure and dynamic process, is the open systems model.

We have also tried in this book to provide students with an understanding of the relationship between research methods and findings.

Without belaboring the issue of methods, we have attempted to make students aware of the relationships between accurate data, operationalization of ideas, careful use of the language of causality, and support of one's generalizations. Our hope is that students sense that doing research really can be exciting work. In this 6th edition, we have continued to provide features on "Doing Research on Religion" to intrigue readers with the exciting process of inquiry. "Critical Thinking" questions are also provided throughout to stimulate engagement with the material and more active reading and learning.

Each chapter of this text has been student-tested for readability and clarity among nonsociologists, and all revisions have been made with an eye to making the material ever more accessible to the nonspecialist. Photos have been selected with great care to illustrate concepts and to heighten interest. At the outset of each chapter, there are inquiry questions to heighten reader curiosity and to help students become more "active readers." While we have made every effort to enhance clarity and to amply illustrate abstract ideas, we have also tried to resist appeals from some quarters to lessen the theoretical sophistication of the text.

The first four editions of this text were a solo "labor of love" by the first author. When we began to look at a new edition of *Religion in Sociological Perspective*, a major obstacle was in the way. The original author was so involved in continual revisions of an introductory book (*Our Social World*, coauthored with Jeanne Ballantine, and now with Kathleen Korgen as well) that he was unable to find the time necessary to complete the necessary revisions. The solution was to bring on board a coauthor. The five selection criteria for finding a coauthor were as follows: (1) effective writing skill in communicating with lay audiences, (2) solid familiarity of the issues in the scholarship of teaching and learning, (3) cutting-edge knowledge of the scholarship in the sociology of religion, (4) a balanced, nonideological approach to

the discipline (with no ax to grind on a particular theoretical paradigm), and (5) being less fossilized than the now-semiretired first author. The two authors had worked together on the editorial board for the American Sociological Association (ASA) journal *Teaching Sociology*, and David Yamane was also the editor of one of the leading journals in this subfield: *Sociology of Religion*. It was an obvious choice, and it has been a superb decision. As with the 5th edition, we have worked together in this revision.

Many of the changes in the 6th edition are matters of updating data and including recent findings. In fact, we have added over 200 new sources to the bibliography. We also continue to take advantage of the ever greater availability of some very important data sets on religion. These include the National Congregations Study, Hartford Institute's Faith Communities Today project, the National Study of Youth and Religion, and many surveys undertaken by the Pew Research Center. These are not just updated data but cover new ground in religious life. Therefore, these data play a major role in several chapters.

Major substantive additions to this edition include greater attention to digital religion, multisite megachurches, prosperity theology and economic inequality, issues of racial integration and sexuality, religious nones and apostasy, religious nationalism and humanitarianism, violence, and peace. We have also added new features on "Illustrating Sociological Concepts" in 9 chapters, "Global Perspectives" in 8 chapters, and "Doing Research on Religion" in 4 chapters. Brand new to this edition are 18 boxed features that point to free online resources available to students, such as downloadable data sets from the Association of Religion Data Archives, data visualizations on global anti-Semitism, denominational histories, and open access scholarly journals dedicated to digital religion.

Some of the material that has been dropped in this edition—on religion and nationalism in Wales, for example—is now available on this book's website at **study.sagepub.com/rsp6e.** Those who may still wish to use it can do so via the web.

There is substantial value to texts that have interchangeable chapters, for they allow the instructor flexibility in designing the course. What a text gains in flexibility, however, it often loses in cumulative development of analytical complexity. While it is possible to vary the order of the chapters in this text, the text is designed to be cumulative. Later chapters are more intricate in their analysis than earlier ones and attempt to stretch students to greater levels of analytical sophistication. Considerable deliberation has been given to building greater analytical complexity as one moves through the book. If an instructor does choose to use these chapters in a different sequence, we recommend that the first three chapters be covered first as a foundation. Chapters 10 and 11 will also make more sense after Chapter 4 has been read. Other chapters may be selected as one wishes.

Resources for Instructors

Unique among sociology of religion texts, *Religion in Sociological Perspective* has a companion website at **http://study.sagepub.com/rps6e** and contains a myriad of supporting teaching resources designed to inspire creative teaching and active learning. Resources were co-written by Keith Roberts who has won both the Hans O. Mauksch Award for Distinguished Contributions to Undergraduate Sociology (given by the ASA Section on Teaching and Learning) and the ASA Distinguished Contributions to Teaching Award (in 2010) and include a comprehensive test bank, more than 200 active-learning instructional strategies, suggested films and videos, term paper projects, expanded chapter material from the previous edition, a sample syllabus, as well as chapter specific non-lecture teaching strategies, simulation games, in-class writing exercises, simple class surveys, small group work ideas, film ideas,

and discussion questions. Our hope is that some of these ideas will serve as a stimulus to each instructor's own creativity.

The test bank includes both essay and multiple-choice test questions for each chapter and essay ideas for a comprehensive final examination. There are 18 to 40 multiple-choice questions and 8 to 12 essay questions per chapter (approximately 500 questions total). All resources are password protected and instructors are required to create an account to access the website. Contact the technical support team at supplements@sage pub.com or call 1(800) 818-7243 ext. 6140 for assistance.

People interested in creative teaching strategies for the sociology of religion may also want to utilize the ASA's teaching resources called TRAILS (Teaching Resources and Innovations Library for Sociology) located at http://trails .asanet.org/Pages/default.aspx. TRAILS does have an access fee, but in our judgement it is well worth the $25. It has creative term projects, innovative teaching strategies, and sample syllabi from many people who teach this course. There are a host of ideas that involve students as active learners. We are convinced that providing a set of choices on term projects increases the quality of the projects. None of us writes well on a task that we do not undertake with some volition, and our students are no different. So we recommend provision of a diversity of active course projects from which students can choose. We know of no better source of ideas than TRAILS, which can be accessed at trails. asanet.org.

A Unique Program Supporting Teaching of Sociology

The first author has been instrumental in the founding of a unique program to support and enhance the quality of college teaching. A new award program—the SAGE Teaching Innovations & Professional Development Award—is designed to prepare a new generation of scholars within the teaching movement in sociology. People in their early career stages (graduate students, assistant professors, newer PhDs) can be reimbursed $600 each for expenses entailed while attending the daylong ASA Section on Teaching and Learning workshop. The workshop is the day before ASA meetings. By 2015, 204 people had already benefited because of donations from royalties of SAGE authors and the generosity of SAGE Publications—a total well over $100,000. This book will also be a cosponsor of this program with contributions from book royalties. To apply for such a scholarship, contact Keith Roberts at robertsk@hanover.edu.

ACKNOWLEDGMENTS

While only two names go on the book cover, a project of this nature is enriched by the labor and support of many people. Keith Roberts is deeply appreciative of the assistance offered by the librarians of Bowling Green State University and Hanover College. Reviewers for the first four editions deserve special comment for their incisive analysis, helpful criticism, constructive suggestions, and encouragement in this project. The reviewers for earlier editions were Charles Bonjean, David Bromley, Dennis J. Cole, James D. Davidson, Barbara J. Denison, Roger Finke, Sharon Georgianna, John W. Hawthorne, Tom Kearin, Fred Kniss, James R. Koch, Les Kurtz, Martin Laskin, Marty Laubach, Harry LeFever, Richard Machalek, Perry McWilliams, Edgar W. Mills Jr., Christine O'Leary-Rockery, Liane Pedersen-Gallegos, Wade Clark Roof, Frank Sampson, John S. Staley, Matthew Vos, David Yamane, Samuel Inuwa Zalanga, and Phil Zuckerman. Reviewers for this edition were as follows:

Susan Cox—Bellevue College

Gerhard Falk—Buffalo State College

Lori L. Fazzino—University of Nevada, Las Vegas

Mary-Paula Nash—Montgomery College

Matthew Sargent—Madison College

Keith also had several student editorial assistants: Jennifer Crye, Rachael Ernst, Emily McDarment, Sarah Opichka, Elise Roberts, and Sarah Sheagley. An exceptional reference librarian, Kelly Joyce, has helped with finding and documenting obscure sources. David Yamane benefited from input and assistance from Nancy Ammerman, Kelly Besecke, Gerardo Marti, Margarita Mooney, Lynn Neal, Roman Williams, and Sandy Stroud Yamane. His fall 2014 Sociology of Religion class at Wake Forest University also helped critique and update the 5th edition of this book. SAGE has been wonderful to work with, including Jeff Lasser (acquisitions editor), Alexandra Croell (editorial assistant), Laura Barrett (production editor), and Melinda Masson (copy editor). While all of the persons just listed have contributed tremendously to the finished product, they are certainly not responsible for its flaws.

Several colleagues who teach at universities with very large classes necessitating objective examinations have shared with us the multiple-choice test banks they have generated for this book. Many of the multiple-choice questions that appear in the test bank originally had been used in classes taught by Roger Finke, David Bromley, and Jeffrey Hadden. Several undergraduate students—Jeremy Castle, Rachel Ernst, Emily McDarment, Sarah Opichka, and Elise Roberts—have also served as assistants in the production of the instructor's manual and test bank. We are indebted to these junior colleagues for their help. Samuel Inuwa Zalanga (Bethel University) has also added a great deal to the instructor's manual by providing additional video suggestions.

Finally, Keith must express his deep appreciation to his wife, Judy, and children, Justin, Kent, and Elise. Judy Roberts has been enormously supportive and has offered helpful comments and criticism at untold times in this project. Keith's progeny contributed to earlier editions through provision of delightful interludes away from the intensity of the project. Now that they are all young adults, their critique of Keith's work and stretching of his thinking has been stimulating, encouraging, and insightful. Elise has also provided some of the photographs for this book from her extensive international travels.

David is blessed with three wonderful children, Paul, Hannah, and Mark, and a generous and loving wife, Sandy, all of whom make this work possible and meaningful.

If you have suggestions for this text or for the instructor's manual, we would be happy to hear them. We can be reached at the addresses below:

Keith A. Roberts
Hanover College
robertsk@hanover.edu

David Yamane
Wake Forest University
yamaned@wfu.edu

About the Authors

Keith A. Roberts is professor emeritus of sociology at Hanover College in Indiana. In 2000, he was awarded the Hans O. Mauksch Award for Distinguished Contributions to Undergraduate Sociology by the ASA Section on Teaching and Learning, and in 2010, his work in the scholarship of teaching and learning was recognized through the ASA Distinguished Contributions to Teaching Award. He continues to update his coauthored introductory book *Our Social World* and does consulting for academic departments.

David Yamane is professor of sociology at Wake Forest University. He has published in the sociology of religion and in the scholarship of teaching and learning. He is completing a 4-year term as associate editor of a leading journal in the field, the *Journal for the Scientific Study of Religion*. In 2007, he was chosen by Wake Forest students to receive the Kulynych Family Omicron Delta Kappa Award for Contribution to Student Life.

PART I

INTRODUCTION TO THE SOCIOLOGY OF RELIGION

Before we delve too deeply into analysis of our topic, we must establish some common assumptions and understandings. The reader need not agree with the authors, but at least the reader should know how the authors are using key concepts and approaching various topics. That is the purpose of these first two chapters; we are laying the groundwork for a shared investigation.

In Chapter 1, we explore what we mean by religion and the importance of different definitions of "religion" as different "ways of seeing" a complex, multifaceted social phenomenon. Then in Chapter 2, we examine what it means to take a *social scientific* approach to the study of religion, including the unique perspectives and methodological assumptions of sociology as a discipline.

1

WHAT DO WE MEAN BY THE TERM *RELIGION*?

HERE ARE SOME QUESTIONS TO PONDER AS YOU READ THIS CHAPTER

- What is religion? What makes something "religious"?
- Why might one's definition of religion create blinders that cause one not to include important phenomena?
- How are religion and magic similar or different?
- What does the concept of invisible religion add to this conversation about definitions?
- How are religion and spirituality similar or different?
- What is critical in your own idea of what is or is not "religion"?

We begin our venture together with a difficult and complex problem: the definition of our topic of study. To students who have never studied the sociology of religion, the definition of religion may seem clear. Certainly, everyone knows what religion is! Let's get on with more important matters! Yet we dare not be so hasty. Some definitions are so narrow and specific as to exclude Buddhism as a religion. Other definitions are so broad and inclusive that many social behaviors may be considered forms of religion—including patriotism, systematic racism, or any other core set of values and *beliefs* that provides an individual or community with a sense of worth and of meaning in life.

We must begin our analysis, then, by exploring the question of what it is we intend to study. What, after all, is religion? We begin to answer this question by recognizing that the way we define our subject matter sets boundaries on what are and are not legitimate topics or groups for analysis—on what will be included in our studies of "religion" and what will be excluded. In this sense, definitions are "ways of seeing" a complex, multifaceted social reality, and as literary theorist Kenneth Burke observes, "Every way of seeing is also a way of not seeing" (Burke 1935:70).

An important implication of this approach is that definitions are not mirrors of reality to be judged as "true" or "false," but are *tools* that can been seen by those who use them as more or less *useful* (Berger 1967). As you read and think about the following ways in which social scientists have defined religion, think about which definitions you find more or less useful and why.

SUBSTANTIVE DEFINITIONS

Many sociologists employ what has been called a *substantive* definition. This approach hinges on identification of the "substance" or "essence" of religion. Edward B. Tylor used this approach in 1873 when he defined religion as "belief in Spiritual Beings" (Tylor [1873] 1958:8). For most of us, a reference to God or gods does seem to be an essential element in religion. The reason Tylor used the term *spiritual beings* is that many nonindustrialized people worship and/or fear their deceased ancestors. They have little or no concern about gods, as such, but their world is peopled with many unseen beings. Hence, spiritual beings seemed to Tylor a more inclusive term than belief in gods. Some other scholars have reaffirmed Tylor's insistence that religion involves a belief in a Being or beings that are not encountered in normal empirical processes (Spiro 1966).

Trying to define the essence of religion is a difficult task, but it becomes more difficult if our definition is to be applied cross-culturally. In the Western world, we tend to feel that religion is essentially a matter of belief. In fact, some social scientists have attempted to measure the religiosity of people—the extent of their "religiousness"—by determining how orthodox they are. (An orthodox person is one who believes the traditional doctrines of a religious tradition.) However, as Robert R. Marett suggested, in many cultures, religion is "not so much thought out as danced out" (Marett 1914:xxxi). That is to say ritual and emotion are primary to religion, and belief is only secondary.

Sam Gill's study of traditional Native American religions has convinced him that these faiths are expressed through tribal practices, prayer, and religious objects, not creeds, dogmas, or theologies (Gill 2004). Scholars studying Orthodox Judaism and Islam have also consistently pointed out that a focus on behavior, rather than on beliefs and attitudes, is characteristic of those faiths (Aslan 2011; Cohen 1983; Moberg 1984). Anthropologists studying other cultures have also insisted that emphasis on belief is a bias of the Western world that causes investigators to miss the underlying thrust of many non-Western religions. For example, several observers have insisted that any concepts of a deity or superhuman beings are peripheral to official Buddhism (Benz 1964; Herbrechtsmeier 1993; Zaechner 1967). On the other hand, most common folks around the world who identify themselves as Buddhists do believe in superhuman beings (Herbrechtsmeier 1993; Orru and Wang 1992; Spiro 1978). So a definition that emphasizes a belief in superhuman beings leaves doubt about whether Buddhism is a religion. Strictly speaking, many Buddhist gurus (who are not concerned with superhuman beings) would not be considered to be practicing religion. Does religion refer only to those who hold a specific kind of belief?

Another definitional approach that tries to capture the essence of religion but that avoids the requirement of a specific belief was first suggested in 1912 by Émile Durkheim ([1912] 1995). Durkheim was fascinated with the cleansing exercises and the change of attitude that in many cultures were necessary before one could enter into religious ritual. Durkheim maintained that a recognition of the division of life into sacred and profane realms allows us to identify religion in any culture. People around the world seem to undergo a psychological shift when encountering holy objects or engaging in religious ritual. This shift involves a sense of awe, a feeling of fear and majesty. The attitude differs from anything one encounters in the everyday life of these people (see Chapter 4).

Durkheim recognized that not all experiences of awe or sacredness by an individual are religious in character. Religion, he maintained, is a communal activity. It involves a social group: "In all history we do not find a single religion without a Church" (Durkheim [1912] 1995:59). The sacred attitude must be fundamentally a group experience if it is to be identified as religion. Durkheim's formal definition, then, is that "religion is a unified system of beliefs and practices relative to sacred things, that is to say, things set apart and forbidden—beliefs and practices which unite into a single moral community

called a Church, all those who adhere to them" (Durkheim [1912] 1995:62).

This approach is helpful in a great many cases, and it avoids the problem of deciding which specific belief is intrinsically or inherently religious. Yet social scientists who have used this approach have often implied (if not asserted) a dualistic *worldview*. That is to say, life has a religious (sacred) dimension and a nonreligious (profane) dimension. For example, Durkheim insisted that

> the religious life and the profane life cannot coexist in the same unit of time. It is necessary to assign determined days or periods to the first, from which all profane occupations are excluded.
>
> ... There is no religion, and, consequently, no society which has not known and practiced this division of time into two distinct parts. (Durkheim [1912] 1995:347)

Mircea Eliade concurred: "For religious [persons], space is not homogeneous; he [or she] experiences interruptions in it; some parts of space are qualitatively different from others" (Eliade 1959:20).

While it is true that many people organize their life experience into separate categories, not all do. The United Society of Believers in Christ's Second Appearing (the Shakers) attempted to sustain an attitude that all of life is sacred. More recently, a deeply religious utopian society called the Bruderhof (who are Anabaptists like the Amish and Hutterites) has also attempted to make *all* life hallowed by de-emphasizing separate sacraments and rituals. The community worked to sustain an attitude that all of one's life is to be lived in the spirit of worship. Based on his observations of their communal life, Benjamin Zablocki wrote, "The Bruderhof is concerned with bearing witness in the simple, everyday acts of living. . . . There are no activities, however trivial, that cannot be permeated by the divine spirit" (Zablocki 1971:31). This community even refuses to erect a church building lest religion be identified with a distinct time and place. As we will see later in this chapter, many sociologists of religion have come to question whether a strong distinction between sacred and profane realms of life is useful or whether it creates a false dichotomy in contemporary society.

Andrew Greeley has employed this criterion of sacredness as a defining characteristic of religion but has avoided the dualism of many writers. Greeley suggested that any being, social process, or value that gives meaning and purpose to life tends to become a source of reverence or profound respect. When Greeley referred to a sacred attitude, he suggested that it is not totally unlike a secular outlook but is a matter of intensified respect. Hence, Greeley's reference to a sacred attitude does not entirely preclude the study of nationalism, worship of the free-enterprise system, or any other example of profound loyalty as a form of religion. However, he did insist that not all experiences of transcendence or profound reverence are religious.

He did not say how one distinguishes religious transcendence from nonreligious transcendence, but the distinction appears to pivot on the degree to which the object of awe is supernatural (Greeley 1972).

An underlying question in this whole debate, then, is whether religion by definition includes only that which has an otherworldly or supernatural dimension. What about people whose ultimate value and deepest commitment is to the United States? They have a deep sense of loyalty to the flag of the United States and will even give their lives to defend it. The American Way of Life and the American Dream provide a sense of meaning, purpose, and value in life. National holidays are celebrated with devotion, and a tear may be shed when the national anthem is played. These individuals may belong to several organizations for the preservation and promotion of patriotism and the glorification of the USA. They love this country

Photo by Elise Roberts

In Islam the inside of the mosque is holy ground, and Muslims recognize this extraordinariness and sacredness by removing their shoes when they enter.

above all else, according it highest value and deepest loyalty. Is this religious behavior? Can nationalism be a form of religion? It is not otherworldly, and it is not essentially supernatural (although the belief structure may include a God who overlooks, blesses, and judges the nation). Certainly these individuals feel a sort of sacredness toward the nation and its primary symbol, the flag. Yet this sacredness does not involve the fear and trembling that Rudolf Otto (1923) and Durkheim ([1912] 1995) describe as part of the sacred attitude. How does the feeling of awe and reverence toward a nation differ from the awe and reverence toward a supernatural being or realm? Is this difference significant enough to call one experience religious and the other not? These are not easy questions to answer. Some scholars feel that nationalistic behavior as described above *is* religious in character and that a broader definition of religion is appropriate. This has even caused one prominent scholar to suggest that we simply focus on the sociology of the sacred, even if the behavior is not "a religion" in the strictest sense, since anything that is considered "sacred" is likely to interest the sociologist of religion (Demerath 2000).

The major criticism of substantive definitions is that they tend to focus the researcher's attention solely on traditional forms of religion. Some writers feel that people in complex and changing societies such as ours are religious in new ways, like Thomas Luckmann's idea of "invisible religion" discussed later in this chapter. Substantive definitions are felt to be too narrow and too tradition-bound, hence blinding researchers to these new modes of religiosity.

FUNCTIONAL DEFINITIONS

An alternative to substantive definitions of religion are functional definitions. These tend to be much more inclusive of differing forms of "religion" and therefore better able to capture some of the nontraditional models of religion the substantive definition misses. Milton Yinger has offered one such definition. He suggested that we focus not on what religion essentially *is* but on what it *does* (Yinger 1970). He proposed that we define a social phenomenon as religious if it fulfills the manifest function of religion.[1] He followed Max Weber in asserting that meaning in life is a basic human need (although the nature and intensity of that need will vary among individuals). Theologian Paul Tillich has described religion as that which is one's "ultimate concern," and Yinger also drew on Tillich's understanding in developing his own definition. The underlying conviction is that a fundamental concern of human beings is to understand the purpose of life and the meaning of death, suffering, evil, and injustice (Tillich 1957). In line with this conviction, Yinger wrote, "Religion, then, can be defined as a system of beliefs and practices by means of which a group of people struggles with these ultimate problems of human life" (Yinger 1970:7). Religion helps individuals cope by offering an explanation for these challenges and by providing a strategy to overcome despair, hopelessness, and futility.

Using this type of definition, the range of phenomena that we consider under the heading *religion* is considerably expanded. Yinger insisted that nontheistic and even nonsupernatural systems of belief and practice can be appropriate subjects of inquiry for the sociologist of religion. "It is not the nature of *belief*, but the nature of *believing* that requires our study" (Yinger 1970:11). Wherever one sees a closing of the gap between fact and hope, wherever one sees a leap of faith that allows a person to assert that suffering and evil will somehow, someday be defeated, there one sees the manifestations of religion. Even a secular faith that science and technology will ultimately solve all our problems

[1]Manifest functions are the *conscious* and *intended* functions of a social pattern or institution. Latent functions are unconscious and unintended (Merton, 1968).

is, by this definition, a religious or quasi-religious phenomenon. Yinger wrote, "A term that already includes, by common consent, the contemplations of a Buddhist monk and the ecstatic visions of a revivalist cult member, human sacrifice, and ethical monotheism may have room in it for science *as a way of life*" (Yinger 1970:12). Intense faith in nationalism, in capitalism, and in many other objects of deep loyalty may become grist for the student of religion if the object of loyalty and belief is expected eventually to solve the ultimate human perplexities over the purpose of life and the meaning of death, injustice, and suffering. Yinger argued that if a narrower definition is utilized, one may misidentify (or even miss entirely) religion in a society, particularly in societies undergoing cultural change.

This functional definition assumes that all people are to some extent religious. Yinger wrote, "To me, the evidence is decisive: human nature abhors a vacuum in systems of faith. This is not, then, a period of religious decline but is one of religious change" (Yinger 1970:vii). The assumption underlying the functional definition of religion does not really invite the question of whether a society is becoming less religious, but rather asks what new forms religion is taking. The sociologist adopting this approach is less likely to overlook nontraditional or alternative forms of religion (see Chapter 14) or new developments in the ways that people practice religion, especially younger generations (see Chapter 5).

Another well-known functional definition of religion is Robert Bellah's view that religion is "a set of symbolic forms and acts that relate [people] to the ultimate conditions of [their] existence" (Bellah 1970c:21). Like Yinger, Bellah's view of religion was influenced by the theologian Tillich's view of "ultimate concern." One problem with these functional definitions is that "ultimate concern" or "ultimate conditions of existence" are difficult phenomena to identify and are even

Photo by Bill Branson for National Institute of Arthritis and Musculoskeletal and Skin Diseases (NIAMS)

In modern society, a sharp distinction is often drawn between religion and science, but Yinger's broad functional definition of religion suggests that faith in and the practice of science may be a form of religion itself, or at least a quasi-religion.

more difficult to measure using the empirical methods of social science (see Chapter 2). Nevertheless, Yinger's and Bellah's definitions suggest that any system of belief and action that fails to address the fundamental questions of meaning in life is not a religion.

In response to these functional definitions, some scholars have argued that a supernatural dimension to the belief system is a fundamental characteristic of religion (Stark and Bainbridge 1996; Stark and Finke 2000). They argue that if a definition of religion does not include a supernatural dimension, the term *religion* may become so inclusive that it is virtually meaningless. They advocate substantive definitions for this reason.

Critical Thinking: Consider your own presuppositions: Is a belief in a God or gods or the supernatural necessary when you use the term *religion*? On the other hand, is it the fact that something is helping individuals address what is of ultimate concern that matters most?

A Symbolic Definition

You may have noticed that the strengths and weaknesses of substantive and functional definitions of religion are to some extent mirror images of each other. Because of this, some scholars have attempted to offer more comprehensive definitions of religion. Their hope is to capitalize on the strengths of substantive and functional definitions and to avoid their weaknesses. Anthropologist Clifford Geertz's symbolic definition of religion is one such effort.

Geertz begins by recognizing that *symbols*— objects, behaviors, or stories that represent or remind one of something else—are powerful forces in human behavior. They are also central to religion. Given the abstract nature of the focal point of religion, symbols become its indispensable medium. Symbols include objects (e.g., the cross, the Star of David), behaviors (e.g., genu-

flecting before the altar; baptizing a convert; touching the mezuzah on the doorpost of a Jewish home before entering; kneeling, facing Mecca, and praying five times a day), and myths or stories (e.g., the creation story, the story of Jesus washing the disciples' feet, legends of ancestors). (All of these elements of religion will be discussed in more detail in Chapter 4.) Geertz was impressed with the way in which various levels of meaning can be communicated through symbols. Moreover, symbols are more accessible to observation than subjective experiences of "ultimate concern." Hence, he used symbols as the starting point for his definition of religion (Geertz 1973).

Not all symbols are religious, of course. A handshake, a kiss, and a wave of the hand are all symbolic behaviors, but they do not normally have religious connotations. Religious symbols are distinct from nonreligious ones in that the former are macro symbolic. *Macro symbols* are those that help one interpret the meaning of life itself and that involve a cosmology or worldview: a cross, circumcision, a loaf of bread and a cup. Because they serve this important function, they tend to acquire a sense of sacredness or profound respect. Many nonreligious symbols are *micro symbols*—that is, symbols that affect everyday interaction with others and that enhance daily communication and cooperation, like a wink or a smile. Micro symbols do not claim to explain the purpose of life and do not suggest values and beliefs that claim highest priority in one's life.

Geertz's symbolic definition is so fully and carefully developed that it deserves a close examination. He wrote,

> Religion is (1) a system of symbols which acts to (2) establish powerful, pervasive, and long lasting moods and motivations in [people] by (3) formulating conceptions of a general order of existence and (4) clothing these conceptions with such an aura of factuality that the moods and motivations seem uniquely realistic. (Geertz 1973:90)

Religion is a "system of symbols which acts" in that the symbols provide a blueprint for understanding the world. These symbols provide a model of the world by helping people understand what the world and life really are. Many people believe, for example, that life is actually a testing ground in which God determines one's fitness to live in the heavenly kingdom. These individuals live their lives with reference to this understanding. Other religious perspectives offer alternative views of what life really is. In any case, these symbols not only suggest a model *of* the world, but they also propose a model *for* the world (Geertz 1973:93). The symbol system describes what life *is* and also prescribes what it *ought* to be. Not only do many Christians assert that life is a testing ground, but they claim access to the answers that will help them pass the test.

This system of symbols acts to "establish powerful, pervasive, and long lasting moods and motivations" in people. In other words, acknowledgment of the symbols affects one's disposition. Religious activity influences two somewhat different types of dispositions: (1) moods and (2) motivations. Geertz suggested that moods involve depth of feeling, whereas motivations provide a direction for behavior. Moods vary in intensity, and they affect our total outlook on life, but they are not aimed at any particular goal. One simply experiences a mood; one does not gain a feeling of obligation about a specific goal to be attained from a mood. Some born-again Christian groups emphasize that to be a Christian is to be joyful, even in the face of adversity. The emphasis is on a pervasive mood that is to characterize the believer, regardless of the specific circumstances.

Some religions may emphasize moods as primary (in Buddhism the focus is on mystical experience), while other religions stress motivations and a system of ethics (the Unitarian–Universalist society illustrates this latter focus). Nonetheless, Geertz suggested that in all religions the symbol system produces moods that intensify commitment and motivations to act in specified ways. In another context, Geertz

referred to the moods and motivations together as the *ethos* of the religion.

Not only do the symbol systems enhance a particular disposition, but they also act to "formulate conceptions of a general order of existence." A distinguishing characteristic of religion is that it provides a worldview, a cognitive ordering of concepts of nature, of self, of society, of the supernatural. Religion not only creates intense feelings but also establishes a cosmology that satisfies one's intellectual need for reasonable explanations. Geertz emphasized that not all intense feelings of awe are religious. One may be overwhelmed by powerful emotions (moods) in viewing the Grand Canyon, but such feelings may be either purely aesthetic or deeply religious. If no explanatory perspective or overview of the meaning of life is involved, the experience is not religious (Geertz 1958).

There are three major challenges that seem to belie the meaningfulness of life, and it is these that a religious worldview must resolve: (1) a sense of coherence and reasonableness of events of life; (2) a sense of meaning in suffering so that it becomes sufferable; and (3) a sense of moral order in which evil will be overcome and that virtue, goodness, and justice will somehow, someday prevail. Symbol systems, then, attempt to "account for, and even celebrate, the perceived ambiguities, puzzles, and paradoxes in human experience" (Geertz 1973:108). The worldview represents an intellectual process by which people can affirm that life makes sense, that suffering is bearable, and that justice is not a mirage—that in the end, good will be rewarded.

Geertz continued his definition by attempting to answer the question of how a particular worldview or set of concepts comes to be believed. The symbols act to "clothe those conceptions in such an aura of factuality that the moods and motivations seem uniquely realistic." How is it, he asked, that despite common sense, everyday experience, and empirical evidence, people will come to believe irrational and unsupportable things? What compels a Christian Scientist to deny the reality of illness, even though the person experiences the symptoms of influenza? Why does a Mormon believe that a new revelation was written to Joseph Smith on golden plates, even though no one could read them but Smith? Why do members of the Unification Church assert that their leader, the Reverend Sun Myung Moon, is the Christ, even though other observers see him as a rather unexceptional man? Why do Christians continue to affirm that Jesus is the son of God who ushered in God's kingdom, even though he died in the manner of a criminal nearly 2,000 years ago? Geertz pointed out that religious ritual often creates an aura in which a deeper reality is said to be reached. Truths are experienced or understood that are more profound than everyday experience provides.

Geertz's definition is both abstract and quite elaborate. In fact, his explanation of the definition is over 40 pages long. A clear strength of his definition, however, is that it offers a contribution to the debate over what distinguishes religion from other cultural phenomena. His central contributions are that religion must have a macro symbol system that acts to reinforce both a worldview and an ethos and that has a built-in system of believability or plausibility.

In the end, Geertz's analysis is really more than a definition. It is an essay on how religion "works" to reinforce itself and on what religion "does" in the society. Because of this focus on what religion does, the symbolic definition may be considered as one type of functional definition (Berger 1974).

Critical Thinking: How do you think symbols, moods, and motivations play a role in religious commitment? What symbols elicit strong moods and motivations for you?

Gerripix via Istockphoto.com

Religion is communal in character and often involves intense emotional experiences. The photo depicts a congregation worshipping with their pastors at a revival meeting. The intense emotional experience acts to clothe the religious concepts in a mystique that makes these concepts seem uniquely realistic.

DISTINCTION BETWEEN RELIGION AND MAGIC

When studying religion, social scientists often find themselves investigating a closely related phenomenon—magic. The two are often found together, but because they serve rather different functions, students of religion should understand the distinction between them.

Many criteria have been used to discriminate between religion and magic. In the listing that follows, some of the differences are juxtaposed. Various scholars have emphasized one or more of these factors (Titiev 1972).

These seven distinguishing factors make a nice, neat picture of magic and religion, but in reality the distinction is not so precise. There are many worship experiences in which the members may not find the ritual meaningful. Many members may attend worship only at critical times in their lives (e.g., funerals, baptisms, marriages, or times of emotional stress for the individual), and

the minister may emphasize utilitarian reasons for belonging (e.g., God's blessing on one's business or promises of good health). Yet the phenomenon hardly seems to be magic rather than religion. Furthermore, the factors listed do not show a high correlation with each other. The distinction between magic and religion remains somewhat foggy. Nonetheless, one factor seems worthy of our attention.

The primary difference between religion and magic has most commonly been defined in terms of the attitude toward the transcendent: Is it considered of intrinsic or utilitarian value? The religious perspective views the object of worship as being of inherent, categorical worth. It is not worshiped primarily because of favors to be returned for performance of the ritual. God is worshiped in the Jewish, Christian, and Islamic traditions—or at least is supposed to be worshipped in those traditions—simply "because God is God." In religion, the object of worship is the center of worth or the epitome of value.

Religion	Magic
1. There is a sense of a "group" of common believers: a church, temple, or mosque.	1. No faith community or "group consciousness" is involved.
2. Moral ethos, or a system of ethics, guides behavior.	2. No moral ethos or systematic pattern of ethics is present.
3. Rites are meaningful: They reinforce patterns of belief.	3. Rites are not necessarily meaningful; they are used to cast a spell or make something happen.
4. Rites occur calendrically (on a regular basis each week, month, and/or year).	4. Rites occur at critical (crisis) times.
5. It functions for both the individual and the structure.	5. It functions only for individuals, not for social structure.
6. Participation is open; a leader leads the entire group in performance of ritual.	6. The leader is the only one to know ritual and how to perform it; others present are passive.
7. The worship of a transcendent Being or Power as intrinsically worthy of one's attention occurs.	7. Manipulation of impersonal, transcendent power occurs for utilitarian reasons.

In the case of magic, the world is believed to be influenced by supernatural forces that control one's destiny. The objective is to get those forces working for you and not against you. Magic involves manipulation of supernatural forces. In a discussion of magic in American culture, George Gmelch pointed out that many baseball players will often follow such patterns as rising in the morning at a specific time, eating only certain foods prior to a game, consistently taking the same route to the stadium, getting dressed according to a specific preset pattern (e.g., always putting on the right sock first), and always stepping on third base on the way to the outfield. The players who follow these rituals seem to feel that they will be jinxed if they break them. Somehow, the unspoken forces of fate will betray them if the proper (nonrational) steps are not taken (Gmelch 1971).

While this may be an unusual example, the worldview of expecting supernatural and impersonal forces to control one's destiny is characteristic of what anthropologists have called magic. The supernatural forces are not personal beings to whom one prays or with whom one develops a relationship. Rather, they have no will of their own. They simply represent laws of the universe that must not be violated and that might be used to one's own advantage. Hence, magic in tribal societies is a supra-empirical means of controlling one's chances of success in any endeavor. Whenever the desire for success is high but the chances of failure are great, people may look for any means possible to ensure success. Bronisław Malinowski wrote, "Magic is to be expected and generally to be found whenever man comes to an unbridgeable gap, a hiatus in his knowledge or in his powers of practical control, and yet has to continue in his pursuit" (Malinowski 1931:638).

Some of the functions of magic are the same as those of religion. In a study of water witching (using a forked twig to locate a source of underground water), Evon Vogt (1952) found some important functions being served. In Homestead, New Mexico, the cost of drilling was high, the chance of failure great, and success in finding water critical. Hence, people turned to a dowser (water witch). The persons investing money in drilling were satisfied that they were doing *something* to increase the likelihood of success. Because the water witch had confidence, the anxiety of the people was reduced, and they were willing to invest more in any given drilling site. They agreed to drill deeper because they were assured that water was there. Vogt insisted that there is no scientific evidence to support the claim that dowsers can actually find water and that mere chance is actually a more reliable means of hitting water than employing a dowser. Nonetheless, farmers continue to use them because doing so lessens their anxiety. The worldview of those farmers is magical in that they assume some supernatural force is at work in helping the witch to locate water. The behavior of people who forward chain letters out of fear of "bad luck" in the next week if they fail to do so—or in expectation of some "blessing" in the next 4 days if they do pass it along—is another example of a "magic" worldview.

Magic provides a concrete action to *control* adverse events. In actuality, magic serves as a form of primitive technology or as a complement to empirical techniques. If we want to control events, but we do not have at our disposal rational means to do so, then we may turn to supernatural methods. In the case of magic, one looks for ways to manipulate supernatural forces for one's own benefit. One does not have to confess sins or otherwise earn a right relationship with supernatural beings. The twig will work regardless of the moral righteousness of the dowser. Magic has no ethos and no "moral community."

It is true that religion is often concerned with mundane adversities, but the method of resolving the problem calls for moral purification, confession, or some other transformation of the person involved. Faith healing, for example, is usually expected to be effective only after the person is in "right relationship with God." If a person is ill and resorts to magic for a cure, it is believed that healing will come if the words are said correctly and the ritual is performed properly. If healing is not forthcoming, the ritual was not performed correctly. However, if a person turns to a religious faith healer for help and the ailment is not cured, the explanation is frequently that the afflicted person or the healer is not in harmony with God.

When studying any one group, the question of whether one is encountering magic or religion may not be as clear and categorical as suggested here. Nevertheless, the primary appeal of magic is to manipulate the world. Science and technology are more rational means of controlling one's environment. As science and technology allow persons to have increasing control over their lives, magic tends to decline. The amount of magic in a society tends to be inversely correlated to the amount of science and technology.[2] As Malinowski said, we do not find magic wherever the pursuit is certain, reliable, and under the control of rational methods.

Critical Thinking: Although you are unlikely to adopt magic as a worldview, are there ways in which you invoke magical thinking to try to control the world, like Gmelch's baseball players do? How does that magical thinking relate to your religious beliefs, if any, and your scientific understandings of the world?

INVISIBLE RELIGION

Another definitional—and, by extension, empirical—issue that emerges in our consideration here is whether private systems of belief are to be called religion. After all, many individuals have

patterns of belief that solve the ultimate meaning issues for them but that are not necessarily shared with others. Yinger insisted, as do most sociologists of religion, that religion is a "social phenomenon: it is shared and takes on many of its most significant aspects only in the interaction of the group" (Yinger 1970:10). An overly social conception of religion, however, runs the risk of overlooking newer forms of religiosity that are not centered on traditional religious groups and organizations. In particular, a number of contemporary scholars have emphasized the modern individualization of religion—the way in which each individual in modern society constructs his or her own meaning system by drawing on many religions. Perhaps the most important work developing this thesis is not that new, though. In 1967, Thomas Luckmann advocated an extraordinarily broad definition of religion, referring to religion as the "symbolic universes of meaning" that infuse all of life with a sense of transcendent purpose. He emphasized worldview as an elementary and universal manifestation of religion (Luckmann 1967). In this respect, Luckmann's definition of religion is similar to other functional definitions (Yinger 1970). However, rather than limiting religion to macro systems of meaning—meaning systems that address death, suffering, and injustice—he sought to understand worldview at all levels of generality and specificity. He insisted that "no single interpretive scheme performs the religious function. It is rather the worldview as a whole, as a unitary matrix of meaning" that defines one's identity and serves as one's religious orientation (Luckmann 1967:55–56). In essence, he pointed to personal identity as "a form of religiosity" (Luckmann 1967:70). A person's sense of identity—his or her values,

---

[2]This does not mean that magic is the primitive substitute for science. Anthropologists have shown that even the simplest society has some empirically validated knowledge (Fabian 1992; Malinowski 1948), and technical skill is never replaced by magic. Malinowski wrote, "Magic, therefore, far from being primitive science, is the outgrowth of clear recognition that science has its limits and that a human mind and skill are at times impotent" (Malinowski 1931:637). Only when technology can ensure success in a task does magic cease.

attitudes, dispositions, and sense of self-worth—is part of his or her religiosity because all these are related to feelings about what makes life worth living. These are "invisible" forms of religion in that they do not have the social manifestations one normally associates with religion.

Luckmann believed that as society has become increasingly complex, and as institutions have specialized their sphere of influence, traditional religions influence a decreasing range of human behavior and thinking. Combined with this is the tendency of traditional religions to freeze their systems of belief so as to make them seem more eternal, absolute, and unchanging. At the same time, technological, political, and economic changes have continued to occur; indeed,

in the modern world, change occurs at ever increasing rates. Luckmann maintained that this has caused traditional forms of religion to become irrelevant to the everyday experiences of many people. He denied that this represents a decline of religiosity. The common person is as religious as ever, but the religiosity of the laity has taken on new forms. Luckmann insisted that claims of a decline in religiosity are due to the fact that sociologists have usually asked questions that measure only traditional religiosity (formal affiliation and attendance, belief in traditional doctrines, frequency of prayer, and so forth).

In the modern world, people derive their sense of meaning by drawing on a wide range of religious and secular philosophies. Each of these

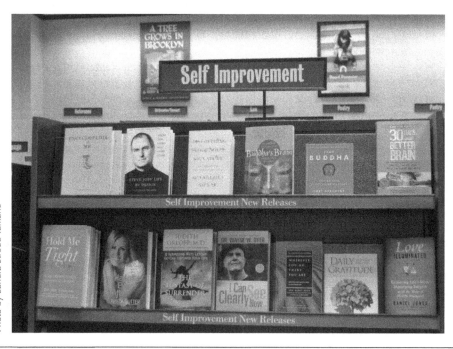

Photo by Sandra Stroud Yamane

Go into any bookstore today, and you will find a large section of books on "self-improvement" or "self-help." Notice how many of these books include religious ideas and ideals like soul, meditation, transcendence, and ecstasy. The tremendous popularity of these books is evidence, from Thomas Luckmann's perspective, of the reality of invisible religion. If we only look at traditional religious organizations, we will miss this distinctively modern form of religion.

competes for the loyalties of the citizen, who is basically a consumer at the marketplace. The product that each philosophy is selling is a worldview—with its own system of values and its own definition of what makes life worth living. Popular religious tracts, *Playboy* magazine, psychological theories expressed in best-selling books and magazines, and underlying themes and values in popular television programs can all affect a person's sense of the meaning of life and one's individual "philosophy of life."

Other organizations, social movements, or businesses also compete in the philosophy-of-life marketplace. Libertarianism is a political movement that exalts the rights of the individual to seek his or her own self-interests without interference. The prime formulator of libertarianism was the late Ayn Rand, whose newsletter was faithfully read by believers and whose public addresses packed houses with enthusiastic followers. Rand stressed individual initiative and the survival of the fittest and believed that altruism was the worst sort of vice. Selfishness, if one followed the logic of her argument, was the most exalted virtue and would ultimately lead to the best type of society. At the opposite end of the political spectrum, Marxism offers a coherent outlook on life and a constellation of values that promises to bring a better life in the future through collective action and collective consciousness. Each of these social movements offers a philosophy of life and a set of values that compete with traditional religions in defining the meaning and purpose of life.

Even business enterprises, like Amway Corporation, seek to motivate by stressing the primacy of financial independence, the ultimate value of free-enterprise economics, and the rewards of close friendship with other distributors. In fact, the regular Amway weekend regional rallies can be analyzed as plausibility structures (see Chapter 8) that operate to reinforce the believability of the values and outlook presented by the corporation. Privatization of religion involves each individual developing a personalized meaning system or philosophy of life by drawing from many sources in

modern life, including secular media, the traditional religions, and popular psychology.

While Luckmann did not see the process as indicative of a decline in religion, neither did he view it as a particularly healthy trend. When individuals must construct their own meaning systems, those systems may seem less eternal and less compelling. The individual may therefore experience anomie or normlessness. Further, those who do construct a sustainable meaning system often develop one that is so privatized that it offers meaning only to the individual—ignoring the larger social structure. Because many privatized meaning systems in modern society exalt the autonomy of the individual (self-realization, individual social and geographic mobility, etc.), the locus of meaning is in the individual biography (Luckmann 1967). With this locus of meaning, individuals may not be likely to make sacrifices on behalf of the larger society. For this reason, the privatization of religiosity could be unhealthy in the long run for the larger society.

Critical Thinking: Readers may find it interesting and worthwhile to reflect on their own sense of meaning and their own system of values. Do all your values evolve out of a traditional religion? Most of them? Some of them? What other sources have affected your outlook on life? What about the sense of meaning and the personal values of your friends and acquaintances? Does it make sense to you to refer to personalized systems of meaning as a form of religiosity? Why or why not? Is it essential for a meaning system to address the meaning of suffering and death in order for it to be called religion?

After garnering significant attention following his initial formulation, over the years fewer sociologists have drawn on Luckmann's concept of "invisible religion." The fundamental concern that motivated Luckmann, however, has not gone away. It lives on most clearly in the concept of "lived religion."

DOING RESEARCH ON RELIGION

Finding Religion in Everyday Life

In a new book on finding religion in everyday life, Nancy Ammerman challenges some dichotomies that have dominated sociological thinking including spirituality *versus* religion and sacred *versus* profane. The way forward she offers centers on the study of lived religion. The idea of lived religion, Ammerman recognizes, has been circulating since the 1990s, but it bears repeating that sociologists need to look for religion "outside the (God) box" (as we say in Chapter 14) and can find it in everyday life, if we have the right sensitizing concepts and methodological tools.

Ammerman argues that religion is sociologically accessible through *spiritual stories* individuals tell about everyday life, and the *spiritual tribes* who are both the audience for and co-creators of those stories. Listening to stories highlights not a monolithic asocial spirituality, but spiritualities (plural) that are culturally patterned. It also draws attention to the ways in which spirituality manifests itself not only in spiritual practices per se or religious communities, but also at home and work, in public life, and in understandings of health and illness. In an interesting parallel to Luckmann's early ideas about invisible religion, lived religion is literally everywhere.

One reason the sociology of religion emphasizes organized religion so much is that it is easy to study religion there. If we want to study the storied nature of religion outside of organizations—spiritual stories in everyday life—how do we do it? In addition to conducting traditional interviews, Ammerman's research team used photo elicitation interviews (PEIs) and daily diaries. Drawing on Douglas Harper's (2012) work, Ammerman gave disposable cameras to respondents and asked them to photograph at least 5 or 6 places that are important to them. After having the photos developed, the photographers were interviewed about the story behind what was depicted.

In addition, adapting social scientific research that has used diaries, Ammerman's team gave digital audio recorders to respondents, asking them to record 5- to 15-minute stories about their thoughts and/or experiences daily for a week and giving fairly extensive instructions and story ideas. Most respondents did 2 to 3 weeklong rounds of recording over several months.

The way these methods come together can be seen in the case of Theresa Collins. A 66-year-old Episcopalian in Boston, Collins expresses what Ammerman calls "theistic spirituality" in her narrative interviews, PEIs, and diaries. At one point she tells her digital recorder, "[The rector] gave a really wonderful sermon that will stay with me always. This week I will really enjoy thinking about it in depth as I do my walk in the morning." Later in the book, Ammerman reproduces a photo Collins took of the front gate of her home. This picture gave Collins occasion to talk about how she starts every day by passing through the gate while walking her collie, Digby, saying "Good morning, world" and then starting her prayers. Still later Collins, again recalling her walks, talks about making "a conscientious effort to be a good Christian, um, and to try and develop a relationship" with a "funny little woman who walks around here" (Ammerman 2014:215). From this Ammerman concludes, "Being friendly, even to a difficult person is as much a part of her spiritual practice as the prayers she recites from the Book of Common Prayer" (Ammerman 2014:216).

Without making any claim that Collins is typical, Ammerman shows in this single example, threaded throughout the book, how spiritual stories are shaped by religious communities (sacred tribes) but also spill over into the world of everyday life, sacralizing the mundane.

Front gate of Theresa Collins's home.

SOURCE: Ammerman, Nancy Tatom. 2014. *Sacred Stories, Spiritual Tribes: Finding Religion in Everyday Life*. New York: Oxford University Press.

Although there is no single, universally accepted definition of lived religion, Meredith McGuire centers her understanding on the distinction between "the actual experience of religious persons" and "the prescribed religion of institutionally defined beliefs and practices" (McGuire 2008:12). Lived religion, much like Luckmann's invisible religion, is *a part of* rather than *apart from* everyday life. The "Doing Research on Religion" box on page 16 shows how one well-known sociologist, Nancy Ammerman (2014), has attempted to explore lived religion.

SPIRITUAL BUT NOT RELIGIOUS?

Another conceptual issue that raises definitional challenges for sociologists studying religion today is that some people consciously reject organized religion in favor of more individualized forms of "spiritual" belief and practice. It is increasingly common to hear people utter the phrase "I am spiritual, not religious." Spirituality in this sense is seen as a quality of an individual whose inner life is oriented toward God, the supernatural, or the sacred. Spirituality is considered primary, more pure, more directly related to the soul in its relation to the divine, while religion is secondary, dogmatic, and stifling, often distorted by oppressive sociopolitical and socioeconomic forces. Some scholars have argued that in the new millennium there is a "divorce" between spirituality and religion with more personal forms of spirituality destined to replace traditional, organized forms of religion (Cimino and Lattin 2002). However, the relationship between spirituality and religion is not quite as simple as that.

Robert Wuthnow argued that "at its core, spirituality consists of all the beliefs and activities by which individuals attempt to relate their lives to God or to a divine being or some other conception of a transcendent reality" (Withnow 1998:viii). There is nothing in this definition of spirituality that makes it inherently antithetical to religion. To the contrary, spirituality has long been historically connected to religion. Even though it is a social phenomenon, individual forms of piety such as prayer, meditation, or other devotions (often with a mystical component) have long been part and parcel of many major religious traditions. Sufism in Islam; Kabbalah in Judaism; and Benedictine, Franciscan, and Dominican spirituality in Roman Catholic Christianity are well-known examples. Given the historical connection between traditional religion and spirituality, it may be better to use the term Eva Hamberg (2009) suggested— "unchurched spirituality"—to refer to religious beliefs and practices that exist outside of traditional religious institutions.

A second important point to consider is that "unchurched" does not mean "not social." Wuthnow pointed out that "spirituality is not just the creation of individuals; it is shaped by larger social circumstances and by the beliefs and values present in the wider culture" (Wuthnow 1998:viii). That is, we construct our spirituality out of the "toolbox" of cultural resources that is available to us at the time we are living.

Courtney Bender highlights this social dimension of spirituality in her study of contemporary spiritual practitioners in Cambridge, Massachusetts. Spirituality for these individuals is not a purely individual project but is learned and practiced in social organizations, just as religion is (Bender 2010). Some of these social organizations are religious, but Bender also finds spirituality produced in a variety of institutions that are typically considered secular, like medicine, art, and even the market economy. Examples include the Mystical Art and Talent Show and the Whole Health Expo. Spirituality among the new metaphysicals Bender studied is also deeply rooted in practices like homeopathic healing, astrology, regression therapy, yoga, past-life regression, Reiki, shamanistic drumming, and spiritual belly dance.

Because of this, Bender suggests that the phrase "spiritual not religious" obscures more than it enlightens. Although they do occupy a different space in the spiritual marketplace than those who dwell in congregational religion, Cambridge's metaphysicals and mystics are inside rather than outside religion. In the end, although it is conceptually distinct, individual spirituality is never far removed from religion. Survey data that investigate the connection between spirituality and religion suggest as much. In a survey of baby boomers—individuals born between 1945 and 1963 who are supposed to be on the leading edge of the revolution in spirituality in American society (see Chapter 5)—Wade Clark Roof asked individuals to identify themselves as "religious" and/or "spiritual." Roof found that nearly 60% of the respondents identified themselves as *both* spiritual *and* religious. Only 15% of the respondents answered that they are spiritual but not religious (Roof 1979).

More recently, the Pew Research Center asked a representative sample of Americans questions similar to Roof's. Rather than asking if people think of themselves as "spiritual not religious," respondents were asked separately whether they considered themselves "religious" and whether they considered themselves "spiritual." The four-fold table constructed from the responses looks very much like what Roof found a decade earlier (see Table 1.1). Only 18% of the sample consider themselves spiritual but not religious, while 3 times as many (56%) consider themselves both spiritual and religious. Only 15% of respondents do not consider themselves religious or spiritual.

These data clearly demonstrate that the majority of Americans do not see religion and spirituality as a zero-sum game where one must be one *or* the other, a fact that other studies have born out (Marler and Hadaway 2002). The diversity of approaches to integrating spirituality into life can be further seen in the "Doing Research on Religion" box on *thoughtful spirituality*.

Table 1.1 Religious, Spiritual, Both, or Neither?

		Do you consider yourself a religious person?	
		Yes	*No*
Do you consider yourself a spiritual person?	Yes	56%	18%
	No	9%	15%

SOURCE: Authors' calculations from Pew Research Center/Religion and Ethics Newsweekly survey (9 October 2012).

DOING RESEARCH ON RELIGION

Thoughtful Spirituality in a Rational Age

Kelly Besecke

The relationship between reason and spirituality has been part of our cultural conversation since the advent of modernity. In recent times, we've seen this conversation play out in public debates over creationism and arguments between religious leaders and representatives of a "new atheism." Meanwhile, ordinary people are engaging this subject on their own terms and in their own daily lives.

One evening, for example, college professor Ron Miller was speaking at Common Ground, a Chicago-area center for interfaith spiritual education. He told his students, "Our culture doesn't support what we do. We all know a lot of people who absolutely think we're crazy for doing what we're doing here today." A Common Ground participant agreed, saying,

"When I tell people about Common Ground, they think it's all froo froo and crystals. So I tell them how smart people are, how well-educated the people are, the teachers are people with PhDs, it's like a lecture. We should talk about this in Common Ground—how to explain Common Ground without sounding froo froo."

A few suburbs over, Gregg Levoy, author of *Callings: Finding and Following an Authentic Life,* was leading a weekend workshop about the challenges and rewards of following a calling—an inner pull to, for example, become a singer or artist, take up a social cause, or explore an interest in spirituality. At one point, Gregg asked participants what they thought other people would say if they decided to follow their calling. Participants responded:

"I always knew there was something flaky about her."

"I always thought you were crazy."

"That's too woo woo for business."

(Continued)

(Continued)

Gregg chimed in with his mother's reaction to his book:

"'Where did you come up with the notion of God, coming from the family you came from?' She was astonished that I had a spiritual life. I heard it as, a spiritual life is so anti-intellectual, so intellectually creepy, so intellectually tacky."

"Crazy." "Flaky." "Woo woo." "Tacky." These are the prejudices of a rationalized society confronted with spirituality. Viewed from a narrowly rationalistic perspective, spirituality comes off as fuzzy, illogical, impractical, and above all, irrational. So to make major life decisions based on an intuited spiritual calling rather than on logic and practical reason, as the Callings workshop participants were thinking of doing, means risking one's status as a reasonable, responsible, sane person. . . .

[This] creates something of a dilemma for educated spiritual seekers, who value both reason and spirituality and see the two as partners, not antagonists, in the search for meaning. A century ago, sociologist Max Weber described rationalized society as "disenchanted"—lacking a sense of deeper meaning, existential purpose, or transcendent possibility. Educated spiritual seekers value reason, but they are frustrated with disenchantment, and they suspect that spirituality is not only important, but also valid. . . .

On one hand, when educated spiritual seekers look out at modern society, they see it as preoccupied with the basest functions of humanity; they see it as a wasteland. On the other hand, they fear that their efforts to introduce some sense of larger meaning and purpose into that society would be dismissed as "woo woo"—too weird, too flaky, and too irrational.

Philosopher Paul Ricoeur once wrote that if we are to bring meaning back into modern society, we need to "struggle with the believable and unbelievable of our time in order to make a place for intelligent discourse." Some educated seekers are trying to do just that. Ron Miller introduced the word "transrational" to Common Ground participants:

"There are three levels: the prerational, the rational, and the transrational. The rational is very important—as a college teacher, most of our task is getting students from the prerational level, where they just have opinions, to the rational. But in our culture, we stop there. We stop with the rational. Other cultures affirm the third step, the level of the transrational, the things that can't be understood in rational language. Our culture doesn't affirm that."

Just because something is *nonrational*, Ron is saying, does not mean that it's *irrational*. In other words, for educated spiritual seekers, reason is only one way of knowing, and a meaningful modern society requires both the rational and the spiritual.

SOURCE: Excerpted from "Woo Woo Versus Doo Doo," first appearing on the blog of Oxford University Press (http://blog.oup.com), which also published Besecke's book *You Can't Put God in a Box: Thoughtful Spirituality in a Rational Age* in 2013.

THE CONCEPT OF RELIGION AS EMPLOYED IN THIS TEXT

In attempting to present a comprehensive sociological perspective on religion, our approach is to be as inclusive as possible. Therefore, rather than dichotomizing religion from nonreligion, the sacred from the profane, we seek to explore anything that provides meaning and purpose in the lives of people. We ask *how* people are religious rather than *whether* they are religious. Hence, the perspective of this book will be most compatible with the comprehensive symbolic definition of Geertz, although we also incorporate the research and the insights of those who use a more narrow substantive definition of religion.

Let us synthesize the debate over definitions by simply highlighting our view of the distinguishing characteristics of religion. First, while spirituality is sometimes quite individual, religion is a social phenomenon that involves the grouping of people around a faith perspective. Faith is an individual phenomenon that involves trusting in some object, event, principle, or being as the center of worth and the source of meaning in life. We sympathize with Yinger's insistence that the "nature of believing" is probably more indicative of religion than the "nature of belief" itself. Hence, a profound commitment to Marxism, intense nationalism, or faith in science and technology as the ultimate solution to our human predicament could be considered at least a quasi-religious phenomenon. Yet religion is also viewed here as a social phenomenon—involving a group of people with a shared faith or a shared meaning system. Beyond being just a social phenomenon, religion has to do with that assortment of phenomena that communicates, celebrates, internalizes, interprets, and extrapolates a faith. As we discuss further in Chapter 4, these phenomena include *beliefs* (myths), *rituals* (worship), an *ethos* (the moods and moral values of the group), a *worldview* (the cognitive perspective by which the experiences of life are viewed as part of a larger and ultimately meaningful cosmology), and a *system of symbols* that serve to encapsulate the deepest feelings and emotion-packed beliefs.

The criteria identified here should be specific enough to distinguish religion from many other cultural phenomena. For example, we have suggested that a worldview and an ethical system are intrinsic aspects of religion. A feeling of awe or sacredness is not considered religious in this text unless it includes a cognitive pattern that helps persons make sense out of life and helps explain the meaning of suffering, death, and injustice.

To summarize, we believe that religion is an interdependent system by which a community of people are bonded

- by a shared meaning system (a faith or a worldview);
- by a set of myths (beliefs), rituals, and symbol systems that sacralize the meaning system for the members;
- by a sense of belonging to a reference group;
- by a system of ethics or values that is directive in the lives of the members; and
- by a set of routinized social expectations and patterns.

At the same time, we hope that these criteria for identifying religion are sufficiently broad so that we do not miss the religious significance of nontraditional groups and even less organized spiritual movements. We will be studying Methodists, Muslims, and Mormons, but this approach also allows us to explore *Star Trek* fandom, Transcendental Meditation (TM), and Scientology as quasi-religious movements that can impact traditional religion and that may well be emerging as new religions in the society.

Taking seriously our own idea that definitions are tools to be judged not as true or false but as more or less useful, in the balance of this chapter we consider other phenomena that share boundaries with religion (like invisible religion or lived spirituality) and in some cases challenge accepted understandings of what religion is and is not. The distinction between religion and magic, "invisible religion," and the relationship between spirituality and religion each remind us of the importance of making conceptual distinctions, but also of being open to new social developments that may challenge our assumptions about what should or should not be considered under the heading "religion."

A FINAL WORD ABOUT DEFINITIONS

One's definition of religion is important, for it specifies what are and what are not appropriate objects of investigation for the sociologist of religion. The discussion in this chapter was designed to help the reader understand the differences in the ways religion has been defined by scholars. We hope that the discussion has stimulated you to think through your own criteria for identifying religion. A consensus among us would be convenient, but a lack of agreement need not cause problems (Lechner 2003). The purpose of this text is not to convert readers to the authors' theoretical persuasion but to help them think more clearly about the relationship between religion, culture, and society.

Before going further, it would be helpful to consider (1) your own assumptions regarding the definition of religion, (2) the defining criteria used by the social scientists discussed in this chapter, and (3) the perspective of the authors. As we noted at the outset of this chapter, and as Yinger has written,

> Definitions are tools; they are to some degree arbitrary. . . . They are abstract, which is to say they are oversimplifications. . . . We must relinquish the idea that there is any one definition that is correct and satisfactory for all. (Yinger 1970:4)

The definition we each use tends to "slice up life" a little differently and causes us to focus on slightly different phenomena as most important. Hence, we have begun by making our assumptions about religion conscious and explicit. For an exercise that can help you take a more reflexive approach to your own assumptions, see the "Illustrating Sociological Concepts" box on designing your own religion.

Although there is no consensus on the definition of religion, there is agreement among sociologists that any investigation of religion must be based on empirical methods of investigation. In the next chapter, we explore what it means to take a social scientific approach to studying religion.

ILLUSTRATING SOCIOLOGICAL CONCEPTS

Design Your Own Religion

Our assumptions about what we mean by the term *religion* are hard for us to see. That, after all, is the nature of assumptions. By outlining various ways of defining religion, as well as highlighting conceptual distinctions between religion and magic and spirituality, this chapter helps students get some critical distance on their assumptions about religion.

An assignment created by Boston University religion professors M. David Eckel and Stephen Prothero offers students an excellent vehicle for further examining their understanding of what religion is, and also what they like and dislike about religion as they understand it. Professors

Eckel and Prothero ask students to design their own new religion and to present it to their classmates. The class then votes on the winners and losers, and the designers of the winning religion earn A's for the presentation portion of the assignment.

If you were to design your own new religion, what would it look like? Professors Eckel and Prothero encourage their students to consider the following questions when undertaking this assignment:

- How does your religion incorporate different dimensions of religion (ritual, myth, experience and emotion, organization, morals/ethics, doctrine/philosophy, material culture)?
- What holidays does it celebrate?
- How does it deal with birth? Death?
- What are its key symbols? Beliefs? Practices?
- How, if at all, does it deal with the problem of evil?
- Does it have any interesting moral teachings? A political ethic? A sexual ethic?
- Does it have a story of creation or of the end of the world?
- What kinds of institutions or activities does it support?
- Finally, what is your religion really about?

Doing this assignment at the outset of your course—whether in writing, as a presentation to your classmates, or just as a mental exercise—will help you begin to surface and engage your assumptions about religion.

At the end of the course, you can also take some time to reflect back on the religion you designed and see what ideas from the course were most helpful in understanding why you designed the religion the way you did. You can also take on some broader questions: Having studied the sociology of religion, what would you change about the religion you designed? What does the particular religion you designed tell you about the current state and future prospects of religion in your society?

SOURCE: Kevin M. Taylor, "Facebookismanity, St. Tupac Shakur, and Lucid Dreaming: What College Students Want From Religion," paper presented at the annual meeting of the Association for the Sociology of Religion, Boston, August 2008.

SUMMARY

Definitions of religion are usually one of two types: (1) substantive (which focus on the substance or essence of religion) and (2) functional (which focus on what religion does). Substantive definitions usually emphasize a specific belief, such as in spiritual beings or in a supernatural realm, or they stress the distinction between sacred and profane realms of experience. Substantive definitions tend to focus attention on the traditional forms of religiosity. Functional definitions identify religion as that which provides a sense of ultimate meaning, a system of macro symbols, and a set of core values for life. They invite an investigation of any profound loyalty or ultimate meaning system as a form of religiosity. Social scientists who are interested in cultural change and the new forms of meaning that emerge in times of cultural transition tend to favor functional definitions. Because they are not overly focused on traditional forms of religiosity, they often view religion as changing rather than as declining.

This text is based on the definition of religion as an interdependent system by which a community of people are bonded (a) by a shared meaning system (a faith or a worldview); (b) by a set of myths (beliefs), rituals, and symbol systems that sacralize the meaning system for the members; (c) by a sense of belonging to a reference group; (d) by a system of ethics or values that is directive in the lives of the members; and (e) by a set of routinized social expectations and patterns. It also views religion as different from, though complexly related to, magic, science, and spirituality.

2

A Social Scientific Approach to Studying Religion

The Sociological Perspective

Sociological Methods
of Studying Religion

   *Survey Research
and Statistical Analysis*

   Interviewing

Participant Observation

Content Analysis

Historical–Comparative Analysis

Experimentation

Triangulation

Summary

HERE ARE SOME QUESTIONS TO PONDER AS YOU READ THIS CHAPTER

- What is unique about the approach social scientists take in analyzing religion?
- If sociologists want to find out if something is true, how do they gather data?
- What is considered "evidence" in sociology—that is, what is considered sound enough to reach a conclusion?
- What are strengths and weaknesses of the different methods of data collection and analysis used by social scientists studying religion?

Ahighly respected sociologist once said of religion, "There are few major subjects about which people know so little, yet feel so certain" (Yinger 1970:2). This seems to be true of both those who are sympathetic to religion and those who are hostile toward it. In light of this, we suggest two characteristics or attitudes that will be particularly helpful in approaching our topic of investigation: a healthy dose of humility and a corresponding openness to new ideas. No one has all the answers on religious behavior, but by listening to one another and by paying close attention to the empirical evidence, we can each broaden our understanding.

In this text, we will be presenting a sociological perspective on religion and explaining some of the discipline's theories and findings. Sociology does not offer the whole truth any more than other disciplines or perspectives, but it does offer insights that can be helpful to those interested in religion—whether they be believers or skeptics or students taking classes on the topic. Our point is that we seek understanding here; a posture of defensiveness—with people seeking only to preserve their own preconceived notions—is counterproductive. Seventeenth-century philosopher Baruch Spinoza's summary of the intellectual life applies equally to our work here: "Not to laugh, not to lament, not to curse, but to understand" (Spinoza [1670] 2009:I §4). Among other things this means that we seek neither to dissuade believers from their faith nor to convince skeptics of the efficacy of religion. Our goal is to gain a new perspective on religious behavior and thereby expand our comprehension of religion.

Sociology offers only one of many possible vantage points from which to view religion. Consider the following analogy: Many people may interact with the same child and yet have quite different perspectives and understandings of that child. An artist may try to capture the child's charm by focusing on his or her unique physical properties such as facial features; body proportions; and shades of coloration in the eyes, skin, and hair. A physician is interested in the physiological needs of the child and the requirements for good health—concentrating on such characteristics as height and weight, immunizations, and the family's history of congenital diseases. A developmental psychologist may study the child not because of an interest in the characteristics of this child but as part of a broader investigation of childhood development. Parents, of course, are interested in the uniqueness and specialness of this *particular* child. Their concern is not one of detached analysis, for their emotional attachment to the child influences their perception. As the people responsible for the child's social and emotional development, they try to be concerned about the child's overall welfare. Because they are so close to the child, some important *patterns* of behavior may go unnoticed. The findings of each of the previous observers may be of interest to the parents as they come to a fuller appreciation of their child and a better understanding of their parental responsibilities. Finally, the child is a unique individual with his or her own self-understanding. The child's subjective experience is unique and important but also has its own biases and limitations.

It would be foolish to ask which of these observers has the "true" understanding of the child. No one perspective is total and complete. In fact, the insights of the psychologist may influence the socialization practices of the parent. The prescription of the physician (e.g., the child needs to wear a back brace) will likely affect the child's behavior and experiences. In each case, the perspective of an outsider may differ from that of the parent or of the child, and that perspective may lead to changes.

Just as people from many fields have unique perspectives on a child—none of which contains the whole truth—so also can religion be understood from many angles. The psychologist analyzes religious experience as a mental and emotional experience of the individual. The concern is not with religion as ideas or beliefs that may hold eternal truth but with the effect of religion on the human psyche. The philosopher of religion approaches the subject by comparing, contrasting, and analyzing beliefs of various faiths, focusing on the ideas of life, death, suffering, and injustice among the many religions of the world. The systematic theologian formulates doctrines about God and about God's relationship to the universe and to humanity, placing what is believed about God (in a particular tradition) into a logically comprehensive and coherent framework. The religious ethicist attempts to define moral responsibility of religious persons, or at least to clarify moral discourse and identify moral dilemmas for members of a faith. The faithful follower understands his or her religion through yet another lens—that of personal commitment. The person's faith is viewed as a source of ultimate truth and personal fulfillment. Members of the clergy also view religion from a vantage point as committed followers, but they are also leaders who seek understanding of religious processes so they can be more effective in guiding others. Hence, they may use the insights of the social scientist, the philosopher, the theologian, and the ethicist in order to understand more fully both their faith and their leadership responsibilities. The sociologist, as we will see, offers a unique perspective that differs from these others and that can contribute to a holistic understanding of this multidimensional phenomenon we call religion.

THE SOCIOLOGICAL PERSPECTIVE

The sociological approach focuses on religious groups and institutions (their formation, maintenance, and demise), on the behavior of individuals within those groups (e.g., social processes that affect conversion, ritual behavior, or decision to defect to another group), and on conflicts between religious groups (such as Catholic vs. Protestant, Christian vs. Muslim, mainline denomination vs. cult). For the sociologist, beliefs are only one small part of religion.

In modern industrial society, religion is both a set of ideas (values, beliefs) and an institution (structured social relationships). We will be looking at both in order to understand how they affect human behavior. We will investigate differences in beliefs not because we expect to prove their truth or falsehood but because beliefs—regardless of their ultimate veracity—can influence how people behave and how they understand the world.

Religious institutions, however, can also affect behavior quite independently of beliefs. In fact, religious institutions sometimes entice people to behave contrary to the official belief system of that religion.

Later in this book, we will discuss the fact that religious organizations may contribute to racism and combat it at the same time. While the belief systems of most mainline Christian denominations proclaim prejudice to be wrong, the institutional structures of the church unwittingly permit it—and sometimes even foster it. Furthermore, religious beliefs themselves can have contradictory effects. While most religions teach that antipathy toward others is wrong, certain other beliefs have contributed—often unconsciously and unintentionally—to racial prejudice, gender bias, and anti-Semitism.

Religious behavior can be either a cause or an effect of other social processes. Although we do not ignore the possibility, there is no assumption in our analysis that religion is always the consequence of other social forces (Stark 2000a). To the contrary, in this book we will examine some approaches that investigate religion as a *causal* variable rather than something that is *caused*.

In short, there are many ways in which religious groups, religious values, and secular social processes can be interrelated. Beliefs are not always at the heart of religious behavior. Social scientists have found that persons sometimes become committed to a new religious group with little knowledge of the group's ideas. They become committed through group pressures and social processes (discussed in Chapters 5 and 6).

Sociologists are convinced that knowing what a group believes provides insights only into one aspect of this complex phenomenon called religion. For a fuller understanding, one must comprehend the social processes as well.

Most Americans believe that the central differences between religious groups have to do with their beliefs, but there are many interesting and important variations between religious groups in historical development, style of worship, and authority structure, among other characteristics (see Chapters 7 and 8). These differences can have a real impact on how members of those groups view life, others, nature, and their own experiences.

Sociology, then, focuses on the *social* dimensions of religion—including the manner in which religion affects society and the ways the society influences religion. Like the developmental psychologist who studies a child to discover the stages of personality development in all children, we will be looking for the common patterns—the general rules—rather than for unique characteristics of each religion. When we do look at unique characteristics, it is to find how those characteristics affect behavior in special ways.

In addition to its particular theoretical perspectives, sociology as a discipline aspires to take a *scientific* approach to the study of religion. A scientific approach is characterized by two fundamental principles: (1) objectivity and (2) methodological empiricism. In the first case, the sociologist tries to be objective. Objectivity does not mean that the sociologist claims to be above error or to have the whole truth; we have already pointed out that no discipline can claim omniscience. Objectivity means that the sociologist tries to prevent personal beliefs, values, or other biases from affecting the study. The social scientist is committed to the search for truth wherever that search leads. Although sociologists as human beings have preferences and commitments, they seek to be open to the data and to avoid prejudgment of any particular religious group, process, or individual. A sociologist may not agree with the views of a group being studied but makes every effort to understand the group on its own terms and to avoid bias in interpreting the data.

Sociologists seek objectivity as a rule of behavior in exercising their discipline. However, this objectivity is not always easy to achieve. Philosopher Leszek Kołakowski once observed that there is no well so deep that leaning over it one does not discover at bottom one's own face (Burawoy 1987:59). There is no standpoint of perfect objectivity from which an observer can see the totality of reality without bias. A sociologist who is active in a church or temple or is otherwise a "believer" is perhaps more likely to be sympathetic to "believers" than is a sociologist who is a committed atheist. As in other areas of study in sociology, those who choose to study religion often do so out of their personal interest in the subject.

The authors of this textbook include an active church member with a theological education (Boston University School of Theology) who was ordained in the United Methodist Church (Roberts) and an adult convert to Roman Catholicism (Yamane). We recognize that our personal commitments may unconsciously affect our perspectives on religion, but we do not abandon the quest for objectivity because of this. To the contrary, we redouble our efforts to be aware of and counter possible biases we bring to our studies. The important point here is that the first step toward objectivity is to identify as clearly and thoroughly as possible any feelings and biases one might have about the object of inquiry. This is not a simple matter of declaring one's group memberships as we just have. It involves an ongoing soul-searching into previously unrecognized feelings and biases and a constant effort to understand each group on its own terms.

In this, we are no different from feminists who study gender in society, Marxists who study class inequality, second-generation Americans who study immigration, or African Americans who study race relations. These personal connections to one's subject matter are not problematic in themselves. We accept the position Max Weber took in early methodological debates in the social sciences over the place of values and the possibilities of objectivity. From a social scientific perspective, values can influence the topics sociologists choose to study and the questions they ask, but they should not affect the data collection and analysis, or the conclusions that are drawn from them (Weber 1949).

Again, this is to some extent idealistic given that sociologists are human beings, but it is a valuable ideal nonetheless. Sociologist Kristin Luker put it well when she wrote, "I see the search for objectivity in the social sciences as something along the lines of Zen enlightenment: I don't personally expect to achieve either of them, but I do find the pursuit worthwhile" (Luker 2008:6).

This leads us to the second fundamental principle of a scientific perspective: methodological empiricism. This principle helps meet the challenge of objectivity just discussed by emphasizing the need to make claims about the social world based on systematically gathered data.

Reliance on empirical data means the social scientist considers only data that are observable through the five senses. A sociologist does not assume that a report of supernatural influence means that supernatural influence is "really real," though it can be real in its influence on the beliefs and behavior of the informant. Like other scientists, the sociologist deals in social facts that can be measured and observed, and addresses claims that can be empirically tested. If a sociologist claims that belief X causes behavior Y, empirical studies can be set up and data gathered to support or refute the hypothesis. For example, if members of certain religious groups are thought to be more racially prejudiced than others, only empirical investigation can establish the validity of that claim. The sociologist is not satisfied with general impressions but seeks reliable data to verify or disprove any generalization.

This is not to say that sociology will ever achieve the precision of measurement or explanatory power of a natural science like physics or chemistry. The object of study in sociology has an inherently subjective element—human beings capable of exercising "agency" (the independent capacity to act)—that the object of study in the natural sciences does not. As many sociologists will tell you, this makes natural science a comparatively "easy" science and sociology the truly "hard" science.

Critical Thinking: What are the key differences between how you have tried to understand religion in the past and the sociological perspective on religion? What aspects of your own personal background might create problems for you in objectively understanding religion?

SOCIOLOGICAL METHODS OF STUDYING RELIGION

An important aspect of sociology's claim to being a science is our use of systematic and rigorous methods of data collection and analysis. Unlike journalists who build stories based on those willing to talk to them, or partisans who only listen to those with whom they agree, or novelists who are free to create their own alternative realities, sociologists (ought to) restrict their claims about social life to those for which they have good empirical evidence. It is essential, therefore, to discuss the methods by which social scientists gather and analyze their data.

Survey Research and Statistical Analysis

Since the middle of the 20th century, the dominant mode of research in sociology generally has been statistical analysis of data from closed-ended surveys of individuals. This is often called "quantitative" research, because the focus is on numbers. Some estimate that

85% of all articles published by sociologists are statistical analyses of survey data. The same is true for sociologists of religion, especially as access to large-scale data sets has expanded in the study of religion. In fact, since 1998, the

Association of Religion Data Archives (www.thearda.com) has made data and other tools and information freely available to scholars and students of religion (see the "Illustrating Sociological Concepts" feature).

ILLUSTRATING SOCIOLOGICAL CONCEPTS

Exploring the Association of Religion Data Archives (ARDA)

The Association of Religion Data Archives (ARDA) was established in 1998 as an online data repository for religion scholars. Its goal is to make the best-quality data freely available in the interest of expanding knowledge on religion.

Among the data sets available are many that are referenced throughout this textbook, including the General Social Survey, the National Congregations Study, and the National Study of Youth and Religion. There are currently almost 900 data sets available on the ARDA, and more are being added all the time.

Being able to access primary data like surveys is important for sociology of religion as a science because it allows more scholars an opportunity to analyze data in new ways and facilitates the replication of existing studies to verify their accuracy. An enterprising student could actually double-check and expand many of the statistics we present in this textbook using data available at the ARDA.

Although it began as a data archive on American religion, the ARDA has since expanded to include international data collections as well as informational resources for journalists and congregations and instructional resources for teachers and students.

If you visit www.thearda.com and click on the tab labeled "The Learning Center," you will see a host of resources including learning modules you can complete, interactive surveys that allow you to compare yourself to the rest of the population, a YouTube channel to explore worship styles of different religious groups, and more.

The key components of this approach are the survey instrument (what questions are asked) and the survey sample (who is asked the questions). In contrast to interviews, which tend to be less structured and more flowing, surveys ask respondents "closed-ended" questions—that is, questions that have prespecified response categories. Here is an example:

How often, if ever, do you pray privately? (Please circle one.)

- *More than once a week*
- *Once a week*
- *Two or three times a month*
- *Once a month*
- *Less than once a month*
- *Almost never*
- *Never*

Responses to these closed-ended questions are easily quantifiable, making survey data amenable to statistical analysis. For example, we can create descriptive statistics like the percentage of people who pray weekly or more. Alternatively, if we have a second question, such as frequency of religious service attendance, we can cross-tabulate and determine the percentage of people who both pray weekly or more and attend religious services at least weekly.

To see the many different ways that sociologists have asked closed-ended questions about religion, see the supplementary online material on "Measuring Religiosity" at www.SAGE.com/rsp6e and the "Measurement Wizard" on the ARDA website.

The most common method of analyzing survey data in sociology is *multivariate inferential statistics*. This simply means that the researcher uses statistics to infer the causal effect of one or more *independent variables* on some *dependent variable*. Independent variables are sometimes called causal variables or explanatory variables; they are believed to cause or explain something else that occurs as a result, which we call a dependent variable. We call them multivariate because the statistical models used to predict the dependent variable have more than one independent variable. For example, we may want to know the causal influence of individuals' gender and social class (and potentially other factors) on how often they pray. Several factors may be influencing whether and how often one prays.

Often these statistical studies also include "control variables"—variables that the investigator is not directly interested in but which could influence the dependent variable and cause a mistaken assumption about the links between independent and dependent variables. Control variables, therefore, need to be held constant in order to assess the real influence of the main explanatory variables being studied. Common variables used in sociological studies of religion—as either control, independent, *or* dependent variables—include age, gender, race, region, education, and income. Causality is central to scientific theories, which is why it is so important to identify independent and dependent variables and to control for other influences. The use of causal language is also important in understanding causality, as indicated in more detail in the expanded chapter material on "Sociology and the Language of Causality" available at www.SAGE.com/rsp6e.

Online Resources: Because computer software can be expensive to develop, the most commonly used statistical analysis packages, like IBM SPSS Statistics (ibm.com/software/analytics/spss) and Stata (stata.com), are only available commercially. Most companies do offer considerable discounts to those affiliated with educational institutions who buy their products directly. Recently, the SAS Institute began making a University Edition of its popular software available as a free download from its website: www.sas.com/en_us/software/university-edition.html. An increasingly common statistical package for advanced users is called R (r-project.org). R is open source software, meaning the underlying code is not copyrighted but is freely available and modifiable.

Creating the questions that will go on a closed-ended survey must be done very carefully, because once the survey instrument is administered to the respondents, the researcher cannot easily change it. The questions should get at the underlying concept in a way that makes sense both to the researcher and (more importantly) to the individuals being surveyed. Social scientists call this process *operationalization*. When we "operationalize" a concept in survey research, we translate conceptual abstractions—like "religiosity"—into specific questions to be answered, such as "How often do you pray?"

Because most survey research seeks to generalize from the individuals surveyed to some broader population, the process of determining who will be given the survey is very important. This is known as the *sampling* technique. The ideal for making generalizations is a simple random sample of the population. In this technique, every member of the population has an equal chance of being selected into the sample. Unfortunately, because there is no list of all adult

Americans from which to draw a simple random sample, most large-scale surveys employ what are called "stratified" sampling techniques. The samples in these studies are segments of the population, which taken together are thought to represent the population as a whole. That is why both simple random and stratified samples are called "representative samples." Using either of these well-established sampling techniques, the researcher can be quite certain (within a few percentage points) that the conclusions drawn from the sample represent the entire population. For example, suppose we want to know the religious beliefs and practices of all adult Americans. We do not have to ask every American; we can ask 1,500 or 3,000 of them, if we use the right sampling technique. Many of the studies we will discuss in this textbook are based on representative

samples of the American adult population, including those conducted by the Pew Research Center, which were already cited in Chapter 1.

Because nationally representative survey samples are very expensive, however, many surveys involve a smaller population base. Examples include a sample drawn from college students at a particular type of institution (such as state universities or private liberal arts colleges), a sample of residents in a particular city or set of cities, or a sample of members of a particular denomination.

Although the units of analysis in survey research are typically individuals, it is also possible to sample organizations. Sociologist Mark Chaves did this in the National Congregations Study. By asking a representative sample of Americans to name the mosque, church, or temple they attend (if any), Chaves and his team

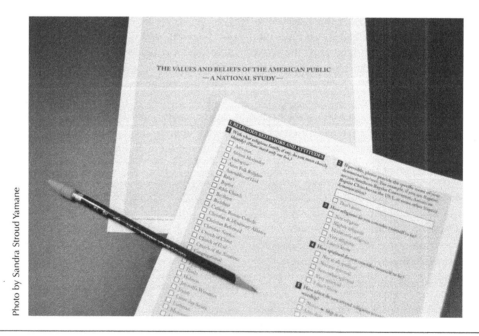

Photo by Sandra Stroud Yamane

Another cost consideration in quantitative research is how to administer the survey. Many closed-ended surveys are conducted by phone. You may have been asked to participate in such a survey yourself. But because telephone surveys are very costly, many surveys continue to be administered by mail. An example of a very prominent survey that switched from phone to mail is the Baylor Religion Survey.

were able for the first time to generate a random sample of congregations in the United States (Chaves, Konieczny, Beyerlein, and Barman 1999). The fruits of this approach are discussed at length in Chapter 8.

Although it is the most common method employed in sociological research, statistical analysis of survey data is not without problems. One difficulty is that although statistical analysis tells us on a large-scale basis which religious characteristics can be found in a population and how they are correlated with which other social attributes, it does not necessarily tell us which factor *causes* which. Does a lower level of education lead one to hold literalistic beliefs about scripture or vice versa? If we observe a correlation between frequency of religious service attendance and frequency of reporting mystical experiences, how can we know which caused which (Yamane and Polzer 1994)? In a cross-sectional survey—that is, a survey of individuals only at one point in time—a great deal of interpretation enters at the point of suggesting causality.

One way of addressing the issue of causality empirically is to do a longitudinal study, surveying individuals at multiple points in time. This helps determine which variable occurs first, though most survey data is not longitudinal because of the high cost of following the same group of individuals over time. The National Study of Youth and Religion (NSYR), overseen by sociologist Christian Smith (2009), is an excellent example of a longitudinal design. In 2003, a nationally representative sample of 3,290 English- and Spanish-speaking teenagers between the ages of 13 and 17 were given a telephone survey asking about their faith and other aspects of their lives. In 2005, researchers were able to re-interview 2,604 of the youth respondents from Wave 1, asking them many of the same questions as before. Data for Wave 3 of the NSYR were collected in 2007–2008, when 2,532 of the original respondents were re-interviewed. The Wave 3 respondents, who were now 18 to 24 years of age, were asked some of the same questions as in

Waves 1 and 2, but also some new questions appropriate to their life stage as "emerging adults." In the end, the NSYR's longitudinal data give social scientists great analytical insight into religious development of American youth and help them make causal inferences (see our discussions in Chapters 5 and 6). A second difficulty is the fact that the data produced by large-scale surveys are characterized by correlations of hundreds of answers to specific questions, which also means that the interpretation of the meaning of the responses for the respondents themselves is sometimes lost. Even a straightforward question like "How often do you pray?" can be hard for a person to answer using the closed-ended response categories given. Furthermore, survey data do not demonstrate the process that an individual goes through; they are static or ahistorical. They do not reveal, for example, the vicissitudes of an individual's prayer life over time, even from day to day or week to week. The respondent could pray more than once a week sometimes and less than once a month other times. What is the "correct" answer for this person, then?

Another difficulty is that sociologists sometimes assume that negative responses to certain questions mean that the respondent is "less religious" than other respondents. The response categories frequently do not allow people to express alternative modes of religiosity and do not account for the fact that what is a core belief or practice in one sect of a religious community may be insignificant or even ridiculous in another sect of the same religion. The presuppositions of researchers are sometimes at work in the formulation and interpretation of the questions and responses, even when they are trying very hard to be neutral. The critical point in this type of research, then, is the objectivity of the questions and accuracy in interpreting the answers.

A final problem with survey studies is a perennial one: What people say is often quite different from what they do (Deutscher 1973). For example, for years major surveys of American adults including the Gallup Poll found that about 40% reported attending religious services in the previous week. When sociologists went and counted individuals actually attending services on any given Sunday, however, they found a much smaller percentage of people actually in church (Hadaway, Marler, and Chaves 1993). The reasons for the discrepancy are not entirely clear, but some believe that it is due to individuals giving socially preferred responses. That is, people believe that going to Sabbath worship is expected of "good people," so when they are asked in a survey context if they attended services last week, they say "yes" whether they did or not. This is particularly problematic if different social groups are more likely to give socially preferred responses than others because it would incorrectly make it appear that there is a correlation between two variables. For example, if evangelical and mainline Protestants are equally likely to have premarital sex, but the evangelicals are more likely to *say* they have not had premarital sex (because they believe that premarital sex is a sin), it will appear in a survey that evangelicals have premarital sex less often than mainline Protestants. Thankfully for survey researchers, some scholars who study these issues have found that even on sensitive issues like sex and sexuality there is no systematic relationship between religion and likelihood of inaccurately self-reporting behavior (Regnerus and Uecker 2007).

More generally, survey information does not involve a direct study of religious experience itself but focuses on reports of religious experience or, more frequently, on the consequences of religious experience. It is a common finding in the social sciences that people often operate on assumptions and respond to symbols of which they are only partially conscious. Hence, the value of survey information is affected by how "hard" (how verifiable, objective, and unchangeable) the data are. Statements about one's religious affiliation or one's political party affiliation provide rather hard data. In such cases, the answers given to researchers are more reliable

(e.g., if you asked the same person 6 months later, you would likely get the same answer, assuming the affiliation had not actually changed). On the other hand, to determine the relevance or the importance of religion to respondents, sociologists sometimes ask the following questions: How significant is your religion to you? How important is religion in your everyday life? The information gathered by such questions is much "softer" in nature. People may say that their religion is very significant to them, and may want it to be so, but it may actually have little influence on their everyday lives. Other respondents may report that religion has very little influence, yet their childhood moral and religious training may significantly affect their daily decisions in unconscious ways. Moreover, a question on the "significance of religion"—as one question among two dozen—does not measure the importance to that person of any specific belief with accuracy. Individuals may say that they do believe in life after death or in the existence of the Devil and that they feel religion is very significant or definitely affects their everyday life. Yet this does not reveal the importance of those particular beliefs. The meaning of the correlations needs to be interpreted with great care. Fortunately, any bias or questionable assumption by the researcher is made manifest in the questions and is accessible to other social scientists to recognize and correct.

Critical Thinking: How we operationalize religiosity in a study is sometimes linked to our research method, but it is also influenced by the way we define religion (discussed in the previous chapter). If you visit www.SAGE.com/rsp6e, you can see some of the ways scholars have operationalized religion in survey studies. Which of these seems to you to get at the heart of what it means to be religious? Which ones seem to have missed something important about religion as you understand it? Why do you think so?

Interviewing

Interviewing as a research method has some similarities with survey research. Indeed, some people call interviews "open-ended" or "semi-structured" surveys. In both cases, a sample of individuals is asked a set of questions, the questions operationalizing some concepts. However, there are some important differences as well, and as with research methods generally, the weakness of one can be the strength of another.

As noted, a weakness of survey research is that the data produced by it do not speak clearly to meaning and process. For example, if a person answers a closed-ended question—for example, "How important is religion in your life?"—by checking the box "somewhat," what exactly does that mean? Here, interviews can be a much better method of data collection than closed-ended surveys because they allow respondents to explain how and why religion is important in their lives.

As with surveys, interviews begin with questions, but they do not prescribe a set of responses from which the respondent must choose. Good interview questions get respondents to begin talking about the topic of interest and then specify certain follow-up questions (called "probes") that the interviewer should use to encourage the respondent to elaborate. The list of questions the interviewer is going to cover with the respondent is called the "interview schedule." An interview schedule with very general questions and few probes is open-ended, and one with more specific questions and more numerous probes is semi-structured.

Consider as an example sociologist Robert Wuthnow's "Spiritual Journals Interview," which was an important part of the empirical basis for his books *After Heaven* (Wuthnow 1998) and *Growing Up Religious* (Wuthnow 1999). The following sample question is a good illustration of a semi-structured interview question:

> Give me a sense, then, of your involvement in religious organizations. Again, start with childhood and work up to the present.

For each one:

Did you like being part of that organization?

What did you like best?

What didn't you like?

So how old were you when you were involved in this?

Then what were you involved in next?

How did you get involved in that?

Did you shop around? What did you look into?

Why did you get involved in this?

So, were there times when you weren't involved at all?

Have religious organizations, then, been an important part of your spiritual journey, or not?

In what way have they been important?

In what way haven't they been important?

This is but 1 of 32 questions in Wuthnow's interview schedule, which runs over 13 printed pages.

Most often interviews are tape-recorded and then transcribed. The transcripts from research interviews can be quite lengthy, ranging from several pages to several dozen pages in length. This makes data analysis challenging in an interview-based study. In analyzing these data, the researcher will seek to identify patterns in the data, often in the types of language individuals use to describe their experiences and understandings. That language is not unique to each individual but is drawn from larger social patterns. As Kristin Luker put it, "The point of interviews . . . is not what is going on inside one person's head, but what is going on inside *lots* of people's heads" (Luker 2008:167). Returning to Wuthnow's example, one of the patterns he identified in his spiritual journeys work was the rise of a new "spirituality of seeking" in contemporary society: an emerging way of thinking about being spiritual that is flexible and less dogmatic.

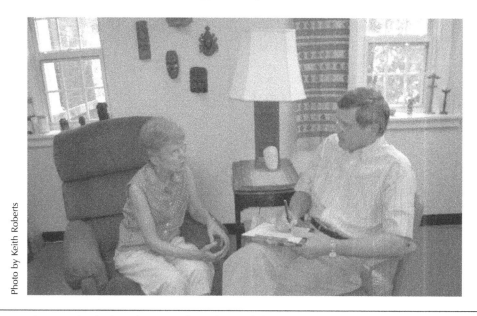

Photo by Keith Roberts

One way to learn in depth about how people understand their faith or their spirituality is to conduct open-ended or semi-structured interviews.

Although social scientists have been using interviewing as a method of data collection for decades, refinements and innovations continue to be made. Recently, sociologist Roman Williams has adapted a technique from visual sociology called "photo elicitation interviewing." This technique involves using photos in interviews to elicit reactions, recollections, and other responses from the interviewee (Williams 2010). Advocates of this technique maintain that it has the potential to get at parts of respondents' memory and consciousness that questions based on words alone cannot (Harper 2012).

Although the source of the photographs used in photo elicitation research can vary, Williams's work is based on the practice of giving respondents disposable cameras and asking them to take pictures of places that are important to them (whether or not it has anything to do with religion). These photographs then provide an occasion for a conversation between the interviewer and photographer, which can begin with a simple open-ended question like "What is the story behind this picture?" In Williams's study (with Ammerman 2014), 57 of 80 respondents took photos of places that were regarded by the researchers as "spaces for God" based on the stories the respondents told about the photos in the interviews.

An example is a photograph of a gazebo taken by Grace Shoemaker, a retired spiritual but not religious lapsed Episcopalian who practices Reiki (Williams 2010:259). Looking at the photograph with the interviewer, Shoemaker explains, "I like to go there and sit when it's quiet, and when I'm at the water, that's when I pray and I talk to God and um, it's a quiet place usually." The photograph, therefore, portrays what for Shoemaker is a "space for God" outside the traditional locations we social scientists look for religion. However, reflecting on the photograph itself in the interview also gives Shoemaker an opportunity to offer her understanding of the role of God or "the spirit" in the world in a way that might never have come up in response to a traditional interview schedule. As we already saw in our discussion of Nancy Ammerman's (2014) work on spirituality in Chapter 1, allowing people to define and document for themselves the location of religion in their lives produces significant insights.

This sort of research is often called "qualitative"—in contrast to statistical analyses of survey data, which are quantitative—because the focus is non-numeric. The richness of the data produced in qualitative research is a clear strength, but there is a downside to this method as well. Wuthnow (1998) reported that the spiritual journeys interviews took an average of 2 hours to complete, and although he does not say, the transcripts made from the interviews must have been quite long. As a result, an interview-based study usually has under 100 respondents, as compared to the thousands that are often found in survey-based studies. Furthermore, those respondents are usually drawn using what is called "convenience sampling" rather than representative sampling techniques. This makes

generalizations from the sample of respondents to a broader population problematic.

Another limitation of interview-based studies is that there is a double interpretation that stands between the reality being investigated and the findings of the study. In the first place, respondents are interpreting their understandings to the researcher. For example, as part of the NSYR discussed earlier, a subsample of survey respondents participated in semi-structured interviews about their religious beliefs and practices. The adolescents who were interviewed were asked questions such as "What is God like?" The youths' responses to this question—for example, "Um, good. Powerful"—reflect an interpretation (Smith 2005:135). In the second place, the researcher has to interpret those understandings in the process of establishing the broader pattern. In Christian Smith's case, he argued that the pattern of responses in the NSYR qualitative interviews reflected a new form of religion operative in the lives of American youth: "moralistic therapeutic

Photo by Grace Shoemaker, used by permission of Nancy Tatom Ammerman

This photo was taken by Grace Shoemaker as part of the photo elicitation interviewing about spirituality in everyday life conducted by Nancy Tatom Ammerman and Roman Williams.

deism" (Smith 2005:118–171). So interviews can speak more to processes than surveys, but that is still not the same as directly observing social processes. To address this particular weakness, we have to look to still another sociological research method: participant observation.

Participant Observation

Also called ethnography—the primary method of data collection employed by anthropologists— participant observation research involves immersing oneself in the situation being studied. The period of immersion can vary from days to months, and the commitment can range from visiting for a few hours at a time to actually living among the people being studied. By participating in the group, a researcher can observe the religious beliefs and behavior of people in a concrete social context. Given ethical concerns about deceiving those being studied, this is almost always done overtly, with subjects aware that the observer is studying them and consenting to be studied.

There are three related advantages of this research method. In the first place, the data that are produced are very "thick" (Geertz 1973). If survey-based research tells you a little bit about a lot of people, the strength of ethnography is the opposite: It tells you a lot about a few people.

Second, the data that are collected in participant observation research are social rather than individual. Although sociologists are explicitly concerned with groups and the social dimension, much research done by sociologists is methodologically individualistic: deriving the data from surveys or interviews with individuals, then drawing conclusions about groups, organizations, or social systems from that. Participant observation research entails observation of the groups and organizations in the first place.

Third, unlike surveys and interviews, which rely on people's self-reporting, in this method sociologists directly observe the phenomena being studied. This allows sociologists to see social processes in action, rather than just hearing people talk about them. As noted earlier, sometimes there is a gap between what people say and what they do.

Consider the case of multiracial congregations as an example (which we cover in depth in Chapter 10). We know that most religious congregations in the United States are racially segregated, so how is it that some congregations manage to integrate racially? Sociologist Gerardo Marti is an ethnographer of religious life who has sought to understand this question. Rather than simply asking people what they think about religious racial integration, he spent considerable time in multiracial congregations observing how people *do* religious racial integration. Through his fieldwork, he eventually identified a three-stage process by which members came to identify with the multiracial religious community (Marti 2009). Although Marti, like most ethnographers, also conducted interviews with those he studied, it is safe to say that a survey or interview alone would have been unlikely to identify these sequential processes. They had to be observed in the situation.

Participant observation allows the researcher to observe subtleties that would not be revealed through responses to a questionnaire or through a 1-hour interview. The quality of the data is rich, but it is also limited to the researcher's observations. This presents two problems with this research method. First, the data are normally limited to one case (for example, one congregation or a single new religious movement). This limits the ability of the researcher to make generalizations. What is true in the one case that is being studied may not be true in others. Case studies permit the researcher to go into great depth in gathering data, but breadth is thereby sacrificed. A large number of case studies is needed before generalized patterns can be identified, and then they are often cataloged by persons who did not have firsthand experience in each group.

A second problem is that the reported data are bound to be somewhat biased by the observer's own "filtering" system. First, not all observers are likely to notice or be interested in the same patterns. Hence, there is the issue of unconscious filtering of data. Second, what the observer chooses to write up cannot possibly include all those observations made. The researcher must consciously choose which data are relevant. This provides a second filtering of data. The same sort of filtering process occurs in all research, but in other sorts of research, it is easier to identify the sources of possible bias by analyzing the nature of questions asked of informants or by checking other available data. Because it frequently happens that only one person is undertaking participant observation on a group at any one time, that observer's data are sometimes the only written record of that particular phase of a group's development. This subjective element in observational studies is a serious hazard.

Recognizing this hazard, many advocates of participant observation have made efforts to make the process of data collection and analysis as methodical as possible. For example, Robert Emerson, Rachel Fretz, and Linda Shaw (1995) have written a 200+-page book on the process of writing ethnographic field notes, which is small compared to the 7-volume, 1,600+-page *Ethnographer's Toolkit* (Schensul and LeCompte 2013). Clearly, participant observation involves more than simply walking into a social setting and looking around. One commonly advocated approach to focusing research using this approach and lessening the random distractions that any given observer might be prone toward is to have a research guide. The "Doing Research on Religion" feature provides a model of how to do participant observation, for students and professionals alike, created by veteran and award-winning ethnographer Nancy Tatom Ammerman.

DOING RESEARCH ON RELIGION

Participant Observation of Local Congregations

So you want or have to observe a congregation? Simply wandering into a synagogue, temple, mosque, or church and looking around is not advisable. Although many congregations welcome visitors, not all do, and some welcome visitors only under certain circumstances. Although not written by or for sociologists or their students, the book *How to Be a Perfect Stranger: The Essential Religious Etiquette Handbook* (Martins and Magida 2003) is an excellent guide to understanding the "dos" and "don'ts" of attending the religious services of various religious traditions.

Also, observing religious services without planning ahead and knowing what one is looking for is likely to yield subpar data. Nancy Tatom Ammerman, a leading sociologist of religion who uses participant observation methods to study congregational life, has written "Observing Congregations: A Guide for First Visits (and Beyond)" to help students sociologically observe congregations in an appropriate and productive way.

Before You Go

- Think about how much you do and don't know about what you may see. How much of a stranger are you? If this group is new to you, consult a source such as *How to Be a Perfect Stranger* (Martins and Magida 2003), and/or ask a more knowledgeable friend to brief you or go along.

(Continued)

(Continued)

- Think about how visible you will be because of ethnic or other differences. The smaller and more intimate the group, even if you look like them, the more you will stand out. Think about how you will explain yourself, and pay attention to the effects of your presence on the group.
- Be sure you are clear about any expectations the group may have about proper dress and limitations on the participation of outsiders.
- Double-check the service times and location.
- Take along a small notebook and pen for jotting notes, as appropriate.

Getting There

- Plan to arrive in the area early.
- Observe modes of transportation. How easy is it to get there via available modes of transport?
- Observe the neighborhood. Walk or drive around. What sorts of businesses, homes, parks, etc., are present? Whom, if anyone, do you see? What does the area feel like? How does the congregation's meeting space fit into its surroundings? Does it look "at home" in the neighborhood, or does it stand out? How?
- Observe the outside of the building. What is your impression as a newcomer—is it attractive and/or welcoming? Is it accessible? Are there signs, and what do they say? What, if any, visible religious symbols are there? Do you know what the symbols mean? Would most people?
- Don't forget to take notes—discreetly. Make sketches for yourself, and make notes about anything you see but don't understand.

Going Inside

- Unobtrusively find a place where you can see as much of the action as possible, while still being part of it. This will usually be near the back or the side of the congregation, but beware of ending up where you can't see or hear what is happening at the front (or being so near the front you can't see the people).
- If people greet you or ask who you are, be open about why you are there. You can say, for instance, that you are doing a class assignment, that you plan to do research on religious groups, or that you are just curious and wanted to visit. Whatever your explanation, be sure to express your appreciation to them for allowing you to visit.
- Read the bulletin. If you are handed a program of any sort, read it.
- Observe what is done where. As you are able, sketch a "function map" in your notes. Where do people mill around and visit? Where do they position themselves to participate in the service (and do different kinds of people—by gender, age, etc.—occupy different spaces)? What spaces do leaders use? Are there multi-use territories? Visible barriers?
- Observe what is displayed. What do the banners and bulletin boards say? Pick up any flyers or other literature that may be available.

Observing the Service

- Observe time. How long does the service last, and does it start on time? Are there clear "segments," and how long are they? Do people seem aware of time?
- Observe leaders. What are they wearing? What are the leadership activities (e.g., singing, announcing, directing, preaching, conducting rituals)? Do different kinds of people (by gender, age, ethnicity, etc.) do different leadership things?
- Observe participants. How are they dressed? What is their demeanor? What do they do at each stage of the service? What physical activities are called for?
- Observe groups and divisions. Who is most involved and who is least involved? Who gathers with whom?
- Observe "artifacts." What special decorations, furniture, clothes, and implements are used? Is there a printed program? Pay attention to any object that does not seem to be "ordinary." If you don't know the meaning or use of something you see, find someone to ask.
- Observe feelings. What emotions do people express? What are your own emotional responses to the service?
- Listen to what is said. Pay attention to announcements and prayers, as well as sermons. Make special note of the picture they paint of their deity, what they say about how people should behave, what they think is good and bad about the world. Listen for what is assumed about people's everyday lives, concerns, and social circumstances. Note also what is said about the congregation's activities and projects, what they are trying to accomplish.
- Take notes, if you can. Be as inconspicuous as the situation will allow. Writing is often possible during the sermon, but avoid writing during prayers or other important ritual moments.

After the Service

- Strike up conversations with anyone who will talk, and pay attention to who seeks *you* out. Remember to be open about who you are and why you are there. Stick around as long as it seems polite to do so.

  - You might start by asking people if they are members or regular attendees and how long they have been coming.
  - Ask how they found out about the congregation and why they first came.
  - Ask what they especially like about this congregation.
  - Ask if there is a part of the service they especially like and why.
  - Ask if they participate in other activities sponsored by the congregation.
  - Ask them to explain things you didn't understand.

- Look around. Either before or after the service, ask someone to show you around other parts of the building. This might be an usher or greeter or perhaps someone you've struck up a conversation with. Note how much space they have, what they do with it, and what sort of condition it is in. Ask about other organizations that use the space.

(Continued)

(Continued)

Back Home

- Go back through the notes you jotted, and make additional notes immediately to remind yourself of the things you couldn't jot down at the time. Start by completing your map of the space and a chronology of the event.
- As soon as humanly possible, preferably before you sleep, type up a full set of notes. Your jottings will be good for jogging your memory for no more than a couple of days; you will need to put flesh on those notes if you need to be able to retrieve the memories weeks and months from now.
- At the end of your notes, jot questions you have for future exploration, and reflect on the particular analytical questions that your project or assignment required.

SOURCE: Used by Permission of Nancy Ammerman.

Despite shortcomings, which all methods have, participant observation has proven to be extremely valuable in the sociological study of religion. In fact, readers may find it enriching to do some participant observation of religious groups different from their own as they read this text. While you will not be trained in participant observation methods, you may find that your observations will provide illustrations and/or questions regarding concepts discussed in this book, especially if you follow Ammerman's systematic guidelines.

Critical Thinking: How is observational research different from just being a visitor and looking around? What makes it more scientific and empirical? What are its strengths and weaknesses relative to other social scientific methods?

Content Analysis

Still another method used by sociologists is content analysis. The name is descriptive of the process: analyzing the content of cultural "texts," where texts are broadly understood to include written documents, spoken words, or other media (including mass media—newspapers, songs, movies, TV programs, cartoons, the World Wide Web). In this instance, the researcher tries to ferret out underlying religious themes or unarticulated assumptions by analyzing written materials. The secular message of American Protestantism can be identified through an analysis of the ways that the parable of the Prodigal Son is preached in different congregations (Witten 1995), or the relative importance of religion and science can be examined by looking at the content of television commercials (Maguire and Weatherby 1998).

An example of using content analysis to understand the relationship between religion and politics is David Yamane's (2000) analysis of legislative hearings before the Wisconsin State Legislature. Yamane examined the way faith-based advocacy organizations like the Lutheran Office for Public Policy, Pro-Life Wisconsin, and Wisconsin Catholic Conference engage in political debate, in particular the type of language they use in justifying their public policy positions. Testimony from these groups was coded for its use of claims to religious authority (e.g., scripture, church documents, and leaders), civil religious claims (the connection between law and morality or national/state identity), and secular justifications (science and socioeconomic analysis). Once the testimony was coded, Yamane could test several hypotheses concerning which groups were more or less likely to use religious versus civil religious versus secular legitimations in making their arguments before the state legislature.

Although content analysis is interpretive in the sense that a researcher has to read and interpret the texts being analyzed, those who use content analysis seek to be as methodologically rigorous as possible. A key issue in content analysis is whether every person using the same coding scheme and instructions would analyze the texts in question the same. This is called *inter-coder reliability*. Ideally, once a coding scheme and instructions are written, a sample of texts will be content analyzed independently by different individuals. Their analysis can then be compared and various statistics can be used to test for inter-coder reliability. In Yamane's study of legislative testimony, for example, the author and a trained student assistant independently coded 10 pieces of testimony using the coding scheme described above. The inter-coded reliability score suggested that the coding scheme was reliable (Yamane 2000).

In the end, reliability of coding schemes and instructions means that the findings of a content analysis are reproducible over time and across coders, which is important to approaching religion from an objective, empirical (that is, social scientific) perspective. An example of content analysis in a cross-national study (on which Yamane based his work) is described in the next "Global Perspectives" feature.

Online Resources: As with software for statistical analysis, there are many computer-assisted qualitative data analysis software (CAQDAS) packages. Wikipedia lists nearly 30, including open source, proprietary, and web-based programs (en.wikipedia.org/wiki/Computer-assisted_qualitative_data_analysis_software). A good example of an open source program licensed by the Free Software Foundation (fsf.org) is AQUAD, from "analysis of qualitative data." From the AQUAD website (www.aquad.de/en/) you can easily download the program, example files, and the user's manual. Of note is that, although we discuss analysis of "texts" in this section, AQUAD and other CAQDAS packages are also able to content analyze audio, video, and pictures.

One difficulty with content analysis in certain types of analyses is its assumption that the texts being analyzed accurately represent the views of the people. Sermons may not reflect the attitudes and values of the people in the pews. Television commercials may or may not appeal to the actual values and interests of the viewers. Those doing content analysis have to be cautious in generalizing from the texts under consideration to wider views in the population.

GLOBAL PERSPECTIVES

Content Analysis of Catholic Abortion Discourse in Four Countries

In "Cultural Differences in Abortion Discourse of the Catholic Church: Evidence From Four Countries," Michele Dillon offers an excellent example of content analysis as a social scientific method applied in a cross-national research project.

(Continued)

(Continued)

Dillon wanted to know whether the institutional Catholic Church used different types of arguments against legalized abortion in different national contexts. To do so, she examined key written statements on abortion issued by the national conferences of Catholic bishops in England, Ireland, Poland, and the United States.

For her content analysis of these documents, Dillon identified two broad categories of arguments that can be invoked by the Catholic bishops to justify their position in the debates over abortion: doctrinal legitimations and cultural legitimations. Doctrinal legitimations are grounded in the Catholic Church's particular teachings on the issue, which include references to scripture, Christian or Catholic teaching, the Second Vatican Council, or Pope John Paul. Cultural legitimations are grounded in secular reasons such as scientific authority, national identity, women's socioeconomic situation, and general views of the relationship between law and morality.

An example of a doctrinal legitimation is the Irish bishops' quoting of the Old Testament Book of Psalms: "For it was you who created my being, knit me together in my mother's womb" (coded as "scripture"). An example of a cultural legitimation is the Polish bishops' declaration, "Voting on legislation regarding the destruction of human life is not only incompatible with human rights but also violates the very order of nature" (coded as "law/morality").

Dillon's content analysis examined the documents using these coding categories to determine the frequency of different types of arguments in the four countries.

One of Dillon's key explanatory variables in analyzing cross-national differences in the Catholic Church's abortion discourse is the insider/outsider status of the Catholic Church as an institution. In Ireland and Poland, the Catholic Church is historically an important source of national identity; in England and the United States, Catholics historically are cultural outsiders. Where the Catholic Church is more of a cultural insider, Dillon expects we might see more use of doctrinal legitimations, as compared to more cultural legitimations where it is an outsider.

In fact, Dillon finds no statistically significant variation in the overall pattern of arguments between the four countries. Although there were some small differences, cultural legitimations were a large majority of the arguments employed by the Catholic bishops in Ireland (84%), Poland (83%), the United States (75%), and England (74%).

There were, however, some statistically significant differences in the type of cultural legitimations employed across the four countries. In England, references to women's socioeconomic situation was the most common cultural argument (52%), while in Ireland and Poland the majority of arguments were based on ideas about law and morality (68% and 57%, respectively). In Poland, the second most common argument was based on national identity (33%), while in Ireland and England there were no references made to this justification. In the United States, a range of cultural legitimations were invoked: law and morality (49%), national identity (27%), and women's situation (21%).

Although her main hypothesis was not supported, Dillon's study shows the importance of bringing empirical data to bear on hypotheses instead of relying on what "everyone knows" or what "common sense" might dictate. She also shows the value of content analysis as a social scientific method for doing research from a global perspective.

SOURCE: Dillon, Michele. 1996. "Cultural Differences in Abortion Discourse of the Catholic Church: Evidence From Four Countries." *Sociology of Religion* (January):25–36.

Historical–Comparative Analysis

Sociologist Kristin Luker made a humorous analogy to help understand historical–comparative analysis when she observed the following:

> As methods go, "historical-comparative methods" are something like that drawer in your kitchen where you put all the useful stuff that doesn't logically go in other drawers. Mind you, I'm not saying that it's the *junk* drawer—quite the contrary. . . . The things in this special drawer are unique, and therefore of high value because they do what they do better than anything else in the kitchen. So it is with historical-comparative methods. (Luker 2008:190)

What historical–comparative methods do better than others is to help us understand what events in the past shaped the present situation in which we are living and why things turned out differently here than in other places.

Max Weber's famous studies of the rise of capitalism in Western Europe exemplify these strengths. Weber sought to understand the connection between religious beliefs and economic practices in parts of the world dominated by different religious traditions. Examining Confucian, Hindu, Buddhist, Christian, Islamic, and Judaic religious ethics, he found that only Protestant Christianity provided the motivation necessary to facilitate the rise of modern industrial capitalism. In this, he explained both the seeds of the world we live in today and why those seeds flowered first in the West rather than some other part of the world (see more in Chapter 9).

Working very much in a Weberian tradition, Philip Gorski (2003) tried to understand the role that religion played not in the rise of modern capitalism but in the modern state (the word social scientists use to describe the entire apparatus of government in a nation). Comparing the Dutch Republic and Brandenburg-Prussia, Gorski identified the key role played by religious beliefs unleashed by the Protestant Reformation in creating the disciplined order needed for the modern state to flourish. As with Weber's study of the spirit of capitalism, Gorski found these beliefs most clearly in Calvinism (as compared to Lutheranism and Catholicism), again helping to explain how and why our contemporary world came into being.

It is important to note that when sociologists use historical material, they have a different emphasis than historians. Historians normally seek to offer a detailed description of historical situations and perhaps to elaborate the specific circumstances that seem to have caused, or resulted from, a particular set of events. Sociologists are likely to be interested in whether a particular social situation is usually accompanied by or followed by some other "typical" situation or circumstances (Nottingham 1971). The sociologist is normally looking for a pattern—a general rule—in the relationship between social events and religious characteristics. The goal is to develop a generalization or theory that explains the relationship—not just in that particular circumstance but in most cases. This approach has led to the development of typologies of religious groups (Chapter 7) and to the development of theories about the evolution and decline of religion in modern society (Chapter 13).

Historical analysis is important, but the danger is a tendency to impose one's own pattern on the data and thereby distort history. The goal of this method is to recognize and uncover historical patterns that are relevant today, but a nonbiased execution of this method is far from simple to accomplish.

Experimentation

The most powerful tool of the social sciences in terms of ability to control variables and therefore isolate causal influences is experimentation. In a pure experimental model, research subjects are randomly assigned to "treatment" and "control" groups. Random assignment to these groups is key because the systematic influence of any confounding variables should be nullified. The only systematic difference between individuals in the two groups is the exposure of the treatment group to the causal force in question. Experimental designs are seen most often in medical research, where members of a treatment group are given a drug and those in the control group a placebo, and the effect of taking the drug can thereby be isolated.

Although it has great explanatory power, experimentation is also the least used research method by sociologists. Experimental research in sociology has been undertaken primarily by social psychologists. Experimental research on religion—even by social psychologists—has been almost nonexistent. Why?

Obviously, one cannot use control groups and treatment groups to experiment on the factors operative in most aspects of religious life. Consider conversion to a new religious organization, for example. We could not experiment on research subjects to test several techniques for converting people to a new religion. In fact, most forms of experimentation regarding people's religiosity would be considered a gross violation of social norms and research ethics. The public would be outraged—and rightfully so. Religion is so intensely personal and deeply felt by so many people that manipulating it for purposes of study would not be tolerated. Institutional review boards or human subjects committees (university bodies that approve research projects involving the study of human beings) would be unlikely to endorse such studies unless participants agreed to the experiment and were fully aware of its nature. On the other hand, informing participants of the full nature of the research would bias the outcomes. Thus, true experimentation on religious behavior has been limited.

Instead, sociologists of religion have tended to employ various types of "quasi-experimental" designs. These are research projects that employ the logic of treatment and control groups without the actual random assignment of individuals to groups. For example, J. M. Darley and Daniel Batson (1973) conducted a quasi-experiment with seminary students in which they tried to measure effects of biblical stories on subsequent behavior. They staged a scene in which they placed a groaning, coughing, sinister-looking man who was apparently in need of help in an alley through which the seminary students passed en route to a location where they were to deliver speeches. Some of the students had recently read the Good Samaritan story and were to speak on that parable. Others were assigned to speak on the role of theological education for nonpastoral occupations. The purpose was to see whether those who had recently read the Good Samaritan story and were to speak on it were more likely to stop and help. Interestingly, Darley and Batson found that they were not more likely to help—although other factors of religious orientation did affect the likelihood that the students would help. In such experiments, the controls on variables are not as strong as in most experimental research, and that is why they are considered only quasi-experimental.

Other quasi-experimental designs based on a pre-test/post-test logic may also be used if one allows an intervening event to be the manipulator of variables (Mark and Reichardt 2009). For example, Daniel Batson (1977) suggested that one could study whether attendance at a revival meeting affected individuals' religiosity by surveying people about their beliefs and values before ("pre-test") and after ("post-test") the meeting. While such a procedure would not conform to all of the normal standards of an experiment, it could offer an important means for establishing the validity or inadequacy of certain theories regarding the effects of religious rituals and celebrations. Most people would probably not object to such tests, for the experimenter would be attempting not to manipulate an individual's faith directly but only to measure the effect of other events on the person. Further, research ethics committees do not usually object as long as the research project does not put subjects at risk of harm.

The fact remains that most research on religion must proceed without this powerful tool of the social scientist. Although the lack of much experimentation on religious behavior is fully understandable, it does limit the research tools available to the sociologist of religion.

Critical Thinking: Although you probably cannot do it practically or ethically, a worthwhile intellectual exercise is to think about how you would design an experiment to test the effect of some causal factor (independent variable) on some religious outcome (dependent variable). What kind of experiment would you design? Can you think of an experimental design in which religion is the causal factor rather than the outcome?

Triangulation

Examples of studies using each of these methods of research—except for the pure experimental method—will be incorporated in this text. We must draw on every method to gain a comprehensive understanding of religion in sociological perspective because each method in itself has its own strengths and weaknesses.

Because the strengths and weaknesses of the different methods tend to be complementary, the weaknesses of each research design used in isolation can be compensated for and overcome. The variety of approaches allows scientists to check the accuracy of their theories from a variety of data sources. Sociologists often quarrel over which research design is most adequate, and most researchers tend to prefer one approach over others. However, our ability to

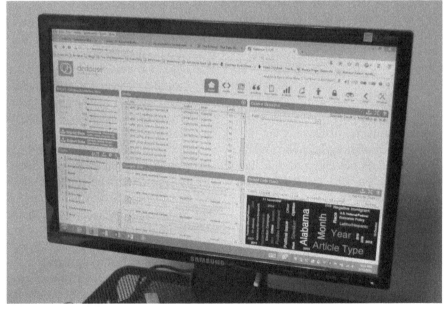

Photo by David Yamane

There is no bright line dividing "quantitative" and "qualitative" research. Quantitative data do not speak for themselves, so they have to be qualitatively (non-numerically) interpreted in order to make sense. Similarly, the words, concepts, or themes that appear in qualitative data—in interview transcripts, field notes, and other texts that are subjected to content analysis—are often quantified so we can appreciate their frequency and structure. In the past, the researcher did this by reading and processing all of the texts by hand. Today, many rely on computer-assisted qualitative data analysis software (CAQDAS) like AQUAD or Dedoose, pictured here, a commercial software package that was developed by scholars at the University of California, Los Angeles.

gather data in several ways provides checks on the weaknesses inherent in any one approach—a process called *triangulation* of the data (Denzin 2009). Together, these approaches allow social scientists to substantiate or dismiss various generalizations about religious behavior.

Critical Thinking: One issue in empirical research involving humans is that of ethics. Researchers must ensure that no one will be hurt—including damage to a person's self-concept or self-esteem. Also, the privacy of subjects must be protected so that information that is given voluntarily does not later jeopardize their social status or their reputations in the community. What kind of ethical problems might be encountered in the study of religion for each of the following research methodologies: Experiment? Sample survey? Observational studies?

SUMMARY

Sociology offers a unique vantage point for viewing religion and religious behavior. While sociology certainly does not claim to offer the whole truth about human behavior, it does provide insights that other approaches may fail to recognize. The sociological perspective focuses on religious groups and institutions or the behavior of individuals within those groups and on conflict between groups. While religious beliefs are seen as important, they are not the exclusive focus of sociologists. In fact, beliefs are viewed as one variable of religion among many—and often beliefs are found to be the effect of other social behaviors rather than the cause. Sociology of religion does not attempt to prescribe how religion ought to work. Rather it attempts to describe accurately the social underpinnings of religious groups and to generalize about common patterns and apparent causal correlations.

Two fundamental principles characterize this sociological approach: (1) objectivity and (2) reliance on empirical data (methodological empiricism). The sociologist is not satisfied with general impressions but seeks concrete, verifiable data to confirm or disprove any empirical generalization about a group. Although sociologists have preferences and commitments of their own, they seek to be open to the data and to avoid prejudgment of any particular group or any particular religious process. Such objectivity is not easy to maintain and serves as an ongoing goal for each sociologist.

Sociology is commonly referred to as a "probability science" because it is not able to make deterministic statements about cause and effect like the natural sciences. Our conclusions about the social world are not etched in stone, and we often recognize multiple paths of causality in the formation of any behavior pattern. The fact that we are very cautious about the use of causal language does not mean that the findings are ambiguous. Indeed, caution allows for greater precision in describing the social world accurately. The unwillingness to make simple and absolute statements of cause is due to the complexity of our subject matter, not to the confusion of sociologists.

In order to understand the world empirically, a number of different methods of data collection and analysis have been employed. Each has its own advantages and disadvantages. Collectively, they can provide checks on errors that any single method might make. Use of two or more methods to be sure the data all point toward the same conclusions is called triangulation.

However, due to the nature of religion as a topic of study, some special problems do arise. This is especially true in the case of experimentation. Ethical considerations prevent many aspects of religious behavior from being tested and analyzed through experimentation. Any other method of research may also be forbidden by research ethics committees if there is any likelihood of someone being hurt or there is no consent given by the subjects.

PART II

The Complexity
of Religious Systems

Integration and Conflict

Religion is a complex phenomenon. It plays a diversity of roles in society and is itself composed of an intricate interplay of symbols, myths, rituals, mystical experiences, and social interactions. In Chapter 3, we take an overview of the multifaceted relationship between religion and the larger society. To do so, we first need to understand two major theoretical perspectives employed by sociology and how each contributes to our overall understanding of societies and social processes. At the end of the chapter, we will explore a theoretical model that attempts to integrate insights from both perspectives. Then in Chapter 4, we turn our attention to the internal complexities of religious systems. In this chapter, we will examine and apply another critically important sociological theory: social constructionism. In both chapters, we will discover ways in which religion can serve as a source of social cohesion or as a major contributor to conflict and divisiveness.

3

RELIGION IN THE LARGER SOCIETY

Macro Perspectives

HERE ARE SOME QUESTIONS TO PONDER AS YOU READ THIS CHAPTER

- How do different macro-level theories analyze the place of religion in a *society*?
- What are the functions and dysfunctions of religion? How might a faith have positive consequences for society and negative consequences for individuals (or vice versa)?
- How might conflict impact a religious group?
- Is religious belief and behavior shaped by the self-interests of the adherents?
- How does open systems theory contribute to our understanding of religion?

The relationship between religion and the larger society is multidimensional and complex. To explore this relationship, we will be engaging in a macro-level analysis. By *macro*, we simply mean an attempt to explain the relationships and dynamics of the society at large. Macro theories look at the *structure* of societies, the overall patterns of organization, rather than at the minutiae of everyday interaction between individuals. The two primary macro perspectives used by sociologists are (1) functional and (2) conflict theories. Each of these has a rather different approach to understanding social behavior, focusing on slightly different aspects of society and illuminating certain elements in the relationship between religion and the larger society. Although the theories are sometimes viewed as incompatible because of these differences, they can complement each other and together can broaden our understanding.

FUNCTIONAL THEORY AND THE FUNCTIONS OF RELIGION

Our first macro perspective is *functionalism*. This perspective emerged out of concern by early social scientists to explain why a few social patterns exist in all societies. Religion, for example, was believed to be a cultural universal, to exist in some form in every culture in the world. Why is this the case? Functionalism sought to answer this question about religion, and to explain social organization and behavior in general, in terms of the consequences it had for society; that is, how it satisfied basic needs.

Although functionalism can be first attributed to Émile Durkheim, it was developed as a systematic method of analysis by anthropologists Bronisław Malinowski and A. R. Radcliffe-Brown. One principle of their approach was that any social pattern or institution that does not serve a function will cease to exist. Furthermore, any pattern found among all people is believed to have its basis in innate human needs. Before focusing on the functions of religion, let us review the development and controversies within functional analysis itself, especially the divergences between Malinowski and Radcliffe-Brown.

Functional and Structural Functional Analysis

Malinowski maintained that all basic human needs or drives must be satisfied in a way that does not cause social chaos. The hunger drive, the sex drive, and the need to relieve oneself of bodily wastes are all satisfied in ways controlled by society. One cannot satisfy one's sex drive with just anyone and everyone. Certain norms specify which persons are or are not potential sexual partners. Sex without consent by the partner (rape) and sex with a close family member (incest) are only two of the more common prohibitions societies set down. Similarly, the society as a whole has a stake in controlling how one procures food and where one deposits body waste. Hence, all societies are made up of institutions—regularized patterns for the satisfaction of human need. Human needs, or drives, are thereby satisfied without creating social conflict or chaos (see Figure 3.1 on page 52).

Malinowski believed that all institutions and regularized patterns of behavior satisfy a basic human need; otherwise those institutions and behaviors would cease. Therefore, the task of the social scientist is to identify which needs, conscious or unconscious, each social pattern serves (Malinowski 1944).

Malinowski maintained that evil and misfortune cause people to feel helpless. Religion allows one to feel that there is a source of power and hope that is greater than one's own resources. Especially important for humans is the need to cope with the anxiety and personal disorganization caused by the death of a loved one. Although the various religions deal differently with death, all religions establish some belief and ritual that functions to reduce anxiety about death.

Figure 3.1 Satisfaction of Human Needs Through Social Institutions

Malinowski traced the function of religion and that of many institutions to basic human needs, drives, and emotions. In this sense, functionalism à la Malinowski tends to be rather individualistic and psychological in character. The bottom line in understanding many social patterns is the needs of individuals (Malinowski 1944).

Radcliffe-Brown developed a different approach to functionalism. He saw the function of most social patterns as traceable not to individual needs but to needs or requirements of the society as a whole. For example, fear of hell and damnation—and perhaps fear of death itself—would not exist if the teaching of religious groups did not instill such fear (Radcliffe-Brown 1939). Religion generally functions not to resolve anxiety but to create, foster, or heighten it.

Why would religion act to enhance anxiety? Some sociologists answer that social stability is important for the survival of the society. Fear of hell, anxiety over offending one's gods, or fear of being bewitched by evil spirits tends to ensure social conformity. Radcliffe-Brown insisted that by making one anxious about breaking cultural rules, religion functions to discourage deviant behavior, and this enhances stability. The function served is not an individual but a societal need. For Radcliffe-Brown the need for social integration and stability is a driving force behind most institutions. Because his emphasis has been on the way social patterns meet societal or structural needs,

Radcliffe-Brown's brand of functionalism has been called structural functionalism.

This structural approach was also used by Émile Durkheim. In 1912, Durkheim maintained that God stands in the same relationship to worshippers as does a society to its members. God transcends the individual in power and scope, is immanent within the individual, and occupies a world that is fundamentally different from the world of the individual. Furthermore, the divine has priority over the individual: Human need must always give way to God's demands. Similarly, society transcends the individual in power, scope, and longevity. Society is contained within the individual in that each member of society has internalized the values and norms of his or her group. The demands and prerequisites of the society have moral priority over the desires of individuals (Durkheim [1912] 1995).

A thoroughly socialized person is one who wants to do that which is necessary for the society to survive. Persons must be motivated to *want* to behave in ways that are good for the society, even when the action may contradict their own desires. If the only argument presented to a person for not engaging in extramarital liaisons was that social stability would be adversely affected, most persons would probably not suppress their desires. However, when the prohibition is presented as a moral principle that is based on divine command, people will more likely internalize that norm. Similarly, people may not curb their desires if they are simply told that incest is wrong because it creates intrafamilial competition, undermines the socialization role of parents, and confuses the lines of inheritance and authority. These may be the functional reasons for the incest taboo, but many people honor the taboo because incest is an unthinkable sin. It is a moral absolute, the violation of which would seem to undermine the laws of the universe.

Durkheim's approach has been referred to as "metaphoric parallelism" (Winter 1977). He believed that the sacred world is a world that parallels the mundane world. Behavior patterns that would cause social chaos are prohibited by fear of sanction from the supernatural realm. That which is structurally dysfunctional is simply made taboo. According to Durkheim, the term *God* is a metaphor for society; worship of God is really worship of one's own society. People are not aware of this projection process, and taboos and moral models become unquestioningly absolute and binding.

Functionalists do not always assume, as Durkheim did, that the belief in God is a mirage. For most functionalists, the existence or nonexistence of God is beyond the capacity of empiricism to prove or disprove. The concern of the functionalists, regardless of the truth or falsity of a belief, is how a belief or ritual operates in the society. What needs does it meet?

Critical Thinking: Do you find that you tend to identify with the functionalists or with the structural functionalists? Does religion *alleviate* anxiety about death, or does it *create* anxiety about death in order to ensure social conformity? Readers might find it instructive to attend funeral services in several different religious traditions. Notice comments made by the clergy who officiate, and listen carefully to the prayers. What emotions do they seem to create? During regular worship services, do prayers and sermons create anxiety about death? If so, how is this accomplished?

Durkheim and Radcliffe-Brown believed the most important functions of religion are structural, while Malinowski focused on individual needs like personal anxiety. George Homans offered a synthesis that attempts to avoid the either/or choice, pointing out instead that both processes may be at work. He used the term *primary anxiety* to refer to the anxiety an individual may feel as a result of the loss of a loved one. Some rituals are designed to alleviate this anxiety or grief; they serve an individual function. On the other hand, rituals may also create anxiety—called *secondary anxiety*; these rituals ensure that society's members will conform to social norms. Hence, they serve a structural function (Homans 1941).

It is possible for a single ritual to relieve primary anxiety while creating secondary anxiety. For example, a Protestant funeral service may emphasize that the departed loved one has gone on to the next world and is in the loving care of God. The virtues of the individual are emphasized. The minister may suggest that the bereaved family members will be united with "Grams" (as she was known) when they, too, pass on. "The best way to honor her is to live our lives with faithfulness to the values she taught and lived," they are assured. Comments that produce fond memories, assurance that the deceased is with us in spirit, affirmation that the bereaved will again see the deceased, and confidence that the deceased is dead only in physical form are all reassuring to the survivors. They help to lessen primary anxiety: grief.

At the same time, persons attending the funeral may be reminded that their own lives have not been as noble or righteous as that of the deceased. The thought of meeting God and receiving one's just reward may heighten their anxiety. The challenge to remember Grams by living a righteous life like hers may increase the listener's sense of humility and inadequacy: How could I ever be as generous and wise as Grams? (One tends to recall primarily the most *positive* qualities of the deceased at that moment.) The funeral service may also cause one to reflect on one's own life and its brevity. This secondary anxiety may cause the person to reaffirm conformity to the mores of that religious group. Hence, the same ritual may reduce primary anxiety and create secondary anxiety. As Homans's synthesis illustrates, the analysis of the function of any institution may be a complex process. Figure 3.2 illustrates the complexity of relationships between individual and structural functions, manifest and latent functions, and dysfunctions. Let us turn now to some of the specific functions of religion and see how modern functionalism is applied.

The Functions of Religion

From our discussion thus far, it should be apparent that religion performs a variety of functions. Religious faith and religious organizations serve a number of needs of individuals and the social structure. However, it can be misleading to offer a general list of the functions of religion, for the way in which a religion functions will vary somewhat depending on the social structure, the culture of the society, and the specific characteristics of the religion itself.

For a group that has immigrated to a new country, religion may take on increased significance as a source of identity. For a group experiencing great suffering, religion may offer a supra-empirical explanation that makes the suffering bearable. In a society experiencing rapid social change, religion may provide a feeling of security and assurance. However, without overgeneralizing, it is possible to point to four types of functions that religion

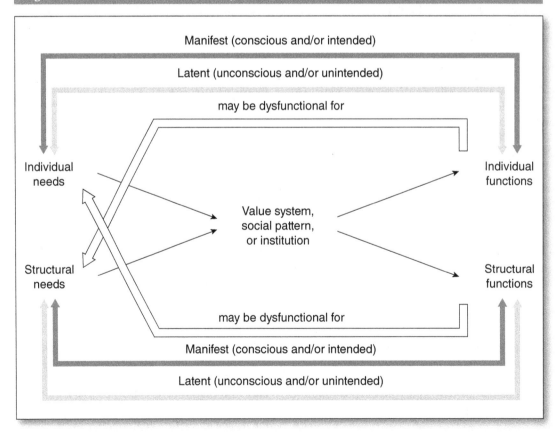

Figure 3.2 Model of Functional Analysis

typically serves: (1) meaning functions, (2) belonging and identity functions, (3) cultural functions, and (4) structural functions.

Individual Functions

Religion functions for individuals in two primary ways: (1) provision of meaning and (2) provision of a sense of identity and belonging.

Meaning Functions. The function most explicitly associated with religion is the provision of a sense of meaning in life. Religion provides a worldview by which injustice, suffering, and death can be seen as ultimately meaningful. Clifford Geertz said when suffering or death has meaning, it becomes sufferable (Geertz 1966). Friedrich Nietzsche said the same thing when he insisted that "he who has a *why* to live can bear almost any how" (cited in Frankl 1963:121).

To meet the meaning function, however, religion must include more than a set of ideas or notions about the world. Abstract philosophical ideas seldom satisfy this function for the masses. Meaning involves both concept (idea) and demand (imperative) (Kelley 1972). The worldview must be presented to the prospective believer in such a way that the person seems to be held by the belief rather than voluntarily holding the beliefs. Philosophical systems of thought seldom address people's emotions in a way that impels them to believe: There is no demand. The communication of concepts through rituals and symbol systems, on the other hand, incorporates both affective *and* cognitive dimensions; this makes the religion seem compelling.

The desire to make sense out of the world seems to be nearly universal. People may be willing to admit that their own worldview is less adequate than another, but they are not willing to give up their interpretation for none at all. They are simply not willing to say that human events are meaningless. It seems that bafflement (lack of explanation) is an extremely anxiety-producing experience; religion acts to combat it. The religious response to "Why?" is answered primarily in terms of values: What does a particular event *mean* in understanding the ultimate purpose or goal of one's life? Another way to say this is that religion locates a specific experience, event, or observation within a larger context of experiences, events, or observations. The larger context is attributed with *ultimate* meaning, and the specific event is viewed as having significance because of its relationship to the "big picture" (Wuthnow 1976b).

Belonging and Identity Functions. A less often recognized aspect of religion is its importance for the sense of identity of the believers. Andrew Greeley argued that denominationalism is so strong in the United States because of the function religion has played in the lives of immigrants. Before coming to the United States, many Italians (for example) did not identify themselves primarily as Catholics. Placed in a new environment, however, with different norms and values, many Italian Americans came to identify strongly with the Catholic Church. Many Italian Catholic congregations became community centers that helped members preserve their sense of roots (Greeley 1972). Similarly, other immigrant groups have shown increased denominational loyalty and intensified religiosity after coming to the United States. The denomination, in effect, became a source of ethnic identity and a bastion of cultural stability for those facing culture shock (Marty 1972). As decades pass, religious services eventually come to be conducted in English, assimilation occurs, and ethnic loyalty starts to fade; religion then becomes the source of identity in and of itself (Warner 1993).

This is not simply a relic of the past for white ethnic groups in the United States. Religion continues to play a role in immigrant incorporation today, though scholars are increasingly attuned to variations in the extent to which religion is a source of meaning and identity for immigrants depending on their country of origin, religious tradition, and the

Photo by Elise Roberts

A core aspect of religion is providing a sense of belonging and identity. Worship is usually done in groups, and one's worship community or prayer group often becomes a central reference group. This photograph is of nuns praying at the start of the day at Mother Teresa's orphanage in India.

character of religious congregations receiving immigrants (Alba, Raboteau, and DeWind 2008; Cadge and Ecklund 2007; Warner and Wittner 1998).

The significant role of religion in the lives of immigrants is not just an American phenomenon. In a world of increasing transnational movement, this phenomenon must also be viewed internationally (see also Chapter 15). A recent collection on religion and migration edited by Glenda Tibe Bonifacio and Vivienne S. M. Angeles included studies of "pathways of integration" for Muslim youth in Berlin and Muslim men in Sydney, Filipina domestic workers in Hong Kong and Filipino Catholics in Philadelphia, Muslim women in Brazil and Brazilian migrants to Japan. The variations are seemingly endless (Bonifacio and Angeles 2010).

As the "Global Perspectives" feature on Margarita Mooney's (2009) study of religion and Haitian immigration to Miami, Montreal, and Paris shows, the context of reception of immigrants—especially the way the host country's government relates to the religious organizations that are so important to them—can significantly affect the ability of religion to function as a source of stability for those facing the challenges of resettlement.

Along similar lines, in Poland, Ukraine, and other Eastern European countries that were dominated by the Soviet Union, the Roman Catholic tradition became a source of identity and solidarity for those opposing foreign control. In Poland, the church contributed a sense of commonality for people of several ethnic groups and gave sacred sanction to their resistance to a government that they viewed as an illegitimate puppet government controlled by Moscow. Unity of the Polish people—based on a common *religious* identity—was an important component of their survival and ultimate success (Tamney 1992).

GLOBAL PERSPECTIVES

Religion and Immigrant Incorporation Cross-Nationally

In her 2009 book *Faith Makes Us Live: Surviving and Thriving in the Haitian Diaspora,* sociologist Margarita Mooney examines how religious beliefs, and especially the relationship between religious organizations and the government, affect the lives of immigrants from Haiti to the United States, France, and Canada.

Although known as the "First Black Republic," having gained independence from French colonial rule in 1804, Haiti has also suffered historically from political dictatorship and economic underdevelopment. (It is the poorest country in the Western Hemisphere). Political repression and economic necessity have driven many Haitians from their homeland. According to the Haitian Diaspora Federation (myhdf.org/the-Haitian-Diaspora.htm), as many as one third of all Haitians today live outside Haiti.

Immigrant incorporation is a challenge all open societies face, but because Haitian immigrants are often poor, black, and undereducated, the challenge is even greater. Mooney's ethnographic fieldwork in the Haitian communities of Miami, Montreal, and Paris paints a vivid portrait of their struggles to assimilate—to find jobs, homes, medical care. She also highlights the centrality of religion in Haitians' coping with their difficult circumstances, which is summarized in the Haitian proverb from which Mooney takes the title of her book: "Faith makes us live."

Religion matters in immigrant incorporation more than just as a coping mechanism for individuals, however. By analyzing the same group of immigrants in three different countries, Mooney is able to say something about the effect of national context on incorporation processes and outcomes. The key variable here is how the governments of France, Canada, and the United States relate to religious organizations.

In all three countries, the government plays a large role in providing social welfare, but in Canada and France the government takes a more "top-down" approach to controlling social services, while in the United States the approach is a more decentralized, "bottom-up" approach. Because the government plays a key role in all three countries, the relationship between church and state is crucial to understand.

In the Canadian province of Quebec, the relationship between church and state is one of conflict, with the government distancing itself as much as possible from religious organizations. In France, the principle of *laïcité* (secularism) attempts to limit any public role for religious organizations, rendering them invisible. In the United States, as in Quebec and France, religion is formally disestablished; however, the "free exercise" clause of the First Amendment to the U.S. Constitution creates a national context much more open to religious voluntary organizations contributing to public life.

As a consequence of these different models of church–state relations, the incorporation of Haitian immigrants in these three societies differs. By not accepting the importance of Haitian immigrants' faith, and hardly working with faith-based aid organizations, the governments of France and Quebec eliminate one key resource that helps these immigrants survive and thrive. By contrast, the more cooperative model of interacting with immigrant organizations, especially faith-based ones, found in the United States results in better adaptation and incorporation outcomes for those living in the Haitian diaspora of Miami.

Even beyond the cases of immigrants or of victims of colonialism, a sense of religious belonging often affects individuals' understanding of whom and what they are. A teenager at a party may forgo alcohol or may refuse to participate in certain activities. The individual may identify herself strongly as a Christian, and according to her definition of what that means, certain activities are unacceptable. Likewise, a young Mennonite, faced with his draft papers for the U.S. Army, may conclude that his identity as a Christian conflicts with his identity as an American. As a Mennonite, he may accept the prohibition against war as categorical. His petition for status as a pacifist may be a profound statement of identity as a Christian. Interestingly, Lori Peek found an increasing religious identification among some young Muslims in the United States after the terrorist attacks on September 11, 2001, a time when one might think that religious identity would be downplayed. This suggests the importance of the belonging function of religion for individuals (Peek 2005). Greeley emphasized that while meaning functions may be primary (in the sense of being closer to the manifest purpose of religion), the belonging functions may actually be prior to meaning in terms of chronology. He wrote, "With some exaggeration we may say that instead of Americans belonging to churches because they believe in religion, there may be a strong tendency for them to believe in religion because they belong to churches" (Greeley 1972:115).

When we first read that statement by Greeley, we thought he was mistaken. After doing a good deal of research on the social psychology of religion, we have come to believe that he is essentially correct. In a rapidly changing society, especially in a society with a high degree of geographic mobility, a sense of belonging is a critical need. If one's kin all live 500 miles away, the need for emotional support during a time of crisis can be intense. Religious groups often serve to satisfy

this need. This is true for both mainline congregations and new religious movements (NRMs) (McGaw 1979; Roof 1978).

Societal Functions

Religion serves the society as a whole by bolstering both the culture and the social structure.

Cultural Functions. In most societies, religion functions to sacralize cultural values. Of course, generalizations about the relationship between religion and morality, or religion and everyday values, must be cautiously made and must take into account the researcher's definition of religion. They are most accurately made with reference to a specific religion in a specific society. Nonetheless, we would concur with Geertz in asserting that for most individuals in most religions in most societies, religion and everyday morality are closely linked. Geertz wrote,

> The tendency to desire some sort of factual basis for one's commitments seems practically universal; mere conventionalism satisfies few people in any culture. However its role may differ at various times, for various individuals, and in various cultures, religion, by fusing ethos and worldview, gives to a set of social values what they perhaps most need to be coercive: an appearance of objectivity. In sacred rituals and myths values are portrayed not as subjective human preferences but as the imposed conditions for life. (Geertz 1958:426–427)

A moral code may not seem entirely compelling to people if it is enforced by nothing more than social tradition. One of the important functions of most religions, then, is to provide a metaphysical basis for the moral order of the social group and to reinforce obedience to norms. Thomas O'Dea's comment seems to be accurate for most cases: "By showing the norms and rules of society to be part of a large supraempirical ethical order, ordained and sanctified by religious belief and practice, religion contributes to their enforcement" (O'Dea 1966:6).

By providing a metaphysical foundation for the culture's values, moral codes, and outlooks on life, a religion helps to combat the confusion, disorientation, and deviance that anomie can generate. This aspect of religion enhances stability for the culture.

Structural Functions. Religion also serves the organizational structure of society. Durkheim emphasized that religion served as a sort of glue to bond together people who otherwise had diverse self-interests; it helped them to define themselves as a moral community with common values and with a common mission in life. This unifying and self-defining function is especially true of religion in nonindustrialized, homogeneous societies. In the pluralistic society of the United States, no single traditional religion can claim that role.

As indicated earlier, religion also enhances social stability by sacralizing (making sacred) the norms and values of the society. This persuasive power of religion can have a number of important consequences. If certain behavior is taboo (so heinous and so dangerous that it is unthinkable), people may conform for fear of the consequences of breaking the taboo. Many Inuit (Eskimos) believe that Sedna, the goddess of the sea, determines one's success or failure in hunting seals. Such believers are not likely to risk offending her by violating one of her rules. Hence, no Inuit kills more than is needed; waste is unthinkable. This conservation ethic is functional for Inuit society, yet it is enforced by religious rather than legislative sanction. In most societies, religion creates an environment of moral obligation to norms that benefit the social structure.

Dysfunctions of Religion and the Diversity of Consequences

Any institution or behavior pattern is likely to have a multiplicity of consequences in a society; it may be both functional and dysfunctional at the same time. In Western culture, religion has often rejected scientific knowledge. Copernicus's claim that the earth revolves around the sun was condemned as heresy, and Galileo was tried by the Inquisition for asserting that he had proved Copernicus correct. Much later, biblical literalists condemned Charles Darwin's theories and insisted that such heresy not be taught in the public schools. The criterion of truth was the Bible, and alternative theories or ideas were to be suppressed. Such an attitude is certainly dysfunctional for scientific inquiry. This may have had positive effects for some individuals by creating an unchanging and stable worldview, but it also stifled creativity and advancement of human knowledge through scientific inquiry.

The stabilizing function of religion itself has more than one consequence. It is interesting that Karl Marx and Émile Durkheim basically agreed on the way in which religion contributes to society. Religion tends to unite people around common values and beliefs. This occurs even when the self-interests of members are contrary. Durkheim ([1912] 1995) admired the way religion functioned for social unity; Marx ([1844] 1977) was appalled by it and referred to religion as the "opium of the people." By claiming that injustice would be rectified in an afterlife or in a reincarnation, religion has served to keep oppressed people in bondage, creating for them "illusory happiness" based on "illusions" about their real material conditions of existence. Religious support of the existing social system may benefit the system while being dysfunctional for the disfranchised members of that society.

We have seen that the sense of belonging that a religious community provides can serve important psychological needs. However, this sense of belonging and strong group identification may lead to extreme parochialism, bigotry, and ethnocentrism. Religion frequently breeds narrow-mindedness and strong group boundaries.

The key point is that we must always be cautious about broad generalizations regarding religion. In order to be precise, we must discuss the functions and dysfunctions of a specific religion for specific individuals or a specific structure in a specific society. We must acknowledge that religion may be functional in one way and dysfunctional in another.

Critical Thinking: How might a religious behavior or religious norm be functional for society but dysfunctional for an individual? How might a religious belief or behavior be functional for an individual but have harmful consequences for the larger society?

Problems With Functional Analysis

Functional analysis is but one lens through which any social process can be viewed and understood. There are, however, distortions in this lens.

1. Functionalism tends to err in the direction of overemphasizing social stability and underemphasizing conflict and change. In so doing, functionalists have often assumed that societies are quite well-integrated systems; the positive functions have been stressed more heavily than the dysfunctions.

2. In stressing functions, one also loses sight of the historical process by which any particular religion established its present character. The contemporary emphasis on historical sociology (or diachronic analysis) in the study of religion is an important corrective to this oversight (Geertz 1968).

3. By emphasizing the critical needs that religion fulfills, one might assume that the traditional forms of religion are indispensable. However, much research in the past three decades has been devoted to discovering new forms of religion or "religion surrogates" (Bellah 1970b, 1975; Bellah et al. 1985; Luckmann 1967; Roof 1999; Wuthnow 1976b; Yinger 1969, 1977). Hence, it is important to avoid the trap of thinking that traditional forms are indispensable.

4. Functionalism has sometimes evolved into a social philosophy rather than a tool of empirical research. As a social philosophy, functionalism has sometimes used circular reasoning to posit and then prove a point. Certain basic needs, whether biological, psychological, or social, have occasionally been set forth as basic and inherent to human society. Any existing social arrangements are said to be *created by* those needs and, in turn, to have the *effect* of satisfying them. This makes a neat theory because it cannot be disproved. The answer is presupposed in the question; satisfaction of some posited need is both cause and effect.

Most sociologists do not accept many of the assumptions of functionalism as social philosophy, but functionalism continues to provide an important methodology. By this, we mean that the basic questions of functional analysis continue to guide much sociological inquiry: What individual and social needs does a particular social pattern serve in a particular society at a particular time? How does a social pattern or institution affect the lives of individuals and influence other social patterns and institutions? What are the social forces that contribute to social integration? As a method of analysis, these questions are asked as open-ended queries and with the realization that the amount of social integration in a society is never total and is always subject to change.

5. Structural functionalists have often evaluated social functions as being primary, while seeing individual dysfunctions as necessary evils. Therefore, some functional theories have operated with a conservative bias. This need not be an inherent problem with functionalism as a methodology, but it has been a tendency of functionalism as a social philosophy. For functionalism as a method of analysis, social order is not intrinsically good or evil but a variable to be assessed in each society.

As a method of analysis, functionalism has certain common concerns with conflict theory, for both seek to discover the social consequences of a particular belief, behavior, or structure. However, many sociologists are principally interested in issues of change, conflict between interest groups, and inequalities in power. Conflict theory addresses these issues more adequately than does functional theory, and it is to this second macro-level theory that we now turn.

CONFLICT THEORY AND RELIGIOUS CONFLICT

Marx maintained that the fundamental reality of history and modern society is a conflict between the classes. The "haves" use every tool available, including coercion and ideology, to sustain their advantageous position over the "have-nots" (Marx [1852] 2008). According to this view, understanding modern industrial society does not necessitate an analysis of cultural values and beliefs. The basic issue is economic conflict. Hence, Marx is often identified as the father of modern conflict theory. He maintained that values and beliefs basically operate (after the fact) to justify the self-interests of various groups.

Accordingly, Marx viewed religion as an ideology that justifies the current social arrangements. It serves as a tool of the upper classes and helps maintain stability. Marx, like Durkheim, viewed religion as a force for social integration. However, for Marx, this had a tragic consequence; religion served to maintain an unjust status quo. Religion acts to unite people of various classes with one another when, according to Marx, the lower classes should be uniting against all those in the upper class. In fact, the ideology that promised rewards in an afterlife for conformity in this world has had as much of a pacifying effect as opium (hence, his comment about religion being the "opium of the people").

Certainly there are many examples that would lend credence to the Marxian interpretation. The Hindu belief in reincarnation has led many lower-caste Indians to conform to the laws of *dharma*. Only by conforming to dharma (which reinforces caste lines) can one expect to be reincarnated in a higher position. Those who

Online Resources: The work of Karl Marx, although foundational for sociology, is often misquoted and misunderstood. Fortunately, thanks to free online resources, you can find and read Marx's ideas about religion for yourself. As part of the Marxists Internet Archive, you can do detailed searches of Marx's writing. Navigate to the landing page of the Marx and Engels section of the archive (marxists.org/archive/marx/index.htm) and enter "opium of the people" in the exact phrase search box, and you will be taken to the text of the "Introduction" to Marx's *A Contribution to the Critique of Hegel's "Philosophy of Right"* (first published in 1844). As you will see, this work begins with another famous phrase: "the criticism of religion is the prerequisite of all criticism."

violate these laws can expect to be reincarnated in some lower animal form. This sort of belief system tends to undermine any impetus to rebel against the social system. Christian beliefs in otherworldly salvation sometimes act in a similar way to pacify the poor and the disfranchised (see Chapter 9).

Conflict as a Source of Social Disruption

Not all conflict theorists emphasize that religion integrates and stabilizes society. In fact, a number of them emphasize that society is not well integrated at all. Society comprises interest groups, each of which seeks the fulfillment of its own self-interests. They believe there is no consensus over values and beliefs that serves to unite the society; rather, modern society is characterized by conflict, coercion, and power plays by various groups. When stability does occur in a society, it is because (a) a temporary balance of power exists between groups or (b) one group has gained enough power to control the others. Stability lasts only so long as the distribution of power remains the same. In this scenario, religious groups are simply viewed as one more set of interest groups in society. Hence, Marx's principle—that self-interest is the key factor in shaping social relationships—is a central emphasis of all conflict theory.

Interreligious Conflicts

Some conflicts involve hatred of those who adhere to a different faith, and this disrupts the working of the society as a whole. Conflicts between Christians and Jews provide a vivid example. Christians and Jews have coexisted in the Western world for nearly 2,000 years. Yet because Christianity has been the dominant religious force in Europe since late Roman times, Christian leaders have determined the nature of the relationship, and the result has often been profound *anti-Semitism*. (Although there are many Semitic peoples historically and linguistically, the term anti-Semitism has come to refer to hatred toward Jews.) For example, the day before Columbus first set out for America, all Jews were ordered to leave Spain. The same thing had occurred in England in 1290 and in France in 1306 (Berry and Tischler 1978).

The Holocaust (1941–1945)—known in Hebrew as the *Shoah*, for "catastrophe"—brought unprecedented attention to the issue of anti-Semitism. Although Adolf Hitler maintained the racial, not religious, superiority of Germans over Jews, the hostile views toward Jews that had been constructed over many centuries in Europe facilitated this state-sponsored killing of 6 million Jews (two thirds of the European Jewish population) by the Nazi regime and its collaborators (Longerich 2010). In 1988, the Catholic Church issued a document in which the Church officially acknowledged 2,000 years of hostility between Christians and Jews and apologized for "the errors and failures of those sons and daughters of the Church" during the Holocaust (Commission for Religious Relations with the Jews 1988). Still, the document fell short of accepting responsibility for helping to create the cultural atmosphere of anti-Semitism that made the Holocaust possible. It also specifically rejected controversial claims that the Pope at the time, Pius XII, did not do enough to challenge the Nazis, making him effectively "Hitler's Pope" (Cornwell 1999).

In the 21st century, anti-Semitism persists. In 2013–2014, the Anti-Defamation League (ADL)—founded in 1913 to defend the civil rights of Jews—conducted an unprecedented global public opinion project designed to measure attitudes toward Jews in over 100 countries (ADL 2014a). The ADL Global 100 includes data on 53,100 adults in 101 countries and the Palestinian territories in the West Bank and Gaza. This project builds on survey research the ADL has been conducting in the United States since 1964, in which respondents are read 11 statements about Jews and asked to indicate whether they think they are "probably true" or "probably false." Among the statements are "Jews have too much control over global affairs" and "Jews talk too much about what happened to them in the Holocaust." Individuals who say at least a majority (6 of 11) of the statements are probably true are counted as having anti-Semitic attitudes.

The ADL Global 100 reports an Index Score, the percentage of the population that is anti-Semitic, overall, for regions of the globe, and for every nation surveyed. The overall rate of anti-Semitism was 26% in 2013–2014. Aggregating these nations into regions of the globe, we find the following Index Scores:

- Middle East and North Africa   74%
- Eastern Europe   34%
- Western Europe   24%
- Sub-Saharan Africa   23%
- Asia   22%
- The Americas   19%
- Oceania   14%

Rates of anti-Semitism ranged from 93% in the Palestinian territories, 92% in Iraq, and 88% in Yemen to 4% in Sweden, 3% in the Philippines, and 0.2% in Laos.

Online Resources: The Anti-Defamation League's ADL Global 100 website (global100.adl.org) includes an interactive map in which you can explore the extent of anti-Semitism in different regions of the world or specific countries. You can also use the "compare" and "shuffle" functions to randomly compare rates between two countries overall or for specific questions.

The United States' Index Score of 9% ranks it tied for 95th (with Denmark) out of 102 countries surveyed. The ADL also reports that the number of anti-Semitic incidents in the United States fell by 19% in 2013, to 751 incidents, continuing a decade-long decline in such incidents (ADL 2014b). These data collected by the ADL are also supported by numbers reported by the Federal Bureau of Investigation (FBI) in its hate crime statistics. In 2013, nearly 6,000 hate crime incidents were reported. Of these, 17.4% were based on religion, compared to 48.5% based on race and 20.8% based on sexual orientation. Jews continue to be the most frequently targeted religious group in the United States for hate crimes, with nearly 60% of religious hate crimes against Jews and Jewish institutions (Federal Bureau of Investigation 2014).

As with anti-Semitism, Islamophobia—fear or hatred of Islam and its followers—has been a part of Christian Europe since Muslim immigrants began arriving in the 14th century. This has persisted to today, and in many cases worsened as Muslims have in many minds become associated with terrorism, especially in the United States since the attacks of 9/11. In the FBI hate crimes statistics just noted, 14.2% of religiously based offenses reported were anti-Islamic. Although Jews are most likely to be victims of hate crimes reported to law enforcement, Muslims in the

Used by permission of the United States Holocaust Memorial Museum

The most extreme expression of antipathy against a religious group occurred in the 1940s, when an estimated 6 million Jews were murdered by the Nazi regime in Germany and its European collaborators. The stated goal of Hitler was to exterminate all Jews. This scene is from the concentration camp at Buchenwald.

United States are most likely to report having experienced religious discrimination. According to a 2010 Gallup Poll, 48% of Muslims reported experiencing religious discrimination in the previous year, compared to 31% of Mormons, 25% of those with no religion, 21% of Jews, 20% of Catholics, and 18% of Protestants (Gallup 2013).

In a 2006 analysis of the sources of anti-Islamic attitudes, sociologist Stephen Johnson found that attending conservative Protestant churches had the biggest effect on holding anti-Islamic attitudes. Sociologist Saher Selod examines some of the results of anti-Muslim sentiment after 9/11 in the "Illustrating Sociological Concepts" box.

ILLUSTRATING SOCIOLOGICAL CONCEPTS

Anti-Muslim Sentiments in the United States

Saher Selod

On September 11, 2001, the United States experienced the largest terrorist attack on U.S. soil. Four airplanes were hijacked by terrorists. Two of the airplanes were flown into the World Trade Center, causing the two buildings to collapse. Another airplane crashed into the Pentagon, and the fourth plane crashed due to a revolt by the passengers on board. The attacks claimed the lives of close to 3,000 Americans. The terrorists were Muslims from Saudi Arabia, United Arab Emirates, and Egypt. These horrific events changed the lives of all Americans, including Muslim Americans and immigrants.

A few sociologists studied the impact 9/11 had on Muslims living in the United States (Bakalian and Bozorgmehr 2009; Cainkar 2009; Peek 2011). Some of the findings revealed that Muslims have become targets for antiterrorist laws and policies that were a part of a government-led campaign known as the "War on Terror" (Cainkar 2009). For example, a little over a month after the attacks, the USA PATRIOT Act (Uniting and Strengthening America by Providing Appropriate Tools Required to Intercept and Obstruct Terrorism Act) was signed into law. This 300-page document restricted the civil liberties of Muslims and any other American who could be connected to terrorism. The document loosely defined terrorism, justifying the surveillance of Muslims due to an inaccurate association of Islam with terrorism. As a result, mass deportations of Muslim immigrants for minor infractions of their visas were hidden from the public through the application of the Patriot Act. There was also an increase in visitations of Muslims by the FBI following 9/11.

Another policy passed after 9/11 was the National Security Entry-Exit Registration System, initiated in September 2002 by the Immigration and Naturalization Service. This law required noncitizen men over the age of 16 from 25 countries (of which 24 were Muslim) to register with the government. Muslim men were forced to submit fingerprints and had their photos taken as if they were potential criminals. One of the consequences of these laws and policies is that they created an environment where innocent people were treated as if they were guilty due to their shared religious identity with the perpetrators of the terrorist attacks. Since 9/11, over a thousand Muslims (mostly noncitizens) have been detained even though no connection to terrorism was determined. Furthermore, these policies have encouraged the distrust of Muslims.

Muslims living in the United States have reported a rise in prejudice and discrimination. Lori Peek's study, *Behind the Backlash: Muslim Americans After 9/11* (2011), highlights the backlash Muslims living in New York City and Colorado experienced in the few weeks after 9/11. Although it has been over 10 years since the terrorist attacks, anti-Muslim sentiments remain strong today. According to a Gallup report, 43% of Americans admitted to feeling some prejudice toward Muslims, and 31% of Americans view Islam unfavorably (Gallup 2009). These rising anti-Muslim sentiments have had a direct impact on the everyday life of the Muslim population. Statistics compiled by the FBI reveal hate crimes against Muslims increased by almost 50% from 2009 to 2010. In August 2012, a mosque in Joplin, Missouri, was burned to the ground by an arsonist. As a consequence of government policies targeting Muslims and the perpetuation of stereotypes and myths that Muslims are a threat to national security and American cultural values, Muslims are living with a new racialized identity.

Organizations such as the Council on American–Islamic Relations (CAIR) strive to counter stereotypes about Muslims and "enhance understanding of Islam, encourage dialogue, protect civil liberties, empower American Muslims, and build coalitions that promote justice and mutual understanding" (CAIR 2014). Working with other organizations, like the American Civil Liberties Union (ACLU), they fight bigotry and discrimination against Muslims living in the United States.

* * * * * * *

Saher Selod is an assistant professor of sociology at Simmons College. Her areas of research are race and ethnicity and sociology of religion—especially the Muslim experience in the United States.

Intrafaith Conflicts

Religio-economic conflict has certainly not been limited to that between Christians and non-Christians. In the United States, Protestants have used their dominant numbers and established positions of power to oppress Catholic immigrants. Because they were here first, Protestants were well established before Catholic immigrants of Irish, Italian, or Hispanic background came to this country. The Know-Nothing Party and the Ku Klux Klan are two examples of American movements that were intensely anti-Catholic and that limited membership to white, American-born Protestants. Some analysts insist that the temperance movement was also essentially an anti-Catholic phenomenon in which

Protestants sought to force their own definitions of Christian morality on Catholics and Jews (Gusfield 1963). The Anti-Saloon League, formed in 1896, specifically attacked the symbol of the urban, ethnic, Catholic, lower-class leisure lifestyle. For many Protestants, the saloon was a symbol of Irish Catholics, who had immigrated in large numbers, were taking jobs, and were beginning to upset the economic and political advantage Protestants had enjoyed. In 1844, the conflicts between Protestants and Catholics actually deteriorated to armed combat in Philadelphia (Shannon 1963).

According to this analysis, Prohibition was largely an attempt to define ethnic Catholic lifestyles as illegal and thereby to label such persons as deviants. Protestants continued to

"Ganges1876." Licensed under Public Domain via Wikimedia Commons

THE AMERICAN RIVER GANGES.

This editorial cartoon in *Harper's Weekly* from 1876 depicts the Vatican in the background and Roman Catholic bishops in the foreground. The bishops appear as crocodiles attacking U.S. public schools and schoolchildren with the support of Irish Catholic politicians.

dominate the top positions in business and finance into the 1950s, with Catholics—regardless of competence or credentials—effectively shut out. For example, Charles Anderson reported that in the mid-1950s, 93% of the top executives in manufacturing, mining, and finance were Protestant and that Protestants held 85% of the highest positions in the 200 largest corporations (Anderson 1970). This was despite the fact that Catholics comprised approximately 25% of the American population (Greeley 1974; Stark and Glock 1968). Fortunately, since then, levels of anti-Catholicity among Protestants and anti-Protestant sentiments among Catholics have declined. Still, Protestants have clearly been an interest group that used a position of power and influence to ensure an economic advantage (see Chapter 9).

Hostility against "those others" varies in large measure with the extent to which lines of religious affiliation are coextensive with ethnic and class lines. When ethnic ties and economic interests act to create social solidarity, religious differences may serve as one more symbol of differentiation.

American and Canadian societies are increasingly characterized by many cross pressures and countervailing forces. People may have group loyalties, friendships, and business partnerships that involve alliances with members of other religious groups, social classes, and ethnic groups. Insofar as this is true, the multiplicity of crossed alliances provides the basis for integration and social stability. Interreligious conflict is less severe in those settings where religious, ethnic, and class lines are not coextensive and where countervailing forces can provide structural integration to the society. In this circumstance, there is less tendency to view members of other faiths as enemies.

Conflicts Regarding
Religious and Secular Authority

Religion may prove divisive in another instance: recognition of what constitutes proper authority. The central value system of a religion may come into conflict with the secular legal system. In this case, people must choose which set of values and norms they will respect. Often this boils down to the issue of which value system is authoritative or which leader (religious or political) is attributed with proper authority. In the late 1960s and early 1970s, a number of religiously motivated individuals violated federal laws in protest of the Vietnam War (Hall 1990). For example, two Roman Catholic priests, Daniel and Philip Berrigan, broke into draft board offices and poured blood on files. They maintained that their Christian conscience would not permit them to remain idle while young men were being drafted for war. Likewise in the 1980s, evangelical Christians bombed and sabotaged abortion clinics, despite the illegality of the act in the civil law (Blanchard and Prewitt 1993), while liberal Christians provided sanctuary to Central American immigrants who— fleeing the war in that region—were in the United States illegally (Smith 1996b). While the movement is less visible in the press and has modified tactics, it reemerged in 2007 as the New Sanctuary Movement. It continues to directly challenge the government over immigration and asylum policy (Yukich 2013). In these and other such cases, a person's theological understanding may generate norms that differ from those the civil laws uphold.

The Amish regulation that their children must not go to school beyond the eighth grade provides another example of conflict between religious and state authorities. When this norm conflicted with state law compelling all children to stay in school until graduation or age 16, some Amish parents in the 1950s and 1960s chose to go to jail rather than obey the law. In 1972, the Supreme Court settled the issue in *Wisconsin v. Yoder*, ruling that a state is in violation of the First and Fourteenth Amendments to the Constitution if it forces the Amish to send their children to high school (Hostetler 1993).

The Mormons also encountered intense conflict with the federal government in the 19th century. In this case, the issue was over which authority, the church or the state, would decide how many wives a man may have. The Supreme Court ruled against the Mormons, and later Latter-day Saints leaders revised their doctrine in conformity with federal law. However, conflict between the Mormon Church and the government had nearly escalated to a small-scale civil war.

In each of these cases, religious norms have conflicted with secular law. The result has been considerable disruption of social harmony and unity. Whether the disruption was good or bad is not our concern here; the point is that religious loyalties sometimes result in discord and conflict in the larger society. Religiously motivated people often march to the beat of a different drummer. Religion, then, may contribute to either consensus or dissension.

Conflict as a Source of Integration

While religious conflict may bring disruption to the larger society, it may also be a source of internal unity for the religious group. Some groups seem to cultivate conflict with the outgroup because conflict is functional to the group's internal solidarity. As we will see in Chapter 5, groups with high boundaries usually sustain stronger member commitment and retention than do those with low boundaries. Some Amish groups shun their deviant members— especially those who marry outside the group or who adopt the lifestyle of the outside. The shunning, or *meidung*, involves a refusal to interact with persons so labeled. In some cases, Amish parents whose child marries outside the group have considered the child to be dead, have refused to speak the child's name, and have refused to acknowledge the child's presence when in the same room. The interesting point sociologically is that those groups that are very strict about practicing *meidung* have greater retention of members than do more liberal Amish groups (Hostetler 1993; Kraybill 2001).

Conflict produces internal cohesion for several reasons. First, repression and hostility by outsiders tend to create a feeling of common plight and common destiny. The more animosity that neighbors direct toward the Amish, the more inner unity is created within Amish communities. In the late 1970s, there were a series of incidents of youths attacking Amish buggies, and at least one person was killed—an Amish infant whose skull was crushed by a rock. Such an attack bonded together Amish communities that previously had been in conflict.

Second, a common rejection of something helps articulate one's own beliefs. Actually, it is usually easier for members of a group to agree that they reject something than it is to formulate a constructive statement about what they do believe. A shared disgust at the actions of a deviant member may provide unity for the conformists (Erikson 1966). Likewise, rejection of worldliness or of some specific religious movement (e.g., satanic cults) may be a significant source of group harmony. For this reason, social conflict and social integration must be seen not as opposites but as different sides of the same coin.

One can see the same phenomenon at work at the national level. When the United States was at war with Iraq over Saddam Hussein's invasion of Kuwait, the sense of patriotism in both countries was greatly strengthened. The same was true following the 9/11 terrorist attacks. Conflict in one situation often creates integration and unity in another. Moreover, the most threatening conflict occurs within the context of a meaningful or important relationship with others. When conflict occurs, it is within a larger system of interrelatedness. Social harmony and social conflict must be understood together (Coser 1954).

Conflict as a Source of Change

Conflict is often a source of change. Clearly, religion is capable of contributing to conflict and to social change. One aspect of religion that most interested Max Weber was the role of the charismatic leader. He found charisma to be fundamentally contrary to social stability and a major source of change (Weber [1922] 1963, 1946, 1947). As a person who is attributed with divine authority, the charismatic religious leader is able to challenge social mores where there is otherwise little room for social and political dissent. (This will be treated further in Chapter 7.)

In the eyes of those who defend the status quo, such conflict is disruptive and therefore dysfunctional. Such conflict is indeed disruptive, but disruption may be needed. Religiously motivated abolitionism was thought to be dysfunctional by slave owners. In terms of the interests of blacks and in terms of the structure of contemporary postindustrial society, abolitionism was clearly a beneficial disruption of the status quo. Religion is capable of disruption because religious values sometimes define social relationships differently than the encompassing culture does. If a religious ideology maintains that all people are equal before God and if the society is rigidly stratified, a dissonance may be created for those who take the religious ideology seriously. By affirming the innate personal worth of blacks, the African American church in the United States provided a foundation for these oppressed people to assert their rights and to insist on social change. As we explain at length in Chapter 12, it was no mere coincidence that Martin Luther King Jr. was both a civil rights leader and a Baptist minister. Whether the contribution is direct or indirect, religion can contribute to the modification of the larger society, for it can provide an alternative worldview and an alternative set of values.

On the other hand, conflict and change in the society itself can also be a major source of religious change. Rapid social change is one factor in the rise of new religious movements. Societies that are stable and highly integrated are not conducive to the emergence and expansion of religious cults, but loosely integrated, changing societies do experience such phenomena with great frequency (Stark and Roberts 1982).

The broad sweep of social change in the direction of secularization has also brought modifications in religion. The advent of rational, scientific, empirically oriented culture has caused changes in the worldviews of many people. Scientific interpretations of such issues as the origins of humanity have induced liberal theologians to reformulate religious ideas so that they are compatible with scientific ones. This, of course, has involved conflicts between modernists and conservatives within religious bodies. Hence, the growth of science as a major institution—an institution autonomous from religious authority—has led to changes and conflicts within religious groups. As will be amply illustrated throughout this text, changes and conflicts in the larger society often result in changes and conflicts within religious bodies.

Conflict as a Pervasive Element in All Social Life

Marxian theory suggests that conflict is pervasive in human life; it can arise not only between groups but also within them. Social behavior is always guided by individuals and groups protecting their self-interests. For Marxian theorists, social animosity and inequality are always the result of a struggle for power, privilege, and prestige. Religious groups experience these processes no less than other groups.

For example, men have dominated the leadership roles in most denominations. In Orthodox Jewish groups, only male members are counted as part of the necessary quorum for prayer meetings. Until recent decades, most Protestant congregations excluded women from the ordained ministry or even from lay positions of leadership (such as

offices of deacon or elder in Congregational or Presbyterian churches). Some conflict theorists have viewed these practices as evidence that men are an interest group—whose members cling tenaciously to their positions of authority and power (see the discussion in Chapter 11).

Intrachurch conflicts between clergy and laity or between theological liberals and conservatives may also be rooted in socioeconomic competition and class conflict. Peter Berger suggested this conflict is actually between two elites in American society that are struggling for power, privilege, and prestige. One is the business elite—a class of people managing industrial production and manipulating business enterprise. This group is more attuned to conservative theology, as is evidenced in the conservatism of most laity. Berger claims that conservative theology tends to justify the self-interests of the business elite.

The "new elite" are those who manipulate symbols and words and who manage the production of ideas. This group includes intellectuals, educators, members of the helping professions, media people, and various social planners and bureaucrats. Highly educated clergy of the mainline denominations are also part of this group, which advocates federal support of education, social welfare, minority rights, and environmental protection. This new class is highly represented in government-supported work, and its members argue for increased business regulation. Hence, this new elite really seeks its own self-interests. Berger insisted that proclamations by the National Council of Churches normally reflect the current interests of this new class. Clergy and modernists are much more likely to support the National Council than are the laity in general and conservatives in particular. Producers of ideas and producers of material objects are viewed as two diverse social classes in a postindustrial society. The conflict between such groups as the Christian Right and the National Council of Churches is interpreted as part of a deeper struggle for access to power and privilege (Berger 1981).

Even the conflict over creationism versus science can be viewed as being, in part, a conflict of self-interests. Christians who are well educated, whose professions are related to scientific investigation, or whose business depends on scientific advances tend to be the ones who dismiss creationism and claim that theology should be reformulated to be consistent with science. In other words, theological modernism can be self-serving. On the other hand, biblical literalism is adhered to largely by the lower- and working-class people—folks whose jobs are sometimes threatened by technological innovations. Furthermore, working-class Americans may be rankled by a perception that many of the persons who occupy high-paying and high-prestige positions—physicians and scientists—are foreign born. Antiscientific views may be interpreted—through a conflict theory analysis—as veiled attacks on those who threaten the jobs and prestige of lower-class Protestants. Although such an

analysis certainly does not tell the whole story, it does raise some interesting questions about the extent to which our behavior—including religious behavior and beliefs—is influenced by our self-interests.

A second contribution of conflict theory is that it focuses attention on issues of change. Religious conflicts can contribute to social change, and social conflicts can cause religious change. Those changes may create social dissension and disruption, but depending on the nature and location of the conflict (external versus internal), they are also capable of contributing to the integration and cohesion of a group.

Conflict theory's tendency to use historical analysis is another strength. In using historical perspective and data, it offers an important corrective to more static theories that ignore the specific causes of a contemporary social pattern.

Most important, perhaps, conflict theory illuminates the many ways in which self-interests

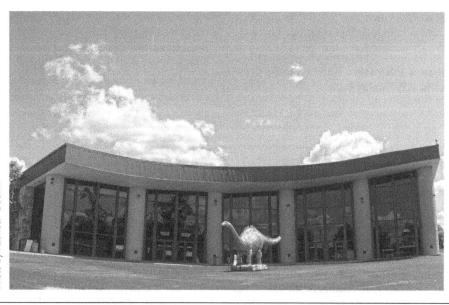

Photo by Kathleen Oberlin

Kathleen Oberlin's (2014) work on the creationist social movement shifts the analysis of long-standing controversies surrounding creationism from courtrooms and textbooks to a new setting: a natural history museum. The Creation Museum in Petersburg, Kentucky, was built in 2007 by Answers in Genesis (AiG). The museum promotes a biblically literalist interpretation of the creation of the universe over an evolutionary view.

affect perceptions and behavior—including religious ideas and (supposedly) religiously motivated behavior.

Critical Thinking: How might your own self-interests have shaped your religious beliefs? Do you think it is true that our economic self-interests may bias or even completely blind us as we seek eternal truths? Why or why not?

Problems With Conflict Analysis

Although conflict theory offers important insights and correctives to functional analysis, it is not without its problems. If functional theory often errs in overemphasizing consensus and harmony, conflict theorists often see only social stress, power plays, and disharmony. Although conflict theory is helpful in illuminating the causes of change, it is less complete in explaining social cohesion and cooperation.

Perhaps the most important criticism of conflict theory is its tendency to view all behavior as motivated by self-interest. For those who believe that religious commitment may call a person to genuine unselfish action, the appeal to self-interests as the ultimate motivator of all behavior is unsatisfactory (Smith 2003a). The response among conflict theorists is that appeals to altruistic motives are simply ways of mystifying or hiding the true motives. However, the willingness of deeply religious persons to sacrifice even their lives for others or for their faith raises questions about this unicausal interpretation. Persons may be influenced by a wide range of motives. Conflict theory correctly points out that self-interests can be pervasive and can influence a wide range of behavior and attitudes. However, when it insists that *all* behavior is determined by self-interests, conflict theory commits the error of reductionism.

Another problem with this emphasis on self-interests is that interests are often interpreted only in economic terms. Although economic self-interests are more encompassing than we once realized, other sorts of self-interests can

also profoundly affect behavior. For example, a calculation of one's spiritual self-interests—such as a desire to attain a heavenly afterlife and avoid hell—could cause persons to behave in ways that are contrary to their economic self-interests. Religious moods and motivations are, to quote Geertz, "powerful, pervasive, and long-lasting" (Geertz 1973:90). They are capable of influencing behavior in ways that are insensitive to economic consequences. Conflict theory does not normally take into account such forces.

Conflict theory stresses conflict and dissension and the role of self-interests in shaping behavior. It de-emphasizes the harmony, consensus, and interrelatedness that so intrigue functionalists. There is no shortage of data on conflict within religious groups, but given all of the conflict that does exist, most groups cohere surprisingly well.

TOWARD SYNTHESIS: AN OPEN SYSTEMS MODEL

Some sociologists believe that no synthesis of the structural functional and conflict perspectives is possible. They do offer very different perspectives on society and on human behavior. However, one effort to combine the insights of both perspectives is promising. That approach is called open systems theory. Variations of systems theory have been used to understand units as small as nuclear families and processes as large as the "world system" of international economic interdependence (Shannon 1989; Wallerstein 1974, 1984). Interestingly, systems theory—especially world systems theory—is often claimed to be an outgrowth of conflict theory, but structural functionalists also claim that the systems approach is an extension of their perspective. Open systems theory is not a panacea; it does not solve all of the problems or discrepancies between the two dominant macro perspectives, but it does offer some overview of how an entire system may be characterized simultaneously by interdependence and by conflicts of interest.

Contemporary systems models stress the idea that societies are both stable and dynamic, depending on whether one focuses on structure or on processes. Structure refers to the organized aspects of a society; this dimension of a social system is resistant to change. The structure can be diagrammed on an organizational chart: statuses, roles, departments, and organizational units each in relationship to one another. Religious denominations have stable sources of income, officers who fill certain roles and responsibilities, and clergy who are responsible to bishops or district superintendents. Local faith communities have commissions and committees that make decisions regarding certain parts of the life of that church or temple: worship, religious education, fund-raising, care of the building, and so forth. These offices or interrelated positions may evolve over a period of time, but generally they remain with similar job descriptions and a consistent set of responsibilities. This is structure.

On the other hand, the process aspect of a social system is characterized by action; nothing is ever fixed or final. The members of committees change; the clergy retire or move to new churches or temples and are replaced in the old ones; and the values and ideas of the congregation are transformed in light of national events (such as a recession), international crises (such as a war in which some members are called to serve and others feel compelled to oppose), or local incidents (such as a hate crime against a homosexual in the community). Such happenings may change the value orientations of members, bring a shift in perceived interests of various groups, or induce a transfer in the allocation of resources within the organization. While it is true that organizations are somewhat stable, it is equally true that they are always becoming something new as they interact with the larger environment.

Structure and process are both necessary parts of any social unit; they cannot be separated. Structure provides the context for action; but action brings the structure to life. Without process, an organization would wither and die; without structure, action would be disorganized and aimless (Ballantine and Hammack 2008; Olsen 1978).

Figure 3.3 illustrates one dimension of the systems perspective on how organizations work. Any organization or institution exists within a field of forces, which it tries to influence and which try to influence it. The model provided here is simplified for our understanding, but it is important to recognize that the "organization" in this diagram might be a nation (e.g., Canada), a national institution (e.g., a particular denomination), a local organization (e.g., a congregation), a unit within a local religious community (e.g., the religious education committee of the congregation), or a subsystem of the education program (e.g., an adult scriptural study class).

One of the first points that we must comprehend is that all organizations have *outputs*. For schools, the outputs are graduates, new ideas, new skills and ways of doing things, and developing cultural values and outlooks. For religious organizations, the outputs or "products" that influence the larger culture include the following: values, attitudes, benevolence or "mission" programs, published instructional materials, broadcast programming, movements to influence the larger society (e.g., peace organizations, antiabortion groups, and movements to have "creation science" taught in the science curriculum of the public schools). Nearly all organizations want to influence, at least in some marginal way, the larger social environment in which they exist. Their outputs are the means through which they do this. Even if influencing the larger culture is not an explicit goal, religious groups are bound to have some impact on the secular society around them as these groups struggle for resources necessary for survival. Also, religious groups typically feel an obligation to engage in benevolent acts, or what they interpret as benevolent acts, for those "less fortunate." This requires outputs beyond the boundaries of their own group.

As the diagram suggests, outputs of any organization will enter and influence the environment—that is, the dominant culture or

Figure 3.3 Open Systems Model

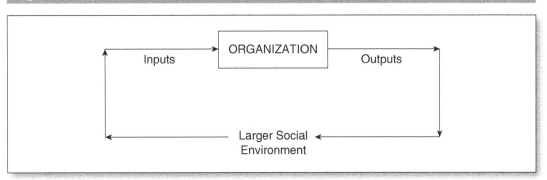

larger society. The extent of influence varies with the goals and purposes of the group and with the amount of power the group wields. Regardless of the intent of the religious groups themselves, segments of the larger society are being influenced by the religious organization and may even be competing with it for resources (including the time, energy, and monetary donations of members) and for the ability to shape central values and beliefs of the culture. Therefore, those in the social environment want to influence the religion itself. So the final dimension of the process is *inputs* into the organization: new members, secular values and beliefs (including nationalistic pride, scientific theories, and definitions of morality), attempts by governments to legislate religious groups (such as financial disclosure requirements to prevent fraud), new ideas (e.g., use of the latest business principles to manage a large congregation), and even new technologies (including computerization of mailing lists and sophisticated technology to record religious services).

Critical Thinking: How might a global event influence a religious community? How could other institutions (e.g., economics, the family, government, sports) affect a religious group? How might a religion influence or impact other institutions in society?

The more the organization is an *open system*, the freer is the flow of both information and resources to and from the surrounding society. In theory, a totally open system would have a completely open interaction with the larger society. In reality, in all environments there are some people who will resist influence from the organization because their own interests are threatened. Further, all systems like to control the input from the community. In fact, in order to develop in a controlled manner, any organization must maintain an appropriate ratio of input and output. Internal needs of the organization demand some filtering of the flow of information (Olsen 1978).

At the other end of the spectrum, some groups are *closed systems*, organizations that try to exclude outside influence as much as possible and whose desire to shape the larger culture is minimal. It is as if the group built an enormous barricade around the organization. That barricade is what sociologists call a social boundary. Especially important for some groups is the building of a wall preventing inputs, often to protect the self-interests of the organization. We will see examples of this resistance to input from the surrounding society later on in this book. No organization, however, is totally closed, for all must live in an interdependent relationship with the environment. For effective adaptation to new circumstances, any organization must have some flow of information into the organization from the environment, but the important point here is that each group is selective about—or at least *tries* to control—what penetrates the organization. Religious liberals and religious conservatives each try to filter the inputs (with varying degrees of success), but both allow inputs of one kind or another.

No one diagram can fully explain all of the complexities of the systems approach. Figure 3.4 illuminates another dimension of the social systems view of society. As Marvin Olsen put it, "Organizations overlap and interlock with each other, forming a gigantic social web, the totality of which is human social life" (Olsen 1978:99). Any organization or system is made up of a number of interdependent parts. A family is made up of the various members who are linked together with a variety of bonds and obligations. Imagine that in Figure 3.4, each dot represents a member of your family and the lines between the dots represent the bonds of love and concern. If one person is undergoing some stress (e.g., chemical dependency, unemployment or job stress, or poor health), the rest of the family might well support that individual by taking up some of his or her roles, by offering emotional support, and by helping in other ways. This stressor on one person might then cause stressors on other family members as they try to help out and "make things work" during this time of special tension.

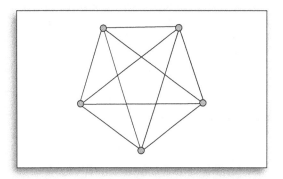

Figure 3.4 Systems Composed of Subsystems

Religious groups are also characterized by interdependent roles and statuses, each dependent upon the other for effective functioning. For the religious education committee to do its job, the stewardship committee must solicit enough money from the congregation to meet the budget. Likewise, the stewardship committee may not be able to be successful if the worship committee and the minister do not function effectively and members find worship unsatisfying and empty.

Yet systems are not just dependent upon each other; each system is related to other systems. The family is linked to and dependent upon many other institutions: health care, the workplace, schools, the religious community, the criminal justice system, the banking system, and so forth. If any one of those systems is not functioning properly, the family experiences pulls and tugs on their own life. If the economy is in recession and the workplace lays off family members, or if the agents of law enforcement are harassing members of your ethnic group, or if your local congregation is wracked with angry conflict and division, the family will likely feel the stress. Likewise, if families are not socializing their children with values consistent with those of the temple or church (or are not functioning at all), or if large numbers of the membership are out of work and unable to pay their pledges because of local industry closings, the congregation and even the denomination will feel the stress.

All of these institutions (and others) comprise an interdependent system that makes up the nation. However, our nation is only one system that is related to many others: Great Britain, Canada, Iraq, Germany, Russia, Somalia, Pakistan, Israel, El Salvador, Nigeria, and so forth (see Figure 3.5). If we have trade relations or diplomatic concerns with another system (which we most assuredly do), then a malfunction in that country or that region of the world may cause stresses on our nation. If war is declared in the Persian Gulf or Afghanistan, stresses are generated on the resources of our country, and they impact families (whose members may be called into combat duty), the economy, the churches (which may have some members advocating peace and others wanting the congregation to support the war effort), and so forth.

Figure 3.5 The Interdependence of Social Systems

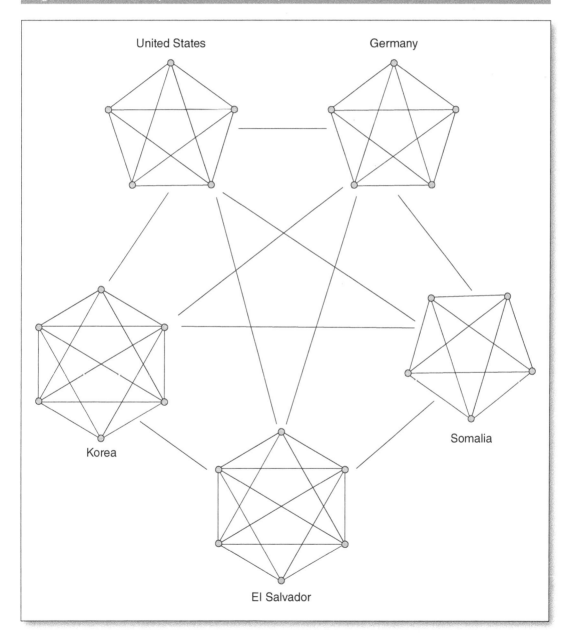

Likewise, an economic recession in Europe or Japan can influence trade and therefore negatively impact certain businesses in other countries; a destruction of rain forests can have devastating effects on the health care community as certain medicines become scarcer.

Some institutions would be influenced directly and profoundly by stresses in the global system; others would experience only indirect impact. The important point is that social systems are interrelated in a variety of ways; this brief discussion greatly oversimplifies the complexity of the ties, but our purpose here is to illustrate the point that social systems are layered. Subsystems exist within subsystems, which exist within subsystems. Sometimes subsystems are parts of two or more overlapping macro systems (Olsen 1978). One example would be a military chaplaincy in which the chaplain is both an officer in the military (and answerable to that hierarchy) and an ordained member of a specific denomination (and responsible to a bishop and/or to denominational policies and values).

Similar to structural functional theory, systems models stress the interrelatedness of society. Unlike functionalist approaches, there is no assumption of harmony and consensus within the system. Indeed, systems often experience conflict and tension as various units pursue their own self-interests. Further, those with power in the larger society are often able to ensure that various institutions (such as religion) serve and legitimize their own positions of privilege. Also contrary to functional theories, systems models view societies as dynamic and changing. While there may be some forces pushing toward coherence and stability, the model is anything but stagnant. The ties between units may be stressful rather than supportive, and that stress is itself not necessarily viewed as negative. Stress may bring change and enhance the health of the organization in the long run. However, at any given period of history, a system may indeed be characterized by fairly high levels of consensus and relative stability. Rather than assuming either

harmony or discord, systems models leave that question open to investigation for the specific system and period of history.

Critical Thinking: In what sense is open systems theory a synthesis of functional and conflict theories?

SUMMARY

Irrespective of the ultimate truth or fiction of a religious ideology, religion has certain kinds of social effects or consequences. These consequences are what most interest sociologists. Functional theorists tend to focus on the beneficial role religion plays. For example, at an individual level, religion may offer a sense of meaning in life, sacralize and give certainty to a system of moral values, and establish a sense of belonging. Religion thereby affects an individual's sense of identity. Furthermore, religion can also serve societal functions. By providing a sense of values and beliefs around which a social consensus is formed, religion may contribute to social coherence and harmony. This is especially true for societies in which there is only one religious tradition.

On the other hand, religion is sometimes characterized by conflict—experiencing internal discord and/or contributing to conflict in the larger society. Dissension itself may be either beneficial or disruptive, healthy or unhealthy. Conflict theorists tend to focus on dissension, disruption, and change. Conflict theorists also tend to emphasize the role of self-interests in human behavior, including supposedly religious behavior.

Conflict and functional theories need not be mutually exclusive. Both offer important insights, and each has blind spots in its views of society. We will be incorporating insights and analysis from both perspectives in this book. No analysis that relies on only one perspective can offer a rounded understanding of the relationship between religion and society.

The central fact to remember is that the balances of harmony versus dissonance and of value consensus versus interest-group coercion will vary from one society to another. Furthermore, the amount of integration or conflict within religious groups varies significantly.

The systems model of social organization attempts to integrate many of the key ideas of both structural functional and conflict theories. Systems approaches stress the fact that the structures of society tend to be rather integrated and stable, while processes of societies are dynamic and action-oriented. Systems are viewed as composed of subsystems, which are composed of subsystems, with the largest systems being global in nature. This view of organizations stresses the interrelatedness of social units, but it does not presume harmony within the system and does not predict that any one element of the system is indispensable. Religion is viewed from this approach as a complex system, linked to other elements of society in intricate ways and often protecting its own self-interests in relationship to the larger society. Open systems theory will be used to understand the dynamics of religion throughout this book.

In the next chapter, we will look at the cultural construction of religion, exploring such elements as belief, ritual, symbol, nonrational transformative experiences, and worldview and examining the complex relationship among them.

4

THE CULTURAL CONSTRUCTION OF RELIGION

Experience, Myth, Ritual, Symbols, and Worldview

HERE ARE SOME QUESTIONS TO PONDER AS YOU READ THIS CHAPTER

- What does it mean to say that religion is culturally constructed?
- What are the characteristics of the sacred *experience* of the holy?
- How do myths, rituals, and symbols interact with one another?
- How do myths, rituals, and symbols support a religious worldview?
- What is the importance of a religious ethos, and how does it relate to one's worldview?
- How does a social constructionist perspective help us understand religion?

Having investigated the ways in which religion operates in society and in individuals' lives, it is appropriate next to examine religion as a cultural system and to investigate the internal interrelationships of its elements. According to sociologist Andrew Greeley, if we want to understand religion, we need to focus not on its prose or "cognitive superstructure" (doctrine) but on its poetry or "imaginative and narrative infrastructure" (experience, symbol, story, community, ritual) (Greeley 1995). For Greeley, "the origins and raw power of religion are at the imaginative (that is, experiential and narrative) level both for the individual and for the tradition" (Greeley 2000:4).

Nonrational religious experience, myths, rituals, symbol systems, worldviews, and ethos are all part of this complex phenomenon we call religion. Scholars are interested in how each of these facets relates to the others, and how they sometimes create integrity and sometimes dissonance in religious groups.

THE SOCIAL CONSTRUCTION OF REALITY

The idea that reality is socially constructed comes from a classic work in sociology by Peter Berger and Thomas Luckmann (1966). Berger and Luckmann wanted to explain how people's conceptions of reality are created and become institutionalized in society. Berger (1967) later applied this perspective specifically to religion.

According to the social constructionist view, "Social order is a human product, or more precisely, an ongoing human production" (Berger and Luckmann 1966:52), one that "continuously acts back upon its producer" (Berger 1967:3). The social order that humans create comes about in a dialectical process of (1) externalization, (2) objectivation, and (3) internalization.

Unlike many animals, humans are "unfinished" at birth due to our underspecialized and undirected instinctual structure. Consequently, humans must make a "world" for themselves, externalizing a world we call culture. In particular, we create symbols (and symbolic acts) that help us to interpret the world around us and communicate with each other. Religious symbols, as we will see, are crucial to this. Examples of symbols include the Star of David, the cross, the star and crescent, the eight-spoked wheel, and the Aum. Greetings are also a good example of externalization, from traditional handshakes or bows to newer forms like "daps" and fist bumps. In creating this cultural "world," humans provide order not only for their society but also for themselves.

The second step in the process of social construction is objectivation: "The transformation of man's products into a world that not only derives from man, but that comes to confront him as a facticity outside himself.... The humanly produced world becomes something 'out there'" (Berger 1967:8–9). Consider social roles, for example—what it means to be a "man" or a "woman," a "father" or a "mother," an "atheist" or a "believer." These roles are socially constructed, but they very much shape and constrain the actions of those playing them.

Similarly, religious symbols have a reality beyond their creators. Who was it that designed the Star of David and gave it meaning? Most people do not know, but they do know what the symbol stands for. They do share with others the meaning of this object. In fact, they may feel intense loyalty to the object. An entire history of a people may be recalled and a set of values rekindled when the symbol is displayed.

This is because other people have internalized the objectified symbol. In this final step, the objectified world is reabsorbed into the individual's subjective consciousness through the process of socialization. For example, when we internalize social roles, we do not simply see ourselves playing a role like an actor (e.g., "I'm not a professor, but I play one on TV"), but we actually identify ourselves in terms of that role. We inhabit the role; we are the role: "I am a professor."

Having briefly introduced the social constructionist perspective, let us begin exploring the roles of religious experience, myths, rituals, and symbol systems and investigating the relationships among them. We also discuss the way in which these specific manifestations of religion are related to the more intangible elements of worldview and ethos.

The Experiential Dimension of Religion

The social construction of reality begins with human experience and the externalizations that grow out of it. It is appropriate, therefore, to begin with a consideration of the experiential dimension—some would say the experiential *core*—of religion.

Many social scientists define religion in terms of the sacred–profane distinction. For these scholars, the essence of religion has to do with a unique and extraordinary experience—an experience that has a sacred dimension and is unlike everyday life. According to some scholars, all religious phenomena evolve out of this seminal experience—the experience of the holy (James [1902] 1958; O'Dea 1966; Otto 1923). Such an experience is often called nonrational, for it is neither rational nor irrational. These nonrational experiences are described by those who have them as being outside the usual categories of logical, systematic reasoning. They are not illogical; they are simply nonlogical. These experiences seem to defy the normal categories of language. Whether a nonrational experience is the essence of all religious behavior may be debatable; that such mystical experience is one important aspect of the complex experience we call religion is not. Émile Durkheim in 1912 was one of the early scholars to discuss characteristics of the sacred. Using a broad description of religious experience that he believed would be applicable in all cultures, Durkheim defined the sacred realm as one that both attracts and repels individuals. The sacred is not only attractive but also repugnant; it is capable not only of being helpful but also of being dangerous (Durkheim [1912] 1995). This ambiguity rests in part in the

This Greek Orthodox painting that appears in the Stavronikita Monastery is typical of the icons throughout Greece. All Orthodox icons show a rather unusual hand configuration with the thumb and the ring finger crossed, the little finger and the index finger pointed almost straight up in the air, and the middle finger slightly bent. When Keith Roberts—one of the authors of this book—asked a priest about it, he was told that this is the symbol of Christianity. He was told this with considerable impatience—as if *anyone* who was Christian would most certainly know that. It is interesting that *all* Greek Orthodox icons of Jesus depict his hand in this posture. At this point, no one knows who created this symbol, but it is so objectified and internalized in the Orthodox Church that it is inconceivable to Greeks that this symbol of Christ has not always existed. Christ is even thought to have used it as a tiny infant, always with the right hand and often with both hands.

attribution of great power to the sacred; because of the overwhelming power that it possesses, it holds the potential for being either beneficial or harmful. Nevertheless, the attraction of the sacred is not based primarily on utilitarian considerations. The sacred is understood as a *nonempirical force* that is considered intrinsically valuable. As such, it places a moral obligation on the worshipper and imposes certain ethical imperatives.

Rudolf Otto explored the nature of the religious experience in his classic book *The Idea of the Holy* (1923). In that work, Otto insisted that there is a tendency of people in Western culture to reduce the holy to rational concepts about God. Otto's contention was that holiness cannot be reduced to intellectual concepts; hence, he attempted to describe solely the human experience of the sacred. He insisted that the experience of the holy is so unique that one can never fully understand his description unless one has experienced it; the experience seems to bring forth a "creative consciousness." A person is profoundly humbled as he or she senses an utter dependency and unworthiness before the holy. (See the "Illustrating Sociological Concepts" feature.) Rational and moral conceptions about religion come only much later, as an outgrowth of the experience itself.

ILLUSTRATING SOCIOLOGICAL CONCEPTS

Personal Accounts of Religious Experiences

I remember the night, and almost the very spot on the hilltop, where my soul opened out, as it were, into the Infinite, and there was a rushing together of the two worlds, the inner and the outer. It was deep calling unto deep—the deep that my own struggle had opened up within being answered by the unfathomable deep without, reaching beyond the stars. I stood alone with Him who had made me, and all the beauty of the world, and love, and sorrow, and even temptation. I did not seek Him, but felt the perfect unison of my spirit with His. The ordinary sense of things around me faded. For the moment nothing but an ineffable joy and exaltation remained. It is impossible fully to describe the experience. It was like the effect of some great orchestra when all the separate notes have melted into one swelling harmony that leaves the listener conscious of nothing save that his soul is being wafted upwards, and almost bursting with its own emotion . . . I could not any more have doubted that *He* was there than that I was. Indeed, I felt myself to be, if possible, the less real of the two. (James [1902] 1958:66)

In that time the consciousness of God's nearness came to me sometimes. I say God, to describe what is indescribable. A presence, I might say, yet that is too suggestive of personality, and the moments of which I speak did not hold the consciousness of a personality, but something in myself made me feel myself a part of something bigger than I, that was controlling. I felt myself one with the grass, the trees, birds, insects, everything in Nature. I exulted in the mere fact of existence, of being a part of it all . . . In the years following, such moments continued to come, but I wanted them constantly. I knew so well the satisfaction of losing self in a perception of supreme power and love, that I was unhappy because that perception was not constant. (James [1902] 1958:303)

SOURCE: James, William. [1902] 1958. *Varieties of Religious Experience*. New York: New American Library.

Otto elaborated on the quality of this experience, which he called the *mysterium tremendum et fascinosum*. He identified five qualities of the *mysterium tremendum*. First, the individual is filled with a sense of awe and fear. The word *tremendum* itself expresses the tremor or terror that Otto felt was part of the experience. The story of Moses awed and frightened by the burning bush provides an example of feelings a religious experience generates.

Second, one feels overwhelmed by the absolute unapproachability of the holy. Durkheim's concept of the sacred as a dangerous force is shared by Otto. The ancient Hebrew prohibition against even mentioning the name of Yahweh because of God's absolute power and unapproachability provides an example. One can also see elements of unapproachability in many "high churches" that allow only the clergy to enter the chancel area.

This leads us to the third characteristic: power, energy, or urgency. Otto claimed that in describing the experience of the holy, people use such symbolic language as "vitality, passion, emotional temper, will, force, movement, excitement, activity, impetus" (Otto 1923:23).

Fourth, the experience of *mysterium tremendum* causes an awareness of the "wholly otherness" of the holy. The mystery of the experience lies in its unfamiliar and nonempirical nature. The holy is utterly unlike the profane.

Fifth, one feels a sense of fascination with and attraction to the holy. Although it is potentially terrifying, it also elicits a sense of wonder and a feeling of ultimate goodness. Hence, it commands a sense of ethical imperative. According to Otto, this experience of *mysterium tremendum* is the universal foundation and source of all religious behavior.

Religiosity is multidimensional. The kind of experience Otto described is vital to religious life for many people, but it is not the only source of religious conviction. Yet he makes the important point that religious conviction is more than ideas. To influence lives in a fundamental way, religion must have an emotional component, something that makes the ideas or belief systems "seem uniquely realistic" (recalling Geertz's definition of religion). A nonrational experience often provides such an impetus to belief.

Andrew Greeley offered clarity to this discussion of the role of sacred experiences. In his analysis of "sacredness" and the extraordinary quality of religious experience, he granted that the sacred is usually removed from everyday existence. Yet, he pointed out that sense of sacredness is not always the same thing as religious commitment. Greeley summarized his argument with an important twist:

> [People have] a tendency to sacralize [their] ultimate systems of value. Even if one excludes the possibility of a transcendent or a supernatural, one nonetheless is very likely to treat one's system of ultimate explanation with a great deal of jealous reverence and respect and to be highly incensed when someone else calls the system of explanation to question or behaves contrary to it. It is precisely this tendency to sacralize one's ultimate concern that might well explain the many quasi-religious phenomena in organizations which officially proclaim their non- or even antireligiousness. The communist, for example, may vehemently deny the existence of a "totally other" and yet treat communism and its prophets, its dogmas, its code, and its ritual with as much respect as does the devout Christian approach [Christianity]. (Greeley 1972:9)

Rather than citing an experience of the sacred as the source of all religious behavior, Greeley suggested that whatever we value very highly, we tend to sacralize (to make sacred). Sacredness, then, may be the *result* of a valuing process rather than the primal *cause* of all other religious activity. Greeley did not suggest that experiences of the holy are always secondary; he merely pointed out that the relationship among values, beliefs, and the sacred may be quite complex. The sacred experience, then, has appeal insofar as it can help persons make sense of the world and feel a sense of belonging to something larger than themselves.

Photo by AllStars Youth is licensed under CC BY-ND 2.0

Although William James and others focused on individual religious experiences, sociologists have long recognized that experiences of "collective effervescence" are facilitated by group interactions, like at this youth ministry camp.

Several conclusions can be drawn regarding nonrational religious experiences. First, they vary greatly in intensity from one person to another. Some people have a "strange warming of the heart" while others have an ecstatic, orgiastic type of experience (Neitz 1990). Second, nonrational experiences vary in frequency. For some, mystic experience becomes a goal in itself and may even take on the form of a full-time occupation, as occur in some Buddhist and Roman Catholic monasteries.

Third, nonrational experiences vary in context. For some people and in some religious traditions, intense experiences of holiness occur to individuals in isolation, as was the case for Plains Indian men who went off by themselves in search of a vision quest. For other people, profound nonrational experiences are primarily social, occurring in a charismatic prayer meeting or during a worship service (Neitz 1990). In either case, social norms usually prescribe how

to achieve such an experience, the value of such an experience, what a sacred encounter "looks like," and how to interpret it when it does occur.

Fourth, they vary in content. The Inuit shaman makes a spiritual journey to the bottom of the sea to visit Sedna and to appease her for violations of taboos (Barnouw 1982). The Lakota (Sioux) holy man experiences a visit by 48 horses that approach in groups of 12 from the four cardinal directions (Neihardt 1961). The Christian mystic may see the Holy Virgin, experience the love of Jesus, or hear the voice of God. The Buddhist mystic may experience "nonbeing" or "utter unity with the universe." The content, or at least the interpretation of the experience, is defined in culturally familiar terms.

Fifth, the people who value and expect a religious experience are those who report having had one. Abraham Maslow insisted that probably everyone has had at least one nonrational "peak experience" but that some people do not value such experiences and therefore dismiss them as insignificant or bizarre or even forget them altogether (Maslow 1964). Other researchers insist that people who desire such experiences may cultivate behaviors and attitudes that make it likely that they will have them (Anthony, Hermans, and Sterkens 2010; Hood, Morris, and Watson 1989; Nelson 2005; Straus 1979; Yamane and Polzer 1994).

In short, a social group's definition of what is normal or desirable influences both the way individual members interpret their own experiences and the kinds of experiences they try to bring about (Nelson 2005; Yamane and Polzer 1994). This is a basic premise of social constructionist theory. The theory is useful in understanding and predicting variations in religious experiences between groups. Roman Catholics are surrounded by much visual stimulation in churches (Stations of the Cross, statues, and stained glass windows). It should not be surprising that Catholics are much more likely than Protestants to have religious experiences that involve visions, while Protestants, whose worship experience is heavily auditory, are more likely to hear voices.

Regardless of variations, some form of nonrational religious experience seems to be at the root of religious behavior for many people. Such an experience gives impetus and emotion to belief systems. However, the assumption (by Otto, Durkheim, and Maslow) that a mystical or nonrational experience is the only source of religious conviction may be overdrawn. As Greeley pointed out, people have a tendency to sacralize the things that they value most highly and that give meaning and purpose to their lives. Because both religion and national symbols elicit a sense of sacredness, they are sometimes intermixed. For example, 64 national flags have religious symbols on them (Theodorou 2014). While there are no explicitly religious symbols on the American flag, note the sense of sacredness that accompanies ceremonial handling of the American flag. The directions that accompany the newly purchased flag emphasize a sense of reverence and awe that should be maintained when caring for the flag. See the "Illustrating Sociological Concepts" feature as an example.

Such sacredness is not caused by a mystical experience but is created in the presence of a valued symbol. The sacralization of objects or beliefs places them above question; it ensures their absoluteness. Hence, that which we value highly tends to be perceived in reverent or sacred terms.

ILLUSTRATING SOCIOLOGICAL CONCEPTS

The American Flag as a Sacred Symbol

The American flag is often treated with a profound respect and reverence, as indicated by the directions for flag etiquette. The mere fact that detailed rules are spelled out so explicitly for the treatment of this symbol and the reality that violation of these rules will infuriate some Americans is testimony to the awe with which this symbol is held. The extreme anger expressed by many Americans over the burning of a U.S. flag is also evidence of its sacredness, though the behavior itself is not the cause of anger. One of the rules of flag etiquette is that a tattered flag should be burned or buried as a sign of respect. The U.S. Flag Code has an extensive list of rules about sacred treatment and what constitutes desecration of the flag. A few of those rules are listed here.

- Display the flag only from sunrise to sunset on buildings and on stationary flagstaffs. The flag may be displayed at night only upon special occasions.
- The flag should not be left outside when it is raining.
- The flag should be hoisted briskly and lowered ceremoniously.

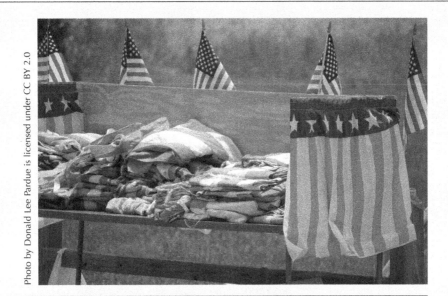

Photo by Donald Lee Pardue is licensed under CC BY 2.0

This is a table of American flags to be ceremonially burned at the American Legion Post 12 in Carthage, North Carolina.

- No other flag or pennant should be placed above or, if on the same level, to the right of the flag of the United States of America, except during church services conducted by naval chaplains at sea, when the church pennant may be flown above the flag during church services.
- The flag of the United States of America should not be dipped to any person or thing.
- The flag should never be carried flat or horizontally but always aloft and free.
- The flag should never be used as a drapery of any sort whatsoever, never festooned, drawn back, nor up, in folds, but always allowed to fall free.
- The flag should under no circumstances be used as a ceiling covering.
- During the ceremony of hoisting or lowering the flag or when the flag is passing in a parade or in a review, all persons present should face the flag, stand at attention, and salute. Men should remove the headdress with the right hand holding it at the left shoulder, the hand being over the heart.
- The flag should *never* be used for advertising in any manner whatsoever.
- The flag should not be embroidered on cushions, handkerchiefs, or scarves, nor reproduced on paper napkins, carryout bags, wrappers, or anything else that will soon be thrown away.
- No *part* of the flag—depictions of stars and stripes that are in *any form other than that approved for the flag design itself*—should ever be used as a costume, a clothing item, or an athletic uniform. In other words, wearing hats and shirts that involve a combination of red, white, and blue stripes and stars in a design that is not a complete flag is officially an offense to the flag.

It is interesting that much of the American public seems unaware of many of the flag code rules regarding sacredness and desecration (Ballantine, Roberts, and Korgen 2016; Billig 1995; U.S. Flag Code 2007).

Anyone who doubts the fact that a firsthand religious experience can be very important need only observe the major surge of born-again and Pentecostal movements in Christianity in the past two decades. The emphasis of each of these movements is the assurance and sense of certainty provided by a personal experience of the holy. Indeed, the recent emphasis on "spirituality" can be seen at root as focusing on personal experience (Yamane 1998). Although an experience of the *mysterium tremendum* may not be the sole source of religious behavior, a sense of sacredness is clearly one important aspect of religion.

Critical Thinking: Is nonrational experience of the holy *necessary* for a vibrant religious faith, or is it mostly a contributing factor? Is experience of the holy *sufficient* to mobilize a religious movement? Why or why not?

MYTH AND RITUAL

When Americans speak of religion, they usually think of a belief system. Indeed, many social scientists have even attempted to measure religiosity by questioning subjects on their agreement or disagreement with certain orthodox religious beliefs. Even the practice of referring to faithful members of a religious group as believers is indicative of this focus. As we will see, however, belief and ritual are interdependent, and in the case of some religious groups, ritual is the more important of the two.

Myth

Religious beliefs are usually expressed in the form of myths. By myth, the social scientist does not mean untrue or foolish beliefs; myths have little to do with legends, fairy tales, or folktales (Borg 2011; Kluckhohn 1972). Myths are stories or belief systems that help people understand the nature of the cosmos, the purpose and meaning of life, or the role and origin of evil and suffering. Myths explain and justify specific cultural values and social rules. They are more than stories that lack empirical validation; they serve as symbolic statements about the meaning and purpose of life in this world. One sociologist of religion has gone so far as to suggest that all religious symbols (including religious myths) are in a fundamental sense true (Bellah 1970a). He did not argue their literal veracity, but he insisted that symbolic systems of meaning are true insofar as they speak to the fundamental human condition. Hence, they need to be taken seriously. Myths have a powerful impact on the subjective or mental orientation of persons because they communicate and reinforce a particular worldview or a particular outlook on life. (See the next "Illustrating Sociological Concepts" feature.)

After undertaking an in-depth study of the Hare Krishna, Stillson Judah insisted that "'myth' is actually the highest subjective reality to the devotee. It is the vehicle [which carries one] to inner integration. [Humans] can only live without 'myth' at [their] peril" (Judah 1974:196). What is important here is a recognition of the emotional power of which myth is capable. For many persons, logical, systematic, and scientific statements do not capture one's imagination so as to mobilize one's emotional resources. The capacity of myths to do this is precisely the reason they have such power in the lives of individuals.

A Netsilik Inuit (Eskimo) myth from central Canada may serve to illustrate. Historically, the Netsilik Inuit believed in the existence of a woman, Sedna, who lived at the bottom of the sea. Sedna was once an Inuit girl. However, contrary to the wishes of her father, she married a very large bird and went to an island to live with her new husband. When her father returned from a hunting trip and found her missing, he came to get her. While the father was returning the girl to

ILLUSTRATING SOCIOLOGICAL CONCEPTS

Myths Can Create Powerful Moods and Motivations in People

The mythology of heaven and hell and the belief that one who is not saved by God will go to hell are vividly expanded by Jonathan Edwards in this passage. By emphasizing this myth and elaborating on it, he sought to create powerful, pervasive, and long-lasting *moods* (awe of God's power, humility, fear of God) and *motivations* (repentance, change of attitudes, and behavior).

> The God that holds you over the pit of hell, much as one holds a spider, or some loathsome insect over the fire, abhors you, and is dreadfully provoked: his wrath towards you burns like fire; he looks upon you as worthy of nothing else, but to be cast into the fire; he is of purer eyes than to bear to have you in his sight; you are ten thousand times more abominable in his eyes, than the most hateful venomous serpent is in ours.

> You have offended him infinitely more than ever a stubborn rebel did his prince; and yet it is nothing but his hand that holds you from falling into the fire every moment . . . There is no other reason to be given, why you have not dropped into hell since you arose in the morning, but that God's hand has held you up . . . Yea, there is nothing else that is to be given as a reason why you do not this very moment drop down into hell.

> O sinner! Consider the fearful danger you are in: it is a great furnace of wrath, a wide and bottomless pit, full of the fire of wrath, that you are held over in the hand of that God, whose wrath is provoked and incensed as much against you, as against many of the damned in hell. You hang by a slender thread, with the flames of divine wrath flashing about it, and ready every moment to singe it, and burn it asunder; and you have . . . nothing to lay hold of to save yourself, nothing to keep off the flames of wrath, nothing of your own, nothing that you ever have done, nothing that you can do, to induce God to spare you one moment. (Edwards [1741] 1966)

Although there is no question that this "hellfire and brimstone" style of sermonizing still exists, Edwards's approach has fallen out of favor in American culture today.

"Old-time religion" has been trumped by American culture that is highly individualistic. Alan Wolfe points out that the emphasis of contemporary worship is increasingly on meeting the needs and interests of members. An attitude of "nonjudgmentalism" accompanies a view of God not as "angry" (Edwards's view) but as understanding and empathetic. This creates moods and motivations of a different sort (Wolfe 2003).

Critical Thinking: Think of the difference between "hellfire and brimstone" sermonizing and the "nonjudgmentalism" Wolfe identifies. What types of individuals do you think would be attracted to the moods and motivations created by one as compared to the other? In your experience, is the happy god of nonjudgmentalism ascendant (or already on top) and the angry god of Jonathan Edwards in decline? Of what consequence might that be for religious mythologies in the future?

her home, Sedna's husband caused a violent storm to arise. Sedna fell overboard, but she hung on desperately to the gunnels of the canoe. To prevent capsizing, the father chopped her fingers off with his machete, and she sank to the bottom of the sea. The pieces of fingers turned into the various sea mammals—whales, seals, and walruses.

The Inuit were constrained by many taboos or moral prohibitions. For example, when seals were killed and brought home, certain behaviors were prescribed (sharing meat with everyone in the village, apologizing to the soul of the seal, using every part of the seal so there was no waste) or were prohibited (e.g., the skins from the sleeping platform could not be shaken out until the seal had been cut up, products from land and sea had to be cooked in different pots, and many other taboos related to food preparation, to giving birth, and to menstruation). If any of these taboos were broken, a vapor was believed to emanate from the body of the violator. That vapor sank through the ice, snow, and water and settled in Sedna's hair as dirt and maggots. Because she had no fingers, Sedna could not comb out this debris. In revenge, she would call the walruses and seals (which were once her fingers) to the bottom of the sea, and the people would face starvation. Salvation came only if a shaman (Inuit holy man) entered into a trance, traveled spiritually to the bottom of the sea, combed Sedna's hair, appeased her, and discovered who the offenders were. When he returned, all offenders were required to confess their taboo violations openly. The seals then returned (Barnouw 1982).

Sedna was not a benevolent deity. She was vengeful and had to be obeyed. She was the cause of much anxiety, fear, and even hostility. The Sedna myth served to create these moods of fear and anxiety in people, which then motivated them toward certain types of behavior (obeying of taboos and prohibitions). This myth reinforced an overall worldview that the world

is a hostile environment, that the future is fraught with danger and may be jeopardized by human acts, that the environment and animals must be respected, and that survival depends on conforming behavior and obedience to rules by everyone. The Sedna myth served to solidify and sacralize the general Inuit outlook on life. Insofar as this view was consistent with the harsh environmental conditions in which the Netsilik Inuit live, the myths may have contributed to adaptation and survival. Further, many of the taboos helped to sustain an environmental ethic, which was important to the survival of the people.

Ritual

Although Americans tend to think of belief as the central component of religion, ritual appears to be equally important. In fact, several scholars have pointed out that *orthopraxy*, not orthodoxy,

Online Resources: If you are unable to attend different religious services in your community to listen to the symbolism of the language used, many congregations today put their services online. You can also visit the Association of Religion Data Archives' Learning Center (thearda.com/learning center). In the "Observational Learning" box, you can access the ARDA's YouTube channel, which, as of this writing, already has over 100 videos of worship services from over 20 religious groups. Pick two groups, for example the United Methodist Church and a nondenominational church like Lakewood. What myths are being played upon in each? What moods do the clergy intend to create with these myths? What motivations are sought? What is the symbolic role of emotionally laden language in these services?

is central to Islam (Aslan 2011; Tamadonfar 2001; Watt 1996). That is, precise conformity in ritual behavior (e.g., prayers five times a day facing Mecca) is what is mandated for the faithful, not total conformity in theological interpretations. Many scholars have also observed that Judaism—especially Orthodox Judaism—and the Eastern Orthodox tradition within Christianity focus much more on concrete behaviors (orthopraxy) than on theological tenets, beliefs, or attitudes (Cohen 1983; Moberg 1984; Vrame 2008).

A careful observation of human behavior is enough to make one aware of the great attraction of humans to ritual experiences. Consider, for example, the elaborate pageantry and ritual of a Shriners' convention, a scouting induction, or the opening and closing ceremonies of the Olympic Games. Football games always begin with the playing of the national anthem, and colorfully uniformed marching bands perform. Many meetings of secular civic groups begin with a ritual pattern: the pledge to the flag and a prayer. Moreover, for many people, marriage is not legitimate unless the couple has been through a ceremony, however brief. The preceding examples do not necessarily involve a sense of sacredness or ultimacy, and we do not suggest that they are particularly religious phenomena. Our point is merely that there is something about human beings to which ritual and pageantry appeal.

Religious ritual usually involves affirmation of the myths and gives emotional impulse to the belief system. Judah pointed to this when he wrote, "The enthusiasm of the devotees leaping in ecstasy with upraised arms . . . can be contagious for many" (Judah 1974:95). Not only is the mood contagious; acceptance and understanding of the belief system may be attained through continual practice of a ritual. Judah cited a number of devotees of the Hare Krishna movement who made comments such as the following: "Although we may not understand something

when it is given to us, it comes to us through faith. It's revealed to us through our continuing [ritual performance]" (Judah 1974:169).

Ritual may involve the enactment of a story or myth, or it may symbolically remind one of the mythology of the faith by moving participants through a series of moods. Perhaps a brief analysis of a ritual familiar to many readers will help illustrate the point.

Biblical theology was based on the idea that God had a covenant (or contract) with the chosen people. If they obeyed the commandments and worked to establish a kingdom of justice and righteousness, then God would protect them and provide for them. The scriptures maintain that the Hebrew people got into trouble whenever they broke the covenant, forgot the demands of justice, and ignored the sovereignty of God. In these circumstances, the prophets called the people back to the covenant. The prophets assured them that if they would repent and renew their covenant, Yahweh would forgive them. The New Testament renews this theme, with Jesus calling the wayward to repent and promising God's forgiveness. The most important sacrament in the Christian church is Communion (alternatively referred to as the Lord's Supper, the Eucharist, or the Mass). In instituting this practice, Jesus claimed to be inaugurating a new covenant. Covenantal theology, then, is a basic Christian mythology or belief system.

Many Protestant Christians are not consciously aware that the liturgy (or ritual) in which they participate is based on this theology. In fact, many laypeople believe that the order of a worship service is rather arbitrary, that the minister randomly intermixes hymns, prayers, a confession, scripture, anthems, and other liturgical devices. Let us look, however, at a consistent pattern that prevails in many American Protestant liturgies. The sample provided in the next "Illustrating Sociological Concepts" feature will serve as an example. While there is some variation in the order

Photo by Dominik Golenia is licensed under CC BY-ND 2.0

Muslims pray to God five times a day at set times, regardless of where they are. They are also required to face Mecca. Conformity to this and other ritual behavior is considered a more important measure of faith than doctrinal orthodoxy.

of mainline Protestant worship services, the majority of such churches in the United States tend to move worshippers through successive movements or moods as shown in this liturgy (Hesser and Weigert 1980; Johnson 1959). Let us examine the relationship between these liturgies and the mythology of the divine covenant.

At the outset of the service, the liturgy is designed to create a mood of awe and praise. The architecture of the building may also enhance this sense. Many church bulletins request that worshippers sit in silence and focus their attention on a rose window, on some other symbol, or on "the presence of God." The prelude is frequently a piece of music that will lift one's spirits. The call to worship draws one's attention to the reason for gathering: to worship and praise God. The congregation then joins together in a

hymn of praise, which is frequently a joyful, uplifting song of adoration.

Shortly after the congregation is made aware that it is in the presence of God, the mood shifts. Although most of the worshippers were in the same place dedicating their lives to God just a week before, the liturgy attempts to make them aware of the fact that they have not always lived in a way consistent with Christian values. They are reminded that in the push and pull of daily living, they have said an unkind word or failed to do a loving deed. The values they professed on Sunday they may have betrayed by Wednesday (if not by Sunday afternoon). Hence, the second mood or theme of this worship liturgy is a service of confession. The prayer of confession is sometimes called an "act of honesty" (between oneself and God). However, this liturgical movement does not end on a note of guilt. Confession

ILLUSTRATING SOCIOLOGICAL CONCEPTS

Order of Worship

First United Methodist Church

Service of Praise

Prelude: Walther

Call to Worship

Hymn of Praise: #432 "Fill Us With Your Love"

Service of Confession

An Act of Honest before God: Confession (in unison)

Lord, we gather on the Sabbath to worship You and to dedicate our lives to Your service. Yet in the strain and hurry of everyday living, we often forget You. We say the unkind word, or we fail to do the loving deed. We betray the values which we profess on Sunday morning, and we do not remember that You are the Center of Life. Forgive us, O Lord, and renew in us a resolve to live Christ-like lives.

Assurance of Pardon

Service of Proclamation

Apostles' Creed

Children's Chat

Anthem: "Different Is Beautiful" Avery/Marsh

Scripture Reading

Hymn of Proclamation: #11 "Immortal, Invisible God Only Wise"

The Sermon

Service of Commitment

Concerns of the Congregation, Prayer of Intercession, Lord's Prayer

Tithes and Offerings   N. Lebegue

Hymn of Dedication: #593 "Here I Am Lord"

Charge to the Congregation and Benediction

Postlude: J. Stanley

is followed by words of assurance, assurance of pardon, or words of new possibility. At this point, the congregation is assured by the minister (often through quotation of a biblical passage) that people who sincerely confess their sins and who renew their commitment to God are forgiven. The covenantal theme of repentance prior to renewal of the covenant is enacted.

The liturgy then moves to a third phase, an affirmation of faith, or service of proclamation. This phase is frequently the major part of Protestant services. The congregation may repeat a creed or covenant, listen to an anthem or other special music, sing a hymn of proclamation, listen to scripture, and hear a message (sermon) delivered by the minister. In this phase of the ritual, the emphasis is on remembering and rehearing the Word of God and remembering the demands of the covenant.

The final movement of most Protestant liturgies is a service of dedication. This part of worship calls for a response to God's word by the congregation. The movement is characterized by a monetary offering (a symbolic act of the giving of one's self), concerns of the congregation or announcements from the pulpit, a hymn of dedication, a charge to the congregation, and a benediction. In some churches, the third and fourth phases of the liturgy (proclamation and dedication) may be merged into one. In this case, some acts of dedication and commitment (such as the offering) may actually precede the sermon. However, the hymn of dedication always follows the sermon. In the more evangelical churches, this hymn may be followed by an "altar call"—a request for members to make a public commitment by coming forward and standing before the altar to commit their lives to Christ.

It should not be inferred that all Protestant worship through history has followed this mood sequence. The pattern described here was initiated by John Calvin. It is noteworthy that much of contemporary Protestant worship emphasizes

proclamation and commitment. The Catholic Mass seems to place more stress on the service of praise. This reflects a fundamental difference in Protestant and Catholic views of worship (Pratt 1964). The Roman Catholic Church has historically taken an objective approach to the Mass. The emphasis is on glorification of God, and the liturgy is designed with that in mind. It is best to have a congregation present at the celebration of Mass, but if no one came, the Mass would go on. On the other hand, a Protestant minister would scarcely think of conducting a full service of worship if no congregation gathered. The more subjective emphasis of the Protestant denominations—especially the ones that have a more informal, low-church tone—is on how the worship affects the worshipers themselves. Hence, the beliefs about worship itself significantly affect the order of a liturgy and the themes it includes.

From the example provided, it may be seen that ritual and belief are often closely intertwined and tend to be mutually reinforcing. That is, they tend to provide an interrelated system. It is noteworthy that sample surveys have consistently found a high correlation between regular attendance at rituals and a high level of acceptance of the belief system of the denomination. However, it is also true that many people are unaware of the logical progression of the worship liturgy and of the theological basis for its order. Hence, the liturgy is viewed by some attendees as just so many hymns, prayers, and scripture readings in random order (Roberts 1992).

Relationship Between Myth and Ritual

Ritual and myth are closely connected. Some scholars have maintained that, in terms of chronological development, ritual emerges first and myth develops later to justify the existence of the ritual (Kluckhohn 1972). However, the process may develop the other way as well. The Mass is clearly an example of a ritual based on a sacred story. Another example is the Ghost Dance, a religious ritual based on a dream or vision by Wovoka, the Paiute holy man whose trance in 1889 regenerated a powerful religious movement among Native Americans. In this case, the interpreted dream provided both a mythology and a command to perform a ritual (LaBarre 1972). Clyde Kluckhohn points out that regardless of which emerges first, "what really is important is the intricate interdependence of myth with ritual and many other forms of behavior" (Kluckhohn 1972:96).

In some cases, both myth and ritual may be viewed as factors dependent on a third component: mystical or nonrational experience. The experience of awe may be so fascinating and attractive that a ritual is established to try to elicit or re-create that experience. Furthermore, a mythology is generated to try to explain or make sense of the experience (O'Dea 1966; Otto 1923; Van der Leeuw 1963).

The image presented here of highly integrated ritual and myth needs a word of caution. The discussion of the Protestant liturgy suggested a high degree of integration and interdependence between ritual and belief system. However, that integration is largely a matter of interpretation— that is, this integration is to a considerable extent in the eye of the beholder. The participant interprets the ritual and myth as mutually supportive— hence it is mutually supportive for that person. However, many cases have been found in which diverse tribal people practice the same ritual but interpret that ritual as expressing very different myths. Likewise, people holding the same belief system may celebrate those beliefs with very different ritual patterns. In summary, we can say that beliefs, ritual, and religious experience are important components of religion, that they are usually interrelated and mutually supportive, and that the integration of the three is itself largely a matter of interpretation by the believer and the community (Batson, Schoenrade, and Ventis 1993).

Critical Thinking: As readers attend religious services in their own communities, they may be interested in asking themselves, What is the rationale for the order of this liturgy? How are myth and ritual intertwined and mutually supportive, or is there no apparent relationship? What does the ritual mean to the *members* of this group?

THE IMPORTANCE OF SYMBOLS

The reason why myths and rituals normally have a close relationship is that they are both manifestations of a larger phenomenon—a system of symbols. Elizabeth Nottingham emphasized the unifying function of symbols:

> [It] is not hard to understand that the sharing of common symbols is a particularly effective way of cementing the unity of a group of worshipers. It is precisely because the referents of symbols elude overprecise intellectual definitions that their unifying force is the more potent; for intellectual definitions make for hairsplitting and divisiveness. Symbols may be shared on the basis of not-too-closely-defined feeling. (Nottingham 1971:19)

Certainly, this is one reason that symbols are important. Clifford Geertz emphasized a slightly different reason for symbols' critical importance: "*Meanings can only be stored in symbols:* a cross, a crescent, or a feather. Such religious symbols, dramatized in rituals or related in myths, are felt somehow to sum up what is known about the way the world is" (Geertz 1958:422, italics added). Edmund Leach's research on the symbolic power of rituals supports this view. Leach has studied rituals as "storage systems" that encapsulate knowledge. He maintained that ritual provides an important form of economical thinking among many tribal people (Leach 1972). Meaningful information and important knowledge are encapsulated in ritual in a way analogous to the loading of computer chips with information in our culture.

Rituals are viewed by Leach as vessels that carry powerful symbols and that authoritatively transmit a worldview and an ethos.

A consideration of certain elements in the Catholic Mass illustrates the power of symbols. As the celebrants come before the altar, they genuflect and cross themselves. Although the act may sometimes be perfunctorily executed, making the sign of the cross acts to remind believers of a particular event. The cross has meaning because it reminds the participant of a sacred story, a particular life, and a divine event. The theological interpretation of the event may vary somewhat from one celebrant to another, but with the regularized pattern of crossing oneself, the centrality of Christ on the cross will not be forgotten. The stained glass windows may have symbols meaningful to the early church or perhaps depictions of Jesus in a well-known scene. These symbolic representations also bring to mind a whole series of events and stories that are part of the sacred myth. At certain points in the Mass, the congregation kneels. This act is a gesture of humility and is to remind one of an utter dependency and humility before God. In each case, the entire story does not have to be repeated in detail. If the myth is well known and if the symbolic meaning of the ritual action is understood by the celebrant, then all that is necessary to elicit certain moods and motivations is to introduce the symbol itself. The symbol stores meaning and can call forth certain attitudes or dispositions.

In the Jewish tradition, one can see the same power of symbols in a religious festival such as the Seder meal. Even a Gentile cannot help but be moved by the symbolic reenactment of the escape from Egypt. The eating of bitter herbs, which actually bring tears to one's eyes, reminds one of the suffering of the ancestors. The unleavened bread, the parsley, and the haroseth (a sweet condiment) have symbolic value in recalling a sacred story. This symbolic reenactment confirms in the minds of the Jews where they have been, who they are, and what task lies before them. A sense of identity and a sense of holy mission are powerfully communicated through the ritual (Fredman 1981).

Geertz's definition of religion articulates very well the important role of symbols: "Religion is a system of symbols which acts to establish powerful, pervasive, and long-lasting moods and motivations in [people] by formulating conceptions of a general order of existence" (Geertz 1966:4). The symbol systems are important in that they act in people's lives. Ritual and myth, then, are important as symbol systems. In this text, we have stressed worldview (conceptions of a general order of existence) and ethos (powerful, pervasive, and long-lasting moods and motivations) as central components of religion. Hence, the next issue before us is the relationships among worldview, ethos, and symbols.

WORLDVIEW, ETHOS, AND SYMBOLS

Worldview refers to the intellectual framework within which one explains the meaning of life. Myths are specific stories or beliefs, the net effect of which is to reinforce a worldview (Wuthnow 1981). A single story may not be sufficient to convince someone that God is in charge of the universe and all is well. However, a series of many such myths may serve to reinforce such an outlook on life. Worldview is a more abstract concept than myth; it refers to one's mode of *perceiving* the world and to one's general overview of life. In this sense, a worldview is more taken for granted and less questioned. Many individuals may not be fully conscious of the alternative types of worldviews, and many never question the fact that their perception is influenced by intellectual constructs. Whether one is optimistic or pessimistic in outlook is strongly influenced by one's worldview. (See the passages from Jonathan Edwards in the "Illustrating Sociological Concepts" feature on page 87.)

A religious worldview is also closely related to a group's ethos, as demonstrated in the next "Illustrating Sociological Concepts" feature. "A people's *ethos* is the tone, character, and quality of their life, its moral and aesthetic style and mood; it is the underlying attitude toward themselves and

Photos by Keith Roberts

Judaism is rich with symbolism, and the symbols often serve on an everyday basis to remind people who they are. The man on the left wears a *yarmulke* like those worn by Jewish men since roughly the 2nd century CE. It symbolizes respect for and fear of God. These caps are also a sign of belonging and commitment to the Jewish community. At the right is a *mezuzah*, a daily reminder of identity on doorjambs of Jews. A parchment inside it has the "Shema Yisrael" (Deuteronomy 6:4–9) written on it, a passage that commands the faithful to keep God in their minds at all times. Whenever Jews pass through a door with a *mezuzah* on it, they kiss their fingers and touch them to the *mezuzah*, expressing love and respect for God and God's commandments. These symbols carry meaning and reinforce identity every day.

their world" (Geertz 1958:421, italics added). Ethos refers to attitudes about life (moods, motivations), whereas worldview refers to an *intellectual* process—thoughts about life (concepts of a general order of existence) (recall Geertz's symbolic definition of religion from Chapter 1).

Both attitudes and concepts are essential to the establishment of a sense of meaning in life. The worldview is confirmed and made to seem objective by the ethos. The set of concepts is placed beyond question and is made absolute by the sacred mood in which it is transmitted. Furthermore, this basic attitude (ethos) is justified and made reasonable by the worldview. So in a well-integrated religious system, the ethos and worldview are mutually reinforcing.

ILLUSTRATING SOCIOLOGICAL CONCEPTS

Native American Ethos: Moral and Esthetic Style and Mood

Sam Gill insists that the moods and motivations of Native American religion are both critically important for understanding Native American religion and often beyond the capacity of rational discourse to explain or describe. In a discussion of the oral tradition of storytelling (myths), he commented on the ethos:

> Ordinarily underlying questions of meaning is the assumption that these oral traditions carry messages and that we need to translate these speech acts into their messages so that we too will know what they mean. After spending much time asking Native American

(Continued)

(Continued)

people questions like "What does this story mean?" and feeling by their lack of response that it must have been a stupid question—or having gained answers completely incompatible with the story—I have had to seek ways of understanding how these stories bear meaning and how we can appreciate them . . .

Perhaps we can approach an understanding by certain olfactory experiences. I cannot smell the odor of juniper smoke without experiencing a series of peculiar images and feelings related to experiences I had while living among Navajo people. If you were to ask me what the smell of juniper smoke means to me, I would at first be confounded, for such a question seems inappropriate to ask. The smell bears no translatable message, although it has an emotional impact upon me; the experience is meaningful but has no meaning at all in the sense of bearing a message. Listening to music evokes similar sorts of meaning by awakening a certain emotion, often a series of images or memories connected with the music through one's personal and cultural history.

Speech acts in Native American cultures . . . have an emotional impact, a significance much more far-reaching. In their performance, they are not simply streams of words whose full significance lies in the information they convey. They are complex symbols, networks of sounds, odors, forms, colors, temperatures, and rhythms. . . .

Consequently any story, any song, any prayer is a stimulus that frees strings of associated images, emotions, and patterns. To ask what they mean and expect a translatable message is often to ask an inappropriate question. Their significance is inseparable from the whole field of symbols which they evoke. (Gill 1982:48–49)

SOURCE: Gill, Sam D. 1982. *Native American Religions*. 2nd ed. Belmont, CA: Wadsworth.

* * * * * * *

The inability to articulate the meaning of a particular myth may be twofold. First, part of why it is meaningful is because of the emotionally laden context in which it is told—the ethos. Second, the myth may reinforce a worldview that is only partially explicit or conscious to the subject. It is taken for granted. The worldview may, for example, assume certain categories of time and certain meanings of the concept of time that are not shared by the interviewer. Without that shared worldview, the informer hardly knows where to begin to explain the "meaning" of the story.

Critical Thinking: Identify a smell or song (perhaps a pop music favorite from your elementary or middle school years) that elicits a strong reminiscence. What does that smell or that tune mean to you? Why is it so difficult to explain? Does the fact that it is difficult to explain indicate that it is insignificant to you? Why or why not?

Symbols play the central role of relating the worldview to the ethos (Geertz 1958). Symbols transform fact into value. The function of sacred symbols is to encapsulate, or summarize, the system of meaning and to deliver that meaning system with power and authority at appropriate times. Geertz discussed the symbolic significance of the circle among the Oglala Sioux as an example:

For most Oglala the circle is but an unexamined lumi-
nous symbol whose meaning is intuitively sensed, not
consciously interpreted. But the power of the symbol,
analyzed or not, clearly rests on its comprehensive-
ness, on its fruitfulness in ordering experience. Again
and again the idea of a sacred circle . . . yields, when
applied to the world within which the Oglala lives,
new meanings; continually it connects together elements within their experience which would otherwise
seem wholly disparate and, wholly disparate, incom-
prehensible. (Geertz 1958:423)

Thus, symbols have power to bind worldview
and ethos into a unified system of meaning.
Durkheim suggested long ago that the experience of anomie—social rootlessness or a lack of
identity and purpose—can be so unsettling that it
can result in suicidal behavior. The feeling of a
firmly rooted worldview, with certain and defi-
nite moral rules and regulations, is a compelling
need for many humans. Geertz insisted that his
tribal-society respondents were quite willing to
abandon their cosmology for a more plausible
one. What they were *not* willing to do was abandon it for no other hypothesis at all, leaving
events to themselves (Geertz 1966).

In line with this emphasis, Mary Douglas has
offered an insightful interpretation of biblical
taboos (such as the taboo against eating pork or
against eating a milk product and a meat product
at the same meal). In the process of socialization,
a child learns to think in terms of categories of
language and in terms of theories or explanations
extant in a culture. When new information is
received, it is interpreted in terms of those
accepted categories of thought. New experiences
and new information are assimilated into the
present worldview. When an experience does not
seem to fit into this mold, the person experiences
dissonance (internal cognitive conflict). Douglas
claimed that many taboos have to do with avoid-
ance of those things that challenge one's worldview (Douglas 1966, 1968).

Anomalies that do not fit one's worldview
are simply abominations that are dirty and to be
avoided. Other aspects of social order may also be
protected or reinforced by taboos. Beliefs about

women being unclean during their menstruation and
in need of purification functioned to remind them of
their inferior social position. The insistence in the
New Testament that women cover their head in
church served a similar function. Men and women
were viewed as fundamentally different. This was
symbolically emphasized by men keeping their hair
short and women keeping theirs long. Anything that
threatened this essential distinction (essential to that
worldview) was an abomination (it threatened concepts of order). Douglas argued that protection and
preservation of the worldview is very important in
understanding much religious behavior.

Sociologist Peter Berger insisted that one's
worldview must seem authoritative, certain, and
compelling. In the midst of alternative paradigms and cosmologies, one's worldview may
become fragile and vulnerable. Hence, the vulnerability of a worldview is concealed in an aura
of sacredness (Berger 1967). Without a basis in a
convincing worldview, social values would not
seem compelling, and social stability itself may
be threatened. Geertz came to the same conclusion through cross-cultural analysis of religion:

[M]ere conventionalism satisfies few people in any
culture. Religion, by fusing ethos and world view,
gives to a set of social values what they perhaps
most need to be coercive: an appearance of objectivity. In sacred rituals and myths values are portrayed
not as subjective human preferences but as the
imposed conditions for life. (Geertz 1958:426–427)

In conclusion, we might simply point to the
complexity of the relationships among the various components of religion. In terms of the integration of these elements into a coherent religious
system, we might summarize with the following
four points:

1. Ritual and myth tend to be mutually reinforcing
as symbol systems.

2. Symbols (including rituals, myths, and artifacts) encapsulate the worldview and ethos of a
people. Hence they can elicit powerful emotional responses and (by repetition) help reinforce a general worldview.

3. The ethos and the worldview are themselves mutually reinforcing.

4. Together, all of these elements provide a compelling basis for social values (see Figure 4.1).

A problem may arise when a religious system is not so well integrated and mutually reinforcing. Geertz has himself described the social and cultural disintegration that can happen when

Figure 4.1 The Meaning System

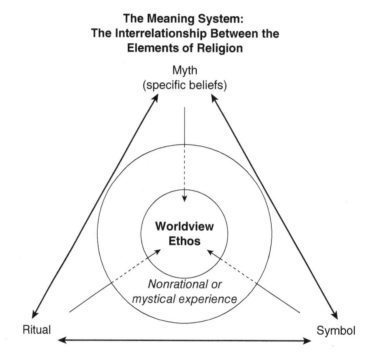

The Meaning System:
The Interrelationship Between the
Elements of Religion

Myth
(specific beliefs)

Worldview
Ethos

Nonrational or
mystical experience

Ritual   Symbol

Worldview and ethos are at the heart of what we mean by "religion." Yet these concepts are abstractions from experience; an individual's worldview and religious ethos (moods and motivations) are so pervasive and so taken for granted that the subject may not be fully conscious of all their dimensions. These abstractions are made concrete and are reinforced by more concrete expressions of religiosity: ritual, myth, and symbols. Each of these is interrelated and acts to confirm the ethos and worldview. Frequently, the entire religious realm seems uniquely compelling because of a nonrational religious experience. Some groups may emphasize some of these elements more than others (e.g., religious experience may be more important than unquestioned belief in the myth). Variations in interpretation of any of these may also lead to considerable conflict within the group. In actual practice, religion always has a good deal more internal inconsistency than this diagram would suggest. Hence, it is important to bear in mind that this model is idealized. It does represent a strain toward integrity that is a very real part of all religion. It is also true that when glaring incoherence in this system and conflict in interpretation of the elements becomes severe, some form of religious change is likely to take place.

ritual, myth, social values, and social structure do not harmonize. Some measure of conflict between these elements can be tolerated and is normal. This is the advantage of symbols: They can unify individuals who each adhere to the symbol but who attach alternative meanings to that symbol. However, some scholars believe that the lack of a common, shared worldview can eventually become a problem for a pluralistic society. Their argument is that lack of agreement on the big picture, the unifying ideology or outlook, leaves the culture without a unifying core (Geertz 1957).

It is a maxim of the social sciences that "facts do not speak for themselves; they must be interpreted." The difficulty in a heterogeneous culture is that there is no agreement on which big theory really makes sense and explains the meaning of life. The overriding, integrating worldview—which religion provides for many cultures—is not a uniting and integrating factor in a pluralistic one. For most science teachers in the past several decades, evolutionary theory has provided the big picture, the overriding theory that explains the relationships among data. The creationist or intelligent design movement, of course, challenges this big picture. It is an interesting question whether a core of common assumptions about the way things are is critical to harmonious social life.

Critical Thinking: Is a lack of a single uniting religious outlook a serious problem for a pluralistic society like Kenya, India, or the United States? Is the result anomie, or can societies be bound together by common interests and interdependencies? Why do you think as you do? What evidence is persuasive? What kind of evidence might cause you to change your mind?

Summary

Social constructionism focuses on the processes by which individuals create and internalize the cultural worlds that they inhabit. By watching how others act in certain circumstances, we define situations—ascertaining what is going on and is appropriate for that situation. Because of its emphasis on the construction of meaning in ambiguous situations, this theoretical perspective has much to offer the study of religion. Clarification of the meaning of life, death, and suffering is fraught with ambiguity and requires interpretation of meaning.

In terms of religion, those worlds include experiences, myths, rituals, and symbol systems. These cultural elements are also related to the ethos and worldview of a religion. Frequently, there is a perceived integrity between these elements, and they are mutually reinforcing. Myths are embodied in rituals and vice versa; rituals facilitate religious experiences, which are shaped by the symbol system; religious experiences reinforce the ethos and worldview of a religion; and so on.

Because of this, it is nearly impossible to identify one as primary—at least when one is referring to religion as a general phenomenon. However, specific groups may emphasize one or more of these and de-emphasize others. Pentecostals emphasize direct, embodied experience of the Holy Spirit more than Presbyterians (Poloma 1989), and African American congregations do so more than white congregations (Nelson 2005). When a religious group begins to undergo change, the relationships between these elements of religion may be less integrated. This may be so disconcerting to believers that the conflict may lead to schisms, a topic to be discussed in later chapters.

PART III

RELIGION IN THE LIVES OF INDIVIDUALS

In this section, we explore religion in the lives of individuals. The various ways that religion manifests itself in the lives of individuals, how people understand themselves religiously, and how they practice religion in everyday life are of intense interest to sociologists. Also, the process by which people acquire faith, change religions, and become committed to religious groups is of great importance to whether a religious group will survive and thrive in the long run. In Chapter 5, we look at some of the recent research on how individuals acquire, develop, and commit to religion in their lives and how that shapes their identity and everyday lives. In Chapter 6, we examine the social psychology of religious conversion and the processes of religious "switching."

5

BECOMING AND BEING RELIGIOUS

HERE ARE SOME QUESTIONS TO PONDER AS YOU READ THIS CHAPTER

- How is religion reproduced and transmitted from one generation to the next?
- How are young people affected by religion, and how are they influencing the trajectory of religious change?
- In what ways does religious involvement change over the life course?
- How might differences in age groups (generations) cause change in religious sensibility or religious affiliation and expression?
- Why do people become committed to a faith perspective and to a religious community?
- How have the bases of individual religious identity changed over history?
- Who are the religious "nones"—those unaffiliated with a particular religious tradition?

In his *Invitation to the Sociology of Religion* (2003), Phil Zuckerman made the point that people become religious through a social learning, or socialization, process. He did so by using two fictitious characters as examples: a Christian believer "Tom" living in the contemporary United States and a devout Muslim "Mustafa" living in Saudi Arabia. Zuckerman observed the following:

> [H]ad Tom been born and raised in Yemen three hundred years ago he would most likely be a devout Muslim . . . Conversely, if "Mustafa" . . . had been born and raised in northern Mississippi two hundred years ago, he would most likely be a Baptist or Methodist Christian. (Zuckerman 2003:51)

From this, Zuckerman concluded, "Ultimately, religious identity and conviction aren't generally so much a matter of choice or faith or soul-searching as a matter of who and what one's parents, friends, neighbors, and community practice and profess" (Zuckerman 2003:51). Put simply, religious engagement is largely an accident of birth (Wuthnow 1999). However, that is not the whole story.

In this chapter, in examining the process of being and becoming religious, we will see that Zuckerman is three-quarters right. Individuals are socialized into their religious identities and orientations, beliefs, and practices by those close to them (Sherkat 2003). This is a fundamental insight of sociology. At the same time, we must be careful to avoid an "oversocialized" conception of human beings that leaves no room for individual interpretation of or deviation from conventional social norms (Wrong 1961). As we will see throughout this chapter, the transmission of religion from a community to its residents, from parents to children, and even from a religious group to its members is not perfect. Religiosity also changes over the course of an individual's life, and this change can be magnified or diminished by broader changes taking place in the individual's sociocultural environment. Some even argue that it is the individual's lived religion, in all its uniqueness, that ultimately matters. Though this approach may lead us to an equally problematic "undersocialized" conception of human beings, it is nonetheless an important position to consider here.

RELIGIOUS SOCIALIZATION AND THE INTERGENERATIONAL TRANSMISSION OF RELIGION

Socialization is defined as the process by which individuals are taught the beliefs, values, and norms—that is, the culture—of their community and society. Religious socialization is no different. It is how religion is reproduced and transmitted from one generation to the next (Guest 2009). The same processes by which individuals are socialized into a culture generally can be observed quite specifically in religious socialization.

For most of human history and in most parts of the world, people have become religious by inheriting their beliefs and practices from their ancestors. In the early stages of social development, religion is inherited from the clan into which the person is born. Here, the clan is the equivalent of an extended family unit, so there is no difference between one's society and one's family (Bellah 1970c). In these early societies, religious beliefs were passed from generation to generation through stories, folktales, ballads, and chants, which were told and enacted in a ritual context. The group's children learned the beliefs and understandings as well as religious practices through this informal form of socialization (Johnstone 2007). Under these conditions, general socialization and religious socialization cannot be distinguished, and the transmission of religion takes place more or less mechanically.

As societies grew in size and became more internally differentiated—during the Industrial Revolution in the West (17th and 18th centuries)—the *nuclear* family emerged as the core unit of "family" (Burgess 1916). Under these social conditions, religious socialization is more distinct from general socialization and becomes primarily the job of parents, in conjunction with other distinct organizations like congregations, youth programs, and perhaps schools. As Nancy Ammerman put it, "Congregations, in tandem with families, are the primary agents of religious socialization in places where religion has been institutionally separated from an integrated culture that carries religious meaning and practices in the warp and woof of everyone's everyday life" (Ammerman 2009:567). Although informal socialization continues, the intergenerational transmission of religion outside the home becomes more formalized. In congregations, Sunday schools and children's ministries proliferate, increasingly supervised by professionally trained ministers and religious educators. Religious primary and secondary schools

also grow in number as parents seek to reinforce their religious teachings in the home, especially as the public schools have become more secular over time (Sikkink and Hill 2006).

Thus, as with scholars studying socialization generally, those studying religious socialization focus on the major agents of socialization in modern society: parents and the family, congregations and religious education, peers and schools (Erickson 1992; King, Furrow, and Roth 2002). The dominant process by which these agents facilitate religious socialization is by serving as models for children to observe and imitate and by offering positive reinforcement for the desired and negative reinforcement for unwanted religious beliefs and behaviors. This perspective on the socialization process is known as social learning theory (Bandura 1977).

Photo by Christopher Futcher/iStock

Family is one place for religious socialization. Parents read scriptures, tell stories, emphasize moral codes of behavior, and celebrate holidays bearing religious significance that become embedded in memory and meaning for youngsters.

Social Learning Theory

Social learning theory suggests that parents are the primary models for and agents of religious socialization, and most research shows that family religious commitment is the most powerful predictor of adulthood involvement in a faith community (Dillon 2007). The first systematic study showing children's religiosity being shaped by their parents' (especially their mother's) attitude toward religion dates to 1937 (Newcomb and Svehla 1937). In general, if parents have a strong religious identity and engage in religious education and practice at home, children will develop and maintain the religious practices to which they were exposed (Myers 1996; Wilcox 2006). There is also evidence that grandparents can influence their grandchildren's religious socialization by taking active roles in the process (Bengtson et al. 2009).

Summarizing the research, Mark Regnerus, Christian Smith, and Brad Smith concluded, "Parent-child transmission of religiosity and religious identity is indeed quite powerful, but it's not inevitable" (Regnerus et al. 2004:28). As we noted at the outset, there is considerable truth to Zuckerman's view of the reproduction of religion from generation to generation, but there is more to it. Several characteristics of parenting and family life have been shown to affect religious socialization outcomes. We highlight three: (1) the quality of relationships, (2) unity of tradition, and (3) stability of family structure.

Quality

Religious socialization is stronger in families characterized by considerable warmth and closeness—where parents enjoy marital happiness and show affection toward their children (Myers 1996; Ozorak 1989). Having parents who are supportive and accepting of their children, rather than judgmental, also appears to affect how well a faith perspective is transmitted to children (Bao et al. 1999). It is likely that in these cases children are generally more receptive to all of their parents' beliefs, values, and preferences, religion included. Research in this area has also shown that higher levels of marital conflict are found in religiously heterogamous couples (Petts and Knoester 2007), which leads to our second point.

Unity

Religious intermarriage—marriage between people of different religious backgrounds or levels of religious commitment—disrupts the religion–family linkage and thereby weakens the socialization of children into a faith. Several studies have suggested reasons for this. In the first place, married couples who share the same faith are more religious than couples with heterogamous marriages and therefore practice religion more frequently and are more likely to want to socialize their children into a faith tradition (Petts and Knoester 2007). Also, families in which the parents share the same religious beliefs give more reinforcing religious cues to children. Parents who come from different religious backgrounds, by contrast, send mixed messages about religion to their children (Wilcox 2006). Religious intermarriage may also lead children to withdraw from religious commitments altogether instead of choosing one parent's religion over the other (Hunt 2007). The research in this area confirms that parents are more likely to transmit religious affiliation and the faith perspective to their children when they have common religious commitments. An illustration is the Navajo and Hopi reservations, where intermarriage means that the parents often speak to each other in English, and the children may not learn the native language—which is essential in order to participate in a Hopi kachina dance or a Navajo healing ceremony. The mixed marriage across native tribal lines may leave the children without full socialization into either one.

Stability

Intact families are more likely to practice religious rituals, attend services, and affiliate with a religious tradition. This translates into stronger religious socialization of children. Studies have shown that children who grow up in intact families are more likely to continue with religious practice as adults than those raised in single-parent households or in stepfamilies (Myers 1996). This is due in part to the fact that single parents are less involved in faith communities than parents in intact families. Also, divorced fathers are less involved in religious socialization than married fathers (Regnerus and Uecker 2006; Zhai et al. 2007).

The recent availability of longitudinal data on youth and religion has allowed some additional subtlety to be added to these analyses. Using three waves of data from the National Study of Youth and Religion (NSYR), Melinda Denton examined the relationship between family disruption and adolescent religiosity. She found that the effect of disruption is different for different religious types.

For those adolescents who are more religious, parental breakup leads to a decline in religiosity. For those youth who are less religious to start with, parental breakup is related to an increase in religious engagement (Denton 2012).

The importance of unity and stability of family life in the intergenerational transmission of religion has significant implications for the future. First, religious intermarriage has dramatically increased in recent decades as social and cultural differences between people from different religious backgrounds have diminished and as social stigmas against religious intermarriage have faded. The rate of religious intermarriage from 1955 to 2005 increased from 12% to 25% for Protestant women, from 33% to 46% for Catholic women, and from 16% to 38% for Jewish women (Rosenfeld 2008). There is no reason to expect a reversal in this trend as religious identification becomes a less and less salient factor in mate selection.

Sol Stock/iStock

Same-sex marriage is being legalized in more of the United States every year, as well as in other parts of the world, especially Europe. The implications of this for intergenerational transmission of religion are something sociologists are watching closely.

Second, rates of marital dissolution have increased significantly in the last century. Just as the rise of the nuclear family had implications for the process of religious socialization, so too will the advent of the "postnuclear" family— divorced or never-married single parents, blended families, cohabiting couples with children, and gay and lesbian couples (Cherlin 2013; Popenoe 1993). The traditional family structure in the United States for much of the 20th century was the two-parent household in which the husband is employed and the wife is not. Only a minority of households today fit that bill, yet this type of family seems to be correlated to high levels of faith transmission. As it is unlikely that rates of cohabitation and divorce will decline or that women will move out of the labor force in large numbers, the future intergenerational transmission of religion may be adversely affected.

Channeling Through Peers and Schools

In addition to direct religious socialization in the family through social learning processes, parents have some indirect influence on their children's peer groups. Parents can facilitate the religious socialization of their children by "channeling" them into groups, settings, and experiences (such as friendships and schools) that reinforce their efforts in the home (Martin, White, and Perlman 2003).

As many of us have experienced ourselves, from childhood to later adolescence friends have an increasing influence on children's lives. This includes their religious beliefs and practices. Two studies using high-quality longitudinal data both found that youth involvement in a faith community was significantly predicted by that of peers. When peers' attendance is low, youth attendance is low, and vice versa (Gunnoe and Moore 2002; Regnerus et al. 2004). This does not mean that parents no longer influence their children but highlights the fact that parents can influence their children's religious beliefs and commitments both directly and indirectly by channeling their other social relationships (Cornwall 1987).

Another extrafamilial agent of socialization over which families have some discretion is schools. The desire to align family socialization with school socialization is a major reason the number of conservative Protestant primary and secondary schools grew to 9,000 by 2006 (Sikkink and Hill 2006) and also explains the choice of many to homeschool their children (Stevens 2003). Although the effect is not as strong as for parents or peers, schoolmates' religious attendance patterns do matter. Mark Regnerus and his colleagues (2004) found that the more one's schoolmates attend services, the more one is likely to attend. Interestingly, they found that it is not being in a religious school that matters but the level of religiosity within the school (regardless of type).

A significant avenue for harnessing the influence of peers on adolescents' religiosity is faith-based youth ministries. Many religious groups sponsor these programs, and many parents eagerly encourage their kids to attend them because of the anticipated positive religious and social outcomes. Beginning with the observation that half of American youth attend these groups at some point, Patricia Snell explored the effect of religious youth group participation on adult support, connections in church, and moral values— mechanisms that can help produce positive outcomes in the adolescent years and later in life. Using data from the first two waves of the NSYR, she found an inconsistent effect of participation in religious youth groups in the first wave of the survey (when respondents were 13 to 17 years old). Looking at the second wave of the survey (when respondents were 16 to 20 years old), the earlier youth group participants were more likely *both* to lie to their parents *and* to believe that morality is based on God's law (Snell 2009). Continued participation in youth groups does have a significant positive effect, however, suggesting that self-selection into youth groups may be the more significant factor, along with religious service attendance, which is also consistently, positively related to these outcomes.

Members of Ignite, West Houston Chinese Church's high school youth group, meet with members of the church's Middle School Fellowship for a game night.

This is just a cursory overview of the many factors that go into childhood religious socialization. We have not discussed the role of individuals like teachers, mentors, coaches, ministers, or pastors; or secular groups like the Boy and Girl Scouts programs; or sports teams. Surely these agents of socialization have an influence as well on how people grow up and understand their faith (Wuthnow 1999). We have also for simplicity's sake kept our focus on childhood socialization, even though sociologists understand that socialization is a lifelong process. Obviously, most children grow up, most partner, most have children, most grow old, and all of them die. Religion continues to have a presence in many people's lives through all of these stages of the life course.

Critical Thinking: How does this discussion of religious socialization apply to your own life? If you have no religious affiliation or faith tradition or a strong one, is the pattern consistent with the explanations presented here? Why or why not?

RELIGION OVER THE LIFE COURSE

Religious conviction and commitment does not proceed in a straight line over the course of life for most people, either upward or downward or straight across. Sociologists have recognized this and have attempted to find the systematic patterns of variation in religious involvement over the life course. As modern society has become more pluralistic, differentiated, and even frag-mented, it has become harder to find those pat-terns (Hunt 2007). We will nonetheless try to bring some order to the chaos and answer the question: How does religion evolve and change as people age and as they experience major "life course" events like high school graduation, mar-riage and child rearing, and retirement?

Adolescence

In discussing religious socialization, we already paid some attention to the period of ado-lescence. It is hard to define strictly in terms of age, but it is typically seen as the transitional period from childhood to adulthood. A broad estimate would be from 13 to 19 years of age. This is the time of life when children are matur-ing physically and seeking independence from their parents socially and therefore is expected to be a period of declining religious involvement.

In part because of the practical difficulties of studying children and in part because many soci-ologists have not been interested in the religion of youth, sociologists have not historically had good data on religion and youth. That has changed considerably lately thanks to the availability of data sets such as the National Longitudinal Study of Adolescent to Adult Health (Add Health; cpc .unc.edu/addhealth), Monitoring the Future (monitoringthefuture.org), and, most recently, the National Study of Youth and Religion (NSYR; youthandreligion.org).

These different data sets tell a similar story about religion and adolescence: that adolescence is a major period of instability. Frequently that instability manifests itself as religious decline, for example in attendance from middle through high school. The NSYR data showed that in the 3 years between ages 13 to 17 and ages 16 to 20 of their data collection, weekly religious service attendance declined by 13% and nonattendance increased by 10% (Denton, Pearce, and Smith 2008). The authors highlighted some interesting caveats, though. First, most adolescents only changed their level of religious attendance slightly over this time period, from weekly to two to three times per month, for example. Second, very few adolescents (7%) went from regular attendance (once/week or more) to non-attendance. Third, 15% of adolescents reported *increased* levels of religious service attendance.

These NSYR data also show that declining levels of religious service attendance are related to events taking place outside the family and religious sphere, such as getting a job and start-ing to have sex (Hardie, Pearce, and Denton 2013). As we will explore more in the next sec-tion on emerging adulthood, leaving home is also related to declining attendance. Parental reli-gious involvement, by contrast, has a "protec-tive" influence on adolescents' attendance (Hardie et al. 2013).

This last finding draws attention to a fact that others have previously noted: that the religious story of adolescence is not simply one of uni-form decline. Rather, some scholars have called it a period of religious "polarization" (Ozorak 1989). In line with this interpretation, Regnerus and Uecker examined the Add Health data and found that 20% to 22% of adolescents showed a decline in some form of religiosity during ado-lescence, but 15% to 18% showed an increase. Those whose involvement in a faith community increased during adolescence tended to come from highly religious families and from conser-vative Protestant traditions, suggesting the con-tinuing importance of religious socialization in the later period of childhood (Regnerus and Uecker 2006).

Emerging Adulthood

In every society, adolescents make a transi-tion into adulthood. In some societies, this involves elaborate (and sometimes dangerous) rites of passage like the Maasai lion hunt in Africa, the Australian Aborigine walkabout, and the Native American vision quest among the Plains "Indians." Historically, many of these rites of passage were conducted in the context of religious celebrations. Even in the modern West, many religious groups mark the transition into religious adulthood with rituals such as baptism (in Protestant traditions), confirmation (Roman Catholicism), and the bar/bat mitzvah (Judaism). However, as these religious transitions typically take place during adolescence (the bat mitzvah coincides with physical puberty, for example), they cannot really be seen as transitions into adulthood in the secular world.

For most American youth today, the passage to adulthood is not clear (Hunt 2007). The age of 18 used to be fairly significant, as it entailed a graduation from high school and entrance into college or the world of work, as well as the right to vote, drink alcohol, and (for men) be drafted into the military. Also, the average age of marriage and childbearing was lower then, so the years of 18 to 22 were a real transition into adulthood. How the times have changed. Today, some young people—especially those higher on the economic ladder—stay connected financially to their parents, delay marriage (or have "starter marriages"), and postpone childbearing longer than ever. A term has even been coined to describe young people who leave home (often for college) and then return home to live with their parents—"boomerang kids" (Mitchell 2006). Where once high school graduation was a passage to adulthood, now college graduation does not even serve that function for all young people.

Jeffrey Arnett has described this new cultural life stage from roughly ages 18 to 29 as "emerging adulthood"—a sort of gray area between adolescence and adulthood. Not surprisingly, like adolescence, the period of emerging adulthood is characterized by considerable instability, but compounded by the flux created by the process of leaving home (Arnett 2004). The effect of this on religion is clear: "Emerging adults are . . . the least religious adults in the United States today" (Smith 2009:102). On measures of service attendance, prayer, and religious importance, emerging adults consistently registered lower levels of religiosity

than older adults. Christian Smith made an important comparative point in putting these emerging adult religious practices in a broader context. Drawing on the work of political scientist Robert Putnam (*Bowling Alone*), he noted,

> Emerging adults are not only less *religiously* committed and involved than older adults but also tend to be less involved in and committed toward a wide variety of other, nonreligious social and institutional connections, associations, and activities. Emerging adults, for instance, belong to fewer voluntary associations, give less money in charitable donations, volunteer less, and read newspapers less than do older adults. (Smith 2009:92)

Emerging adults who attend college are no less likely to have religious involvements than those who do not seek further education (Smith 2009). Thus, it is not the secularizing effect of college that lowers emerging adults' religiosity but their general detachment from broader social associations, activities, and concerns (Smith 2009). This makes sense because it is exactly the lack of stability in work and personal relationships that is definitive of emerging adulthood as a developmental stage.

Online Resources: To see how your religious beliefs and practices compare to those of others, go the Association of Religion Data Archives' online interactive surveys and quizzes (thearda.com/learn ingcenter) and choose the "Compare Yourself Survey." There are both youth and adult interactive surveys. The youth survey allows you to input an age between 13 and 20 and compares your responses to data from the National Study of Youth and Religion. The adult survey allows you to choose age categories from 18 to 35, 36 to 55, and 56+ and compares your responses to the Baylor Religion Survey. What interesting similarities and differences do you find? Are you surprised by them?

Mature Adulthood

Mature adulthood is characterized for most people by two of the most significant life course events: (1) marriage and (2) childbearing. Both of these family formation events are related to higher levels of religious practice. Of course, these are not the only family cycle events that can take place during this time. Both divorce and cohabitation are increasingly common and generally reduce religious activity (Myers 1996; Stolzenberg, Blair-Loy, and Waite 1995).

Some interesting caveats apply in this stage of the life course. The exact timing of these family formation events mediates their influence on religious behaviors. For example, research shows that people who have children in mature adulthood (their late 20s or early 30s) increase their religious participation while those who rear their children earlier do not (Stolzenberg et al. 1995). This may be due to the fact that when people marry and have children at the later ages associated with mature adulthood, they benefit more from the social support provided in religious organizations.

Also, unlike emerging adulthood, mature adulthood is often fraught with responsibilities and other stressors that can negatively affect religious involvement (Hunt 2007). For middle-class mature adults, especially those who buy into the ideology of "competitive parenting," weekends may no longer constitute a Sabbath (day of rest and time of worship) but a time to take their children to swim meets, soccer games, dance recitals, art exhibits, tennis tournaments, photography classes, college campus visits, and the like. Stress may be work related, like increasing responsibility on the job, job-related relocation, the threat of "downsizing," or the possibility of being overtaken by younger workers. Alternatively, stress may be family related, like concern for aging parents, saving for retirement, and children's education (Hochschild 2001). That said, some stressful experiences in mature adulthood, like personal illnesses, may be inducements to seek consolation in religion (Ferraro and Kelley-Moore 2002).

Later Life

Studies consistently show that religion increases in old age. For example, in his summary of the research on religion and aging, Neal Krause noted that 79% of people between the ages of 65 and 74 claim that religion is very important, 52% attend a worship service, and 89% of older people pray during the typical week (Krause 2006). Christian Smith, in his study of religion and youth, contrasted emerging adults' low levels of religiosity with older adults' high levels: 42% of young adults pray daily or more often compared to 76% of those over 75 years old, 22% of emerging adults characterize their religion as "strong" compared to 53% of older adults, and 15% of emerging adults attend religious services at least weekly compared to 40% of older adults (Smith 2009).

One explanation for the rise in religiosity in later life is that religious participation provides a system of social, emotional, and spiritual support (Krause 2006). As people age, they lose social ties, and their role in society changes. They retire and lose friends. The social ties of religious congregations help to fill this void. Many religious communities also still believe in the concept of respecting one's elders. As shown by prevalent ageism in contemporary society, this is not necessarily true in the secular world. Older adults are also encouraged to perform volunteer work through religious organizations. This provides social ties and an opportunity to participate in important productive activities.

In addition to the benefits of involvement within a religious organization stated previously, there is evidence that being involved in a religious community as an older adult has health benefits. A 2001 study by Krause suggests that people in active social networks have better mental and physical health. People with stronger support systems like those found in churches, temples, and mosques also live longer (Hummer et al. 1999). The difference that occurs in the religious setting as opposed to secular social ties is the component of spiritual support. Unlike other social ties, religious ties are uniquely suited to relieving the fear and uncertainty of death (Siegel and Shrimshaw 2002).

Critical Thinking: Does this description of change over the life course, including modifications in religious sensibility, seem consistent with older members of your family or with other people you know? If not, what might be different to have altered the outcomes?

AGE, COHORT, AND GENERATIONAL EFFECTS ON RELIGION

In our review of religiosity at various stages of the life course, we focused our attention only on different age groups (13- to 18-year-olds, 18- to 20-year-olds, and so on). We specified how religiosity fluctuated according to age or age-based life course events (e.g., leaving home, marriage). These are called "age effects" on religiosity. Although this offers an important developmental perspective on variations in religiosity, it assumes that the effects of aging on religiosity are constant over time. For example, emerging adults have low levels of religious involvement *now*, but when they are 40 and married with kids, their engagement with a faith community will *increase*, and when they are 70 and facing death, it will be *even higher*.

This assumption would be sound if age effects were all that mattered in explaining religiosity over time. It seems unlikely, however, that someone experiencing adolescence in the 1920s or 1930s (the Great Depression era) would experience religion or faith tradition over the life course in the same way as someone coming of age in the 1940s (the World War II era) or 1960s ("The Sixties"). The age effect in all of these cases combines with the effect of living

through a specific period in history (called, not surprisingly, a "period effect") to produce what sociologists call a "cohort effect." A cohort effect is the combined effect of being a certain age at a certain period of time.

Cohort analysis reminds us that cultural context shapes the expectations of age-related behavior. In fact, although we discussed it as an age-based developmental stage, "emerging adulthood" may in fact be more properly characterized as a cohort phenomenon: It is the particular way that early adulthood is experienced by those who came of age in the last 10 to 15 years. "Emerging adulthood" as a part of the life course did not exist 50 years ago, and it may not exist 50 years from now. This highlights the importance of looking at cohorts but also the difficulty of separating age and cohort effects in any particular analysis.

At this point, you might be saying to yourself that this sounds like an extremely complex way of describing a commonsense idea: "generation." To some extent, you would be right. Karl Mannheim long ago stressed the importance of understanding how shared formative experiences forge in a collection of individuals particular worldviews that they carry with them the rest of their lives. He called his paper "The Problem of Generations" (Mannheim 1927). So, generations and cohorts are closely related. A generation is typically seen as encompassing several cohorts (Ryder 1965).

A good example of how age and cohort/generation can independently affect religious participation is Michele Dillon's (2007) summary of her analysis of data collected by UC Berkeley's Institute for Human Development (IHD) in the 1920s (see also Dillon and Wink 2007). The study contains longitudinal data over a 60-year time span, including two cohorts born 8 years apart (the older in 1920 and 1921 and the younger in 1928 and 1929). The older subjects were children of the Great Depression, old enough to serve in the military during World War II, and experienced the social upheaval of The Sixties when they were in their 50s. The younger subjects did not experience the deprivation of the Great Depression, were not old enough to serve in the military during the war, and were almost to middle age during the 1960s. In Dillon's view, the drastic differences in experiences of the subjects represent not just different cohorts but also different generations.

Results of the IHD study showed that religious involvement did not follow a linear trend across the life course but was described as a U-curve. Religious commitment was high in adolescence and in later life and generally lower in middle adulthood. That the pattern of high religiosity at the beginning and end was the same for both of the generations suggests that age effects might be at work rather than cohort effects. On the other hand, the timing of the post-adolescence decrease differed between the generational groups. The younger generation declined in religious commitment in their 30s, while the older generation declined much later, in their late 40s. The different timing of these drops suggests a cohort or generational explanation. Given their different experience—the Depression and World War II compared to the 1950s and '60s—members of the older group *as a generation* remained more committed to social institutions, including religion, for a longer period of time.

Using more contemporary data, generational analysis in the sociology of religion has grown increasingly popular in the past 25 years as the "Baby Boom Generation" has worked its way through the life course, spawning Generation X and Generation Y (also known as "Millennials" or "Echo Boomers"). Table 5.1 illustrates how age and period come together to forge these cohorts into recognizable generations for sociological analysis.

Critical Thinking: Examine Table 5.1, and determine the generation with which you would be identified. Do you feel a part of that generation? Do you think of yourself in those terms? Look at the period influences that have shaped your generation. Do those influences shape the way you approach religion, or do you feel your religion is pretty typical for a person your age, regardless of the time period?

Table 5.1 Recent Generations of Interest to Sociologists of Religion

Generation	Birth Years	High School Class	Age in 2016	Some Period Influences
Silent Generation	1928–1945	1945–1962	71–88	World War II, nationalism, McCarthyism (anticommunism), strong confidence in American institutions (including government, business, religion, and family), television becomes ubiquitous
Baby Boomers	1946–1964	1963–1981	52–70	The Sixties (Vietnam War, civil rights movement, sexual revolution, drugs, rock and roll, Kennedy–King–Kennedy assassinations, Stonewall riots), *Roe v. Wade*, OPEC oil crisis, Watergate, Nixon resignation, drugs–disco, stagflation
Generation X (Baby Bust)	1965–1980	1982–1997	36–51	Disco dies, MTV born, beginning of cable TV, Iran hostage crisis, Ronald Reagan/George H. W. Bush, energy crisis and recession followed by unprecedented stretch of economic growth, HIV/AIDS, end of Cold War/fall of Berlin wall, hip-hop, PC revolution, creation of the World Wide Web, cell phones

(Continued)

Table 5.1 (Continued)

Generation	Birth Years	High School Class	Age in 2016	Some Period Influences
Millennials (Generation Y, Echo Boomers)	1981–2000	1998–2017	20–35	Ubiquity of computers, cell phones, iPods and MP3 players, e-mail/IM/texting, Facebook and YouTube ("digital natives"—see Chapter 14); globalization and pluralism; Harry Potter; hooking up; sex scandals; 9/11 and war on terror; dot-com bubble burst (2000); U.S. housing bubble burst (2008); global financial crisis (2008–)
Homeland Generation (New Silent Generation)	2001–	2018–	16 and under	Also digital natives, plus "War on Terror," global financial crisis, ISIS, torture, Sandy Hook, lockdown drills in school, first African American president, same-sex marriage legalized

NOTE: There is no definitive dating of these generations. For ease of presentation of data, we follow the Pew Research Center's definitions.

The key to a generational analysis of religion is to understand how the period influences fundamentally shape the outlook of individuals who live through them at a key developmental moment (typically adolescence). That unique outlook then shapes the specific way the generation members understand and practice their faith. Wade Clark Roof was among the first to do this for Baby Boomers. In *A Generation of Seekers: The Spiritual Journeys of the Baby Boom Generation* (1993) and *Spiritual Marketplace: Baby Boomers and the Remaking of American Religion* (1999), Roof argued that the particular generational experiences of Baby Boomers led them to fundamentally reorient themselves to religion by adopting the posture of spiritual seekers. Having come of age largely in the 1960s and 1970s—fully exposed to the cultural ferment of the time as well as the authority damaging revelations of the Vietnam War and Watergate—the Boomers Roof studies feel authorized to choose their own religious path, emphasize the experiential aspect of religion over the doctrinal, and are skeptical of traditional religious organizations. They created the idea of being "spiritual, not religious."

This brings us back to cohorts. According to Ryder (1965), "cohort replacement"—the replacement of older cohorts (through death) by younger cohorts—is a fundamental engine of social change. Roof's argument that Baby Boomers are remaking American religion is based in part on this idea: Cohorts of Boomers and their children—who they will socialize into this new seeker orientation toward religion—will gradually replace older cohorts who were oriented toward more traditional expressions of religion.

Of course, for this transformation of American religion to take place, Boomers need to effectively socialize their children into their spiritual seeking orientation. Have they done so? No comprehensive study of Millennials—sometimes called Echo Boomers because they are generally the children of Baby Boomers and hence also a larger generation in number—yet exists. However, some scholars have begun to grapple with the religion of those born after the Baby Boomers. Richard Flory and Donald Miller, for example, highlighted the spiritual quest of the post-Boomer generation. They argued that, like the Baby Boomers, Echo

Boomers have formative experiences that are specific to their time and place and that influence their orientation to religion (Flory and Miller 2008). Among the formative experiences is that as children of Boomers, they inherit an ethos of questioning institutional authority and focusing on the personal journey. This has been reinforced by unethical and hypocritical actions of some major institutions, including business scandals like Enron and religious malfeasance like the Catholic Church's handling of pedophilia by priests. Another major influence on Echo Boomers is the increasing pluralism of the world, whether they experience it directly in their neighborhoods and schools or indirectly through the ubiquitous "new media" these "digital natives" employ (Palfrey and Gasser 2008). This leads to an attitude of tolerance and acceptance of difference.

How do these cultural influences and generational responses affect the practice of religion or faith traditions? Flory and Miller argued that Echo Boomers approach religious institutions with some suspicion and so focus on the quality of relationships within the institution instead of the institution itself. They also emphasize experience and embodiment in their religious practices (Flory and Miller 2008). Although they are in the spiritual marketplace created in part by their parents' generation, they are not content simply to browse and buy (consume). They want to have a hand in the production of the religious goods to be consumed. The authors call this combination of these elements "expressive communalism."

Table 5.2 highlights some major differences in the religious practices of Americans by generation. Whether we look at religious affiliation, self-claimed importance of religion, service attendance, or prayer, there is a correlation between generation and religion. Although we need to be aware of the life-cycle effects discussed above—that people become more religious as they age—the Pew Research Center Forum on Religion and Public Life (2010, 2014) reports on which this table is based show that at each successive generation the starting point of religiosity gets lower and lower. So, even if Millennials become increasingly engaged in a faith community and practices as they age, unless there is some dramatic change, they will not surpass the levels of previous generations. This suggests the significance of considering cohort effects alongside the age effects discussed above.

Table 5.2 Religious Beliefs and Practices by Generation

Generation	Religiously Unaffiliated	Religion Very Important in Lives	Weekly Religious Service Attendance	Daily Prayer
Millennials	29	40	18	41
Generation X	21	52	27	54
Baby Boomers	16	60	32	62
Silent Generation	9	67	44	71

SOURCES: Column 1 from Pew Research Center Forum on Religion and Public Life, *Millennials in Adulthood: Detached From Institutions, Networked With Friends* (March 7, 2014). Columns 2–4 from Pew Research Center Forum on Religion and Public Life, *Religion Among the Millennials* (February 2010).

According to Wade Clark Roof, generational patterns not only have significance in terms of individual-level beliefs and practices but also have implications for the religious organizations that have to adapt to generational shifts. Faced with children of Baby Boomers who have no strong attachment to particular religious institutions but who, as "digital natives" (those who have never lived in a world without digital technology), are strongly attached to their smartphones, religious organizations must respond. They are scrambling to figure out ways to harness the power of new media in order to connect with these Millennials (Roof 2009).

As we will discuss in Chapter 14, use of the Internet is one of the areas of fastest growth for congregations recently, but much of that use is simply informational, not interactive. In the "Illustrating Sociological Concepts" feature, we learn about a Lutheran minister, Rev. Keith Anderson, who is more actively engaging the social media interests of his digital native congregants. "You can try to keep [teens] off Facebook for as long as you want, but this is the world they are living in. They are native to it," Anderson says. "So instead of saying, 'It's the devil; stay away from it,' I'm here to show them faith has a role in it. God has a role in everything" (Wellington 2014).

A Multidimensional Model of Commitment

At the core of religion is commitment, for religious organizations are voluntary groups in the modern world. This raises questions about how people become and remain committed; what is the social psychology of the process of devoting one's life to a movement, a group, or a system of meaning? Analytically we can gain significant insights into this issue by looking at groups that are outside the mainstream. In this section, we utilize insights from Rosabeth Kanter's study of how commitment develops and is sustained in utopian communities and communes, suggesting how those same processes can be seen in more conventional religious groups and even nonreligious groups that require commitment (Kanter 1972).

Utopian communities provided a good test for Kanter's model of commitment because these groups attempt to create a radically different social order, and it must compete with the broader society for followers' loyalties. Clearly, living an austere lifestyle with all things shared in common demanded a high level of commitment. The result of Kanter's research was to identify a number of mechanisms of commitment found in successful communities. These commitment mechanisms apply to a variety of different types of organizations—Kanter's work has been cited in over 1,000 other studies of businesses, nonprofits, and social movement organizations over the past four decades—but the model is particularly applicable to religious movements.

Kanter found that commitment occurs on three different levels: (1) commitment to the organization (*instrumental commitment*); (2) commitment to other persons in the group (*affective commitment*); and (3) commitment to the rules, regulations, ideas, and mores of the group (*moral commitment*). Any group or institution may elicit one or more of these types of commitment (Kanter 1972). Although they are interrelated, they are also distinct aspects of social organization that can be analyzed separately, for they are forms of commitment to the meaning system, the institutional system, and the belonging system, respectively—the three subsystems we found to make up a religion. According to Kanter, each of the three types of commitment involves two mechanisms that enhance commitment.

Moral Commitment

Moral commitment refers to commitment to the norms and values of the group—indeed, to the meaning system of the religion. If the group is to

ILLUSTRATING SOCIOLOGICAL CONCEPTS

Digital Disciples

Elizabeth Wellington

Twenty-six teenagers dillydally on smartphones, sending instant messages, scrolling through news feeds, liking statuses and posting updates on social media sites Twitter, Facebook and Instagram while intermittently gazing at farmland images beaming from a digital projector. New Age tunes echo through the room courtesy of online music service Spotify.

Despite the tech-rich environment, these youths aren't meeting at an urban cybercafe or taking a class at an Apple store. They are congregating at the Upper Dublin Lutheran Church fellowship hall in the Rev. Keith Anderson's weekly catechism class. The day's focus is on the third commandment: Remember the Sabbath day and keep it holy.

But Anderson sees no irony in allowing his students to noodle around online as part of a discussion on God's rules of rest. Indeed, this is their Sabbath.

"When we were planning this class, we debated whether or not we would let them use their smartphones during the 20-minute in-class Sabbath time," said Anderson, the 39-year-old pastor of Upper Dublin Lutheran, a 1,000-member church family in Ambler, Penn.

"And then we decided, yes we should. This is how they relax. This is what they would do to relax. This is how they experience Sabbath," he said.

Over the last five years, Anderson has built a national reputation in Christian circles as a social media expert—especially as the technology relates to teens and tweens. He is best-known for the 192-page paperback "Click 2 Save: The Digital Ministry Bible," which he co-wrote with Elizabeth Drescher, a professor of religious studies at Santa Clara University.

More than a gimmick to spark the teens' interest, Anderson says, social media can be used as a tool to convey the ancient teachings of the church in the formation of a new generation of Christians. It can help break down barriers, reach across fractures in teens' lives, and engage teens in the spaces—digital or otherwise—where they live.

"How do we equip them to take care of themselves in this space, and be people of faith, if we aren't in this space?" he said.

In his own church, he is incorporating technology and social media into the everyday life of faith, including youth formation. It's more than just letting the students text during breaks; as part of the class's fall Ten Commandments project, Anderson asked his students to Instagram pictures of their ideal forms of Sabbath. They've discussed Christlike behavior on the Internet, and what it means to be a "digital disciple."

Anderson's social media philosophy is simple: God is everywhere, even in the Twitterverse. If the church fails to embrace that, it stands to lose its future members.

"[Social media] isn't just a tool you can use in formation, like the way we used a slide show in the 1960s and '70s," said Drescher, Anderson's co-author. "The church is slowly starting to acknowledge that social media is the landscape of communication," Drescher said. "This is the medium where spiritual growth is happening, so we have to be working in that medium."

SOURCE: First published in the Faith & Leadership blog (www.faithandleadership.com), Duke University Divinity School, January 14, 2014.

develop in a coherent way and have some sort of consistency in ideology, members must grant some authority to the leaders and buy into the consensus. Because leaders of religious groups do not have total control over their members, they must depend on voluntary compliance. The control issue is especially problematic for groups that have messages that deviate from the dominant (secular) society. Hence, the meaning system—the theology—of the group must seem compellingly true, eternal, and just. There are two mechanisms that can enhance the moral commitment of devotees: *mortification* and *transcendence.*

The mortification process places heavy emphasis on the willfulness, egotism, selfishness, and conceit of people, and this generates a sense of profound humility. This is often done by emphasizing that without this group or this faith, the members would be hopeless degenerates. Often the message is on how sinful or unworthy human beings are, and this is hammered home in sermons and hymns. Many groups have frequent confessions of sins—some make them public confessions in front of everyone else in the group—and this enhances humility. However, surprisingly, this procedure often releases feelings of exhilaration. Kanter writes,

[T]he use of mortification is a sign that the group cares about the individual, about his thoughts and feelings, about the content of his inner world. The group cares enough to pay great attention to the person's behavior, and to promise him warmth, intimacy, and love . . . if he indicates he can accept these gifts without abuse. (Kanter 1972:105)

The act of being emotionally naked before others whom one trusts tends to engender ecstatic feelings of intimacy and union with one's associates. The feeling of worthlessness is also important in understanding why people follow the leadership of the group with intense loyalty.

Many groups could be identified as having mechanisms to induce feelings of individual insignificance and even submissiveness. Regardless of variations in the way different religious groups engender the attitude, a sense of personal worthlessness is very functional for the group. When people are convinced that they are truly insignificant as individuals, they are more humble and more willing to obey their superiors.

Humble people are also less likely to assert themselves in conflict with peers, and deference to others enhances harmony and cooperation. Note that if Roberts and Yamane (your authors) have huge egos and they disagree about something, each may dig in his heels and insist that the other is just plain wrong. It could get nasty if it were in a public setting. If, on the other hand, they have some measure of humility, each may figure that the other is a bit smarter than himself. In such a case, it is amazing how well they can get along. Humility helps groups cohere, and mortification mechanisms foster that humility.

This leads to the second process: transcendence—the sense of ultimate purpose and meaning. Although the person may feel worthless as an individual, his or her life has ultimate and eternal meaning as a member of the group. The group offers a hope of final victory that obliterates the meaninglessness of mundane existence. The group offers "The Truth." This, in turn, builds a secondary self-esteem *as a member of the group.* This generates a sense of mystery and a feeling of awe for the leaders and/or for the myths, symbols, and rituals of the group. These processes of de-emphasizing the individual, glorifying the group, and creating a sense of awe about the group's ideology are the foundation stones of moral commitment.

Instrumental Commitment

Instrumental commitment means the individual must be convinced that continued association with the group or organization is worth the time and effort it demands. Hence, the individual engages in a sort of cost–benefit analysis. At the cognitive (thinking) level, the committed individual must conclude that the profits associated with continued participation are significant and well worth the time and energy expended. Furthermore, if individuals feel that there would be substantial cost associated with leaving the group, the institution stands to gain in its *retention* of members. Two organizational mechanisms tend to enhance instrumental commitment by influencing this cost–benefit ratio. They are *sacrifice* and *investment*. "Sacrifice means that membership becomes more costly and is therefore not lightly regarded nor likely to be given up easily" (Kanter 1972:72).

Members of religious movements are sometimes asked to make substantial sacrifices. Many times a comfortable life has been sacrificed for the rigor of an austere lifestyle, in which numerous popular recreational and social activities are denied. Devotees may be forbidden alcohol, drugs, or coffee, and they may find that movies and other secular entertainments are disallowed. For example, Stillson Judah wrote regarding the attitude of a new religious movement he studied: "The devotee must be ready . . . to give up something that he strongly desires, while accepting something he does not like" (Judah 1974:91).

Even being active in the local religious community may mean one cannot sleep late on the Sabbath morning (a sacrifice, indeed) and one may be expected to fast (go without food) on certain holy days. Attitudes of asceticism or self-denial are especially common among sectarian and cultic groups. Kanter showed that this sacrifice is quite functional for commitment:

> Once members have agreed to make the "sacrifices," their motivation to remain participants increases. Membership becomes more valuable and meaningful. Regardless of how the group induces the original concessions or manages to recruit people willing to make them, the fact is that those groups exacting sacrifices survive longer . . . The more it "costs" a person to do something, the more "valuable" he will consider it. (Kanter 1972:76)

Sacrifice causes a person not to want to leave because leaving would be to admit that the sacrifices were not worthwhile. Whether consciously or unconsciously, people do not like to admit that they have made foolish sacrifices. Hence, once a part of the group, demands for self-denying behavior act to increase and sustain members' commitment.

The other mechanism that enhances instrumental commitment is investment. Although people sacrifice by not using their time, energy, and resources in activities they might otherwise find enjoyable, they are expected to invest that time, energy, and money in the group. Many vibrant religious movements require at least a tithe (usually 10% of earnings), and some new religious movements (NRMs) require that for full membership the devotee turn over *all* of his or her earnings to the organization. If the donation of all one's worldly goods is irrevocable, the investment becomes even more important, for it deters one from leaving the group later. Most people will continue their association with a group rather than to admit to themselves that they have been foolish.

The devotee may also be required to invest substantial amounts of *time* in the group. The expectation of the Church of Jesus Christ of Latter-day Saints (the Mormons) that young men devote 2 years proselytizing or missionizing is a good example. Likewise, hours of public chanting required of new members of the Hare Krishna enhanced their commitment (Judah 1974). Members of many religious communities will spend untold hours in meetings, service activities, and other time-expensive activities.

The important factor in understanding retention of members is that a group that requires little investment and little or no sacrifice is likely to elicit little instrumental commitment. Persons may be committed at other levels, but commitment to the organization itself will be low. In conventional religious denominations, the *costs* of joining a conventional group are much less severe than in groups like utopian movements. Regardless, some measure of instrumental commitment is important for any organization, for the organization needs the time, the talents, and the financial resources of members if it is to thrive.

Affective Commitment

Affective commitment refers to an emotional dependence on the group. The group's members become one's primary set of relations. Many sects and cults work to become the *only* reference group of the members, but affective ties are important in conventional religious groups as well. A number of studies have shown that the vitality of any local religious community is profoundly affected by the number of small, intimate groups in which people share their lives with one another (Berger 1999; Miller 1997; Wilson et al. 1993; Wuthnow 1994b). Affective commitment is of central importance in religious behavior. Andrew Greeley suggested that while meaning functions may be *primary*, the belonging functions are often chronologically *prior* (Greeley 1972). We see this clearly as we explore the commitment and conversion processes in the NRMs that scholars have been able to track from their early periods. For example, "warmth and friendship among the devotees" was one of the reasons most frequently cited by members for original attraction to the Hare Krishna movement (Judah 1974:153–154). The Moonies consciously looked for signs of isolation or symbols of transiency—like backpacks—to identify prospective converts (Bromley and Shupe 1979). Such persons are less likely to have other affective commitments and are more likely to be in need of a group that can offer emotional support.

The affective commitment process involves two mechanisms: (1) detachment or *renunciation* of former ties and (2) *communion* with the new group. Many NRMs demand that new recruits not contact their families, especially for the first few weeks or months. Judah reported that for the group he studied, "progress depends on willingness to give up the company of anyone who is not a devotee" (Judah 1974:91). Renunciation of one's former friends, family, and social groups typically involves defining outsiders as evil or as insignificant. Other groups reject the secular world itself as sinister.

Among the Amish, the Bruderhof, the early Christian church, the early Mormon church, and many holiness groups, we find high boundaries and a tendency to define nonmembers as degenerate, evil, or confused. Hence, contacts with outsiders are limited and are controlled by norms that make those interactions rather formal, ritualized affairs. The process of becoming committed to NRMs has to do with a complete change of reference groups. Note that many groups enhance commitment by heightening the boundaries between "us" and "them": Think about Greek houses on campus.

The second affective mechanism is communion—emotional solidarity with others. While new recruits are removed from former reference groups, they are warmly embraced and provided with a high degree of emotional support in the new reference group. The Moonies were very intentional about this process, which they called "love bombing." Particularly for isolated persons, transient people, or loners, this intensity of concern and emotional warmth may be the most significant experience of family that the individual has known. Many communes—as well as many religious groups—refer to themselves as family, for the group actually becomes a surrogate family for the members.

It is not necessary to focus only on unconventional groups to see the importance of this process. Most of the more conservative churches and temples with high retention rates have extensive meetings and social events. If a person attends morning worship on the Sabbath, has another worship experience on Sunday evening (perhaps preceded by a potluck dinner), attends the men's prayer breakfast or the women's prayer group on Tuesday morning, goes to Bible study on Wednesday evening, and serves on a committee of the congregation, he or she has little time or energy for other social commitments. The other persons attending those functions become one's primary social relations.

Prayer groups build an intense sense of intimacy and belonging. In prayer groups, people develop trust and display vulnerability—sharing weaknesses, confessing faults or failings, and asking for prayer on these matters. The group is likely to be supportive rather than judgmental, and other members reciprocate with confessions of matters where they need support. A very intense sense of belonging develops—thus enhancing affective commitment.

As mentioned in the photo of the young people praying, prayer groups often share deeply within the group and become tightly bonded. Still, many congregations of mainline denominations do not seem to elicit high levels of commitment; many are lacking programs that develop close and supportive interpersonal relationships among members. In fact, members of NRMs frequently cite a lack of meaningful friendships in their original religious group as a reason for leaving that faith (Bromley and Shupe 1979; Judah 1974). The feeling of communion—of truly belonging, being cared for, and caring for others—is an extremely powerful commitment mechanism.

Once recruits become a part of the group and begin to identify its members as their best friends, they may come to realize that the group has an internal stratification system. Some people are more highly respected than others. Because one wants to be liked and respected by one's new friends and colleagues, following the group's rules becomes important. As one receives responsibilities and is recognized for contributions to the group, one has begun to climb the stratification ladder. Having taken a step or two up the ladder, the individual has made an initial investment in the group. Hence, affective commitment leads naturally to instrumental commitment. Commitment to the group members and commitment to the organization are intertwined—as indeed, the belonging and institutional subsystems of religion are linked.

Retention of members also depends on an ongoing set of primary relationships with believers. Bromley and Shupe reported that when Moonie devotees are not harbored in supportive environments, defections are very high. The insistence on endogamy (marriage only to individuals within the group) is one way to ensure interlocking relationships. By ensuring endogamous marriages, as Reverend Moon did by arranging marriages among the Moonies, a set of interlocking and mutually reinforcing relationships is created. Cross-religion marriage is, after all, one of the strongest predictors of low religious practice. It all has to do with in-group affective ties (Bromley and Shupe 1979).

Table 5.3 summarizes the types of commitment and the processes that enhance each type.

Regardless of how liberal or conservative or radical the group, research indicates that affective commitment usually comes first, followed by instrumental commitment to the organization and then moral commitment to the ideas and beliefs of the group. The sequence is not absolute, but when Greeley said "instead of Americans belonging to churches because they believe . . . there may be a strong tendency for them to believe . . . because they belong" (Greeley 1972:115), he was describing a typical scenario. Note that we are born into groups and feel belonging from infancy. No wonder that most people stay in the religious group of their birth and come to believe (accept) the meaning system that it affirms.

Table 5.3 Kanter's Commitment Theory

Type of Commitment	Processes That Enhance This Commitment
Instrumental commitment (Commitment to the organization)	1. Sacrifice 2. Investment
Affective commitment (Commitment to the members)	1. Renunciation 2. Communion
Moral commitment (Commitment to the ideas as spelled out by the leaders)	1. Mortification 2. Transcendence

A Commitment Dilemma for Liberal Faith Communities

Some of the mechanisms that contribute to commitment in sects and cults are antithetical to many mainline denominations and more progressive faith communities. First, the doctrine of the "priesthood of all believers" in some religious communities is contrary to the "spiritual hierarchy" of certain other groups that seek submission. Second, the emphasis on open-mindedness and tolerance toward others in more liberal faith communities counters the sectarian emphasis that one's group has the whole truth, the only truth, and the exclusively held truth. The high boundaries of "us" and "them" have been falling away in the more moderate and progressive denominations and congregations as they have stressed cooperation and ecumenism. Third, and perhaps most importantly, clergy in more liberal mainline denominations have tended to emphasize the importance of self-esteem, thereby reversing the denigration of one's self. Liberal clergy, especially, see a positive self-image as essential to mental health and well-being and maintain that religions encouraging dependency are not allowing individuals to nurture their God-given creativity (Clinebell 1965). People who respect themselves and their own ideas are more likely to engage in independent and critical thinking, but this does not enhance commitment to the group's ideology. Hence, liberal religious groups may have lower levels of commitment because they emphasize individuality and personal self-esteem. It is no wonder that conservative groups lose fewer members.

Many different types of groups and organizations use one or more of the commitment mechanisms discussed by Kanter. The unique quality of nonconventional religious groups (like most NRMs) is that they must elicit and sustain a very high level of commitment, for they need many resources from their limited membership. The NRMs and sectarian groups that survive are those that use all—or at least most—of the commitment processes discussed here.

Commitment, then, can be commitment to the ideology and the moral rules of the group (the meaning system), to the organization (the institutional system), or to the group members with whom one has strong emotional ties (the belonging system of religion). Often, commitment at one level will lead to commitment at another. Although it is possible for people to be committed at only one level (the old man who gives thousands of dollars to the church or temple but never attends), religious groups usually need commitment at multiple levels, for the subsystems that compose a religion are linked together in ways that mutually affect one another. This is yet another way that the religion as an interconnected system operates as a system: Meaning, belonging, and institutional structure are all related.

Critical Thinking: In your own religious tradition, which type of commitment do you think *usually* comes first as people become committed members? Why do you think so? Can you think of people in your congregation or people you know for whom the sequence is different from the one you think is typical?

RELIGION AND IDENTITY

When a person is deeply committed to something, it often shapes that individual's sense of self and identity. So we look now at the link between religion and identity. Identities are people's conceptions of who they are and where they belong in the world. Some of these are very individually idiosyncratic (e.g., I am a sensitive, new age guy), while others are connected to various group identities (e.g., I am an Asian American professor) (Postmes and Branscombe 2010). Not surprisingly, given the belonging dimension of religion that we stress in this textbook, religious groups have historically been among the most important identity groups for people. A person's religious identity, then, can be understood (at least initially) as the religious group with which a person identifies (including behaviorally and in terms of attitudes). For example, "I am a Methodist," "I am a member of First Baptist Church in Mocksville," or "I am a druid."

Most sociologists of religion, usually implicitly, have adopted this approach to identity, perhaps because it is particularly conducive to the closed-ended survey method of data collection that dominates the field. In these quantitative studies, religious identification or "affiliation" is typically measured using a two-step question. For example, since 1972, the National Opinion Research Center's General Social Survey (GSS) has been asking Americans the following questions: "What is your religious preference? Is it Protestant, Catholic, Jewish, some other religion, or no religion?" Those who respond "Protestant" are then asked this: "What specific denomination is that, if any?" From this we know, for example, that 51.1% of the American population in 2008 identified as Protestant, and 4.3% of Protestants identify as United Methodist.

Online Resources: The Association of Religion Data Archives has a "Measurement Wizard" that allows you to select a concept and see how it has been measured in different surveys (thearda.com/mawizard). In this case, you want to explore the concept "Denominational/Religious Identification." From there choose the category "Denomination, Affiliation to." You should find that there are over 300 questions in the ARDA database that measure some aspect of denominational affiliation. Using the options on this results page, you can refine your search by year, geographic scope, survey frame, and survey type. Explore the various survey questions and results to get a sense of the similarities and differences in the way social scientists have measured this aspect of religious identity.

In 1990, the American Religious Identification Survey (ARIS) took a radically different approach to religious identity. Rather than offering people predetermined response categories, ARIS simply asked, "What is your religion, if any?" Although interviewers did have a list of many different religions that they could mark as responses, they were specifically instructed not to read the list to respondents. As with other surveys, ARIS had a second follow-up question: "If 'Christian' or 'Protestant,' which denomination is that?"

The first ARIS survey had a sample size of (an astounding) 113,723 cases (Kosmin and Lachman 1993). (By comparison, most nationally representative survey samples are 1,000 to 2,000 respondents.) The survey was replicated in 2001 with 50,281 respondents and again in 2008 with 54,461 respondents (Kosmin and Keysar 2009).

The benefit of having these very large sample sizes is that very small religious groups can be identified and analyzed. For example, in the 2001 ARIS, 4 respondents identified themselves as "druid" (Kosmin and Keysar 2006). Table 5.4 summarizes the ARIS findings regarding religious identity in the United States in the nearly 20 years from 1990 to 2008.

Although there are many interesting developments represented in this table—for example, the rising number of Buddhists, Muslims, and other Eastern religions due to immigration (see Chapter 15)—the most significant in terms of changing patterns of religious identification are as follows: (1) The proportion of the American population that self-identifies as Christian in one form or another declined from 86% in 1990 to 76% in 2008. (2) The proportion of the American population self-identifying as mainline Protestants (Methodist, Lutheran, Presbyterian, Episcopal, and United Church of Christ) declined by nearly 6% in the last 20 years. At the same time, there has been a 40-fold increase in the number identifying as nondenominational Christians, from an estimated 194,000 in 1990 to over 8 million in 2008.

This represents a nearly 3.5% increase in the proportion of Americans whose religious identity is nondenominational. (We discuss the former development at greater length in Chapters 6 and 8.) (3) The number of Americans who identify themselves as having no religious preference ("nones") continues to grow dramatically, as does their proportion of the American population. From 1990 to 2008, the proportion of the American population self-identifying as nones increased from 7.5% to 13.4%. Note that this explicitly excludes those who self-identify as agnostic or atheist. As we discuss later in this chapter, about half of these estimated 34 million Americans are religious but choose not to identify themselves as having a religious affiliation—that is, their religious identity is not connected with a particular religious group identity.

These data can be read in light of our previous discussion of generational change, as well as our discussion in Chapter 1 of invisible religion, lived religion, and spirituality. As older cohorts of Americans, who identified themselves according to traditional denominational labels, are replaced in the population by Baby Boomers, GenXers, and Millennials, who have more fluid religious identities, the population who identify as nones will likely continue to grow. In the spiritual marketplace, which has been developing for the past 50 years, religious consumers are increasingly shopping for religious identities that are not closely tied to historic religious groups (Roof 1999). They are increasingly individualized in their tastes and preferences for religious identity (Cimino and Lattin 2002). These data can also be read in a larger historical context as reflecting the flowering of what Phillip Hammond called the "third disestablishment" in American religion (Hammond 1992). The formal disestablishment of religion in the First Amendment to the Constitution of the United States encoded an open market for religion into the DNA of the country (Warner 1993). That open market

Table 5.4 Religious Self-Identification of U.S. Adults, 1990 and 2008

	1990	*2008*	*Change*
Religious Identity	%	%	%
Catholic	26.2	25.1	−1.1
Baptist	19.3	15.8	−3.5
Nones/No Religion	8.2	15.0	+6.8
Christian Unspecified	4.6	7.4	+2.8
Methodist	8.0	5.0	−3.0
Lutheran	5.2	3.8	−1.4
Nondenominational Christian	0.1	3.5	+3.1
Pentecostal Unspecified	1.8	2.4	+0.6
Protestant Unspecified	9.8	2.3	−7.5
Presbyterian	2.8	2.0	−0.7
Mormon/Latter-day Saints	1.4	1.4	—
Jewish	1.8	1.2	−0.6
Episcopalian/Anglican	1.7	1.1	−0.6
Evangelical/Born Again	0.3	0.9	+0.6
Eastern Religions	0.4	0.9	+0.5
Churches of Christ	1.0	0.8	−0.2
Jehovah's Witness	0.8	0.8	—
Muslim	0.3	0.6	+0.3
Buddhist	0.2	0.5	+0.3
Assemblies of God	0.4	0.4	—
United Church of Christ	0.2	0.3	+0.1
Church of God	0.4	0.3	−0.1
Agnostic and Atheist	0.7	1.6	+0.9

SOURCE: Kosmin, Barry A. and Ariela Keysar. 2009. *Summary Report: American Religious Identification Survey (2008)* (March). Hartford, CT: Trinity College. Retrieved from commons.trincoll.edu/aris.

allowed for—and perhaps even promoted—considerable religious vigor in the early decades of the new republic, including revivalism and even the birth of new, distinctively American religions like Mormonism (Finke and Stark 2005). Still, American culture remained steadfastly Protestant during this time. It was not for another century—the early 20th century—that cultural disestablishment of American (Protestant) religion took place, aided in particular by internal divisions between fundamentalists and modernists within Protestantism and by waves of Catholic immigrants who challenged Protestant hegemony (cultural dominance) in politics, education, and elsewhere. Hammond called this the "second disestablishment" of American religion (Hammond 1992).

Will Herberg famously argued in the mid-1950s that a moderate pluralism existed that allowed for Protestants, Catholics, and Jews to be seen as equal contributors to the "American Way of Life." In the decades that followed World War II, this moderate Protestant–Catholic–Jew pluralism would give way to the seemingly unlimited diversity of religious options in the present-day United States (Herberg 1955). Religion as an integrative force and source of collective identity began to give way to a more individualized approach to faith that centered on personal autonomy (Hammond 1992). This is the "third disestablishment" of American religion (see also Roof and McKinney 1987). It is driven by structural and cultural changes in American society. Increasing geographic mobility (especially suburbanization), social mobility (driven by rapidly expanding higher education), and familial mobility (rising rates of divorce and blended families) all acted to loosen the connection between place, family, and inherited faith (Hammond 1992; Wuthnow 1998).

Alongside and related to these structural changes was a profound cultural change that significantly increased the centrality of individualism and individual choice in religion. Religious identity went from being "ascribed"—a characteristic someone is born with—to being "achieved"—something a person earns or chooses. This was the social and cultural environment (the "period") in which the Baby Boom Generation came of age. The danger of this for traditional religious identification was obvious to scholars from the start. In their analysis of mainline religion in the United States in the 1980s, Wade Clark Roof and William McKinney concluded that "the enemy of church life in this country is not so much 'secularity' as 'do-it-yourself religiosity'" (Roof and McKinney 1987:56).

For many Americans, religious authority lies in the individual rather than in the Bible, the historical tradition of the faith, or the hierarchy of clergy. Each person is expected—even required—to pick and choose what he or she believes to be true. This has two consequences. First, some religious leaders begin to "market religion" (explored in more detail in Chapter 8). A second consequence is that religion comes to be viewed as a matter of "opinion," which can be easily modified or discarded. The idea of religious conviction or commitment along the lines that Rosabeth Kanter described comes to be replaced with the more noncommittal notion of religious "preference." The salience of social identity connected to religious groups is diminished.

Reginald Bibby suggested that the same process is very much at work in Canada. Canadians do not switch denominations very often but have begun to treat their religion as casually as a menu choice in a restaurant:

> Canadians are still eating in the restaurants [i.e., mainline denominations]. But their menu choices have changed. . . . [Many] are opting only for appetizers, salads, or desserts [funerals, weddings, and baptisms], rather than full course meals [of full commitment and weekly Sunday worship]. The minimum charge has been lifted—it is now possible to skip the entree page altogether. (Bibby 1987:133–134)

Bibby also believed that such privatized religion is very vulnerable because it lacks the sanction and support of a group. The ideas set forth by the community may have less plausibility—less staying power—without the context.

At the same time that Americans have nearly unlimited discretion to choose and an unprecedented number of religious identity options to choose from (including no religious identity), they frequently opt for *convention*. Indeed, the main chronicler of the spiritual quest of the Baby Boom Generation, Wade Clark Roof, documented that 59% of American Baby Boomers are "born-again Christians" or "mainstream believers" and only 14% are "metaphysical believers" or "spiritual seekers" (Roof 1999:178). Christian Smith has extensively documented this conventionality in his work on American religion. In his recent studies of American youth, for example, he found the following:

> [T]he vast majority of American teenagers are *exceedingly conventional* in their religious identities and practices. Very few are restless, alienated, or rebellious; rather, the majority of U.S. teenagers seems basically content to follow the faith of their families with little questioning. (Smith 2005:120)

In explaining the vitality of American evangelicalism, Smith went so far as to argue that choice in fact is key to a stronger religious identity: "Moderns authenticate themselves through personal choice. Therefore, modern religious believers are capable of establishing stronger religious identities and commitments on the basis of individual choice than through ascription" (Smith 1998:104).

In terms of religious identity, we may be seeing a dividing up of the American population into two great camps: (1) those whose religious identities are more social and (2) those whose religious identities are very personal. Like the individual mentioned earlier whose self-identity is "the sensitive, new age guy," more and more people may craft identities that do not exactly fit the established group categories. How does this Boomer influence echo through the culture into the outlook of the Millennials?

One answer to this question that is readily accessible to many readers of this text can be found on Facebook. A cursory scan of the expressed religious views on the profile pages of the junior author's Millennial Facebook friends finds identities such as "I play dreidel for fun," "'love is my religion'—ziggy marley," and "everybody love everybody." Even those who seem to be expressing a conventional religious identity do it in an unconventional, or at least non–group-oriented, way: "follower of Jesus Christ," "he's beside me every step of the way," "Appropriating Grace through Existential Faith." Very few people use Facebook's option for expressing conventional, group-based religious identities like "Christian–Catholic" or "Christian–Baptist." If you have access to Facebook, try collecting your own systematic data on Facebook religious identity according to the guidelines in the next "Illustrating Sociological Concepts" feature.

ILLUSTRATING SOCIOLOGICAL CONCEPTS

Exploring Religious Identity on Facebook

Is religious identity becoming increasingly personalized? Although Facebook has nothing formally to do with religion, it does allow users to specify their "religious views." Looking at individuals' presentation of their religious views on Facebook is a way to explore this.

In the spirit of sociology's methodological empiricism (Chapter 2), systematically examine your Facebook friends' religious views, as follows (you obviously need to have a Facebook account to do this):

(Continued)

(Continued)

1. When you are looking at your Facebook profile, on the left-hand side you will see a grid of your "friends." Click on friends to reveal your friend list.

2. Select every third "friend" in the list to get a sample of your friends to study.

3. On each friend's profile page, click "About" and "Contact and Basic Info" to reveal his or her "Religious Views" (if any).

4. Write down the individual's religious views, or note with an X if the person does not list religious views (an interesting finding in itself).

5. Keep recording until you get 10 friends who list some religious views. Note how many friends you had to investigate to get 10 who listed religious views.

What does this exercise reveal about religious identity today (especially among young people)? To analyze what you have just observed, think about issues of personal versus group identities, being "spiritual, not religious," and the like. For example, how many friends did you have to look at to find 10 who even listed religious views? Did those who listed religious views tend to use "conventional" labels (e.g., "Roman Catholic," "LDS"), other theological characterizations ("follower of Jesus Christ"), or perhaps more unconventional, even silly, ones ("I play dreidel for fun")? Are your Facebook friends' religious identifications similar to or different from your own (if you even have one)? What does it even mean for people to list religious views on Facebook?

RELIGIOUS "NONES"

As noted earlier in this chapter, one of the most important developments in religious identity in recent decades is the growing number of people claiming no religious preference—that is, religious "nones." In 1968, Glenn Vernon characterized these individuals as "a neglected category." This was perhaps understandable at the time, because in the 1950s and 1960s, the proportion of Americans claiming no religious preference was just 3% to 4% (Condran and Tamney 1985). Today the situation is much different. The proportion of Americans claiming no religious preference in survey studies is nearly 1 in 5 (Pew Research Center Forum on Religion and Public Life 2012a). Surprisingly, this puts the United States very close to the global average for religiously unaffiliated population, as the "Global Perspectives" box discusses.

GLOBAL PERSPECTIVES

The Religiously Unaffiliated and the Culturally Religious

It will surprise many readers to learn that the percentage of the world's population that is religiously unaffiliated is only slightly lower than in the United States. According to the Pew-Templeton Global Religious Futures Project (globalreligiousfutures.org), 16.4% of the world's population does not identify with a particular religion (compared to 19.6% of the U.S. population). As they are in the United States, those with no religious affiliation are one of the largest groups in the world. As it is in the United States, having no religious affiliation is not the same as being an atheist.

Of course, statistical averages are useful for making generalizations, but they can also cover over very important diversity. The unaffiliated population varies considerably among the 232 countries and territories included in the study (Pew Research Center Forum on Religion and Public Life 2012b).

The religiously unaffiliated are heavily concentrated in Asia and the Pacific region. Although only 6 out of 232 countries have a majority of their population religiously unaffiliated, 4 of those 6 countries are Asian/Pacific: North Korea (71%), Japan (57%), Hong Kong (56%), and China (52%). In fact, the 62.2% of all the religiously unaffiliated *in the world* live in China: 700,680,000 estimated population in 2010. The 10 countries with the most religiously unaffiliated populations together constitute 85.8% of all the religiously unaffiliated in the world. The other 222 countries combined have only 14.2% of the world's unaffiliated population.

The areas of the globe that have the smallest proportion of unaffiliated are sub-Saharan Africa (2%) and the Middle East and North Africa (less than 1%).

As in the United States, high rates of unaffiliation do not mean the religious nones have no religious belief or practice. For example, the Pew Research Center report observes that in China, "44% of unaffiliated adults say they have worshipped at a graveside or tomb in the past year" (Pew Research Center Forum on Religion and Public Life 2012b).

There is also some evidence that the reverse is true—that low rates of unaffiliation should not be taken to mean high rates of religiosity. For example, the Global Religious Futures country page for Denmark shows only 11.8% of the population to be religiously unaffiliated and 83.5% to be Christian. Yet Phil Zuckerman claims in his book *Society Without God* that Denmark is one of "the least religious countries in the world, and possibly in the history of the world" (Zuckerman 2008:2).

Zuckerman argues that affiliation with the Lutheran Church in Denmark—which includes paying taxes to the church—is a purely secular act. Danes baptize their children, they get married in church, and they have funerals there, but only 3% attend church weekly—among the lowest rates in the world. Danes' affiliation with Christianity, then, is underpinned by cultural rather than religious beliefs.

Sociologist Grace Davie used the phrase "believing without belonging" to describe persistent belief accompanied by falling rates of religious practice in Britain after World War II (Davie 1994). Zuckerman turns this phrase on its head, arguing that Danes "belong without believing" (Zuckerman 2008:150). This represents what he calls "cultural religion": *"the phenomenon of people identifying with historically religious tradition, and engaging in ostensibly religious practices, without truly believing in the supernatural content thereof"* (Zuckerman 2008:155).

Taken together, the broad-sweeping quantitative Global Religious Futures Project and Zuckerman's fine-grained qualitative study of Denmark highlight the complexity of the way religion manifests itself in the modern world. They also remind us of the importance of definitions (Chapter 1) and the benefits of triangulating data (Chapter 2) when social scientists attempt to wrestle with that complexity empirically.

An important part of Vernon's analysis—replicated many times in subsequent research—was that religious "none" is not synonymous with "not religious." Many nones believe in God, pray, participate in religious services, and report having religious experiences. The Pew Research Center Forum on Religion and Public Life (2012a), therefore, distinguishes among three types of religious nones among the 19.6%:

Atheist	2.4%
Agnostic	3.3%
Nothing in Particular	13.9%

Although 27% of the unaffiliated say they do not believe in God or a universal spirit, only 1 in 10 describe themselves as atheists (along with another 17% who use the label agnostic). This is likely due to the continued hostility in American society toward nonbelievers. For example, Penny Edgell, Joseph Gerteis, and Douglas Hartmann found atheists are less accepted than a long list of other groups, including Muslims and homosexuals (Edgell et al. 2006).

So, religious nones are much less religious than the religiously affiliated. However, they are not completely secular (Chaves 2011). Many of the unaffiliated describe religion as either somewhat important (19%) or very important (14%) in their lives. Indeed, 5% of religious nones attended religious services weekly or more, and 22% attended monthly or yearly (Pew Research Center Forum on Religion and Public Life 2012b). For these religious nones, it is not that they are not religious; they simply are not part of an existing religious community.

How are we to understand the rising number of Americans who claim no religious preference? According to sociologists of religion, religious nones have not only been increasing over the years, but the reasons for nonaffiliation also seem to be changing. Previously, "structural" reasons for nonaffiliation were dominant. For example, as Condran and Tamney argued in 1985, some people were geographically or socially isolated and so had little connection with religious institutions (e.g., people living in rural areas). Today, "cultural" or ideological reasons appear more important.

One cultural explanation for the change is cohort replacement. As older, more religiously affiliated cohorts die off and are replaced by younger, less religiously affiliated cohorts, the overall proportion of unaffiliated in the population will increase (Hout and Fischer 2002; Schwadel 2010). The data shown in Table 5.2 support this explanation. Of Millennials, 29% are unaffiliated, compared to 21% of Generation X, 16% of Baby Boomers, and just 9% of the Silent Generation.

A second explanation is that a growing percentage of people who seldom or never attend services are willing to call themselves nothing in particular—as opposed to claiming the religious affiliation of their youth, for example. According to Chaves (2011), this is itself indicative of an important cultural change. In addition, Michael Hout and Claude Fischer (2002) observed that individuals who were raised with no religion were less likely to affiliate in adulthood than had been the case historically, perhaps because they find themselves enmeshed in social networks with others—spouses, friends—who are also nones (Baker and Smith 2009).

Hout and Fischer have also advanced a novel ideological explanation for the change. They found that the growth in religious nones was heavily influenced by individuals with liberal political identities becoming alienated from organized religion due to the alignment of religion and conservative politics by the "religious right" (Hout and Fischer 2002). In an updating of their study using data through 2008, Hout and Fischer again found "unaffiliated believers" to be a significant segment of religious nones, and symbolic protest against the cooptation of religion by conservative Protestants to be an important explanation of their unwillingness to identify themselves as having a religious preference (Hout and Fischer 2009).

As the percentage of individuals claiming no religious preference continues to grow, we might expect that this trend will continue into the future, especially since one of the strongest predictors of being a religious none is having parents who are religious nones. Although some of these individuals will be atheists or agnostics, many of them will be unaffiliated believers. They may be the Americans who are most likely to describe themselves as "spiritual, not religious" (discussed in Chapter 2). In the next chapter, we will also consider "apostasy"—the process by which individuals abandon or renounce religion. In any event, what the continuing increase in Americans with no religious preference means for the future of American religion is an open question that sociologists of religion will be grappling with for some time.

Critical Thinking: Some well-educated young adults say they are disaffected with their denomination's conservative stance on homosexuality or other issues that they see as matters of social justice. How important do you think social positions of denominations have been in the exodus of younger adults from formal religious communities? What other factors might be at work?

Summary

In this chapter, we have examined some of the dimensions of individual religiosity: belief, practice, commitment, and identity. We have also considered how religion is lived out over the life course, with attention to differences in generational experiences. As we analyze religion in the lives of individuals, we find remarkable diversity and complexity. Efforts by sociologists to understand the complex social configurations require simplification, and that always means risk of oversimplification. Still, some patterns of religious behavior and affiliation are clear.

We see this in our studies of religious socialization and of the role of faith over the life course. Religion is transmitted from one generation to the next via certain recognizable social patterns, even though there are variations on and exceptions to those relationships. Family is the main influence on religious socialization of children. Children exposed to active and devoted parents tend to continue that tradition and remain religiously engaged as young adults and beyond. Mature adulthood is usually a time of heightened religious involvement as family formation events drive connections to religious values and institutions. At some points, however, the demands of adult life make religious responsibilities difficult to fulfill. Adults may leave their religious community with the possibility of a return when life becomes less demanding. They may also reengage with religious communities as a result of aging. For adults in late life, the benefits of religious engagement include social, emotional, and spiritual support.

Religious commitment is both a property of individual religiosity and an important factor in the survival and prosperity of religious organizations. Interestingly, the three types of commitment also relate to the three interrelated subsystems that make up a religion: (1) meaning, (2) belonging, and (3) institutional/instrumental. In any case, successful religious commitment is related, in large part, to the formation of a particular religious identity. When one says "I am a Muslim" or "I am a Catholic," that says something about his or her loyalty to that religious organization or tradition. However, in modern society, religious identity has become more personal and less group oriented, resulting in multifaceted and idiosyncratic identities for some modern people—including the complex category of religious "none" domestically and globally. We have focused on individuals becoming and being religious—how one grows into a faith perspective and how one comes to have particular religious commitments, practices, and networks. The next chapter also looks at religion in the lives of individuals but focuses on the processes of religious transformation or change, which we know as "conversion" and "switching."

6

CONVERSION AND SWITCHING

HERE ARE SOME QUESTIONS TO PONDER AS YOU READ THIS CHAPTER

- Are many of the new religious movements (NRMs) involved in *brainwashing*? (What *is* brainwashing, and how do we know whether some religious movements do it?)
- Is there any typical order or sequencing of contributing factors in bringing about intense religious commitment?
- Is a decision about religious commitment driven by the same forces as secular economic decisions: a cost–benefit analysis in which people seek that which is in their own self-interest?
- What social forces are at work today in people switching from one religious community or denomination to another?
- What is the story and the trend line regarding religious "nones"—those with no religious preference?

In Chapter 5, we explored the process by which individuals are socialized into and practice religion throughout their lives. Yet most religions give considerable attention to the process of personal change or transformation. In this chapter, we investigate the change of worldviews that is expected and even anticipated by religious practitioners: the conversion process. We also explore the patterns of religious change in individuals' lives when they switch from one religious group to another ("switching") or from religion to no religion ("apostasy"). The increasing diversity and voluntarism in American religion discussed in the last chapter creates a context in which religious choices like conversion, switching, and apostasy are more likely.

CONVERSION, BRAINWASHING, AND THE NEW RELIGIOUS MOVEMENTS

The term *conversion* refers to a process of "turning around" or changing direction in life. It often is viewed as a sudden crisis event, but the process can also be a gradual one. In any case, conversion represents a transformation in a person's identity or self-image. The change is often symbolized by a change of name (e.g., the Hebrew Saul became Paul when he converted to Christianity, and, in the 20th century, the boxer Cassius Clay became Muhammad Ali when he converted to Islam).

Research on conversion in the sociology of religion flourished from the 1960s through the 1980s, coinciding with the rise in prominence of nonconventional religious groups known as "new religious movements" (NRMs, see Chapter 7). Perhaps this is to be expected. Conversion to a group that affirms the basic values of the dominant society does not seem as mysterious and

puzzling to most people as conversion to a "cult."[1] People who convert from Methodism to Catholicism have not engaged in terribly unconventional or "abnormal" behavior, and in some cases the change may not even be dramatic enough to warrant the term *conversion*. Individuals who depart from their Episcopal heritage to join a congregation of Reform Jews are of somewhat more interest because the change involves adherence to a different religion and an acceptance of minority group status. However, people who give up all of their possessions to join a religious commune are even more of an enigma. Indeed, this behavior can be terribly puzzling and somewhat frightening to many. In any case, these most extreme cases can teach us something about radical religious transformation.

Because conversion to an NRM carries a potential stigma for both the convert and the convert's friends and family, the charge of "brainwashing" has sometimes been a ready explanation for this otherwise inexplicable behavior. Most people have little idea what brainwashing actually is. The term originated during the Korean War (1950–1953) to explain how American prisoners of war (POWs) were allegedly made to cooperate with their captors. Brainwashing refers to a process by which persons are *involuntarily* caused to adopt a belief system, a set of behaviors, or a worldview. To force such a change, one must have total physical and psychological control over the individual. Even in such a total control situation, however, only small numbers of American soldiers yielded to the brainwashing techniques of the North Koreans in the 1950s. Furthermore, most of the acquiescence was merely verbal. The Americans were eager to return to their previous culture as soon as the total control situation was alleviated. No more than a dozen men, and probably fewer, were permanently converted by North Korean

---

[1]Although the term often has a negative connotation, as social scientists we understand cults as the nascent organization of new religions. They often experience hostility because they involve a break from the traditional religions in a society and the creation of a nonconventional form of religion (Stark and Bainbridge 1979). The term *cult* will be treated in more detail in Chapter 7.

thought reform out of thousands that experienced the severe treatment (Farber, Harlow, and West 1951; Lifton 1954).

The questionable reality of brainwashing in the Korean War notwithstanding, when large numbers of (especially younger) Americans began to be attracted to NRMs, brainwashing was often invoked, especially by those in the anti-cult movement (Bromley and Shupe 1981). The controversies over whether brainwashing exists are not just academic questions. Individuals like Ted Patrick were hired by families to rescue their loved ones from cults through what became known as "deprogramming" techniques. Patrick was one of the founders of The Parents' Committee to Free Our Children from the Children of God (FREECOG) in 1971 and is known as the "Father of Deprogramming." FREECOG eventually became the Cult Awareness Network, the major anti-cult organization from 1978 until it went bankrupt in 1996. Others like sociologist Richard Ofshe and clinical psychologist Margaret Singer—who had interviewed Korean POWs after their release in the 1950s—regularly served as expert witnesses in suits against NRMs accused of brainwashing (Shupe and Darnell 2006).

By invoking the word *brainwashing,* these anti-cult groups and activists imply that NRMs manipulate the minds of potential recruits and current members so that they are unwitting and somewhat passive victims of the process. The majority of actual studies of conversion and commitment suggest otherwise. For example, Roger Straus insisted that the recruit is usually actively involved in choosing to be converted.

> The act of conversion, we find, is not a terminal act. Rather, guided by the principle that the way to be changed is to act changed, the new convert works to make conversion behaviorally and experientially real to self and others . . . It is not so much the initial action that enables the convert to experience a transformed life but the day to day actions of living it. (Straus 1979:163)

Rather than a passive victim, researchers find that recruits are active seekers who want the

conversion experience and go to considerable effort to cause it to happen (Balch 1980; Staples and Mauss 1987; Straus 1979). In short, "new religions" do not induce people into some sort of hypnotic trance (Barker 1984; Beckford 1985; Levine 1984; Stark and Bainbridge 1985). Thirty-nine members of the Heaven's Gate movement committed suicide in 1997 as a way to be transported via a flying saucer to the "next level," but recent studies conclude that while some odd group dynamics were at work and some strange beliefs were held by the members, "brainwashing" was by no means part of the process (Balch and Taylor 2002).

Why, then, has there been so much talk of brainwashing, or "mind control"? Thomas Robbins and Dick Anthony (1978) pointed out that the brainwashing term has been used as a weapon to suppress these nonconventional groups. Anson Shupe and David Bromley (1978) even insisted that the anti-cult movements have distorted information to the point that the attacks are actually very akin to the witch hunts of an earlier era. Stigmatization of NRMs by established forces are common throughout history. Although we do not often think of it, the Jesus movement that became Christianity was just one of many NRMs at the time (Theissen 1978). When Christianity was still an NRM, pagans claimed that the Christian movement was a dangerous one because Christians worshiped an ass's head, murdered children as sacrifices, and committed other atrocities (Baroja 1964:41). As recently as 60 years ago in the United States, Roman Catholics were characterized as subversives who committed all sorts of abominations (Bromley and Shupe 1981). The mainstream view among sociologists of religion today is that the charge of brainwashing is primarily a way of discrediting NRMs and making them appear illegitimate and dangerous.

Stigmatizing unconventional groups makes them appear more dissimilar from conventional religions than they really are. As we will see in this chapter, the processes by which individuals convert to NRMs are fundamentally social and do not involve any forms of recruitment or socialization that we would not also expect to find among more mainstream religious groups. Moreover, the birth of large numbers of NRMs in the latter part of the 20th century created a unique opportunity to study conversion and recruitment at the critical period when a religious group is just getting started.

PROCESS MODELS OF CONVERSION

For the first six decades of the 20th century, conversion was viewed by social scientists as a single event that brought radical change in the orientation of an individual. Subsequent analyses have tried to identify a process or series of steps involved in conversion (Richardson 1985). In the first real process model—based on a study of conversion to the Unification Church (then called the Moonies after founder Sun Myung Moon[2])—John Lofland identified a sequence of factors that operate to move a person from nonmember status to committed devotee. Lofland's theory posits that a social movement or process may best be understood by identifying "successively accumulating factors." According to this perspective, it is the cumulative effect of many different factors that gives rise to specific types of behavior (Lofland 1977).

According to Lofland, only persons who experience all of these conditions are likely to convert to a new religious group. Hence, these conditions help determine who will convert and who will remain uninvolved. "The sequential arrangement of the conditions may be conceived as a funnel"; that is, they "systematically reduce the number of persons who can be considered available for recruitment" (Lofland 1977:31). A large portion of the population may experience stress or tension, the first condition. A somewhat smaller portion of the population may adopt a religious problem-solving perspective, the second condition. The third condition may

apply only to a segment of *that* population, and only a few who experience the first three conditions may confront the fourth. Hence, the number of converts, and who those converts are, is largely a function of the proper combination of events in the lives of individuals (see Figure 6.1 on page 136). Lofland maintained that three *predisposing conditions* (dispositions, attitudes, outlooks) and four situational factors incline the individual to be attracted to a new and innovative religious group. The predisposing conditions are attributes of individuals that exist *prior* to contact with the religious group.

Predisposing Conditions

Tension

It is a commonly accepted maxim of the social sciences that personal change is generally the result of some felt need for change—a dissatisfaction with the current situation. In societies such as our own that undergo a great deal of change, persons often experience anomie or normlessness. They feel that they are without roots. This anomie creates a great deal of stress in persons. Anomie is, of course, only one source of stress that can cause discontent. Further, while Lofland viewed tension or dissatisfaction as necessary, it is certainly not sufficient by itself to cause a religious conversion. Dissatisfaction may be worked out in a psychiatrist's office, in a political campaign designed to change social conditions, or in any one of a dozen different ways.

Religious Problem-Solving Perspective

The second personal characteristic is an inclination to solve problems by turning to religious leaders or methods rather than to political or psychiatric ones. Only when a person begins to attach religious or spiritual meaning to events

[2]According to Virginia Commonwealth University's World Religions and Spirituality Project entry for the Unification Church, "While Unification Church members initially embraced the name 'Moonie,' in recent years they have come to view this term as pejorative" (www.wrs.vcu.edu/profiles/FamilyFederationForWorldPeaceAndUnification.htm). Because Lofland was writing during the early history of Unificationism in the United States, we accept his use of the label *Moonie.*

Figure 6.1 Lofland's Process Model of Conversion

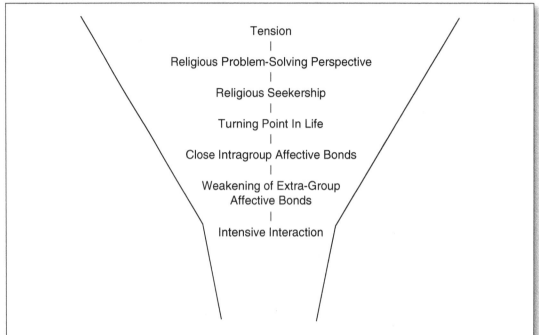

Tension
|
Religious Problem-Solving Perspective
|
Religious Seekership
|
Turning Point In Life
|
Close Intragroup Affective Bonds
|
Weakening of Extra-Group
Affective Bonds
|
Intensive Interaction

One might view Lofland's model as a "filtering" of people. Each step involves a filtering out of some people and a filtering or even funneling in of others. Those who have experienced the first six filters become "verbal converts." They must go through the seventh step as well to become "total converts." Total converts really believe the theology or ideology of the group. Verbal converts feel committed to the members of the group, and they verbally assent to belief, but they are not yet really committed at a "moral level."

does the individual become amenable to the message of religious groups. Otherwise, one will seek political, psychiatric, or other resolutions to problems. For example, young people were not favorably inclined toward the Divine Light Mission until they first sensed that religion was a viable problem-solving route (Downton 1979). Hence, Lofland posited that a spiritual outlook is necessary before someone will take seriously the message of a religious group.

Religious Seekership

Lofland insisted that among the Moonie converts there was a dissatisfaction with the conventional religious groups and a feeling of being a religious seeker. Virtually all converts had drifted from one religious group to another. They had already concluded that the worldview of the religion in which they were raised was inadequate. The new converts had identified themselves as seekers of truth. However, not all seekers were converted. There must be a certain amount of "cultural conduciveness" between the worldview of the group and that of the recruit. To illustrate, in the 19th century, the Ghost Dance religion spread rapidly among Native American nations. However, it failed to attract the Navajo. The Ghost Dance religion predicted the rise of the dead, but the Navajo were afraid of ghosts. Hence, rather than celebrating such a future event, they refused to have anything to do with this movement. Likewise, Lofland suggested that for a person to be a likely candidate for Unificationist recruitment, he or she must already hold some attitudes that are consistent with Unificationist theology. Uniform congruence of beliefs is not required, but a general compatibility of outlook seems to be necessary for a potential recruit to become an actual convert.

Situational Contingencies

If these predisposing conditions are operative, the *situational contingencies* become relevant. Situational contingencies are circumstances that influence the social interaction between a potential convert and a recruiter to a religious group.

Turning Point in Life

The converts to the Unification Church had reached important turning points in their own lives. Lofland put it this way:

Each had come to a moment when old lines of action were complete, had failed, or . . . were about to be disrupted, and when they were faced with the opportunity or necessity for doing something different with their lives. (Lofland 1977:50)

Potential converts had recently migrated, had lost or quit a job, or had completed or dropped out of college. On the other hand, Lofland found that marital dissolution and illness seldom served this turning-point function. Apparently, some types of turning points stimulate the meaning and belonging needs more profoundly than do others. Nonetheless, persons who are not at turning points in their lives are less likely to be responsive to proselytization—especially to proselytization of unconventional groups. Turning points are times of new beginnings when investment in the status quo is minimal.

Close Intragroup Affective Bonds

In Lofland's study of the Unification Church, almost all recruits were gained through preexisting friendship networks. The group learned that

cognitive appeals to ideology (with a focus on the moral commitment level) did not win converts. As they became aware of this, they gradually began to modify their recruitment strategy. Lofland emphasized that they "learned to start conversion at the emotional rather than the cognitive level" (Lofland 1977:308). In other words, they learned that affective levels of commitment precede moral levels of commitment.

Weakening of Extra-Group Affective Bonds

Because of migration away from one's family or because of disaffection from it, an individual may experience isolation, alienation, or loneliness. Such a person is more in need of emotional support as he or she faces a turning point than is one who has a close network of friends and family. As we have mentioned previously, Unificationists seeking recruits consciously looked for signs of transiency (backpacks, individuals who were alone). The person who has no other immediate reference group is less likely to have someone oppose or intervene in the conversion process. Without another individual or group to offer an alternative interpretation of the group, the individual is more likely to be drawn into that group.

Intensive Interaction

Lofland maintained that some Unificationists were only verbally committed—that is, they were not yet totally committed. This seventh condition solidifies commitment to the group through intensive interaction among members. In this way, "moral-level commitment"—meaning—is enhanced by providing "communion" with the group. Once the intensive interaction provides a sense of unity and oneness, the devotees actively *want* to believe the ideology. By consciously working on strengthening their faith, they come to believe the ideology, to feel a sense of awe about the leader, and to uphold the group's values. The conversion becomes total, and engagement becomes intense in all three modes of commitment.

Even members of some of the relatively recent groups who have gone to their deaths for the sake of the group, an act that represents extreme commitment, seem to have been motivated by these processes. Recent studies of Heaven's Gate, the California group that involved the suicide of 39 members, and the Branch Davidians, who died in a massive fire at their Waco, Texas, compound, indicate that these same processes of intense bonding were at the core of the movements (Balch and Taylor 2002; Hall 2002).

Critique and Evolution of Lofland's Process Model

Several scholars have voiced reservations about the applicability of this particular "process model" to all groups. One study of an American Buddhist movement indicated that several of the stages may not be universal even among NRMs (Snow and Phillips 1980).

> Having a religious problem-solving perspective, for example, was not a prerequisite to persons becoming members of some religious communities. Likewise, the question about whether one was at a turning point in one's life at the time one encountered a religious group is a matter of interpretation. Looking back retrospectively at one's pre-conversion experience, one may note something as a turning point that otherwise would not be. (Snow and Phillips 1980:439)

The importance of weak extra-group affective bonds may depend on the extent to which the group's values represent a break from the values and perspectives of one's family. If group membership does not involve a transformation of the values one shares with one's family, then alienation from family is unnecessary. If the group is not stigmatized, then the strategy of alienating members from nonmembers is also less important.

Still, most researchers have found affective bonds and intensive interaction to be central to conversion (Cornwall 1987; Greil and Rudy 1984; Kox, Meeus, and Harm't 1991; Stark and Bainbridge 1985), and the *lack* of intensive interaction has been linked to deconversion or apostasy (Jacobs 1987). While the idea of a sequential

cumulative process seems to be a fruitful way to think about conversion, with various factors contributing, at this point there is no consensus about which factors are *necessary*.

Actually, Lofland and a colleague have offered a modification of his original theory. They now suggest that there appear to be several conversion processes and that different types of groups tend to employ different processes. Lofland and Norman Skonovd discussed six different conversion patterns or "motifs," each involving a slightly different series of factors. Some conversions are induced by nonrational experiences, others involve a more intellectual process of study, and still others stress affective ties and belonging functions (Lofland and Skonovd 1981). Lofland and Skonovd also hypothesized that different conversion patterns may be more common in different epochs of history. Hence, the heavy emphasis on nonrational experience by William James and Rudolf Otto early in the 20th century (discussed in Chapter 4) may have been due to the fact that mystical modes of conversion were more common then, while affective modes have been more widely employed by groups in the past 50 years. It is interesting to note, however, that of the six conversion motifs outlined by Lofland and Skonovd, four emphasize belonging and group participation *prior to* belief. Intense affective involvement normally precedes total conversion. In the case of contemporary sects and cults, this sequence seems to be nearly universal.

RELIGIOUS CHOICES AND COMMITMENTS: A RATIONAL CHOICE MODEL

In the past two decades, a new paradigm has emerged in the sociology of religion: rational choice theory. Rational choice theory in much of sociology evolved from exchange theory, a longstanding micro theory that focuses on individual decision making and interaction between individuals and within small groups. However, rational choice theory in the sociology of religion has drawn heavily on macro- and micro-economic theories as well (Iannaccone 1995). We will begin by looking at the early contribution of rational choice theory to the study of conversion, then turn to broader issues of commitment.

The Convert and Active Choice

Historically, many social scientists have explained conversion using a rather passive model of human behavior. Conversion was an event that happened to the individual because of unconscious psychological processes or compelling social tensions (Richardson 1985). Certainly, the "brainwashing" hypothesis is consistent with this perspective. The process models of Lofland and others represent a break from this determinism. A series of events are believed to be at work—events in which the participant has some choice and makes some decisions. However, several researchers believe that even these models have too much of a passive view of the convert, that these models depict conversion as the result of various social pressures *outside* of the individual.

Several social scientists have set forth a view of conversion in which the individual is an active agent purposefully making choices and seeking conversion (Balch 1980; Balch and Taylor 1976, 1977; Dawson 1990; Finke and Stark 1992; Kilbourne and Richardson 1989; Richardson 1985; Straus 1976, 1979; Warner 1993). This activist perspective stresses that individuals are seeking meaning in life, and they consciously join groups that they believe may fulfill their needs. To give the faith a fair chance, they thrust themselves into the roles and behaviors of the group.

Critical Thinking: In what ways does the "activist" model differ from other conceptions of conversion? Do you think people always make deliberate and conscious choices, or do social factors often incline people toward identification with a certain group or toward a particular outlook on life and death?

Religious Choices: Costs and Benefits in a Supply and Demand "Market"

Rational choice theory (RCT) applies economic principles of behavior to all areas of social life. The basic idea is that the kind of decision making that people use in economic choices is also at work with religious choices: the goal is to maximize benefits and minimize costs. (This is known in economics as "utility maximization.") The benefits, of course, are nonmaterial when it comes to religious choices—sense of meaning, assurance of an afterlife, sense of communion with God, and so forth. This approach views religiously engaged people as consumers of "products" that provide these benefits and religious organizations (churches, sects, denominations, NRMs) as "firms" competing with each other in the religious marketplace to supply those products (Finke and Stark 1992; Iannaccone 1994).

As in neo-classical macro-economics, the major approach to RCT in the sociology of religion focuses on *"supply-side"* explanations (Sherkat and Ellison 2001). Supply-side theory stresses the way in which religious communities produce religious "commodities" (rituals, meaning systems, sense of belonging, symbols, and so forth) to meet the "demand." Since the overall demand for religion in a society is believed to be stable, it is the number and type of religious organizations producing that interest supply-side theorists. The more firms there are, the more competition there will be between firms in the marketplace. Competition requires firms to produce better and more specialized products, thereby meeting more of the demand for religion in society. Firms generally develop a specific kind of "product"—a specific type of theology and a particular style of worship, for example—and these "products" usually appeal to people who have a specific socioeconomic status, ethnicity, geographic identity, or other traits.

Therefore, in contrast to theorists who argued that religious pluralism would be corrosive to

Rational choice theorists would call this local church a "franchise" that is part of a larger "firm" that produces a particular "product." In this case, the "firm" is the Evangelical Lutheran Church in America.

religiosity (Berger 1967), RCT holds that religious pluralism will increase rates of religious consumption, creating a more vibrant religious marketplace in a society (Finke and Stark 1992; Iannaccone 1994, 1995; Stark and Bainbridge 1996; Stark, Finke, and Iannaccone 1995; Warner 1993). By contrast, when there is a religious monopoly—that is, less diversity of religious options in the society because an established religious organization is supported with tax dollars—religion may become less vigorous. When there is a state-supported religion, the monopoly firm does not have to compete for members, and clergy do not have to "sell" their product in order to earn a living. This supply-side theory has been used to explain the low rates of religious practice in countries like England and Sweden, which have officially established national churches, and high rates in the United States where religion is deregulated (Stark and Iannaccone 1994). The "Global Perspectives" box highlights a recent analysis of rates of conversion in 40 countries that is based on RCT.

One can readily see that this perspective is quite compatible with the open systems model we have used in this text. The outputs of the religion can influence the society. The "supply" of religious options or "products" can influence how highly religious a society becomes. On the other hand, characteristics of the society, such as how pluralistic the society is and how competitive the faith marketplace is within the society, can shape the nature of religious "firms" or the behavior of ministers and local congregations.

As we will see later in this chapter, RCT makes some predictions about the growth and decline of particular religious bodies in a competitive religious market. For now let's consider the micro-level implications of RCT for individual religious change. Individuals develop "religious human capital"—that is, knowledge and familiarity with hymns, myths, memorized creeds, and insider language—according to the religious tradition in which they are raised. It is more efficient, therefore, for these individuals to conserve their religious human capital by consuming the religious products of (i.e., participating in) firms that are within those same religious traditions (Iannaccone 1990). This explains why many people do not change religions, or if they do change, they are more likely to do it when they are younger—before they have accumulated so much religious capital that switching is more costly than staying. Moreover, if people do change religions, it is likely to be to other firms that are quite similar in beliefs and practices, so that their religious capital is still valuable. Examples would be changing affiliation from the United Methodist Church to the Presbyterian Church USA (PCUSA), or from the Roman Catholic to the Episcopal Church. However, for someone who has invested 40 years accumulating the "knowledge, skills, and sensitivities" associated with the United Methodist Church, the cost of associating with the PCUSA is still quite high (Iannaccone 1997). Because longer-range conversions—a Christian converting to Judaism or Islam, an individual joining an NRM—are more costly for the individual, there

GLOBAL PERSPECTIVES

Religious Conversion in 40 Countries

The increasing availability of high-quality data based on comparable closed-ended surveys administered cross-nationally is allowing social scientists to make useful international comparisons. Two examples are the International Social Survey Programme (ISSP) (issp.org), which began in 1984 and currently includes 49 countries, and the World Values Survey (WVS) (www.world valuessurvey.org), which began in 1981 and has included nearly 100 countries over the years.

Robert Barro, Jason Hwang, and Rachel McCleary (2010) use these two data sets to explore and explain conversion in 40 countries. Most studies of individual religious change focus on the individual level in a single country, the United States. They contribute to the understanding of religious conversion by making comparisons across a number of countries and by looking at *national rates* of conversion rather than individual conversions. They adopt a rational choice framework to understand how national context affects the costs and benefits of religious conversion and thereby decreases or increases a country's rate of conversion.

The authors predict that certain national-level policies and countrywide characteristics will be associated with higher national rates of religious conversion because they decrease the costs of that decision for individuals within the country. These include higher level of religious pluralism, recent shift toward more pluralism, and higher average educational attainment. Legal and religious restrictions on conversion and a history of Communism are associated with lower national rates because they increase the cost of conversion.

The ISSP asks respondents to identify their current religion and the religion in which they were raised, with any change interpreted to mean a conversion has taken place. The WVS asks directly whether the respondent has ever had a different religion. Rather than looking at the less dramatic forms of individual religious change ("reaffiliation" of a faith or religious "switching" of similar denominations), the authors examine more significant religious changes—shifts between any two of eight major religious groups: Catholic, Protestant, Muslim, Hindu, Eastern religion (including Buddhists), Jewish, Orthodox (sometimes called "Eastern" as opposed to "Roman" Catholic), and other religions. The conversion rate is the number of individuals aged 30 and over who have changed their religion divided by the total number of religious individuals in that society.

Conversion rates so defined vary considerably from country to country, "ranging from near zero for Spain, Italy, and many former Communist countries in Eastern Europe to over 10 percent in the United States, Canada, Chile, and New Zealand" (Barro et al. 2010:33). The question is, do they vary in the ways predicted by the rational choice model?

In their multivariate statistical analyses, the authors find religious conversion rates—as predicted—are positively related to aspects of the national context that reduce the costs of change (religious pluralism and levels of education), and negatively related to those aspects that increase the costs of change (government restrictions on religious conversion and a history of Communism).

The authors conclude that their findings support the macro-level understanding of religious economies proposed by Finke and Stark (2005). A more open religious marketplace will allow for a better fit between individuals' religious preferences and what is available to "consume" religiously.

SOURCE: Barro, Robert, Jason Hwang, and Rachel McCleary. 2010. "Religious Conversion in 40 Countries." *Journal for the Scientific Study of Religion* 49(1):15–36.

must be a dramatic drop in one's religious benefits for the individual to make such a decision. Still, when the costs of staying outweigh the benefits, a change is more likely to occur according to this rational choice approach.

As David Yamane has observed in his study of adult converts to Roman Catholicism, RCT also suggests that in cases of religious intermarriage there is pressure to have one spouse convert. Without such a conversion, the couple faces several inefficient options (Yamane 2014). Consider a hypothetical couple, Pat and Kim. Prior to their marriage, Pat attended First Baptist Church, and Kim attended Our Lady of the Pillar Catholic Church. One option for them would be to continue to attend their respective churches. Although they would continue to derive religious rewards from their participation in their respective churches, this would come at the cost of time they do not spend together and possible disagreements over how to allocate their resources (time, money, and talents) in their different churches. These costs become even greater when children enter the equation. Option 2 would be for Pat and Kim to attend both churches. This option, too, has significant costs in terms of time and money. Option 3 is for both to join a third church; however, in doing so they would both forfeit their accumulated religious capital. Option 4 is to discontinue religious participation altogether, which reduces the costs significantly but also eliminates the benefits. The fifth and common response to religious intermarriage would be for Pat to become Catholic and join Our Lady of the Pillar or for Kim to become Baptist and join First Baptist. As Stark and Finke have observed, "When mixed marriages occur, the couple maximize their religious capital when the partner with the lower level of commitment reaffiliates or converts to the religion of the more committed partner" (Stark and Finke 2000:125). This pattern was so commonly seen that it has been dubbed by some "Greeley's Law," after the sociologist Andrew Greeley, who first observed it (Greeley 1970).

Critique of Rational Choice Theory

The mechanical nature of these "utility maximization principles" of the rational choice model is not above criticism. RCT generally has been criticized for neglecting the changing cultural contexts within which religious decisions are made. Cultural contexts are crucial because they shape motivations for action and render action meaningful for the individual. For example, religious homogamy—marriage between individuals who are religiously similar—has been strongly supported historically by cultural norms for marriage within one's religious tradition, and for changing affiliations in the event of religious intermarriage. A 1951 Gallup Poll found 54% of Americans agreeing that "two young people in love who are of different religious faiths—Protestant, Catholic, or Jewish—should not get married" (Putnam and Campbell 2010:151). Not surprisingly, in 1955, only 12% of Protestant women and 16% of Jewish women married someone of a different faith. Since then, religious intermarriage has dramatically increased as social and cultural differences between people from different religious backgrounds have diminished and as social stigmas against religious intermarriage have faded. By 2005, the rate of religious intermarriage increased to 25% for Protestant women and 38% for Jewish women. During this same time period, the percentage of Catholic women who married non-Catholic men rose from 33% to 46% (Putnam and Campbell 2010:145–152).

The rational choice theorist would explain the increased rate of religious conversion after intermarriage as maximization of household religious capital. However, Putnam and Campbell find that over the past several decades marital switching as a proportion of all switching is going down and nonmarital switching is going up. They estimate that today about 60% of Americans marry someone from another religious tradition (including from two different Protestant traditions). Of these, roughly two thirds are still mixed (Putnam and Campbell 2010). The failure to take into account changing culture conditions is part of a broader critique of RCT's failure to take meaning into account in understanding religious decision making. This is particularly interesting because one motivation claimed for adopting a rational choice perspective was that religious people and religious commitments were not being taken seriously by other theoretical perspectives. At least one rational choice scholar has taken other sociologists of religion to task for not treating religious people and their decision making with respect (Stark 2000a). Yet this strictly utilitarian/economic analysis of religion seems to be counter to the way most religious people understand their own behavior, which is much more complex. As Meredith McGuire put it,

> It is one thing to describe a person's decision to join a church *as if* the person were trying to maximize his or her benefits; it is something different to claim that the person's *actual* thought in joining measured his or her potential gains against potential losses. It is impossible to demonstrate that people actually think this way (and few people would admit to doing so). Empirical motivations are much more complex than the rational-choice approach allows. (McGuire 2002:298–299)

Although the rational choice perspective does provide a surface-level explanation for some empirical regularities observed in patterns of individual religious change, it cannot account for many of the complexities we see in studies of religious conversion.

To take but one example, Yamane's (2014) study found that people clearly do convert to Roman Catholicism for spousal reasons, but there is no simple relationship between getting married and switching. Among the individuals he studied, Yamane found the length of marriage ranged from 2 months to 42 years, with an average length of 10.8 years. The presence of children in a family is also connected with the decision to become Catholic; however, there is

no "one size fits all" explanation for when and how children factor into the decision to become Catholic. The decision may come when they are pregnant, or when their children are baptized, start Sunday school, enroll in Catholic schools, or receive their first communion. For others the critical point may be when their children ask them to, when their children get married, or even when they are babysitting their grandchildren! How can we understand the varying timing of these decisions to convert from the rational choice perspective? RCT would suggest that the decision to convert comes when the benefits of changing outweigh the costs of remaining, but that is a thin sort of explanation.

RCT has been very controversial in the field for some time (Bruce 1999; Hamilton 2009; Lechner 2007; Lehman 2010; Spickard 1998; Young 1997). Some of those controversies will be explored later in this text (see Chapter 13). However, it has clearly generated a new approach and an active research agenda as scholars seek to explore religious commitment as a form of consciously made choices based on costs and benefits. Unlike many theories, it also makes contributions at both the macro and micro levels of analysis.

Critical Thinking: In what way does the rational choice approach seem to you to make sense of religious behavior? If you find this approach appealing, how do you respond to the charge that it shows disrespect for the self-definitions of religiously motivated people? If you find it unconvincing, what reasoning or what evidence seems to you compelling in rejecting this approach?

The activist perspective that RCT offers serves as a useful corrective to viewing the convert as a passive participant, who is the unwitting "victim" of social processes beyond his or her control (Dawson 1990). The recruit is a participant in the definition of his or her situation. Most sociologists do not view humans as robots who are totally controlled by outside stimuli. People are active agents who must respond to, but also help to shape, their environments. If theorists lose sight of either side of this dual character of the relationship between individuals and society, their theories will be simplistic and distorted.

RELIGIOUS "SWITCHING"

Changes in religious affiliation have become fairly common in the United States. According to the Pew Research Center Forum on Religion and Public Life,

> More than one-quarter of American adults (28%) have left the faith in which they were raised in favor of another religion—or no religion at all. If change in affiliation from one type of Protestantism to another is included, 44% of adults have either switched religious affiliation, moved from being unaffiliated with any religion to being affiliated with a particular faith, or dropped any connection to a specific religious tradition altogether. (Pew Research Center Forum on Religion and Public Life 2008b:5)

As expected by rational choice theorists, the American religious marketplace is very open and therefore very dynamic. Some scholars call this change in religious affiliation "everyday conversion" to distinguish it from the more dramatic forms of conversion we discussed earlier (Suchman 1992). Others use the term *switching* to refer to this religious change that does not necessarily involve a major "turning around" or changing direction in life (Loveland 2003). Because it does involve a change in organizational membership, the term *reaffiliation* is often more accurate than conversion (though there are times when reaffiliation *does* involve a deeper conversion).

The Pew Forum's U.S. Religious Landscape Survey, based on responses from a representative sample of 35,000 Americans, charts these patterns of religious switching. Every religious group has gained some members and lost some members due

to religious switching. Table 6.1 shows the percentage of the U.S. adult population that reports growing up in a particular denomination and the percentage currently a member of those same denominations. The table shows that the biggest "winners" in the American switching game are nondenominational Protestants and the religiously unaffiliated (more on them later). The biggest "losers" are Catholics, Baptists, Methodists, and Presbyterians. Many groups, however, essentially break even, with roughly equal numbers of individuals entering and leaving the religion.

Table 6.1 shows the overall pattern of people's switching from the faith communities of their youth to new ones or to no churches. Table 6.2 on page 146 elaborates that pattern by showing the original religious tradition of respondents and their current religious tradition. Among the interesting findings in this table is that Hindus are the least likely to switch faith traditions, and Protestants leave that faith tradition to become, among other things, Jehovah's Witnesses (one third of whom were raised in Protestant households), Buddhists (32% former Protestants), or another Protestant tradition. It is interesting that 44% of all unaffiliated adults were raised Protestant, double the number of unaffiliated who were raised without religious identification (21%). Note also that being unaffiliated is a much less stable religious identity than most others.

Critical Thinking: As you study Table 6.1, what patterns do you see in members switching between religious groups? Do the patterns seem to suggest a move toward more conservative and evangelical groups, toward disaffiliation with denominations, or toward dissatisfaction with religion entirely? Why?

Explaining Religious Switching

What accounts for switching among the 44% of Americans who have changed their religious affiliation? The Pew Forum has not done complex statistical analyses necessary to make causal

Table 6.1 Changes in Religious Affiliation From Childhood to Present Among Adults in the United States

Religious Group (Listed in Order of Increase to Decrease as Percentage of Population)	Childhood Family Religious Affiliation (Percentage)	Current Religious Affiliation (Percentage)	Total Change (Percentage)
Unaffiliated ("nones")	6.6	12.1	+5.5
Nondenominational Christian	1.5	4.5	+3.0
Agnostic	<0.3	2.4	+2.1
Protestant (nonspecific)	3.4	4.9	+1.5
Lutheran	5.5	4.6	+1.1
Atheist	0.5	1.6	+1.1
Other faiths	0.3	1.2	+0.9
Pentecostal	3.9	4.4	+0.5
Holiness	0.8	1.2	+0.4
Buddhist	0.4	0.7	+0.3
Jehovah's Witness	0.6	0.7	+0.1
Adventist	0.4	0.5	+0.1
Muslim	0.3	0.4	+0.1
Congregationalist (United Church of Christ)	0.8	0.8	0.0
Orthodox	0.6	0.6	0.0
Hindu	0.4	0.4	0.0
Reformed	0.3	0.3	0.0
Other Evangelical/Fundamentalist	<0.3	0.3	0.0
Anabaptist	0.3	<0.3	0.0
Pietist	<0.3	<0.3	0.0
Friends (Quakers)	<0.3	<0.3	0.0
Mormon	1.8	1.7	−0.1
Restorationist	2.3	2.1	−0.2
Jewish	1.9	1.7	−0.2
Anglican/Episcopal	1.8	1.5	−0.3
Presbyterian	3.4	2.7	−0.7
Methodist	8.3	6.2	−2.1
Baptist	20.9	17.2	−3.7
Catholic	31.4	23.9	−7.5

SOURCE: Pew Research Center Forum on Religion and Public Life. 2008b. *U.S. Religious Landscape Survey*. Retrieved from http://religions.pewforum.org

Table 6.2 Retention and Switching: From What Groups Are People Exiting?

Current Religion (Listed by Highest Retention)	Unchanged From Childhood	Percent Who Were Raised:			
		Protestant	Catholic	All Other Faiths	Unaffiliated
Hindu	90	2	4	4	2
Catholic	89	8	NA	1	2
Jewish	85	5	2	3	5
Orthodox	77	12	5	1	4
Mormon	74	13	7	1	5
Muslim	60	24	4	5	8
Protestant	54	29	9	2	6
Within Protestant		To other Protestant			
Historic black Prot.	69	21	4	1	4
Mainline Prot.	54	30	9	2	5
Evangelical Prot.	51	31	1	2	6
Jehovah's Witness	33	33	26	1	8
Buddhist	27	32	22	6	12
Unaffiliated	21	44	27	8	NA
Other Faiths	9	50	23	7	11

SOURCE: Pew Research Center Forum on Religion and Public Life. 2008b. *U.S. Religious Landscape Survey*. Retrieved from http://religions.pewforum.org

Online Resource: The Pew Research Center Forum on Religion and Public Life, whose data appear in Tables 6.1 and 6.2, also conducted a major survey of Hispanics living in the United States in 2014. The survey found that 32% of Hispanics have switched from the religion in which they were raised. Of those raised Catholic, 69% are still Catholic, and of those raised Protestant, 66% are still Protestant, but of those raised unaffiliated, only 47% remain unaffiliated. The Pew Forum's website provides an interactive chart on "Religious Switching Among Hispanics" that graphically displays this and the other paths taken by these individuals. See pewforum.org/2014/05/07/hispanic-religious-switching/.

inferences about religious switching, but earlier sociologists have done so on other data sets. The two most consistent predictors of religious switching in these studies are intermarriage and education.

As noted above, individuals who marry outside their religious tradition are more likely to switch to bring their affiliation in line with their spouse's. This comprises a significant proportion of religious switchers (Loveland 2003; Musick and Wilson 1995; Suchman 1992). One reason that Roman Catholics, Orthodox Jews, and conservative Protestants tend to have higher retention rates than do liberal Protestants is that the former are much more likely to marry within their own denominations (Sherkat 2014:58).

The more general principle explaining switching, one observed also by Lofland in his studies of conversion to NRMs, is that individual religious change tends to run along network lines

(Stark and Finke 2000). Darren Sherkat argues that this also helps to explain why individuals who experience geographic mobility are more likely to switch religions, especially if they move to an area in which one type of religion predominates. Moving disrupts the existing social network connections the individual has and creates the possibility of forming new social ties with individuals from different religious backgrounds (Sherkat 2014).

This network understanding of religious switching can even be used to explain why education level has historically been a very strong predictor of religious switching. What happens is that people tend to worship with others of a similar socioeconomic class. As people are upwardly mobile, they often change their denominational affiliation (Sherkat and Wilson 1995). It is not always clear whether the move to a denomination of higher status is usually a planned "image-enhancing" strategy or merely a function of joining a religious group where one has a friendship network (coworkers and colleagues). In any case, the move to higher-status churches is commonly a move to a more modern or liberal theology, for the high-status churches tend to be more modern in theology. For someone who is in a professional occupation or who has moved up the social ladder, the more modern, more secular theology may be appealing. A worldview that accepts the advances of science may provide more personal coherence and meaning to a highly educated scientist than does a worldview that rejects Darwin. Further, religions of the have-nots tend to condemn materialism and the accumulation of possessions as signs of depravity. This may be comforting to the dispossessed, but it can be most uncomfortable to those who are affluent. Liberal theology tends to embrace *this* world more completely than do orthodox traditions that stress rewards in an afterlife. Regardless of reasons, changes in socioeconomic status do seem to be a significant source of denominational switching (Hoge and Carroll 1978; Newport 1979).

In addition to these network-based factors, there are aspects of an individual's personal background that increase his or her likelihood of switching. In particular, instability in individuals' connection to religion makes them more likely to switch. Loveland (2003) found that not formally joining a faith community and having a lapse in religious practice are both significant predictors of religious switching. Along these same lines, having one's parents divorce in childhood increases the likelihood of religious reaffiliation (Lawton and Bures 2001).

It is clear that denominational switching is not the same as an internal conversion experience. Much of the change from one denomination to another is a matter of merely changing organizational membership. Yet the feeling of belonging—because of friendship networks or because of socioeconomic homogeneity—seems to be the primary influence in this decision to switch. Reginald Bibby's summary of the research on recruitment among Canadian evangelicals seems to apply equally well to American faith communities of all kinds: "If they are serious about recruiting 'real live sinners,' the best approach is either to befriend them or marry them. For this is how the majority of outsiders are actually recruited" (Bibby 1987:30).

Critical Thinking: How or why is "switching" between denominations *similar* to "conversion"? How is it *different* from conversion experience?

Switching and the Growth or Decline of Religious Bodies

Beyond the individual causes of religious switching, some scholars have been interested in its potential social consequences. They want to know why some religious groups are growing and others are declining and whether switching is a primary factor in the change of fortunes of various religious groups.

Dean Kelley's book *Why Conservative Churches Are Growing* (1972) was one of the first to explore this phenomenon. Kelley's thesis was that people are attracted to churches that have strict standards of membership and that expect members to invest much of their time and resources in the group. He pointed out that conservative (fundamentalist, charismatic, and evangelical) churches like the Churches of God, Nazarenes, Seventh-day Adventists, Jehovah's Witnesses, Southern Baptists, and Mormons are growing rapidly while liberal denominations like the United Methodist, United Presbyterian, and Episcopal churches are declining. Data on denominational growth and decline 40 years later show the same pattern as Kelley sought to explain (see Table 6.3).

With the exception of Catholicism, all of the denominations in Table 6.3 that are growing in membership are conservative varieties of Protestant Christianity, and all of the denominations that are shrinking in membership (with the exception of the conservative Lutheran Church—Missouri Synod) are mainline Protestant. In the United States today, there are now more Jehovah's Witnesses than there are Congregationalists (United Church of Christ) and more members of the Pentecostal Assemblies of God than mainline Presbyterians. Mormons today have higher membership numbers than every mainline Protestant denomination except the United Methodists.

Kelley explained this trend by arguing that people are leaving more liberal denominations and switching to more conservative denominations. This view was later complemented by Laurence Iannaccone who offered a rational choice explanation for why strict churches—those that are more theologically conservative—are stronger than liberal churches. He argued that religion is a "collectively produced commodity" in which the participants share in creation of an experience (such as a worship service) and they each benefit from that collective experience (Iannaccone 1994). However, some people "give" a great deal to the creation of the experience and support of the collective enterprise, while others may be "free riders"—people who benefit from the experience but are not as committed. Iannaccone held that this results in resentment or demoralization by those who give a great deal, and it reduces commitment by everyone. Strict churches force high levels of commitment by everyone, so the "free riders" are forced to leave; thus, the argument goes, strict churches remain more vigorous and vibrant (Iannaccone 1994).

However, Kelley's and Iannaccone's interpretation of the data has been repeatedly challenged. Analyses of General Social Survey (GSS) data show only 10% of Americans born after 1970 and raised in mainline churches switched to a conservative one (Chaves 2011). Chaves identifies four major factors to explain conservative church growth.

First, basic demographic phenomena like fertility play a major role in the fortunes of religious groups. The conservative denominations that are growing have much higher fertility rates than the mainline denominations that are shrinking. By Chaves's estimate, 80% of the pattern of growth and decline is due to differential fertility (Chaves 2011). Over 30 years ago, Dean Hoge and David Roozen (1979) reported that, over time, birthrates have been the most consistent correlate with growth and decline of church membership. Conservative denominations "grow on their own" because of the higher fertility rates and earlier childbearing among women in conservative denominations (Hout, Greeley, and Wilde 2001).

A second explanation for the growth of conservative denominations and decline of liberal ones is that it is much less common than it used to be for individuals to switch from conservative to liberal as they experience upward social mobility. Although, as noted above, people do still switch as they experience upward mobility, this is not as common as it once was. Chaves's observations about upwardly mobile individuals raised in conservative Protestant traditions are instructive here. Among those born before 1931, 28% switched to a more liberal Protestant denomination; among those born after 1950, only 12% switched (Chaves 2011).

Table 6.3 Membership in 13 of the Largest U.S. Denominations in 2009, Compared to 1998

Denomination	Characterization	1998	2009	% Change
Jehovah's Witnesses	Millenarian restorationist Christianity	825,570	1,162,686	+34.9
Church of God (Cleveland, TN)	Holiness Pentecostal denomination, conservative theology	870,039	1,076,254	+23.2
Church of Jesus Christ of Latter-day Saints	American upstart denomination, conservative theology	4,923,100	6,058,907	+21.3
Roman Catholic Church	Historically White, increasingly Latino	62,018,436	68,503,486	+9.8
Assemblies of God	Pentecostals, conservative theology	2,687,366	2,914,669	+7.9
Southern Baptist Convention	Historically Southern and White Baptists, conservative theology	15,729,356	16,160,088	+3.2
United Methodist Church	Mainline Protestant	8,400,000	7,774,931	−6.5
Lutheran Church—Missouri Synod	Theologically conservative Lutherans	2,594,404	2,312,111	−9.9
Evangelical Lutheran Church in America	Mainline Protestant	5,178,225	4,542,868	−10.5
Episcopal Church	Part of Worldwide Anglican Communion, Mainline Protestant	2,300,461	2,006,343	−10.6
American Baptist Churches in the USA	Mainline Protestant	1,507,400	1,310,505	−11.7
Presbyterian Church (USA)	Mainline Protestant	3,595,259	2,770,730	−20.9
United Church of Christ	Mainline Protestant	1,421,088	1,080,199	−21.8

SOURCES: 1998 data collected in 1999 and published in Eileen Lindner, ed., *Yearbook of American and Canadian Churches, 2000* (Nashville, TN: Abingdon Press). 2009 data collected in 2010 and published in Eileen Lindner, ed., *Yearbook of American and Canadian Churches, 2011* (Nashville, TN: Abingdon Press).

*Three historically black churches—Church of God in Christ, National Baptist Convention USA, and National Baptist Convention of America—are reputed to be among the largest denominations in the country, but they have not reported new membership figures to the *Yearbook* in many years, and the numbers previously reported were unsubstantiated self-reports. Therefore, we have excluded them from this list.

Third, Chaves points to conservative denominations' ability to retain their youth better than mainline denominations. Conservative churches typically have more commitment mechanisms (discussed in Chapter 5), and these tend to enhance retention. The early research indicated that Jehovah's Witnesses, Seventh-day Adventists, Southern Baptists, Pentecostals and holiness groups, and Mormons had some of the highest retention rates. However, conservative fundamentalist and evangelical sects, whose members are largely of lower socioeconomic class, have had some of the worst retention rates (Roof and McKinney 1987). Interestingly, the recent Pew Forum research is not showing strong retention among Jehovah's Witnesses or the Baptists (Pew Research Center Forum on Religion and Public Life 2008b). Although these groups have many commitment mechanisms, they foster values and outlooks—especially on a range of issues related to gender—that are in conflict with the larger societal trends. Although these conservative groups do lose members, they do not lose as many as the mainline groups.

Fourth, Chaves highlights a cultural factor in these trends. Conservative Protestant denominations have adopted a strongly countercultural position on certain issues of sexual morality, in particular premarital sex and homosexuality. As more and more of the American public has increased tolerance for these phenomena, conservative Protestant denominations have continued to resist them (as we will see in Chapter 11). This highlights their distinctiveness and motivates those who are already members to remain members. By contrast, in embracing these changes, mainline Protestant denominations blur their distinctiveness from the culture in general and give members one less reason to stay.

Of course, declining numbers in a denomination does not mean decline in every congregation that is part of that denomination. One study of a mainline congregation in the United States that was growing at a very healthy rate in the 1990s revealed that the key to its success was largely in a strategy of implementing affective and instrumental commitment mechanisms—small support groups for emotional bonding, eliciting a commitment of time and energy in the organization by new members, and so forth (Wilson et al. 1993).

There are many trends within trends, but it does appear that in the United States certain conservative groups and congregations are gaining a larger overall proportion of the *active, religiously affiliated population*. On the other hand, the category that has grown the most is believers who have left religious communities entirely and those who have moved to nondenominational congregations (Pew Research Center Forum on Religion and Public Life 2008b). Insofar as some very conservative churches have grown, this is clearly the result of a complex mix of factors: higher birthrates, higher percentages of endogamous marriages, more commitment mechanisms, higher overall retention of members, and less ambiguity about authority. Their numerical success is not due primarily to switching of members from liberal faith communities to conservative ones or to recruitment of large numbers of people from among the unaffiliated. The old mainline denominations in the United States, on the other hand, seem to be suffering from apathy and dropping out more than from massive out-migration to other denominations. Indeed, those who leave mainline churches are increasingly likely to answer the "religious preference" question on a survey form with "none."

Critical Thinking: Why do you think people are leaving mainline churches and disaffiliating? What social factors might explain the trend?

Photo provided by Justin W. Roberts

This young lawyer and most of his friends grew up in churches—in his case, a United Methodist church. However, he and his friends have disaffiliated in their 20s and 30s. They seek spirituality, but the main thing alienating them from childhood religious groups is the stance of so many Christian churches with highly conservative social positions—positions they find morally unconscionable. One of these is the stand of many religious bodies against same-sex marriages.

APOSTASY

The debates over the growth of some religious groups and the decline of others should not overshadow something we highlighted at the end of Chapter 5 and that is amply demonstrated in Table 6.1: the growing number of people in the United States with no religious preference. If any group has shown consistently dramatic growth in recent times, it is the "nones." Although many of these are religious people who do not adopt particular religious labels for various reasons, some of them are truly secularists, atheists, or agnostics. The growth in the number of people in American society who are not religious is a real development. A "wind of secularity" is blowing across the religious landscape (Zuckerman 2012:3). As younger cohorts are more likely to leave religion than older cohorts, it is a wind that may continue to blow for some time into the future (Sherkat 2014).

As Table 6.2 shows, only 21% of those raised unaffiliated remain unaffiliated as adults. Therefore, many seculars are converts from religion to no religion. In a word, they are apostates. As Zuckerman notes, apostasy comes from the Greek word *apostasia,* meaning "a defection or revolt." He quotes another scholar as describing it as "disaffection, defection, alienation, disengagement, and disaffiliation from a religious groups" (Zuckerman 2012:4).

As is evident from the different words used to describe apostasy, the same continuum we see in other religious change—from dramatic, life-altering conversion to more mundane denominational switching—also occurs in change *from* religion to no religion. Drawing on open-ended interviews he conducted with 87 individuals, Zuckerman develops a three-dimensional typology of apostasy.

First, he distinguishes between *early* and *late* apostasy. Early apostates are those adolescents and emerging adults who leave the religion into which they were socialized as children. As was suggested in our discussion in Chapter 5 of declining religiosity in early adulthood, Zuckerman finds early apostasy to be common among seculars as they leave their childhood homes and establish more independent identities. Late apostasy involves an individual accepting religion as an adult (independent of his or her childhood commitment) and subsequently rejecting it. It is much rarer than early apostasy (Smith 2010).

Zuckerman next distinguishes between *shallow* and *deep* apostasy, which he saw in equal proportions in his qualitative study. Shallow apostates are those who have rejected the religion that they previously associated with, but are not willing to go all the way

and call themselves atheists. These include the "spiritual, not religious" (see Chapter 1), as well as "open-minded agnostics" (Zuckerman 2012:7). Deep apostasy involves the complete rejection of religion, and anything that seems like religion, including spirituality. These are the true "atheists."

The third dimension is *mild* versus *transformative* apostasy. Mild apostasy is when someone who has little faith leaves it behind. There is a change in the person's religious identification but not a major change in his or her fundamental identity, since religion was never a major part of the person's identity. Transformative apostasy is when a strongly religious person rejects that religion. As Zuckerman describes it, "For such a person, apostasy is a true personal revolution, a life-altering transformation. It involves not only a massive psychological reorientation from a religious to a secular worldview, but it also often entails a loss of close friendships, alienation from a strong community, and even rejection by one's family" (Zuckerman 2012:7).

For an example of an individual who exemplifies late, deep, and transformative apostasy, see the story of Nathan in the next "Illustrating Sociological Concepts" feature.

ILLUSTRATING SOCIOLOGICAL CONCEPTS

An Apostate's Tale

As in sociology generally, most studies of apostasy are based on closed-ended surveys, but as Phil Zuckerman observes, "apostasy is a story that takes place in a person's life." In the introduction to *Faith No More*, Zuckerman introduces readers to one of his 86 interviewees, Nathan.

Nathan is a 42-year-old college professor in Alabama who was raised in an African American Pentecostal church in Philadelphia. So deep was his involvement in the church that his family called him "little Jesus." His religious involvement continued into his 20s. He attended Oral Roberts University, majored in evangelism, started a prison ministry, did mission trips in the summers, and attended graduate school at Christian institutions. In Zuckerman's telling: "Nathan's entire life was his faith and his church and his Bible" (Zuckerman 2012:8).

Then it wasn't.

Here is part of Nathan's story of apostasy, in his own words:

I was really active in the church . . . I got really serious as far as religion . . . I mean, my worldview was totally that God is in control of everything.

I remember the day that I rejected Christianity . . . It's weird . . . but one day I was driving to the gym to work out and I thought about a good buddy of mine who was in a wheelchair. He was a brilliant guy. I thought to myself: "If Rick ever got up out of that wheelchair, it would be on CNN. . . . If a blind person got healed, it would be on CNN." I watch CNN every day, and I've never seen a story about a paralyzed person or blind person . . . so then I thought: God doesn't heal. I had already kind of come to that conclusion, but this way of thinking in terms of it is a fact in my mind that the God of the scriptures that claims to be a healer does not heal today. . . . Then I concluded that if God doesn't heal, then the God of the Bible does not exist. If the God of the Bible does not exist, then I don't believe in God. It was really that simple.

Nathan's adjustment to life as an apostate was not as simple as his realization that he was one.

I had to learn how to be a non-Christian. There was a lot of sort of angst in that. Here I am now, 26 years old, 27—I don't remember the exact age—and I've been pretty much a Christian all that time. A serious Christian. So I have to now learn . . . there was a lot of sorrow in the fact that I now was in a world, a dangerous world, where I didn't feel I was protected by anything, where I was on my own and things were just kind of random. . . . So I had to kind of like learn this new worldview. So on the one hand there was a lot of angst and frustration and a lot of—but that didn't last long. The freedom, the tremendous freedom overcame the frustration—the sorry and the loss, I overcame it because I'm a free thinker. . . . Here I am now, I can be whatever I want, I can re-invent myself, I can do whatever I want, I can create my own moral system, and I don't think I ever looked back. I got to the point where I really embraced the freedom. So this period of frustration, of loss of regret, of how am I going to make it . . . was superseded by the tremendous, almost worship of freedom. . . . I worship freedom now instead of God. (Zuckerman 2012:8–10)

SOURCE: Zuckerman, Phil. 2012. *Faith No More: Why People Reject Religion.* New York: Oxford University Press, pp. 8-10.

Having described apostasy, how do we explain it? Not surprisingly, just as we have moved away from thinking of religious conversion as a result of a particular moment of insight—Saul being struck down on the road to Tarsus—deconversion from religion should be thought of the same way. Based on his interviews, Zuckerman concludes that the process of apostasy in general is gradual (taking place over a period of years at times) and "the result of numerous factors, working in conjunction with one another, steadily compounding over time"

(Zuckerman 2012:151). Not everyone exactly fits this mold, but it serves as a useful heuristic to guide our studies, much like Lofland's process model of conversion to NRMs we discussed earlier in this chapter.

Zuckerman identifies nine common reasons people give for their apostasy:

1. Parents: As we observed in Chapter 5, an intact two-parent family that faithfully practices the same religion will produce children who more faithfully practice religion. Zuckerman finds the opposite is true also: Family disruption and nonpracticing parents produce religious nones.

2. Education: To the extent that higher levels of education require individuals to think more critically about the world and themselves, this can lead to a weakening of previous assumptions including religious ones.

3. Misfortune: One of the best-selling religious inspirational books of all times is called *When Bad Things Happen to Good People*. It was written by Rabbi Harold Kushner to answer the question "Why me?" in response to the death of his 14-year-old son due to a genetic disease. Essentially, Kushner addresses the issue of "theodicy"—if God is good, why is there evil in the world?—by reasserting faith. Some people, however, have the opposite reaction to personal misfortunes.

4. Other Cultures, Other Religions: Being exposed to other religious traditions, through education or travel or media, leads some people to reflect critically on the religious tradition they chose or (more likely) inherited. This can weaken faith. As Peter Berger (1967) argued long ago, exposure to religious pluralism undermines the "plausibility" of religious belief because individuals can see their way is not the only way.

5. Friends, Colleagues, Lovers: We noted above that both religious conversion and switching social networks are a central mechanism. According to the network theory of conversion, "conversion is about bringing one's religious behavior into alignment with that of one's friends and family members." Thus,

"conversion tends to proceed along social networks formed by interpersonal attachments" (Stark and Finke 2000:117–118). So, too, deconversion or apostasy.

6. Politics: For some politically liberal apostates, being religious in the United States is synonymous with being politically conservative, and so they opt out. This reason is in line with the demographic analysis of Hout and Fischer (2002), who argued that growth in religious nones is due in part to individuals with liberal political identities becoming alienated from organized religion due to the alignment of religion and conservative politics by the "religious right" (see Chapter 5).

7. Sex: If most religious traditions are hostile toward sexual behavior, or very proscriptive of "who one can have sex with, as well as when, where, and how," individuals who are pro-sex or sexually active, or whose sexuality is nonnormative (homosexual, bisexual, transsexual, etc.), are more likely to opt out of religion entirely (Zuckerman 2012:160). (We discuss sexuality and religion in Chapter 11).

8. Satan and Hell: Some apostates who were taught to fear Satan and threatened with suffering in the fires of hell have very negative associations with those religious traditions. At some point they can react against those feelings by leaving those religions.

9. Malfeasance of Religious Associates: Whether friend, relative, priest, rabbi, imam, lay minister, or some other religious person, the bad actions of religious associates can have a profoundly disillusioning effect on people, in some cases leading to apostasy.

Zuckerman is careful to note that the *reasons* people give for their apostasy are not the same as *causes*. The social world is not mechanical in the way the natural world is. If variable X (say, education) goes up a certain amount, it is not guaranteed that variable Y (faith) will go down a certain amount. Yet the factors that Zuckerman (2012) identified may increase the likelihood that someone will become an apostate, especially if there are conjunctions between them.

To better address in a systematic and generalizable way the social correlates of apostasy, we need to look to statistical analyses of closed-ended surveys based on representative samples (recall Chapter 2). Darren Sherkat has taken advantage of the fact that the GSS has been asking individuals to specify their current religion and their religion at age 16 since its inception. Recognizing that not all "nones" are not religious, he defines apostates as those whose current religion is unaffiliated but who claimed a religion in their youth (Sherkat 2012).

The factors that most increase the likelihood of apostasy in Sherkat's quantitative analysis are similar to the reasons identified by Zuckerman in his qualitative analysis, but the quantitative analysis allows us to identify specific levels of likelihood. For example, married people are 33% *less* likely and divorced people are 13% *more* likely to be apostates compared those who have never been married. Each child you have decreases your likelihood of apostasy by 9%. A person with 2 children is 18% less likely, a person with 3 children is 27% less likely, and so on. Having more education than the average member of the religious denomination in which you were raised also makes you 18% more likely to leave a faith community (Sherkat 2014:75).

Geographic mobility is something that Zuckerman alludes to but Sherkat investigates specifically. Whether looking at intrastate or interstate, urban-rural, or southern-nonsouthern migration, in every case geographic mobility is associated with higher rates of apostasy (Sherkat 2014:77). This makes sense as geographic mobility—like educational or status mobility—disrupts existing social networks and plausibility structures that support faith.

Finally, of all the status and life course effects on apostasy that Sherkat included in his statistical model, gender has the largest effect. As we discuss further in Chapter 11, women are more religious than men, and one way this manifests itself is in their lower likelihood of apostasy.

Sherkat (2014) finds women are 42% less likely to be apostates than men.

This combination of qualitative and quantitative description and analysis of apostasy shows the benefits of the methodological triangulation we advocated in Chapter 2. It helps to paint a more comprehensive portrait of a significant and growing segment of the American religious landscape.

Critical Thinking: Have you or has someone you know left religion? If so, do Zuckerman's and Sherkat's explanations for apostasy help explain that change? If not, why is apostasy something that is not close to you, even though it is becoming more common? Can sociological explanations of apostasy shed light on people who stay in religion?

SUMMARY

Conversion and switching are complex processes, and there is much we do not know. What does appear entirely clear at this point is that the NRMs are not engaged in brainwashing as was once charged by the anti-cult movement and by the media.

While the idea of a sequential cumulative process first advanced by Lofland seems to be a fruitful way to think about conversion, with various factors *contributing*, at this point there is no consensus about which factors might be *necessary* ones or what precise sequence might be most typical. Most conversions probably involve a complex interplay between factors.

Rational choice theorists stress the activist role of actors in the process of making choices. Whether the focus is on converts or on the action of religious "firms" acting through local "franchises" and "entrepreneurs," this form of analysis stresses the role of decisions that are based on a religious market. The "winners" are those who are aware of market forces of supply and demand and the interplay of costs and benefits in individual religious commitments.

Switching among denominations also seems to be a result largely of affective factors. Friendship networks and marriages across denominations appear to be the most powerful factors, but other factors are at work as well. Interestingly, the conservative Christian churches and nones are the fastest-growing. The growth patterns among conservative groups are because birthrates are very high; strict membership rules in those organizations may also contribute to higher levels of retention.

The largest growth and arguably the most important development in American religious affiliation is among those with no religious preference. Scholars studying apostasy approach the issue of conversion or switching *from* religion in much the same way as scholars studying conversion or switching *to* religion.

In this and the previous chapter, we have sought to understand socialization into and commitment to religion, as well as religious conversion and denominational switching. In the next section, we will explore other factors that are necessary if a religious group is to survive over time, examining religion at the organizational level.

PART IV

FORMATION AND MAINTENANCE OF RELIGIOUS ORGANIZATIONS

In the previous chapters, we explored two of the three interrelated subsystems that comprise the larger system we call religion. We have investigated the meaning system (e.g., the network of myths, symbols, rituals, ethos, and worldview), and we have pointed to the importance of the belonging system (e.g., the network of friendships and affective ties). We have learned something about the processes by which individuals become and remain committed to a faith and a faith community, as well as patterns of changing religious affiliations.

The question of the organizational bases and forms of religion will be a central focus of this unit.

In Chapter 7, we examine the major typologies that sociologists have used to categorize religious organizations: church, sect, denomination, and cult (or new religious movement [NRM]). As part of that consideration, we examine the process of institutionalization that is necessary for any religious group to survive and grow. In Chapter 8, we turn our attention more narrowly to American religion and examine two distinguishing characteristics of the social organization of religion in the United States: denominationalism and congregationalism. Included in our consideration of congregations is the rise of megachurches, new paradigm and seeker churches, and the marketing of religion.

7

ORGANIZED RELIGION

Churches, Sects, Denominations, and "Cults"

HERE ARE SOME QUESTIONS TO PONDER AS YOU READ THIS CHAPTER

- What is a charismatic leader, and how does this kind of leadership influence a group?
- How does institutionalization of religion figure into a group's survival?

- What dilemmas does institutionalization create for a group?
- What are the core characteristics of a church, denomination, sect, or cult?
- What kinds of social conditions help to create a new religious movement (NRM) or a sect?
- What forces cause a fledgling religious movement to evolve into denominations of an existing religion or a new religious tradition?
- Are the ideas of ecclesia, denomination, sect, and NRM the best way to think about religious groups and movements?

Adequately socializing young members, gaining new members, and maintaining a high level of commitment from existing members is necessary for a religious group to survive. The commitment of individual members, however, is not sufficient to ensure the group's ongoing viability. Religions are not simply collections of individuals, but are organizational realities that are greater than the sum of their parts. In this chapter, we look at the organizational development of religious groups from their beginnings as fledgling "cults" or NRMs to their status as established and stable religious organizations.

Ever since Max Weber first developed the proposition that NRMs generally start out as cults headed by a charismatic leader, much of the sociological work in religion has evolved around the concept of charisma. However, Weber insisted that charisma is inherently unstable; if the group does not institutionalize, it will die shortly after the founder dies. Many NRMs never make the transition and therefore never develop into viable religions. Even if a group does institutionalize, the process of institutionalization is itself fraught with dilemmas, usually causing changes in the religious movement. In this chapter, we explore the role of charismatic leaders in the emergence of NRMs, discuss the importance of institutionalization in the survival of these movements, and examine problems that this institutionalization creates for the group.

Having examined the changes religious organizations undergo in the process of institutionalization, we turn our attention to the various ways that sociologists of religion have classified religious organizations. "Church," "sect," "denomination," and "cult" (or "NRM") are the most common categories used, though the precise definitions of each and their relation to one another have been the source of considerable debate, as we will see. (We will be considering denominationalism more fully in Chapter 8.)

CHARISMA AND THE CHARISMATIC LEADER

Weber was the first sociologist to write extensively on the importance of charismatic leadership. He maintained that new religions generally get their impetus from the attraction of a charismatic leader, a dynamic person who is perceived as extraordinary and set apart from the rest of humanity. Weber wrote,

> The term "charisma" will be applied to a certain quality of an individual personality, by virtue of which (s)he is set apart from ordinary [people] and treated as endowed with supernatural, superhuman, or at least specifically exceptional powers or qualities. These are such as are not accessible to the ordinary person, but are regarded as of divine origin or as exemplary, and on the basis of them the individual concerned is treated as a leader. (Weber 1947:358–359)

The charismatic leader is able to use this power to mobilize followers and to create within them a sense of mission.

Weber insisted that charismatic leadership is not to be judged as intrinsically good or evil, for it could be either. The point is that some individuals come to be regarded as exceptional and perhaps even divine by followers or disciples. Although the followers do not necessarily experience the *mysterium tremendum* in quite the way it is described by Rudolf Otto (see Chapter 4), they do become convinced that their charismatic leader is a direct agent of God, or perhaps God incarnate. Believers may feel a sense of mystery and awe in the presence of such a leader. The feelings of members of the Unification Church for the Reverend Moon provide one example. He is believed to be the new Christ, God incarnate. Whatever he says is believed to be true simply because he said it.[1] Likewise, whatever Jesus Christ said is true for Christians because he is, in their eyes, God incarnate (God in the flesh). Jesus is a classic illustration of a charismatic leader who began a new movement.

One element of charismatic leadership that Weber thought to be especially important was its antiestablishment and revolutionary tendencies. Weber believed that charismatic authority is intrinsically unstable and is antithetical to social order:

> Charismatic authority is specifically outside the realm of everyday routine and the profane sphere. In this respect, it is sharply opposed both to rational, and particularly bureaucratic, authority and to traditional authority. . . . Both rational and traditional authority are specifically forms of everyday routine control of action; while the charismatic type is the direct antithesis of this. Bureaucratic authority is specifically rational in the sense of being bound to intellectually analyzable rules, while charismatic authority is specifically irrational in the sense of being foreign to all rules. Traditional authority is bound to the precedents handed down from the past and to this extent is also oriented to rules. Within the sphere of its claims, charismatic authority repudiates the past and is in this sense a specifically revolutionary force. (Weber 1947:361–362)

Weber was emphatic in asserting that the Old Testament prophets were not spokesmen for some economic group. Their interests were explicitly religious, although there were social and economic implications to their messages. Weber was interested in the power of ideas in bringing social change. Research in the latter half of the 20th century focused on why people attribute superhuman powers to others. This line of research stressed the fact that adherence to a charismatic leader and the development of an NRM is likely when certain social conditions prevail, and it occurs in stages by which the leader comes to be elevated to sacred status (Wallace 1972).

Nonetheless, once the charismatic leader has emerged and developed a following, it is necessary for the group to undergo a transformation. Charismatic leadership is not only revolutionary but it is inherently unstable. Hence, the movement undergoes a process that Weber referred to as the "routinization of charisma."

Critical Thinking: How does the experience of awe before a charismatic leader differ from the experience of awe in a nonrational *mysterium tremendum* encounter? How are these experiences similar? How might these two types of intense religious encounter result in different social consequences?

The Routinization of Charisma

If the religious movement is to survive for any significant period of time, a stable set of roles and statuses must be established and a consistent pattern of norms generated and practiced. Hence, the nature of the charismatic authority is transformed. Weber wrote,

> In its pure form charismatic authority has a character specifically foreign to everyday routine structures. If this [religious movement] is not to remain a purely transitory phenomenon, but to take on the

character of a permanent relationship . . . it is necessary for the character of charismatic authority to become radically changed. Indeed, in its pure form charismatic authority may be said to exist only in the process of originating. (Weber 1947:363–364)

The community gathered around a dynamic leader must evolve into one with a stable matrix of norms, roles, and statuses. This process of *routinization* (developing stable routines) is commonly referred to by sociologists as institutionalization. Any group that fails to institutionalize its collective life simply will not survive.

Institutionalization serves both ideal and material interests of followers and leaders. The ideals of the group can be furthered only if it survives and only if it mobilizes its resources. Hence, institutionalization serves the ideological interests of adherents. Yet the followers and the leaders also have a material stake in the survival of the group. Insofar as they have invested time, energy, and financial resources in the group, they are likely to feel that they have a vested economic interest in its survival and success. Therefore, the inherent forces working for routinization are strong.

Perhaps the most critical test of a group's routinization is the way it handles the issue of succession. When the charismatic leader dies, the group may quickly disperse. However, many people have a vested interest in the survival of the group and will seek to ensure its viability. The problem is, who will provide the group with leadership? Equally contentious is how that decision will be made.

The transfer of power to the next designated leader has important implications for the subsequent evolution of the group. First, the charisma that was once identified with a personality must be associated with the religious ideology and with the religious organization. The group, the body of beliefs, and perhaps a written record (a scripture) become sources of veneration. This more stable source of authority in itself changes the character of the group. Second, the decision-making process itself becomes sacralized as the divinely appointed method of choosing the successor. This method may involve the designation of a successor by the original leader, some form of divinely sanctioned and controlled election, the drawing of lots, a hereditary succession, or any one of a number of other procedures. In any event, the followers must recognize the new leader(s) as the legitimate heir(s) to leadership. Otherwise, the group may be torn by schisms as various splinter groups identify different persons as the rightful leader.

© Brigham Young Family Association

Joseph Smith was the founder of the Church of Jesus Christ of Latter-day Saints (also called the Mormon Church), but when he was murdered in Illinois in 1844, Brigham Young (above) became the president and leader of the group. He was already the president of the church's leadership core—the Quorum of the Twelve Apostles—and second in command after Smith. Young led the migration west, established church settlements throughout the western states, founded Salt Lake City, and served as territorial governor of Utah. For 33 years, Brigham Young was the leader of the church, further stabilizing the resource base and leadership of the group. Without this smooth transition of leadership—part of routinization—the church may have split or simply died without its charismatic founder, Joseph Smith.

The new leader or group of leaders is not likely to possess the same sort of unquestioned authority that was vested in the personhood of the original leader. Some of the awe and respect will have been transferred to the teachings and to the continuing organization itself. The rules and values of the group must be attributed with transcendent importance in and of themselves. Commitment is now to the organization and to the ideology of the movement, and the authority of the *new* leader(s) may be restrained by these stabilizing forces. No longer are the sayings of the leader taken as true simply because that person said them. They must be evaluated in light of what the original leader said and did. In short, the new leader is usually an ideological leader rather than a charismatic one.

Another issue of routinization has to do with provision of a stable economic base. If some members are to devote full-time to the service of the leader and the movement, then a continuing and consistent source of income must be provided. This may come from some obligatory payment to the organization by members who are employed in secular positions (a tithe), from members begging or soliciting (as some NRMs in the 1970s and 1980s did), or from the establishment of some industry sponsored by the organization (as in the Bruderhof production of *Community Playthings* or, in the mid-19th century, Oneida's production of steel traps). However accomplished, this provision of a stable source of income is a critical part of the routinization process. Without this financial base, there can be no full-time clergy, administrative staff, or other regular employees. If there are no career opportunities within the organizational structure, instrumental commitment may begin to wane. Furthermore, some type of full-time administrative staff may be necessary if the group is growing and expects to continue expanding.

Sometimes routinization is a slow process that occurs largely after the death of the leader. After the death of Jesus, his disciples were a band of frightened and discouraged individuals. Through a series of experiences, they became convinced that Jesus had risen from the dead, and their faith was renewed. However, it was the new convert Paul (previously known as Saul of Tarsus) who was responsible for the expansion of the group, for he universalized the faith and recruited Gentiles on an equal basis with Jews. Paul also established organizational links between the various congregations. He collected money from his Gentile converts, which was given to the parent organization in Jerusalem, and he traveled from one congregation to another forging a bond between them and creating a loyalty to himself. In fact, the parent Christian group in Jerusalem often sought to undermine his authority, and Paul constantly had to work at maintaining his position of leadership.

Paul established norms and expectations that were spelled out in his teachings and in his epistles. He often "corrected" local congregations because they had begun to follow norms that had emerged spontaneously out of the group. He assumed authority and was sought out as the person to resolve conflicts and to define customs and mores (e.g., whether women could worship without a head covering, and what format the love feasts should follow). He also authorized teachers at various churches. In fact, in his later epistles, he even referred to bishops and deacons. These officials appear to have been local ones at the time, but eventually the roles expanded to be more centralized, with broad supervisory functions. The routinization process was by no means complete by the time of Paul's death, but it was well under way. It is clear that Paul was the organizational genius who initiated the institutionalization process; it was his organizational initiative that eventually resulted in that bastion of European religious life, the Roman Catholic Church.

So in some cases, a later organizer initiates institutionalization of the faith after the death of the charismatic founder. In other cases, the charismatic leader also happens to be an excellent organizer. In any event, the routinizing function must be performed.

Perhaps the most important test of the routinization of charisma is that of determining leadership succession. However, normalization of roles and statuses, establishment of relatively stable norms, and provision of a stable economic base usually have to be addressed long before succession becomes an issue. If routinization does not occur, the viability of the group for any substantive period after the death of the original leader is unlikely.

There have been thousands of NRMs that are spawned but do not survive. One example is the California group known as Heaven's Gate. The group had two leaders, a woman and a man called "Ti" and "Do"—as in the musical notes. Studies indicate that when Ti died in 1985, there was a major crisis. Because there had been two leaders, the community rallied behind Do. Ti had been the more charismatic figure, but they worked together, and when she died, followers came to believe that Do had direct communication with Ti on a regular basis. As Do began to enter his 60s and he experienced some health problems, it was clear that the group would not survive his death intact. The group had failed to fully institutionalize and was still dependent upon primary charisma. Ultimately, of course, the group did not survive the leader since almost all members committed suicide with him. This was the only way they could join Ti in a spaceship on the other side of comet Hale-Bopp, thus ascending to the "Next Level" (Balch and Taylor 2002).

There are many other examples of collapsed religious movements that failed to institutionalize, but few have as dramatic an ending as Heaven's Gate, whose group suicide made international news in March 1997. Indeed, the reason most people cannot name many groups that did not institutionalize is precisely because they failed to survive as a group. They are relegated to the history of religious movements.

Many scholars believe that most, if not all, religions begin as charismatic cultic movements. However, if a new group is to prosper and survive, it must undergo a process of institutionalization.

The extent and form of institutionalization will vary from group to group, but some routinization must take place. Beyond this, institutionalization itself creates new problems or dilemmas.

Critical Thinking: *Refute* or *support* the following statement, providing your reasoning for your position: "When religion becomes 'organized religion,' it ceases to be real religion."

DILEMMAS OF INSTITUTIONALIZATION

As Thomas O'Dea put it, "religion both needs most and suffers most from institutionalization" (O'Dea 1961:32). Although institutionalization is necessary, it tends to change the character of the movement and to create certain dilemmas for the religious organization. O'Dea elaborated five such dilemmas.

The Dilemma of Mixed Motivation

When the enthusiastic band of disciples is gathered around the charismatic leader, there is a single-minded and unqualified devotion to the leader and to his or her teachings. The followers are willing to make great sacrifices to further the cause, and they willingly subordinate their own needs and desires for the sake of group goals. However, with the development of a stable institutional structure, the desire to occupy the more creative, responsible, and prestigious positions can stimulate jealousies and personality conflicts. Concerns about personal security within the organization may cause members to lose sight of the group's primary goals. Mixed motivation occurs when a secondary concern or motivation comes to overshadow the original goals and teachings of the leader. Conventions of clergy sometimes debate pension plans and insurance programs more heatedly than statements of mission (O'Dea 1961).

It is important to recognize the dilemma in this process. Religious institutions do need to provide for the economic security and well-being of their full-time professionals if they expect them to maintain high morale and commitment. Likewise, if those professionals are to be satisfied and fulfilled by their work, they need to feel that they can really use their creative talents and abilities. These secondary concerns are important to the individuals in question. The problem for the organization is that these secondary matters can take on primary importance for some members and subvert the original sense of mission.

Such secondary concerns may come to the surface while the charismatic leader is still alive. For example, the New Testament reports that at the time of the Last Supper, Jesus's disciples got into an argument over who was the most important and who would have the most exalted position in the kingdom of God (Matthew 18:1; Mark 10:37). However, such self-oriented motivations can be rather easily overcome by a simple command of the charismatic personality. Mixed motivation is more likely to develop when the group's sense of security is institutionally based rather than charismatically based. Later generations are much more likely to belong to the group for reasons that are unrelated to the teachings of the charismatic leader.

Mixed motivation may also involve a more subtle form of goal displacement. Max Assimeng studied six millennial and Pentecostal Christian mission groups in Africa, which began with a goal of converting people to their own faith. Their focus was otherworldly and theological. To attract converts and to demonstrate their concern for people, some groups started schools; others established hospitals. While the religious message itself was not always well received, the hospitals and schools were enthusiastically embraced (Assimeng 1987). Indeed, promises of offering such this-worldly services were often necessary before the government authorities would allow these groups to proselytize in their country. It is natural, one might suggest, for people to repeat those behaviors that are successful and well received. The enthusiastic and warm

response to this-worldly benevolent aid was an enticement for missionaries to focus more and more of their energies on provision of those services. Goal displacement began to occur in the allocation of time and resources because the areas in which success did occur provided ego gratifications for the individuals involved. Such goal displacement did not occur equally in all groups or in all regions of Africa; for a variety of reasons, some missionaries were more effective than others in resisting goal displacement. Still, the original goals in many mission stations were displaced. Success can be intoxicating and alluring and can cause one, consciously or otherwise, to redefine one's goals.

The Symbolic Dilemma: Objectification Versus Alienation

In Chapter 4, we explored the importance of symbols in religion. For a community to worship together, a common set of symbols must be generated that meaningfully expresses the worldview and the ethos of the group. However, this process of projecting subjective feelings on to objective artifacts or behaviors can proceed to the point that the symbols no longer have power for the members. O'Dea wrote,

> Symbolic and ritual elements may become cut off from the subjective experience of the participants. A system of religious liturgy may come to lose its resonance with the interior dispositions of the members. . . . In such a case the forms of worship become alienated from personal religiosity. (O'Dea 1961:34)

Variant interpretations of a symbol in a religious community can clearly have divisive effects. Yet according to O'Dea, symbols may also become utterly meaningless to members of the religious community. Many Christian churches have stained glass windows that depict a fish. This was a powerful symbol to the early Christians. In Greek, the first letters of each word in the phrase "Jesus Christ, Son of God, Savior" spelled the word *fish*. The fish came to be used as a coded symbol of insiders: A drawing of a fish identified one as a Christian to other believers without giving one's Christian identity away to Roman soldiers. Hence, a representation of a fish became an important symbol of solidarity and conviction for Christians, a highly persecuted group. Most modern-day worshippers do not know the origins of the fish as a symbol of faithfulness, and the symbol does not particularly enhance the worship experience or bond the members together. In this case, the symbol is treated with indifference rather than with hostility. In any event, the fish is no longer a powerful symbol that acts to create powerful moods and motivations and reinforce the worldview.

In other cases, the symbols may come to be seen by some as a barrier to communication with the transcendent. The anti-symbolism of the Puritans, who rejected stained glass windows and identified Roman Catholic Stations of the Cross as "idols," provides an example. In the minds of these people, visual symbols had come to symbolize an overbearing bureaucratic organization rather than a transcendent experience. Such alienation from established forms, symbols, and rituals can lead to either apathy toward religion or radical revolt and reformation of the faith.

The process of developing objective, observable symbols that express a deeper subjective experience is part of the process of institutionalization. Symbols are necessary to bind a group together and to remind group members of a common faith, but that very objectification of experience into symbols may eventually create problems. If the symbols lose their power and meaning for members, either the group must create new symbols, or it will face internal problems of meaning and belonging.

The Dilemma of Administrative Order: Elaboration of Policy Versus Flexibility

As a religious group grows and institutionalizes, it may develop national offices and a

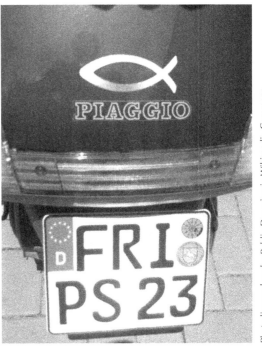

As on this scooter in Germany, some people have the "Jesus fish" symbol ("Ichthys") on their vehicle bumpers or wear it as jewelry to indicate they are Christians. Many people have little idea of the real origins of why a fish is a symbol of Christianity. This scooter is also interesting because PS23 on the license plate stands for Psalm 23 in the Hebrew Scriptures, also known as "the Shepherd Psalm." It is a contemporary way of signaling to others familiar with these scriptures that the owner is a person of faith.

Photo licensed under Public Domain via Wikimedia Commons

bureaucratic structure. In so doing, a set of rational policies and regulations may be established to clarify the relationships between various statuses and offices in the organization. Like the federal government or any other bureaucratic structure, these rules and regulations and the plethora of interrelated departments and divisions may create an unwieldy and overcomplicated structure. Ecclesiastical hierarchies are no less susceptible to red tape than any other bureaucratic structure. As O'Dea pointed out, attempts to modify or reform the structure may run into severe resistance by those whose status and security in the hierarchy may be threatened. Resolution of the dilemma of administrative order may be impeded by the existence of mixed motivation. Many persons within the hierarchy may view reorganization as a threat to their own security or positions of power and prestige.

Again, the dilemma must be recognized as such. Students sometimes see unwieldy organizational complexity and excessive rules and regulations as silly and unnecessary. However, people in complex organizations frequently feel a profound need for guidelines for decision making. The search for concrete policy in the face of some new problem is common in any large, formal organization. If no policy has been clearly established, people look to the resolution of similar cases in the past. The precedent often then becomes an unwritten rule. The development of elaborate and sometimes overly complex policy is a natural outgrowth of the desire of people to know how to solve problems and deal with unusual cases. People at lower levels in the organization do not feel comfortable making decisions without the sanction of those with more authority. Yet, this felt need for clearly articulated policy can mean that an organization is run entirely by rigid rules and regulations. Not only is this uncomfortable and frustrating, but it also greatly reduces flexibility.

A group of clergy appointed to a committee to screen candidates for ordination and ministry may not feel authorized to establish their own standards for ordination. They want to know what guidelines have been set by the denomination as a whole. If none are available, they would likely seek to have some guidelines formally approved to help them make decisions. The guidelines that are adopted may specify a college degree and a seminary education from an accredited university and theological school, respectively. However, years later an ordination-screening committee may encounter a case in which an individual brings impressive experiential credentials and enthusiastic letters of reference but holds degrees from non-accredited institutions. Does the committee have the authority to waive the national guidelines in this case? Whatever the members decide, their decision may be seen as a binding precedent for future cases. Policy continues to be elaborated, but it may also restrict a group in its ability to be flexible with new circumstances.

The Dilemma of Delimitation: Concrete Definition Versus Substitution of the Letter for the Spirit

In the process of routinization, the religious message is translated into specific guidelines of behavior for everyday life. The general teachings about the unity of the universe or about the love of God must be translated into concrete rules of ethical behavior. If this is not done, the religious belief system may remain at such an abstract level that the ordinary person does not grasp its meaning or its importance for everyday living. The meaning of many of Jesus's teachings was not understood even by his disciples until he gave specific illustrations or elaborated through parables. In the ancient Hebrew tradition, the covenant that Abraham had made with God was comforting, but to understand the human obligations in it, specific ethical codes were spelled out. The Torah, the first five books of the Hebrew Bible, is a record of this religious law; it includes the Ten Commandments as the best known such code in the Western world.

In the process of translating the outlook of the faith into specific rules, however, something may be lost. Eventually, the members may focus so intently on the rules that they lose sight of the original spirit or outlook of the faith. The religion may then degenerate into legalistic formulas for salvation and/or may become moralistic and judgmental in a way inconsistent with the original intent of the founder (O'Dea 1961). The legalism and ritualism of the late classical period

The substitution of the letter for the spirit of a set of beliefs is illustrated in this linocut by Robert O. Hodgell. Some religious people seem so intent on literal interpretation of the written word that the spirit of the faith seems to be lost; there seems to be little love, compassion, or joy in such religion.

of Pharisaic Judaism provides one example. The fundamentalistic and rule-bound interpretations of Islam by some of the leading Shiite ayatollahs of Iran provide another example; their posture is clearly inconsistent with the central thrust of Islam—love, compassion, and peace. The linocut print by Robert O. Hodgell expresses more eloquently than words the problem created when the letter of the religious ethical code becomes more important than the spirit of that code. The image could apply equally well to some types of

Protestant Christians, to Islamic fundamentalists, or to Hasidic Jews (at least as the Hasids are seen by Reformed Jews).

Hence, the dilemma is created: The abstract moods, motivations, and concepts must be made concrete so that common laypeople can comprehend their meaning and implication for everyday life. However, by translating the spirit of the faith into specific moral rules and ritual requirements, the possibility is established that later generations may become literalistic and legalistic about those rules and may miss the central message.

The Dilemma of Power: Conversion Versus Coercion

If a religious group is to stay together and sustain its common faith, conformity to the values and norms of the group must be ensured. Although occasional deviation from established norms may not threaten the group, most of the beliefs, values, and norms of the faith must be adhered to most of the time. In its early stages, the religious group is composed of members who have personally converted to the group. They feel a personal loyalty to the charismatic leader, they have had a nonrational conversion experience, or they have been motivated to internalize the faith through some other process. By contrast, later generations who have grown up within the religious organization may never have personally experienced anything that compelled them to accept the absolute authority of the faith in their own lives, or to accept the authority of the religious hierarchy to interpret the faith. They may be inclined to challenge official interpretations. Although such challenges can also come in the first generation, internalization of the authority structure is usually more complete in the first generation of believers than in later ones (O'Dea 1961).

To maintain the integrity of the organization and ensure consensus in their basic worldview, religious organizations may resort to coercive methods of social control. Excommunication is one procedure. When Sonia Johnson, a Mormon, took a public stand in 1979 in favor of the Equal Rights Amendment for women, the Mormon hierarchy informed her that her stance was heretical. When she refused voluntarily to accept the position of the Mormon Church and the authority of its leaders, she was excommunicated. Likewise, other religious bodies have excommunicated members who failed to conform to basic doctrinal or ritual standards. Of course, in some periods of history, the unorthodox were subject to torture and death. Regardless of the specific methods used, the maintenance of conformity through coercion rather than conversion is significant. Conformity due to internalization of norms is much more powerful and lasting than the use of coercion, but voluntary internalization of the norms by all members is difficult to sustain. Therefore, an institutionalized religious organization may come to rely on coercive methods as a last resort to maintain conformity and consensus.

Edward Lehman pointed out that in democratic, pluralistic societies such as the United States, religious organizations have little coercive power over their members. In fact, it is the members who have some control over their churches; they may threaten to withhold financial support. Thus, churches in the modern world have much less clout to enforce and maintain their interpretations of the faith (Lehman 1985).

Institutional Dilemmas and Social Context

Milton Yinger (1961) pointed out that O'Dea's discussion of institutional dilemmas failed to specify the conditions under which the dilemmas are most and least likely to occur. Indeed, O'Dea suggested that the dilemmas are inherent, unavoidable, and inevitable. If they *are* inevitable, it seems clear that in some cases it may take several generations, and perhaps several centuries, to occur.

James Mathisen (1987) analyzed the Moody Bible Institute in Chicago, tracing its 100-year history, with attention to how it has dealt with these institutional dilemmas. Several of the dilemmas appear not to have occurred, and the movement seems to have coped fairly effectively with most of the others. Mathisen's analysis highlights the fact that some social organizations and some social conditions may be more conducive than others to the occurrence of certain dilemmas.

It appears from Mathisen's study that the symbolic dilemma is less likely to occur in groups that stress intense emotional conversion experiences and that have strong mechanisms to sustain the plausibility of the worldview and the symbol systems. Alienated or marginal groups in the society may also be less susceptible to this dilemma because the religious symbols may serve to enhance group boundaries. Conflict with outsiders provides a context in which symbols gain emotional force and relevancy for the members.

Likewise, the dilemma of delimitation (concrete definition versus substitution of the letter for the spirit) may be less of a problem in circumstances where the group perceives itself to be a persecuted or vulnerable minority group. Having a clearly defined set of "fundamentals" by which to measure faithfulness may become a source of strength for the group and may be defined as a virtue. Not only was this the case for fundamentalists running the Moody Bible Institute, but it also appears to be operative among Orthodox Jews in North America as well. Both groups are minority movements that are substantially concerned with maintaining clear boundaries between themselves and the larger society. If concrete definition sometimes does lead to a problem for the group, it is clear that this is not always the case.

The dilemmas of mixed motivation and of power may also be lessened in circumstances in which many commitment mechanisms are used. As we saw in Chapter 5, commitment mechanisms heighten one's commitment to the needs and interests of the group by causing one to identify self-interest with group interests. This would lessen the likelihood of mixed motivation and would reduce the need for coercion as a means of social control. These generalizations are at this point reasonable hypotheses that need to be tested empirically. Continued research is needed regarding the conditions under which the dilemmas are most and least likely to occur.

Dilemmas of institutionalization do plague organized religion, but the five dilemmas outlined in this chapter are not necessarily "inevitable," and it is clear that they need not be fatal. Margaret Poloma conducted research on the Assemblies of God, a Pentecostal denomination that celebrates the unexpected and the spontaneous messages of God through nonrational experiences such as glossolalia ("speaking in tongues"). Unlike Weber, she finds the Assemblies of God have insisted that charisma is dispersed among all of the people, not just a charismatic leader (Poloma 1989). Poloma has studied how the group has institutionalized over time but has fought against lessening of spontaneous nonrational euphoria and inspiration by members of the group. She finds that the dilemmas of institutionalization have played a role in the institutional life of the Assemblies of God, but that they have found ways to affirm charisma and to slow the eroding effect of rationalization (bureaucratization) and rationalism. It does appear that the dilemmas are more pronounced when the organization is a majority religious movement than when it is a minority protest movement preoccupied with tensions with the larger society.

Once created, institutions take on a life of their own and may focus more on their own survival than on anything else. Anson Shupe found that denominations would often try to cover up clergy malfeasance (including sexual misconduct by ministers) because of a concern for how publicity might hurt the church as an organization. Survival and health of the religious organization became more important than ethical misconduct and injury to members of the church (Shupe 1998; Shupe, Stacey, and Darnell 2000). This was abundantly evident in the Roman Catholic Church hierarchy's complicity in the

Bernard Law was Roman Catholic Archbishop of Boston, Massachusetts, from 1984 to 2002. When the Catholic sexual abuse scandal in Boston came to light, groups such as the Survivors Network of those Abused by Priests (SNAP) and Voice of the Faithful accused Law of complicity (Bruce 2011). Although he resigned his position as Archbishop, Pope John Paul II appointed him Archpriest of the Basilica di Santa Maria Maggiore in Rome, where he served until his retirement in 2011.

sexual abuse of children by priests over a period of decades—including paying hush money and emotionally manipulating the abused—which came to light dramatically in an exposé by the Investigative Staff of the *Boston Globe* (2002).

Thus, the process of institutionalization is a mixed blessing—or perhaps a necessary curse—for religion. If an NRM does not institutionalize, it is not likely to last long. The absence of routinization will mean that the group will expire with the death of the charismatic leader. The particular pattern of routinization will vary from group to group, and some organizations become more bureaucratic and centralized than do others. For example, some religious bodies have successfully routinized without establishing a professional clergy, while others have highly trained professionals as ministers and a hierarchy of area ministers, bishops, and archbishops. The student of religious organizations will find considerable variation in the extent and style of institutionalization, but some form of routinization is essential.

Critical Thinking: Make two lists: one enumerating the benefits of institutionalization for religious groups and the other identifying problems that institutionalization creates. How do you evaluate the net impact of institutionalization on religious groups?

CLASSIFYING RELIGIOUS ORGANIZATIONS

To conduct research on religion and make generalizations about religious behavior, social scientists have categorized groups with significant similarities into types, comparing and contrasting characteristics of churches, sects, denominations, and cults (the latter now usually called NRMs). Max Weber called such groupings *ideal types.* By this, he did not mean that they were "the best" or somehow preferable, but only that these classifications exist entirely in the world of ideas (Weber 1949). For example, if there are seven typical characteristics of a dysfunctional family, the ideal type would list all seven of these. However, most troubled families may only have some combination of four or five of the features.

Generalizations about any social behavior can be made only by comparing and contrasting phenomena that are in some respects similar. However, it is essential that the conception of various types be as clear and accurate as possible.

Otherwise, the concepts themselves may cause faulty generalizations. In fact, the concepts of church, sect, and denomination have been used in a variety of ways by various researchers, and this causes some confusion. Nonetheless, many scholars continue to try to work with these concepts because they feel that they continue to be valuable as analytical tools. As we explore the ways in which terms such as *church, sect, denomination,* and *cult* have been used, it is important to keep in mind that they provide only one of many possible ways to organize the data and to think about religious groups. Readers must always be sure they understand how a given study is using the terms (Dawson 2009).

THE CHURCH–SECT TYPOLOGY

Classical Distinctions

Most discussions of the church–sect typology begin with the work of Max Weber and his student, Ernst Troeltsch. Weber emphasized that the sect is an exclusive group. To be a member, one must meet certain conditions such as adherence to a particular doctrine or conformity to particular practices (like adult baptism or abstinence from alcohol). For Weber, the sect involved three characteristics: (1) Membership is voluntary, (2) it is limited to those who "qualify" for membership, and (3) it involves a substantial commitment by the members. The church, on the other hand, is depicted as (1) a group that one is typically born into rather than choosing, (2) inclusive—that is, encouraging all members of the larger society to join, and (3) requiring minimal commitment to remain a member (Weber [1922] 1963).

Troeltsch and American theologian H. Richard Niebuhr, who each wrote much more extensively on this topic, included Weber's defining criteria but expanded the concept to include many other factors. For them, the central characteristic of the church is its acceptance of the secular order—including even reproduction of the larger society's hierarchy of prestige within the church itself. In short, the church "compromises" Christian values and makes accommodations to the secular society. The sect, on the other hand, tends to reject the social order and to maintain a prophetic ministry—a ministry concerned with justice in the society and helping the disfranchised. While this was their central emphasis, Troeltsch and Niebuhr generated multivariable typologies, with *many* distinguishing characteristics of church and sect (see Table 7.1).

Table 7.1 Characteristics of Sects and Churches as Delineated by H. Richard Niebuhr

The Sect	*The Church*
1. Volitional membership (emphasis on adult conversion and commitment).	1. Volitional membership (emphasis on adult conversion and commitment).
2. Exclusive membership policy.	2. Inclusive membership—may coincide with national citizenship or geographic boundaries.
3. Particularism—judgmental attitude toward those who do not accept the one true path; self-image that of the "faithful remnant" or the "elect."	3. Universalism—acceptance of diversity and emphasis on the brotherhood and sisterhood of all humanity.
4. Small faithful group.	4. Large, bureaucratic organization.
5. Salvation achieved through moral purity, including ethical austerity or asceticism.	5. Salvation granted by the grace of God—as administered by church sacrament and church hierarchy.
6. Priesthood of all believers; clergy de-emphasized or nonexistent; lay participation high.	6. Leadership and control by highly trained professional clergy.
7. Hostile or indifferent to secular society and to the state.	7. Tendency to adjust to, compromise with, and support existing social values and social structures.
8. Fundamentalistic theology—only the original revelation is an authentic expression of the faith.	8. Either orthodox or modernist theology—formulations and interpretation of the faith in later periods of history are legitimate in their own rights.
9. Predominantly a group of lower-class persons or those otherwise socially disfranchised. (Worldly prestige is rejected.)	9. Membership composed of upper- and middle-class people, but with professional classes controlling most leadership positions.
10. Informal, spontaneous worship.	10. Formal, orderly worship.
11. Radical social ethic—emphasizing the equality of all persons and the necessity of economic equality.	11. Conservative social ethic—justifying the current socioeconomic relationships.

H. Richard Niebuhr elaborated Troeltsch's suggestion that the sect and the church are *stages* in the evolution of a religious group, adding a new type: the denomination. He also moved beyond Troeltsch by identifying factors, including internal structural characteristics, that cause a group to move from one end of the continuum to the other (Niebuhr [1929] 1957).

These two scholars believed the division of churches into different (and often exclusive) groups was rooted in socioeconomic inequalities and ethnic prejudices and was therefore contrary to core religious teachings. As Niebuhr put it, "The inequality of privilege in the economic order appears to contain a fundamental denial of the [religious] principle of brotherhood" (Niebuhr [1929] 1957:8–9). For Niebuhr, the emergence of the "church" is caused by a deterioration of religious ethics and adoption of secular definitions of human value. The reemergence of a sect is an attempt to recapture and reassert the faith commitment to social justice and the equality of all people under God.

Sectarian reaction against "compromises" of the faith results in renewal and revitalization. The first generation of sect members stresses adult conversion and commitment, but they also establish religious education programs for their children. Eventually, the children are accepted into full membership on the basis of their knowledge of the faith (memorized scriptural passages and so on) rather than personal conversion and dramatic life changes. Often the later generations also experience upward social mobility and are no longer disfranchised. The sect gradually institutionalizes at the same time it assimilates secular outlooks. In emphasizing the process of evolution, Niebuhr developed the concept of denomination, another type of religious group that represents a midpoint in the continuum between sect and church (Figure 7.1). Formality and orderliness (lack of spontaneity) were also marks of the trend to denominationalism—a reflection of institutionalization. This was even reflected in the tendency to a more sober, literate, intellectual, and orderly style of worship as opposed to the emotional expressiveness of sectarian worship.

Niebuhr especially stressed that the existence of different denominations is not due to mere ideological differences, as is often believed. He asserted that religious ideology is often used to justify economic self-interests and pointed out

Photos by Keith Roberts

John Wesley began a renewal movement in the Church of England. He wanted to call people back to the basics of the faith. His evangelical revival called followers to lead Christian lives through a method of strict discipline—prayer, worship, study, and mutual support groups. Hence, the name *Methodists* arose. Today, Methodists have become one of the largest Christian bodies and a mainstream denomination in the United States. The photo on the left is a United Methodist Church in a medium-sized town in Ohio. Eventually, as the Methodist church became more prosperous, more open, and more institutionalized, there were reform schisms—such as the Wesleyan Church (right photo), which is now institutionalizing.

Figure 7.1 The Continuum Between Sect and Church

that groups from different social classes tend to develop different theological outlooks. The stratification of society affects both the social organization and the theology of a religious group. The real source of the schism that eventually creates new denominations, then, is *social* rather than theological. This was a radical idea at the time.

The formulations of Troeltsch and Niebuhr assumed a high level of correlation among many diverse factors. Although their descriptions may have been accurate for many religious groups of their days, we can point to many groups now that have some features of the sect and some of the denomination. For example, many of the more emotional, conversion-oriented Christian groups of today (born-again Christians) have many traits of a sect, but many of them support the current economic system (the economic status quo) and defend the national values of the larger society. They are well acculturated. Niebuhr and Troeltsch would probably assert that they are not manifestations of early Christianity but further forms of compromise: They fail to restore the original social ethic of Christianity. So the problem of the church–sect model is the problem of all ideal types: A significant number of groups do not seem to fit *all* the characteristics of any one type. The question becomes this: Which characteristics are most important in classifying a group?

Although many religious groups do fit Niebuhr's sequential model—with new groups returning to the purity of the original faith and then gradually assimilating to the dominant culture—some groups do not. Several scholars

(Cohen 1983; Steinberg 1965) have analyzed the emergence of Reform Judaism from Orthodox Judaism as a reform group resembling the church model. Reform Judaism did not represent a protest against the "perversion of true religion" and did not call for a return of the "old ways." Rather, it represented a fuller acculturation or modernization of the faith. This new group was rejecting what its adherents considered an excessive tie to the past on the part of the parent body. The reforming body sought greater assimilation—in effect, more openness as a system. Likewise, Mauss and Barlow (1991) documented a shift in Mormonism *away* from assimilationism and toward a deliberate religious traditionalism, an evolution opposite that predicted by Niebuhr. Finke and Stark (2001) pointed toward evidence of movement toward higher levels of tension with the larger culture in the United Methodist Church during the 1990s as well. Therefore it is important to remember that Niebuhr described the predominant trend, but the sequential evolution of sect-denomination-church and revolution back to sect is not universal.

Critical Thinking: Why is Niebuhr's diachronic (or historical) model of analyzing sects and denominations an improvement over simple synchronic (nonhistorical) typologies? That is, what are some advantages of seeing sect, denomination, and church as evolving patterns rather than stagnant, unchanging "types"?

The Church and Sect as Open and Closed Systems

While most of the scholars discussed in this chapter do not talk about open and closed systems in explaining the difference between church and sect, the model can be useful (see Figure 7.2a). Most church/sect typologies essentially depict the church as an open system, with fairly free flow of influence *into* the larger society (outputs such as symbols, benevolent actions, definitions of morality, and so forth) and *from* the larger society (inputs such as new members, ideas from education, science and business fields, predominant economic attitudes and assumptions, and even reproduction of the secular system of social stratification—with high-income professionals being more highly respected church members and more likely to be elected to church offices). The danger of openness for the church is that "the salt may lose its flavor"—the uniqueness of the religious perspective may be endangered as the church becomes just another social club. No religious group can allow this to happen, so all religious groups do *some* filtering of inputs. Nonetheless, the filter used by churches allows much to pass through it into the faith system and the life of the congregation.

The sect chooses to protect its uniqueness at all costs, barricading itself against the secular culture, carefully screening any inputs. It is a much more closed system, though few systems can be totally closed and still survive (see Figure 7.2b). They need members and resources and even technology

Figure 7.2a The Church as an Open System

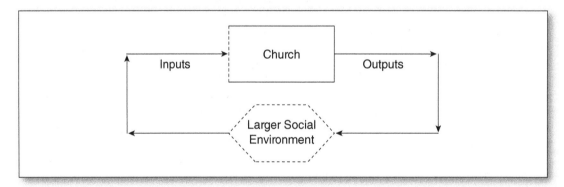

Figure 7.2b The Sect as a Closed System

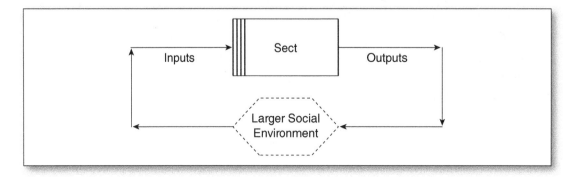

to enhance efficiency, provided by the larger society. The sect allows inputs, but these inputs must pass through a dense filter. The danger of this choice is that the group may risk becoming so isolated that its message may seem anachronistic and irrelevant to the larger society. The closed system also risks stagnation as little that is new or innovative can enter the system.

It is useful to think of open and closed systems not as categorically different types, but as opposite ends on a continuum. Any given religious group can be closer to one end than the other. As you read various ideas about sects, denominations, and churches, it may be helpful to keep in mind the idea of more open and more closed social systems. Further, each group may make different choices as to what kinds of things are threatening: Some will find certain economic ideas incompatible with their worldview; others will reject modern technologies; still others may find definitions of sexual morality or scientific theories especially threatening. Finally, keep in mind that open and closed systems have their own advantages—and their own problems.

Yinger's Multilinear Evolution Model

Like many contemporary scholars, Yinger held that Troeltsch's concept of church and sect includes too many variables, many of which are not highly correlated in actual groups. Yinger suggested three social factors that seem to him to be central, and he established a model that lends insight into types of groups and their evolution. The three defining criteria suggested by Yinger are as follows:

1. The degree to which the membership policy of the group is exclusive and selective or open and inclusive.

2. The extent to which the group accepts or rejects the secular values and structures of society.

3. The extent to which, as an organization, the group integrates a number of local units into one national structure, develops professional staffs, and creates a bureaucracy. (Yinger 1970:257)

Yinger pointed out that in actual cases, the first two variables are very closely correlated. Those groups that reject secular values are likely to be exclusive and selective in their membership policies—indications of a closed social system; those groups that accept secular values are likely to be inclusive and open in their membership—indications of an open social system.

By using the first two factors as one axis of variation and the extent of institutionalization as the other, Yinger developed a model that suggests several different types of groups. (See Figure 7.3. on page 176). This two-dimensional model is capable of showing a progression from sect to church, but it also demonstrates that increased institutionalization may occur somewhat independently from membership policy and from the acceptance of secular values. There are pressures that cause groups to evolve generally from the types in the lower left side of the grid toward those in the upper right side. Nonetheless, the rate, the direction, and the extent of this evolution are not inevitable.

Whether a group stabilizes as an "established sect" or continues to acculturate to the stage of "institutional denomination" or "ecclesia" has to do with the group's belief system. A group that focuses on the sin and salvation of individuals will acculturate rather easily. Sects whose primary concern is social evils and injustices—reformative and transformative movements—are more likely to become established sects and may never become ecclesiastical or denominational bodies (Wilson 1970; Yinger 1970). Ronald Lawson found that a number of other elements of a sect's ideology may shape its trajectory toward becoming established. Passionate commitment to pacifism, and thus an internationalism in the face of warfare, was one factor that has kept Jehovah's Witnesses more sectarian. Meanwhile, the Seventh-day Adventists (which came from the same Adventist movement in the 19th century) have embraced patriotism and become more mainstream in the society. The refusal to embrace jingoistic values during war

Figure 7.3 Yinger's Schema for Types of Religious Organizations (Adapted)

Inclusiveness of Membership Extent of Acceptance of Dominant Society Values

	Low --➤ High		
Null (No known examples)	Rare (Seventh Day Adventists)	Institutional Denomination (Church of God)	Institutional Ecclesia (Episcopal Church)
Null (No known examples)	Established Institutionalized Sect (Old Order Amish)	Diffused Denomination (Beachy Amish; Mennonite)	Diffused Ecclesia (Christian Scientist)
Sect Movement (The Bruderhof)	Established Lay Sect (Amana Church Society)	Rare	Rare
Charismatic Sect (The Way)	Null. (No known examples)	Null. (No known examples)	Null. (No known examples)

*Extent of Organizational Complexity** — vertical axis from High (top) to Low (bottom)

*The criteria for determining placement on the vertical axis are (1) whether local religious units are integrated into a national organization, (2) whether there are religious professionals, and (3) whether there is a bureaucratic structure with rules and procedures that govern group decisions. A yes to all three questions places the group at the highest level.

SOURCE: Adapted from Yinger, J. M. 1970. *The Scientific Study of Religion.* New York: Macmillan.

has also led to persecution for the Witnesses, further alienating them from the dominant society in a way that Seventh-day Adventists never experienced (Lawson 1995, 1996, 1998).

The existence of sects and denominations is a phenomenon of pluralistic societies. In fact, scholars have maintained that the pure form of "Church" described by Troeltsch is impossible in a democratic and pluralistic society. Moreover, it may be the case that in a very open, pluralistic society, the distinction between sect and denomination also becomes less important as all groups converge on a single denominational model. We explore the possibility of such a "denominational society" in the next chapter.

We have found Yinger's conceptualization to be helpful, for he reduced the number of variables to be considered while he shows how different social forces can result in several different types of groups. The primary value of his schema is in identifying several possible patterns in the evolution of groups.

SOCIAL CONDITIONS THAT GENERATE EACH TYPE OF GROUP

We might summarize this discussion of churches, denominations, institutionalized sects, and sects by reviewing the factors that seem to cause the emergence of new groups. Niebuhr pointed to four factors.

First, when Christian denominations begin to ignore the original concern of the faith regarding poverty and inequality, sectarian groups are likely to arise. As members of those sects (who are disproportionately from the lower classes) begin to achieve some affluence, the sect begins to accommodate secular values and becomes comfortable with the status quo. The group begins to denominationalize. Those persons who are still economically disfranchised are likely to break again from the group and reject social inequality as contrary to the original ethic of the faith. To put it in other terms, the poor may reject worldly affluence—defining it as depraved—and seek otherworldly compensation. By affirming asceticism and condemning the comforts of this world, the sect tends to alienate persons who are affluent (Stark and Bainbridge 1985). One cause of sectarianism, then, is the existence of socio-economic inequality.

Second, some groups are expressions of ethnic values and national loyalties. In such cases, the belonging function operates to separate German Methodists from Welsh Methodists and Italian Catholics from Irish Catholics. One analysis of sectarian movements concludes that approximately 21% of American sects were founded almost entirely on the basis of racial or ethnic identity (Stark and Bainbridge 1985). The sense of ethnic belonging, then, has been a source of organizational diversity in religious groups (Greeley 1972; Niebuhr [1929] 1957; Roof and McKinney 1987).

Third, churches and denominations often become bogged down in bureaucratic structures. Some sect movements are expressions of a desire for religious groups that are smaller, more informal, and less under the control of a professional clergy. Individuals may become alienated by the institutional constraints and formalized structures of large denominations. Sectarianism then is sometimes an expression of rebellion against complex organizational structure.

Fourth, sectarian movements are sometimes spawned by a desire for more spontaneity and more emotional expression in worship. Worship in the denominations tends to become formal, orderly, and highly intellectual. Some people find that stifling and inauthentic as a way to worship God.

Of course, sectarian schisms can also occur over seemingly trivial issues. Max Assimeng (1987) pointed out that Seventh-day Adventists split from other Adventists largely over the issue of whether the Sabbath should be on Saturday or Sunday.

Whether and how a sect develops into a denomination also depends largely on how the larger society responds to this new group. If the sect challenges values that are central to the dominant society, if the host culture does not have a tradition of religious freedom and tolerance, and if the strategy of the sect is aggressive militancy (rather than withdrawal), the group either will be crushed or will further establish its antiestablishment posture. If the group does manage to survive, its acculturation is likely to be very slow. In fact, such a group may remain forever an established sect. On the other hand, if the sect rejects values that are tangential to the dominant society and if there is a tradition of religious tolerance in the host culture, the group may accommodate and become acculturated rather quickly. The movement from sect to denomination is determined in large degree by outsiders' response to the group (Redekop 1974).

In a comparison of Protestantism in the United States and Canada, Harold Fallding suggested that separation of church and state also contributes to the emergence of sects. Canada, with state-established religion, has generated far fewer religious sects than has the United States and has historically shown a greater trend toward denominational mergers. The struggle for religious liberty and disestablishment from government structures may unwittingly result in intensification of boundaries between groups and an environment conducive to religious innovation and independence (Fallding 1980). Rational choice theorists point out that in an environment where the state does not control religion, there will be more religious vitality simply because there will be more religious "firms" started. They see the increased numbers of sects as a sign that more religious niches in the religious market will be filled.

The internal belief system of the group can be another factor important in the evolution of a group. If a sect's definition of evil and corruption is individualistic (matters of personal decision making and individual determination), then acculturation and accommodation are likely. If evil is considered to be social in nature, if the structures of the society are defined as incompatible with religious values, then the group is less likely to denominationalize. The Quakers (Religious Society of Friends) have a very strong social ethic, which includes a rejection of any participation in warfare. This position often puts them at odds with the larger society when international conflicts arise. Although they are not currently persecuted in American society, Quakers remain an institutionalized sect. In this case, the resistance to denominationalizing is internal (based in their own social ethic) rather than external.

Bryan Wilson (1959) argued that some types of sects are more likely to denominationalize than are others. Groups that have a theological orientation encouraging a simple ascetic lifestyle are more likely to generate an affluent membership, for their lifestyle leads to savings and accumulation of resources. Affluence often leads to accommodation. Wilson believed that those sects that lack this emphasis on asceticism are less likely to accommodate. Wilson also demonstrated that the movement toward denominationalism is strongly influenced by an expanding economy. As members become more affluent, they tend to acculturate to the values of the dominant society and lose their fervor for revolution or reform. Because opportunities for upward mobility are most likely in a climate in which the

economy is growing, the state of the economy may affect the likelihood of a group becoming a denomination or stabilizing as an institutionalized sect. Stagnant economic conditions are more likely to generate permanent sects. Lawson (1995, 1996) agreed that both internal and external factors are at work, showing that upward social mobility, organizational openness, ideological rigidity, urgency of expectation of the end of the world, the intensity of the indoctrination of converts, relations with the state, and the extent to which the group was stigmatized and persecuted all affect a sect's trajectory.

The formation and evolution of any group is the result of many interacting processes: the social standing of members, ethnic factors, survival forces that impel a group to institutionalize, responses of outsiders to the group and its message, the belief system of the group, and the state of the economy in the host society. Both internal and external forces determine its evolution.

Critical Thinking: Using sociological perspectives and insights, *refute* or *support* the following statement: "Denominations are functional to society and to the groups' members, but sects are disruptive and dysfunctional."

Thus far, we have discussed only the development of sects, institutionalized sects, denominations, and churches. What is meant by a religious "cult"?

New Religious Movements, aka "Cults"

The term *cult* is used by sociologists in two distinct ways—and by the popular media in yet a third way. Sociologists feel that the popular usage has terribly misconstrued and distorted a useful sociological concept. The popular media and many anti-cult movements define a cult as a religious group that holds esoteric or occult ideas, is led by a charismatic leader, and uses intense and highly unethical conversion techniques. (See the discussion in Chapter 6 of the charges of "mind control" or "brainwashing" in NRMs.) The group is almost always depicted as totalitarian, capable of bizarre actions, destructive of the mental health of members, and a threat to conventional society. The tag "cult" is often used in this context as a stigmatizing label intended to discredit a group rather than as a nonjudgmental technical term that describes a social unit (Zuckerman 2003). This view of cults is explicitly rejected by sociologists of religion, but this media use has managed to cause confusion about NRMs and about the very concept of "cult," as is shown in the "Doing Research on Religion" box on media constructions of cult stereotypes.

Critical Thinking: When you hear the word *cult*, what comes to mind? Are your thoughts positive or negative? Where do these ideas come from? Reflect on the extent to which your ideas about and understanding of these new religious movements are direct versus mediated. What difference does that make?

DOING RESEARCH ON RELIGION

Media Constructions of "Cult" Stereotypes

Most people have little direct experience with new religious movements (NRMs). Our ideas about them, therefore, are often based on stereotypes. Religion scholar Lynn S. Neal highlights the crucial role of the media, especially television, in disseminating "cult" stereotypes in her article "They're Freaks!"

Given how much Americans watch TV, it is not surprising that scholars find it plays an important role in circulating ideas and ideals about all aspects of religion. Especially for less known and more marginal religions (like NRMs), televisions act as "a powerful mechanism for the dissemination of stereotypical views" (Neal 2011:85). Although many focus on TV news as delivering the key information, Neal highlights that fictional TV programs also shape our understandings of NRMs—and our judgments of good and bad, normal and abnormal.

Although in the 1960s NRMs were largely seen as benign and perhaps even exotic, by the end of the 1970s, negative sentiments came to predominate. The mass homicide involving Jim Jones's Peoples Temple in "Jonestown," Guyana (on the Caribbean coast of South America), in 1978 solidified most of the negative stereotypes about cults. Cults were seen to have deceitful leaders who used brainwashing techniques to manipulate individuals into becoming fanatical disciples, as well as bizarre beliefs and practices (especially sexual).

Neal conducted a content analysis (see Chapter 2) of five popular fictional television shows that aired from 1998 to 2008. Although she does not analyze a random sample of programs, she does make a concerted effort to select episodes from different genres and from different networks.

The five episodes she analyzes are "The Joy of Sect" (*The Simpsons,* comedy, 1998, FOX), "The Cult" (*Everybody Loves Raymond*, comedy, 2002, CBS), "Charisma" (*Law and Order: Special Victims Unit*, drama, 2004, NBC), "Shooting Stars" (*CSI*, drama, 2005, CBS), and "Minimal Loss" (*Criminal Minds*, drama, 2008, CBS).

(Continued)

(Continued)

Neal identified several anti-cult themes circulating in these programs. Three of the five episodes showed cult leaders engaging in fraudulent practices, such as a preteen being pregnant by her husband, a cult leader. In two of the programs, brainwashing is invoked as an explanation of conversions of people. The dramas associated cults with violence, including teen suicides.

Beyond these stereotypical associations, cult members are portrayed as "abnormal" and destructive of mental health.

Interestingly, when cults are in play, even "happiness" can become a marker of deviance— a sign of being delusional. Much that marks cult as destructive involves depictions of sexual exploitation as worship, mass suicide, and murder—highlighting that cults are not only different but deviant.

Fictional television programs do not create cult stereotypes out of nothing. There is plenty of cultural material for them to draw on, including using elements from actual situations in which cult deviance captured the public imagination like the Peoples Temple, Heaven's Gate, and the Branch Davidians. Cult stereotyping becomes a problem when it is the *only* portrayal of NRMs seen on TV. It is a one-sided exaggeration and reification of cult deviance, and it becomes a vicious circle of beliefs circulating in our culture. According to Walter Lippmann, who coined the term *stereotype* in 1922, "when a system of stereotypes is well fixed, our attention is called to those facts which support it, and diverted from those which contradict it" (Neal 2011:95).

SOURCE: Neal, Lynn S. 2011. "'They're Freaks!' The Cult Stereotype in Fictional Television Shows, 1958–2008." *Novo Religio* 3:81–107.

The predominant sociological approach is to define the cult as the beginning phase of an entirely new religion. The group may be loosely structured or it may demand tremendous commitment, but it must provide a radical break from existing religious traditions (Nelson 1968; Stark and Bainbridge 1985; Yinger 1970). Many sociologists now recommend that the meaning of the term *cult* has become so muddled and tainted by media misuse that it should be abandoned entirely. Because of the misunderstanding, most sociologists now use *NRM* (new religious movement) in place of *cult* (Bromley 2009; Robbins and Lucas 2007). We have tended to use the phrase *NRM* through much of this book, but since the word *cult* is still frequently used, students should be aware of its proper sociological meanings.

In an effort to distinguish cults or NRMs from sects, Stark and Bainbridge wrote,

Because sects are schismatic groups, they present themselves to the world as something old. They left the parent body not to form a new faith, but to reestablish the old one, from which the parent body had "drifted." Sects claim to be the authentic, purged, refurbished version of the faith. . . . Whether domestic or imported, the cult is something new vis-à-vis the other religious bodies of the society in question. If domestic—regardless of how much of the common religious culture it retains—the cult [NRM] adds to that culture a new revelation or insight justifying the claim that it is different, new, "more advanced." Imported cults [NRMs] often have little common culture with existing faiths; they may be old in some other society, but they are new and different in the importing society. (Stark and Bainbridge 1985:25–26)

This emphasis distinguishes an NRM from a sect in that the latter attempts to renew or purify the prevailing religion of the society, whereas the cult or NRM introduces a new and different religion. Sometimes it is difficult to determine whether a religious movement is attempting to renew or replace the traditional religion, for a new religion often tries to gain legitimacy and acceptability by exaggerating its continuity with existing faiths. Nonetheless, the issue of whether a group is trying to purify or to replace the traditional religion of a society is central to this concept of cult.

Because they are in part defined by their relationship as outsiders to the core faiths of a particular culture, NRMs pose particular challenges for researchers. Access is perhaps the greatest issue. Researchers are seeking access to observe the new religious groups for scholarly purposes, and the groups are often struggling for legitimation in the society. Tensions can sometimes arise because of this, and scholars studying NRMs have in the past done things that would be considered inappropriate or unethical among social scientists generally today.

In the early stages of his study of the Unification Church (discussed at length in Chapter 6), John Lofland (with Rodney Stark 1965) undertook "covert" research to understand the process of conversion. That is, he did not make his research subjects aware that he was conducting observational research on them. Similarly, Robert Balch and David Taylor (1977) posed as potential converts to a UFO cult in order to get access to parts of the movement's activities from which they might otherwise be excluded (Gregg 2014).

Not gaining informed consent of research subjects is severely discouraged today by institutional review boards, which are charged with overseeing the ethical procedures of researchers to protect the health and safety of human subjects. (These boards review research from the biomedical sciences and social sciences alike, as noted in Chapter 2.) Although doing "covert" research can be considered unethically deceptive, it cannot be denied that studies like Lofland's on the Unification Church and Balch and Taylor's on a UFO (unidentified flying object) cult—which turned out to be Heaven's Gate—produced interesting findings that might not have been possible otherwise (Gregg 2014).

There are many documented cases of scholars attempting to study religious movements overtly and being rebuffed by the groups (Bromley 2007). Amway, which we discussed in Chapter 1, has resolutely refused to allow scholars access to its meetings. The Church of Scientology also has a long-standing hostility toward overt researchers. Indeed, it famously demanded and won inclusion of a rebuttal in the form of an appendix to Roy Wallis's pioneering book, *The Road to Total Freedom* (1977). The group also harassed Wallis after the results of his study became known to them (Arweck and Stringer 2002).

Online Resources: One way to begin to understand the challenge of studying controversial religious groups is to compare the online presentation of the groups by the groups themselves, by "anti-cult" groups, and by scholars studying the groups (Barker 2007). Take Jehovah's Witnesses, for example. First visit their official site (jw.org) and get an understanding of what the group is about. Next find information about Jehovah's Witnesses on the website of the Watchman Fellowship (watchman.org). Last visit the Jehovah's Witnesses page at the World Religions and Spirituality Project (wrs.vcu.edu), which is overseen by respected scholar of new religions David Bromley. How do the presentations of the Jehovah's Witnesses differ between the sites, and what do you learn about studying religion from visiting them?

Another challenge of studying NRMs that results from their marginality in society is that people can have very strong negative feelings about their family members joining NRMs, and some ex-members can have similarly strong negative feelings when they leave the groups. Consequently, some of the main "informants" that a researcher would typically interview to understand a religious group are strongly biased. Bromley (2007) and other scholars of new religions insist that not all former members are bad informants, but recommend "triangulation" of data from multiple sources whenever possible (an approach we advocate in Chapter 2).

The Unification Church (sometimes called "Moonies") provides an interesting example of an NRM. The members of this group believe that Sun Myung Moon is the Messiah. They accept his doctrine that Jesus was supposed to have been the Son of God but that he failed in his mission and got himself killed. Jesus provided a partial salvation (purely spiritual), but he failed to redeem the social, economic, and political structures of this world. Because Jesus failed in the total task that was assigned to him, God has now blessed and empowered Reverend Moon to fulfill this divine role. Obviously, such a doctrine is a sharp break from traditional Christianity. While the organizational structure and the conflict with the predominant societal values cause the Moonies to appear to be a sect, the development of a new and unique religious doctrine distinguishes them from the sects. To gain legitimacy and acceptance, however, the Unification Church has downplayed these radical doctrines and has stressed its endorsement of traditional American values (pro-capitalism, pro-family, and so forth).

The early period of the Church of Jesus Christ of Latter-day Saints (Mormons) provides another example. Although they believe that Jesus was the Messiah and they believe in the Bible, Latter-day Saints also have a second book that they hold as sacred scripture. The new scripture (*The Book of Mormon*) came from Joseph Smith's "translation" of some golden plates, which he found in upstate New York. Smith taught that prophets in the early Americas had made a written record of messages from God and of the visit that Jesus made to North America. The last of these prophets buried the written record on golden plates, and Smith was told in several visions where to find them and how to translate them.

The Mormons emphasize that they are a branch of Christianity, but many of their theological innovations are not accepted as Christian doctrine by other Christian groups (such as the belief that unmarried individuals do not attain the celestial kingdom, the highest of their levels of heaven). It seems fair to say that at least the early Mormons were an example of an NRM rather than a case of sectarian reform (Johnson and Mullins 1992; Shipps 1985; Stark 1984). Whether it is driven by a desire for legitimacy or is a reaction to gross misrepresentations of their faith, many Mormons reject the NRM designation (Barlow 1991). The same was true of the initial decades of Christianity; the first Christians tended to think of their group as a faction of Judaism rather than the beginnings of a new religion. The difference is that Christianity eventually made a clean break and developed on its own path quite independent of its parent group; Mormons have in some ways moved closer to traditional Christianity in the 20th century rather than asserting independence and stressing differences. Is the modern-day Church of Jesus Christ of Latter-day Saints just another denomination of Christianity, or a new religion that evolved out of Christianity? The dominant scholarly interpretation seems to affirm the latter pattern (Shipps 1985; Stark 1984; Warner 1993), but the issue remains controversial, especially among Mormon scholars.

Although the matter of whether a group is initiating a new religion is the central issue, there are several other characteristics that are common in NRMs. While sects often place a strong emphasis on the authority (perhaps even literal authority) of scripture, NRMs frequently stress mystical, psychic, or ecstatic experiences. There is not a categorical difference between the two groups on this, but NRMs seldom use previously existing scriptures as a sole source of truth. In fact, it is not uncommon in the United States for NRMs to generate their own scriptures. The Mormons are one example. The Unification Church also generated a written record that seems to have the aura of sacred scripture. This penchant for scriptural basis is probably caused by the scriptural (written record) orientation of American culture. NRMs in other cultures do not ordinarily generate new scriptures. Hence, if the traditional religion emphasizes the role of scripture, the NRM is likely to develop its own alternative form of "written word."

Another pattern that prevails in many NRMs is the centrality of a charismatic leader (Bromley 2009). As discussed earlier in this chapter, a charismatic leader is a person who is believed to have extraordinary insights and powers. Such a person is attributed with certain divine qualities and is believed to have direct and unique contact with the supernatural. It is the unique insights of these individuals that are the basis for the alternative faith.

Although most NRMs are founded by charismatic leaders, some sociologists believe that they can also develop in a more spontaneous way—through "spontaneous subcultural evolution" (Bainbridge and Stark 1979). Such movements, like the groups that focus their faith on the saving power of UFOs, are usually more loosely structured and more democratic. Stigmatization and hostility by outsiders may force adherents of such a group to draw more closely together and raise boundaries against outsiders. They usually start out as nonreligious subcultures but may eventually emerge into esoteric cultic groups with a worldview and ethos that contradicts that of the dominant society (Nelson 1968; Bainbridge and Stark 1979). Social scientists are therefore not in agreement on the necessity of a charismatic leader in the

formation of an NRM, since it appears that some evolve through subculture evolution.

Externally, the sect and the NRM look much alike, although NRMs tend to appeal to the middle and upper classes, while sects have generally appealed to the lower classes (Stark 1986). However, both rebel against the predominant cultural values, both lack trained professional leaders and a bureaucratic structure, and both insist on a stringent membership policy that requires significant commitment (although the NRM may not require this in its very earliest stage of development). The NRM, like the sect, is also capable of institutionalization. In fact, some institutionalization is necessary if the group is to outlive its founder. (For an extended discussion of the process of institutionalization that is necessary for religious group survival, see the supplemental materials available at www .SAGE.com/rsp6e.)

The evolution of sects and NRMs is comparable as indicated in Figure 7.4 on page 184. This diagram, while oversimplifying the process, does suggest the parallel manner in which these two types of groups may evolve. If we allowed for the two-dimensional analysis Yinger proposed (Figure 7.3), we would have a more accurate picture: Institutionalization and accommodation to secular values do not necessarily occur at the same rate. Sects and NRMs, then, tend to evolve along parallel lines.

To understand fully the evolution of a sect or NRM, however, we must give attention to the hostility toward the group by traditional religious groups in the society and to the strength of the desire for legitimacy within the new group. In other words, we must take into account the pressures at work on a group as it attempts to mobilize its resources and to counter opposition to its existence. Bainbridge and Stark (1979) insisted that hostile forces may cause a sectarian group to evolve into an NRM; as its beliefs are modified to define its separateness and to cope with being made "alien," it develops a unique worldview. Jim Jones's Peoples Temple of

Figure 7.4 Evolution of Sects and NRMs

Sect →	Established Sect →	Denomination →	Church
Cult →	Permanent Cult →	Centralized Cult →	New Religion
Dependent on charisma of leader, minimal organization	Routinized charisma at a local level, but has no national organization or bureaucratic structure; able to survive independently of charismatic leader	Charisma routinized; national office and bureaucratic structure established	Centralized national office and bureaucratic structure established; recognized by nonmembers as a legitimate or conventional form of religiosity

SOURCE: Nelson, G. K. 1968. "The Concept of Cult." *Sociological Review* 360 (November). Used by permission of Routledge and Kegan Paul Ltd.

Jonestown is an example of this sect-to-NRM movement. With this added variable that affects the development and self-image of a group, our view of sect and cult emergence becomes more complex. (See Figure 7.5.)

A central point here is that both sects *and* NRMs lack organizational complexity and both reject at least some of the values of the secular society. However, the sect views its role as one of purifying the traditional faith by calling members back to what are believed to be core principles. NRMs (or cults) represent the nascent stages of the development of a new or a syncretistic religion. Other factors may affect the evolution of a sect or an NRM, but the institutionalizing and accommodating tendencies frequently cause sects to become denominational in form. The cult usually either dies out or institutionalizes into a new religion. The debate previously discussed regarding whether Mormonism is an NRM or another denomination of Christianity is an argument about how that group has evolved.

If all of this seems terribly complex, it is because the evolution of religious groups *is* complex. Various scholars have focused on different aspects of religious group evolution and therefore have defined such terms as *sect, cult,* and *church* in alternative ways. This is an important point for the new student of religion to bear in mind when reading a study that discusses sects and cults. Readers should always be sure they understand how a given author defines his or her terms and how those terms were operationalized or measured.

It is important to note that the terms *sect, cult, established sect,* and *denomination* are normally not ones that can be permanently assigned to a group. They simply describe organizational characteristics of a group at a particular moment in its history. With this in mind, church–sect theory can enable us to describe the normal process of organizational change in religious collectivities. One interesting application of church–sect theory is the use of the adjectives *sectlike* and *churchlike* to describe

Figure 7.5 Social Forces and the Sect–Cult Transformation

the predominant religiosity of individuals—regardless of the groups to which those individuals belong (Demerath 1965). This has yielded fruitful insights, but students encountering such a study should be sure they understand how *churchlike* and *sectlike* were defined and measured.

In short, if one seeks to generalize about how most groups evolve and the stages they go through, the concepts of church, sect, and denomination can be helpful. However, if one seeks to understand a specific group, one must learn that group's characteristics on each issue. One must discover various dimensions of the group, including theological orientation, relationship with the secular society, amount of formality of the ritual ("high church" being very formal, elegant, and decorous and "low church" being informal, unpretentious, and spontaneous), appeal of the ritual (with a "Dionysian" appeal to emotions or an "Apollonian" appeal to reason), and the extent of organization (the complexity of the structure; whether there are official clergy and whether the clergy are formally trained; and the relative restrictiveness of membership policy). Other

elements may also be included in this analysis (Greeley 1972). Looking at each issue separately rather than constructing a typology is sometimes called "choice point analysis" (O'Dea 1968; Winter 1977). Because these elements do vary somewhat independently of each other, analyzing these dimensions without reference to sectlike or churchlike categories can sometimes be very useful.

Critical Thinking: Using sociological perspectives and insights, respond to the following statement: "Cults are inherently evil and are led by dangerous, dictatorial leaders."

SUMMARY

Many religious movements appear to get started through the dynamism of a charismatic leader (Jesus, Muhammad, Sun Myung Moon, Ann Lee). The individual is viewed as an agent of God or perhaps as God incarnate (in the flesh). What that person says is held as true simply because he or she said it. However, Weber held that charisma is inherently unstable, and if a group is to survive, it must routinize—that is, it must develop norms, roles, and statuses; it must transfer the sense of awe from the individual personality to the teachings and the organization; and it must make provisions for succession of the leader when he or she dies. As these policies are spelled out and various statuses gain specialized job descriptions, the movement is taking its first steps toward institutionalization. Many decades later, the group may be highly bureaucratized.

Regardless of the cause of institutionalization, it brings many changes in the religious movement itself. Bureaucracies take on a life of their own, somewhat independent of the lay members, and tend to influence the workings of the whole organization. Over time, the institutionalized religion is likely to face the dilemmas that routinization creates. Institutionalization is a necessity, but it has mixed consequences for the group.

In attempting to classify different styles of religious groups, various scholars have described different types of religious groups—sect, denomination, and ecclesia (church)—and have examined the typical mode of religious group evolution.

The lack of precise correlation of the many variables in multidimensional formulations has led to efforts to simplify the number of factors that are used to define each type of religious group. This procedure has contributed to the identification of alternative paths of religious group evolution, depending on the extent to which a group institutionalizes and accepts the values of the dominant society.

The concept of cult or NRM has also been added to the types of religious groups. Although the concept of cult has been used in various ways by different scholars, we have (with Nelson, Yinger, Bainbridge and Stark, and others) distinguished the cult as a new (or imported) religious movement in a society (also frequently called an NRM to avoid the stigma of popular usage given to *cult*). This type of group is differentiated from the sect, which represents the regeneration of a traditional religion in that society. The NRM, like the sect, goes through processes of institutionalization and modification. However, if it survives and eventually gains legitimacy in the society, the cult becomes a new religion rather than a denomination of an existing religion. As in the case of the sect, many social forces affect the development of the NRM and shape its style and character. The extent of institutionalization, pressures to be "legitimate" in the society, experiences of rejection and stigmatization by the traditional religions, and the extent to which the group seeks to be an "open social system" are just a few of the key factors shaping the evolution of a religious group.

8

ORGANIZED RELIGION

Denominationalism and Congregationalism

HERE ARE SOME QUESTIONS TO PONDER AS YOU READ THIS CHAPTER

- What factors—social and theological—have caused the fission (schisms) and fusion (mergers) of denominations?
- Why have denominationalism and congregationalism become the central features of organized religion in the United States?

(Continued)

(Continued)

- What are the ways in which denominations organize themselves?
- How do congregations work, and how do megachurches differ from the typical local congregation?
- Is marketing religion—selling it like any other product—a perversion of the faith, or is it a normal and healthy process?
- What are "new paradigm" churches, and how are they using marketing ideas to grow at phenomenal rates?

In the previous chapter, we looked at some important aspects of organized religion, including the various ways that sociologists have tried to categorize different types of religious organizations (church, sect, denomination, and new religious movement [NRM]). In this chapter, we continue to think about the way religion is organized, taking a distinctly American focus as we consider denominationalism and congregationalism as central organizing principles of religion.

Recall that church–sect theory was initially developed by Max Weber and Ernst Troeltsch, both Germans and well aware of the tradition of state-established religions, which was a central part of German (and European) history in the early modern period. In reality, the concept of "church" as Weber and Troeltsch imagined it is not possible in a democratic and pluralistic society like the United States. Not surprisingly, it was an American, H. Richard Niebuhr, who introduced the concept of "denomination" into the church–sect equation, and another American, J. Milton Yinger, who elaborated the concepts of sect and denomination even further (identifying various types of sects and denominations). This expansion of the original model has led some to conclude that church–sect theories have become such a hodgepodge of approaches that the typology has lost its utility (Goode 1967; Greeley 1972).

At least in the modern American context, it may be wiser to begin understanding the organization of religion from different starting points. The unique history of religious development in the United States has led one observer to describe the country as a "denominational society" and to specifically "reject the notion that denomination is a compromise or halfway house between sect and church" (Greeley 1972:71). Another focuses his organizational lens even closer to the ground by looking at congregations (local churches, synagogues, mosques, and temples) and arguing that the central organizing principle of American religion is "de facto congregationalism" (Warner 1993, 2005). To understand organized religion, from this point of view, we have to understand denominations/denominationalism, congregations/congregationalism, and the relationship between the two.

Although religious establishments existed in the American colonies, the United States as a nation is constitutionally diverse in two senses: (1) Multiple religious groups have been woven into the fabric of American life from its founding, and (2) this pluralism became embodied in the disestablishment of religion in the U.S. Constitution. Disestablishment allowed for free exercise of religion—religious voluntarism—which has taken organizational form in the proliferation of religious groups in the United States. In the terms of the "religious economies" perspective (Stark and Finke 2000), American religion is a free market in which religious organizations—from corporate giants like the Roman Catholic Church to entrepreneurial start-ups like New Church North Carolina (profiled later in this chapter)—compete for the attention of religious consumers. As we saw in Chapter 6, there are winners and losers in this marketplace. This religious pluralism in a free religious market-place raises the issue of religious marketing, which we discuss in this chapter.

As Nancy Ammerman has argued, both denominations and congregations are part of larger "organizational fields," and as we would expect from the open systems perspective, they are susceptible to influence from this larger field (Ammerman 2006:355). Hence, both denominations and congregations from all religious traditions have a tendency to become like each other. Organizational theorists call this propensity to morph into similar forms *institutional isomorphism* (DiMaggio and Powell 1983).

One major development in the organizational field of religion that has the potential to influence both denominations and congregations through this process of isomorphism is the rise of very large congregations known as *megachurches*. In addition to understanding the rise, structure, and spread of megachurches, we will also consider their implications for the marketing of religion, especially to the unchurched and religious "seekers."

THE DENOMINATIONAL SOCIETY

Denominationalism is a unique and recent way of organizing religion in the long history of human society (Ammerman 2006). In his famous work on the evolution of religion, Robert Bellah maintained that the early stages of religious development are characterized by an undifferentiated religious worldview, so that individuals experienced the world as a single cosmos in which religion was diffused through all of life. Under these conditions, religious community and society are one and the same (Bellah 1970c).

In the course of societal development, religion becomes symbolically differentiated from other social institutions; in particular, the political and distinct religious organizations arise. Initially, a single religious organization dominates a particular geographic area. This is evident in the domination of Europe by the Roman Catholic Church. Over time, the religious sphere itself comes to be internally differentiated. In the Western world, the Reformation era (1517–1648) brought about the emergence of different "confessions" that were doctrinally and organizationally distinct: Catholicism, Lutheranism, and Calvinism (Gorski 2000).[1]

Although this gave rise to some religious pluralism between societies, each confession attempted to align itself with the political powers to become the officially sanctioned church in its territory. Thus, Lutheranism became the official religion in Scandinavia and parts of Germany (e.g., Saxony). Calvinism predominated in Switzerland, the Netherlands, and southern Germany. Roman Catholicism continued to have official status in France, Spain, and Italy. In each case, political citizenship and confessional identity were linked. Consequently, conflict rather than peaceful coexistence dominated the scene, and religious persecution was prevalent. As Gorski observed, "The sixteenth and seventeenth centuries witnessed mass movements of religious refugees, a sort of confessionally driven *Völkerwanderung* [migration of peoples] in which Protestants drove out Catholics, Catholics drove out Protestants, and everybody drove out the Baptists and other sectarians" (Gorski 2000:157–158).

Some of those driven out of Europe for religious reasons were followers of the Calvinist Puritan movement who were seeking to reform the Church of England. They ended up founding the New England colonies and creating Congregationalist religious establishments of their own in Connecticut, Massachusetts, and New Hampshire. In six other colonies, the Church

---

[1]These are called "confessions" because they have distinct "confessions of faith." A confession of faith is a particular religious group's doctrinal statement. Among the most significant of these historically are the Augsburg Confession (1530), written by Martin Luther and severing ties with the Roman Catholic Church, and the Geneva Confession (1536), originally credited to John Calvin (Pelikan 2003).

of England was established (Georgia, Maryland, New York, North Carolina, South Carolina, and Virginia). Rhode Island, Delaware, New Jersey, and Pennsylvania had no religious establishment, the latter three being among the most religiously diverse colonies. As noted, the result of this situation was that no single confession dominated the American religious scene.

Religious disestablishment and religious freedom are key social structural preconditions for denominationalism to flourish. When Greeley refers to the United States as "the denominational society," he means a society that is characterized neither by an established church nor by dissenting sects but by religious bodies or associations of congregations that are united under a common historical and theological umbrella, that are presumed equal under the law, and that generally treat other bodies with an attitude of mutual respect. As a consequence of this "social organizational adjustment to the fact of religious pluralism" (Greeley 1972:1), there are hundreds of denominations in the United States. Indeed, the *Handbook of Denominations in the United States* lists 29 Baptist denominations and 18 denominations in the Calvinist/Reformed tradition alone (Mead, Hill, and Atwood 2010). This denominationalism has also become a global phenomenon; the *World Christian Database* (worldchristiandatabase.org) reports over 9,000 denominations within Christianity worldwide.

William Swatos observed this isomorphic trend of religion in the United States:

Although, strictly speaking, denominationalism is a Protestant dynamic, it has become fully accepted in principle by all major religious groups in the United States; in fact, one could say that the denominationalizing process represents the *Americanizing* of a religious tradition. (Swatos 1998:135)

In this understanding, other Christian religious traditions like Roman Catholicism, Mormonism, and Seventh-day Adventism are also considered denominations. Beyond Christianity, some have even written about Jewish "denominationalism" in reference to the four branches of Judaism—

Orthodox, Conservative, Reform, and Reconstructionist (Lazerwitz et al. 1998). The Nation of Islam and American Society of Muslims are distinctively American Islamic denominations (though the former is often viewed negatively by traditional Muslims). In fact, the American Society of Muslims evolved from the Nation of Islam under the leadership of Warith Deen Muhammad and once established saw a splinter group calling itself the Nation of Islam break from it with Louis Farrakhan as head (see Chapter 12 for more details).

If Swatos's observation is correct, we could in time expect to see Sunni and Shiite Islamic organizations develop as distinctive Islamic denominations, perhaps with a national twist: Nigerian Sunni Muslims of America, American Federation of Pakistani Shiite Mosques, the Association of Indonesian Sunni Mosques in America, and so on. Buddhism and Hinduism also have different branches or schools, though like Islam they were brought to the United States in large numbers only recently, so time will tell whether there will be an evolution of those branches into recognizable denominations.

Theology and Social Processes in the Proliferation of Denominations

The development of this diversity of American denominations has been the result of theological differences and disputes, theological innovations by religious entrepreneurs, and fundamental social processes such as immigration and racial conflict.

Race

Methodism, for example, has been heavily influenced by theological differences and race. The denomination itself began as a revitalization movement in the Church of England under the direction of John Wesley (an ordained minister of the Church of England) whose preaching emphasized personal holiness. As the movement spread, it eventually broke from the Church of England when the Methodist Episcopal Church in the United States was organized in 1784. By 1816, the African Methodist Episcopal (AME) Church was founded by African American congregations seeking independence from white Methodists, and not long after, the AME Zion Church ordained its first bishop, symbolizing its split from the larger (white) body of the Methodist church. In 1844, the Methodist Episcopal Church, South split from the Methodist Episcopal Church over the issue of slavery and later amicably split with the Colored Methodist Episcopal (CME) Church in 1870. In 1939, the two historically white Methodist Episcopal denominations, along with the Methodist Protestant Church, reunited to form the Methodist Church, which was joined in 1968 by the Evangelical United Brethren Church to become the United Methodist Church—the second largest Protestant denomination in the United States. All these splits and mergers were related to issues of race, not theological differences.

Other denominations were also affected by racial differences and differences over racial issues. Presbyterians were split over the issue of slavery, dividing in the mid-19th century between the United Presbyterian Church in the USA and the Presbyterian Church in the United States ("Southern"). The Southern Baptist Convention was formed in 1845 when Baptists in the South—who held to a biblical defense of slavery—split to form their own denomination. Free slaves after the Civil War founded the National Baptist Convention in 1895, creating yet another race-related schism.

Immigration

Lutheranism has been a predominantly white denomination in the United States, owing to its historic establishment in parts of Germany and Scandinavia. Its history, therefore, has been shaped less by race than by immigration and theological disputes. When Lutherans immigrated, they brought their national churches with them, as well as their particular languages and cultural practices, which prevented unity among groups that shared many religious views in common. Lutheran denominations (typically called "synods" or "churches"), therefore, proliferated

Official White House Photo by Pete Souza

The African Methodist Episcopal (AME) Church as a denomination was founded by Reverend Richard Allen in Philadelphia, Pennsylvania, in 1816 in response to racial discrimination in the Methodist Episcopal Church. It is the oldest and one of the largest African American denominations in the United States, with over 1 million members and over 4,000 congregations. President Barack Obama and First Lady Michelle Obama attended a church service at Metropolitan African Methodist Episcopal Church in Washington, D.C., on Inauguration Sunday in 2013.

in the late 19th and early 20th centuries as Lutheran immigrants flowed into the country. For example, Swedes founded the Augustana Evangelical Lutheran Church in 1860, Danes started the American Evangelical Lutheran Church in 1872, Finns established the Finnish Evangelical Lutheran Church of America in 1890, and Norwegians spawned the Lutheran Free Church in 1897.

Over time, as these immigrants assimilated into American society, theological differences became more prominent than differences of nationality. This is reflected in the current state of Lutheran denomination in the United States. Currently, there are 10 Lutheran denominations organized in the United States. The three largest of these are the Evangelical Lutheran Church in America (ELCA), Lutheran Church–Missouri Synod (LCMS) (est. 1847 by Germans), and Wisconsin Evangelical Lutheran Synod (WELS) (est. 1850 by Germans). (The word *synod* in Lutheran usage can refer either to an entire religious body like the LCMS or a local administrative region like the Texas Synod or Iowa Synod.)

Important theological differences and religious practices exist among these three groups (e.g., over the interpretation of scripture, ordination of women and gays, and the role of women in lay authority positions), with the ELCA being the liberal or mainline Lutheran church, the LCMS more conservative, and WELS the most conservative.

The history of denominations is one not only of division and schism but also of mergers and consolidation (Chaves and Sutton 2004). For example, the largest Lutheran church in the United States, the ELCA, was formed out of a complex series of mergers beginning in the early 20th century. It was formally established in 1987 with the merger of three Lutheran denominations, each of which was formed from the merger of several other Lutheran denominations, which were themselves formed from mergers of various Lutheran denominations and synods.

These developments are not just remnants of a historical past. In the dynamism of the American "religious economy," denominations are continually developing and dying, splitting and merging. As we discuss at greater length in Chapter 11, the ELCA voted in 2009 to ordain noncelibate gay clergy, and in 2010, the first gay Lutheran ministers were welcomed onto the church's clergy roster. As a consequence, 185 ELCA congregations have left the denomination, and a new Lutheran denomination was established in 2010: the North American Lutheran Church (thenalc.org).

In the opposite direction, some of the historical race-based differences between Methodist denominations are being challenged. Hood Theological Seminary in Salisbury, North Carolina, is a good example. It began in 1906 as part of Livingstone College, which is operated by the AME Zion denomination. The AME Zion Church was formed under the leadership of James Varick in 1821 due to racial discrimination in the Methodist Episcopal Church. Still sponsored by the church, but operating independently of the college since 2001, Hood today is a racially integrated theological seminary. It is recognized by a successor to the Methodist Episcopal Church, the United Methodist Church, as an "approved graduate theological seminary" where United Methodist ministerial candidates may be prepared for ordination (hoodseminary.edu). Also, in 2012, five black denominations entered into an agreement with each other and with the predominantly white United Methodist Church to recognize each other's churches, sacraments, and ministers (called a full communion agreement) (Banks 2012).

Online Resources: As noted in Chapter 2, an excellent, free online resource for information on American denominations, including profiles, membership statistics, and family trees, is the Association of Religion Data Archives (thearda.com). On the ARDA website you will also find in the College Modules of The Learning Center an exercise on "Exploring Denominations in the United States" where you can download detailed instructions on how to track the history of any denomination on the ARDA site.

Innovation

A final significant source of new denominations in the United States is the theological innovations of religious entrepreneurs. Joseph Smith founded the Church of Jesus Christ of Latter-day Saints (the Mormons) in the 1820s, Charles T. Russell the Jehovah's Witnesses in 1870, and Mary Baker Eddy the Church of Christ, Scientist, aka "Christian Science," in 1879. All of these groups are innovative developments of the Christian tradition.

Although they were attacked early on as "cults" (in the negative sense sociologists reject), they have since grown to relatively large and respected denominations (Jenkins 2000). As we saw in Chapter 6, Mormons and Jehovah's Witnesses in particular have experienced amazing growth.

As we will see later in this chapter, associations of congregations like the Vineyard Movement, fellowships of churches like Calvary Chapel, and church planting networks like Acts 29 may eventually develop more formal denominational structures, especially to help manage continual growth and the diversity that comes along with it.

Critical Thinking: Of the three processes of denominational formation discussed—race, immigration, and innovation—which do you think will play the biggest role in the future? Do you think another social process will be more important in the future? Is it possible for future religious entrepreneurs to have the success that Smith, Russell, and Eddy had in the 19th and 20th centuries?

BEYOND DENOMINATIONS?

Although the United States is still a "denominational" society, there are some significant developments in American religious life that suggest the importance of looking beyond denominations. These include transdenominational evangelicalism and nondenominationalism.

Transdenominational Evangelicalism

By all accounts, one of the most dynamic sectors of the American religious economy—and, indeed, the global religious economy—is evangelical Christianity. Although still in the minority, evangelical Protestantism has made significant inroads in Africa, Latin America, and Asia (Freston 2007). In the United States, individuals belonging to evangelical traditions now constitute over half of all Protestants (Pew Research Center Forum on Religion and Public Life 2012a).

For ease of identification in survey-based studies, some scholars define individuals as evangelicals according to their denominational affiliation, such as the Southern Baptist Convention and Churches of God. However, most recognize that evangelicalism is a movement, not a denomination or even a collection of denominations. It is, in fact, a *transdenominational movement* that had its origins at a specific place and specific point in time: with the founding of the National Association of Evangelicals in April 1942 in St. Louis, Missouri (Marsden 1991). According to sociologist Christian Smith, "Evangelicalism is not primarily denominationally based but ... 'a transdenominational movement in which many people, in various ways, feel at home.' ... Institutionally, this transdenominational evangelicalism is built around networks of parachurch agencies" (Smith 1998:135). These agencies include seminaries like the Moody Bible Institute, publications like *Christianity Today*, colleges like Wheaton, and publishing houses like Zondervan.

Associations or networks of churches and denominations do contribute to the movement—the Vineyard Christian Fellowship, Calvary Chapel, Korean Presbyterian Church in America, and Church of God (Cleveland, Tennessee) are examples. Some observers have also noted the influence of the evangelical movement within otherwise mainline denominations (Kosmin and Keysar 2009). Nonetheless, Smith and others are right to say that evangelicalism in the United States is not fundamentally denominational.

Evangelical Protestantism's transdenominational character may be one of the sources of its strength today. The theoretical issue of interest with respect to evangelical strength has to do with the plausibility of traditional religious worldviews in the modern pluralistic world. One widely respected sociologist of religion, Peter Berger, has devoted much of his writing to the exploration of *plausibility structures* (Berger 1967; Berger and Luckmann 1966). These are social interactions and processes within a group that serve to protect and sacralize the shared meanings and outlooks of the group. Much of Chapter 4 was concerned with this issue, and the emphasis in Chapter 5 on the importance of affective commitment in maintaining moral commitment (adherence to ideology) points to the same phenomenon. Berger's view is that belief systems, if they are to survive, must be rooted in a plausibility structure. An understanding of the religious group as a reference group is particularly critical to any analysis of plausibility. Individuals are capable of accepting all sorts of "strange" beliefs if enough other people seem convinced. It is a basic maxim of social constructionism that individuals look to others for a definition of the situation if they are uncertain themselves. When dealing with issues of the meaning of life, with the supernatural, and with the ultimate cause of perplexing events, ambiguity is a given. Plausibility structures—which include rituals, symbols, music, architecture, reference groups, and self-validating beliefs— are critical in making beliefs credible, especially if they run counter to those of the larger society. Moreover, plausibility is especially problematic in a pluralistic society where people are constantly exposed to meaning systems and believers who seem to contradict their own ideas. Thus, for Berger, pluralism itself undermines the plausibility structures that support religious belief. He felt that religion provided a large protective "sacred canopy" for its system of meaning, and that canopy protected aspects of the larger society as well (Berger 1967:152).

In his analysis of American evangelicals, Smith took issue with Berger's argument. He maintained that "American evangelicalism as a religious movement is thriving . . . very much because of and not in spite of its confrontation with modern pluralism" (Smith 1998:1). Smith proposed a *subcultural identity theory* of religious strength in modern society that accords well with the understanding of religion we suggest in this textbook: "Religion survives and can thrive in pluralistic, modern society by embedding itself in subcultures that offer satisfying morally orienting collective identities which provide adherents meaning and belonging" (Smith 1998:118).

Part of evangelicals' collective identity has to do with their distinguishing themselves from non-evangelicals as a negative reference group ("outgroup") and thereby creating some boundaries, but at the same time keeping the boundaries somewhat permeable so as to not cut themselves off entirely from the wider society (as fundamentalists often do). By doing so, they create the social basis (plausibility structure) necessary to support their religious beliefs. About this Smith concluded the following:

> We would like to suggest, however, that in the modern world, religion does survive and can thrive, not in the form of "sacred canopies," but rather in the form of *"sacred umbrellas."* Canopies are expansive, immobile, and held up by props beyond the reach of those covered. Umbrellas, on the other hand, are small, handheld, and portable— like the faith-sustaining religious worlds that modern people construct for themselves. We suggest that, as the old, overarching sacred canopies split apart and their ripped pieces of fabric fell toward the ground, many innovative religious actors caught those falling pieces of cloth in the air and, with more than a little ingenuity, remanufactured them into umbrellas. In the pluralistic modern world, people don't need macro-encompassing sacred cosmoses to maintain their religious beliefs. They only need "sacred umbrellas," small, portable, accessible relational worlds—religious reference groups—"under" which their beliefs can make complete sense. (Smith 1998:106)

Evangelicalism as a transdenominational movement helps provide the plausibility structures that support individuals' beliefs and that help make evangelical Protestantism one of the strongest traditions in American religion.

Nondenominationalism

A second religious development that takes us beyond denominations proper is the rise of nondenominationalism, in the form of both nondenominational congregations and individual religious identities. We have already seen in Chapters 5 and 6 the increasing number of Americans who choose not to identify their religion according to a denominational label (including those who specifically say "nondenominational" but also those who are "just Christians" and the "religious but unaffiliated").

Organizationally, nondenominational congregations are the single largest category of faith community in terms of affiliation and are a growing percentage of all congregations. As Figure 8.1 shows, in 1998, roughly 18% of congregations in the United States were nondenominational. That proportion had grown by 2006–2007 to 20.4% and in 2012 to 23.5%, a statistically and socially significant change in less than two decades. In terms of individual membership, Mark Chaves has observed the following: "If the unaffiliated congregations were all in one denomination, they would constitute the third-largest U.S. denomination in number of participants" (Chaves 2004:25).

Figure 8.1 Decreasing Denominational Affiliation in National Congregations Study

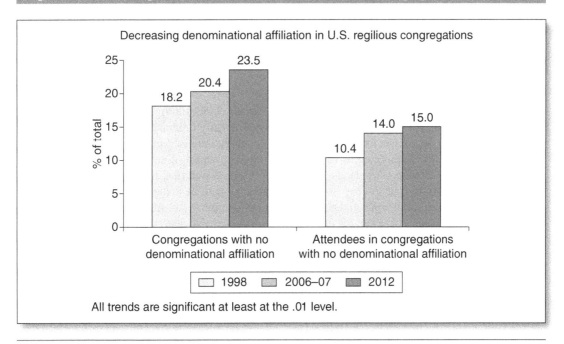

SOURCE: Chaves, Mark, and Shawna L. Anderson. 2014. "Changing American Congregations: Findings from the Third Wave of the National Congregations Study. *Journal for the Scientific Study of Religion* 53 (December): 676–86.

As we will see later in this chapter, there is a strong connection between nondenominationalism and the megachurch phenomenon, as well as "new paradigm" and "seeker" churches. According to the Hartford Institute for Religion Research's online database, four of the five largest megachurches in the United States identify themselves as nondenominational (hartfordinstitute.org/megachurch/database.html). A 2011 survey of churches with over 1,800 regular attendees found that 54% were nondenominational (Bird and Thumma 2011).

Nondenominationalism is actually related in part to evangelicalism, and vice versa. In one survey, 20% of evangelicals reported attending nondenominational churches (Smith 1998). Another study—the American Religious Identification Survey (ARIS)—found that from 1990 to 2008, most of the growth in the Christian population occurred among those who would identify only as "Christian," "evangelical/born again," or "nondenominational Christian." Taken altogether, these three groups grew from 5% of the population in 1990 to 11.8% in 2008. Looking to the future, Kosmin and Keysar observed in 2009 that among all Christians, these generic Christians have the youngest age composition.

In the press release announcing the release of ARIS 2008, Mark Silk (director of the program that sponsors ARIS) suggested that a "generic form of evangelicalism is emerging as the normative form of non-Catholic Christianity in the United States." If this is true, it may soon be possible to view nondenominational and transdenominational evangelicalism as a sort of "denominational label" (Ammerman 2006:364)—a category people can use to identify themselves as holding certain beliefs and engaging in certain practices in common with others across the United States and, perhaps, around the world.

Critical Thinking: When you think of religious groups and individuals, do you tend to think in terms of denominational labels? Is it important for you to know if someone is an Orthodox or Reformed Jew, an ELCA or WELS Lutheran, a Southern or an American Baptist, and so on? What do you make of people who say they are "just Christian"? Why do you think as you do?

DENOMINATIONS AND DE FACTO CONGREGATIONALISM

Organizationally, denominations are a group of congregations linked through centralized bodies to which congregations grant some overriding authority and to which individuals direct some loyalty as members. Although denominations are an organizational reality in American society and people often use denominational labels to describe themselves, no one actually "belongs" to a denomination. People are members of particular congregations (Chaves 2004). These congregations are usually, though decreasingly as we saw, affiliated with denominations, but most people's experiences of denominations are wholly mediated by the local congregation to which they belong. This is what R. Stephen Warner described as the bias of American religious life—"de facto congregationalism" (Warner 1993:1066). Even churches that are hierarchically organized by church law become "congregationalist" in fact. Regardless of the formal structure of authority in a denomination or religious tradition, local congregations tend to have a significant measure of autonomy to do their own thing (Ammerman 2006).

The way that denominations *officially* relate to local congregations is determined by the denominational "polity" structure. Three ideal type polities have been identified: *congregational*, *episcopal*, and *presbyterian* (Moberg 1984).

In a congregational polity, the authority of the local congregation is supreme. For example, although the thousands of Baptist congregations in the United States are typically part of various denominations (like the Southern Baptist Convention or American Baptist Churches), they are nonetheless formally independent. They choose their own pastors, control their own finances, own their own property, and so on. This is not to say that some denominations that are formally organized as congregational polities do not exercise influence on their member congregations. As Ammerman observed, at the height of its power, the Southern Baptist Convention "provided such comprehensive programmatic support that local congregations from Atlanta to Dallas bore strong resemblance to each other" (Ammerman 2009:574).

The Roman Catholic Church provides a good example of the episcopal polity. Also called "hierarchical," this type of church polity places ultimate authority over local churches in the centralized hands of bishops (the Greek word is *episkopos*). Each of the Roman Catholic Church's nearly 20,000 congregations in the United States (called "parishes") is geographically defined and clustered into a "diocese," which is under the authority of the local bishop and, ultimately, of the Bishop of Rome (i.e., the Pope). This does not mean, however, that de facto congregationalism does not exist in Catholic churches. In fact, there is a great deal of diversity and difference between parishes. In his survey of Roman Catholicism in the United States, theologian Chester Gillis observed that "differences in composition of the parish community, leadership, interests, preaching, programs, worship, and organization can make one parish, even in the same diocese or city, very different from one another. . . . To this extent, all Catholicism is local" (Gillis 1999:32).

De facto congregationalism is evident in how local dioceses and parishes implement—or choose not to implement—universal rites promulgated by the church hierarchy (Yamane and MacMillen 2006). It is also seen on Sunday mornings when Catholics across the country "church shop," floating from their geographically defined parish to their parish-of-choice, often passing several other Catholic churches on the way (Warner 2005). Catholics choose their parishes because Catholic parishes have their own

local cultures and identities through which official church policies are interpreted (McCallion, Maines, and Wolfel 1996). Indeed, one of the major conclusions of the Notre Dame Study of Catholic Parish Life in the 1980s was that "relative to the life of the rest of the church, parishes seem to have a life of their own" (Gremillion and Castelli 1987:47). This remains true today.

Other denominations that have some form of episcopal polity, with a bishop having some authority over the churches, include Eastern Orthodox, Anglican, Episcopalian, Methodist, AME, AME Zion, and some (but not all) Lutherans. Many of these denominations are also affected by congregationalism and local authority. For example, the United Methodist "General Conference," where policy is decided, has an equal number of ordained clergy and laypeople who vote representing their congregations. Likewise, the local United Methodist church building is actually owned by the larger denomination but maintained by the local congregation. So power and responsibility are shared.

Presbyterian is a kind of intermediate polity, between the congregational and episcopal, which is derived theologically from the Swiss reformation. Like episcopal polities, it is hierarchical; like congregational polities, it gives some authority to the local church. Some say it was a model for the U.S. Constitution's federal system of government. Like the U.S. government, there are typically levels of governance: Local churches are grouped into larger assemblies sometimes called presbyteries, which are grouped into synods, which are brought together in general assemblies. General assemblies have authority to set policy for the denomination, but decisions at that level must be filtered down through the lower levels of governance for final approval. Local congregations have authority insofar as they elect members to represent them at the higher levels of the denomination's governance structure. Not surprisingly, denominations like the Presbyterian Church USA (PCUSA) and Presbyterian Church in America (PCA) are organized in this fashion. Yet, as Warner wrote, many Presbyterian congregations use hymnals other than the ones authorized by the denomination and choose ministers trained at seminaries other than denominationally sponsored ones. This de facto congregationalism means that the "label *Presbyterian* on the door no longer conveys a great deal of information to the first-time visitor to a local church" (Warner 2005:163).

Although the idea of a congregation comes from Christianity, de facto congregationalism means that this organizational form is not limited to the Christian tradition. Scholars studying the Muslim community in the United States have found convergence toward the congregational model, even though most of the nearly 2,000 mosques (*masjids* in Arabic) in the United States are relatively new, with 87% having been founded since 1970 and 62% since 1980 (Bagby 2003). According to Islamic scholar Ihsan Bagby, "Most of the world's mosques are simply a place to pray. . . . A Muslim cannot be a member of a particular mosque" because mosques belong to God, not to the people (Bagby 2003:115). The role of the imam—the minister—is simply to lead prayers five times a day and to run the services on the Sabbath, including delivery of a sermon. The imam does not operate an organization and does not need formal training at a seminary, unlike most Christian and Jewish clergy. Mosques were historically government supported in other countries, so they had to make major changes in how they operate in North America. Because they could not depend on government funding, Islamic mosques needed to adapt to the congregational model: Members who were loyal to a particular mosque would support it. They also began to put more emphasis on religious education (which had been done largely by extended families in the "old country"), religious holidays at the mosque rather than with families, socializing (potlucks and coffee hours), and life cycle celebrations (birth and marriages solemnized, conducting funerals) (Waugh 1994). This is a major change in the role of the mosque and the imam for many Muslims.

This same pattern of transformation from the religious structure of the homeland to a congregational structure in the United States has been seen in other religious communities founded by non-Christian Asian immigrant groups in recent years, including Indian Hindus (Kurien 1998) and Japanese, Korean, and Laotian Buddhists (Warner 2005). For example, Carl Bankston and Min Zhou reported on a fieldwork study of a Laotian community in New Iberia, Louisiana, in the mid-1990s. The Theravada Buddhist temple constructed there reproduces the festivals and rites of the home country, but its organizational functioning has also been transformed by the American context (Bankston and Zhou 2000). In the home country, the community of monks has authority over the temple, and all men at some point in time are expected to become monks at least for a period of time. In the United States, the authority is dissolved into the local congregation, and being a monk becomes a specialized, professional status. Lay members of the temple "call" the monk to service in their community (a very "Baptist" or "Congregational" idea). The Korean Buddhist Kwan Um Sa temple in Los Angeles grew in membership when it began offering the types of social services often found in American congregations: "marriage and youth counseling, hospital arrangement, hospital visits, arrangement for Social Security benefits, . . . transportation for elderly members" (Yu 1988:90). The Japanese American Jodo Shinshu Buddhists call their place of worship a "church" and sit in church pews rather than on traditional Japanese mats (Warner 2005).

De facto congregationalism is a structural reality of American religious life. It reflects principles of the open systems model: Organizations are influenced by inputs from the larger social environment. In this case, the key aspect of the environment is the pattern of organization constituted by other religious congregations. That environment exerts influence particularly under conditions of uncertainty for new organizations, like those founded by immigrant religious communities. As Warner argued, "organizations that copy other organizations" (Warner 2005:168) have a "competitive advantage," and "reliance on established legitimated procedures enhances organizational legitimacy and survival characteristics" (Warner 2005:155; see also DiMaggio and Powell 1983). This all reflects the fact that religious groups tend to become like the dominant religious organizations in any geographical region.

CONGREGATIONAL DEMOGRAPHY

No one knows how many congregations exist in the United States today, but most educated observers estimate that there are over 300,000 (Ammerman 2009). Most "congregational studies" have been qualitative case studies. Indeed, sociology of religion students are often asked to do case studies of congregations—visiting a congregation and writing or presenting about what they observed—as one of their class assignments. The "Doing Research on Religion" feature on page 39 in Chapter 2 offers students some suggestions from a veteran sociologist on how to observe congregations sociologically.

The most important recent contribution to the study of congregations in the United States is the National Congregations Study (NCS). The NCS uses a technique pioneered in the study of other organizational fields to draw a representative sample of U.S. congregations: It asks individuals participating in a nationally representative study of Americans to name their congregation (Chaves and Anderson 2014). To date, there have been three waves of data collection; the first in 1998 had a sample of 1,234 congregations, the second in 2006–2007 had 1,506 congregations, and the third in 2012 had 1,331 congregations. The longitudinal design of this ongoing study allows

Online Resources: All three waves of data from the National Congregations Study (NCS) are available at the Association of Religion Data Archives (thearda.com). You will also find in the College Modules of the ARDA Learning Center an exercise on "Exploring Congregations in America" with detailed instructions on how to explore the NCS data. The website of the NCS itself also provides tools that allow you to do basic analyses of the NCS data (www.soc .duke.edu/natcong/explore.html).

scholars to track continuity and change in congregational life (Chaves and Anderson 2014).

Analyzing a representative sample of congregations at three points in time has yielded many insights. The first insight from the NCS has to do with the demography of congregations, and the curious relationship between looking at congregations from the perspective of the organization as compared to congregational experiences of individuals. As Chaves wrote, "although most *congregations* are small, most *people* are associated with large congregations" (Chaves 2004:18). In 2012, the median *congregation* had just 70 regular participants (including children), down from 80 in 1998, but the median *person* attended services at a congregation with 400 regular participants.[2]

One way to understand this "double aspect" of congregations is to think about lining all congregations up from largest to smallest. The median congregation is the one in the very middle (see Figure 8.2 on page 200). Using data from the first wave of the NCS, Chaves observed that if you walked from the smallest congregation toward

---

[2]In statistics, *median* is one way of understanding the *average* value in a collection of values. It refers to the value that is in the middle of a distribution, where half of the values are above it and half of the values are below it. Like the more commonly used *mean* (or arithmetic mean or simple mean), it is a measure of central tendency, but has the benefit over the mean of eliminating the influence of outliers (very large or very small cases). For example, median income is often reported because the income of the superrich like Bill Gates would skew the mean. Similarly, Chaves looks at the median size of congregations to eliminate the excessive influence of the few extremely large congregations that exist. We consider these megachurches more fully later in this chapter.

Figure 8.2 Double Aspect of Congregations' Size of Distribution

Organizational Perspective
Median congregation had 75 regular participants

The smallest 50% of congregations contain 11% of all participants

50% of all participants are in the largest 10% of congregations

Individual Perspective
Median person is in a congregation with 400 regular participants

the largest and stopped in the middle, you would be at a church or temple with 80 regular participants. The proportion of the total population who attend the congregations you passed would only be 11% (Chaves 2004). In other words, 89% of regular attendees are in the 50% of congregations that are above the median.

Looking at it from the individual perspective, if you walked from the largest religious communities toward the smallest, once you walked past half of all the people who attend religious services regularly, you would be at a congregation with 400 members. The proportion of all of the congregations you have passed, however, is just 10%.

There are significant denominational differences in congregation size also between the organizational and the individual perspectives. Data from the 2012 NCS show that only 5.5% of all congregations in the United States are Roman Catholic, but 27.7% of people attend Catholic churches. By contrast, over twice as many congregations are Methodist (12.8%) as Catholic, but only one third as many people attend Methodist churches (7.9%) compared to Catholic churches.

One consequence of this "double aspect" of congregations is that when you ask people to estimate the average size of a congregation, they almost always estimate well over 70. As we can see, this overestimate is based in their individual experiences with congregations. The average size of a congregation *is* larger from the individual perspective than it is from the organizational perspective. Also, if you ask Catholics to estimate average congregation size, they are likely to give a higher estimate than a Methodist. Catholic congregations are, on average, much larger than Protestant ones.

Critical Thinking: Thinking about your own experiences with religious congregations, if you have any, did you see the "double aspect" of congregations that Chaves observes? What religious traditions were the congregations? What would you have estimated the average congregation size to be based on your experience?

What Do Congregations Do?

As one of the most prevalent voluntary organizations in American society, congregations do many things. As we have already seen (Chapter 5), they are central to the socialization of children. They are the organizational center for the belonging function that we have identified as central to religion. As such, they play a key role in community formation (Ammerman 2009).

Because communities can be exclusive, there is a dark side to this, as we will see in Part V when we consider religion and social inequality. The segregation by people according to economic class (Chapter 9) and race (Chapter 10), as well as inequalities of gender and sexuality (Chapter 11), are organizational realities of religious life.

The flip side of this same segregation coin is that congregations can also be the main community-based organization involved in the preservation of ethnic or racial minority cultures and therefore important organizational bases for survival and empowerment. This is why religious communities have historically been so important to immigrant populations (as discussed in this chapter and in Chapter 15 on globalization). We discuss at length the reality of churches as the core institution of African American communities in Chapter 12.

This segregation notwithstanding, when the "imagined community" is drawn more widely, congregations perform many valuable social services that benefit individuals well beyond their memberships (Chaves and Tsitsos 2001; Trinitapoli 2005). They feed the hungry, clothe the naked, welcome the stranger, care for the sick, visit those in prison, give comfort to the abused and elderly, tutor the young, and so on. For all of their difficulties in terms of recent membership declines, mainline Protestant churches are the most active congregations in providing social services to their local communities (Ammerman 1997, 2005).

Finally, congregations are very active in political life. Using the 1998 NCS data to look at seven different types of political involvement—from distribution of voter guides to demonstrations and marches to voter registration drives—Kraig Beyerlein and Mark Chaves found that 41% of congregations had engaged in at least one political activity in the previous 12 months. NCS data from 2012 show considerable consistency in these same political behaviors. Congregations from different religious traditions tend to be drawn to different types of activity, though. More than others, Catholic congregations are involved in demonstrations, marches, and lobbying. Mainline Protestant congregations more often organize discussion groups. Black Protestant congregations register voters. Mainline and Black Protestant congregations host political candidates, while evangelical and Black Protestant congregations distribute voter guides more than other congregations (Beyerlein and Chaves 2003).

These various and important activities of congregations notwithstanding, at the heart of congregational life is worship (Ammerman 2005). As Chaves put it, "Congregations' central purpose is, of course, the expression and transmission of religious meaning, and corporate worship is the primary way in which that purpose is pursued" (Chaves 2004:127). There have been many fascinating case studies of congregational worship, especially changes in worship style to more contemporary forms (see Wolfe 2003). As we will see later in this chapter, much recent attention has been paid to the nontraditional worship services held at megachurches, especially those that are seeker-oriented.

A particularly insightful study is Timothy Nelson's analysis of Eastside Chapel, an AME church of some 300 members in Charleston, South Carolina. More than some other AME churches, Eastside Chapel is Pentecostal in orientation, emphasizing the "gifts of the spirit." Eastside Chapel members believe they can and should have relationships with God, Satan, and other spiritual beings; they are an objective reality for them, as consequential as human beings

(Nelson 2005). Nelson showed how the Pentecostal beliefs and the ritual structure in Eastside Chapel's service work together to organize and direct what otherwise seem to be spontaneous, enthusiastic outbursts from the members in worship. Jumping up and down, raising hands, shouting out, and even moving out into the aisles to dance are all governed by social norms prescribing what can be done, by whom, and when.

As with any case study, Nelson's offers great insight into the substance and process of worship. However, the question of representativeness also arises: How typical is Eastside Chapel? However,

Table 8.1 Frequency of Worship Elements, From Perspective of Congregations and of Individuals, 1998, 2006–2007, and 2012

Elements	% of Congregations With Element (1998)	% of Congregations With Element (2006–2007)	% of Congregations With Element (2012)	% Change in Congregations With Element (1998–2012)
Singing by congregation	97	97	96	−1.0
Sermon/speech	95	95	96	+1.0
People call out "amen"	61	71	67	+9.8
Applause	55	61	65	+18.2
Written order of service (program)	72	68	62	−13.9
People other than leader raise hands in praise	45	57	59	+31.1
Singing by choir	54	44	45	−16.7
Organ	53	–	42	−20.8
Visual projection equipment	12	27	35	+191.7
Drums	20	33	34	+70.0
People speak in tongues	24	27	30	+25.0
Electric guitar	22	34	29	+31.8
Adults jump/shout/dance spontaneously	19	26	26	+36.8

SOURCE: National Congregations Study Wave 1 (Chaves 2004, Table 5.1, p. 132), NCS Wave 2 (Chaves and Anderson 2008, Appendix B, pp. 433–434), and NCS Wave 3 author calculations. By permission of the Association for the Sociology of Religion.

NOTE: All elements are found in most recent main service, except for speaking in tongues, which was any time in the past year. Percentages are rounded to the closest integer, using the round half-to-even rule for 0.5 percentages.

because it is a national sample of congregations, the NCS provides a national sample of worship. This first wave of the NCS explored worship according to a "repertoire" of worship elements that can be assembled by congregations in different ways (Chaves 2004). The second and third waves asked about many, but not all, of those same elements. Table 8.1 shows the frequency of 14 different worship elements in 1998, 2006–2007, and 2012, as well as the percentage change in frequency from 1998 to 2012.

As Table 8.1 indicates, there are two nearly universal elements in congregational worship: singing and preaching. In 2012, 96% of congregations (housing 98% of attenders) included singing in their weekly worship services, and 96% (with 98% of attenders) had a weekly sermon or speech. The average congregation's worship service was 75 minutes long, of which 30 minutes were devoted to a sermon and 20 minutes to music.

Beyond singing and preaching, other elements of worship were less universal, but the direction in which they changed from 1998 to 2012 is significant. One of the most notable changes between the first and third waves of the NCS is the increasing informality of worship (Chaves and Anderson 2014). For every element of worship the study measured, those that are more formal are becoming less common. As the last column in Table 8.1 shows, the use of written programs decreased by 14%, singing by choirs declined 17%, and the use of organs dropped by 21%. These declines in formal worship elements are mirrored by even larger increases in informal ones. In just 16 years, the percentage of congregations that report using visual projection equipment has increased by nearly 200%. Drum use is up by 70%. Jumping, shouting, and dancing increased by 37%. People raising their hands in praise increased by 31%.

Photo by Tamuka R. Hwami

Use of visual projection equipment (rather than hymnals), praise bands, and praying with hands upraised in praise are on the increase in many congregations. While this type of emotionally intense worship was once associated with a particular social class, it is spreading through the culture, in part due to megachurches and televangelism. Oasis Church, pictured here, was the subject of sociologist Gerardo Marti's 2008 book, *Hollywood Faith*.

Indeed, every spontaneous and demonstrative element listed in Table 8.1 became more common by 2012.

Chaves notes that this growing informality of worship is not equally distributed through all religious traditions. Catholic churches have not adopted informal practices as quickly as Protestant churches, and certain informal styles like jumping shouting and dancing are still more concentrated among black churches (Chaves 2011). This latter observation suggests the generalizability of Nelson's (2005) observation of the enthusiastic style of worship at Eastside Chapel.

What explains the increasing informality of worship? Analyzing the first wave of the NCS study, Chaves highlighted "a long-term trend toward informality in several cultural domains, including clothing, manners, and naming" (Chaves 2004:158, citing Lieberson 2000). The open systems perspective suggests that these broader cultural shifts cannot help but influence religious organizations.

Critical Thinking: Do you agree or disagree with the general assessment of a "long-term trend toward informality" in society? What evidence do you have for or against this claim? In what ways do you see (or not see) this reflected in religious practices, both inside of churches (as we discuss) and outside of them?

Another explanation for the spread of informality in worship is the growing number and influence of megachurches, especially those "new paradigm" and "seeker" churches that use contemporary marketing strategies to reach bigger and bigger audiences. We turn our attention to these very large and influential religious communities next.

MEGACHURCHES

One of the realities in American religious life is the concentration of worshippers and resources (money and staff) in large congregations. Although a big part of this is due to megachurches, as we will see, it is important to recognize a broader trend as well. For both denominations that are growing like the Assemblies of God and those that are declining like the Episcopal Church (recall Chapter 6), the number of very large churches is growing. Moreover, across a number of denominations, the percentage of individuals who are concentrated in the largest churches is also growing. Put simply, "religious concentration is intensifying" (Chaves 2011:65). Beginning in 1970, the percentage of individuals attending the largest 1% of churches has grown dramatically. This is especially true of the Assemblies of God, Southern Baptist Convention, United Methodist Church, PCUSA, Reformed Church in America, and Church of the Nazarene—all of which have over 10% of their followers attending the largest 1% of their churches (Chaves 2011). This is the broader context within which to understand the megachurch phenomenon, as "the very biggest churches also have become even larger" (Chaves 2011:65).

Stories about megachurches in the popular news media abound. For example, a 2005 *New York Times Magazine* cover story on "The Soul of the New Exurb" reported on Radiant Church in Surprise, Arizona (Mahler 2005). Although it was only founded in 1997, the church had since grown to 5,000 weekly attendees in a new 55,000-square-foot church with five 50-inch plasma screen TVs, a bookstore, a café (including drive-through), Xboxes for the kids, and Krispy Kreme doughnuts at every service (the doughnut budget is $16,000 per year). The story quotes the church's pastor, Lee McFarland, as saying, "We want the church to look like a mall. We want you to come in here and say, 'Dude, where's the cinema?'"

More recently, the website of *Forbes* magazine reported on megachurches using Second Baptist Church of Houston (est. 1978) as an example. Second Baptist is the 13th largest megachurch in the United States, claiming

A view of the drive-through coffee shop at Radiant Church in Surprise, Arizona.

53,000 members, over 20,000 weekly attendees, and an annual budget of more than $50 million. It does not just have a building with a sanctuary; it has five *campuses* that house fitness centers, bookstores, coffee shops, and an auto repair clinic. Of course, it does have a building for worship, which it is currently refurbishing to the tune of $8 million. It will seat 6,500 under a six-story-high dome (Bogan 2009).

Other well-known megachurches include North Point Community Church in Alpharetta, Georgia (average attendance 30,629), the Willow Creek Community Church in South Barrington, Illinois (average attendance 25,743), and LifeChurch.tv of Edmond, Oklahoma (30,000), not to mention the megachurches associated with famous pastors like Joel Osteen's Lakewood Church in Houston (43,500), Rick Warren's Saddleback Valley Community Church in Lake Forest, California (22,055), T. D. Jakes's The Potter's House in Dallas (16,140), and Creflo Dollar's World Changers Church International in College Park, Georgia (15,000).

Online Resources: Although megachurches are geographically concentrated in the Sunbelt, there are megachurches in almost every state. The Hartford Institute for Religion Research maintains an interactive database of megachurches in the United States on its website: hartfordinstitute.org/megachurch/database.html. You can sort the Hartford list by congregation, denomination, or size. You can also look at megachurches by state. What megachurches in the database are near where you live? Have you ever attended one of these megachurches? If so, how did your experience compare to what is described in this chapter?

By any measure, megachurches are a significant social phenomenon. According to Scott Thumma and Warren Bird, megachurches are "Protestant congregations that draw 2,000 or more adults and children in a typical weekend (attendance not membership)" (Thumma and Bird 2008:1). (Due to their organization into geographic "parishes" rather than congregations of people who specifically joined that church, Catholic parishes are excluded from this definition.) Thus defined, the best estimate is that the total number of megachurches in the United States has increased from 50 in 1970 to over 600 in 2000 to more than 1,200 by 2010. Even though this is a small segment of the 300,000+ congregations in the United States, the average megachurch has weekly attendance of between 3,000 and 4,000 persons, compared to 70 in the average congregation. This means that over 6 million people attend services weekly in megachurches, giving them a disproportionately large influence (Bird and Thumma 2011).

As noted previously, four of the five largest megachurches in the United States identify as nondenominational: Lakewood, North Point Community, Gateway (Southlake, Texas), and Willow Creek. (The third largest megachurch, LifeChurch.tv, is part of the Evangelical Covenant Church.) Over half of all megachurches are nondenominational (up from 29% in 2000), and 71% self-identify as theologically evangelical (up from 48% in 2000) (Bird and Thumma 2011; Thumma and Bird 2008).

The ever-present singing and preaching we find in congregations generally are translated in the megachurch ritual vernacular into electric guitars (often or always used in 96% of megachurches), drums or other percussion instruments (98%), and visual projection equipment (97%). Megachurches are also leading the way in terms of informal, demonstrative, and upbeat contemporary worship styles. Ninety-four percent of megachurch leaders describe their worship as "joyful" and 92% as "inspirational," compared to only 46% who say their worship is "reverent" (Bird and Thumma 2011:9). As a flier from Radiant Church sent to the residents of Surprise, Arizona, put it: "You think church is boring and judgmental, and that all they want is your money? At Radiant you'll hear a rockin'

band and a positive, relevant message. Come as you are. We won't beg for your money. Your kids will love it!"

Critical Thinking: What megachurches are near where you live? Have you ever attended one of these megachurches? If so, how did your experience compare to what is described in this chapter? Even if the megachurch experience is not to your taste, what do you think attracts so many people to these very large churches?

Although Protestant megachurches are clearly riding the wave of significant changes in the ecology of religious organization and the informalization of culture, not all megachurches are "new." As Bird and Thumma document, almost half of all megachurches (47%) were founded before 1970. Another 27% were founded from 1970 to 1989. Thus, only one in four (26%) megachurches were founded after 1990 (Bird and Thumma 2011). Many of the older megachurches, however, have adopted newer approaches to attract members. Some sociologists have argued, and many megachurch pastors would readily admit, that everything done in megachurches is done intentionally for the purpose of attracting new attendees and retaining existing ones. In this view, many (and perhaps most) megachurches can be considered "new paradigm" or "seeker churches," as we discuss later in this chapter.

MULTI-SITE CHURCHES

The idea of having a single church with multiple sites is not new. This is the model of the "universal church" held by Roman Catholicism, in which the entire globe is divided up into geographic regions (dioceses) and those regions into geographic subdivisions (parishes) managed by an elaborate hierarchy of Cardinals, Bishops, and priests, all headquartered in Rome at the Vatican.

Similarly, more hierarchical denominations consider themselves a single religious body with multiple churches. Still, the term *multi-site church* has a distinctive contemporary meaning that captures a very new development on the religious landscape. By multi-site church is meant a single *congregation* that meets in two or more locations but maintains a single organizational structure (leadership and finances) (Bird 2014).

This organizational form is quite new in the long history of religion. According to an early study of the phenomenon, in the 1980s there were fewer than 100 multi-site congregations in the United States, and by the 1990s there were no more than 200 (Surratt, Ligon, and Bird 2009). The 2000s, then, were a time of dramatic expansion. According to the 2012 NCS, 3.4% of all congregations (with 10.3% of all attenders) have worship services in more than one location, with a median number of locations of three. This suggests that there are over 10,000 multi-site congregations in the United States—almost all of them Protestant, and most of those evangelical Protestant—with upwards of 5 million attendees.

Many megachurches are also multi-site. According to Bird and Thumma (2011), 46% of megachurches hold services at more than one location, averaging 3.6 locations, and another 20% are considering expanding sites. By the time you read this passage, a multi-site organization will probably be the norm for megachurches in the United States—and perhaps globally as well. Although this chapter focuses on developments in the United States, as the "Global Perspectives" box suggests, both megachurches and multi-site churches are global phenomena.

In the same way that no one starts a megachurch as a megachurch, most congregations are not founded as multi-site. They become multi-site. According to Bird, this happens on average when attendance reaches 1,200 and is growing. For congregations with weekly attendance below 1,000, 5% are multi-site and average 2.6 "campuses," compared to 81% of congregations with 15,000 or more weekly attendance, which

average 8.5 campuses (Bird 2014). (The question of "internet campuses," or "online church," will be discussed in Chapter 14.)

Some multi-site churches operate just in one geographic area and follow something like the Catholic parish model where everyone can attend a "neighborhood church" instead of driving for miles to get to the home campus. Bird gives the example of The Summit Church, which has eight campuses in the Raleigh-Durham, North Carolina, metropolitan area. According to Pastor J. D. Greear, "We can bless people when we are closer to them. That's why we plant campuses—to bring ministry closer to home" (Bird 2014:3). Another pastor wrote, "Multisite fits with our vision as we take church to neighborhoods. In many cases people walk to their worship gathering" (Bird 2014:7). Multi-sites are not just an urban phenomenon. Forty-seven percent of multi-sites have a campus in a small town or rural area (Bird 2014).

Other multi-site churches have a much longer reach. LifeChurch.tv, for example, has its main location in Edmond, Oklahoma, but also has campuses in Florida, Kansas, New York, Tennessee, and Texas (lifechurch.tv/locations). Saddleback Church is even more expansive. Saddleback was founded in 1980 in Lake Forest, California, by Rick Warren. It now has nine locations in Orange County as well as campuses in Berlin (Germany), Buenos Aires (Argentina), Hong Kong (China), and Manila (the Philippines) (saddleback.com).

Given that preaching and music were the two nearly universal elements of congregational worship (Table 8.1 on page 202), how does worship work in a practical sense at multi-site churches? In terms of preaching, multi-site churches must decide between having sermons delivered live (as a live feed from the home campus) or by prerecorded video, or some combination of the two. Bird found that as the number of campuses grows, the likelihood of delivering sermons by video alone increases. For churches with more than six campuses, two thirds of the messages are prerecorded, typically at an earlier service that same day (Bird 2014).

Although not the exclusive domain of multi-sites, these congregations are very involved in a practice called "church planting." Rather than creating a new campus of their own church, church planting involves helping others to start their own churches. Church planting is not a new phenomenon; denominations have planted churches for centuries. However, in the 1980s Calvary Chapel and the Vineyard established this as a pattern outside of denominations (Miller 1997). The vast majority of multi-sites are involved in church planting in some form or fashion; only 19% report no involvement on any level. Forty-nine percent of multi-sites directly sponsor new churches, and 36% are part of a church planting networks like Acts 29 (acts29network.org) and LAUNCH (launchstrong.com) (Bird 2014).

As should be evident even from this brief description, like megachurches, multi-site churches frequently have a very proactive orientation toward growth. They frequently do this by orienting themselves toward meeting consumer demand through a clear strategy to market their products in novel ways and to individuals who are unchurched or alienated from traditional churches.

GLOBAL PERSPECTIVES

The World's Largest Churches

Warren Bird is a sociologist of religion who has the imposing title of "Director of Research and Intellectual Capital Support" at the Leadership Network, a nonprofit founded in 1984 to help Christian leaders foster innovation and growth. He has been a significant player in researching American megachurches and multi-site churches. He is also responsible for an online list of the largest churches in Africa, Asia, Europe, Oceania, and Latin America and the Caribbean. The list is available as a downloadable Google spreadsheet on the Leadership Network's website (leadnet.org/world).

As with the Hartford Institute for Religion Research's database of megachurches in the United States, Bird's global database lists Protestant churches according to attendance, not membership. It counts all attendees regardless of age, at all weekend services and all campuses (excluding Internet campuses). Multi-site congregations are counted as one church if they share the same theology, name, leadership, and finances.

At the end of 2014, the 20 largest Protestant churches in the world, according to Bird's database, were:

1	Yoido Full Gospel Church	480,000	Seoul	Korea
2	Deeper Christian Life Ministry	75,000	Lagos	Nigeria
3	Mision Cristiana Elim Internacional (Elim Central Church)	75,000	S. Salvador	El Salvador
4	New Life Church	70,000	Mumbai	India
5	Onnuri (All Nations) Community Church	65,000	Seoul	Korea
6	Victory Metro Manila	65,000	Manila	Philippines
7	Jesus Celebration Center	60,000	Mombasa	Kenya

8	Pyungkang Cheil Presbyterian Church	60,000	Seoul	Korea
9	Ministere du Combat Spirituel	50,000	Kinshasa	Congo
10	Living Faith Church (Winner's Chapel)—main campus	50,000	Lagos	Nigeria
11	Apostolic Church	50,000	Lagos	Nigeria
12	Yeshu Darbar (Royal Court of Jesus)	50,000	Allahabad	India
13	Nambu Full Gospel Church	50,000	Anyang	Korea
14	Bethany Church of God	50,000	Surabaya	Indonesia
15	New Life Assembly of God	50,000	Chennai	India
16	Igreja de Paz (Church of Peace)	50,000	Santarém	Brazil
17	Evangelical Cathedral of Santiago (former Jotabeche Church)	45,000	Santiago	Chile
18	Comunidad Cristiana Agua Viva	42,000	Lima	Peru
19	Redeemed Christian Church of God	40,000	Lagos	Nigeria
20	United Family International Church	35,000	Harare	Zimbabwe

As this table shows, these very large churches are widely distributed over the globe—from Indonesia and the Philippines to Kenya and the Congo to Chile and Brazil. Still, it is hard not to notice that four of the churches are in Nigeria (total population 174 million) and four are in Korea (total population 50 million). The largest megachurch in the United States (total population 317 million)—Joel Osteen's Lakewood Church in Houston, with 43,500 attendees—would barely make the top 20 globally.

The attendance figure for Yoido Full Gospel Church is not a typographical error. The church actually has nearly half-a-million weekly attendees. The Assemblies of God congregation was started in 1958, and in 1973 it opened a new church with a seating capacity of 12,000. Twenty years later, attendance topped 200,000, and Yoido began opening satellite churches in Seoul and beyond. At the start, this Pentecostal church was a missionary outpost in a Buddhist country. It now sends missionaries itself to over 60 countries as well as receiving so many international visitors that each of its services is translated into 16 languages.

Critical Thinking: Visit the Yoido Full Gospel Church website at english.fgtv.com and compare what you see there to Lakewood Church's website (lakewoodchurch.com). What are the similarities and differences between how these two megachurches present themselves?

"New Paradigm" and "Seeker" Churches: Congregations With a Marketing Strategy

Some newly founded and very rapidly growing religious communities have been extremely deliberate about marketing strategies, including virtually all megachurches. They have identified a "market segment" that they believe to be undersupplied or for which they believe a demand can be created. They assess the demographic characteristics of the population and seek to provide a service (pun intended) that will "sell." Not all of these congregations are huge, but they do tend to grow quickly. Donald Miller called these churches geared to marketing the "new paradigm churches." Indeed, he believed these religious organizations are so significant that they represent the first wave of a new reformation that will shake the foundations of religion as we know it (Miller 1997). The data we just examined from the NCS on trends in worship styles suggest that these churches are indeed making some inroads.

Miller called these "new paradigm churches" because they seem to break many of the rules for reform movements. These religious organizations are unlike previous renewal or reform movements within Christianity. Some of the unique aspects can be summarized as follows:

- Unlike most reform movements, these churches are less interested in revising the *message* of the dominant religious establishment (that is, a rethinking of the meaning system) and more focused on a radical transformation in *medium* of delivery (for example, breaking away from stodgy 16th-century hymns accompanied by a pipe organ and presenting the faith through the music and technology of the youth culture).
- Whereas previous renewal groups have rejected the dominant culture and presented an image of world rejection, the new paradigm churches have assimilated greatly to the larger culture, adopting most of its technology and *some* of its values. This defies the typical sect-to-church-to-sect renewal pattern.
- As these organizations have developed, they have been remarkably "postmodern" organizations, with more emphasis on energetic activity than on hierarchy—more characterized by networking than by formal structures that control people's behaviors within the organization.

The new paradigm churches have 12 common features, according to Miller:

1. They were all started after the mid-1960s.
2. The majority of congregation members were born after 1945.
3. Seminary training of clergy is optional (indeed, there is fear that seminary training may taint one's pure spirituality).
4. Worship is contemporary.
5. Lay leadership is highly valued.
6. They have extensive small group ministries.
7. Clergy and congregants usually dress informally.
8. Tolerance of different personal styles is prized.
9. Pastors tend to be understated, humble, and self-revealing.
10. Bodily, rather than merely cognitive, participation in worship is the norm.
11. The "gifts of the spirit" (a phrase that normally embraces "speaking in tongues") are affirmed.
12. Bible-centered preaching predominates over topical sermonizing. (Miller 1997:20)

Kimon Howland Sargeant did a study of a similar (but not identical) phenomenon, a group of loosely connected Christian churches designed very specifically to market the faith to the unchurched. She looked at very rapidly growing churches, many of which either are or are becoming megachurches (Sargeant 2000). These religious movements are referred to as "seeker churches" because they are designed to appeal to religiously alienated "seekers." The population they address, the adoption of modern media, the insistence on upbeat messages, the ideas of marketing the faith through paying attention to method of delivery, the willingness to modify aspects of the faith to meet consumer demand, and the leadership by innovative (and often theologically untrained) religious entrepreneurs makes these organizations relevant to our focus on marketing of religion. For example, Sargeant said that "seeker church experts often proclaim the shopping mall, Disney, and other customer-sensitive companies as models for the twenty-first-century church" (Sargeant 2000:8).

We will draw from the literature on both new paradigm and seeker groups in the remainder of this chapter. With Miller, we will consider "seeker-sensitive churches" as one type of new paradigm church. As you read the following sections, consult the "Illustrating Sociological Concepts" feature at the end of the chapter for an extended case study of a new paradigm seeker church, New Church North Carolina.

The Audience: Targeting Markets

Like any good business that pays attention to marketing, seeker and new paradigm churches have focused on specific target markets. They analyze the characteristics of their target group and make adjustments to attract that population. Indeed, they sometimes hire consultants to conduct surveys of interest and needs of the local population and to develop market strategy action plans (Sargeant 2000). It is important to realize what a profound shift this represents in evangelism. It would never have occurred to Great Awakening preachers like Jonathan Edwards to target the market. He simply preached what he believed to be the truth and trusted it would fall on receptive ears. While later evangelists such as Charles Finney, Dwight Moody, and Billy Sunday introduced a marketing perspective (Sunday calculated the "efficiency" of revivals by determining the cost per convert and advocated "scientific management in the pulpit"), they did not focus explicitly on target markets or market shares.

While there are variations on the theme, new paradigm churches have largely targeted middle- to upper-middle-class families, especially those who were part of the Baby Boom Generation and are college educated. Often the targeted group is "the unchurched," but since white Baby Boomers, young adults, and the college educated are the least likely folks to be active in a church, and

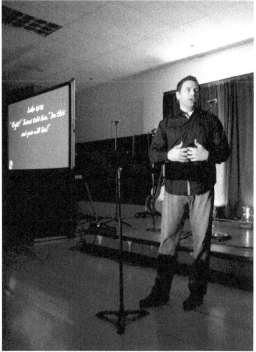

T. J. Ward is the founder and pastor of a new paradigm church in North Carolina. Shown here casually preaching in jeans and an untucked dress shirt, he exemplifies all of the characteristics of new paradigm clergy highlighted by Donald Miller.

since Baby Boomers are a very large segment of the population, the target quickly becomes this same cohort. People who fit that profile generally have certain characteristics in common, and the new paradigm clergy are highly sensitive to those traits.

Thus, a key element of new paradigm churches is the desire to be *culturally relevant*. Miller wrote, "Simply put, if the message is going to communicate with an intended audience, it must be culturally appropriate" (Miller 1997:28). He further quoted a new paradigm minister as saying, "If [nonbelievers] are going to reject the message I preach, let them reject it, but let them reject the message and not all the peripheral things that are secondary" (Miller 1997:66). Market-sensitive churches therefore try to appeal to people through themes that have cultural currency with middle-aged, well-educated Americans:

- They use the language of the therapeutic community (though they may reject the narcissistic elements of that subculture).
- They stress individualism.
- They are intensely antiestablishment (opposed to bureaucracy, but not necessarily antagonistic to the dominant culture, per se).
- They employ the metaphors of consumerist America, with the mall as a model of the good life.
- They appeal to the cultural styles that are current with the targeted cohort, such as music styles.

What this means is that direct requests for money are carefully avoided and offerings are unobtrusive (sometimes as minimalist as a box at the exit for contributions). Because "product loyalty" is very weak (including loyalty to a denomination), any affiliation to a denomination—if it does exist—is downplayed. Most new paradigm churches are independent, and those that *are* affiliated with a mainline denomination do not indicate that affiliation on their signs or their literature. This seems to be in keeping with the anti-bureaucracy attitudes of the Baby Boomers. Music is decidedly contemporary and upbeat, with a very strong preference for vocal and band music over the ponderous melodies of Bach played on an organ. Indeed, as was noted, guitars are everywhere, and meeting houses in the early years of a church's growth are likely to be rented space in a mall, a renovated warehouse, or a rented auditorium with no stained glass or other accoutrements of traditional religious settings. Baby Boomers by and large have a negative image of "organized religion," so the setting and the attire are not conventional "high church." People dress very casually—including the ministers in many such congregations. Pastor Lee McFarland was pictured in the *New York Times*

Magazine preaching in a Hawaiian shirt. This target group wants direct access to spirituality, not a mediated experience through ordained clergy. They are often free with bodily expression in worship, reaching levels of euphoria that would be embarrassing in mainline churches.

The historical Protestant idea of the "priesthood of all believers" resonates well with the members of new paradigm churches. Lay leadership is encouraged, pastors are understated in their leadership styles (even though they may be very much in charge behind the scenes), and members are invited to make their own interpretations of the meaning of scripture to their lives.

Sargeant wrote, "One might describe the dominant characteristic of this cultural ethos as consumerism. People today, especially middle-class baby boomers, expect, even demand, choice in their workplace, home, shopping options, *and* their religious commitments" (Sargeant 2000:42). If religious individuals are the consumers in this equation, then religious communities are the producers of religious products that must be appealing in a competitive marketplace.

Creating an Appealing "Product"

Many unchurched people who are white-collar professionals are more comfortable in a business or consumer environment than in a traditional religious one. Thus, the huge Willow Creek Community Church near Chicago has developed a campus of new buildings that look more like a modern community college or a corporate training center than a faith community. Indeed, a mall is often explicitly used as a model of what these churches should be like, once they become large enough to build their own facilities. Sargeant wrote,

Every aspect of the church's facilities emulates the best of corporate America in quality, design, and style. Willow Creek's aim is to reduce or minimize any cognitive dissonance between the religious realm and the working and shopping world of sub-urban middle-class Americans. (Sargeant 2000:19)

Many seeker-sensitive churches are even afraid of making people uncomfortable with too much religious symbolism, so a surprisingly high number of these evangelical churches do not even have a cross in the worship auditorium or in any prominent place (Sargeant 2000).

Tradition is often avoided as well. Sargeant reported that "seeker churches have taken a very low view of tradition in all of its various meanings. Tradition, according to many pastors, poses an unnecessary barrier for seekers. . . . Tradition, in short, represents the old paradigm, an outdated way of doing things that is largely ineffective in the current religious environment" (Sargeant 2000:63). So eager are such churches to be user-friendly to the unchurched that American holidays are often highlighted over Christian holy days. In roughly a fourth of the seeker-sensitive congregations, there is not even any communion as part of worship, despite the fact that these are led by emphatically evangelical Christians (Sargeant 2000). In the interests of recruitment, these churches have jettisoned aspects of organized religion that alienate young adults and baby boomers (Miller 1997).

Services are designed to appeal to the cultural preferences of the target group; the pre-worship music is often light rock or soft jazz "because rock music has played such an important role in the lives of baby boomers" (Sargeant 2000:65). The music style helps to define what kind of people a faith community wants to attract. Praise music is often written locally and is very rhythmical and upbeat. An important point is that these sounds are *love songs to God* rather than lyrics *about* God. Miller even describes the musical portion of the services as "a form of sacred love-making" to God (Miller 1997:87). They are easy to sing and are emotionally evocative.

Of course this is also a population that seeks the novel and the innovative, so spontaneity prevails over ritual and contemplation;

the services are often designed to surprise and intrigue attendees. Baby Boomers generally do not cope with boredom patiently. Innovation is the name of the game. Drama is often employed as a major element of the morning service, as are multimedia entertaining "shorts." Everything is very carefully choreographed and rehearsed, with timing as important as in a Broadway theatrical production. The pastor, while giving the image of a down-home sort of person, is actually performing as a CEO in a major corporation (Sargeant 2000).

Seeker-sensitive churches try to present the gospel in a way that is relevant to the lives of attendees. Unlike many new paradigm churches that have sermons based on verse-by-verse explication of the Bible, the explicitly "seeker-sensitive churches" present messages that are topical and pragmatic. Message titles include "Fanning the Flames of Marriage," "Authenticity," "The Art of Decision Making," and "Energy Management" (Sargeant 2000:18). Sargeant pointed out that one danger of emphasis on "relevance" is that "the audience and not the messenger, determines, at the very least, the topics and tone of the message" (Sargeant 2000:81).

There is a danger in marketing religion, however, which brings us back to the issue of mixed motivations in a complex organization. In her study of televangelism empires, Frankl found that like any other institution, a religious corporation can face dilemmas that can compromise the original mission of the organization. The survival of a huge organization requires generation of large amounts of money to keep the organization going. Organizational maintenance of the huge financial enterprise may lead to goal displacement so that even the core beliefs of the group may be modified (Frankl 1987). According to Frankl, the content of religious programming in a market-driven religious enterprise often becomes transformed; it is based no longer on the message of the founder but on rationally calculated economic needs of the "business" to prosper.

In today's media world, content must be simple, fast-paced, and entertaining—not complex and thought-provoking—so the message itself may have to be truncated to meet the market needs. The message of Christianity may undergo scrutiny for its marketability and be modified accordingly. If a message is popular with the public, it "sells" well: The money pours in. So there is a temptation to preach only on those things that are profitable and to avoid preaching on those things that do not yield a financial reward. So the marriage of Christian message with marketing can sometimes change the message itself. The marketing process—changing the message to adapt to the market—may distort the message that the founder intended. This is a worst-case scenario that you may consider as you learn about marketing a faith and efforts to avoid compromising it.

In this way, the church becomes a place for therapeutic comfort or for maximizing one's full potential. God is *immanent* (a nearby source of comfort) but not a *transcendent* being who sets standards for a life lived in covenant with the divine. As Sargeant put it, "Seeker church pastors de-emphasize God's inscrutability, God's mystery, and God's ultimate judgment" (Sargeant 2000:85). These things just do not "sell" well with this population.

Sin is recast as preventing realization of one's potential as a human being. The measure of profound spirituality remains: "Is your soul being satisfied?" By contrast, First and Second Great Awakening evangelists believed that God had chosen the elect and God's satisfaction was all that mattered; using human subjectivity as a standard of authentic Godliness would have been offensive and profoundly un-Christian to them. However, we live in a different time. Sargeant summarized it this way: "For today's religious consumers, the search for meaning and fulfillment is as important—and initially even more important—than the search for God. . . . God becomes the means toward our fulfillment, rather than the end toward whom we owe our allegiance" (Sargeant 2000:98, 121).

In addition to the worship hour being adapted, two other types of programs cater to the needs of the congregation. These seeker-sensitive churches are not necessarily different from other congregations, but they are clearly more intentional and more focused. First, they provide a wide range of entertainment and social opportunities: movie nights, marriage renewal weekends, family camping retreats, basketball and softball leagues, handball tournaments, and so forth. These are sometimes called the "side doors" of recruitment by church-growth consultants, since they are ways of attracting people to the church other than the historically preferred "front door": the Sunday morning church service (Mahler 2005).

Second, small groups are at the core of the ministry. Opportunities for deep intimacy are rare in a competitive capitalist society, and feelings of alienation from the structures and from other people are common. People in a dog-eat-dog, rapid-paced modern society need to feel human connection. New paradigm churches provide this. Indeed, they consider small groups to be the "*real* church experience," not the Sunday morning worship hour. Virtually every member is urged to join at least one small group, for "this is a movement built on relationships" (Miller 1997:36).

Sargeant cited the adage among leaders of these churches that "the church only grows bigger by growing smaller" (Sargeant 2000:118). These small groups can be Bible study groups, prayer groups, exclusively men's or women's gatherings, healing or therapeutic clusters, or other topical groups. However, they remain small, they challenge people to apply faith principles to their lives, they invite individuals to share intimately with one another about their lives, and they become potent reference groups. Many studies have shown that in churches of all sizes and denominations, small intimate groups are at the core of local church vitality, for we live in a society that atomizes and isolates us (e.g., see Wuthnow 1994b).

Critical Thinking: New paradigm and seeker-sensitive churches are being very self-conscious about their marketing strategies to draw members. Yet Max Weber insists that people have always been more likely to join churches where there is "elective affinity" to their social, cultural, or economic circumstances. Is this any different? Does it make a difference whether the leaders unintentionally draw people with similar cultural values or interests or intentionally target an audience and modify the message to have greater appeal? Why?

Pragmatism About Methods and an Uncompromising Message

New paradigm clergy believe that they have changed the medium or the methods of delivery, but not the message. Scholars who study these groups are less sanguine that they have been successful in not compromising the message itself. Sargeant concluded that "changing the *method* can not only change your results; it can also change your *message*" (Sargeant 2000:131). A basic principle of marketing, of course, is that the product *ought* to change in order to meet the demand.

We have seen that marketed Christianity tends to become infused with local or national values—embracing consumerism, shying away from asking the larger ethical questions about the consequences of one's behavior on others or on the natural environment, and even blessing a certain amount of self-absorption. Yet leaders of these new paradigm churches have tried to be self-conscious about what they believe to be the core of the faith—what is *not* open to compromise. It may be that their decisions about what is the kernel and what is chaff may differ from yours or mine or the mainline minister down the street, but there are some things on which they will not budge.

The centrality of Jesus Christ is affirmed, as is the importance of a personal relationship with

Jesus. The notion that human depravity is part of the human condition is affirmed, even if it is given a soft sell and is sold as a matter of self-actualization. Interestingly, a central theme in the Baby Boom Generation is tolerance for others who are different—an openness to acknowledging that what is right for me is not necessarily right for you. This is perhaps the first generation of Americans in which the majority affirms that there are multiple paths to God, each with equal legitimacy. Indeed, at the turn of the 21st century, a Gallup Poll reported that of Americans who identify with a religious group, 82% said other paths to God are as legitimate as their own path (Gallup Organization 2000). However, new paradigm churches are quite uniform in rejecting this notion. They proclaim that Jesus offers the exclusive access to God. This is an issue that for them is a core belief and is not to be compromised.

Another core belief is the authority of the Bible. This is a firm affirmation. Yet the new paradigm churches have avoided stridency or the appearance of intolerance on this issue. This seems to be related to the fact that they "are doctrinal minimalists," according to Miller (1997:121). "Their emphasis is on one's relationship to Jesus Christ, not on whether one believes [specific dogmas]. New paradigm Christians view doctrine as being of human origin." Miller continues,

> What typically gives stridency to biblical literalism is its use in the service of doctrinal dogmatism, as the justification for an attack on other beliefs. However, the deemphasis of doctrine by new paradigm Christians puts a different spin on the way scripture is utilized. Although they view the Bible as authoritative, there seems to be a certain modesty in terms of the conclusions that one should draw. (Miller 1997:131).

While the authority of scripture is affirmed, the intolerance that middle-class Baby Boomers find offensive is avoided. This rather "soft" approach to interpretation is consistent with new paradigm principles of priesthood of all believers in interpreting the meaning of the faith. In this case, compatibility with target-group values is achieved without compromise of basic principles.

The new paradigm ministers try to keep clarity about the message, the model, and the market: how these interact, which are most important, and which cannot be compromised. They do not all agree on where the lines should be drawn. Indeed, while some leaders in new paradigm churches actively utilize the language of the business world, not all are comfortable with this. Sargeant quoted a minister of music in one Baptist church: "People may think because we are a church, maybe we shouldn't market. But any organization, secular or otherwise, if [it's] going to grow, [it's] got to get people to buy into the product" (Sargeant 2000:5). On the other hand, Miller found that most new paradigm pastors do not use the rational choice language about "selling a product." They generally avoid the crass utilitarian terminology of the marketplace. Still, the leaders of these new paradigm churches are "entrepreneurs" in the sense that they innovate freely and seek to meet demand in the marketplace, but their purpose is spiritual. Ultimately a faith community is not a business seeking economic profits. For pastors and members, the purpose is spiritual, and that makes a huge difference in standards of conduct. It is mostly social scientists using marketing perspectives who are likely to refer to individual congregations as local "franchises."

Critical Thinking: Is "marketing" of religion intrinsically a problem that causes distortions of religion, or does competition in the marketplace of ideas add vitality and intensified commitment to religion? Why do you think as you do?

ILLUSTRATING SOCIOLOGICAL CONCEPTS

New Church North Carolina as a New Paradigm Seeker Church

David Yamane

In January 2011, as I was sorting through my junk mail for the day, I noticed yet another glossy cardstock mailer advertising yet another store's greatest sale event that I would surely not attend. This one caught my eye because it boldly proclaimed in all caps with fireworks in the background, "GRAND FREAKING OPENING." Imagine my surprise when I turned the mailer over to find that it was advertising the grand opening of "New Church" in Winston-Salem, North Carolina. Reminiscent of Radiant Church in Sunrise, Arizona, the card read: "It's a new year, and we're starting a New Church with friendly people, excellent children's environments, and practical teaching! We realize there is no shortage of churches in this area, but we also understand it takes different types of churches to reach different types of people. If you aren't currently involved in church, we would like to invite you to our Grand Opening!"

I arrive at the large YMCA complex for the first service a bit nervous, not quite knowing what to expect. I was immediately put at ease by a warm welcome from a member of the "host team" at the front of the building who gave me a bubble gum cigar to thank me for helping to celebrate the "birth" of New Church. I walk past the front desk of the "Y" and into a fitness class studio that has been transformed into a worship space by pipe-and-drape barriers, portable light standards, folding chairs, and yards of cables and wiring.

Photo by Sandra Stroud Yamane

Screens on either side of the stage project a countdown timer. When it reaches 0:00 the band launches into "Happy Day," a popular contemporary Christian song. "The greatest day in history / Death is beaten, You have rescued me / Sing it out, Jesus is alive / Oh, happy day, happy day / You washed my sin away / Oh, happy day, happy day / I'll never be the same / Forever I am changed." The four-piece band includes a drummer playing on an electric kit, a guitarist, and banjo and bass players. Bassist Jeremy Martin leads worship. He looks young with his shaggy hair and untucked shirt, until he is joined in singing by his wife Martha, who looks even younger in her jeans, New Church T-shirt, and nose ring. Sitting in the back row, I can feel the drumbeats in my chest, though later the guy working the audio board tells me the sound-level meter reading of 95 decibels was just what they were looking for.

Twenty minutes into the service, Pastor T. J. Ward takes the stage. His uniform is neat, but casual—dress jeans and a button-up shirt, tucked in for this special occasion. Wearing a wireless microphone, he places his iPad on a simple black music stand and invites people to open their Bibles if they have them. In my row, no one pulls out a printed text, but one person uses an iPad and another studies her smartphone Bible.

In green and black to match the New Church color scheme, Ward's plaid shirt accentuates his stocky build. I am not surprised to learn at the beginning of his sermon that he loves football (he played in college) and hates rice cakes. For the next 20 minutes, Ward preaches about "New You," moving effortlessly back and forth between references to scripture—always projected onto the screens in front—and to everyday life. They key passage from which New Church derived its name and vision is 2 Corinthians 5:17: "Therefore, if anyone is in Christ, he

(Continued)

(Continued)

is a new creation; the old has gone, the new has come!" He pairs this with a story about an outlaw biker who commits his life to Christ.

By the end of the service just before 11:00 a.m., I count 125 to 150 people, a very respectable turnout considering that the average congregation in the United States has just 70 regular participants. As quickly as the service ends, New Church volunteers get to work breaking down and storing every seat, sign, stand, cable, table, light, projector, and instrument, and any other object that is not a part of the permanent structure, so the YMCA can open for business at noon.

Reflecting on what I had experienced on my drive home, I thought about how New Church shares many of the 12 common features of new paradigm churches enumerated by Donald Miller. Moreover, observing the church over the next four years, I continued to see many ways in which it aspires to be a "seeker-sensitive" church, especially targeting "markets," creating an appealing "product," and combining pragmatic methods with an uncompromising message.

Targeting Markets. At first glance, it seems odd to "plant" an evangelical Protestant church in the middle of the Bible Belt, but New Church did not end up in Winston-Salem, North Carolina, by accident. T. J. Ward consulted with several church planting organizations, one of which suggested there could be a need for a nontraditional church in Winston-Salem, and the church planting arm of the Baptist State Convention of North Carolina helped with additional information and training.

Having grown up in a staunchly traditional Southern Baptist church in Jacksonville, Florida, Ward understands that it is entirely possible for people to be unchurched or alienated from church even in areas saturated with them—or *because* they are saturated with them. He understands how people can be turned off by traditional forms of church, church politics, and clique-iness. His goal is to market to this felt need of the community for some faithful alternative to these alienating forms of church. As the New Church motto puts it: "it's church . . . just different."

Although New Church expects and hopes for regular attendees, time is set aside at the beginning of every service to welcome new guests and to explain what they can expect from the service. Not only is there no expectation that all attendees will be "members" of New Church (indeed, it does not even have any type of formal membership), there is not even an expectation that those attending will be Christians. When Ward or the student minister Josh Black preach, it is common to hear phrases such as "If you are new to church . . ." or "If you are a Christian . . ." The "ifs" here are telling. According to Ward, "I hope we never have a Sunday when everyone in there is a Christian because that is not what we are called to do."

Not everyone agrees with this calling. Some people let him know they were praying for him after receiving the "GRAND FREAKING OPENING" mailer, and another person cut up a different mailer and sent it back to the YMCA. The way Ward handles criticism of New Church's approach is telling. He simply replies: They are not our audience. Instead, he focuses on the incest survivor who coped for years by abusing alcohol and sex, but found Christ during New Church's series called "NC Ink" (see below). This, after all, is the bottom line: to help as many people as possible to develop a relationship with Christ, the only avenue for salvation.

Creating an Appealing Product. Perhaps the most conventional aspect of New Church is its structure of worship. Across all congregations in North America, there are two universal elements of worship: singing and preaching (see Table 8.1). In an hour-long Sunday service at New Church, two thirds of the time is given over to music and a sermon. Within those universals, however, there is considerable variation from congregation to congregation, and it is in that variation that we see the desire to create an appealing product at New Church.

In targeting the market of people who are unchurched or alienated from traditional churches, New Church tries to make attending church a fun and uplifting experience. Contemporary music, a come-as-you are atmosphere, and positive sermons on practical topics are par for the course. No one is scandalized when the band shows up pierced and tattooed, or T. J. Ward shows a clip from *Meet the Fockers* to make a point, or Josh Black preaches wearing a fitted ball cap, or their flip-flop–wearing neighbor ambles in 10 minutes into the service drinking a Starbucks Pumpkin Spice Latte.

The attempt to create an appealing product can be seen most clearly in how New Church celebrates baptism. Traditional Protestant theology maintains that baptism, along with Communion, is one of the two ordinances (prescribed practices) instituted by Jesus Christ for the church. Just because Christ prescribed it does not mean it cannot be fun. To the contrary, because it symbolizes individuals' acceptance of Jesus Christ as Lord and Savior, it is the greatest cause for celebration.

Hence, from the start New Church has had a line item in its budget: "baptism parties." Twice a year, New Church has a *party* during which its leaders baptize people. In the YMCA's parking lot, along with a cattle trough large enough to accommodate full-body immersion, you will find party accessories like a DJ, a bounce house, face painting, and food. The baptisms themselves are greeted by cowbells and clappers in the audience, and the baptized wear T-shirts reading "I took the PLUNGE at New Church."

Bringing people to Christ is the most important thing to T. J. Ward and his team at New Church. It is evidence that they have successfully targeted an underserved market and created an appealing product. At the church's first anniversary service in January 2012, Ward reflected on the previous 12 months and proudly noted that 77 people at New Church placed their faith in Christ, including 18 who were baptized. An appealing product is never an end in itself. It is a means, a vehicle, pragmatically chosen to reach the end.

Pragmatism About Methods and an Uncompromising Message. T. J. Ward has learned a lot from Craig Groeschel of the Oklahoma-based megachurch LifeChurch.tv. Part of the staff meetings I attended in the first weeks of New Church's existence were given over to discussion of Groeschel's book and companion DVD, *It: How Churches and Leaders Can Get It and Keep It*. It is not surprising then that Ward has often invoked the LifeChurch.tv motto: "We will do anything short of sin to reach people who don't know Christ."

This was abundantly evident in one of the most controversial teaching series in the brief history of New Church: NC Ink. Not a year into its existence, New Church sent over 25,000 mailers to postal addresses in a 5-mile radius of the YMCA offering the opportunity to "WIN A FREE TATTOO AT CHURCH." The purpose was to announce a new four-week teaching series

(Continued)

(Continued)

on how people are "marked to make a difference." It was hard for many to ignore the drawing for a free tattoo that had been donated to New Church by a local artist.

Ward used the obviously provocative campaign to make the point that it is totally acceptable to "use culture to redeem culture," and that tattoos with Christian symbols are examples of this. According to Ward, the basis for all truth is the Holy Bible, and there is nothing in the Bible that says tattoos are sinful. The ceremonial laws expressed in certain parts of the Old Testament are not binding, while the moral laws represented in the New Testament are. The pragmatism of using a tattoo to draw attention to the church is thereby combined with an uncompromising message based in scripture.

The New Church website (newchurchnc.org) lists the four non-negotiable core beliefs of the church: (1) The Bible is without error, (2) believers have a Trinitarian view of God (Father, Son, and Holy Spirit), (3) humanity is alienated from God by original sin, and (4) salvation is only available through repentance of sin and faith in Jesus Christ. These core beliefs have certain consequences for understandings of controversial issues such as abortion (no), same-sex marriage (no), and any sex outside of marriage (no).

Ever the optimist, however, T. J. Ward would much rather talk about what New Church is *for* rather than what it is *against*. New Church is about creating an opportunity for people to come to Christ who otherwise might not. When it celebrated its fourth anniversary in January 2015, New Church was averaging over 300 attendees at its two Sunday services, had three full-time and two part-time paid staff members, and had helped facilitate the salvation of over 150 souls.

SUMMARY

Denominationalism was born as a fundamentally American phenomenon, rooted in the pluralism of the new continent and the new country. Separation of church and state became central principles of the founders as they realized that religious tolerance and public policy need to be based on rational deliberation. This is the way the best interests of the country can be served in a culturally and religiously diverse society. In this environment, each religious group had to organize without state tax support. As congregations with similar outlooks or similar issues and cultures looked for ways to provide mutual support, denominations became the vehicle to do so.

When religious groups that did not organize themselves into larger umbrella groups immigrated to the United States (Muslims, for example), they have tended to follow the pattern of "institutional isomorphism"—becoming like other religious communities in the environment. Moreover, this pattern of denominationalism has now spread around the globe to other places that are religiously and culturally diverse. Still, as we enter the third millennium, denominationalism seems less compelling as people organize around religious special purpose groups. Nondenominational Christian churches are now the largest "brand" of religious congregation in the United States.

Congregationalism—in which local congregations have a good deal of power and authority and no bishop controls policy—is also preeminently American. Even the more hierarchically organized churches—those with episcopal or presbyterian polities—have elements of congregationalism when they are in the United States. Congregations do vary in many ways: When we compare congregations, the median size of a congregation is 70, but because some congregations are huge, the typical American attends a congregation of about 400. Regardless of size or style of worship, congregations provide a range of resources and support to their members.

The most notable phenomenon in the past three decades has been the rise of megachurches, congregations of more than 2,000 attendees, and the related rise of multi-site congregations, single congregations that meet in multiple locations. These developments are closely associated with the broader movements toward increasing nondenominationalism and transdenominational evangelical Protestantism.

Also associated with these megachurches is a relatively new phenomenon—the explicit and intentional marketing of the faith so it will "sell" and so the organization can grow and thrive. This marketing involves finding target "markets" where there is a need and producing a "product"— a religious product—that will sell to that market. Critics claim that this includes a truncating and distortion of the message, but adaption of a faith to a new environment is hardly new or innovative. It has existed for a very long time.

One of the ways that religion is modified is that it must meet the needs for meaning of people in different socioeconomic circumstances. Thus we turn next to the issue of religion and inequality—how religion affects economic development and how it is affected by economic factors in the environment.

PART V

RELIGION AND SOCIAL INEQUALITY

In the next three chapters, we examine the interactive relationship between religion and the social structures and processes of the larger society. These chapters are designed to illustrate the sociological method of analysis; they are certainly not exhaustive treatments of the influence of religion on other social structures or of other social structures on religion.

One of the important elements of social structure is the stratification system. Four main dimensions of social stratification in contemporary society are (1) social class, (2) race, (3) gender, and (4) sexuality. Therefore, in Chapter 9, we investigate the interrelationships between social class and religion. Chapter 10 considers race and religion; and Chapter 11 examines gender, sexuality, and religion. In each case, religion is examined as both a dependent and an independent variable.

In Chapter 12, we address an important issue regarding religion and social status that arises from the considerations of inequality in Chapters 9 through 11, the relationship between religion and social activism aimed at redressing social inequality.

9

RELIGION, ECONOMICS, AND SOCIAL CLASS

HERE ARE SOME QUESTIONS TO PONDER AS YOU READ THIS CHAPTER

- Can religion influence economic behavior and socioeconomic status? If so, how?
- Did religious beliefs have any role in the formation of capitalism as an economic system?
- What specific aspects of religious commitment might influence one's economic conduct or circumstances?
- How might socioeconomic status influence religious behavior or beliefs?
- Which is more likely to influence the other: religion or economics?

One of the most important factors in shaping the life chances and life experiences of people is economics. In this chapter, we explore how socioeconomic circumstances affect religion and how religion, in turn, impacts economic behavior. We begin by investigating the role of religion as a causal variable that affects one's economic behavior.

RELIGIOUS ETHICS AND ECONOMIC ACTION

Weber's Protestant Ethic Thesis

Among the important factors determining the social status of individuals in any society are the economic behavior of those individuals and the nature of the economic system itself. Many scholars have wondered about the extent to which religion affects economic behavior: To what extent is religion an independent variable influencing economics? The landmark study on this issue has been Max Weber's seminal work, *The Protestant Ethic and the Spirit of Capitalism* ([1904–1905] 1958a), for it has generated an incredible amount of research and discussion.

Weber's study was undertaken in response to two issues. First, he was interested in the relationship between religion and economic activity. This study was one of a series of comparative studies of religion and its effects on economic development (Weber [1920–1921] 1951, [1920–1921] 1952, [1920–1921] 1958b, [1922] 1963).[1] In the opening sentence of *The Protestant Ethic*

([1904–1905] 1958a), Weber pointed out that Protestants tend to be more affluent than Catholics and to occupy the higher-status positions in virtually all industrialized societies. He was interested in the relationship between religious affiliation and social stratification, including the differential effects of various faiths.

Second, Weber wished to address a larger theoretical issue. He hoped to provide a corrective to the simple economic determinism of Karl Marx. Marx had maintained that one's economic status was the principal determining factor in all behavior. He felt that it was fruitless to try to understand human behavior as an expression of values, ideals, or beliefs. Marx believed that beliefs and values are a *result* of economic forces, that one's ideas and ideals act to justify one's economic fortunes—or to compensate one for a lack thereof. Religion served to justify and sacralize the current social arrangements. Because of this, it helped reinforce the status quo and served to retard change. For Marx, values, beliefs, and ideals do not serve as primary causal forces; they are secondary factors that result from economic forces.

Marx recognized that beliefs—including religion—could serve as *proximate* causes, even as he insisted that they are not *ultimate* causes. He acknowledged that humans are active agents and that beliefs organize and propel one's actions. It was for this reason that he stressed the importance of the working class changing from "false consciousness" to "class consciousness." He also emphasized that religion often served as an opiate of the masses—again revealing his

---

[1] Weber's interest in accounting for the distinctive pattern of development in the modern West, especially the rise of modern capitalism, was a key concern of the founders of the discipline of sociology. *The Protestant Ethic* (Weber [1904–1905] 1958a) was one part of a planned multivolume work on the religions of the world. Weber did not ultimately complete the project, but three volumes were published in 1920 and 1921: *Ancient Judaism* (Weber [1920–1921] 1952), *The Religion of China* (Confucianism and Taoism) (Weber [1920–1921] 1951), and *The Religion of India* (Hinduism and Buddhism) (Weber [1920–1921] 1958b). His thesis in this massive comparative–historical project was that civilizations outside the West could not internally generate a "spirit of capitalism." The "inner-worldly asceticism" of Protestantism in the West thus played a key role in helping motivate and diffuse the spirit necessary for capitalism to arise.

awareness of the influence of beliefs and ideas on action. Without ignoring this awareness, it is also accurate to say that Marx believed ideas are powerfully conditioned by material (or economic) circumstances. Economic forces were viewed as the principal factors in shaping human behavior; ideas, values, and beliefs were only proximate influences and were themselves largely shaped by economic forces. Religion, which deals in values, ideals, and beliefs as its primary currency, was viewed as a relatively unimportant force—at least for those interested in the principal factors that cause social change or ultimately shape human behavior.

Some writers have claimed that Weber's study was intended as a direct refutation of Marx, but this clearly was not the case. Weber agreed with Marx's contention that economic self-interests have a powerful effect on the beliefs and values of people. Yet, Weber viewed this position as only a partial truth. He insisted that while economics can affect religion, religion can also affect economics. In fact, he held that Protestantism (especially Calvinism) was a significant force in the formation of capitalism as an economic system. Rather than being a refutation of Marx, Weber viewed his study as a modification or corrective to the overly simplistic analysis by Marx. Although he accepted Marx's view that people behave in ways that enhance their own self-interests, Weber felt that perceptions of self-interest were not limited to the economic realm. A religious self-interest (e.g., concern over salvation) could also motivate people.

In *The Protestant Ethic and the Spirit of Capitalism* ([1904–1905] 1958a), Weber attempted to identify how religious beliefs and self-interests had affected economic behavior. In focusing on the Protestant "ethic," he was really referring to the overall perspective and sense of values of Protestantism. He felt that the breakthrough from the feudalistic to the capitalistic economic system was substantially enhanced by this particular worldview. In sum, he felt that ideas could be important factors that facilitate social change, including changes in the economic system.

For capitalism to thrive, several conditions had to be met. There had to be a pool of individuals with the characteristics necessary to serve as entrepreneurs. They had to be individualistic and had to believe in the virtues of hard work and of simplicity of lifestyle. Protestantism tended to create a supply of such people. Although economic self-interests create such people today, Weber maintained that the original pool was formed largely by people motivated by religious beliefs and self-interests.

One of the primary concerns of people in the 15th and 16th centuries was their eternal salvation. One way to be assured of salvation was to serve God directly. If one was called by God to the priesthood or to holy orders in a monastery, one seemed to have a better chance of eternal salvation. However, taking a new slant, Martin Luther stressed the "priesthood of all believers" and insisted that one could be called by God to a variety of occupations that served humanity. This new concept of a calling is referred to as his *doctrine of vocation*, for the word *vocation* means calling. According to Luther's teachings, one may be called to many types of secular positions, as well as to the priesthood. Because secular positions were also viewed as service to God, any form of work could be a means of expressing one's faith. Hard work became a way of serving and glorifying God. Idleness or laziness, by logical extension, came to be viewed as a sin. Although Luther initiated this concept of vocation and held to it in principle, it was the Calvinists who fully implemented it. In fact, John Calvin even suggested that when a person was hard at work, he or she was most in the image of God.

Industriousness was an essential quality for the emergence of a class of entrepreneurs, and this quality was a central virtue among Calvinists. However, it was not enough for people simply to develop an ethic of hard work. The rational investment of earnings was also critical. Weber believed that the Protestant emphasis on asceticism and on *delayed gratification* served to enhance this aspect of capitalistic enterprise. Asceticism was a major theme in the preaching of a number of reformers, for the pleasures of the world (gambling, drinking, secular forms of entertainment, and luxuries) were all viewed as sinful and evil. God required a simple, even austere, lifestyle. Calvin even described self-discipline as the "nerves of religion"; hence, self-denial became a central virtue. This denial of present desires was accomplished because of the principle of delayed gratification. Believers were willing to forgo pleasures now for the promise of much greater rewards in the future. In the case of reformers, the future rewards were anticipated in the afterlife. Nonetheless, the principle of delayed gratification is an important one for the development of economic capital in *this* world. In fact, Weber defined capitalism as the systematic investment of time and resources with the hope of significant returns in the future (profits). The idea of denying one's immediate desires in the hope of a greater return in the future was basic both to Calvinism and to capitalism.

Among many of the early Protestants—and especially among Calvinists—hard work was a moral and religious duty, but because income from one's industriousness was not to be spent on luxuries or sensual pleasures, the only thing to do was to invest it. Among Methodists and certain other Protestant sects, excess income was to be given to the poor, but according to R. H. Tawney, the Calvinists felt that people who were impoverished were poor simply because they were lazy. Not wishing to contribute to this wickedness, Calvinists were not inclined to donate much of their income to the needy. Most of their profits were available for investment. This created a situation in which increased amounts of capital were available in the society and economic growth was enhanced (Tawney [1924] 1954).

Other characteristics of Calvinism were also significant. One of the important doctrines in Calvin's theology was that of *predestination.* According to this doctrine, God has already decided who is saved and who is damned. One's fate is predetermined, and there is really nothing a person can do about it. This doctrine might easily have resulted in a sense of fatalism, despair,

and despondency, but in this case, people coped with their anxiety about whether they were saved by acting as if they were. Of course, this would not improve their chances, but any impious or un-Christian behavior would only ensure to themselves and others that they were damned. Righteous behavior would be an outward and visible sign (to one's neighbors) of one's eternal status. Being righteous, thrifty, hardworking, and ascetic was a way of hedging one's bets.

Furthermore, this predestined state placed one in a position of radical individualism. One was not saved because of anything others did or because of the groups one belonged to. One was strictly on one's own in this matter of salvation. Weber wrote,

> In what was for the man of the age of the Reformation the most important thing in his life, he was forced to follow his path alone to meet a destiny which had been decreed for him from eternity. No one could help him. . . . the Calvinist's intercourse with his God was carried on in deep spiritual isolation. (Weber [1904–1905] 1958a:104–107)

Because an attitude of rugged individualism was important for the entrepreneur, the sense of religious individualism provided a compatible outlook. In fact, Weber suggested that the religious individualism may have partially predated and thereby contributed to the attitude of economic individualism. Economic individualism, in turn, means that individuals make rational economic decisions based on their own self-interests. Once capitalism is formed, according to Weber, it is capable of sustaining its own individualistic motivations. Still, he suggested that religious self-interests and beliefs may have contributed to the *original formation* of capitalism.

Finally, Calvin emphasized that the proper aim of humanity is not personal salvation but the glorification of God through the sanctification of this world. This focus created a strong this-worldly component to the theology, for one's labors in transforming this realm—the here and now—were the best indicators of one's devotion to God. Later Calvinists (Puritans) reinforced a this-worldly orientation even further by suggesting that one's socioeconomic status was an indicator of one's spiritual grace and eternal destination. Delayed gratification and asceticism became increasingly this-worldly and rational (i.e., based on concrete self-interest).

Due to certain beliefs, then, 15th-century Europe was supplied with an increasing supply of capital for investment and a pool of individuals who had the values and attitudes appropriate to becoming entrepreneurs. Although these characteristics were not *sufficient* to bring on the development of capitalism, they were *necessary*, and Weber believed that religion had contributed to the formation of the capitalistic system of economics by supplying these characteristics. He maintained that a religious outlook had influenced the economic behavior and financial fortunes of individuals (Protestants becoming more affluent than non-Protestants) and also had contributed to the development of a new economic system. Contrary to Marx, Weber felt that religion was capable of being a cause of economic conditions—not just a result.

Weber's thesis has been highly controversial and in the decades following its publication generated a large number of essays and research projects, some historical and some focused on efforts to measure a "Protestant ethic" in the modern world. Some scholars have argued that Calvinism had little to do with the development of capitalism. Some insist that the beginning of colonialism (with its influx of new capital resources) and changes in post-medieval technology sparked the advent of capitalism. Others emphasize the fact that capital was available for entrepreneurs through Jewish and Catholic bankers in urban areas. In these cases, the concurrent rise of capitalism and Protestantism is seen as a simple coincidence (Samuelsson [1957] 1961). The outlook described as the Protestant ethic is viewed by these scholars as

Photo by Sandra Stroud Yamane

When he traveled to the United States in 1904, Max Weber stayed for a time with relatives at this house in Mount Airy, North Carolina. While there, he attended a Methodist service and a full immersion baptism in a mountain brook by a Baptist church. In his book, *Max Weber in America* (2011), Lawrence Scaff argues that Weber's time in the United States profoundly influenced his understanding of religion and capitalism. In the foreground is a plaque that was dedicated in 1995 and reads in part, "To commemorate the visit of German scholar Max Weber here in 1904. Max Weber is a central founder of the discipline of sociology."

insignificant—or at least its uniqueness to Protestants is denied (Hudson 1949; Fanfani 1936; Green 1959; Robertson [1933] 1959; Samuelsson [1957] 1961).

Other writers have basically agreed with Weber but have suggested modifications in his thesis. For example, R. H. Tawney suggested that most contributions of Protestantism to the development of an individualistic and laissez-faire economic system were entirely latent (unconscious and unintended). He pointed out that in the Middle Ages, the Catholic Church held usury (lending money for interest) to be on a par with adultery and fornication. Not only was lending money at interest considered immoral, but prosperity itself was viewed as a source of spiritual corruption. Both of these attitudes were carried over in the teachings of the reformers (Tawney [1924] 1954).

Luther, who represented a rural peasant orientation, was particularly opposed to self-interested individualism and to laissez-faire policies. Furthermore, he felt that it was immoral to make money through investments, lending, or any form of speculation. He held to the idea that one should be rewarded financially only in proportion to the labor one actually performs.

Calvin, on the other hand, was much more urban and secular in background and orientation. Although he was no defender of laissez-faire capitalism, he did believe that capital investment was essential to a healthy economy. Hence, he insisted that there was nothing inherently evil about investing or lending money at moderate interest. On the other hand, he did insist that no interest should be charged the poor, and he put strict ethical guidelines on economic activity. He also remained deeply suspicious of the spiritual effects of economic prosperity. At one point he commented, "Wherever prosperity flows uninterruptedly, its delight corrupts even the best of us," and at another time he suggested that "prosperity is like rust or mildew." In fact, Calvin's distrust of the influences of money is revealed in his considerable ambivalence about usury. One English

clergyman who studied Calvin's theology commented that "Calvin deals with usury as the apothocarie doth with poyson" (cited by Tawney [1924] 1954:94). It seems clear that at the manifest level both Protestants and Catholics believed that "the spirit of capitalism is foreign to every kind of religion" (Samuelsson [1957] 1961:19).

The reformers explicitly preached against certain practices that were later taken for granted as an integral part of the free enterprise system. In fact, Tawney insisted that the massive accumulations of wealth that were acquired by later industrialists were not the result of the Protestant ethic or of thriftiness. Such capital was acquired by unscrupulous exploitation of people. He agreed with Weber that Calvinistic theology and ethics subtly contributed to the advent of the free enterprise system, but he felt that early Protestant ethics were quite incompatible with the free-for-all capitalism of the 18th, 19th, and 20th centuries. Moreover, Tawney felt that capitalism would probably have made its entrance even without the contribution of Protestantism.

The most recent attempt to test the Weber thesis involved an effort to reduce Weber's broad-ranging theory to 31 specific hypotheses. These were then tested by examining journals of 17th-century Puritan entrepreneurs, the writings and sermons of 17th-century Puritan clergy, and previous analyses for data that might be relevant. Sociologist Jere Cohen concluded that some of Weber's assertions are supported by the evidence, but some specific hypotheses are not confirmed. In other words, the theory is not correct in all respects, but the entire thesis cannot be dismissed as invalid (Cohen 2002).

Cohen pointed out that religion may influence people either by direct impact on their individual behavior or by shaping the larger cultural values over time. In the latter case, specific ideas from a theology may be selectively adopted and modified. Moreover, in this latter case it is all people in the culture who come to be influenced, not only those who belong to the group that spawned the ideas. Cohen found rather weak support for direct behavioral effect of the Protestant teachings on economic behavior. On the other hand, he believed a strong case can be made that Protestant ideas were selectively used and adapted in ways that legitimated certain economic behavior in the culture itself. So Protestantism seems to have had an impact mostly through cultural diffusion. For example, Protestantism seems to have strengthened the work ethic that had been a part of the Judeo-Christian tradition, but it was not the first or the only such force.

Moreover, even if a religious group does have a strong Protestant ethic, its members will not necessarily become highly affluent. Access to natural resources, willingness to use technology and other efficient sources of energy, and economic opportunities that are available to the group within the larger social structure all affect economic circumstances. For example, maintaining a very intense work ethic and an ascetic lifestyle has not been sufficient to bring extraordinary prosperity among the Old Order Amish—who reject modern technology such as tractors. No amount of asceticism and work ethic among African Americans has fully counteracted the structural discrimination they have experienced. A profound work ethic combined with an emphasis on asceticism may contribute to affluence, but it is certainly not sufficient.

So, Protestant theology was, at best, only one of many forces for capitalist expansion. Weber himself recognized this in his mature work in which he emphasized institutional developments over religious ideals. Shortly before he died in the summer of 1920, Weber delivered a series of lectures in which he developed an institutional theory of the development of capitalism. These ideas were never published in his lifetime, but were brought together from lecture notes and published as *General Economic History* (Weber [1923] 1961). Sociologist Randall Collins has called this work of Weber "the most comprehensive general theory of the origins of capitalism that is yet available" (Collins 1980:926).

In his systematization of Weber's theory into a sequence of causal conditions, Collins places the rationalized economic ethic (of which the Protestant ethic was the archetype) alongside calculable law as one of two intermediate conditions leading to rationalized capitalism. However, these two conditions were also caused by more fundamental factors. Institutional developments such as the bureaucratic state and legal citizenship are background determinants of calculable law. Christianity's evangelical impulse brought the faith out into the world, and its universalizing impulse broke down barriers between different clans. In doing so, it was an ultimate cause of both citizenship and the economic ethic focused on this world, which was manifest in the Protestant Reformation sects that Weber initially studied. As Collins summarizes the role of the Protestant ethic thesis in Weber's mature theory:

> Protestantism is only the last intensification of one of the chains of factors leading to rational capitalism. Moreover, its effect now is conceived to be largely negative, in the sense that it removes one of the last institutional obstacles diverting the motivational impetus of Christianity away from economic rationalization. For, in medieval Christianity, the methodical, disciplined organization of life was epitomized by the monastic communities. . . . As long as the strongest religious motivation was siphoned off for essentially other-worldly ends, capitalism in general could not take off. Hence, the Reformation was most significant because it abolished the monasteries. The most advanced section of the economy would, henceforth, be secular. Moreover, the highest ethics of a religious life could no longer be confined to monks but had to apply to ordinary citizens living in the world. (Collins 1980:924)

In the end, Weber's understanding of modern capitalism is sophisticated in identifying both the institutional and motivational conditions necessary for its rise. In this sense, he complements and extends Marx's economic determinism rather than disproving it.

The Amish of Pennsylvania, Ohio, and Indiana have a very strong work ethic and live a simple life, but they do not become extremely affluent by contemporary American standards. They reject modern technology, such as tractors, and they define success in terms of faithfulness, community, and intragroup solidarity. The strong Protestant ethic has not been sufficient to create great wealth.

Critical Thinking: Does Max Weber's argument— that religious ideas can cause social change— make sense to you? Why or why not? What do conflict theorists tend to say about the role of religious ideas in a society? Do you agree? Why?

The Prosperity Gospel and Modern Capitalism

As we have seen, Weber sought to explain the role of religious values in the *rise* of modern industrial capitalism. He recognized, however, that once it was established, this economic system did not require the same religiously based ethic:

The Puritan wanted to work in a calling; we are forced to do so. For when asceticism was carried out of monastic cells into everyday life, and began to dominate worldly morality, it did its part in building the tremendous cosmos of the modern economic order. This order is now bound to the technical and economic conditions of machine production which today determine the lives of all the individuals who are born into this mechanism, not only those directly concerned with economic acquisition, with irresistible force. Perhaps it will so determine them until the last ton of fossilized coal is burnt. (Weber [1904–1905] 1958a:183)

What advanced capitalism requires, then, is not asceticism but consumerism. It does not simply need people to save and invest their money; it needs people to spend their money buying all of the goods and services that are produced in a capitalist economy (Bell 1976).

Colin Campbell described the culture of consumer capitalism as one of extreme self-gratification:

The revolution of rising expectations means that everyone not only expects to "better" himself but it is considered "immoral" not to strive to do so; this means an obligation to seek out and satisfy new "wants." . . . The obligation to satisfy want is linked to a money market economy embodying the principle of consumer sovereignty and mechanisms to guarantee the perpetual stimulation of new wants. (Campbell 1983:281)

Extreme self-gratification has certainly not been one of the historical virtues of any of the world's religious traditions, and it has been antithetical to much of Christian teaching. Thus, in a reversal of the Weberian causal ordering—in which a religious ethic helped give rise to an economic spirit—it seems that today modern consumer capitalism in the United States has given rise to a religious ethic that suits and supports it. A contemporary "Maxine" Weber studying American society might title her book *The Prosperity Ethic and the Spirit of Consumer Capitalism.*

In 2006, *Time* magazine ran a cover story called "Does God Want You to Be Rich?" (van Biema and Chu 2006). The photo on the cover of the issue showed the front of a Rolls-Royce with a cross replacing the traditional Spirit of Ecstasy hood ornament. The story was about the rising number of American Christians who were adherents to what is known as "prosperity theology" (aka the "prosperity gospel" or the "health and wealth gospel"). At the heart of this ethic is the idea that God provides material prosperity for those God favors. As the *Time* magazine story put it, "In a nutshell, it suggests a God who loves you does not want you to be broke" (van Biema and Chu 2006).

Although its roots can be traced back to the 19th-century United States (Bowler 2013), the recent history of prosperity theology is found in the Pentecostal tradition of preachers promoting spiritual healing through faith and prayer. The most important evangelist of the movement was Oral Roberts, the Tulsa, Oklahoma–based healing minister. Roberts became a leading televangelist of the 1970s and '80s and is perhaps best

known for declaring once that if his followers did not meet an $8 million fund-raising goal, God would "call him home." Jim and Tammy Faye Bakker of the PTL (Praise the Lord) Club were among the most prominent promoters of prosperity beliefs in the 1980s, until a sex scandal forced Jim Bakker to resign in 1987 (see Chapter 14 on televangelism).

Kate Bowler argues that the prosperity movement's survival of these scandals was aided by the "soft prosperity" approach of more contemporary preachers and televangelists like Joel Osteen, Joyce Meyer, and Paula White, as well as the rise of black megachurch pastors like T. D. Jakes, Eddie Long, and Creflo Dollar. The prosperity gospel today has broken free of its Pentecostal roots and often finds an organizational home in megachurches, which shun any historic denominational affiliation (Bowler 2013).

Not surprisingly, a national poll taken for the *Time* story found that prosperity theology beliefs are widespread:

- 17% of Christians surveyed said they considered themselves part of such a movement.
- 61% believed that God wants people to be prosperous.
- 31%—a far higher percentage than there are Pentecostals in the United States—agreed that if you give your money to God, God will bless you with more money.

Further analyses of these same poll data by sociologist Bradley Koch found African Americans and the less educated were particularly drawn to the prosperity gospel (Koch 2014).

Scott Schieman and Jong Hyun Jung have also quantitatively studied adherence to prosperity gospel beliefs (Schieman and Jung 2012). In a 2006 Pew Research Center survey, a representative sample of American adults were asked how much they agreed with two statements meant to represent the wealth and the health sides of these beliefs: "God will grant material prosperity to all believers who have enough faith" and "God will grant good health and relief from sickness to believers who have enough faith" (Schieman and Jung 2012:743). Response categories were a 4-point Likert scale ranging from "completely agree" to "completely disagree." As in the *Time* survey, Schieman and Jung find prosperity gospel beliefs to be widespread. Of all respondents, 48.5% affirmed the wealth belief, and 56.6% affirmed the health belief. Interestingly, Pentecostals—the denominational group most associated with the prosperity gospel—are those on the *lowest* end of the economic spectrum. Also, those social groups that are most disadvantaged in U.S. society—African Americans and Latinos—adhere to the prosperity gospel more than others (Harrison 2005; Schieman and Jung 2012). This gives credence to Marx's view that religious ideas serve to legitimate the status quo. As Marx would suggest, the belief that hard work will lead to God's favor and hence success serves to justify the current economic system. Individuals adhering to these beliefs, even if they are economically disadvantaged, will never rise up against the system. The belief becomes, in effect, an "opiate."

At first blush, like their Calvinist forebears, adherents of the prosperity gospel seem to look to material success as a sign of their "chosen" status: a sign of their righteousness in the eyes of God. Unlike the progenitors of the Protestant ethic, however, outward signs of material success are embraced by adherents to the prosperity gospel. They focus on the accumulation, not the ascetic self-denial. As Koch explained, adherents

> tend to interpret the New Testament as portraying Jesus as a relatively rich figure who used his wealth to feed the masses on several occasions and to finance what they argue to have been a fairly costly itinerate ministry. As such, Prosperity adherents argue that we should model our lives after Jesus' by living lavishly. (Koch 2014:1)

Thus, it is not uncommon to see preachers of the prosperity gospel driving Rolls-Royces and flying in private jets.

Although it has not been a historical affirmation of the Christian faith, the gospel of prosperity has become a central message of a number of American evangelists. For the financially successful, prosperity theology embraces affluence and consumerism, and provides sacred permission to engage in lavish consumerism. For the disadvantaged, it provides the hope of upward mobility and motivation to take action toward that end. Because of this, prosperity theology has been successfully exported to developing countries around the world.

One of the strengths of prosperity theology in an increasingly capitalist world is that it fulfills both functions Stephen Vaisey attributed to religious culture: *motivation* for those seeking "heath and wealth," and *justification* for those who achieve it (Vaisey 2009). The Yoido Full Gospel Church in South Korea (discussed in Chapter 8) exemplifies this. The prosperity teaching of Yoido's founder, Paul Yonggi Cho, was attractive

TB Joshua Ministries
4 hrs ·

This Money shall be placed into your hands on 31st in Jesus' name!
#TBJoshua

Claim this Prayer: Type Amen and Share" it shall come to pass on 31st.

Like   Comment   Share   262   575   189

This "name it and claim it"–inspired Facebook wall post by Lagos, Nigeria–based minister T. B. Joshua was shared by one of the authors' relatives in the United States just after Christmas in 2014.

to Koreans during the difficult years of war and recovery in the 1950s and '60s, and continues to be attractive now that South Korea is one of the wealthiest countries in the world.

The message is becoming global. The gospel of prosperity has been successfully exported to every continent and is found in some of the world's largest and most prominent churches. In addition to Yoido, there is Singapore's City Harvest Church, Australia's Hillsong Church, Brazil's Universal Church of the Kingdom of God, and Nigeria's Winners' Chapel.

Although many have criticized prosperity theology—as departing dramatically from the historic Christian message and ethic—some have highlighted the attractiveness of the perspective (Coleman 2000). "The prosperity movement offers a comprehensive approach to the human condition," writes Bowler (2013). "It sees men and women as creatures fallen, but not broken, and it shares with them a 'gospel,' good news that will set them free from a multitude of oppressions" (Bowler 2013:232). See the "Global Perspectives" box on the prosperity gospel in Africa for an example of a sympathetic view

Critical Thinking: Based on your understanding and possibly even experience, does a Weberian argument about religious motivation or a Marxian argument about religious suppression better explain the attractiveness of the prosperity gospel to those who are more disadvantaged?

Global Perspectives

Two Cheers for the Prosperity Gospel in Africa

Arriving in East Africa with only preconceptions about the prosperity gospel, Oxford University graduate student in religion and politics Grant Brooke quickly found abundant evidence of this American export. He soon realized that much of his understanding was based on caricatures of the movement as seeking to enrich pastors at the expense of impoverished followers. So he asked himself, "What if the prosperity gospel in its worldwide Pentecostal form actually hastens development, fosters upward social mobility, and makes great strides in establishing a middle class in impoverished nations?" In short, what if the prosperity gospel works—at least economically? This is an empirical, sociological question, not a theological one.

Without ignoring potential liabilities, Brooke focuses on four positive outcomes in making a sociological case for the benefits of the prosperity gospel in Africa (and, by extension, the developing world generally):

1. Educational Opportunity. Some prosperity gospel churches promote the kind of education that is likely to lead to upward mobility for individuals and economic development for nations. This can be in the form of classes taught on the church on computing or bookkeeping or marketing, or in church-sponsored college scholarships.

2. Market Individualism. As Brooke puts it, "poverty fosters substance abuse, sexual abuse, and higher crime rates. Prosperity churches present a God that does not tolerate this behavior if one wishes to earn his blessing, an exchange that creates safer, more dependable and ambitious individuals."

3. Fiscal Soundness. Much like the Reformation sects in Weber's account, adherents to the gospel of prosperity look for economic rewards as a sign of their position among the "elect" (the saved as opposed to the damned). This encourages them, according to Brooke, "to save, live debt-free, and create businesses"—actions that are likely to foster individual and community economic development.

4. Secular Mentality. Weber argued that once capitalism was established, it no longer needed the motivational underpinning provided by the Protestant ethic. Brooke makes a parallel argument for the prosperity ethic in the developing world. Third-generational Pentecostals in the developing world tend to be more secular than other Christians, and consequently "these newly secular individuals tend to be members of the middle class, be better educated, and have better health outcomes than their religious counterparts."

In proposing the "heretical" idea that there may be something good about the prosperity gospel, Brooke recognizes he is not alone. In 2008, the eminent sociologist of religion Peter Berger visited Rhema, a prosperity megachurch outside Johannesburg, South Africa. He reports: "The message from the preacher had two major themes. One: God does not want you to be poor! And two: You can do it! That is, you can do something about the circumstances of your life. Should one quarrel with this message? I'm inclined to think not." Berger sees a parallel between the contemporary prosperity gospel and Weber's Protestant ethic in the emphasis on hard work, family, and education (albeit without the ascetic self-denial) and predicts that those who adhere to this ethic will earn upward social mobility for themselves, or at least for their children. As Brooke concludes, belief in prosperity can become a self-fulfilling prophecy.

SOURCE: Brooke, Grant. 2011. "The Case for the Prosperity Gospel." *Huffington Post*, May 25.

SOCIAL CLASS AND RELIGIOUS INVOLVEMENT: INTERACTIVE PROCESSES

Religion and Social Class Stratification

According to Ballantine, Roberts, and Korgen, "Social stratification refers to how individuals and groups are layered or ranked in society according to their access to and possession of valued resources" (Ballantine et al. 2016:196). What resources are valued varies from society to society, but in most modern societies these include political power, education, income, occupational position, and wealth. For analytical purposes, we can treat these as separate stratification outcomes, but in the real world they tend to be found together (Domhoff 2013).

Recall that Weber began his inquiry into the connection between religious beliefs and economic action by noting that Protestants tended to have higher class positions than Catholics at the time. This interest in the relationship between religion and social class stratification was brought into the American context by theologian H. Richard Niebuhr, who was influenced by Weber's student Ernst Troeltsch. Niebuhr wrote about the *social* sources of denominationalism in American society—in particular the tendency of sectlike denominations to draw from the lower classes and churchlike denominations to draw from the upper classes (Niebuhr [1929] 1957; see also Chapter 7). Understanding religion in part in terms of social stratification has been central to the sociology of religion from the start (Park and Reimer 2002).

The ranking of faiths according to social class in the United States is as old as the country itself. In the United States, the Episcopalians, Congregationalists, and Presbyterians are the denominations that have been established for the longest period of time. In fact, members of these denominations so dominated business and politics that they were known as "The Protestant Establishment" (Davidson and Pyle 2011). Lutherans, who occupy higher status in certain European countries, represent somewhat more recent arrivals in this country. The highest-status positions were already occupied in North America when German and Scandinavian immigrants arrived, and the latter have had to work their way up the social ladder from the bottom. Roman Catholic immigrants from Europe in the late 19th century experienced the same pattern as Lutherans, and Catholic immigration from Latin American countries continues to shape the overall economic and educational achievement of Catholics.

There are notable exceptions to this pattern. Jews, with some exceptions, are more recent immigrants than the long-established Protestants, but they have obtained higher socioeconomic status than one might expect for fairly recent arrivals. Hindus as a group are even more recent immigrants than Jews and seem to follow the same pattern. Their variation from the earlier immigrant pattern can be explained in part by the fact that they are more likely to be professionals or to have higher levels of education and capital *when they enter the country* than have most immigrants.

Muslims prove to be an interesting reversal of the Catholic pattern. Of the over 2 million Muslims living in the United States, 65% are foreign-born, and 35% are native-born. Despite the fact that over half of foreign-born Muslims have immigrated since 1990, foreign-born Muslims on average have higher levels of both education and income than native-born Muslims (Pew Research Center Forum on Religion and Public Life 2007b). This is due to the fact that a high percentage of native-born Muslims are African American converts to the tradition. The lower social class position of African Americans in general, and of those who are inclined to convert to Islam, explains the reversal in historic pattern for Christian immigrants from Europe.

Although there has been some mobility in the religious stratification system in the United States over the years, overall the socioeconomic inequality in the U.S. religious system has been "quite persistent and stable" (Smith and Faris 2005), whether we look over the past 20 years (Pyle 2006) or the past 200 (Davidson and Pyle 2011). In the following sections, we examine three specific social class stratification outcomes—income, occupation, and wealth—and then seek to explain those outcomes sociologically.

Religion and Social Stratification Outcomes

Although the situation is more complex today than 200 years ago, there remains a connection between denominational affiliation and social class. This is shown in Table 9.1, which looks at two key measures of social class—income and education—for the major denominations in U.S. society. Before examining this table, it is important to recall the discussion of denominations and congregations in Chapter 8. At the local level, congregations tend to be even more class-segregated than denominations as a whole. For example, a large downtown Baptist church in a southern community may have a large percentage of upper- and middle-class people from that town. On the edge of town or in a nearby community, a smaller Baptist church may be attended almost entirely by working- and lower-class persons. Probably no local congregation is totally class-exclusive, and some congregations are relatively well integrated in terms of class. Nevertheless, the tendency is for local congregations to be somewhat more segregated by social class than Table 9.1 indicates.

Table 9.1 Socioeconomic Profiles of American Religious Groups

Religious Group	Educational Level (% With at Least a College Degree)	Religious Group	Annual Household Income (% Over $100,000)
Hindu	74	Jewish	46
Jewish	59	Hindu	43
Episcopal Church in USA	57	Episcopal Church in USA	35
Unitarian	51	Presbyterian Church USA	28
Buddhist	48	Orthodox	28
Presbyterian Church USA	47	Atheist	28
Orthodox	46	Unitarian	26
United Church of Christ	42	Buddhist	22
Atheist	42	United Methodist	22
United Methodist	35	Disciples of Christ	20
Disciples of Christ	35	Catholic	19
Evangelical Lutheran in America	30	United Church of Christ	18
Nondenominational	29	Nondenominational	18
Latter-day Saint (Mormon)	28	**U.S. Average**	**18**
U.S. Average	**27**	Evangelical Lutheran in America	17
Catholic	26	Muslim	16
Muslim	24	Latter-day Saint (Mormon)	15
Southern Baptist	21	Southern Baptist	15
Seventh-day Adventist	21	Religious but Unaffiliated	12
Religious but Unaffiliated	17	Seventh-day Adventist	11
Historically Black Baptist	15	Jehovah's Witness	9
American Baptist	14	American Baptist	8
Assemblies of God	12	Assemblies of God	8
Other Pentecostal	11	Historically Black Baptist	8
Jehovah's Witness	9	Other Pentecostal	7

SOURCE: Pew Research Center Forum on Religion and Public Life. 2008b. *U.S. Religious Landscape Survey*. Retrieved from religions.pewforum.org.

Clearly there are unmistakable differences between the denominations that call for some explanation. Relative to Weber's argument, we note that this hierarchy of denominations *cannot* be classified according to ascetic values and practices based in Protestant theology. The top two groups in terms of both education and income are Hindus and Jews. Only 6 of the 13 denominations that are above the U.S. average for annual household income are Protestant. We do, however, see the historical legacy of the Protestant establishment in the relatively high ranking of Episcopalians, Presbyterians, and Congregationalists.

Another important measure of social stratification is differences in occupational position. Occupations are important not only because different jobs allow people to earn more or less income. Occupations are also stratified according the amount of prestige or status that people associate with them. People in certain occupa-

tions have higher social standing in their communities than others. There are additional nonmonetary ("intrinsic") rewards associated with different types of occupations, such as the variety and creativity of the work, autonomy and flexibility, sense of accomplishment, and so on (Hodson and Sullivan 2012).

In general, professional jobs have more "extrinsic" rewards (pay and other material benefits), status, and other intrinsic rewards than other jobs (Hodson and Sullivan 2012). Darren Sherkat has examined religious stratification in terms of occupations. He examines the differences between religious groups in six occupational classifications in the General Social Survey: (1) science, education, arts, and medicine; (2) engineers and technicians; (3) business and management; (4) clerical workers; (5) other laborers; and (6) agriculture (Sherkat 2012). Sherkat considers the first three occupational classifications as professional. For the sake of simplicity, in Table 9.2 we present the

Table 9.2 Religion and Occupational Stratification

Religious Tradition	Professional Occupations	Other Occupations
Jewish	67.6%	32.4%
Liberal Protestant	53.1%	46.9%
Other Non-Christians	50.5%	49.4%
No Religious Identification (None)	44.2%	55.8%
Other Protestant	41.6%	58.4%
U.S. Average	**38.2%**	**61.8%**
Moderate Protestant	38.1%	61.9%
Catholic	37.8%	62.1%
Sectarian Protestant	27.5%	72.5%

SOURCE: Adapted from Sherkat, Darren E. 2012. "Religion and the American Occupational Structure." Pp. 75–102 in *Religion, Work and Inequality*. Edited by L. A. Keister, J. McCarthy, and R. Finke. Bingley, UK: Emerald.

NOTE: Data are from the General Social Survey, 1972–2008 cumulative file.

data only in terms of professional occupations versus other (nonprofessional) occupations.

Using the General Social Survey, Sherkat cannot present as much detail about smaller religious groups as was possible for education and income using the Pew Religious Landscape Survey. He groups different Protestant denominations according to their theologies and histories. Liberal Protestants are the historic Protestant Establishment of Congregationalists (UCC), Episcopalians, and Presbyterians. Moderate Protestants include other "mainline" denominations such as Lutherans, Methodists, and Disciples of Christ. Sectarian Protestants are those sectlike denominations of which Niebuhr wrote, including Baptists, Pentecostals, and Churches of Christ. Other Protestants are those who did not specify a particular denomination. The other non-Christian category includes all Buddhists, Hindus, and Muslims (Sherkat 2012).

Table 9.2 reveals very clear differences in attaining a professional occupation by religious group. This is particularly evident at the top and bottom of the hierarchy. Over two thirds of Jews and over half of liberal Protestants and other non-Christians have professional occupations, while nearly three quarters of sectarian Protestants have other (nonprofessional) occupations. Moderate Protestants and Catholics are below the national average for professional occupations, but only very slightly.

A final stratification outcome of interest here is wealth. Relative to other measures of inequality, wealth has been comparatively understudied by sociologists, but in a series of influential papers and books, sociologist Lisa Keister (2003, 2005, 2007, 2008) brought the issue of wealth and wealth accumulation more to the fore. This culminated in a book titled *Faith and Money: How Religion Contributes to Wealth and Poverty* (Keister 2011).

Wealth is typically measured as "net worth"—that is, the total value of all assets minus total liabilities (usually at the household rather than the individual level). Typical assets are a home, automobiles, stocks and bonds, savings accounts, and retirement funds. Typical liabilities are home mortgages, car loans, student loans, and credit card debt. Wealth is unequally distributed in U.S. society, even more than other resources like income or education. As Keister highlights, the richest 1% of Americans control 33% of all the country's wealth, and the richest 10% control 70%. At the bottom, 16% of U.S. households have zero or negative net worth—that is, they owe more than they own (Keister 2012).

Although related to education, income, and occupation, wealth has some properties that make it uniquely valuable. According to Keister, wealth "provides a buffer against income interruptions, medical emergencies, and other crises such as accidents and natural disasters. Wealth can create more wealth when it is reinvested, and it can generate income in the form of interest or dividends" (Keister 2012:132). Wealth can also be passed down directly from generation to generation.

Keister (2011) draws on a variety of data sources in her work to document wealth inequalities by religious tradition. Because the pattern of inequality is basically the same in all of these data sets, in Table 9.3 on page 240 we show Keister's (2012) results from the Health and Retirement Study (HRS), a longitudinal panel study of older Americans whose average age in 2006 was 68.

Like Sherkat, Keister groups denominations into broader classifications according to theology and history. Conservative Protestants include Southern Baptists, conservative Lutherans, Pentecostals, and nondenominational Christians, further subdivided according to the race of the respondent (African American or white). Black conservative Protestants also include those naming historic African American denominations like the African Methodist Episcopal Church. Mainline Protestants include United Methodists, moderate and liberal Lutherans and Presbyterians, and Episcopalians (Keister 2012).

Table 9.3 Household Wealth by Religious Tradition

Religious Tradition	Net Worth	% of Average
Jewish	$705,564	283%
No Religious Affiliation	$384,172	154%
White Catholic	$356,999	143%
Mainline Protestant	$322,142	129%
Other Religions	$269,857	108%
All Respondents	**$249,243**	**100%**
White Conservative Protestant	$189,088	76%
Hispanic Catholic	$58,188	23%
Black Conservative Protestant	$50,692	20%

SOURCE: Adapted from Keister, Lisa A. 2012. "Religion and Wealth Across Generations." Pp. 131–150 in *Religion, Work and Inequality*. Edited by L. A. Keister, J. McCarthy, and R. Finke. Bingley, UK: Emerald, p. 136.

NOTE: Data are from the 2006 Health and Retirement Study (HRS) (hrsonline.isr.umich.edu).

Using this classification of religious groups, Keister finds Jews to have by far the most wealth of any religious group in the United States—over $700,000 on average, which is nearly 3 times the national average of $250,000. Religious nones, white Catholics, and mainline Protestants also have approximately 30% to 50% more wealth than the overall average, while white conservative Protestants, Hispanic Catholics, and black conservative Protestants all have lower average wealth. In the case of black conservative Protestants, the average net worth of just over $50,000 is just 20% of the national average net worth. How are we to explain, therefore, this religious stratification? Does religion continue to play a role, or are secular factors more important in producing this hierarchy? In explaining religious group stratification in the United States, we need to examine several factors, some of which can be considered predominantly secular factors and some more truly religious factors.

Explaining the Connection Between Religion and Social Stratification

As Figure 9.1 shows, the same basic model can be used to explain the clear correlation between religious background and social stratification based on income, occupation, and wealth (Fitzgerald and Glass 2014). The key mediating variables are social networks, family formation processes, and education. Each of these factors affects stratification outcomes for everyone, so a key question is how these mediating factors are affected by religion.

In this model, the cultures of different religious groups matter because they shape the decisions people make about their educations, their families, and with whom they associate. All of these decisions are consequential in terms of social stratification. They help us to explain why Jews do so consistently well in U.S. society (despite the anti-Semitism discussed in Chapter 3), why certain

Figure 9.1 Model of Religion and the Intergenerational Transmission of Social Class

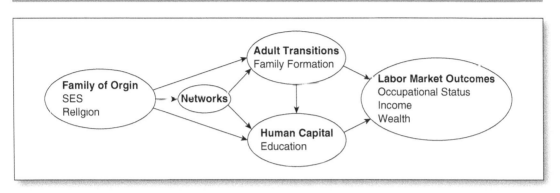

SOURCE: Fitzgerald, Scott T., and Jennifer L. Glass. 2014. "Conservative Protestants, Normative Pathways, and Adult Attainment." Pp. 97–118 in *Religion and Inequality: Research and Theory on Religion's Role in Stratification*. Edited by L. A. Keister and D. E. Sherkat. Cambridge: Cambridge University Press, p. 100.

Protestant groups fare so poorly, and why some groups like Catholics experience upward social mobility over time.

Education

Education is a key vehicle for upward mobility in modern societies across the globe, and the United States is no different (Sewell and Hauser 1975). Understanding how religion affects educational decision making and outcomes, therefore, is crucial.

As Table 9.1 shows, the lowest positions in the education hierarchy are dominated by Protestant denominations that are sectarian in orientation and fundamentalist in belief. These groups are well known to demonstrate hostility toward secular education and an anti-intellectual orientation that reduces educational achievement (Beyerlein 2004; Darnell and Sherkat 1997; Sikkink 1999). Moreover, sectarian Protestant affiliation is also negatively related to verbal ability—at all levels of education—which can impede occupational success (Sherkat 2010).

The exact opposite is the case for Jews, who are at or near the top of the education hierarchy in the United States. Some argue that Rabbinic Judaism promoted knowledge and learning, which translated into a positive embrace of schooling and literacy. Furthermore, "skills initially acquired for religious purposes (e.g., literacy in Hebrew) enhanced Jews' ability to acquire economically useful skills (such as literacy in local languages)" (Burstein 2007:215).

Similarly, the Protestant elite (Episcopalians, Congregationalists, Presbyterians) have long been highly supportive of and tightly networked into the elite institutions of secondary and postsecondary education (Baltzell 1964; Karabel 2005). This includes some very prestigious prep schools like Groton, St. Albans, and National Cathedral School.

The upward economic mobility of Roman Catholics in U.S. society has been due in no small part to their upward educational mobility (Keister 2007). Catholic children frequently exceed the educational attainment of their parents. The system of parochial schools the Catholic Church developed over the years has been important to this process. Attending Catholic high school is associated with higher rates of both high school and college graduation (Neal 1997). In some areas, the Catholic high school is known as the "college prep" high school. Not surprisingly, then, like the boarding schools of the Protestant elite, some Catholic high schools like Georgetown Prep in Maryland, Delbarton in New Jersey, and Woodside Priory in California are among the best in the country.

In contrast to Jews, the Protestant mainline, and Catholics, sectarian Protestants have often founded schools that stressed faith development over academic development, or opted out of formal schooling altogether in favor of home-schooling. These Protestant high schools and religious homeschooling produce lower levels of educational achievement in terms of test scores, quality of higher education enrollment, and degree completion (Pennings 2011).

Family Formation Processes. Another explanation of educational differences between religious groups, which also has a direct effect on stratification outcomes, has to do with family formation processes—marriage and childbirth. Scott Fitzgerald and Jennifer Glass argue that different religious groups uphold different "normative pathways" (i.e., appropriate steps) to these adult responsibilities. Some of these pathways are conducive to higher levels of educational and economic achievement and some to lower levels (Fitzgerald and Glass 2012).

Fitzgerald and Glass use data from Wave IV of the National Longitudinal Study of Adolescent to Adult Health (Add Health) to compare the social class origins of individuals to their social class standing in early adulthood (ages 24–32). This allows them to assess what role religion and family formation processes play in the transition to paid employment in the labor market.

Online Resource: Public use data from the National Longitudinal Study of Adolescent to Adult Health (Add Health) is available for download in several formats from the Inter-university Consortium for Political and Social Research (ICPSR). Go to www

.icpsr.umich.edu/icpsrweb/ICPSR/studies/21600. For some of the data sets, it is also possible to run simple analyses right from the ICPSR website. Individuals have some access to these data, but if you attend an institution that is an ICPSR member, you can access even more data. Click on "Membership in ICPSR" to see if your institution is one of the 700+ members.

For all individuals, earlier family formation results in less educational attainment, lower-status jobs, and less income in the short run, and less wealth in the long run. Higher-paying jobs in our postindustrial economy now call for higher levels of education and freedom from the responsibilities of child care. Those who marry early and have children early retard their ability to pursue these opportunities.

Fitzgerald and Glass observe that those who have children early also tend to have more children. Because they begin from a lower social class position, they have fewer resources to help care for these children, and (for women) this often leads to lower levels of labor force participation. When women who have children young do participate in the labor force, they often must take lower-paying jobs with fewer opportunities for upward advancement. They also are less geographically mobile, which can also impair upward mobility (Fitzgerald and Glass 2012).

These patterns are reflected in Table 9.4, which compares the marital and parental status of conservative Protestants to other religiously affiliated men and women, as well as income differentials. These data show that conservative Protestant men and women aged 24 to 32 are more likely than others to be married and to have children. They also earn considerably less income on average. Fitzgerald and Glass describe these income differentials as "cumulative financial penalties" of absorbing the religious culture of conservative Protestantism and making earlier family formation transitions (Fitzergald and Glass 2012:60). This includes leaving school earlier, which is not shown in Table 9.4.

Although Fitzgerald and Glass focus on the effect of family formation on educational outcomes, recent research by Uecker and Hill suggests that education can be the independent variable—affecting family formation timing. Using data from the Cardus Education Study, a nationally representative sample of high school graduates who are currently 24 to 39 years old, Uecker and Hill found that those who graduated from evangelical Protestant schools tended to have earlier marriages and first births than public school graduates. By contrast, those who graduated from Catholic schools had later first births (but not later marriages) than public school graduates. The authors suggest that these religious schools reinforce religious culture: putting marriage and family first in the case of the evangelical schools, and putting education and work first in the case of Catholic schools (Uecker and Hill 2014).

Networks. A final way that religion can affect social stratification outcomes is through social networks. Social networks are valuable because they help individuals to generate social capital. Social capital can be used to generate human capital (through education) and also economic capital (through jobs) (Putnam 2000). Thus, the number and nature of social network ties individuals have are significant.

Robert Putnam and David Campbell (2010) highlight the positive relationship between religious practice and social capital–generating activities. Being involved in a religious community promotes social trust, information sharing, and emotional support—all significant predictors of human capital development (Coleman 1988). This is one of the reasons that parental religiosity is related to children's later educational and economic success (Eirich 2012).

Of course, the number of an individual's social ties is not the only factor. The nature or quality of those ties matter, too. If a person is tightly networked, but those ties are with individuals who do not value education, or who privilege early family formation over education, then that social capital will not be productive in creating human capital. Young people in

Table 9.4 Transitions to Adulthood and Social Class Differences by Religious Affiliation

	FEMALES		MALES	
Outcome Variable	Conservative Protestant	Other Religiously Affiliated	Conservative Protestant	Other Religiously Affiliated
Proportion Married	28%	23%	18%	13%
Proportion Parents	66%	54%	53%	39%
Income	$22,615	$31,608	$36,182	$43,585

SOURCE: Adapted from Table 1 in Fitzgerald, Scott T. and Jennifer L. Glass. 2012. "Conservative Protestants, Early Transitions to Adulthood, and the Intergenerational Transmission of Class." Pp. 49–72 in *Religion, Work and Inequality*. Edited by L. A. Keister, J. McCarthy, and R. Finke. Bingley, UK: Emerald.

NOTE: Data are from the National Longitudinal Study of Adolescent to Adult Health (Add Health) Wave IV Respondents, Ages 24–32 (www.cpc.unc.edu/projects/addhealth).

congregations with higher levels of education and income (Jewish, mainline Protestant, and white Catholic) are more likely to develop networks with people who can be mentors and models in the professions. This is yet another way that conservative or sectarian Protestantism restricts social mobility and those with higher educational levels can enhance it (Keister 2008; Sherkat 2010).

Critical Thinking: Which of the factors connecting religion to socioeconomic status just discussed do you think is most influential? Are these factors likely to have an influence in the future? Are there factors the authors have failed to consider?

Socioeconomic Status and Style of Religiosity

Turning the table around from considering the effect of religion on economic action, we can ask, what is the effect of economics on religious action?

There has been some research that has focused on ways in which one's social class seems to affect one's style of religiosity. Some of the early studies on religion and social class used attendance as the prime indicator of religious commitment. Because upper-class people tend to be more regular in attendance at worship, it appeared that the upper and middle classes were more "religious" than were the lower classes. When researchers began to use multidimensional measures of religiosity, a rather different pattern emerged. One analysis found that among Congregationalists, people who ranked high in socioeconomic status also scored highest for religious knowledge (biblical teachings and the theological orientation of the denomination). On the other hand, lower-class members scored higher on devotionalism (personal religious experience, daily prayer, etc.) than did higher-status members (Fukuyama 1961). (See Figure 9.2.)

A range of research strategies involving various groups continue to support these observations. For example, Joseph Baker, using a nationally representative sample of Americans, showed the nearly linear inverse relationship between income and prayer frequency (Baker 2008; see also Figure 9.2). The connection between class and devotionalism remains strong. Studies of youth suggest that this connection may persist into the future. Research by Philip Schwadel, using data from the National Study of Youth and Religion, shows that poor teenagers score high on devotionalism (they are especially likely to pray, read religious scriptures, and report high levels of personal faith) at the same time they are much less likely to participate regularly in organized religious activities (Schwadel 2008).

Steven Cohen reported similar differentials among Jews. Highly educated Jews were more likely to have institutional affiliation and participation at the synagogue but were less likely to observe private family rituals (Jewish devotionalism) than were lower-class Jews. Family income was also positively correlated to institutional affiliation but negatively related to private family observances (Cohen 1983).

N. J. Demerath III also found a connection between social class and style of religious commitment. He began by distinguishing two types of religiosity: (1) "churchlike" and (2) "sectlike." Demerath found from his study of five Protestant denominations that *within* any given denomination, an individual's style of religiosity is highly correlated to his or her socioeconomic status. More important, Demerath suggested that members of different social classes who belong to the same congregation may be active in different ways and may have quite different needs met by the same local church. The higher a Lutheran's social status, the more likely he or she is to participate in churchlike ways. The lower the social status, the more likelihood there was of sectlike participation (Demerath 1965). The same pattern held for the other four denominations as well (Congregationalists, Disciples of Christ, Baptists,

Figure 9.2 Percent Praying at Least Daily by Income

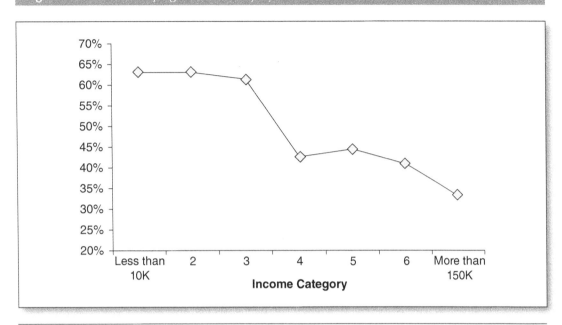

SOURCE: Baker, Joseph O. 2008. "An Investigation of the Sociological Patterns of Prayer Frequency and Content." *Sociology of Religion* 69:169–185, used by permission of the Association for the Sociology of Religion.

and Presbyterians). Other empirical studies have also found both churchlike participation and sect-like participation within each denomination—and have found socioeconomic status to be the critical variable affecting a member's orientation (Stark 1972; Winter 1977).

Moreover, the bulk of empirical research on social status and religiosity suggests that persons with high status are more likely than lower-class persons to be committed at an instrumental level—through investment of time and money in the formal structure (Estus and Overington 1970). Lower-status persons are more likely than higher-status persons to be committed at the affective level—through close friendship networks. So differences in religiosity between the social classes are not ones of *degree* of involvement so much as ones of *kind* or *style* of involvement.

Critical Thinking: Does it make sense that style of religiosity would be influenced by socioeconomic status? Why or why not? Do the findings seem to apply to your own style of religiosity?

Religious perspective and moral standards can influence individuals in their economic choices in still other ways. Robert Wuthnow also found that people whose moral values are shaped by theistic beliefs are less likely to compromise their conduct on the job than are those with other value orientations. People who are "theistic moralists" were less likely to bend the truth, cover for someone else who was not performing appropriately, or use office equipment for personal business. Further, people who were in religious fellowship groups were considerably more likely to have high standards of personal ethical behavior on the job (Wuthnow 1994a). While Wuthnow concluded that religious orientation has less impact on economic behavior than religious officials would hope, it was clear from his study that religion is far from irrelevant to the way people behave and think about their work. Indeed, 30% of Americans feel they are called by God to their present line of work, and 46% of those who are frequent attendees expressed this sentiment. Religiously committed people therefore had more concerns about materialism and its consequences for society, for they saw other purposes that they thought transcended financial success. In another study, Wuthnow concluded that religious ideas provide an alternative way of thinking about economic behavior, a standard that contrasts with the simple utilitarian or "rational choice" approach of the larger secular society (Wuthnow 1996).

In conclusion, the sacralization of specific values or outlooks may affect one's economic behavior. While one's religious perspective may not be sufficient to change one's socioeconomic position, it may contribute to such a change. Religious ideas and communal networks can be an independent variable influencing socioeconomic behavior and circumstances. In the end, expressions of religious commitment tend to be significantly affected by socioeconomic status in a variety of ways. Not only do people of different social classes tend to affiliate with different denominations, but members of the same denomination who are of different socioeconomic status tend to participate in the life of the religious community in different ways and for different reasons. Furthermore, the overall socioeconomic level of a local congregation affects the style of religiosity of that group, and members may be affected in their religiosity as they conform to the norms of their local congregation (Davidson 1977). Socioeconomic status is certainly not the only factor affecting one's style of religiosity, but it has been an important one.

Throughout this text, we have pointed to religion as an open system, a system of meaning, belonging, and structure that impacts the larger society through outputs and is influenced via inputs from the larger society. This principle holds for socioeconomic processes as well as for other aspects of religion. Religion is both a dependent and an independent variable as it relates to the stratification system of the society.

Critical Thinking: Do you think religion is more an *independent* variable influencing socioeconomic standing of members of religious communities, or mostly a *dependent* variable that is shaped by socioeconomic conditions? Why do you think as you do? What evidence is most compelling to you?

SUMMARY

Religion is correlated to socioeconomic status as both a dependent and an independent variable. According to Weber's thesis, one's values and one's worldview may contribute to one's rise or decline in the socioeconomic system. If one is taught a sacred ethic that requires hard work and simple living, this may enhance eventual accumulation of wealth. However, other social conditions must be present for such social mobility to take place. The debate continues on the importance of a particular theological orientation having influenced the original formation of capitalism as a system. In the modern world, it is certainly very possible that certain religious values and perspectives may serve as contributing factors to upward mobility. Theological orientation is neither necessary nor sufficient, however, for economic prosperity.

Religion is also very much influenced by the socioeconomic circumstances of its adherents. People in the lower classes tend to have different styles of religiosity than do coreligionists of the upper classes. This variation shows up not only between denominations serving different socioeconomic groups but also between people of different socioeconomic status within the same denomination.

Religion both influences and is influenced by the socioeconomic system. At this point, the strong consensus among social scientists is that economics is the more powerful variable. In other words, a person's religiosity is significantly affected by his or her position in the stratification system. The effects of religion on the socioeconomic behavior of most people are considerably less pronounced. The Marxian perspective is that economic self-interests affect religion more than religion affects economic behavior. Much to the chagrin of many religious people, the empirical evidence tends to support this view. However, even the Marxian view is too simplistic, for religious principles do influence people's behavior on the job and in the marketplace.

10

RELIGION AND RACE

HERE ARE SOME QUESTIONS TO PONDER AS YOU READ THIS CHAPTER

- How is religion connected to race and ethnicity?
- Why is there so much racial segregation in congregations?
- What is the relationship between religious conviction and racial prejudice? Is religious commitment contrary to ethnic or racial bigotry?
- How might meaning systems, belonging systems, and institutional systems of a religious community contribute to racism in different ways?
- How might religion foster prejudice at the same time it combats it?
- Does religion cause bigotry or merely *justify* social inequality and discrimination after the fact?

Writing in *The Souls of Black Folks* at the beginning of the 20th century, the pioneering sociologist W. E. B. Du Bois asserted, "The problem of the twentieth century is the problem of the color line" (Du Bois 1903:283). Over a century later, much has changed in American society. Racial minorities have increased their standing in almost every aspect of life, aided considerably by the civil rights struggles of the 1950s and 1960s (many of which were led by religious leaders as we will see in Chapter 13). For some, this racial progress culminated in 2008 when Barack Obama was elected president of the United States, though racial tensions are still evident as of this writing with nationwide protests surrounding the police killings of black men in Ferguson, Missouri, and Staten Island, New York.

Despite some progress, racial inequality persists. For example, African Americans overall still have lower levels of educational attainment than whites (more without a high school degree, fewer with college and professional degrees), as can be seen in Table 10.1 (page 250). They also continue to earn significantly less than whites, even if they have the same level of education. Further, at each higher level of education, the ratio of white to black income increases, from 1.08 for those without a high school degree to 1.25 for those with a professional degree. Consequently, whites are not only twice as likely to earn professional degrees as blacks (1.4% vs. 0.7%), but they also earn 25% more income when they do.

Online Resources: Published continuously from 1878 to 2012, the *Statistical Abstract of the United States* is a comprehensive source of official statistics about all aspects of American society (from agriculture to wholesale trade), including race. Most of these annual volumes have been digitized and are available on the website of the U.S. Census Bureau at www.census.gov/compendia/statab. Unfortunately, budget cuts led the Census Bureau to eliminate the department that compiled the abstract in 2012. Library information services company ProQuest (proquest.com) has taken up where the government left off by publishing *Statistical Abstracts* going forward. Of course, online access to this new version will be more costly and more restrictive than previously.

This economic inequality has a religious dimension. As we saw in the last chapter, denominations with a high proportion of African American members are lower on the socioeconomic hierarchy than historically white denominations. Indeed, the very fact that we can talk about black and white denominations suggests the reality (or at least legacy) of religious racial segregation. Civil rights leader (and sociology major) Martin Luther King Jr. wrote,

> It is appalling that the most segregated hour of Christian America is eleven o'clock on Sunday morning, the same hour when many are standing to sing, "In Christ there is no East or West." Equally appalling is the fact that the most segregated school of the week is the Sunday School. (King 2010:207)

King then went on to quote Liston Pope, who lamented, "The church is the most segregated major institution in American society" (King 2010:207; Pope 1957).

In this chapter, we ask and answer the question, is the same true today? If so, what accounts for that religious racial segregation? Further, what is being done to overcome it?

Table 10.1 Income by Race and Education Level, Percent of Population With Highest Degree Earned in Parentheses, and Ratio of White to Black Income by Education Level

Education	White	Black	Ratio of White to Black Income
Not a high school graduate	$20,457 (11.4%)	$18,936 (14.9%)	1.08
High school graduate	$31,429 (29.9%)	$26,970 (33.5%)	1.16
College graduate	$57,762 (20.4%)	$47,799 (14.1%)	1.21
Professional degree	$127,942 (1.4%)	$102,328 (0.7%)	1.25

SOURCE: Income from U.S. Census Bureau. 2012. *Statistical Abstract of the United States*, Table 232. Retrieved from www.census.gov/compendia/statab. Educational Attainment from U.S. Census Bureau. 2013. *Current Population Survey, 2013 Annual Social and Economic Supplement*. Retrieved www.census .gov/hhes/socdemo/education/data/cps/2013/tables.html.

NOTE: Income figures are for 2009, individuals 18 years old and over with any earnings. Educational attainment figures are for 2013, individuals 25 years old and over.

RACE, ETHNICITY, AND
RELIGIOUS IDENTIFICATION

A key starting point here is to look at religious self-identification by members of different racial and ethnic groups.[1] We use data from the Pew Research Center Forum on Religion and Public Life's U.S. Religious Landscape Survey to examine this issue. These data highlight the considerable differences in religious identification by race and how those differences are reflected in denominational racial composition (Pew Research Center Forum on Religion and Public Life 2008b). For example, Table 10.2 shows that more than three quarters (78%) of blacks are Protestant (including evangelical, mainline, and historically black churches), compared to just over half of whites (53%) and

about a quarter of Asians (27%) and Latinos (23%). Of all Americans, 24% are Catholic, but 58% of all Latinos are Catholic, compared with 22% of whites and only 5% of blacks.

Looked at from the perspective of religious traditions in Table 10.3 on page 252, we see large concentrations of whites in Judaism, mainline Protestantism, Orthodoxy, Mormonism, and evangelical Protestantism. In addition to the historically black churches, African Americans are also overrepresented among Jehovah's Witnesses and Muslims, and Asians are dramatically concentrated in the Buddhist and Hindu traditions. Latinos are overrepresented among Catholics and Jehovah's Witnesses. Looked at either way, there continues to be a strong correlation between race/ethnicity and religion in American society.

[1]Race refers to a supposed biological difference that distinguishes a group, and although there is no scientific concept of race, it remains a social distinction because people treat certain physical differences as though they matter. An ethnic group is a group with a cultural difference—variations in language, symbols, norms, values, and beliefs.

Table 10.2 Religious Identification by Racial Group—Reported in Percentages

	U.S. Population	White	Black	Asian	Other/ Mixed	Latino
Evangelical Protestant	26	**30**	15	17	**34**	16
Catholic	24	22	5	17	14	**58**
Mainline Protestant	18	**23**	4	9	15	5
Historically Black Churches	7	<0.5	**59**	<0.5	2	3
Secular Unaffiliated	6	7	3	11	7	4
Religious Unaffiliated	6	5	8	5	9	8
Jewish	2	2	<0.5	<0.5	1	<0.5
Mormon	2	2	<0.5	1	2	1
Atheist	2	2	<0.5	3	1	1
Agnostic	2	3	1	4	3	1
Buddhist	1	1	<0.5	**9**	1	<0.5
Jehovah's Witness	1	<0.5	1	<0.5	1	1
Muslim	1	<0.5	1	**4**	1	<0.5
Orthodox	1	1	<0.5	<0.5	1	<0.5
Other Faiths	1	1	<0.5	1	5	<0.5
Hindu	<0.5	<0.5	<0.5	**14**	1	<0.5
Other World Religions	<0.5	<0.5	<0.5	2	<0.5	<0.5
Other Christian	<0.5	<0.5	<0.5	<0.5	1	<0.5
Total	100	100	100	100	100	100

SOURCE: Pew Research Center Forum on Religion and Public Life. 2008b. *U.S. Religious Landscape Survey.* Retrieved from http://religions.pewforum.org.

NOTES: Due to rounding, figures may not add up to 100%.

We added the bold font for emphasis to key numbers.

Critical Thinking: What additional pattern do you see in Tables 10.2 and 10.3 that might be relevant to understanding race, ethnicity, and religion?

These cross-sectional data do not reveal changes in religious affiliation by race or ethnicity over time, but using other research strategies, scholars have suggested that despite consider-able stability in African American religious identification there has been some loosening of the connection between African Americans and specific denominational affiliations. For example, the American Religious Identification Survey (ARIS) found a decrease from 50% to 45% in African Americans identifying themselves as Baptist, from 12% to 7% in those identifying with the "Mainline Protestant" tradition, and

Table 10.3 Racial Composition of Religious Traditions—Reported in Percentages

	White	Black	Asian	Other/ Mixed	Latino	Total
U.S. Population	**71**	**11**	**3**	**3**	**12**	**100**
Jewish	95	1	0	2	3	100
Mainline Protestant	91	2	1	3	3	100
Orthodox	87	6	2	3	1	100
Mormon	86	3	1	3	7	100
Atheist	86	3	4	2	5	100
Agnostic	84	2	4	4	6	100
Evangelical Protestant	81	6	2	4	7	100
Other Faiths	80	2	1	13	5	100
Secular Unaffiliated	79	5	4	4	8	100
Other Christian	77	11	0	8	4	100
Catholic	65	2	2	2	29	100
Religious Unaffiliated	60	16	2	5	17	100
Buddhist	53	4	32	5	6	100
Jehovah's Witness	48	22	0	5	24	100
Muslim	37	24	20	15	4	100
Hindu	5	1	88	4	2	100
Historically Black Churches	2	92	0	1	4	100

SOURCES: Pew Research Center Forum on Religion and Public Life. 2008b. *U.S. Religious Landscape Survey*. Retrieved from http://religions.pewforum.org/.

Pew Research Center Forum on Religion and Public Life. 2007b, May 22. *Muslim Americans: Middle Class and Mostly Mainstream*. Retrieved from www.pewresearch.org/pubs/483/muslim-americans.

from 9% to 6% in those seeing themselves as Catholic. These declines were offset by gains in the "Generic Christian" category from 9% to 15%, and in the "none" category from 6% to 11% (Kosmin and Keysar 2009). This is not to say that African Americans are becoming less religious, because even among "nones," African Americans affirm religious convictions. The Pew Research Center Forum on Religion and Public Life's (2008b) U.S. Religious Landscape Survey found that 71% of African American "nones" report that religion is very important or somewhat important in their lives, compared to only 41% of all "nones." Thus, most African American nones are what the Pew Research Center Forum on Religion and Public Life (2009) would call "religious unaffiliated."

Latinos in the United States are increasingly drawn away from Roman Catholicism and toward evangelical Protestantism. Of Hispanic evangelicals, 51% are converts, and of that group, more than 80% are former Catholics (Pew Research Center Forum on Religion and Public Life 2007a). This mirrors a worldwide trend, one that is especially prominent in the historically Catholic countries of South America (Martin 1993; Stoll 1990).

In Chapter 9, we noted that looking at socio-economic differences at the denominational level obscures the higher levels of inequality at the local congregational level. The same is true for racial differences. The level of racial segregation we see at the level of denominational identification is even more pronounced in terms of congregational membership.

RACIAL SEGREGATION IN CONGREGATIONS

The leading scholar investigating congregational segregation is Michael Emerson. In a series of studies, books, and articles, Emerson has documented the persisting religious racial segregation in American society (Christerson, Edwards, and Emerson 2005; DeYoung et al. 2003; Emerson 2006; Emerson and Smith 2000). Emerson and his colleagues operationalized racially segregated congregations in two different ways: *binary* and *continuous*.

First, they operationalized racially segregated congregations in a binary (either/or) fashion. Those in which 80% or more of the members are of the same race are considered segregated (or homogenous), and those in which less than 80% are of the same race are considered multiracial (racially mixed) (Emerson 2006). This percentage is not arbitrary but is based on studies of organizations which find that 20% is a sort of tipping point from tokenism to having enough of a critical mass to make a difference in the organization. It is also

based on a mathematical reality that in an organization with at least 20% diversity, under random conditions the probability of interracial relationships is 99% (Emerson 2006; Edwards, Christerson, and Emerson 2013).

Using data from a nationally representative sample of American congregations, they found that 93% are racially homogenous by this definition. Only 7% are multiracial. What about even more extreme cases of racial segregations? Emerson and Kim also found that 9 out of 10 American congregations have 90% of their members coming from one racial group, and roughly 4 out of 5 congregations have 95% of their membership from a single racial group (Emerson and Kim 2003).

Second, they examined racially segregated congregations in a continuous fashion by looking at the likelihood that any two randomly selected members of the congregation will be from different racial groups (Emerson 2006). The method is called continuous because there is no single point at which we can say "this is a segregated congregation, and that is not." Instead, we get a continuous string of probabilities called a "heterogeneity index," which ranges from 0.0 (complete homogeneity) to 1.0 (complete heterogeneity). Put concretely, if a congregation has 50% of its members from one racial group and 50% from another, then the probability that any two randomly selected members will be of different racial groups is 0.5. The more diverse a congregation is, the higher the probability will be, and the less diverse the lower the likelihood. So, if there are four racial groups, each constituting a quarter of the membership, then the probability will be 0.75.

How do congregations fare in terms of this heterogeneity index? Not well. The average probability of randomly selecting two members of a congregation from different races is just 0.02—a 2% chance. This makes congregations far more segregated than even schools or neighborhoods. The heterogeneity index for schools in the United States is 0.40 and for neighborhoods is 0.20. Thus, Emerson, Mirola, and Monahan concluded, "religious congregations are *10 times less diverse* than the neighborhoods in which they reside and *20 times less diverse* than the nation's schools" (Emerson et al. 2011:161).

Recent data from the third wave of the National Congregations Study (NCS) reveal some improvement in the direction of more racial diversity in congregations. As Figure 10.1 shows, the percentage of Americans who attend congregations that are racially mixed (defined by Emerson's 80% rule) grew from 15.3% in 1998 to 19.7% in 2012. This same figure also shows that the percentage of individuals who attend all-white congregations

dropped by nearly half from 19.7% to 11.0%. Even within those congregations that are more than 80% white, there has been movement toward greater diversity (even if they are not yet considered "multiracial"). Of attendees, 69% are in congregations with at least some blacks (up from 57.4% in 1998), 61.7% with at least some Hispanics (up from 54.2%), and 48% with at least some Asians (up from 41.4%) (Chaves and Anderson 2014).

It must be said, however, that the movement toward multiracial congregations is almost always a one-way street with racial minorities

Figure 10.1 Increasing Ethnic Diversity of Religious Congregations in the United States

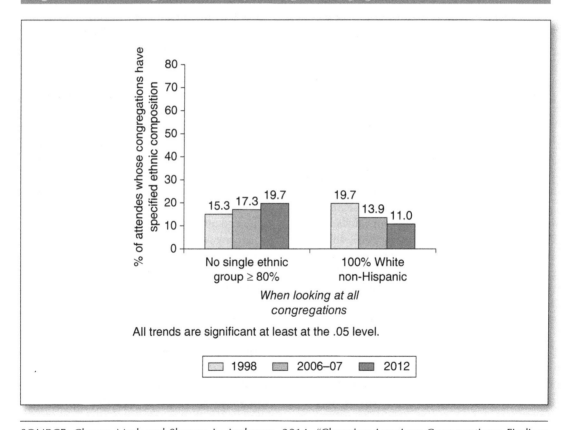

All trends are significant at least at the .05 level.

1998   2006–07   2012

SOURCE: Chaves, Mark and Shawna L. Anderson. 2014. "Changing American Congregations: Findings From the Third Wave of the National Congregations Study." *Journal for the Scientific Study of Religion* 53(December): 680.

having to assimilate into the dominant majority culture. Korie Edwards's research, which combines ethnographic observation of a multiracial congregation and quantitative analysis of NCS data, finds that multiracial congregations look much more like predominantly white congregations in terms of activities and practices (Edwards 2008). Thus, we should not mistake "multiracial" for "multicultural." Becoming multiracial often means "Anglo-conformity."

Even recognizing these limitations, these changes did not take place without some concerted efforts. Scholars studying this issue would no more claim American religion to be racially integrated than they would American society in general (Edwards et al. 2013). The bottom line of Emerson's studies is that no matter how you operationalize congregational racial segregation, Martin Luther King's and Liston Pope's observations about religion being the most racially segregated institution in American society (and religious education the most segregated schooling) are just as true today as they were 50-plus years ago.

EXPLAINING CONGREGATIONAL RACIAL SEGREGATION

As with racial segregation in society generally, explaining religious racial segregation is challenging in its complexity. We briefly highlight several explanations for congregational homogeneity and for movements in the direction of greater congregational diversity, and then turn to a more extended consideration of the relationship between religion and racism.

In the first place, individuals often choose to associate with people like themselves. As the saying goes, birds of a feather flock together. This is known as "homophily" (McPherson, Smith-Lovin, and Cook 2001). As noted in Chapter 9, this often takes place along social class lines, but it happens all the more so along racial lines. However, as sociological investigation has discovered, flocking together is not always a completely voluntary choice. Racial segregation in congregations, then, is a classic example of the mix of choice and constraint. As Karl Marx said, "[People] make their own history, but they do not make it just as they please; they do not make it under circumstances chosen by themselves, but under circumstances directly encountered, given, and transmitted from the past" (Marx [1852] 2008:15). This fundamental sociological insight is highly applicable to this issue. The "black church" in the United States is a case in point, as we will see more fully in Chapter 12. It is an integral part of the black community in the United States, valued by its members and chosen by many of them. Still, the emergence of the black church is rooted in slavery and racial discrimination in the 19th century, not simply preference by blacks to be around people like themselves. Indeed, some have called the black church a "semi-involuntary institution" for this reason (Nelsen, Yokley, and Nelsen 1971).

Immigrant groups have also often chosen to form and maintain segregated religious congregations when faced with language barriers and other forms of social exclusion (recall Chapter 3). Historically, many Lutheran, Methodist, and Catholic congregations in the United States conducted worship services in German, Welsh, and Italian, and going to worship was a comfortable reminder of the home country. This pattern is also evident today in the vast number of Asian immigrant religious communities across the country, such as First Chinese Baptist Church (Walnut, California), Korean-American Calvary Baptist Church (Seattle, Washington), and Chinese American Family Bible Church (Virginia Beach, Virginia). Incredibly, in Columbus, a midsize city of 250,000 people in southwestern Georgia, there are four separate Korean Protestant congregations, including two Presbyterian congregations: the Korean Full Gospel Church, Korean Presbyterian Church, Hallelujah Korean Presbyterian, and Korean Peace Baptist Church. Like the African American church, these Asian ethnic congregations also exemplify the principle of choice under constraint.

Whereas many Asians in the United States *become* Christian upon their immigration, other immigrants bring their religion with them (Yang 1999). For some of these groups, it is impossible to separate their racial/ethnic identity from their religious identity. This is the case for Hindus from India. Consequently, peering into a Hindu temple in the United States today one is likely to find mostly individuals of Indian descent (Emerson and Kim 2003).

Uniracial congregations are not only created but also perpetuated by people's homophilous social networks. Since we already know that most people are recruited into religious groups through family and friendship networks (Chapter 6), and because family and friendship connections tend to be racially homophilous, recruitment into religious groups will also be racially homophilous.

How, then, do we explain the change over the past two decades in the direction of greater diversity in congregations? First, individuals who tend to have racially heterogeneous friendship networks or who live in racially diverse neighborhoods will be more likely to attend racially diverse congregations. This can be a sort of catch-22, however, because the most common way people *meet* their diverse friends is in church (Emerson 2006).

In the same way that demographic imperatives help create racially segregated congregations, they can also contribute to the movement toward multiracial ones. Non-European immigration has diversified American society as a whole in the past half-century, and this becomes reflected in all institutions over time. Edwards and her colleagues observe that from 1970 to 2010, the Latino population in the United States grew from 6.4% to 16.3%, and the Asian population grew from less than 1% to nearly 5% (Edwards et al. 2013). Although they often initially migrate to ethnic enclaves, over time as they become more assimilated into the population they also can find their way into white congregations, helping them to become more diverse.

Marriage across racial lines has also increased considerably in recent years. In 1980, 3.2% of all marriages and 6.7% of new marriages were interracial. By 2010, 8.4% of all marriages and 15.1% of new marriages were interracial (Wang 2012). To the extent that married couples worship together—and as we discussed in Chapter 6, they do very often—this will also make religious congregations more diverse.

These explanations for racial homogeneity apply to congregations from all religious traditions, so the processes that underlie them are not unique to any one faith tradition. On the other hand, racial homogeneity in congregations is not equally distributed across religious traditions. According to Emerson, Catholic parishes are three times more likely to be multiracial than Protestant congregations (15% vs. 5%). This is due both to the geographical reach and very large size of most Catholic parishes and to a cultural embrace of diversity (Emerson 2006).

Because of this, Catholic parishes are also most likely to be multicultural. A recent study has identified over 6,000 Catholic parishes (35.9% of all U.S. parishes) that serve a particular racial, ethnic, cultural, or linguistic community (Gray, Gauthier, and Gaunt 2014). Of Catholic parishes, 29% celebrate at least one Mass per month in a language other than English, and 4% celebrate Masses in two or more non-English languages (Gray et al. 2014). In the Archdiocese of Chicago, Masses are celebrated in English, Spanish, Polish, and 46 other languages including Tagalog (for Filipinos), Vietnamese, and Haitian French Creole. Of course, the majority of multicultural Catholic parishes (69% nationally) serve Hispanic or Latino Catholics. To take one example that is close to home for one of your authors, Our Lady of Mercy Catholic Church in Winston-Salem, North Carolina, is home to a large community of Mexican Americans and Mexican immigrants. Each Sunday, Masses are said in English and

Spanish, and the two-year process of confirmation puts white and Mexican American/Mexican immigrant adolescents together in the same experience. During the Mass at which they receive the sacrament of confirmation, the instructions, prayers, readings, and songs are in both English and Spanish.

Despite—or perhaps because of—the fact that so few Protestant congregations are multiracial, the most conscious efforts to become more diverse are seen among these churches. Beginning in the 1990s and accelerating in the first decades of the 21st century, efforts have included books, Facebook pages, blogs, Twitter accounts, organizations, and conferences, all "explicitly committed . . . to the imperative of diversity, further encouraging pastors and congregations to actualize successful integration" (Edwards et al. 2013:216). Many congregations are attempting to focus on changing the type of music they play to attract more diverse attendees. The next "Doing Research on Religion" box explores the connection between worship music and multiracial congregations and finds the relationship may not be what it seems.

DOING RESEARCH ON RELIGION

Worship Across the Racial Divide

Some believe that the lack of multiracial congregations has to do with the preferred styles of worship in various racial communities, especially tastes for different kinds of music. If worship music were more diverse, so too would be the worshippers. Sociologist Gerardo Marti set out to investigate this question: What role does music diversity play in making congregations more inviting to people of different backgrounds? For example, if a white congregation wants to be more inviting to African American congregants, should it play more Gospel music or African American spirituals? If a congregation wants to attract more congregants of Mexican descent, should it play more Latin music? What if it wants to attract more Asian or South Asian or African congregants?

In *Worship Across the Racial Divide: Religious Music and the Multiracial Congregation*, Marti reports on his study of 12 racially integrated congregations in Southern California. *Racially integrated* here is understood in the common way (all of the congregations have at least 20% of the members coming from a different racial group than the majority), and the congregations in the study come from a range of different denominational and theological traditions. Marti's conclusions are based on two years of ethnographic observation and over 100 interviews with church leaders, musicians, and worship leaders.

Marti's basic finding is that music does matter in multiracial congregations, but not necessarily in the way most people think it will. Playing distinct genres of music for diverse groups can actually reinforce boundaries rather than breaking them down. It can become a sort of tokenism that highlights differences rather than transcending them. For example, an otherwise white congregation putting "Go Tell It On the Mountain" or another African American spiritual into their rotation of hymns is not going to attract more African Americans just by doing that.

(Continued)

(Continued)

What is important in building multiracial congregations, therefore, is not the music itself, or even the quality of the musical performance. What matters are the social processes and social relationships that go into making music. Music itself does not make people feel a part of a religious community, but the time spent together making music and the friendships that develop during that time do. In Marti's words, integrated congregations are successful at "stimulating cross-racial interaction through music worship practices."

In addition, Marti finds that it is important for "racialized ritual inclusion" for there to be a diverse group of individuals leading worship. Successfully integrated congregations actively recruit—even at times pay for—a diverse group of individuals to be involved. Of course, relationships must also be built in the process of making music for that diversity to solidify. In the end, Marti wants to highlight that becoming a multiracial congregation does not happen by chance, luck, or magic. Communities of all sorts, including multiracial religious congregations, are born of intentional efforts to foster personal relationships across social differences.

SOURCE: Marti, Gerardo. 2012. *Worship Across the Racial Divide: Religious Music and the Multiracial Congregation*. New York: Oxford University Press.

Insofar as racial or ethnic segregation of religious groups is related to we/they categories and thinking, there are important issues raised about the role of religion in transcending or fostering racism. This brings us to a robust body of research on the relationship between religion and racism.

Critical Thinking: What seems to you to be the most important factors in racial and ethnic segregation? What empirical data or studies support your position? What data or research provides the greatest challenge to your position? What might be some *consequences* of this segregation for the larger society?

RELIGION, RACIAL PREJUDICE, AND RACISM AS A WORLDVIEW

Religion and Prejudice

In the 1950s, empirical studies showed that religiously affiliated people were more racially prejudiced than nonmembers. Despite the fact that Christianity claimed to enhance fellowship and love among people, the research indicated a correlation between Christianity and bigotry. In the 1960s, several survey studies that were better designed revealed that although church members were more prejudiced than nonmembers, the most active members were less prejudiced than any other group. The earlier studies had lumped together all members without regard to level of commitment or amount of participation in the life of the religious community. Because there are larger numbers of marginal members in most religious groups than there are active members, the statistics were weighted heavily in the direction of marginal member attitudes. The evidence indicates that infrequent attenders are more prejudiced than nonattenders but that frequent attenders are the lowest of all on scales of prejudice (Allport 1966; Gorsuch and Aleshire 1974; Perkins 1983, 1985). A cross-national study that compared prejudice in 11 European countries also found that adherence to the doctrinal beliefs of the Christian church was related to low levels of prejudice (Scheepers, Gijsberts, and Hello 2002).

The relationship between religion and racial prejudice is complex, with studies finding that type of theological orientation and other factors play a role in racial and ethnic attitudes. In the remainder of this chapter, we explore the possibility that religion may simultaneously contribute both to tolerance and to bigotry.

Critical Thinking: Why did the figures on the relationship between religion and racial prejudice change when more complex measures of religious commitment were introduced?

RACISM AS A WORLDVIEW

The belief that some categories of human beings are biologically or genetically less human than others is actually a modern phenomenon (Jordan 1968; Kelsey 1965; Mosse 1985). Of course, people throughout history have believed that those who had different values, beliefs, or styles of life were stupid or inferior. Ethnocentrism (prejudice based on differences in cultures) is a universal phenomenon. One can also find occasions in history when "outsiders" have been excluded because they were not of the same lineage. The articulation of a systematic philosophical and "scientific" statement that divides humans into higher and lower orders of being, however, has been given credence only since the 18th century (Jordan 1968; Mosse 1985). George Kelsey did an incisive analysis of the modern racist worldview and its fundamental difference from the basic worldview of Christianity (Kelsey 1965).

The important characteristic of racism is that a person's inherent worth is judged on the basis of his or her genes. The philosophical foundations of racism are naturalistic. For the racists, a person's value is understood in terms of that which is below themselves—their animal nature

and, specifically, their genes. The quality of a person's life is determined by ancestry and genetic structure. Persons who are racist feel superior to or of greater worth than someone who has a "less human" genetic structure (different skin color, hair color, facial features, etc.). In other words, their sense of worth is centered on their genes (Kelsey 1965).

H. Richard Niebuhr, who uses a broad definition of religion, points out that faith focuses on that which makes our life worth living. He insists that whatever provides one with a sense of worth and meaning is properly termed one's "god" (Niebuhr 1960). Elsewhere, he talked of faith as "trust in that which gives value to the self" (Niebuhr 1960:16). In fact, the term *worship* refers to a celebration of the center of worth or the center of all other values. Literally, the word *worship* means a state or condition of worth. Kelsey cited Niebuhr's definition of faith and went on to explain how racism serves as a faith or worldview:

> The racist relies on race as the source of his [or her] personal value. . . . Life has meaning and worth because it is part of the racial context. It fits into and merges with a valuable whole, the race. As the value-center, the race is the source of value, and it is at the same time the object of value. (Kelsey 1965:27)

Kelsey contrasts this with the worldview of Christian theology. The source of personal worth for the Christian is found not in one's biological nature but in one's relationship with God. In this sense, Christian theology has allowed for only one distinction between persons: that between the regenerate and the unregenerate. The means of saving or improving human life is not through biological controls but through divine grace. Humans have worth because of their relationship with that which transcends them, not because of something they inherit through their genes. By contrast, racism assumes some segments of humanity to be defective in their essential being and thereby incapable of full regeneration (Kelsey 1965). The assumed defect is not one of character or spirit but a defect of creation: Biologically, some people are less human.

Of course, many persons in American society are racist and still consider themselves Christian. Kelsey suggested that such persons are, in fact, polytheists; they worship more than one god. The question is which center of worth predominates in any given situation? Such persons do not have a single worldview that gives unity, coherence, and meaning to life. Most of them are unaware of and unconcerned with theological contradictions in their outlook or the fact that they are actually polytheists.

The official position of all major denominations in the United States is that Christianity and racism are mutually exclusive. Racism is viewed as a form of idolatry (worship of a false god) that is utterly incompatible with Christian theology. The line of argument generally follows the same pattern Kelsey outlined. Yet, despite the fact that racism and Christianity involve assumptions that are logically contradictory and incompatible, the two ideologies have historically existed together and have even been intertwined. Let us investigate some of the ways that Christendom may have unconsciously contributed to racist thinking and actions.

Critical Thinking: George Kelsey argued that racism is a religion and that many Americans are polytheists—having more than one "center of worth" that makes them feel valuable and that guides their evaluations of others. Does his argument have merit? What is your rationale for your judgment?

SOURCES OF RACISM IN CHRISTIANITY

Christianity may have unwittingly contributed to racism through its meaning system, its reference group influences (belonging factors), or its organizational strategies (institutional factors). In the following pages, we explore how each of these types of factors may be conducive to the formation and/or the persistence of racism.

Meaning Factors

We will explore four meaning factors in Christianity that may have affected the development and persistence of racism, but first it is necessary to make a distinction between types of racism. In his psychohistory of white racism, Joel Kovel identifies two types of racist thinking. *Dominative racism* is the desire by some people to dominate or control members of another group. It is usually expressed in attempts to subjugate members of the out-group (Kovel 1970). This is the sort of racism that historically was predominant in the southern United States. White slave owners, for example, would live and work in close proximity to African Americans, even assigning black women to breast-feed and care for their children. White men also visited slave row for sexual purposes. Whites did not mind associating with blacks on a daily basis and having contact with them—as long as blacks knew their place! African Americans were not to get "uppity" or self-assertive.

This sort of racism is quite different from the racism of the North, where the racism was of the aversive variety. *Aversive racism* is expressed in the desire to avoid contact with African Americans rather than the desire to subjugate them. In fact, northerners have often been quite moralistic about the dominative racism of the South, while they were systematically restricting blacks to isolated neighborhoods and ghettos. Part of the reason that school desegregation has been more difficult in the North than in the South is that aversive racism has resulted in more isolated housing patterns. Therefore, desegregation has required a more significant cost. Meanwhile, with the decline of dominative racism in the United States in recent decades, other expressions of racism have been on the rise (Bonilla-Silva 2009; Farley 2010; Yancey 1999).

Most measures of racism have not controlled for these two types of racism, but those studies that have made the distinction have found aversive racism even where people reject more blatant dominative racism (Gaertner and Dovidio 1986; Yancey 1999). Today, few Americans think it is acceptable to discriminate against a person on the job because of the color of her or his skin. Yet although survey data point to growing acceptance of the principle of interracial dating and marriage (Newport 2013), only 26.4% of whites in the 2012 General Social Survey said they would favor a close relative marrying a black person (Djamba and Kimuna 2014). The only study on religion and racial prejudice that controlled for aversive types of racism found lower levels of aversive prejudice among people who attend interracial congregations (Yancey 1999). Unfortunately, as we have already seen, that is a very small percentage of the faith communities in North America.

Moral Perfection and Color Symbolism

The distinction between dominative and aversive racism is significant because Christian groups may at times contribute to aversive racism even while it fights against dominative racism. Gayraud Wilmore has suggested that certain strains of Protestant theology have placed heavy emphasis on the moral purity and perfection of the "saved." The desire for moral purity was especially strong among New England Puritans and later among the Perfectionists. An important aspect of this Puritanism was the desire to avoid contact with anything that was evil or could be polluting.

Wilmore related this to the cultural symbolism of European and American society. Perhaps this is most vividly seen in the color symbolism of the European languages, which is especially noticeable in English (Wilmore 1972). For example, prior to the 16th century, the definition of *black*, according to the *Oxford English Dictionary*, included the following:

Deeply stained with dirt; soiled, dirty; foul. . . . Having dark or deadly purposes, malignant; pertaining to or involving death, deadly; baneful, disastrous, sinister. . . . Foul, iniquitous, atrocious, horrible, wicked. . . . Indicating disgrace, censure, liability to punishment, etc.

In discussing this phenomenon, historian Winthrop Jordan went on to say, "Black was an emotionally partisan color, the handmaid and symbol of baseness and evil, a sign of danger and repulsion. Embedded in the concept of blackness was its opposite—whiteness. . . . White and black connoted purity and filthiness, virginity and sin, virtue and baseness, beauty and ugliness, beneficence and evil, God and the devil" (Jordan 1968:7). Even much of the artwork of this period showed the Devil as dark-skinned and the saintly figures as white. This color symbolism cannot be traced particularly to Christian teachings, but Christian responses to persons with dark skin may have been influenced by this symbolic association. Use of language in shaping attitudes may be especially important in the case of children (Van Ausdale and Feagin 1996).

Interestingly, there is empirical evidence supporting this claim of color symbolism. Athletic teams that wear black uniforms have more penalties called on them than teams with lighter-colored uniforms (Frank and Gilovich 1988; Lidwell 2013). No one argues that this is a conscious process—in sports or in religion—but the association of blackness with something sinister (an association that does *not* occur in all languages or cultures) may have affected the way religious people perceived people with dark skin.

Wilmore argued that areas of the United States that have been especially strongly influenced by Puritanism and Perfectionism are more likely than other areas to have strong aversive racism. Ownership of slaves was often condemned by these groups because it might compromise the moral righteousness of the owner—and moral purity was essential to these pietists. However, many of these same pietists did not want to have to associate with these dark-skinned people. Although the source of the feelings was probably only partially conscious to the individuals, they often felt that blacks were unclean—in body and in soul. They simply wished to avoid contact. Dominative racism was condemned; aversive racism was not.

This statue of Mary and baby Jesus is at the front of the sanctuary in Our Lady of the Sioux Chapel at St. Joseph's Indian School in Chamberlain, South Dakota. Jesus and Mary are clearly Native American, and the crucifix behind the altar at this same chapel has a Christ who looks very much like a Sioux on the cross. Europeans and Americans have done the same thing, making images of Jesus with white skin, classical Greek features, and even straight blond hair and blue eyes. Jesus was obviously Semitic and no doubt had rather dark skin and other Jewish features. Many people seem to be more comfortable with religious heroes who look like themselves.

Used by Permission of St. Joseph Indian School

Jordan showed that, among some of the religious groups that opposed slavery, the opposition was based largely on concern for how slaveholding might corrupt the soul of the owner. In this case, the ultimate goal is the purity and righteousness of the dominant group member more than concern for minority group members who were suffering (Jordan 1968). For example, one of the primary reasons for the abolitionism of Quaker John Woolman in the mid-1700s was that slaveholding created a feeling of superiority and pride in the owners. Pride—considered the most heinous of sins—was a source of evil. Slavery was bad for the slave owners, and by 1776, the Society of Friends was excommunicating any Quaker who owned slaves (Jordan 1968).

The Quakers were more effective than most groups at setting up programs to educate African Americans and to provide them with resources for economic independence. Their stance against dominative racism was unparalleled among religious groups. Yet, Quaker pietism may have created an unconscious aversive form of racism among some members of this group, which sought purity above all else (Jordan 1968).

The Protestant emphasis on moral purity or perfection is perhaps the most important unwitting contributor to the formation of racist attitudes among American Christians. However, this doctrinal emphasis contributed primarily to just one type of racism and only in the context of certain other cultural attitudes and structural circumstances. Pietism in the modern United States may not have the same effect. There are other aspects of Christian thought, however, that may contribute to the *persistence* of racism in American society.

Critical Thinking: Wilmore argued that when color symbolism of European languages combined with puritanical pietism, the result was *aversive* racism. What is most and least convincing about this argument? How would a conflict theorist critique this argument?

Freewill Individualism and Failure to Recognize Institutional Discrimination

Rodney Stark and Charles Glock, among others, have pointed to the importance of the Christian emphasis on free will and a radial individualism before God. The doctrines of sin and salvation are based on the assumption that humans are free and responsible beings. After all, if a person was entirely predetermined in his or her behavior, one could not hold him or her responsible or guilty for an act. Guilt implies freedom of choice, with the wrong choice having been made by an individual. One implication of this view is that each individual is viewed as getting his or her just deserts in society because one's circumstances are considered a result of personal choices, lifestyle, and willingness to work hard. Stark and Glock put it this way:

> Christian thought and thus Western civilization are permeated with the idea that [people] are individually in control of, and responsible for, their own destinies. If I am really the "captain of my soul" and "the master of my fate," then I have no one but myself to thank or blame for what happens to me. (Stark and Glock 1969:81)

This doctrine is significant in race relations because some Christians put the blame for disadvantage on those who are disadvantaged. Although there is no evidence that the doctrine of freewill individualism contributes to the *formation* of prejudicial attitudes, it may disincline those who are affluent to help those who have been subjected to poverty and discrimination (Stark and Glock 1969). The doctrine reinforces the attitude that those who are down and out are probably getting what they deserve. Persons who hold such a view are not likely to want to change the institutional structures of society that systematically discriminate. In fact, they are not likely to recognize the existence of institutional discrimination at all. *Institutional discrimination* refers to policies that discriminate against members of a particular group, even if those enacting the policies

are not themselves prejudiced (Bonilla-Silva 2009; Merton 1949). Frequently, such policies are not intentionally directed against members of a particular group, but because members of that group are disproportionately represented in a certain socioeconomic position, they are disproportionately affected.

One example of intentional institutional discrimination is the California Alien Land Law of 1913, which specified that foreign-born individuals could not own farmland unless they were American citizens or were eligible to become citizens. This in itself does not seem to discriminate unduly against any particular group. However, Congress had previously passed a law that specified that people of Japanese origin were not eligible for citizenship. Likewise, there were the literacy tests that required a person to be able to read and write before he or she was allowed to vote in certain southern states in the 1950s. Such laws were disproportionately disfranchising to blacks. African Americans were not the only ones who could not vote, nor were *all* blacks prohibited, but there is no question that illiteracy was higher in the African American community and that African Americans were disproportionately affected. Restricting the right to vote almost always has a greater impact on minorities by disfranchising them.

Sometimes discrimination in one institution affects discrimination in another. This is called *indirect institutional discrimination*. For example, discrimination in education has often led to discrimination in the job market. Because African Americans, Native Americans, and Hispanics have poorer educational backgrounds (with poorly funded and staffed schools in their neighborhoods), they do not meet the job qualifications for the better-paying jobs in our society. The employer is not purposefully discriminating against members of these ethnic groups, but the net effect is that racial and ethnic minorities are underrepresented in the professional positions in our society. Institutional or systemic discrimination is discriminatory in effect, even if not in intent. This is a major reason for the substantial income gap between blacks and whites reported in Table 10.1.

Stark and Glock found that those who hold to traditional Christian doctrines of total free will, individual responsibility, and moral retribution (punishment for lack of adherence to moral standards) are more likely to believe in rugged individualism and are less likely to work for the reduction of institutional discrimination.

Hence, a particular religious belief (freewill individualism) may contribute to apathy about racial discrimination. It is not at all clear that religious beliefs cause complacency. In fact, it is likely that these beliefs simply justify complacency rather than cause it. They allow people to ignore structural inequality and to benefit from their own unacknowledged privileges without feeling guilty (Farley 2010; Kinder and Sears 1981; Lewis 2003; Rothenberg 2012). The religious beliefs do not contribute to the formation of racism, but they do contribute to its persistence. Many scholars who study race and ethnic group relations believe that the more virulent form of racism in American society is the color-blind claim that refuses to recognize the way in which racism operates at the macro levels of society as part of the structure and can therefore exist and affect lives entirely independently of individual prejudices (Ballantine, Roberts, and Korgen 2016; Bonilla-Silva 2009; Farley 2010; Rothenberg 2012). This is called "symbolic racism," and it is the most common form of racism in the United States today (Farley 2010).

Particularism and Antipathy to Outsiders

Another set of religious beliefs is also correlated with certain kinds of prejudice. This set revolves around the assumption that one's own religion is uniquely true and legitimate and that all others are false. Only members of one's own group are expected to be saved. Glock and Stark referred to this orientation as *particularism*.[2] Not all religious people are particularistic. However, some groups teach that persons who are members of any other denomination or any other faith are damned (Glock and Stark 1966). Glock and Stark found that among Christians particularism is highly correlated with anti-Semitism. It is also highly correlated with antipathy toward atheists and agnostics (Glock and Stark 1966). However, they did not find a correlation between particularism and white–black prejudice (Stark and Glock 1969). This is no doubt due to the fact that both blacks and whites in the United States are predominantly Christian, though as we have seen, there is a substantial portion of the Muslim community in the United States who are African American. Moreover, as discussed further in the "Global Perspectives" box, cross-national studies of attitudes in European countries have found religious particularism to be a strong predictor of prejudice against ethnic "others" (Scheepers et al. 2002).

Further, since the terrorist events of 9/11, there have been high levels of animosity toward any Arab Americans who are assumed to be Muslim (Farley 2010). In many communities, the terrorist attacks of 9/11 resulted in two countervailing actions. Some people engaged in hate actions directed at Muslim people living in North America. The "we versus they" thinking was heightened, and polarities between those identifying with Christianity and Islam were widened. Some churches offered adult education classes to warn people of the dangers of Islam and to stress that only the followers of Christ are chosen for heavenly rewards.

However, another interesting response was also widely seen following 9/11. Aziz Khaki, a prominent leader in the Islamic community in Vancouver, reported to Reginald Bibby that he

---

[1]Particularism is a form of ethnocentrism—a concept that may be more familiar to sociology students.

Global Perspectives

Religious Particularism and Prejudice in Europe

Prejudice has been an enduring problem in Europe for centuries, and is particularly powerful when ethnicity and religion align. The Holocaust is a clear example, but the civil war in the former Yugoslavia in the early 1990s is a more recent case of "ethnic cleansing." In Bosnia-Herzegovina, Eastern Orthodox Serbs led by Slobodan Milošević sought to ethnically cleanse the territory of all Roman Catholic Croats and Muslim Bosniaks. Within this broader Bosnian War, a Croat-Bosniak War erupted when Croatians turned on their former allies the Bosniaks (Toal and Dahlman 2011). In the end, the Muslim Bosniaks suffered the greatest losses: two thirds of the more than 100,000 total killed and over 80% of the civilians, including at least 8,000 massacred in July 1995 in the "Srebrenica genocide" (Sito-Sucic and Robinson 2013).

Although not all prejudice is taken to this extreme, studies of religion and prejudice in Europe have found that religious particularism—the belief that the respondent's own religion is the one true religion—is associated with higher levels of prejudice (Eisinga, Felling, and Peters 1990; Scheepers et al. 2002). The ethnic cleansing in Bosnia, however, reminds us that racism and we–they categories are not just a characteristic of individuals. They also exist on a macro level as a result of intergroup conflict. When different groups in society perceive themselves as in competition, negative out-group attitudes can form, especially among dominant groups in society that may feel threatened by rising groups (Ekici and Yucel 2014).

Photo by Kathleen Franklin is licensed under CC BY 2.0

The Srebrenica Genocide Memorial was dedicated in 2003 in remembrance of more than 8,000 victims of "ethnic cleansing" at the hands of Eastern Orthodox Bosnian Serbs. Most of the victims were Bosnian Muslims, also known as Bosniaks.

(Continued)

(Continued)

Tufan Ekici and Deniz Yucel tested this group threat theory by exploring data from 37 countries that participated in the 2008 European Values Study (www.europeanvaluesstudy.eu). Their measure of prejudice—aversive racism—involved responses to this question: "On this list are various groups of people. Could you please sort out any that you would not like to have as neighbors?" Among the possible responses was "other races." Of the nearly 30,000 respondents, 16% were racially prejudiced. The extent of prejudice varied widely from country to country. Northern Cyprus (55%) and Turkey (42%) had the highest levels of racial aversion, while Hungary (1.1%) and Macedonia (3.4%) had the lowest levels (Ekici and Yucel 2014).

As in previous studies, Ekici and Yucel found that religious particularism is a significant predictor of racial animosity. The more individuals believe their religion is the "one true religion," the less likely they are to want people of other races as their neighbors.

In terms of the macro-level predictors of racial prejudice, Ekici and Yucel have found less support for the group conflict theory. Country-level characteristics measuring group competition did not predict racial prejudice in the multivariate statistical models. This includes per capita gross domestic product, the unemployment rate, population density, and the ratio of immigrants in the population.

The flip side of group conflict in this study is "generalized trust"—how much people in society trust other members of the society. Higher levels of generalized trust in a society have been associated in many previous studies with benefits at both the individual level (e.g., well-being) and the national level (e.g., higher rates of economic growth) (Carl and Billari 2014). Ekici and Yucel found that the percentage of respondents in each country who say they "trust people in general" is related to racial prejudice: The more generalized trust, the less racial prejudice.

Consequently, in addition to the direct effect of religious particularism on racial prejudice in Europe, different aspects of religion and religiosity at the national level could affect racial relations indirectly by promoting or inhibiting generalized trust. Some research has suggested, for example, that Scandinavian countries like Denmark and Sweden with low levels of religiosity and liberal Protestant religious traditions also have higher levels of social trust (Delhey and Newton 2005). This continues to be a very active area of scholarship.

was as appalled as anyone by the terrorist attacks. Khaki affirmed that no one who is truly Islamic could do such a thing. However, he also said that "from the beginning I was contacted by people from a variety of groups, including those who were Roman Catholic, United, and Anglican, who said they wanted to meet with me, that they stood in solidarity" (cited by Bibby 2002:245). In this case, religiously motivated people responded with compassion and sought to reach across the barriers that often separate one group from another. Education courses have been offered in some churches to stress that Christians, Jews, Muslims, and people of other faith traditions are fundamentally alike as children of God.

So the tragedy of 9/11 can be understood in ways that enhance tolerance or bigotry. In their role of explaining the meaning of events, religious communities have an extraordinary responsibility. Churches, mosques, and temples are capable of encouraging polarities between peoples, especially through particularism, or building bridges between people by downplaying differences.

Hence, particularism is a potential contributor to racial prejudice in certain circumstances, and it was definitely operative in the *formation* of racism in this country—especially before blacks were converted to Christianity (Jordan 1968). However, particularism does not currently seem to be a significant factor in negative sentiment toward African Americans.

Despite the fact that official Christianity manifestly opposes racism and encourages a sense of the brotherhood and sisterhood of humankind, certain beliefs may have the effect of increasing certain kinds of prejudice. The meaning function of religion can bring bigotry or can build bridges between people. This brings us to the second process by which religion may contribute to prejudice: reference group loyalties and we–they categories of thought.

Critical Thinking: How might religious *particularism* affect relations with minority groups other than African Americas, such as Asians, Native Americans, and Muslims?

Belonging Factors

Religion may contribute to prejudice through its sense of community and the feeling of belonging. As the religious community becomes a major reference group, people want to conform to the norms of the community in order to feel accepted. Furthermore, as they begin to identify closely with the group, they develop a sense of "us" and "them." In fact, we discovered in

Chapter 5 that the creation of strong group boundaries was one technique used to enhance commitment to a religious group (see the discussion of Kanter's theory of commitment, especially affective commitment). Now we explore two factors that may mean the belonging dimension of religion relates to intolerance toward ethnic minorities.

Informal Group Norms

The informal community of believers that provides individuals with a sense of belonging is a very important part of religion. However, the community develops unwritten norms and expectations—some of which may conflict with official religious policy. In an attempt to conform, members may adhere to the informal norms of the community rather than to the official policy of the formal religious organization. It is noteworthy that Gerhard Lenski found that "communal" members (who are influenced through the belonging function) were much more likely to be racially prejudiced than were "associational" members (who were formal members). Informal norms and values of the community may be contrary to the official ones, but they may be vigorously enforced through informal sanctions (Lenski 1963). A group of Lutheran laity at a Sunday afternoon picnic may tell ethnic jokes or may subtly reinforce negative images of blacks, regardless of the minister's sermon that morning to the contrary. The reference group norms are often more powerful in influencing behavior than are the idealized norms in the ideology. The friendship networks and unofficial norms may be more significant than official statements of religious bodies or messages from the pulpit.

Group Boundaries and Identification With the In-Group

Another major theory of racial and ethnic prejudice is based on the tendency of people to accept those who are similar to them and to be suspicious of anyone who is defined as "different." This view of the cause of prejudice is sometimes called the we–they theory, perhaps best illustrated by an empirical study conducted by Eugene Hartley (1946). Hartley used a variation of the Bogardus Social Distance Scale, an instrument designed to measure prejudice toward various ethnic groups. A list of ethnic groups is provided, and respondents are asked to rate the closest relationship that they would be willing to have with a member of that group. Seven categories are provided, ranging from "would marry a person who is a member of this group" and "would be willing to have a member of this group as a best friend" to "would allow only as visitors to my country" and "would exclude from my country entirely."

Hartley adapted the Bogardus instrument by adding three fictitious groups: (1) Danireans, (2) Pireneans, and (3) Wallonians. Using a random sample of college students at eight northeastern universities, he attempted to measure ethnic prejudice, including prejudice toward these fictitious groups. Hartley found a high level of prejudice toward these three nonexistent groups: More than half of the respondents expressed a desire to avoid contact with these people, and some respondents wanted them expelled from the country. Moreover, nearly three fourths of those who were prejudiced against blacks and Jews were also prejudiced against Pireneans, Wallonians, and Danireans. He used these data as evidence that prejudice is not caused by *stereotypes* (stereotypes are rigid and exaggerated images of a particular group or category of people). After all, no one has a negative stereotype of a group that does not exist. The negative feelings of respondents toward Danireans, Pireneans, and Wallonians were based on the fact that these groups sounded unlike the respondents. In other words, their negative reaction was based simply on whether the people sounded similar to or different from the respondents; the name *Pireneans* sounded more like one of "them" than one of "us." Empirical studies by

social psychologists have supported this we–they theory of the causes of prejudice (Farley 2010).

The fact that a number of Christian groups place a strong emphasis on particularism adds to the in-group sense of superiority and to the distinction between "us" and "them." The belonging function of religion, then, is capable of contributing to antipathy.

The development of religiously based we–they prejudice is especially likely in situations where racial boundaries and religious boundaries are coextensive (see Figure 10.2). The importance of its influences is illustrated by several empirical studies that show high levels of prejudice against people with differing beliefs (e.g., atheists or Jews), often surpassing prejudice against those of another race (Byrne and McGraw 1964; Jackson and Hunsberger 1999; Rokeach 1968; Smith, Williams, and Willis 1967). Moreover, if "they" practice a different religion and also look different, the exclusionary tendencies are reinforced even further.

The white Christians who encountered blacks from the 15th to the 18th centuries were meeting people who were different on several counts. In fact, in the 18th century, the words *white*, *Christian*, and *civilized* were used by many European writers as synonyms for "we," while the terms *black*, *heathen*, and *savage* were used interchangeably with "they" (Jordan 1968). At that point, much of the denigration of blacks was because they were not Christians. We–they religious distinctions, then, may have contributed to the *formation* of racial prejudice, even if these factors are not a primary cause of racial prejudice today. Nonetheless, one can see the application of religio-racial we–they categories in contemporary KKK literature and in various types of anti-Semitic materials.

To summarize, the belonging functions of a particular religion may enhance antipathy toward others in at least two ways. First, the informal community may develop norms that encourage discrimination, despite the official position of the larger religious organization. Second, the development of high boundaries between groups

Figure 10.2 Lines of Differentiation Between "We" and "They"

Parallel or coextensive
lines of differentiation

Cross-cutting lines
of differentiation

Imagine that each line represents a division in the society between groups. These divisions might be based on religion, ethnicity, political party, economic status, language spoken, skin or hair color, or other factors. Parallel lines of differentiation all divide people in each conflict along the same lines. Cross-cutting lines of we/they cut the differences so that people who were part of "them" in a previous antagonism become part of "we" in the present discord. This lessens the likelihood of deep and permanent hostilities within a social unit.

can reinforce we–they categories of thought, and at least historically in North America, "we" among those in power included only whites who were also Christians. Currently, black–white distinctions in North America are not related to difference in religion. Still, persons of Arab background are often stigmatized, and this polarization is especially strong when those Arabs are also Muslim, as we saw in the essay on anti-Muslim sentiments in the United States in Chapter 3. Religion can be related to hostility toward certain groups insofar as it creates and/or sanctifies we–they thinking.

Institutional Factors

Religion as an institutional structure can affect social behavior somewhat independently from the meaning (belief) system or the reference group factors. This is perhaps best illustrated by a study of the clergy of Little Rock, Arkansas, in the midst of a major racial crisis.

Ernest Campbell and Thomas Pettigrew studied the role of Protestant ministers in the school desegregation controversy. They found that ministers of small working-class sects were supportive of segregation and that most of the clergy of mainline denominations were sympathetic to integration (Campbell and Pettigrew 1959). However, very few of the ministers of mainline denominations spoke out or got actively involved in the conflict. The official positions of their denominations, their professional reference system (other mainline clergy), and their own personal convictions all supported integration. Still, they did not take an ethical or prophetic stance as one might expect.

When they did speak out, it was often in generalities, with references to "deeper issues" or with other techniques that would prevent anyone from taking offense (or from taking their statements too seriously). A controversial ethical view can be moderated and made more palatable when a minister begins by saying something such as this: "Everyone has to make up his or her own mind on moral questions. My opinion is simply the opinion of one person, and there is certainly room for other views." Such statements allowed ministers in Little Rock to speak briefly to the issue of segregation without raising too much opposition or offending people too deeply. Members of the congregation were, in effect, invited to ignore the comment or to view it as one opinion among many. This technique allowed ministers to feel that the issue had been addressed. Hence, they could avoid feeling guilty for having ignored the issue. They felt they had not compromised their principles.

One reason that the clergy avoided discussing segregation very forcefully was because their congregations overwhelmingly supported it. Because their congregations were important reference groups to the pastors, they were caught between reference groups (professional colleagues on the one hand and the congregation on the other). Such factors were no doubt part of the reluctance of clergy to take a strong stand, but the most important factors were institutional in character.

Although the official statements of most Christian denominations condemn segregation, the working propositions of the church bureaucracies are such that rewards come to those who do not "rock the boat." Concepts of success in the ministry are related to improvements in membership and in financial prosperity. The addition of a new educational wing or the need to build a new and much larger sanctuary are often viewed as signs that the pastor must be doing something right. Moreover, ministers often view harmonious, satisfied congregations as evidence of success. The minister whose church is racked with conflict and is declining in membership is certainly not a prime candidate for promotion to a larger congregation. Whether the minister is part of an episcopal system (where a bishop appoints clergy to a congregation) or of a congregational system (where a pulpit committee from the local congregation seeks out a pastor to hire), a reputation for controversy and

uncompromising conscience is not usually an asset. The minister who wants to advance in his or her career keeps the congregation united, the funds flowing, and the membership stable and/or increasing.

This process provides an excellent illustration of Thomas O'Dea's "dilemma of mixed motivation." Clergy were torn between two motivations: (1) being faithful to the prophetic ethnical teachings of the denomination on the one hand and (2) enhancing their careers by doing that which was necessary to be "successful" on the other. Many felt that they would work on one of the goals first (building their careers) and would later take on the hard task of speaking their consciences forthrightly. Yet some observers have been skeptical of such a strategy. One Little Rock minister who did speak out had this to report:

> I talk to the young ministers and I ask them why they aren't saying anything. They say no one will listen to them, they aren't known and their churches are small. But wait, they say, until we get big churches and are widely known. We won't be silent then. Then I turn to the ministers in the big churches and I listen to them trying to explain why they have done so little. Their answer is a simple one; they say they have too much to lose. Only recently, one such man said to a group I was in, "I've spent seventeen years of my life building up that church, and I'm not going to see it torn down in a day." (Campbell and Pettigrew, 1959:120–121)

A complex set of factors plays on a minister and affects decision making. Some of these factors may create pressure that calls for contradictory behavior. Just understanding the belief system of a religion is by no means sufficient to understanding the behavior of religious persons. In the case of racial bigotry in Little Rock, the official position of most denominations called for prophetic forthrightness by the clergy, but at the same time they provided concrete rewards (promotions to bigger congregations) for taking the road of least resistance. In effect, the institutional procedures operated to reward those who were restrained in their comments or even complacent about the entire matter. The silence by the clergy, in turn, created an environment in which it seemed that everyone shared the same view. Conformity to norms of prejudice was easy, for few people were saying anything to challenge the norm. In such a case, religion is *not* a factor in *causing* prejudice, but in failing to oppose prejudice forthrightly, religious communities contributed to the *persistence* of racism.

A study by Harold Quinley found similar patterns among Protestant clergy in California. He explored variables affecting the willingness of ministers to take prophetic stands on controversial social issues. The issues in California were civil rights legislation, support for a war or advocacy of peace, and organization of farmworkers (Quinley 1974). Quinley found that support for progressive prophetic ministry depended on at least three variables: (1) the relative liberalism or conservatism of the congregation, (2) the liberalism or conservatism of the denominational leaders, and (3) the organizational structure of the denomination (congregational, presbyterian, or episcopal). He did find, however, that regardless of denominational structure, congregational members have more control over most of the minister's actions than do the denominational hierarchy. While the hierarchy may control appointments and removals from office in episcopal systems (with a bishop), the local congregation controls salary in virtually all Protestant denominations. So support from a powerful and like-minded denominational hierarchy could enhance the tendency to have a progressive prophetic ministry, but in this study local congregations frequently had a moderating effect on the activism of clergy. Most parish ministers believed that their careers would suffer if they engaged controversial public issues. Ethical convictions regarding civil rights and other matters are often muted by institutional-maintenance concerns. These same forces were also found to be at work among clergy during conflicts in Rochester, New York (Martin 1972), and in Boston (Thomas 1985).

Of course, religious institutions are also very capable of using their influence to combat racism. For example, the Roman Catholic Church was instrumental in starting a program known as Project Equality. This involved churches using their buying power to reduce racial discrimination by requiring all their suppliers to adopt affirmative action policies. Many national Protestant denominational offices supported

Photo by Keith Roberts

When the controversy about desegregation of this high school in Little Rock, Arkansas, arose, all major denominations had endorsed the position that racism is contrary to Christianity. Still, ministers in Little Rock were disinclined to speak out because they thought it would reduce membership in their congregations, damage the financial health of the church, and adversely affect their own careers. So despite official positions of the national denomination, pastors remained silent. The second statue on the right, above the front doors of Central High School, is named "Opportunity"—precisely the thing that was being denied African Americans.

Project Equality. A few local congregations did as well, but it was mostly national denominational hierarchies that supported the program for nearly 50 years. This suggests only one of many ways in which religious groups have used their corporate influence to bring change, particularly at the level of the national denominational office. In fact, several studies have indicated that the more insulated the official hierarchy is from the local congregation, the more likely it is to emphasize egalitarian stances. Southern Catholics, for example, have historically been less likely to discriminate than members of congregationally based Protestant churches in the South. This has been largely because bishops, who are not directly responsible to the local congregation, have been willing to uphold the official position of the denomination (Beck 1978; Wood 1970, 1981).

Our point is that institutional factors may work to enhance racial prejudice and discrimination or to combat it. Simply knowing the official position of the denomination does not give the whole picture. Just as the religious meaning system may have countervailing influences within it, so also may the religious institution provide motivations and influences that run counter to the official doctrine. It is simplistic to say that religion contributes to bigotry or that it contributes to tolerance. First, it is necessary to know what interpretation of Christianity one is talking about: pietist, fundamentalist, orthodox, liberal, and so on. Second, any given religious group may be contributing to tolerance in some respects while contributing to exclusivity and bigotry in other ways. The meaning, belonging, and institutional subsystems that comprise religion may work at cross-purposes.

Our focus on ways that religion sometimes contributes to bigotry is only part of the picture. Religious prejudice is frequently an expression of other conflicts within the society at large. On the one hand, bigotry within religious communities may be due to their being open social systems rather than the religion being the cause of bigotry (see Figure 10.3). In addition, some scholars argue that religious prejudice is frequently a consequence of other social forces (such as conflict over resources) rather than the cause of bigotry. This is a contribution of the conflict theory.

Critical Thinking: In this chapter, the investigation has focused on racism directed by white Christians against African Americans. How might the causes of religious prejudice against Jews be different? Which theories might become more relevant for understanding this bigotry? Why? Which might be less relevant? Why?

SOCIAL CONFLICT AND RELIGIOUS EXPRESSION: THE CONFLICT PERSPECTIVE

It often happens that religious prejudice is actually a reflection of larger social conflicts rather than their cause. In this case, religion may be acting purely as a justification for discriminatory behavior; the out-group is defined as spiritually inferior so that members of the in-group do not feel guilty about their blatantly unjust behavior. This perspective is an important contribution of the Marxian theory of social conflict. Marxian analysts look to nonreligious causes of prejudice, although they recognize the role of religion in maintaining social inequities.

Perhaps the most important theory of racial and ethnic discrimination is that which insists that prejudice and discrimination are caused by conflict over scarce resources. Some items in any society are scarce and nondivisible or nonsharable (or at least are viewed as such). The best jobs, the best housing, the best educational opportunities (admittance into a professional school), and social status are examples of items that are viewed as scarce and over which there may be conflict.

Three variables are central in discrimination and prejudice (Farley 2010; Noel 1968). First,

Figure 10.3 Open Systems Model and Bigotry Within Religious Organizations

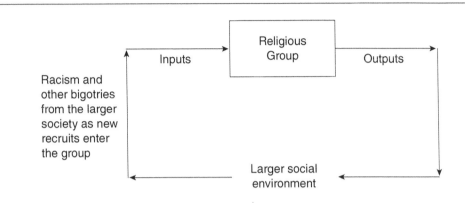

James Wood has suggested that prejudice within religious communities may be due to inputs from the larger society. Christian churches often try to recruit new members who are unchurched. Further, members of any religious community are bound to be profoundly influenced by attitudes in the larger society—their social attitudes shaped by mass media, work colleagues, and friendship networks outside the religious body rather than by the theology of the denomination. So, while much of the discussion thus far in this chapter has focused on ways that religion might influence the society, Wood's idea suggested that racism is an alien value that infiltrates the religious community.

when the two groups are visually distinctive either physically (skin color, facial features) or culturally (dress, language, beliefs), prejudice may occur, but it is not inevitable. Symbolic distinctions between groups may foster feelings of "we" and "they," but there is not necessarily hostility between the groups. Second, if those two groups are in conflict over some scarce resource, the likelihood of prejudice is very high. It is interesting to note that the contemporary high levels of anti-Arab sentiment in the United States began after the energy crisis came to awareness in the 1970s (with Arabs controlling oil resources). Likewise, anti-Asian sentiment is highest in industries where extremely qualified Japanese or Chinese Americans are hired over whites in competitive high-tech jobs. Third, where one of the groups has more power

to control access to scarce and valued resources, discrimination and prejudice are nearly universal. The more powerful group uses its power to control the resources. It then develops stereotypes of the out-group in order to justify discriminatory behavior and to make its own behavior seem morally right. Religion is frequently a part of this moral justification.

An important point here is that prejudice and discrimination are enhanced if the groups in question differ not only in their economic interests but also in their physical appearance, their language, their culture, and their religion. In cases where two groups differ in all of these ways, it is common for the conflict to be justified and highlighted in religious terms. Native Americans were freely exploited and their lands taken from them because they were "heathens" who supposedly needed to be "civilized" (which usually meant "Christianized"). Likewise, many southern states had laws that forbade conversion of slaves during the early period of the slave trade. The slave owners were afraid that, if blacks held the same religious beliefs as whites, owners would be forced to free their chattel. Eventually, justification for discrimination came to be based more intensely on color than on religious affiliation.

The central point is this: When lines of differentiation between people in racial characteristics, cultural backgrounds, language, religious orientations, and economic self-interests are coextensive and mutually exclusive, antipathy is likely to occur (Farley 2010). Although religion is one cause, it is not necessarily the primary cause. However, religion may be used as the primary justification for hostility. After all, if "they" are immoral infidels or heretics, treating them with something less than respect seems quite reasonable and moral. Thus, what seems on the surface to be religious prejudice may, in fact, be caused by conflicts between groups that seek control over the same scarce resources. The source of the conflict is primarily economic.

The conflict in Northern Ireland represents a situation in which economic, religious, and ethnic boundaries have been coextensive or parallel. The Protestants are the landowners and are of Scottish descent. The Catholics tend to be poor laborers who have long been fiercely loyal to the concept of an independent and united Ireland. The conflict is referred to as one between Protestants and Catholics, but religion is not the sole or even the primary cause of the conflict. The medieval crusades of Christians against the Moors were also justified on religious grounds, but the conflict was rooted in economic and ethnic interests as well.

The contrary situation is where lines of demarcation are crosscutting. In social circumstances, where members of an ethnic group are not necessarily of the same social class or the same reli-

gious group, the likelihood of religiously based prejudice is reduced (revisit Figure 10.2). Likewise, where members of a particular religious group do not share the same ethnic background or economic interests, the likelihood of prejudice is somewhat diminished, and religious justifications for discriminatory behavior are also reduced. Hence, religion often acts to reflect larger social conflicts. The student of religion must be wary of overgeneralizing about religion as a *cause* of social conflict. In any given situation, religion may well be a cause of conflict, but each case must be evaluated in terms of the specific social setting and the specific worldview of the religious group.

Critical Thinking: What, in your opinion, are the four most important factors in the existence of racism among Christians? Explain how these factors work and provide your rationale for why you think these are the most important variables. Do you think any of these variables are necessary or sufficient, or are they all just contributing factors? Why?

SUMMARY

Michael Emerson, William Mirola, and Susanne Monahan summarized their findings this way: "Forget the color line. When it comes to religion in the United States, we have a color wall" (Emerson et al. 2011:161). There is a strong correlation between racial identity and religious preference, and that translates at the local level to extremely high levels of racial segregation in congregations. There are many explanations for this racial homogeneity, but given the history of race in American society, we cannot overlook the importance of racial prejudice in driving religious racial segregation.

Christianity may contribute in subtle ways to the development and persistence of racism and other ethnic prejudice, even if its official posture mitigates against such intergroup hostility. Although there are differences between members of different denominations and between theological liberals and conservatives, for the most part, the most religiously committed people tend to rank lower on scales of racism than less active members or than those disaffiliated with religion. Further, the logic of Christian theology is such that racism is really incompatible with Christianity; racism is, in fact, a theology with its own internal logic and value structure. Despite all of this, Christianity has sometimes contributed, even unwittingly, to the formation and continued existence of racism.

First, aversive discrimination may have been unconsciously fostered through a meaning system that linked concern with purity to color symbolism (with blackness associated with evil). Other beliefs emphasizing individual autonomy and free will may also have contributed to the persistence of racism because of a failure of Christians to recognize the realities of systemic or institutional racism.

Second, prejudice may be passed on through the we–they boundaries and through informal norms of the community. The belonging function of religion can be a source of exclusivity and hostility.

Finally, formal institutional structures may contribute to the *persistence* of prejudice by rewarding behaviors other than adherence to the official teachings of the faith. Ministerial or organizational definitions of success may reward (with promotions and professional advancements) those whose style is noncontroversial and unobtrusive.

In short, the three subsystems of religion may sometimes work at cross-purposes, contributing simultaneously to tolerance of others and to bigotry.

Not only is Christianity capable of contributing to racial prejudice, but religious prejudice is also often a reflection of larger conflict in the society. This is especially true if color lines, socioeconomic stratification, political parties, and religious boundaries are coextensive and mutually exclusive. In any case, our discussion points to the interactive relationship between religious values and the social conditions at large. We have also found that religions are themselves complex entities that can have many countervailing forces within them.

11

RELIGION, GENDER, AND SEXUALITY

HERE ARE SOME QUESTIONS TO
PONDER AS YOU READ THIS CHAPTER

- Does religion—and Christianity in particular—contribute to negative attitudes and discriminatory treatment of women?
- How can the meaning systems of religion contribute to gender equity and gender bias?

- Why do structural components and meaning systems of a religion sometimes have contradictory effects relative to gender equity?
- Why do some women actively choose religious communities that have high gender barriers and limited roles for females?
- How do religious systems relate to homosexuality, homophobia, and heterosexism?
- How are same-sex marriage and ordination of gays and lesbians playing out in religious communities?

When examining the relationship among religion, gender, and sexuality, one confronts an interesting paradox. Religion is historically connected to sexism and gender inequality, and yet in most cases women exhibit higher levels of religiosity than men. Why would this be the case, and why would members of a group whose identity is stigmatized in most major religious traditions—the LGBTQ (lesbian, gay, bisexual, transgender, and queer or questioning) community—remain religiously active, oftentimes in religious communities whose teachings stigmatize them?

Women's groups that are committed to changing gender roles and attitudes have often charged that religion perpetuates traditional role expectations of men and women. Historically, many groups have refused to ordain women—barring them from the major leadership positions in the religious group. A few denominations continue to maintain this position today. Studies have suggested that this is not only true of the established religious bodies; women have often been singled out and accused of sexual weakness, sinfulness, and impurity in the new religious movements (NRMs) as well (Jacobs 1987). Some pagan religious traditions, such as Wicca, have a much more positive attitude toward the feminine, with female gods and leadership positions for women. However, as John Hawley concluded, "Theological appreciation of the feminine does not necessarily lead to a positive evaluation of real women" (Hawley 1986:235). Moreover,

religious ideas about gender and religious standards of sexual ethics have often influenced attitudes toward same-sex relationships. In the following pages, we explore the role of religion in sacralizing gendered behaviors and roles and in shaping attitudes toward LGBTQs.

To keep the scope of this chapter manageable, we again focus primarily on the relationship between Christianity and gender prejudice. Although the coverage is not comprehensive of all religious traditions, students should be developing skills in analysis and should gain a sense of how sociologists approach the issue for any religious tradition. We begin by exploring the empirical evidence about whether organized religion really does stigmatize women and legitimate male dominance.

GENDER AND RELIGIOUS INVOLVEMENT

We begin by documenting and explaining the higher levels of religious involvement among women. Table 11.1 on page 278 shows the gender difference in identification by religious tradition. The most heavily female religious traditions are the historically black churches and Jehovah's Witnesses. The members of the largest religious traditions in the United States also are more than half women: Catholic (54%), Mainline Protestant (54%), and Evangelical Protestant (53%). Indeed, over three quarters of Americans belong to religious traditions in which the majority of members are women.

Table 11.1 Gender Composition of Religious Groups in the United States (by percentage)

	Women	Men	Share of Total U.S. Pop.
Historically Black Churches	60	40	6.9
Jehovah's Witnesses	60	40	0.7
Mormon	56	44	1.7
Catholic	54	46	23.9
Mainline Protestant	54	46	18.1
Orthodox	54	46	0.6
Evangelical Protestant	53	47	26.3
Overall Total	**52**	**48**	
Jewish	48	52	1.7
Religious Unaffiliated	48	52	5.8
Buddhist	47	53	0.7
Muslim	46	54	0.6
Secular Unaffiliated	40	60	6.3
Hindu	39	61	0.4
Agnostic	36	64	2.4
Atheist	30	70	1.6

SOURCE: Pew Research Center Forum on Religion and Public Life. 2008b. *U.S. Religious Landscape Survey*. Retrieved from http://religions.pewforum.org.

Men, by contrast, dominate among the nonreligious: atheists (70%), agnostics (64%), and secular unaffiliated (60%). Men are also the majority of members in the major non-Christian traditions in the United States: Jewish, Buddhist, Muslim, and Hindu.

Beyond religious affiliation, women also exhibit higher levels of religiosity than men across a number of measures. As Table 11.2 shows, in terms of religious participation, women attend religious services weekly at a 22% higher rate than men and pray at least daily

62% more than men. Women also report 30% higher levels of belief in God and 300% lower levels of atheism. All of these differences are considerable, and they hold true across almost all religious affiliations (and non-affiliation). In addition, D. Paul Sullins found similar gender differences in religiosity in over 65 countries, suggesting this is not a uniquely American phenomenon (Sullins 2006).

There is no definitive explanation for this gender difference in religion. Some argue that differential gender roles explain the gender gap in

Table 11.2 Gender Differences in Religiosity (by percentage) and Gender Gap

	Women	*Men*	*Gender Gap*
Knows God exists	67.8	52.1	30%
Doesn't believe in God	1.5	4.5	−300%
Prays at least daily	66.8	41.4	62%
Never prays	5.3	16.1	−304%
Attends worship services at least weekly	36.3	29.8	22%
Takes part in other religious activities (beyond worship) at least monthly	26.5	20.0	32%

SOURCE: Authors' calculations from 2006–2012 General Social Surveys.

religion (Levitt 1995). Women are responsible for child rearing, so the argument goes, and this encourages greater religious affiliation and involvement. Although it is true that parenthood has a positive effect on religiosity, the effect of parenthood on religiosity is stronger for men than for women; parenthood alone does not fully explain the gap. Others argue that not being in the labor force gives women more free time for attention to faith issues. This is also partially true. Full-time employment does have a negative effect on religiosity, but the gender gap persists even when controlling for women's employment status. In other words, women who work full-time are more religious than men who work full-time.

In the next two sections, we consider two other ways of understanding the gender gap in religion: a more cultural approach that focuses on the "feminization" of religion and an approach grounded in a rational choice perspective that focuses on the relationship between religion and risk tolerance.

Feminization of Religion

Although women were viewed for centuries as spiritually more vulnerable to sin and corruption than men and as a source of evil influence, an interesting shift occurred in the United States in the 19th century. As opposed to the sternness and harshness of 18th-century American Christianity, the sentimentality of the 19th century was clearly more "feminine" in tone. Barbara Welter, who referred to this as the "feminization of American religion," wrote, "When . . . a more intuitive, heartfelt approach was urged, it was tantamount to asking for a more feminine style" (Welter 1976:94). Welter pointed out that the most popular hymns written at that time stressed passive and accepting roles. Such hymns as "Just As I Am, Without One Plea," "To Suffer for Jesus Is My Greatest Joy," and "I Need Thee Every Hour" illustrate a pattern in hymnody of exalting dependency, submissiveness, and a willingness to suffer without complaint as Christian virtues. These were also viewed as feminine characteristics and as feminine virtues in 19th-century American culture. In contrast, the ideal characteristics of the male were embodied in the aggressive, independent, self-sufficient industrialist. This transformation of American religion was perhaps most noticeably seen in the imagery of Jesus. In the 18th century, he had been viewed as the stern taskmaster and as the exalted ruler of God's kingdom. In the 19th century, the major characteristics attributed to Jesus were loving self-sacrifice, tenderheartedness, and willingness to forgive those who injured him.

Given the mixed signals that men were receiving about masculine and Christian virtues, it is not surprising that male church attendance dropped off and religion came to be viewed as a woman's concern. As depicted in almost any popular novel or sermon of that day, women were more spiritual, more noble, and more generous than men. As Welter put it, "Womanhood was believed to be, in principle, a higher, nobler state than manhood, since it was less directly related to the body and was more involved with the spirit; women had less to transcend in their progress" (Welter 1976:95). Religion also came to be viewed as less rational (Ruether 1975). Rationality was associated with science, technology, and industry—all of which were male-dominated spheres. Women came to be viewed as more religious than men and as the transmitters of morality but still not as highly rational. The clergy, who were still almost entirely male, were sometimes viewed as naive, unknowing, and incapable of understanding business practices. As religion was feminized, the leaders of the church were also attributed with feminine virtues and vices (Ruether 1975).

Although women came to be seen as more spiritual, this happened at a time when religion was having decreased influence on the affairs of the world. Commerce and politics were increasingly secular and governed by principles of secular rationality. At the very time when women were being identified with religiosity, religion was being demoted to a less influential position in society. In fact, the feminization of religion may have occurred precisely because religion was being dislodged from direct access to political power; it was becoming identified as a concern of the home, the hearth, and the individual. This loss of social power was equated to taking on a more feminine role in society. To state it in its most negative form, to be religious was to be unknowing, lacking in power, and guided by naive sentimentality rather than by realism and reason. The stereotypes of women as irrational and emotional had remained constant, but the role of religion in society—and hence its image—had changed significantly from its image prior to the 1800s.

Research from the 1990s indicates that persons—male or female—who have more "feminine" value orientations (valuing feelings and expressiveness) tend to rate higher in various measures of religiousness than persons of either sex who have more "masculine" (instrumental) orientations. In fact, gender orientation in one's values is a better predictor of religiousness than is the sex of the person (Thompson 1991). At least in the contemporary United States, religion continues to have feminine overtones, despite the fact that it has often been less than sympathetic to women.

Critical Thinking: Do the faith traditions with which you are familiar have more feminine than masculine values—stressing cooperation, support, nurturance, and relationships as central, rather than competition and individualistic achievement? If so, does this explain why fewer men affiliate and attend services?

Religion and Risk Tolerance

Sociologists Alan Miller and John Hoffman developed a rational choice explanation for the higher levels of religiosity of women relative to men that focuses on risk aversion. Recall that the basic premise of the rational choice perspective is that in making decisions people try to minimize their costs and maximize their benefits. In terms of deciding whether to engage in religious practices, one of the potential benefits of being religious is the possibility of a better next life, and one of the potential costs of irreligion is the possibility of eternal damnation. From this perspective, *irreligion is risky behavior*. Because women have a lower tolerance for risk than men, this approach argues they are more religious (Miller and Hoffman 1995).

Much of the research in this area since the original statement of the theory has focused on trying to understand the origins of risk tolerance and aversion. Not surprisingly, the major competing explanations are *nature* and *nurture*, biology and socialization. On the side of nature, Miller and Stark tested socialization explanations of gender differences in risk preference and concluded that "physiological differences related to risk preference appear to offer the only viable explanation of gender differences in religiousness" (Miller and Stark 2002:1401). This position argues that men have a biological propensity for risk taking owing to higher levels of testosterone.

Others have focused on nurture, examining how socialization processes could lead to a gender difference in religiosity. One promising line of explanation is based on what is known as "power–control theory" (PCT). PCT was originally developed to explain gender differences in propensity to engage in risky behavior—such as committing crime. PCT maintains that variations in the social control of sons and daughters within a household are linked to risk preference and behavior outside the household. In more patriarchal households, daughters are more subject to social control than sons, and so sons develop more preference for risky behavior than daughters. In more egalitarian households, there is less of a gap in the risk preference between sons and daughters, just as there is less gender-based difference in the freedom or control of children.

Jessica Collett and Omar Lizardo applied PCT to the gender difference in religiosity and found, in line with PCT, that gender differences in religiosity are greater for individuals raised in "traditional" (patriarchal) households than those raised in more gender-egalitarian households. They also found that women raised in more egalitarian households tend to be less religious than women raised in more patriarchal households (Collett and Lizardo 2009). These findings suggest that there could in fact be a connection

between the socialization of women into risk tolerance or aversion that affects their subsequent levels of religiosity.

Although the gender difference in religious commitment is one of the most consistent findings in the sociology of religion, we still have no solid explanation for it. The explanations previously given have been suggested but not definitively confirmed. Socialization explanations for the gender difference and the connection between risk preference and gender have both been challenged (Freese 2004). In the end, this remains a finding in search of an explanation.

Critical Thinking: Do religious affiliation and behaviors by women seem to you to be more about female risk aversion (fear of consequences), or does socialization seem to be the better explanation for gender differences? Why? Which explanation best takes into account the fact that *male* involvement is higher than that of females among Jews, Buddhists, Muslims, and Hindus?

SEXISM IN THE RELIGIOUS MEANING AND BELONGING SYSTEMS

As we noted at the outset, one of the interesting paradoxes we encounter when examining religion and gender is women's higher levels of religiosity *despite* the historical connection between religion and sexism.

One might expect George Kelsey's thesis that racism and Christianity are incompatible (explored in Chapter 10) might apply to sexism and Christianity as well. After all, Christian theology has stressed that one's worth is founded not in one's chromosomes but in one's relationship to God. Basing one's sense of self-worth on gender rather than on skin color would seem to be no less a form of idolatry. Indeed, logic would seem to require such a position. However, the history of sex bias is much longer than that of racial bias. Sexism is not a modern phenomenon; it is deeply rooted in the religious and philosophical traditions of the Western world. Sexual differences have been viewed as creations of God, and sexual inequality has frequently been viewed as God-ordained.

Hence, the meaning system has often reinforced both definitions of gender (concepts of "masculinity" or "femininity") and gender roles (tasks designated as "women's work" or "men's work"). Because inequality based on a person's sex is so much a part of the history of the Western world, it is appropriate that we briefly explore sex-role attitudes in Western philosophical and religious thought. Obviously we can only scratch the surface in the space we have here, but it is instructive to note some of the views held at various points in history by influential religious and philosophical thinkers and by religious bodies.

A Historical Overview of Gender Attitudes in Western Christianity

Because of the increase of women theologians and biblical scholars, more attention has been given in the last four decades to gender role and gender assumptions in the biblical tradition. Familiarity with the original Hebrew, Greek, and Aramaic has allowed feminist scholars to find patterns that were previously overlooked. For example, the Hebrew language has two different words that have commonly been translated as *man*. One of these words, *'adhám*, is a generic term that refers to all of humanity. The other word, *'ish*, refers specifically to males. Because both terms have been translated into English as *man*, some of the subtle implications are lost in translation of biblical verses. The passage in the first chapter of Genesis that says that God created man is written with the term *'adhám*. Hence, it should read "God created humanity in his own image, male and female God created them." Here the scriptures are less sexist than some people assume when they are limited to English versions (Bird 1974; Trible 1979).

Elsewhere it is clear that the scripture was written for males, as in the books of law (Bird 1974). The legal code is divided into apodictic law (moral commandments) and casuistic law (case law). The apodictic law is written primarily to men in that the literary voice and the examples are relevant to males. The Tenth Commandment provides a good example: "You shall not covet your neighbor's house; you shall not covet your neighbor's wife, or his manservant, or his maidservant, or his ox, or his ass, or anything that is your neighbor's." Not only does the passage specify *wife* rather than the more general term *spouse*, but the wife is included in a list of property that was owned exclusively by men. Furthermore, the Hebraic second-person pronoun, which we translate as *you*, had masculine and feminine forms (similar to the way our third-person pronoun has masculine and feminine forms: *he* and *she*). In the Ten Commandments, as in most of the apodictic law, the masculine form of the second-person pronoun was used. Note as another example the audience that is being addressed in Exodus 22:22–24: "You shall not afflict any widow or orphan. If you do . . . then your wives shall become widows and your children fatherless." The intended audience, in much of the Bible, was clearly male.

Similar assumptions are part of the casuistic law, in which punishments for committing proscribed acts are spelled out. Most casuistic law begins with the formula "If a man does X, then . . . ." However, the term *man* here is the masculine term *'ish* that is used. In those instances in which laws were articulated for women, they often served to remind them of their inferior position. Women were defined as unclean during their menstrual period and were unfit to enter the temple for 7 days after the birth of a son and for 14 days after the birth of a daughter. Such contamination was not normally associated with the natural bodily processes of men.

Of course, attitudes toward women are not consistent in the Hebrew Bible (called the Old Testament by many Christians), for it was written over a period of many centuries and contains many types of literature. The book of Proverbs, for example, depicts women as sources of great wisdom. There are also ancient stories about women, such as Ruth, Esther, and various women in the Book of Judges, that depict women as strong and courageous. Still, the overall effect of the Hebrew Bible is that women are subordinate. Even much of the symbolic action is limited to males; the primary symbolic act that represents the covenant with God is circumcision. Hence, only men could be ritually inducted into the covenanted community of God's people. Clearly, there were elements of intrinsic sexism in the early biblical period. Such attitudes are taken particularly seriously today by those Christians who accept the totality of the Bible as literally true.

Christian thought has, of course, been more than just a continuation of ancient Judaism; historically, it represented a synthesis of Hebrew and Greek worldviews. Many of the early theologians drew heavily from Greek philosophers. The Greek tradition was actually more explicitly sexist than was Hebrew culture. Aristotle's biological and political sciences, for example, depicted free Greek males as the embodiment of rationality. Such rationality was to be the ruling force in the good society, and the "spirit people" (males) were obligated to subjugate the "body people"—slaves, barbarians, and women (Ruether 1975). Furthermore, Aristotle taught that every male seed should normally produce its own image in another male. Females were the result of an accident or aberration in the womb in which the lower material substance of the female womb subverted and warped the higher characteristics of the male. Women, clearly, were viewed as defective human beings (Ruether 1975).

Even before Aristotle, Plato and other thinkers maintained that reason and affectivity were mutually exclusive and were associated with good and evil, respectively. Moreover, reason and spirituality were identified with males; emotion and the natural world were associated with females.

This sort of dualistic worldview is characteristic of nearly all philosophical systems in classical Greece. Religious historian Rosemary Ruether sees the problem as *hierarchical dualism,* an outlook that divides all of life into two distinct realms, one of which is higher than the other (this world/other world, darkness/light, carnality/spirituality, emotion/reason) (Ruether 1975). Reuther maintained that this sort of dualism is universally associated with sexist thinking (Shields 1986). Women are invariably associated with the "lower" processes and with worldliness. Women are viewed as the cause of passion and are believed to be preoccupied with it; furthermore, they are identified with worldly creation because of their biological function in childbirth. Ruether insisted that dualistic thinking—in which the empirical world is defined as evil and the spiritual world is viewed as good—has an inherent sexist bias. Ruether maintained that much of the sexist bias in Christian history comes from the Greek, not the Hebrew, legacy. She wrote that, unlike Christianity and Greek philosophy, "Hebrew religion, especially in its preexilic period, is not a religion of alienation that views nature as inferior or evil" (Ruether 1975:187).

The New Testament Gospels depict a much more positive view of women (Parvey 1974; Ruether 1975). Jesus himself violated many of the gender role taboos of his day. He allowed women to join his traveling group (Luke 8:1–3) and encouraged them to sit at his feet and learn (traveling and studying with a rabbi were viewed as very improper for women in that day). Jesus disregarded a number of gender taboos of his day (Mark 5:25–34; Matthew 9:20–22; Luke 8:43–48; John 4:27). He frequently contrasted the faithlessness of the religious leaders with the profound faith of poor widows and outcast women. In that day, unattached women were considered suspect and were to be avoided. His comments would certainly have been insulting and sacrilegious to many people (Luke 4:25–29).

Jesus taught that the role of the faithful was one not of glory and fame but of service. He capped his ministry by washing the feet of his disciples, a task normally assigned to women or servants, and at the time of his greatest disappointment outside the gates of Jerusalem, he described himself as feeling like a "mother hen"—an interesting analogy because of its feminine connotation.

The New Testament epistles are more ambivalent regarding gender. Some people have a view of Saint Paul as one of the world's worst misogynists. He ordered women to obey their husbands, he told them not to speak in church, and he held to the old Hebrew belief that women serve men and only men could serve God. Much has been written on these passages; they are frequently used today in some congregations and denominations to reinforce traditional roles. However, there are numerous references to women preachers who were sent by Paul or who accompanied him. In actual practice, he did not prohibit women from leadership roles. He also asserted that in Christ, "There is neither male nor female," a statement affirming egalitarian values.

The ancient Greek view that women are defective humans found its way into the Christian New Testament. The Apocalypse (the Book of Revelation) describes the procession of the redeemed as a company of virgin *men* "who have not been defiled with women." Women were viewed as lesser beings who were not capable of being saved and might even interfere with men being saved.

Still, it was Paul who emphasized so heavily the sin of Adam and Eve, and he believed that the responsibility for original sin lay with Eve. The implication is that women are an easier mark for the forces of evil. Interestingly, the idea that Eve introduced original sin is discussed only in the first few chapters of Genesis; it is never mentioned again in the Hebrew Bible. Yet, centuries later this was to become a major theme in the teachings of many Christian evangelists and theologians. Tertullian, one of the early Christian leaders, picked up on this theme and continually reminded women that each one of them was an Eve, "the first deserter of the divine law" (Bullough 1973:114). At a much later time, Martin Luther also emphasized that a woman was responsible for the Fall. Although he generally opposed ridicule of women in public, he did on one occasion follow his comments on the story of humanity's Fall with the directed observation, "We have you women to thank for that!" (cited in Bullough 1973:198). So it was that the Adam and Eve story became a much more important justification of misogynism in Christian history than it ever was in the ancient Hebrew tradition.

Saint Augustine, a theologian who has influenced Christian thought for centuries, held to the Platonic view that passion was evil and that the sexual act lowered humans to the frenzied and unthinking level of beasts. So appalled by passion was Saint Augustine that he held the male erection to be the essence of sin. Moreover, if an erection was the essence of sin, it was clear who was responsible for causing it: women (Ruether 1974a). This sort of projection of sexual lust on women and a general view of women as temptresses were common among Christian theologians (Bullough 1973).

This sort of sexism has been integral to the official teaching of the Roman Catholic Church for centuries (Schoenherr 2002), and continued in the Protestant Reformation. It can be seen in the writings of Martin Luther, John Calvin, John Knox, and other prominent reformers. In fact, *The First Blast of the Trumpet Against the Monstrous Regiment of Women* was published by John Knox (the founder of Presbyterianism) in 1558 and stands to this day as one of the most misogynistic statements in Christendom. Moreover, the removal of Mary as a primary religious figure of adulation left Protestantism without a major saint or model who was female (Douglass 1974; Ruether 1975).

Critical Thinking: There are strong anti-female images and rules in both Christianity and other faith traditions, but there are also affirmations of the dignity of all children of God. How important is the *meaning system* in creating and preserving gender inequality? Why?

RELIGIOUS BELONGING SYSTEMS AND GENDERED "WE" VERSUS "THEY" THINKING

When members of conflicting ethnic or racial groups also belong to different religious groups, the likelihood of religiously based prejudice increases. However, in the industrialized world, men and women are not segregated as happens with race. Men and women are members of the same families and the same religious organizations. Hence, it might seem that "we" versus "they" distinctions would not occur. Nonetheless, these distinctions are often given sanction in religious groups. Among Orthodox and Hasidic Jews, men and women sit separately during worship. The same pattern has prevailed among certain Protestant groups in the United States, such as the Shakers and the Old Order Amish, and among the Eastern Orthodox in places like Greece. Such religiously sanctioned segregation of the sexes would seem to reinforce we–they distinctions that are part of the larger culture. The nature of belonging is shaped by one's gender, male or female.

Beyond the issue of gender segregation, informal norms within the religious community may cause people to adhere to prejudicial attitudes in order to feel accepted—regardless of the position of the clerical hierarchy or of official denominational theology. To feel included—a sense that one belongs—one may feel compelled to laugh at jokes about someone out of the "proper" gender role. The penalty for ignoring the informal, unwritten standards is social exclusion; the reward is a sense of belonging. The official positions of the denomination—which may downplay

gender difference and gender roles—frequently lack such immediate and concrete reinforcements. Hence, the informal culture of a local congregation and the desire to belong may be more important in shaping attitudes than the group's formal or official doctrines.

The belonging function of religion, then, may foster sexist attitudes in several ways. Insofar as the religious outlook stresses the fact that males and females are utterly different, the sense of "we" versus "they" may be heightened, and the sense of belonging may be tied to sex group rather than to faith community. This may lead to suspicion and prejudice. Beyond this, the informal community that provides the sense of belonging may have informal norms that foster sexism. This leads to the next major way in which religion may enhance sex bias—the formal organizational structure itself.

RELIGION AND INSTITUTIONAL SEXISM

Perhaps the most vexing problems of religious prejudice toward women lie in institutional patterns—the structural dimension of religion. After a study of Christianity and Islam, Bullough concluded, "Regardless of what a religion teaches about the status of women, or what its attitudes toward sex might be, if women are excluded from the institutions and positions which influence society, a general misogynism seems to result" (Bullough 1973:134). We have already seen that denigration of women became part of the theological system (meaning system) of Western Christianity. This would be less likely to have occurred if women had been in positions to formulate and shape the official theology of the faith community. For this reason, denial of ordination becomes a significant issue. Furthermore, as long as a significant distinction is made between clergy and laity and as long as the clergy are looked up to as leaders, as those most in tune with God and as the legitimate messengers of God, the denial of ordination to women affirms their inferior position among the "people of God."

Ordination of Women

Many women scholars have seen ordination of women as a key issue: "By this exclusion the church is saying that the sexual differentiation is—for one sex—a crippling defect which no personal qualities of intelligence, character, or leadership can overcome" (Daly 1970:134; see also Ruether 1975). When the Church of Jesus Christ of Latter-day Saints (Mormons) refused to ordain African Americans—a policy in place until 1978— it was widely recognized as a statement about the inferiority of black people. Yet, some of the same denominations that were critical of the Mormons have opposed ordination of women. In this latter case, the argument that denial of ordination was a statement of inferiority was vigorously denied. Theologically trained women who have sought ordination have not found the denial convincing. Furthermore, the lack of women in leadership positions can subtly influence attitudes, especially of small children. The absence of women in important positions often communicates to children— much more vividly than any words to the contrary—the social inferiority of females.

The reasons for exclusion of women from ordination are noteworthy. Some scholars trace this exclusion back to Saint Paul who, in keeping

Photo by Keith Roberts

This clergywoman was ordained into the Presbyterian Church USA (PCUSA) in 2008. Ordination of women is an important issue because when women are in leadership positions and involved in formulation of the official theology, there is much less likelihood of misogynistic policies and ideologies. Within the Episcopal tradition, ordination of women into the priesthood was so controversial that it led to the only schism in the Episcopal Church and the founding of the conservative Anglican Church in America.

with the contemporary attitude toward women, wrote that women were not to speak in church. However, he did not vigorously follow that policy himself, and he stressed that gender was unimportant "in Christ." At least one historian has traced the original restriction on ordination to Constantine. When Christianity became the official religion of the Roman Empire, it came under some of the cultic attitudes then prevalent. Specifically, religious leaders were to maintain ritual purity. Because women were viewed as unclean at particular times of the month because of menstruation, they were unfit for ministry (Cox 2009; Ruether 1975). Because males dominated the priesthood and formulated the theology, women were continually defined as unfit. In fact, in the 13th century, Thomas Aquinas adopted Aristotle's view that women are defective males—biologically, morally, and intellectually. Hence, he reasoned that only men could fully represent Christ (the perfect human being) in the ministry. Such a rationale would not likely have occurred if women had been part of the hierarchy all along.

Interestingly, although the Catholic Church does not ordain women as priests, many of the most active members of Catholic parishes are women, and women "religious" ("nuns") have long played a key role in Catholic life (Fialka 2003). Even more dramatically, in some small parishes today, where the church cannot supply a priest, women sometimes act as functional equivalents of priests at the local level. Indeed, Ruth Wallace found that in some Catholic churches, these women are called "pastor" (Wallace 1992). Given the declining number and advancing age of Catholic priests in the United States, if the church continues to deny ordination to women, there may be more and more women acting as de facto leaders of their Catholic congregations (Schoenherr 2002).

Most major denominations now ordain women, and the official pronouncements of most churches reject sexism and endorse equality for women at all levels. There is also a willingness

by rather large majorities of members of congregations to have a female minister (Lehman 1980). Despite all this, few theologically trained women are receiving appointments to large congregations. They continue to be placed in positions as assistant ministers, as directors of religious education, or as the sole minister in small, struggling congregations that have very low salary scales.

If the official position of these church hierarchies is that women are equally competent and should be placed in positions of leadership, why is this not happening? The answer seems to lie in the inherent biases and goals of complex organizations.

The Organizational Survival Impulse and Women Clergy

Once an organization is in existence, it tends to take on characteristics and needs of its own, the most important being viability. If the organization is to survive, it must mobilize and control critical resources: the financial support of members; the skills, time, and energy of members; and so on. However, in such voluntary organizations as churches and temples, people must be convinced rather than coerced into compliance. Members who are not convinced can simply withdraw their support from the organization.

Although Edward Lehman's research on American Baptist and Presbyterian churches indicated that a majority of church members had no objection to having a woman minister, many believed that *other* members were opposed to having a woman pastor. The primary concern was that having a woman as minister would cause controversy and conflict, and such conflict might result in members leaving the church or withholding financial support. Because this sort of action could threaten the continuation of the entire organization, the controversy is studiously avoided. In virtually all churches, the pulpit committee or search committee is elected from representative areas of the church life. In almost all cases, the members of the committee are chosen from among the most active members in the church—people who have made an investment in the church and care about its health and survival. Hence, pulpit committees normally have a built-in bias to avoid anything that might threaten its vitality or viability—including conflict (Lehman 1981, 1985, 1987a, 1987b).

In a follow-up study, Paul Sullins has argued that conflict-aversive behavior is more severe in religious communities than in other types of organizations. The reason for this is that faith communities are more like families than they are like typical bureaucratic organizations—with sensitivity to feelings of others and concerns about not alienating anyone being a core value of the organizational culture. This makes churches, temples, and mosques more change resistant than most organizations, despite what their meaning system may say about equality of treatment (Sullins 2000).

Although the official position of the denomination may encourage local congregations to accept women in positions as senior pastors, organizational concerns regarding viability often play against that. The local congregation is simply more interested in promoting and maintaining its cohesiveness and stability than in responding to denominational resolutions. The needs of the structural system trump the proclamations of the meaning system.

In the 21st century, ordination of women and the frequency of women clergy lag far behind the involvement of women in other professions, such as law and medicine. While the ratios of men to women in law and medicine and ministry were very comparable up until 1970, there are now significant gaps. Roughly 34% of lawyers (U.S. Bureau of Labor Statistics 2009) and 32.3% of physicians and surgeons are women (U.S. Bureau of Labor Statistics 2006); by contrast women are only a bit more than 10% of the clergy (Chang 1997). Women are the primary ministers of about 8% of congregations, while roughly 5% of American Christians attend a congregation led by a woman (Faith and Leadership 2010). While the numbers vary considerably by denomination, women clergy in virtually every denomination still lag behind the numbers of women in most other professional fields, and they rarely are appointed senior pastor of a large church. In a recent analysis, Mark Chaves has offered an insightful analysis, one that is consistent with our open systems model (Chaves 1997).

Open Systems, Comparison Communities, and Religious Gender Roles

Chaves discussed ways in which outside forces may shape or have inputs into decision making in religious organizations. Chaves started with the issue of legitimacy of organizations in a society:

> [W]hen an organizational practice or structure becomes commonly understood as a defining feature of a "legitimate" organization of a certain type, organizational elites feel pressure to institute that practice or structure. If there is a cultural norm that says "In order for an organization to be a good organization, it must have characteristic X," organizations feel pressure to institute characteristic X. (Chaves 1997:32–33)

The more an organization is assimilated into the mainstream of the society, the more pressure it experiences to conform to the norms of other legitimate organizations and corporations. When the larger society did not stress gender equality and when patriarchy was the norm, it was often the more avant-garde or more sectarian groups that violated social expectations by recognizing women as ministers; the mainstream faith communities conformed to the patriarchal model. Of course, in the 19th century, ordination of women even among sectarian groups was not linked symbolically as a statement of gender equality as it is now. Sectarian groups simply did not care about credibility in the eyes of the secular society. The mainstream religious groups did.

As greater gender equality has become the norm, there is greater pressure on organizations that care about legitimacy in the dominant secular society to accept women as equals. This would cause us to predict a greater likelihood of ordination of women among Unitarians, Congregationalists (the United Church of Christ), United Methodists, Lutherans, Presbyterians, Episcopalians, and Reconstructionist and Reform Jews than among more sectarian or isolationist groups. This is indeed what the evidence shows. As ordination has come to symbolize a secular principle (gender equity), the sectarian groups have become more resistant to it, and mainline groups have become more open.

One reason that ordination and numbers of active female clergy lag behind other professions is the role of the state. Discrimination against women can be prohibited by the state in the fields of medicine and law. By contrast, Chaves wrote, "Religious organizations, as a population, are slower than other types of organizations to institute formal gender equality because of their greater autonomy from the state" (Chaves 1997:42). In Norway, Denmark, and Sweden, where the state church is run by the government, sex-based restrictions on ordination were banned by the parliaments. In the United States, where there is a separation of church and state, ordination of women has occurred mostly during one of the two great waves of the women's movement: the first beginning with the Women's Rights Convention in Seneca Falls, New York, in 1848 (peaking in the 1880s) and the second beginning in the 1960s (hitting full stride in the 1970s). Indeed, more denominations began to ordain women in the 1970s than during any other decade in the previous 40 years. The cultural climate of the larger society involved "inputs" into the cultural and structural system of religious communities, even if the government was not mandating it. Indeed, even in denominations that oppose ordaining both genders, the terms of the debate have changed so that women's inferiority is no longer an acceptable argument. The women's movement has changed the grounds for the debate even in those associations that resist female clergy (Chaves 1997).

Furthermore, most denominations think of themselves as similar to certain others; they tend to form alliances and even formal organizations of denominations. Denominations or local churches that are very evangelical or fundamentalist do not generally use the United Church of Christ or the PCUSA as models of how to do things. Indeed, the more liberal denominations are often vilified and used as anti-models by very conservative groups. Chaves suggested that in very broad terms we can identify three sorts of Christian religious organizations that look to one another as comparison communities:

(1) mainstream liberal denominations (United Church of Christ, PCUSA, United Methodist, Evangelical Lutheran, American Baptist, and the majority of groups that belong to the National Council of Churches),

(2) scriptural inerrancy churches (Southern Baptist, Church of God, Assemblies of God, Missouri Synod of the Lutheran Church, and virtually every other group that belongs to the National Association of Evangelicals or the Council of Bible Believing Churches), and

(3) sacramentalist churches (predominantly Roman Catholic and Eastern Orthodox, but to some extent Anglican, Episcopalian, and Lutheran).

When they adopt new policies, denominations often do research on other churches; however, their search is often limited to churches "like" themselves. Thus, groups seek credibility in large measure in relationship to other groups in the same general family. Even if their histories are quite different in origin and organizational style, religious communities are aware of their kinship with other groups that share much in the way of theological outlook.

An issue, then, is the symbolic meaning of ordination of women within a denomination. For scriptural inerrantist churches, literal reading of certain selected passages of the scripture has defined what is or is not acceptable, and ordination of females is interpreted to be beyond the pale. While many of those passages could be interpreted in several ways, faith communities tend to be influenced by the interpretations of kindred groups. Indeed, a number of Christian denominations that believe strongly in the inerrancy of scripture—but that are not highly integrated into the fundamentalist denominational subculture—do ordain women and have done so for more than a century (Evangelical Covenant Church, Church of the Nazarene, Salvation Army, Church of God—Anderson, and Pillar of Fire). They simply focus on different scriptures that stress gender equality, believing that the churches prohibiting ordination of women are out of line with scriptural teachings. Most inerrantist churches, however, have defined ordination as unbiblical, with the central issue being that to be a Christian is—in their eyes—to be antimodernist (Chaves 1997). Those fundamentalist religious bodies that do ordain women typically began doing so in the 19th century—before the matter was defined as an issue of gender equality (a secular and therefore modernist theme).

Sacramentalist churches have historically insisted that the person distributing the elements in the mass or Eucharist (communion) is symbolically in the role of Christ and therefore must be "like" Christ. Now there is no compelling reason that gender must be the defining feature of being "like" Christ, since each person has many qualities that are quite unrelated to her or his sex. However, the Catholic Church has defined sex as highly salient, and other Christian groups with sacramentalist leanings have tended to follow the lead of the Vatican. As one bishop said during the National Conference of Catholic Bishops in 1992, "A woman priest is as impossible as for me to have a baby" (quoted by Chaves 1997:88). Indeed, Chaves believed that sacramentalism has historically been characterized by a measure of antimodernism, and since gender equality is a key element of modernism, rejection of that symbol of modernism becomes an affirmation of orthodoxy. The fact of the matter is that churches that deviate from the expected norm within a family of denominations may be threatened with a kind of "excommunication" from that family of churches. The pressures on denominations from other denominations are sometimes quite overt, as when the Roman Catholic Church has made it explicit to other sacramentalist religious organizations that ordination of women would destroy any prospects of ecumenical union in the future (Chaves 1997).

A key element of Chaves's analysis is that we cannot understand ordination of women as solely an internal decision within a denomination. It is influenced by "inputs" by the larger society (norms about the conduct of business within legitimate organizations) and by pressures from comparable religious groups. Most ordinations of women occurred during one of the two major waves of women's rights activism, demonstrating the influence of secular social movements within religious social systems (Chaves and Cavendish 1997). As open systems theory would predict, any organization exists in dynamic interaction with its larger environment.

The current trend (at least as it is expressed in the official resolutions of most major denominations) is in the direction of ordaining and appointing clergywomen. Some denominations continue to deny ordination to women, the most notable example being the Roman Catholic Church and the Southern Baptist Convention. The first Protestant denomination in North America to ordain women was the Congregational Church (now called the United Church of Christ) in 1853 (Chaves 1997). The first African American group to ordain women was the African Methodist Episcopal (AME) Zion Church in 1898 (Lincoln and Mamiya 1990). The last three U.S. Protestant denominations to ordain women were the Protestant Episcopal Church in 1976, the Reformed Church in America in 1979, and the Christian Reformed Church in 1995. As we have seen, however, even in those denominations that have been more aggressive in endorsing ordination of women, clergywomen have a hard time gaining positions in larger churches, unless they settle for an assistantship or a directorship of religious education. The problem is not one of outright prejudice as much as one of organizational goals and assumptions taking precedence over other considerations. In short, the church has been guilty of institutional sexism. Clergywomen have encountered an "invisible ceiling" that limits their opportunities. The ceiling is invisible because it is an *indirect* result of policies and attitudes within the church.

One fact is highlighted by this exploration of institutional factors: Religion is both a worldview (set of beliefs, attitudes, and outlooks) and an institution in society. Understanding religious behavior can never be limited to one or the other. As organizations in society, religious bodies are often influenced by purely organizational considerations. In many ways, the organizational considerations take precedence. Hence, a strictly philosophical analysis of belief systems can never provide anything more than a partial analysis of religious behavior. It is precisely the interplay between social forces and belief systems that fascinates the sociologist of religion.

The central theme of this unit thus far has been that Christianity has often contributed to sex bias through its meaning system, its belonging system, and its institutional structure. Many denominations are currently trying to reverse these trends, but the countervailing forces of gender inequality are deeply embedded. Still, the empirical question remains regarding the connection between the outlooks and policies of religious organizations and the values and perceptions of individual members of those organizations. Further, some women intentionally join groups that appear to be oppressive to them. These create intriguing questions for sociologists.

Critical Thinking: How can religious organizational structures combat gender inequality while simultaneously contributing to it?

RELIGION, INDIVIDUAL GENDER ROLE ATTITUDES, AND THE SOCIAL CONSTRUCTION OF DIFFERENCE

The Catholic Church officially has remained steadfastly opposed to the ordination of women, and yet the majority of individuals who identify as Catholic support women's ordination (Baggett 2009; D'Antonio, Dillon, and Gauthier 2013; Dillon 1999). This suggests that sexism in the teachings and the institutional practices of churches, temples, and mosques may not simply translate to sexist attitudes in individual members. In fact, over the past half-century or more, attitudes toward traditional gender roles have changed dramatically throughout the world, but especially in Europe and the United States (Davis and Greenstein 2009; Inglehart and Norris 2003; Voicu 2009).

How this overall change relates to religion and religiosity is a question sociologists continue to investigate. We have much less empirical research available on the connection between religion and gender attitudes of individual members than we have on religion and racial attitudes. Most of the studies available contrast the religiously affiliated with the unaffiliated, or they compare gender role attitudes between denominations. Nonetheless, researchers have turned up some interesting findings over the years.

In spite of the broad shift in the direction of more egalitarian gender ideologies, religion remains a strong predictor of traditional sexist gender ideologies. That those who are active members of particular faith communities are the most sexist has been documented in the 1970s (Mason and Bumpass 1975; McMurry 1978), 1980s (Hertel and Hughes 1987; Petersen and Donnenwerth 1998), 1990s (Gallagher and Smith 1999; Gay, Ellison, and Powers 1996), 2000s (Bang et al. 2005; Hoffman and Bartkowski 2008), and 2010s (Whitehead 2012).

Although some studies indicate that conservative or evangelical Christians are increasingly negotiating gender role expectations (Bartkowski 2001; Gallagher 2003), they continue to subscribe to the most traditional gender ideologies (Bang et al. 2005; Denton 2004). By contrast, active members of liberal denominations like the United Church of Christ, Episcopal Church, and Presbyterian Church USA are more supportive of gender equality.

Related to this is the connection between particular religious beliefs and gender ideologies. Those who believe that their holy scriptures are the literal word of God and/or without error ("inerrant") are more likely to hold traditional gender role attitudes (Chaves 1997; Denton 2004; Whitehead 2012). In an interesting study of a little understood ethnic group in the United States, Jen'nan Ghazal Read found that both Arab American Muslims and Arab American Christians who believed in scriptural inerrancy scored higher on her gender traditionalism scale (Read 2003). Another recent line of work looks at the effect of different "images of God" on individuals' attitudes and actions (Froese and Bader 2010). Among the images that are included in survey studies are active, distant, critical, angry, and loving. A less examined image of God is as a "He." Andrew Whitehead has recently explored the relationship between a masculine image of God and traditional gender ideologies using data from the Baylor Religion Survey. Recalling Geertz's definition of religion in Chapter 1, Whitehead observed:

> Cultures containing religions that worship a "male" God are influenced by the "moods" and "motivations" created by . . . religious symbols that legitimate and perpetuate social inequality. (Whitehead 2012:143)

He in fact found that the more strongly individuals held a masculine image of God, the more traditional were their gender role attitudes. Masculine image of God was a stronger predictor than either Biblical literalism or religious practice.

Online Resource: Paul Froese and Christopher Bader argue strongly for the explanatory power of people's different images of God in their book, *America's Four Gods* (2010). On the website of the Association of Religion Data Archives, Froese and Bader have made available additional information about the images of God idea, as well as an interactive "God Test" (thearda.com/whoisyourGod/index .asp). Click on "The God Test" link, and you will be asked a series of questions about yourself and how you imagine God. When you complete the test, you will see your results as well as a comparison between your views and those of others.

Perhaps not surprisingly, women—who stand to benefit more from gender equality—hold more egalitarian attitudes toward gender roles (Davis and Greenstein 2009; Whitehead 2012). Despite this, some women intentionally join faith communities that have high boundaries between men and women and seem to offer limited options for females. This in itself is intriguing, and we look at it more closely in the next section.

Critical Thinking: How is religiously based differentiation similar in the cases of racial and sex-based inequality? How is it different?

Negotiating Gender Barriers in Religious Communities

Of course, social reality is more complex than closed-ended surveys of religion and gender role attitudes can capture. Several scholars have used qualitative research methods such as ethnography and open-ended interviewing to understand in greater depth the process by which women negotiate gender barriers in organized religion. Women are not simply pawns of patriarchal religious leaders but actively engage conservative religion in a way that leads them to find personal fulfillment and empowerment.

Lynn Davidman sought to understand why young, secular women—women who have come of age since the feminist revolution of the 1960s and 1970s—would choose to convert to Orthodox Judaism, a tradition with very restrictive gender roles for women. To do so, she immersed herself in the lives of those she wanted to understand by joining a Hasidic community in Minnesota and an Orthodox synagogue in New York City. In addition to this participant observation, she also formally and informally interviewed over 100 women who were turning to Orthodox Judaism (Davidman 1991). The title of Davidman's book based on this study, *Tradition in a Rootless World: Women Turn to Orthodox Judaism*, captures her main argument: Orthodox Judaism is attractive to women who feel a lack of fulfillment in the contemporary world and seek to become grounded in an ancient tradition. Part of that grounding is in the clarity of the gender roles Orthodox Judaism provides, but that combines with the rootedness of those roles in long-established religious traditions and family life. This contrasts with the gender role confusion in contemporary secular society and the emptiness of working life in the modern corporate world.

Following Davidman's work, several scholars interviewed conservative Protestant women about their understanding of the subservient role of women in their religious traditions' theology and practices. In *Godly Women: Fundamentalism and Female Power* (1998), Brenda Brasher reported on her ethnographic study of women in two conservative Protestant churches in Southern California. Like Davidman's converts to Orthodox Judaism, these fundamentalist women (also largely converts) were seeking refuge from a secular world in which the competing demands of work and home were often overwhelming. Fundamentalist teaching offered some relief to these women by providing clear dictates to focus on the domestic sphere. The women responded to

their exclusion from formal positions of power by erecting a "sacred wall of gender" behind which they created single-sex ministries that ultimately became sites of empowerment for them. They were able to develop supportive bonds and exercise leadership in the women-only settings.

That sacred wall of gender is writ even larger in *God's Daughters: Evangelical Women and the Power of Submission* (2000), R. Marie Griffith's two-year-long ethnographic study of Women's Aglow Fellowship International—the world's largest interdenominational evangelical women's organization. In observing this sex-segregated organization, Griffith found that when it was at its best, the women experienced considerable psychological healing, satisfaction, and even transformation from the group processes of prayer and testimony.

Christel Manning's research covers some of the same ground as the previous studies but has the advantage of putting women in conservative religious traditions in a comparative frame. Manning spent two years observing conservative Catholic, Evangelical Protestant, and Orthodox Jewish women in three Los Angeles–area congregations. In each case, the women in these patriarchal religious traditions see themselves not as victims, but as active agents in defining gender roles for themselves (Manning 1999). Catholic women are excluded from the priesthood, but they look to the many women saints in the Catholic tradition as role models for their own leadership. Evangelical Protestantism strongly professes the submission of women to men, but the Protestant tradition also emphasizes the individual relationship of each believer to Jesus Christ, which can be used to justify women's empowerment. Likewise, Orthodox Judaism requires sex-segregated worship in the synagogue, but it gives women a central role in the domestic rituals that are so important to the Jewish tradition. In the end, although they would never accept the label, the women Manning studies are in certain ways feminists. Indeed, one of Manning's points is that in the contemporary

United States, even patriarchal religious traditions must engage feminist ideas, since these ideas have become mainstream.

The negotiation of gender and religion takes place in every religious tradition, as is shown in the next "Illustrating Sociological Concepts" feature. The bottom line is that we cannot simply assume a mechanical relationship between patriarchal religious teachings and the acceptance or interpretation of those teachings by individuals, especially in the American context where voluntarism is strongly emphasized.

Illustrating Sociological Concepts

Is Veiling Oppressive to Muslim Women?

As the number of Muslims in American society has increased, so has the visibility of the traditional veil (known as a *hijab* in Arabic). In a society that values clothing as a form of personal expression and individuality—indeed, even as a right—the veil is profoundly countercultural. Because only women are required to veil in Islam, it is seen by some observers to be an oppressive means of controlling Muslim women.

Africa Images via istockphoto.com

Recent research in the sociology of religion, however, has called into question outsiders' view of the *hijab*. Scholars are taking seriously the experiences of Muslim women who choose to veil, and their findings are quite surprising.

Women in fundamentalist Muslim societies are separated from men (except for fathers and brothers) in work and in worship, and they generally remain covered. When they come to North America, the women are often accustomed to the practices and continue with them in the new country. *Purdah*, meaning curtain, refers to practices of seclusion and separate worlds for women and men. Screens in households and veils in public enforce female modesty and prevent men from seeing women who are not part of their families (Ward and Edelstein 2006).

Today, some Muslim women argue that the headscarf they wear is for modesty, for cosmetic purposes, or to protect them from stares of men. They see it as a statement of identity as a Godly person and as a protection against intrusion by men. It is often a way to negotiate between the ethnic identity of their parents and the open, free, and sexually promiscuous society around them. It becomes a symbol of transition and dual identity, with some feeling that wearing a *hijab* is part of their free expression at the same time it expresses their moral standing.

Interestingly, Williams and Vashi also found that the style of wrap around the head, the material and color of the scarf, and the way it drapes over shoulders becomes a "fashion statement." So while some people claim that the veil is a symbol of oppression and subservience, Orthodox Muslim women often do not experience it the same way (Bartkowski and Read 2003; Knickmeyer 2008; Read and Bartkowski 2000; Williams and Vashi 2007).

Critical Thinking: So far in this chapter, the focus has been on ways that religion might be a causal or contributing factor in gender inequality. However, religion may sometimes simply be the arena in which larger social conflicts are expressed and justified. In this case, religion is primarily a *reflection* of conflict rather than a *cause*. A number of scholars feel that this perspective is more helpful in understanding the witch-burning craze of Europe, which you may explore on the website for this book at www.SAGE.com/rsp6e. Which causal sequence—religion as cause of bigotry or religious attitudes as effect of other social conflicts—seems more plausible to you? Why?

RELIGION AND SEXUALITY

A number of commentators have noted that *homophobia* (intense fear and hatred of homosexuality and homosexuals) is related to sexism, for homophobia is highly correlated with and perhaps a cause of traditional notions of gender and of sex roles (Shaw and Lee 2005). Homophobia, a concept from the discipline of psychology, suggests that fear or hatred of gays and lesbians is a personality trait or even an abnormality (Weinberg 1973). *Heterosexism*, a more sociological concept, is the notion that the society in many ways reinforces heterosexuality and marginalizes anyone who does not conform to this norm. Heterosexism focuses on social processes that sacralize heterosexuality and define LGBTQ people as deviant (Gender Equity Resource Center 2013; Oswald 2001; Wilcox 2003).

Most established religious groups have had a strong assumption about the normality of heterosexuality. Marriage is sanctified by ceremony in all major religious groups, but it has only been recently that some denominations have even openly debated the possibility of officially authorizing weddings for gays and lesbians. Regardless of whether we focus on psychological or sociological approaches, same-sex marriage and ordination of LGBTQ persons have become hot issues in faith communities, threatening to split some denominations.

Religious Divisions Over Homosexuality

The liberalization of Americans' attitudes toward homosexuality in the past half-century has been dramatic (Loftus 2001; Saad 2012). Most Millennials today have no memory of a world in which consensual same-sex sexual activity was illegal and police would raid bars to arrest people who were cross-dressing (Carpenter 2012). Yet acceptance of LGBTQ people is far from universal even today. At the extreme end is the 20.8% of hate crimes in 2013 that were based on sexual orientation. This is the second highest category, next to racial hate crimes at 48.5% (Federal Bureau of Investigation 2014). More mainstream, however, is the 50% of the American population who believe that homosexual behavior is sinful (see Table 11.3).

The dominant story, then, is growing overall acceptance of homosexuality along with considerable polarization in attitudes. The polarization is strongly associated with religion, and also exists on a global scale as discussed in the "Global Perspectives" feature.

Global Perspectives

Religion and Heterosexism Cross-Nationally

As in the United States, the liberalization of laws governing same-sex marriage globally is quite recent. According to the Pew Research Center Religion and Public Life Project (2015), at the beginning of 2015 there were 18 countries (out of 196 in the world) that allowed same-sex marriage nationwide. The Netherlands was the first country to grant marriage equality (in 2000), and Scotland and Luxembourg are the most recent (in 2014). Five countries in the Southern Hemisphere allow same-sex marriage: Argentina, Brazil, New Zealand, South Africa, and Uruguay.

In the vast majority of the world, therefore, heterosexism prevails. Some societies ignore or deny the existence of LGBTQ members of their national communities. Some consider them to have psychological illnesses or forms of depraved immorality. Some societies even consider these forms of sexuality a crime. This is true in 38 out of 54 African nations today (as it was in most of the United States during much of the 20th century). In the worst case, to be accused of homosexuality can result in the death penalty in Sudan, Somalia, Mauritania, and the northern part of Nigeria (Nossiter 2014).

The status of homosexuality in nations around the world is heavily influenced by the extent of religiosity in those countries. In fact, one study of 39 countries by the Pew Research Center Global Attitudes Project (2013) found a correlation of −0.78 between level of religiosity and acceptance of homosexuality (where 1.00 is a perfect correlation). The negative correlation means that as one variable goes up (religiosity), the other goes down (acceptance of homosexuality).

The dominant religious group in these societies matters also. Muslims overwhelmingly believe that homosexual behavior is morally wrong, including 99% of Muslims in Thailand and Cameroon, 98% in Ethiopia, 97% in Ghana and Lebanon, and 96% in Jordan and Kenya (Pew Research Center Forum on Religion and Public Life 2013).

By contrast, historically Catholic countries in Western Europe are among the most accepting of homosexuality. Only 19% of Italians, 14% of French, and 6% of Spaniards say it is morally unacceptable, suggesting the extent to which the official teachings of the Catholic Church have waned in influence in these countries. In fact, 50% of French respondents said homosexuality is not even a moral issue at all (Pew Research Center Global Attitudes Project 2014).

More secularized societies whose dominant religious heritage is Protestant are most receptive to homosexuality and to same-sex marriage. This is evident in the legality of same-sex marriage in the heavily secular and historically Lutheran Scandinavian nations of Denmark, Norway, and Sweden, as well as their Nordic neighbor Iceland.

Since 1973, the General Social Survey (GSS) has asked: "What about sexual relations between two adults of the same sex . . . do you think it is always wrong, almost always wrong, wrong only sometimes, or not wrong at all?" In 1973, 70% of respondents answered always wrong, and only 10.8% answered not wrong at all. By 2008, only a minority answered always wrong (49.8%), and over one third said never wrong (35.9%). This trend has continued through the most recent year of the GSS available: Almost equal portions of the U.S. population say that homosexual activity is always wrong (43.4%) and not wrong at all (41.6%). There is a significant difference, however, in attitudes toward homosexuality by gender. In 2012, 48.6% of men held that same-sex sexuality is always wrong, and 48.3% of women answered that it is not wrong at all (Smith and Son 2013).

There are also strong age and cohort effects in attitudes toward homosexuality. In every year of the GSS, younger respondents are more accepting than older respondents. In 2012, 53.1% of those 18 to 34 thought that homosexual behavior is never wrong, and 62.6% of those 65 and older said it is always wrong (Smith and Son 2013). Even though older generations of Americans are also becoming more liberal in their views of homosexuality, Millennials and GenXers are still more accepting of LGBTQ people than are Baby Boomers and the Silent Generation (Pew Research Center 2014a).

The key division in attitudes toward homosexuality that concerns us here, of course, is religion. As Table 11.3 on page 298 shows, there is significant variation by religious tradition. Nearly 8 in 10 Buddhists and Jews agree that homosexuality should be accepted by society, compared to fewer than 3 in 10 Muslims, evangelical Protestants, Mormons, and Jehovah's Witnesses. About half as many mainline Protestants as evangelical Protestants see homosexual behavior as sinful, despite the fact that they draw on the same religious tradition. Although the data are not as complete, the second column of data in this table highlights the clear connection between seeing homosexual behavior as sinful and not accepting homosexuality in society.

Mainline Protestants are more likely to be theological liberals. They tend to assume that homosexuality is an inborn trait, and so the issue is one of prejudice against persons for a characteristic that is immutable. Evangelical Protestants (as well as black Protestants) are more likely to be theological conservatives. They tend to see homosexuality as a behavior that is acquired through socialization, and therefore as a choice that has moral implications. The positions themselves are interesting in that they reverse the assumptions liberals and conservatives tend to make about gender and social roles. Conservatives are more likely to posit that gender is innate and inborn, whereas liberals argue that gender and the social roles associated with each gender are learned.

In any case, religious conservatives tend to see liberal notions about homosexuality and gender roles as a threat to the viability of society and as clear debasement of the moral social

Table 11.3 Attitudes Toward Homosexuality

Religious Groups in the United States	% agreeing homosexuality should be accepted by society (2008)	% who say homosexual behavior is sinful (2014)
Buddhists	82	ND (No Data)
Jews	79	ND
Catholics	58	44
Mainline Protestants	56	42
U.S. Average	**50**	**50**
Hindus	48	ND
Black Protestants	39	77
Muslims	27	ND
Evangelical Protestants	26	82
Mormons	24	ND
Jehovah's Witnesses	12	ND

SOURCE: for acceptance of homosexuality: Pew Research Center Forum on Religion and Public Life. 2008b. *U.S. Religious Landscape Survey.* Retrieved from religions.pewforum.org.

SOURCE: for homosexuality sinful: Pew Research Center. 2014. *Public Sees Religion's Influence Waning.* Retrieved from www.pewforum.org/2014/09/22/public-sees-religions-influence-waning-2.

NOTE: The Pew Research Center did not publish data for attitudes on homosexuality as sinful for every religious group.

order. By contrast, liberals often feel that sexuality within a committed relationship is not a moral issue at all. Indeed, it is lack of tolerance of other lifestyles that liberals deem morally reprehensible.

These liberal–conservative differences *between* different religious traditions can also be seen *within* traditions. For example, the official teaching of the Catholic Church is that homosexuality is "objectively disordered" and that LGBTQ people should refrain from sexual activity (as should anyone who is not married). This view is supported by organizations of lay Catholics (not members of the church's official hierarchy). Two examples are Catholic Answers

(catholic.com) and the Catholic League for Religious and Civil Rights (catholicleague.org), both of which seek to explain and defend the Church's teachings on all issues including sexuality. In contrast are groups of lay Catholics like New Ways Ministry (newwaysministry.org) and DignityUSA (dignityusa.org), both of which challenge those teachings by advocating and providing a safe haven for LGBTQ Catholics. As Michele Dillon observed in her study of Dignity, these Catholics remain faithful to a religious organization that marginalizes their sexual identity by using the Catholic tradition itself to critique the tradition's teachings (Dillon 1999; see also Baggett 2009).

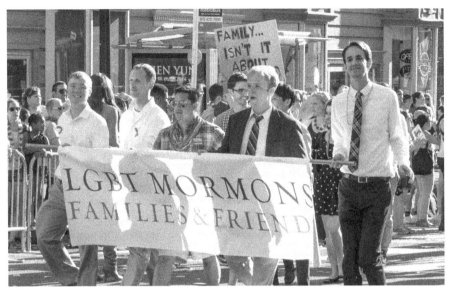

Photo by Tim Evanson is licensed under CC BY-SA 2.0

Among the many religious groups marching in the Washington–Capital Pride parade in 2014 were LGBTQ Mormons, despite the fact that the Church of Jesus Christ of Latter-day Saints officially teaches that homosexual behavior is sinful.

Rather than fighting for a place within existing denominations, some gay and lesbian Christians have opted to establish their own denomination: the Universal Fellowship of Metropolitan Community Churches (UFMCC). The UFMCC, which has 172 local congregations in 37 countries, is a "gay/lesbian positive" church that affirms homosexuality as a legitimate lifestyle for Christians (mccchurch.org).

See the next "Illustrating Sociological Concepts" feature for some history of this denomination. One study conducted on a UFMCC congregation in New York found that gays and lesbians who are affiliated with this church have exceptionally positive personal adjustment; they are more likely to have an integrated self-concept both as gay people and as religious people (Rodriguez and Ouellette 2000).

ILLUSTRATING SOCIOLOGICAL CONCEPTS

Origins and Development of the Metropolitan Community Church

One of the hallmarks of American religion, according to R. Stephen Warner, is that it is a locus of individual and group empowerment. Religious involvement, he writes, "has historically been one way that groups have improved their lot" (Warner 1993:1068). Warner goes on to observe that "the gay liberation movement is itself a practitioner of the art of church-based

(Continued)

(Continued)

mobilization" and that the Metropolitan Community Church is "the organizational center of the attempt to legitimate gay culture in the United States" (Warner 1993:1068–1069).

The Metropolitan Community Church began in 1968 with a gathering of 12 people in Reverend Troy Perry's living room. Perry had pastored Pentecostal churches in Florida, Illinois, and California. Then in the early 1960s, Reverend Perry was defrocked as a minister by a Pentecostal denomination. The issue was that he is gay. He spent several years struggling to reconcile his commitment to Christianity and his sexual inclination.

Some years later he had a bout with depression—a deep despair in which he questioned the very meaning of life. In that context, his religious faith was unable to help him. After recovering from a nearly successful suicide attempt, he began to experience a renewed sense of his own spirituality. When a friend was arrested as part of a familiar pattern of police harassment in gay bars, his friend commented that no one, not even God, cared for gay and lesbian people. Perry was inspired by this incident to mobilize a church that served the homosexual community. He writes that "God wanted me to start a new church that would reach into the gay community, but that would include anyone and everyone who believed in the true spirit of God's love, peace, and forgiveness" (Perry 2010). This was to be not a gay church but a Christian church.

Given the individualism and independence of the LGBTQ community, his friends were skeptical that anyone would come. Further, the longstanding hostility of the Christian church to gays and lesbians created a huge barrier—for many people felt they could not be LGBTQ and a child of God. Still, many members of that community had grown up in religious homes, and the liturgy and hymns of Christianity were a deep part of their memories and their identities.

The first worship service in 1968 was deeply moving to those who came, and the gatherings grew. In less than three months the attendees had tripled—too many for his residence. The worshippers had come from many traditions, and the services needed to appeal to their childhood traditions, but the diversity meant that they could not be limited to one particular faith community. Perry developed a synthesis of prayers, hymns, and liturgies drawn from Episcopal, Presbyterian, and Lutheran denomination resources. Still, Perry believes it was not the mechanics of worship that drew people, but the authenticity for the feeling of worship and the deep sense of belonging that was compelling in the lives of the new members. Perry commented, "People came out of the shadows, out of the closets, out of the half-world. They were drawn to the Metropolitan Community Church. For what? Some were curious. Some were incredulous. We were new. We were a novelty. We were an item in the gay world. . . . We excluded no one. We welcomed everyone. We still do." Indeed, roughly 20% of the membership is heterosexual.

The new movement was so novel that it got a good deal of press within the LGBTQ community, and in 40 years the group has expanded to 43,000 adherents and 300 congregations. It is a vivid example of a denomination being created in response to experiences of rejection and stigma—similar to other ethnic religious communities.

SOURCE: Metropolitan Community Church. 2004. *History of MCC*. Retrieved from http://mcchurch .org/overview/history-of-mcc/

Religious people who are LGBTQ and members of theologically more conservative religious traditions tend to experience less sense of integration in their self-identity. One way that conservative Christian gay men have attempted to reconcile these competing identities is through ministries that counsel them on how to change (or at least restrain) their sexual orientation (Wolkomir 2006). This is sometimes called "sexual reorientation therapy," "conversion therapy," or "gay cure." Tanya Erzen conducted an ethnographic study of one such organization: New Hope Ministry, a residential "treatment" center in California. She found that individuals who completed the program experienced a sort of religious conversion in terms of strengthening

their Christian identity, but did not often have less same-sex attraction (Erzen 2006).

Given the marginalization of sexual minorities in most religious traditions historically and many religious traditions today, it is not surprising that nearly half of LGBTQ people opt out of religion altogether. In Chapter 6, we highlighted Zuckerman's finding that those whose sexuality is non-normative (homosexual, bisexual, transsexual, etc.) are more likely to become apostates (Zuckerman 2012). A survey of a representative sample of LGBTQ adults in 2013 found that 48% of all LGBTQ adults are unaffiliated, compared with just 20% of the U.S. adult population as a whole (see Table 11.4). The difference is even more dramatic when looking at those aged

Table 11.4 Religious Affiliations of LGBTQ Adults and U.S. Population Compared

Religious Groups in the United States	% of LGBTQ Adults	% of All Adults
Unaffiliated	48	20
Atheist/Agnostic	17	6
Nothing in Particular	31	14
Catholic	14	22
White Mainline Protestant	12	15
Hispanic, Black, Other, or Mixed Race Protestant	9	14
Other Faith	8	4
White Evangelical Protestant	6	19
Jewish	2	2
Mormon	1	2
Don't Know	1	2
TOTAL	100	100

SOURCE: Pew Research Center. 2013. *A Survey of LGBT Americans: Attitudes, Experiences and Values in Changing Times.* Retrieved from www.pewsocialtrends.org/files/2013/06/SDT_LGBT-Americans_06-2013.pdf.

NOTE: Totals do not add to 100 due to rounding.

18 to 29. Of LGBTQ young adults, 60% are unaffiliated, compared to 31% of all young adults. For every other religious tradition except "other faith" and Judaism, LGBTQ adults are underrepresented relative to the adult population (Pew Research Center 2013).

In recognition of this alienation of LGBTQ people from religion, some Christian denominations have taken more positive steps to be officially hospitable and supportive. These movements go by various names: More Light (Presbyterian), Open and Affirming (United Church of Christ and Christian Church), Reconciled in Christ (Lutheran), and Reconciling Ministries (Methodist). Official numbers are hard to come by for some of these traditions, but, for example, the More Light Presbyterian (MLP) website (mlp.org) lists 192 member churches in the United States that affirm the MLP mission statement:

> Following the risen Christ, and seeking to make the Church a true community of hospitality, the mission of More Light Presbyterians is to work for the full participation of lesbian, gay, bisexual, transgender and queer (LGBTQ) people in the life, ministry and witness of the Presbyterian Church (USA) and in society.

This represents just under 2% of the 10,038 PCUSA congregations in the United States. Similarly, only 649 United Methodist congregations (or 2% out of more than 30,000 congregations) are part of the Reconciling Ministries Network within that tradition (rmnetwork.org). A little over 5% of the Evangelical Lutheran Church in America congregations (550 total) are "Reconciled in Christ" (ReconcilingWorks 2015). The United Church of Christ was not only the first to have an open and affirming policy; it has the most congregations (1,235 or 23% of UCC churches) opting for being Open and Affirming (Schuenemeyer 2015). The UCC was also the first Christian congregation, in 1972, to intentionally and openly ordain a LGBTQ clergyperson (www.ucc.org/lgbt_about).

Although just a small percentage of congregations within these denominations officially align with these LGBTQ-friendly movements, many more attempt to be welcoming on their own. Data from the National Congregations Study (NCS) allow us to see the pattern of change in acceptance of gays and lesbians at the congregational level from 2006–2007 to 2012. (The wording of the questions in the NCS does not allow us to comment on views of individuals who identify as bisexual, transgender, or queer/questioning.) As Figure 11.1 shows, over this brief five-year period, the percentage of congregations in the United States that would permit an openly gay or lesbian couple in a committed relationship to be full-fledged members increased by 28% to nearly half of all congregations (48%). The 26.4% of congregations in 2012 that also allow these couples to hold any volunteer leadership position in the church represents a nearly 50% increase in five years (Chaves and Anderson 2014).

As Chaves and Anderson note, however, not all congregations are accepting of gays and lesbians. Liberal Protestant churches have the highest rates of acceptance of gays and lesbians as both members (76%) and volunteer leaders (63%). Conservative Protestant churches have the lowest levels of acceptance: 24% for membership and just 4% for church leadership positions. Catholic parishes fall in between these two other traditions, but also show a pattern contrary to the overall trend. In 2006–2007, 74% of Catholic parishes accepted gays and lesbians as members, and 39% accepted them as volunteer leaders (Chaves and Anderson 2014). Five years later, the proportion of parishes dropped to 53% for members and 26% for volunteer leaders—a reduction in openness. Chaves and Anderson speculate that these declines could represent an organizational backlash against the spread of legal same-sex marriage in the United States during this period of time.

As we noted in the beginning of this section, attitudes toward sexuality (heterosexism) are related to attitudes toward gender (sexism).

Figure 11.1 Increasing Acceptance of Gays and Lesbians Within U.S. Religious Congregations

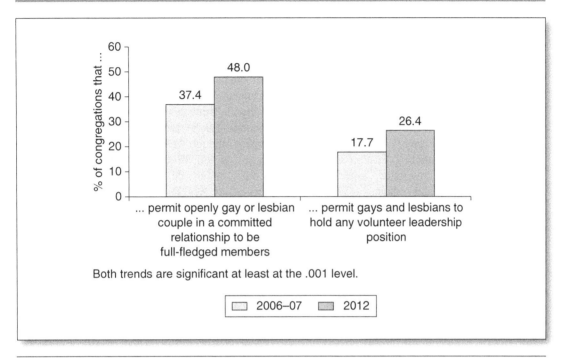

SOURCE: Chaves, Mark and Shawna L. Anderson. 2014. "Changing American Congregations: Findings From the Third Wave of the National Congregations Study." *Journal for the Scientific Study of Religion* 53(December): 681.

Whitehead explores this connection at the organizational level by analyzing the 2006–2007 wave of the NCS. He finds that whether a congregation would allow an "otherwise qualified . . . woman . . . [to be] the head clergyperson or primary religious leader of your congregation" is a significant predictor of whether the congregation accepts gays and lesbians as members or leaders within the congregation (Whitehead 2013). While half of congregations that allow women to be leaders accept gays and lesbians as members, only one quarter of congregations that do not allow women to be leaders do so. The difference is even more dramatic for acceptance of gays and lesbians as volunteer leaders: 32% of congregations that allow women to be leaders compared to just 7% of congregations that do not (Whitehead 2013).

The relationship between the nature of congregational leadership and sexuality suggests a further division between and within various religious traditions: whether clergy themselves must be heterosexual.

LGBTQ Clergy Controversies

One of the most controversial issues in several mainline denominations is over ordination of gays and lesbians as ministers. A divide between the Global North and Global South countries has arisen on this issue within some denominations. For example the election of a gay clergyman as bishop in 2003 caused a major schism, with congregations in the United States and Canada breaking away to form a new denomination and African leaders in that denomination deciding to sever their communion with the mother church (discussed below) (Anglican Church in North America 2015; Zaimov 2013).

A Gallup poll taken in the late 1990s already showed a shift toward acceptance of homosexual clergy by the majority of Americans: 53% approving in 1996 as opposed to 36% in 1977 (Gallup and Lindsay 1999). Nonetheless, in most religious traditions, the issue of ordaining openly practicing LGBTQ individuals as clergy is a nonstarter. This is true of Roman Catholics, Eastern Orthodox Catholics, Evangelical Protestants, Orthodox Jews, Muslims, Mormons, and Jehovah's Witnesses. Even in a more moderate tradition like United Methodism, the official position of the denomination is to deny ordination to "self-avowed practicing homosexuals."

In those denominations in which LGBTQ ordination has been considered, controversy has raged. The case of the PCUSA is instructive here. The ordination issue among Presbyterians focuses on what is called the "fidelity and chastity amendment" to the Book of Order passed in 1996. This amendment addresses sexually appropriate behavior for ministers, insisting that clergy must either be faithful within heterosexual marriages or remain celibate in singlehood. Four times since 1997—including a 373 to 323 vote in June 2010—the PCUSA General Assembly (the denomination's highest legislative body) has voted to repeal the ban on noncelibate homosexual clergy. In each of the first three instances, a majority of individual presbyteries (associations of congregations in a geographic area) did not ratify the General Assembly vote, and so the old standard remained in place. In the case of the 2010 vote, a majority of presbyteries approved. As a consequence, nearly 300 congregations have left the PCUSA, many of them affiliating with the more conservative Presbyterian Church in America (PCA) or the newly formed ECO: A Covenant Order of Evangelical Presbyterians (eco-pres.org).

The Evangelical Lutheran Church in America (ELCA) has become the largest Protestant body in the United States to ordain noncelibate gay clergy (Goodstein 2010). Its path to this position was many years in the making. The denomination appointed a task force in 2001 to study the issue and debated the issue over the following eight years before voting in 2009 to allow noncelibate but monogamous gays and lesbians to be ordained. In July 2010, the first seven LGBTQ Lutheran ministers were welcomed onto the denomination's clergy roster and approved for service, though the decision to hire individual clergy is left to the congregation. In 2013, another major development came when the openly gay Rev. Dr. R. Guy Erwin was elected bishop of the Southwest California Synod of the ELCA. These decisions have not come without some cost to the denomination. In the five years from 2009 to 2013, 675 ELCA congregations disaffiliated from the denomination (out of nearly 10,000 total congregations). As in the Presbyterian Church, a coalition of theologically conservative Lutheran churches have formed a new denomination—the North American Lutheran Church—in response (recall our discussion of schisms in Chapter 8).

In the Episcopal Church, an even bigger step was taken when in 2003 the Right Reverend V. Gene Robinson—an openly gay Episcopal priest—was consecrated as bishop in New Hampshire. This created great controversy. Some Episcopal congregations and even some dioceses have withdrawn from the denomination and the worldwide Anglican Communion (the global network of Anglican ecclesiastical groups with which the Episcopal Church has a long-standing connection) and have also rebuffed the liberal U.S. church. African Anglican bishops were especially upset by the decision, and many have severed ties (Harrison 2007). The Episcopal Church has not faltered in its support for Bishop Robinson, however, and in 2009 yet another diocese elected the Reverend Mary Glasspool to be their next bishop, believing that her openly lesbian identity was irrelevant. That appointment was approved by a majority of dioceses in the

United States, and she was consecrated as the bishop for the Los Angeles diocese in May 2010. Churches and dioceses that have been displeased by the decision and have left the Episcopal Church have usually affiliated with the conservative Anglican Church of North America.

Religious Divisions Over Same-Sex Marriage

A seemingly logical extension of acceptance of homosexuality is the granting of LGBTQ people the same rights as heterosexuals. The biggest and one of the most contested areas of change here has to do with same-sex marriage. Although same-sex marriage is legal in many countries (including the Netherlands, Spain, Canada, Norway, and Argentina), in the United States, jurisdiction on this issue resides with individual states. Therefore, the issue has been debated and decided on a state-by-state basis, beginning with the decision of the Supreme Court of Hawaii in 1993 that laws denying same-sex couples the right to marry violated their constitutional rights to equal protection under the law (a decision overturned by the voters of

Hawaii in 1998). Alaska had a similar scenario in the 1990s. In 2004, following a state supreme court ruling, Massachusetts became the first state in the nation to allow same-sex marriage. As of the beginning of 2015, 37 states and Washington, D.C., are issuing marriage licenses to same-sex couples. Although the majority of these states (24) have same-sex marriage by court decision, 8 have adopted it through their state legislatures (Delaware, Hawaii, Illinois, Minnesota, New Hampshire, New York, Rhode Island, and Vermont), and 3 by popular vote (Maine, Maryland, Washington).

The same patterns we saw with respect to acceptance of homosexuality in society, we see in terms of attitudes toward same-sex marriage. The overall trend is toward greater support for same-sex marriage, especially among women and younger cohorts, though the American populace remains quite divided (Emerson and Essenburg 2013). The GSS is again instructive here. Beginning in 1988 it asked respondents how they felt about homosexual couples having the right to marry. In 1988, only 10.9% of American adults agreed or strongly agreed that they should have the right, while 68.9% disagreed or disagreed

Issues of homosexuality, especially same-sex marriage, have resulted in passionate responses on both sides. In the left photo, Mayflower Church (UCC) performed a "flash mob" (where people assemble suddenly in a public place, perform an unusual act for a brief time, and then quickly disperse) in a Minneapolis park. Their singing and dancing occurred the week before the November 2012 elections to encourage voters to support same-sex marriages. The right photo shows a counter protester at a "marriage equality" rally at the U.S. Supreme Court in 2013.

strongly. By 2012, support had grown to 48.4%, and opposition had fallen to 38.7%. Indicative of polarization, the two most common responses were strongly agree (24.9%) and strongly disagree (24.7%) (Smith and Son 2013).

Although every age group is becoming more liberal in its attitudes toward same-sex marriage, change in the youngest cohorts has been particularly dramatic. According to the GSS, in 1988 only 13.2% of young adults (aged 18–34) agreed or strongly agreed that LGBTQ citizens should have the right to marry. By 2012, this had increased by almost fivefold to 61.7% (Smith and Son 2013).

As with views of homosexuality generally, religion is a significant predictor of attitudes toward same-sex marriage. According to the Pew Research Center, 77% of the unaffiliated, 60% of white mainline Protestants, and 57% of Catholics favor same-sex marriage, compared to just 31% of black Protestants and 21% of white evangelical Protestants. For all of these religious traditions, support for same-sex marriage has increased since 2001 (Pew Research Center 2014a).

The legal expansion of the right to same-sex marriage and the growing popular support in certain quarters has made the issue of performing marriage ceremonies an issue in some churches. Marriage is sanctified by religious ceremony in all major religious groups, but only some religious bodies officially sanction weddings for same-sex couples. Most of the nation's largest denominations (e.g., Roman Catholicism, Southern Baptist Convention, United Methodist Church, Mormon Church) define marriage as between a man and a woman. However, a growing number of smaller denominations have begun to allow same-sex weddings. The Unitarian Universalist Association of Congregations sanctioned them in 1996 and the United Church of Christ began to perform same-sex marriages in 2005. Both the Conservative Jewish movement and the Reform Jewish movement sanction same-sex marriages. At their general assembly in 2014, members of the PCUSA voted to allow their clergy to perform same-sex marriages, making the denomination one of the largest to sanction them.

Of course, just because a denomination does not allow its clergy to perform these ceremonies does not mean that its clergy do not do so. Another aspect of the United Methodist Church (UMC) controversy has centered on ministers who have performed holy unions (a commitment ceremony for gays or lesbians that is similar to a marriage ceremony). A number of ministers have been performing these ceremonies, and the UMC's official position is that a clergyperson can be defrocked from the ministry for doing so.

Further, whether the national denomination officially sanctions same-sex marriage or not, many denominations face internal structural divisions. The UMC illustrates this as well. The governing document for the UMC states that "homosexuality is incompatible with Christian teaching." This statement has been used to prevent same-sex marriages and ordination of gay and lesbian clergy. After the church's national legislative body voted to keep that line in church policy, the West Coast regional organization issued a statement of "Gospel Obedience" that, in keeping with Christian faith, the West Coast Methodist church would act as though that policy "does not exist." Thus, same-sex marriage is affirmed by Methodists in at least one region of the country (Western Jurisdictional Conference 2012). Methodists in southern states, in particular, are outraged by this stand. One study has found that religious affiliation and religiosity continue to be powerful predictors of public opinion about same-sex marriage, so the position of one's denomination does seem to play a role in attitudes (Olson, Cadge, and Harrison 2006; Whitehead 2010).

A helpful perspective on this issue is the open systems analysis. Open systems theory says that religious organizations influence society (in this case, creating more traditionalism and therefore more resistance to homosexuality) and that the larger society influences the religious group.

Chaves argued that attitudes toward gender issues are shaped by other similar denominations; each denomination looks around to comparable others to see what is defined as acceptable in those denominations (Chaves 1997). From this point of view, very conservative organizations are less likely to change because the other conservative denominations serve as "comparison communities"; however, the PCUSA's recent change in its policies may well have a liberalizing effect on the United Methodists since they tend to see themselves as similar. That the PCUSA moved toward a more open policy after the United Church of Christ is not surprising as liberal Presbyterians tend to see the Congregationalists as a comparison community.

Moreover, attitudes in a local community or a region of the country would be expected to influence attitudes within a congregation—irrespective of the positions of the official denomination (Koch and Curry 2000). People living in a local community are in regular contact with neighbors, friends, and coworkers, and the attitudes of those community people are likely to shape outlooks of those within a religious community. In addition, many new recruits to a congregation involve people whose views were shaped—prior to their joining the faith community—by local customs. One study that sought to test this open systems proposition found that most resolutions to the Presbyterian synod seeking to restrict sexual behavior to heterosexuality come predominantly from congregations located in religiously conservative regions (Koch and Curry 2000). Likewise, we could predict that regions of the country with more liberal attitudes are more likely to have "Open and Affirming" or "More Light" congregations.

While this chapter has focused on gender and sexuality issues within the Christian tradition, the same sorts of issues face many religious traditions. For example, Mary Jo Neitz (2000) and Helen Berger (1999) found that some American spiritual communities within Wicca were highly focused on heterosexual tension and attraction, emphasizing the polarity and complementarity

of the genders. So even Wicca has sometimes assumed the normality of heterosexuality and provided a sacralization of such relationships. However, one of the major annual celebrations of Wicca has undergone significant change in the past decade as homosexuality is becoming more visible and more accepted within the movement (Neitz 2000). Some Wiccan covens are exclusively female, and lesbian relationships have come to be more normalized. All religions experience influence due to inputs from trends and issues in the larger society.

Critical Thinking: How is hostility toward LGBTQs similar to, and how is it different from, negative attitudes toward women? Do you think homophobia contributes to sexism? Is it fair to say that religion sometimes fosters heterosexism and homophobia? Why or why not?

SUMMARY

Although the ways Christianity fostered racism were for the most part subtle and indirect, Christianity has encouraged sexism much more directly. Except for the most liberal churches and temples in the United States, traditional images of women are correlated to high levels of congregational involvement and religiosity. Christianity has contributed to inequality and stereotypes of women in a variety of ways. First, women have been conceived as subordinate citizens in the meaning systems of most religions and philosophies of the Western world, and Christianity is no exception. Second, we–they thinking is sacralized in some religious communities, and informal norms of the community that communicate women's inferiority may actually trump official statements of the denomination or the theology. Finally, formal institutional concerns, such as concern for maintenance of the health and vitality of the local congregation, can predispose lay leaders against having a clergywoman. When women are not ordained and in leadership positions, there is a greater likelihood that the meaning systems will develop with a strong bias against women. The fact of the matter is that ordination itself has become a symbol of modernity, for equal treatment of women is increasingly expected—defined as rational behavior—in secular organizations; this adds pressure for ordination of women on those religious groups that want legitimacy in the eyes of secular institutions. By contrast, antimodernist groups reject the idea precisely because it symbolizes modernism.

One cannot make generalizations about Christianity as a whole on any of these characteristics. Some Protestant Christian groups, for example, have been remarkable for their lack of sexism. The Shakers believed in a female Christ figure (Mother Ann Lee), and the Christian Scientists were founded by a female charismatic leader (Mary Baker Eddy). One also cannot conclude that sexual segregation of men and women into monasteries and convents in the Roman Catholic tradition was always bad for women. It did allow for leadership roles otherwise denied to women.

The foregoing discussion should serve to illustrate the complex way in which any given religious body can have countervailing influences. This is precisely why the sociologist who studies religion is not satisfied with an investigation only of the beliefs of a religious group. Religion can influence human behavior in a variety of ways.

Just as gender equality has become a hot issue, so has homosexuality become a tinderbox. The questions of ordination of gays and lesbians and performance of sacred ceremonies to celebrate same-sex marriages divide some denominations and local congregations. Religions have historically sanctioned only heterosexual conduct and commitments. As the society comes to see this as discriminatory, conflict reigns in many groups. Some denominations now ordain gay and lesbian clergy, and some support same-sex marriage, or at least holy unions. Clearly, religious values and behaviors are intertwined with social conditions in the larger society. Moreover, religious organizations affect secular ones, and secular organizations influence religious ones: The causal connection runs in both directions.

12

RELIGION, INEQUALITY, AND SOCIAL ACTIVISM

HERE ARE SOME QUESTIONS TO PONDER AS YOU READ THIS CHAPTER

- How is one's position of privilege or disprivilege related to one's theology?
- Is the fact that affluent and disfranchised people have different theological explanations of their circumstances a matter of *elective affinity*, or is theology used as a tool to prevent social activism?

(Continued)

(Continued)

- Does religion mobilize minorities to protest against an unjust system, or does it act as an opiate to pacify them?
- What are some unique features of African American Christianity?
- How has religion served as a resource to minorities in coping with oppression?

In this section, we have been exploring the relationship between religion and social inequality, but an important issue regarding religion and social status remains: What is the relationship between religion and social activism aimed at redressing social inequality?

Karl Marx set a tone for much sociological work on this question when he asserted that religion "is the sign of the oppressed creature, the heart of a heartless world, and the soul of soulless conditions. It is the opium of the people" (Marx [1844] 1977:131). In his view, religion served to pacify individuals so that they did not come to see the true basis of their oppression, which for Marx was economic. Religion, therefore, was viewed as inherently conservative because it serves to legitimize an unequal social order (recall Chapter 3).

At the same time, history has repeatedly shown that religion can play an important role in motivating people to address social inequities. As Christian Smith has put it, religion can be "disruptive" of the status quo. We see this in the case of abolitionist (antislavery) and civil rights movements in the United States, the antiapartheid movement in South Africa, the Solidarity movement in Poland, liberation theology in Latin America, and others (Smith 1996a).

As with most issues, then, the ultimate answer is not that religion is an opiate or a stimulant, but that under certain social circumstances religion can act in either capacity. Thus, the general question previously posed suggests several more specific questions: How does theology serve as a social ideology appropriate to one's economic circumstances? How

is the religion of the affluent different from that of the poor? What are the consequences of the religions of the affluent and of the disfranchised for social stability or transformation? How does the religion of the disfranchised affect the larger society? Does it always act to justify the status quo, or does religion sometimes inspire oppressed people to militant resistance and advocacy of change? Why do affluent people sometimes become proponents of change that would reduce inequality—and support policies for diversity? We address these questions in this chapter.

THEOLOGY AS SOCIAL IDEOLOGY

Early in this study, we discovered that one of the functions of religion is to address issues of meaning. When people experience suffering or encounter injustices, they want to know why— or why me? Why is it that the good often seem to encounter suffering and hardship, while the evil seem to flourish like the green bay tree? On the other hand, when a family member or a good friend meets tragedy or death, people sometimes question, "Why couldn't it have been me?" The arbitrariness of suffering causes people to want an explanation; the world should make sense—it should have some ultimate meaning. If these events do not make sense, then life somehow seems a cruel joke. Any belief system that attempts to explain the reasons for evil, suffering, and injustice by placing them in a divine master scheme is referred to as a *theodicy*.

In trying to make sense out of the world and out of human experience, religious ideologies frequently provide explanations for the inequalities that exist in the social system. Sometimes religious beliefs endorse the current social system as established under divine will. For example, the present social arrangements may be viewed as God's divine plan, or the structures of this world may be viewed as a testing ground established by God to determine the truly faithful. Alternatively, the structures of this world may be viewed as the province of an evil force (e.g., Satan). Because people living in poverty or under oppression are more likely to experience frustrations with the existing social system and to feel it is unjust, they are likely to have a rather different theodicy—one that views current social arrangements as something other than God's will. Max Weber maintained that the lower their social class, the more likely people are to adhere to an otherworldly faith system (Weber [1922] 1963).

Alignment of Theodicy and Economic Position

The theodicies of the disfranchised are essentially "theodicies of despair" or "theodicies of escape," whereas those of the upper classes tend to be theodicies of "good fortune." People who are socially oppressed and who are experiencing a great deal of suffering need some explanation of a deeper justice or a deeper meaning that will ultimately prevail. While patterns are somewhat similar across religions, they are expressed differently, and in this discussion we will use Christian patterns for the analysis and application. In many lower-class religious groups, financial affluence is often defined as the root of avarice and as a sign of evil. Human experience is divided into worldly and spiritual realms, and attachment to the latter requires a rejection of worldly success. This rejection makes economic deprivation much easier to bear, for deprivation is espoused as a noble choice; it is made a virtue. In fact, a frequent text for preachers in

Christian sects serving the least affluent is the saying by Jesus, "It is easier for a camel to go through the eye of a needle than for a rich man to enter the kingdom of heaven." The saying is likely to be understood literally and as applicable to the present day. (In affluent churches, this saying is often treated as a comment directed specifically at the rich young ruler Jesus was addressing or strictly at the rich people of Jesus's day and age. Its application to today's world is minimized.)

Other devices can also be used to make deprivation and suffering meaningful. When the ancient Hebrews were exiled from their homeland and were made slaves of the Babylonians, their plight seemed hopeless, and many of them felt their God had forsaken them. These people awaited a Messiah who would rescue them and take them back to their homeland. (The expectation of a Messiah was a distinctly Jewish theodicy.) The Messiah, they believed, would be a military general who would show forth the power of God and liberate them from captivity. However, the Messiah did not rescue them from defeat and exile to Babylonia. Eventually, a prophetic genius came along who reformulated the theodicy. He insisted that the ultimate victory would come not through military power but by the ability to endure suffering. The suffering of the Jews was part of God's master plan to provide salvation to all of humanity. The Messiah was recast as a "suffering servant." Suffering was not meaningless; indeed, it was a high calling. Release from the suffering would come in Yahweh's time—only after the divine purposes had been fulfilled. The idea of being a chosen people was preserved by being redefined. Rather than being chosen for privilege, the Jews were chosen for service. They were handpicked to be God's tools to transform the world. Jews have been persecuted and oppressed for 2,500 years, yet their theodicy of suffering has sustained them and held them together. Second Isaiah (Isaiah 40–55) was the first to articulate a theodicy for their oppression.

This provides only one of many possible examples of religious groups that recast their theology and worldview to fit their social circumstances. Groups that are composed of members of the privileged class also develop theodicies to justify their good fortune. As Weber put it, "the fortunate is seldom satisfied with the fact of being fortunate. Beyond this one needs to know that one has the right to good fortune, . . . that one 'deserves' it" (Weber [1922] 1963:107). Elizabeth Nottingham elaborated the idea:

> Almost equally important for a society [as a theodicy of disprivilege] is a morally acceptable explanation of its successes. Since a successful society often enjoys its worldly accomplishments at the expense of less fortunate peoples, its members are frequently driven to find a moral formula that will not only provide positive meaning for their own good fortune but also will help diminish any guilt they feel about the less happy situation of other groups. (Nottingham 1971:126)

One reason for differential denominational affiliation by social class may be that the theodicy of one denomination may have a better fit with the needs and concerns of those in certain circumstances. Weber introduced the concept of elective affinity, the tendency for members of certain social and economic groups to be drawn to certain religious beliefs (Weber 1946).

As we found in Chapter 3, Karl Marx believed that economic self-interests are the driving forces of social behavior. He was convinced that the economic self-interests of the rich—those who own the industries and corporations—caused them to develop a religious view that justified their wealth and alleviated any sense of guilt. Because those with wealth and power can do much to control the belief systems of the society, Marx viewed religion as a system that sacralized the current forms of inequality and even oppression. For conflict theorists, theodicies of privilege are not so innocent as to be called an "elective affinity." They are, instead, insidious tools of the "haves" that "mystify" the true causes of inequality and serve to keep an unfair social system in place.

Whether the theodicy of privilege simply attracts the affluent because of compatibility with their own circumstances or is a consciously developed instrument of the wealthy to help them maintain their privileged position, the theological virtues and vices of the different socioeconomic groups do tend to be different. Liston Pope found that for lower-class Protestant mill workers the world is a battlefield where God and Satan struggle for each individual soul. The sacrificed "blood of Jesus" and Bible reading by the faithful are the critical elements that allow God to be victorious in any given situation (Pope 1942). Moreover, the concept of the deity among oppressed peoples is typically one of a comforter, protector, and savior. The role of God is to take care of His people—who are powerless to do much in this world of woes (Niebuhr [1929] 1957).

The chief decisions that control the lives of unskilled laborers occur at a level that they cannot control directly. They are often bystanders as the owners of corporations close plants, move factories to new locations, and make other decisions that profoundly shape the lives of wage laborers. Likewise, Pope found that mill workers viewed their role in the supernatural realm as one of observer, cheerleader, and marginal supporter. The battle is viewed as one between superpowers (God and the Devil), and it is largely the action of a third party (the sacrifice of Jesus) that will determine the outcome. This passive observer posture is typical of lower-class religiosity, especially for those groups stressing a theodicy of escape. Note the impact of this on people's sense of efficacy to bring change. A content analysis of hymns used in lower-class congregations illustrates the emphasis on dependency, alienation from this world, and blood sacrifice. Notable also is the negative concept of human character and of one's self-evaluation ("such a worm as I"). (See the next "Illustrating Sociological Concepts" feature for examples.)

ILLUSTRATING SOCIOLOGICAL CONCEPTS

Hymns in Churches of the Less Affluent

In churches of the less affluent, the hymns frequently depict the world as a place of suffering and hardship, and the inherent worth of the individual is viewed rather dimly. A major focus is comfort in this world combined with hope for the next. Finally, the decisive action that determines one's changes is accomplished not by the individual but by some external force or action (e.g., the sacrificial blood of Jesus).

"Nothing but the Blood"

What can wash away my sin? Nothing but the blood of Jesus;

What can make me whole again? Nothing but the blood of Jesus.

Oh! precious is the flow, That makes me white as snow;

No other fount I know, Nothing but the blood of Jesus.

Nothing can for sin atone, Nothing but the blood of Jesus;

Naught of good that I have done, Nothing but the blood of Jesus.

Oh! precious is the flow, That makes me white as snow;

No other fount I know, Nothing but the blood of Jesus.

"Remember Me"

Alas! and did my Savior bleed? And did my Sov'reign die?

Help me, dear Savior, Thee to own, And ever faithful be;

Would He devote that sacred head, For such a worm as I?

And when Thou sittest on Thy throne, Dear Lord, remember me.

"No One Understands Like Jesus"

No one understands like Jesus, He's friend beyond compare;

Meet Him at the throne of mercy, He is waiting for you there.

No one understands like Jesus, Ev'ry woe He sees and feels;

Tenderly He whispers comfort, And the broken heart He heals.

No one understands like Jesus, When the days are dark and grim;

No one is so dear as Jesus—Cast your ev'ry care on Him.

Moreover, for the disfranchised it is not simply the individual who needs saving but the whole social system that is corrupt. In fact, sin is thought of not just as wrong actions but as a pervasive depraved condition that infects and becomes an inherent quality of both the individual's soul and the fabric of society.

In the upper classes, different ideas about sin and the social order generally prevail. Economic prosperity is defined as a blessing of God or even as a sign of divine favor. Note that members of the upper classes are accustomed to controlling their own destinies. Their outlook stresses individual accomplishment, a positive assessment of their ability to control things in this world, and a high valuation of individual initiative. In fact, Niebuhr suggested that the American middle and upper classes characterize the deity as "energetic activity" or "dynamic will," and God expects the same sort of productive activity from humans. This set of values is vividly illustrated by the hymns that are typically sung in upper- and upper-middle-class churches (see sample verses in the next "Illustrating Sociological Concepts" feature).

ILLUSTRATING SOCIOLOGICAL CONCEPTS

Popular Hymns in Affluent Denominations

In upper- and middle-class churches, the hymns frequently express a positive value of this-worldly activity, an affirmation of individual self-worth, a high valuation of individual initiative and accomplishment, and a sense that persons are in charge of their own destinies. In one of these hymns, Jesus is depicted as an *example* to humankind rather than as a bloodied sacrificial Lamb. Furthermore, the saints of God are depicted in one hymn as common folks rather than as a highly committed elect.

"O Brother Man, Fold to Thy Heart"

O brother man, fold to thy heart thy brother;

Where pity dwells, the peace of God is there;

To worship rightly is to love each other,

Each smile a hymn, each kindly deed a prayer.

"I Sing a Song of the Saints of God"

I sing a song of the saints of God

Patient and brave and true,

Who foiled and fought and lived and died

For the Lord they loved and knew.

And one was a doctor, and one was a queen,

And one was a shepherdess on the green:

They were all of them saints of God,

And I mean, God helping, to be one too.

They lived not only in ages past,

There are hundreds of thousands still:

The world is bright with the joyous saints

Who love to do Jesus's will.

You can meet them in school, or in lanes, or at sea,

In church, or in trains, or in shops, or at tea;

For the saints of God are just folk like me,

And I mean to be one too.

"Rise Up, O Men of God"

Rise up, O men of God!

Have done with lesser things;

Give heart and soul and mind and strength

To serve the King of kings.

Rise up, O men of God!

The Church for you doth wait,

Her strength unequal to her task:

Rise up, and make her great!

Equally important is the way in which conventional secular norms and values are embraced among upper-class Christians. In middle- and upper-class religious communities, individuals are encouraged to cultivate a sense of self-worth and self-esteem; members do not often sing on Sunday morning about how the blood of Jesus was shed "for a *worm* such as I." Such negative self-images are characteristic of the hymnody of the disfranchised. Thus, a theologian who has strong appeal to the more affluent and well educated can write about sin:

I believe a careful examination of Biblical sources will indicate that humanity's most debilitating proclivity is *not* pride. It is *not* the attempt to be more than human. Rather it is sloth, the unwillingness to be everything humanity was intended to be. (Cox 1964:xi)

As one reviews the hymns in the previous two features, one can see this difference in emphasis. These distinctions are not a categorical or exclusive difference between the more and least affluent. Clearly, there is wide variation of religious expression and theology within denominations and between persons of the same social class. Here we describe some broad patterns to understand that socioeconomic status does affect religiosity and how one is likely to try to change society, if at all.

Theological and Class Realignments in a Postindustrial Age

The specific issues have changed over time, but differences continue between the faith communities of the privileged and those of the least privileged. In the modern economies of the United States and Canada, the working class has had some successes, and while they are not highly prosperous, they are able to feed, clothe, and shelter their families. Many even have some luxuries, such as a boat or a camper. The society looks less menacing, and they have interests that they do not want threatened. On the other hand, as we will see, diversity and openness to change has come to serve the interests of at least some relatively affluent people, including many in the professional classes. Interestingly, the positions of religious groups parallel some of these shifts.

In the postindustrial United States, the religious bodies of the less affluent are those who are normally identified as "conservative." They include Southern Baptists, Churches of Christ, Nazarenes, Pentecostal and Holiness sects, Assemblies of God, Churches of God, Adventists, Jehovah's Witnesses, and various evangelical and fundamentalist groups. Conservative white Christians tend to define the moral issues of our day as secular humanism and moral relativism, which includes the ban on prayer in the schools; the teaching of evolution rather than creationism in the schools; changing roles of women; increases in the divorce rate; and the new morality (which includes nonmarital sexual behavior, legalization of abortion, tolerance of pornography, and tolerance of homosexuality). The U.S. government—which is viewed as too secular and too supportive of diversity and pluralism—is seen as too permissive to have any say in moral issues.

These conservative churches stress absolutism and obedience to rules. However, notice the congruence of that view with low-prestige jobs. People in lower- and working-class jobs usually find that obeying rules of the workplace and adhering to the instructions of the employer or supervisor are qualities that are central to success on the job. Lack of conformity can have serious consequences, and parents socialize their children to develop those attitudes and behaviors that they believe will serve their children well in life (Bowles and Gintis 1976; Kohn 1989; MacLeod 2008). Further, if one works in an occupation where brute strength is essential and often gets the job done, one may look for clear, decisive, and forceful solutions to religious problems as well (Batson, Schoenrade, and Ventis 1993). Clearly if one is to become a conservative activist, the core value issue is not social inequality, but secularization and permissiveness.

On the other hand, the most affluent Christian churches in the United States are also those that are the most theologically and ethically liberal: Unitarian, Episcopalian, United Church of Christ (UCC), and Presbyterian. (Methodist, Lutheran, Disciples of Christ, American Baptist, and Reformed churches serve as a middle-class buffer and are often referred to collectively as "moderate Protestants.") The moral issues of our day for these churches—at least as identified by their clergy and their official denominational boards and agencies—tend to be war and peace issues; protection of the environment; social justice (defined largely in terms of elimination of discrimination against women and minorities and support for more diversity); and the lack of tolerance of those who are "different" (including those from other cultures and often those with different sexual orientations). Pluralism and tolerance seem to be central moral themes of the churches of privilege (Roof and McKinney 1987).

It is important to note that many affluent professional people are paid to be divergent thinkers—to be creative and to solve problems. They often manage organizations and are frequently rule makers. They will not do well in their fields if they merely obey rules. They must respect divergent or nonconformist thinking because creativity and innovation are often necessary to solve new problems. Acknowledgment of ambiguity and utilization of careful analysis of problems are essential (Batson et al. 1993; Bowles and Gintis 1976; Kohn 1989). It should not be surprising that in a postindustrial world, the conception of good and evil among the affluent embraces tolerance of differences and condemns rigidity, absolutism, and conventionalism.

These people also are self-conscious about socializing their children to develop those characteristics that they believe will help their progeny in the world of work—including openness to diversity of all types. Experience tells these professionals that critical thinking, creativity, and even a streak of independence are valuable

characteristics. This becomes a part of what they expect in their religious life as well. Their social values are congruent with their financial self-interests, and both are served by more progressive theologies.

Table 12.1 on page 318 illustrates the divergence in social and political attitudes between religious traditions in the United States. The table includes two measures of tolerance (liberal attitudes on abortion rights and homosexuality) and two measures of political liberalism (self-described ideology and view of government's role in enforcing moral views). In every case, more affluent traditions (Jews, Buddhists, Hindus, and mainline Protestants) are more tolerant and liberal than less affluent traditions (Black Protestants, Evangelical Protestants, Mormons, and Jehovah's Witnesses)—in some cases by wide margins.

Like many professional positions, being a scientist requires tolerance for ambiguity, creativity, and divergent thinking in order to solve complex problems and to be successful in their careers. This acceptance of uncertainty and respect for diverse views often carries over into what they expect in their spiritual lives and their religious communities.

Table 12.1 Social Attitudes of Members of Various Religious Groups (in percentages)

U.S. Religious Traditions	Abortion should be legal in all or most cases	Homosexuality should be accepted by society	Government is too involved in morality	Political views are liberal or very liberal
U.S. Average	51	50	52	20
Buddhists	81	82	67	50
Jews	84	79	71	38
Hindus	69	48	45	35
Mainline Protestants	62	56	58	18
Catholics	48	58	49	18
Muslims	48	27	29	24
Black Protestants	47	39	42	21
Evangelical Protestants	33	26	41	11
Mormons	27	24	39	10
Jehovah's Witnesses	16	12	36	17

SOURCE: Pew Research Center Forum on Religion and Public Life. 2008b. *U.S. Religious Landscape Survey*. Retrieved from http://religions.pewforum.org.

Theology and Financial Self-Interests in Conflict

Of course, this discussion would be incomplete if we pointed merely to economic self-interest as the sole determinant of religious ideologies. An important and interesting phenomenon in today's world is the fact that many denominations whose members are affluent have directly and rather aggressively challenged the structures of inequality and privilege—as their scriptures and religious traditions urge them to do. For example, Congregationalists, Presbyterians, Unitarians, Episcopalians, and Catholics all have commissions or task forces on racism, poverty, and social inequities. Some task forces do not just attack the problem at an individual level; they challenge the very structure of society and point to systemic causes of poverty and racism. They issue statements calling for change—sometimes for radical change—in the basic social and economic structures of society.

Many—but by no means all—relatively affluent members are highly supportive of denomination programs that challenge the status quo (Wuthnow and Evans 2002). This concern for the less privileged among affluent congregations appears to be stimulated by religious teachings. The prophets of the Bible consistently called for social justice as the primary indicator of true religious expression. James Wood has found that congregations will often act collectively in ways that members would reject individually. This is largely because the clergy are able to call on beliefs that are commonly held but that do not coincide with the self-interests of the members. In the context of a group that they view as important, these members will support policies and actions that might not benefit their own financial portfolios (Wood 1981).

An ethical or prophetic theme is also central to the Reform branch of Judaism. Although Jews are generally among the more affluent members of American society, they have often championed the cause of blacks and other minorities. For example, Jews were instrumental in founding the National Association for the Advancement of Colored People (NAACP) and the National Urban League, two organizations that have had crucial roles in fighting for equal rights for African Americans.

Migrant farmworkers (predominantly poor Mexican Americans) have received support from affluent Christian and Jewish congregations, which send financial aid to the United Farm Workers and encourage their members to participate in boycotts of grapes, lettuce, and other products. The boycotts end only after wages are increased, conditions have improved, and a union contract is signed. However, this usually means increases in the cost of the produce. In other words, members of affluent congregations knowingly boycott goods with the ultimate result that they must pay higher prices. Such behavior is not in the narrow self-interests of these affluent individuals, yet they persist in this behavior because they are convinced that it is the moral thing to do. If faith is truly the organizing principle of one's life, it can inspire actions beyond self-interest.

The theodicy that people adopt may be related to their own socioeconomic standing, but the theodicy is also related to their inclination to social activism on issues of social inequality. In the following section, we will see how a theodicy may mobilize people to action or encourage

passivity. Since racial and ethnic minorities experience special issues of disfranchisement and destitution, we focus here on the role of religion in how they cope with inequality.

Critical Thinking: Theology often seems to parallel the economic circumstances and even the self-interests of people. What factors do you think best explain the correlation? Equally intriguing is when people are motivated by faith and moral convictions to do something that is directly contrary to their self-interests. What factors might explain that pattern?

RELIGION AND MINORITY STATUS

Is Religion an Opiate for the Oppressed?

A good deal of sociological research has focused on whether religion among the disfranchised acts as an opiate of the masses or inspires the dispossessed to militancy. As we have seen, Karl Marx maintained the former: that religion gave the poor a feeling of solace and a hope of compensation in the afterlife so that they would not rebel in the present. They were, in essence, drugged. Those who hold to this position insist that religion serves as a tool of control for the dominant economic class and ethnic group. Critics of religion have maintained that when European missionaries went to regions that were later colonized, they had the Bible while the natives had the land. As Gary Marx observed, when the missionaries left, the natives had the Bible, and the Europeans had the land (Marx 1967). Although examples of this view that religion is a tool of exploitation abound, examples neither provide proof nor establish causality.

One landmark empirical study of the effects of religion on blacks in the United States was conducted by Gary Marx (1967). Marx found that infrequent religious attendance was positively correlated with militancy or activism.

When he combined all his factors into an overall index of religiosity, he found a negative relationship between religiosity and militancy. Furthermore, the finding held even when he kept certain key variables constant: age, sex, denomination, and region of the country in which the respondent was raised. Marx concluded that there apparently is an "incompatibility between piety and protest."

Other researchers point to contrary data, such as the facts that most civil rights leaders have been members of the clergy and that high percentages of the members of civil rights groups attend worship services every week. Many historical analyses have also found that black religion was frequently a motivating force in slave revolts, since religion asserted the intrinsic human worth of slaves and raised their hopes for more dignity in life (Lincoln and Mamiya 1990; Wilmore 1972). Scholars from several disciplines have used a variety of research methods to clarify the relationship between religion and activism regarding social injustices. Our treatment in this section focuses on the function of religion in minority groups—specifically ethnic minorities.

Eric Lincoln and Lawrence Mamiya maintained that regardless of the belief system, African American religious structures have enhanced resistance to subjugation. These scholars insist that faith communities can empower people simply by establishing stable institutions, fostering networks, and forging a sense of common identity in suppressed peoples (Lincoln and Mamiya 1990). Regardless of the intent of the religious group, those interested in change are able to use the networks and sense of common interest to mobilize a social movement. Since religious bodies were the first black organizations locally and the first national institutions, they contributed to social activism and sense of potency. Religious institutions spawned various types of protest organizations by providing networks, leadership training in organizational management, and an overall sense of organizational competence (Morris 1986). This sort of

contribution by religion to the civil rights movement is not assessed by survey research like that of Gary Marx.

Follow-up studies have indicated a varied effect of black religiosity, demonstrating that African American religion sometimes does stimulate social change (Nelsen, Madron, and Yokley 1975). For example, African Americans who are churchlike in their religiosity are more likely to be inspired to militancy than are African Americans who are sectlike (Hunt and Hunt 1977; Nelsen and Nelsen 1975). When this variable is held constant, the inverse relationship between militancy and religious attendance disappears. Still, some black "sects" are highly militant (Baer 1984). A more in-depth understanding of the worldview or the theodicy of a subjugated group is necessary before one can predict passivity or militancy.

Critical Thinking: In what ways can religion be an "opiate" to oppressed people? What kinds of evidence support this view of religion? In what ways can religion mobilize suppressed people to greater self-respect and to work for social change?

Theodicies and Levels of Activism

The worldview of many sectarian groups is otherworldly. The reality or at least the importance of this world is denied except for its function as a testing ground. Only the faithful will be saved and will reach heaven in the afterlife; only the true believers will have "pie in the sky in the sweet by and by" (as it is sometimes referred to affectionately by believers and derisively by skeptics). This afterlife experience is expected to commence for each individual immediately after death. This sort of otherworldly religion is frequently associated with passivity in this-worldly affairs. Members of the dominant social groups are usually more than happy to have their subordinates believe that vindication will come only after death. Slave owners in this country often had that sort of doctrine preached to their slaves and coupled it with warnings that the saved would be those who lived out their status in this world without causing any trouble.

Another sort of worldview is eschatological. In the eschatological worldview, the ultimate victory over suffering and death will commence at some future time in history—in *this* world. Eschatology may be expressed in either of two forms: (1) progressivism or (2) millenarism. Furthermore, millenarism sometimes has a subtype known as *apocalypticism.*

In the progressive view, the day of perfection will be reached when God and humanity have worked together to attain it. This involves a gradualistic concept of social evolution. The view is based on the idea that God is the creator and rules over the earth. God's master plan is for the evolution of the world into an ever more humane, just, and godly kingdom (the kingdom of God on earth), but it is believed that God will not establish this without human effort and participation. Believers are to look for signs of God at work in this world and are to become actively involved in the political affairs of this world. Progressive eschatology was characteristic of much of the Social Gospel movement in the United States at the turn of the 20th century. In a somewhat modified form, this sort of outlook—with its positive view of this world—continues to be a force in many mainline denominations and is the predominant view of Reformed Jews. If God expects human participation in creating the "kingdom," it becomes an obligation for believers as well as a way of creating a heaven on earth for all. Therefore, a progressive view of history is often tied to liberal activism by some people who are affluent. The progressive view of history is depicted in Figure 12.1.

A progressive view of history—with a perception that things are getting better and more fair—does not fit the experiences of the dispossessed. Other views of history resonate better with their experiences. Another form of eschatology, millenarism, is more compatible with lives of social outcasts, assuming as it does that the transformation of the world will be sudden rather than gradualistic and will be inaugurated primarily by supernatural powers. Norman Cohn, a historian who has done extensive comparative studies of millenarism, points to five defining characteristics of these movements. The millenarian vision is as follows:

1. Collective, in the sense that it is to be enjoyed by the faithful as a group;

2. Terrestrial, in the sense that it is to be realized on this earth and not in some otherworldly heaven;

3. Imminent, in the sense that it is to come both soon and suddenly;

4. Total, in the sense that it is utterly to transform life on earth, so that the new dispensation will be no mere improvement on the present but perfection itself;

5. Accomplished by agencies that are consciously regarded as supernatural (Cohn 1964:168).

The word *millennium* means a thousand years and refers to the new era to come. Although the term originates from the New Testament prediction (in the Book of Revelation) that Jesus will return and rule for 1,000 years, the word is also used to refer to non-Christian groups with this sort of worldview. Hence, millenarians are those people who await a future event by which the kingdom of God or the new era will begin. Many millenarian Christians have their own life-after-death scenario. This involves a bodily resurrection of the dead at the time the new kingdom begins. This is a rather different concept from the belief that eternal life for an individual begins immediately after death and that the spiritual world is coexistent with the material one. Nonetheless, many people hold some combination of both beliefs and are not much troubled by the need for coherence and consistency in their theodicy.

Figure 12.1 The Progressive View of History

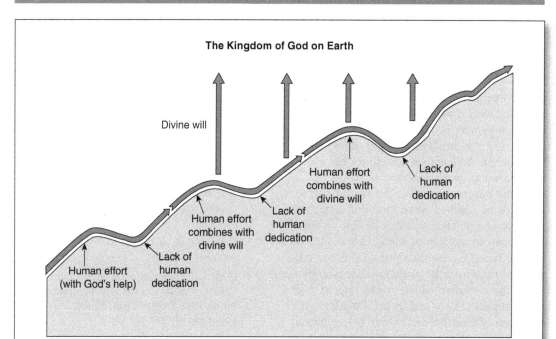

The Kingdom of God on Earth

Divine will

Human effort combines with divine will

Lack of human dedication

Human effort combines with divine will

Lack of human dedication

Lack of human dedication

Human effort combines with divine will

Human effort (with God's help)

The concept of salvation for millenarians, then, is time-oriented, terrestrial (although life on earth in the new era will be quite different from present life on earth), and collective (rather than individualistic). Although the transformation will ultimately be accomplished by supernatural forces, humans do have an active and important role in preparing the way. Life in this world is viewed as a time of suffering and of being tested, but the new era will mean the advent of a new social order where justice prevails.

For disadvantaged groups, the millenarian view offers great hope for the future (see the next "Illustrating Sociological Concepts" feature). Groups that hold this view frequently become fanatical in their efforts to inaugurate the new kingdom. Hence, it is not uncommon for millenarian groups to precipitate active revolt against the established authorities (Talmon 1965).

Talmon pointed out that millenarism has enjoyed popularity at all levels of society at one time or another—including relatively affluent middle- and upper-middle-class people. Nonetheless, it has normally appealed to deprived people—oppressed peasants, the poorest of the poor in cities and towns, and populations of colonial countries. The millennial outlook usually develops as a reaction to especially severe hardships and suffering. Talmon wrote, "Many of the outbursts of millenarism took place against a background of disaster—plagues, devastating fires, recurrent long droughts that were the dire lot of the peasants, slumps that caused widespread unemployment and poverty and calamitous wars" (Talmon 1965:530). In most cases, millenarism is a phenomenon of ethnic groups that have endured sustained subjugation.

Unlike the progressives who see the present order as good and getting better, millennial

ILLUSTRATING SOCIOLOGICAL CONCEPTS

Millenarian Anticipation Expressed in Hymns

These two hymns express vividly the revolutionary and earthly expectations of the millennial vision. The first stresses the collapse of the present social order and the destruction of kingdoms. The second expresses a mood of waiting until the supernatural does its work. Compare the messages to those in the hymns in earlier boxed features.

"Jesus Comes"

Watch ye saints with eyelids waking, Lo, the pow'rs of heav'n are shaking;

Keep your Lamps all trimmed and burning, Ready for your Lord's returning.

Kingdoms at their base are crumbling, Hark, His chariot wheels are rumbling;

Tell, O, tell of grace abounding, Whilst the seventh trump is sounding.

Lo! He comes, lo! Jesus comes; Lo! He comes, He comes all glorious!

Jesus comes to reign victorious, Lo! He comes, yes, Jesus comes.

"Our Lord's Return to Earth Again"

I am watching for the coming of the glad millennial day

When our blessed Lord shall come and catch His waiting Bride away

Oh! my heart is filled with rapture as I labor, watch and pray

For our Lord is coming back to earth again.

Then the sin and sorrow, pain and death of this dark world shall cease

In a glorious reign with Jesus of a thousand years of peace;

All the earth is groaning, crying for that day of sweet release,

For our Lord is coming back to earth again.

Chorus

Oh! our Lord is coming back to earth again,

Yes, our Lord is coming back to earth again,

Satan will be bound a thousand years,

We'll have no tempter then,

After Jesus shall come back to earth again.

movements usually seek total transformation of this world—which they view as unjust or even inherently evil. Many groups that begin with a rational approach become progressively more strategic as they begin to meet with success. This is illustrated by the tendency, which Seymour Lipset described, for religious movements to spawn radical political movements and the political movements, in turn, become more secular (Lipset 1960). Of course, for sociologists who insist that a worldview may be religious without being supernaturalistic, these secular political movements are no less religious than their predecessors. They simply have this-worldly and rationalistic systems of faith.

To complicate matters further, there are actually two types of millenarism. Within Christian circles, *postmillenialism* holds that Christ will come to reign over the earth, but only *after* humans have prepared the way. This is sometimes thought to involve a 1,000-year period of justice and peace prior to Christ's arrival.

Obviously, this stimulates this-worldly activism and is what has been described so far.

The other type of millenarism is common among the most destitute—those who feel utterly vulnerable in relationship to another group of people. This form emphasizes much more strongly the idea that the world is evil and controlled by Satan. Contrary to the evolutionary eschatology, this view describes human history as being on a hopelessly downward spiral. Ironically, this depressing circumstance is viewed as a sign of hope because it indicates that the end is near. God will intervene in history and bring forth the new era. Nothing humans can do will significantly alter the course of history. The believer can only be ready for the day of judgment, preparing his or her own soul and perhaps engaging in mystical ritual action, such as dancing around a fire (the Ghost Dance). This extreme form of millenarism is called apocalypticism, or *premillenialism* (see Figure 12.2). This latter phrase means that Christ will come before the 1,000-year period of justice, peace, and divine rule.

Figure 12.2 The Apocalyptic (Premillenial) Worldview

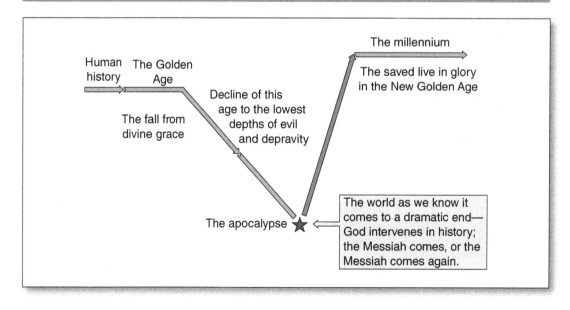

Within Christianity, apocalypticism is normally based on a literal interpretation of the Book of Revelation. Its utter rejection of the present age and present world disallows any attempt to bring change. For this reason, it usually leads to passivity in terms of the social structure. Groups or individuals are more likely to adopt this posture and this worldview if they are powerless and utterly despairing. One must simply wait for a greater power—God—to intervene.

Christianity, then, has within it several theodicies, which in numerous ways are quite different. Some congregations and some denominations stress one of them exclusively. Most congregations have some people who do not believe in a Second Coming or in an imminent end to the world; rather, they believe in a spiritual world that is coexistent with this world and that is attained by individuals if they have a right relationship with God. Others do not believe in life after death, at least not immediately after death; rather, they expect the millennium to occur sometime in the future.

Some Christians believe a little bit in each of these outlooks but have no coherent explanation of how the views fit together. The important point is that, depending on which worldview is stressed among an oppressed minority group, one may expect very different levels of activism for change. Those whose hope lies in a coexistent spiritual world that is attained by individual means are frequently passive. Those who hold an apocalyptic view are also usually passive. However, millenarians are frequently activist and militant. For them, religion is not an opiate; it is the inspiration that gives them hope, provides them with vision, and shores up their courage. The progressive view, with its suggestion that the present social system is already a good one and is constantly improving, has little appeal to the oppressed. This view is frequently held by social activists in more affluent religious groups.

Judaism also has within it several theodicies. Reform Jews await a "messianic age," which

they believe will be established by combined human and divine effort. Orthodox Jews hold to a belief in a coming Messiah who will bring the kingdom of God into being, will reunite the Jews, and will rebuild the temple. This millenarian view has been especially emphasized in times of Jewish history when oppression of Jews was most severe. A belief in resurrection from the dead was introduced to the Hebrews through the Persians nearly 2,000 years ago and is now part of the messianic expectation as well. Another theodicy—the belief in life after death in heaven or purgatory was also introduced about 2,200 years ago. Some Jews affirm this doctrine as well, even though it represents quite a different theodicy from the more this-worldly messianic expectation. Jews vary a great deal from one congregation to another in which of these theodicies they emphasize.

Reform Judaism (at least in its official form) does not accept the beliefs in resurrection or in heaven and purgatory. Its members are messianic, but they anticipate a messianic age—a time of peace and justice—which will be inaugurated due to the work of God and of many people. They do not expect a single individual to arrive who will solve the world's problems. The confidence of Reform Jews that human action can be effective in bringing significant change is itself a product of a people who are not destitute and powerless. The social circumstances of Reform Jews have allowed for and encouraged this modification of the traditional theodicy. Likewise, the theodicy has justified and encouraged social activism. The Reform branch of Judaism is often noted for being especially prophetic and activist in its attention to social and political change, with a focus on social justice.

The Jews have been subjugated and persecuted throughout much of their history, and the theodicies that they have developed have usually been ones of disprivilege. Sometimes the theodicies have motivated Jews to militancy and activism (such as the times of the escape from Egypt and the Maccabean Revolt), and sometimes they have called for passivity—waiting for the Messiah. There can be little doubt, however, that these theodicies have served to bond the Jews together and have helped to sustain them through incredible hardships.

What we have found is that oppressed people frequently adhere to a worldview that is either otherworldly or is millenarian; the answer to life's frustrations is sought in a transformed future or in a different realm of existence. Given the subjugation of women throughout the history of the Western world, the role of women in millenaristic movements is especially interesting. Cohn pointed out that millennial movements are common when there is a substantial group of wealthy, leisure-class women who are still second-class citizens by virtue of their gender. He pointed out that a number of millennial reformers during the Reformation were able to survive because they were sheltered and supported by women of the nobility (Cohn 1964). These women were experiencing extreme status inconsistency; they had high social status in terms of wealth and family political prestige, yet as individuals they had no respected function and could demand little personal prestige or respect. Weber also noted that women showed a great receptivity to all religious prophecy except that which is exclusively military in orientation. He emphasized that prophets challenge the status quo and are usually rather egalitarian in their relationships with women (Weber [1922] 1963). Jesus and Buddha are both cited as examples of charismatic figures who ignored many traditional gender role norms. The point here is that women—like many oppressed groups—are disproportionately attracted to world-transforming charismatic religious leaders and movements. This should not surprise us since women have actually experienced minority status—a position of less power—across the world.

One conclusion can safely be drawn from our foregoing discussion: The experience of social and political disprivilege can have a significant impact on one's worldview and on one's style of religious expression. Likewise, the worldview and sacred ethos of a group may have a significant effect on how its members respond to the experience of social and political subordination. To understand better the workings of religion in the experience of a specific subjugated group, let us turn to a brief overview of religion in the African American experience.

Critical Thinking: If you were a dictator who had total power—which you did not want challenged—what kind of theological orientation and what sort of theodicy should you encourage among the people? What would be the ideal theological system and the most powerful sacred justification to preserve the status quo? What kind of theology would be most threatening to your power and privilege?

RELIGION IN THE AFRICAN AMERICAN COMMUNITY

The vast majority of African Americans who are religiously affiliated are Christian (85%), and most of those are members of historically black churches (69%). Identification of African Americans with the big seven historically black denominations (African Methodist Episcopal or AME, AME Zion, Christian Methodist Episcopal, National Baptist Convention, National Baptist Convention, U.S.A., National Baptist Convention of America, and Progressive National Baptist Convention) has decreased over the years, but two thirds of the members of historically black churches still identify with the Baptist tradition. Churches in the Methodist tradition, as well as Pentecostal churches like the Church of God in Christ, also constitute a large share of the black church (Pew Research Center Forum on Religion and Public Life 2008b). Nonetheless, one must be cautious about making generalizations about African American religion in the United States, for there is tremendous diversity of religious expression among African Americans. There is a strong local autonomy emphasis in the independent black denominations, and this means that local churches within the same denomination may vary considerably in theology and in style of ritual. Of course, there is also wide variation in the white denominations, but these denominations tend to be somewhat more centralized. The local bias of black churches tends to facilitate local variations and to exaggerate diversity within a denomination.

In Cincinnati in the 1930s, only 10.6% of the population was black, but black churches accounted for 32% of all churches in that city. The same pattern was true in Detroit and Philadelphia (Wilmore 1972). More recently, in his study of the predominantly African American Four Corners neighborhood of Boston in the 1990s, Omar McRoberts found 29 churches in a half-square-mile area (McRoberts 2003). Studying the 98% black Eastside neighborhood of Charleston, South Carolina, in the same time period, Timothy Nelson identified 15 active black congregations in an area 1 mile long and a half-mile wide. These large numbers illustrate the high degree of divisiveness and separation that often exists in the black religious community (Nelson 2005).

Perhaps the most important variation in black religiosity is that due to socioeconomic standing. The lower-class religious groups are characterized by emotionalism and fundamentalism, and the minister is unlikely to have had any formal theological training. On the other hand, the religious expression of the black professional class is quite similar to the religiosity of the white middle class. It is characterized by orderly and rational worship conducted by a well-educated, theologically trained minister. Beyond the variations of Christianity in the African American community, there also exist a large number of black new religious movements (NRMs). Regardless of variations, we can still safely say that African American religiosity tends to be more emotional in character than white religiosity (Chaves 2004; Nelson 2005).

We are able to discuss the existence of black religion as a distinct phenomenon in large part because the vast majority of African Americans do belong to all-black churches. This is due not to theological differences but to the castelike nature of American society relative to African Americans. During the time of slavery, black Christians were required to occupy the balcony while whites were seated on the main floor. This allowed slave owners to keep track of their slaves and ensure that religious meetings were not used to incite rebellion. Gradually some "trusted" black preachers were allowed to meet separately with slaves to have religious services. This was virtually the only official leadership role slaves were allowed, and it should not be surprising that the African American pastor enjoyed tremendous prestige and occupied the primary leadership position in the black community for more than two centuries (Lincoln and Mamiya 1990).

However, it was free blacks who actually founded the first independent all-black denominations. In Philadelphia, two African American clergymen, Richard Allen and Absalom Jones, started the AME Church in 1794, and a group of free blacks in New York started the AME Zion Church in 1820 (Wilmore 1972). The segregation in the white churches was unbearable for free blacks. To Allen and Jones, it seemed to be a direct contradiction of the Christian faith. Furthermore, predominantly white denominations were very little concerned about the needs of African Americans. The ability of all-black churches to minister effectively to the social and religious needs of their people resulted in a tremendous increase in the membership of these denominations and eventually in the spawning of others. The result is that most African American Christians have continued to this day to worship in segregation from European American Christians. As we noted in Chapter 10, the most segregated hour of Christian America is eleven o'clock on Sunday morning. It is precisely this separateness that makes it possible to speak about African American religion and the African American church as distinctive.

The Unique Character of the Black Christian Experience

There are two different schools of thought regarding the origins and central character of African American religion. One group of scholars believes that the conversion of blacks was a final step in obliterating any remnant of African culture among the slaves. The experience of being torn from their homelands and their families and being involuntarily relocated on a new continent was a stunning experience for the first generation of African Americans. Furthermore, slaveholders frequently had policies that slaves from the same African culture or who spoke the same African language were not to be placed on the same plantation. Hence, no common language, religion, or culture could enhance communication and solidarity among slaves. In fact, members of enemy societies were sometimes thrown together in the most unhappy of circumstances.

At first, the white masters refused to allow preachers access to their slaves, for most Christian denominations maintained that a Christian could not own another Christian. Hence, if a slave converted, the master would either have to give up his or her own church membership or would have to free the converted slave. For this reason, slave owners prohibited proselytization. Because many Christian missionaries wanted to preach to the Africans, they gradually compromised their position: Conversion did not automatically require manumission. Eventually, slave owners found that religion could be a powerful tool for controlling slaves, for they could use the aura of sacredness to reinforce desirable behavior patterns: submissiveness, industriousness, and obedience. By providing blacks with a worldview that is profoundly otherworldly, slave owners hoped to replace the last vestiges of African hopes for freedom with a sacred system that the whites could control.

E. Franklin Frazier (1957, 1963) and Arthur Fauset (1944) first developed the thesis that the Christianization of African Americans was the final step in the deculturation of Africans. However, they also pointed out that these African converts used the imagery of Christianity to forge a religious expression appropriate to their own needs. In this view, Christianity became functional for the slaves in that it established a common base for unity and solidarity among otherwise disparate peoples. This view of African American religiosity stresses the fact that slave religion was a synthesis of white religion and black experience, and it developed its own unique character and history. The emotionalism that is characteristic of African American churches is attributed to the fact that it was mostly Baptists and Methodists who evangelized the slaves. Because the revival-meeting style of those denominations was highly enthusiastic and emotional, it is not surprising that black Christianity was also revivalistic. Furthermore, poorly educated and economically impoverished groups are frequently more emotional in religious expression than are more educated and affluent coreligionists. This would also add to the highly emotional tenor of African American religion (Baer 1984).

Other scholars, such as Melville Herskovits (1958), Gayraud Wilmore (1972), Joseph Washington (1972), Peter Williams (1980), and Eric Lincoln and Lawrence Mamiya (1990), have insisted that slave religion was influenced by certain patterns of religiosity that are common to many African religious ceremonies. According to Herskovits, the tendency to turn to religion rather than to political action to alleviate frustrations is typical of African cultures. Moreover, the rhythm and motion that characterize the singing, preaching, and congregational responses in black churches are also common in Africa. Hence, the style of religiosity of the African American church is viewed as a survival of previous cultural patterns in much the same way that the sentence structure of

"Ebonics" (the African–English dialect) is viewed by linguists as a survival of African languages. The specific religious belief systems are granted to be a product of the new world and of contact with white missionaries, but the mode of expression is viewed as uniquely African.

The debate continues between those holding each of these views. We cannot expect to resolve the issue here, but we do want to highlight the significance of the alternative views. For those who deny that African culture had any real influence on slave religiosity, the characteristic features of the African American church are thought to originate in socioeconomic subordination. If this view is correct, the emotionalism of black religiosity may fade, even in all-black churches, as members of those congregations improve their socioeconomic standing.

On the other hand, African American religiosity will continue to have a different flavor from European American religiosity if the variation is rooted in ethnic differences that are preserved in segregated religious organizations. There is empirical evidence to support both views, but we do not believe that one can fully understand the religiosity of the first slaves without some understanding of their previous experiences of religion. Through the transmission of religion from one generation to the next, the remnants of African religiosity have been passed down to the contemporary black church. Our expectation is that the unique, expressive style of the black church will continue.

Regardless of the causes of black religious patterns, there is a consensus that African American religion in the United States does have a unique character (Cone 1972; Johnstone 2007; Lincoln and Mamiya 1990; Washington 1964, 1972; Wilmore 1972; Winter 1977). In fact, Washington referred to black Christianity in the United States as a form of folk religion. First of all, the Christianity that was preached to blacks was a truncated and manipulated version of Christian theology; it was designed to help pacify and compensate them for their inferior position in life (see the next "Illustrating Sociological Concepts" feature). Furthermore, religion became the means by which slaves could express their frustrations and their hopes—both of which emanated from their subordinate standing in society. Other scholars point out that all world religions adapt to local needs and that while African American Christianity has its unique character, it is no different from other expressions of Christianity in adapting a local flavor. Like Christianity in Poland, Brazil, or Anglo America, African American Christianity has both folk elements and strong universalistic themes (Lincoln and Mamiya 1990).

Critical Thinking: Which argument is more convincing to you: African American religious style is rooted in religious patterns and styles of Africa, or it is shaped by socioeconomic circumstances? Why is this position more persuasive to you?

ILLUSTRATING SOCIOLOGICAL CONCEPTS

Excerpts From a Catechism for American Slaves

These questions from a catechism designed for slaves illustrate the way Christianity was twisted to serve the interests of the powerful group. Several denominations established special catechisms for slaves, which were, at best, truncated interpretations of the faith.

(Continued)

(Continued)

Question:	What did God make you for?
Answer:	To make a crop.
Question:	What is the meaning of "Thou shalt not commit adultery"?
Answer:	To serve our heavenly Father, and our earthly Master, obey our overseer, and not steal anything.

SOURCE: Wilmore, Gayraud S. 1972. *Black Religion and Black Radicalism*. Garden City, NY: Doubleday.

Religion of the Oppressed and Coded Messages: The Black Spiritual

One of the characteristic expressions of this African American religiosity was the black spiritual. Surprisingly, few African American spirituals were Christ-centered; in fact, many do not even mention God (Wilmore 1972). The message of most spirituals was an expression of hardship and a hope of freedom. Those spirituals that do focus on Jesus stress his suffering, his experience of being scorned, and his role as liberator. Some spirituals were based on biblical stories (such as "Joshua Fit the Battle of Jericho"), but many were commentaries on contemporary events. "Oh, Lord, What a Morning, When the Stars Begin to Fall" emerged right after Nat Turner's insurrection (1831) when slaves were under the tightest scrutiny. The slaves hoped for that day when the Apocalypse would come, the revolution would be successful, and the sky would fall on slave owners. Washington insisted that slaves used the vocabulary of white ministers and of the Bible and that whites believed the slaves were being socialized in the values that owners wanted. However, content analysis of these hymns, combined with reports from former slaves on the role of the spirituals, has suggested a different interpretation. Washington wrote the following:

The popular view that [the] spirituals are of Christian origin is based upon the preponderance of otherworldly themes, Biblical words, and the instruction and messages of the missionaries. These were the tools the [slaves] had at hand, but this view assumes the credulity of the slave. It overlooks the awareness of [blacks] that religion was methodically used to hold them in check, and their capacity to use it for other purposes than worship. Thus, the distinction between spirituals being forged from materials presented by Christians and forged from the Christian faith itself is essential. (Washington 1964:218)

Scholars have found that many spirituals were, in fact, "code songs" that communicated one thing to blacks, while white masters sat by—content that their slaves were getting a heavy dose of otherworldly religion. For example, the spiritual "Let Us Praise God Together, on Our Knees," which is included in the hymnbooks of many mainline white denominations, was actually a call to a secret meeting of slaves at dawn. The chorus of that spiritual is as follows: "When I fall on my knees *with my face to the rising sun,* Oh, Lord, have mercy on me." Likewise, when a slave working in the fields began singing "Steal away, steal away home; I ain't got long to stay here," he or she was indicating *this-worldly* intentions to other slaves. Participation of the other slaves in the chorus was a way to wish the person well and a promise to try to cover for the slave's absence as much as possible. Some of the spirituals were rather thinly veiled codes, such as the one that went like this:

> I am bound for the promised land;
>
> I am bound for the promised land;
>
> Oh who will come and go with me?
>
> I am bound for the promised land!

"Canaan, Sweet Canaan" did not point only to an otherworldly realm, but it referred to Ohio, Illinois, Pennsylvania, and even Canada. Similarly, references to the Jordan River usually meant the Ohio River. "Swing Low, Sweet Chariot" provides an example. When the Underground Railroad was ready to take another group of escapees north, African Americans could let others at a worship gathering know about it without giving themselves away to white attendants who came to ensure that nothing subversive happened at these religious gatherings. Someone would begin to sing, with great emotion:

> I looked over Jordan [the Ohio River] and what did I see;
>
> Coming for to carry me home;
>
> A band of angels [Harriet Tubman or another conductor of the Underground Railroad] coming after me;
>
> Coming for to carry me home
>
> Swing low [deep into the South] Sweet Chariot [the Underground Railroad]
>
> Coming for to carry me home [freedom in the North].

The slaves at those worship services understood the symbolism and double meanings very well (Cone 1972). In some cases, a biblical theme was being rehearsed, but contemporary characters were clearly identified with historical figures in the story. The spiritual "Go Down, Moses" emerged at the time when Bishop Francis Asbury of the Methodist Church was instrumental in formulating antislavery planks in the Methodist code of discipline. Asbury had himself referred to South Carolina as "Egypt" when he had been there to preach (Washington 1964), and that theme was expressed in the chorus of this popular hymn:

> When Israel was in Egypt's land, let my people go;
>
> Oppressed so hard they could not stand, let my people go.
>
> Go down, Moses, way down in Egypt land;
>
> Tell old Pharaoh, "Let my people go!"
>
> Oh let us all from bondage flee, let my people go;
>
> And let us all in Christ be free, let my people go.
>
> Go down, Moses, way down in Egypt land;
>
> Tell old Pharaoh, let my people go.

It does not take much imagination to figure out who represented "Moses," "the Israelites," and the "Egyptians" in the eyes of those slaves.

The use of religious language for coded communication is certainly not a new phenomenon, for there are other reports of oppressed people communicating in a similar manner. Most biblical scholars believe that the Apocalypse (the Book of Revelation) was a coded message from John the Elder (a prisoner on the island of Patmos) to his people in the churches of Asia Minor. At that time, one was required to worship the emperor of Rome. Because Christians refused to do so, they were persecuted. The Book of Revelation is an encoded book that is very difficult to translate because many of the symbolic meanings of that day have been lost. An understanding of the double meanings requires fluency in Aramaic and Greek. The book was not destroyed by the Romans, for they viewed it as a harmless fantasy about another world. They never recognized the political references that abound in the book and that served as a resounding criticism of Rome.

All of this simply serves as a warning against facile generalizations regarding the otherworldliness of the religion of the oppressed. Of course, some blacks did understand Christianity in other-worldly terms, and it served to compensate them and to discourage any rebellion in this world. They believed they would get their just deserts in the next world. The important point here is that slave religion was not a simple adoption of white Christianity; it was a reworked Christianity that had its own character, style, and outlook.

Much of the black church today has been influenced by this heritage. Even where the message is otherworldly, political issues have never been entirely foreign to black churches. Indeed, a comment attributed originally to Mahatma Gandhi—"Anyone who thinks that religion is not political understands neither religion nor politics"—is likely to resonate deeply in the African community (quoted in Spickard 2005:341). Most black Christians today feel that it is utterly appropriate to use the faith community for political purposes: 92% of African American clergy surveyed nationally support the idea of churches expressing their opinions on social and political questions, 91% of black laity believe it is appropriate for clergy to participate in civil rights protests, and nearly a third of the black churches house civil rights organizations and/or voter registration programs. The African American church has historically been much more involved in political affairs than its white counterpart (Lincoln and Mamiya 1990; Wilmore 1972). It has been a source of activism.

Critical Thinking: Slave owners used religion to manipulate and control slaves, while slaves used religion as a coded system to help them with escape plans. Is it at all troubling to you that religion was used as a tool to prevent or to stimulate change? Why or why not?

The Leadership Role of the African American Minister

One reason the African American church has been involved in political matters has been the fact that the black preacher was the main spokesperson for the African American community. During the period of slavery, the role of plantation preacher was often the only leadership role afforded Africans in the American South. Hence, it became a position of considerable prestige within the African American community. Following emancipation, this position continued to be the most important leadership role; the black preacher became the spokesperson for the community and the liaison between the dominant white class and the subordinate black one. Because whites often owned the buildings where blacks worshipped and could impose various sanctions on the black community, the black preacher had to be sensitive to the interests of both whites and blacks. This liaison role was certainly not just religious in character; it was often explicitly political.

The preacher's role as the central spokesperson for the community has largely survived to this day. The African American church has served since emancipation as the heart of that ethnic community. It has sponsored social and cultural affairs, established insurance programs for members who did not qualify for insurance under white-controlled corporations, started schools and colleges to educate young people, sponsored political debates held in church sanctuaries, initiated economic recovery and growth programs for African Americans, and generally served as a community center. In fact, Gunnar Myrdal called the African American church a "community center par excellence" (Myrdal 1944:938). The preacher was the person who gave impetus to most of these programs and thus came to be highly esteemed in the community.

Because the preacher held a position that afforded leadership opportunities and offered status in the community, his was a highly coveted position. Hence, there have often been young would-be preachers waiting in the wings to have their chance to preach and start their own congregations. Perhaps this is another reason for the large number of small black churches, each with its own semiautonomous preacher. The ministry was attractive to energetic African Americans because other professions were essentially closed to them. However, there has been a significant decline over the past 50 years in the ratio of blacks in the ministry (per 10,000 people in the population). Increasing numbers of African Americans now enter law, medicine, politics, and other professions. The black minister no longer holds a monopoly on leadership and status as was once the case. Nonetheless, the preacher still holds a more substantial position within the African American community than does his or her white counterpart. Many African American political figures have begun their careers as ministers.

Partially because of the acceptance of clergy being involved in political affairs, ministers in the black community were able to gain ready acceptance as civil rights leaders. Martin Luther King Jr. provides a particularly good example. King's civil rights speeches were constructed and delivered in the style of African American preaching. His nonviolent resistance strategy of the 1950s and 1960s required resistance to injustice but forbade participants from using violence. He insisted that blacks would change social structures by appealing to the conscience of the nation and by economic boycotts. If a white police officer struck a black protestor, African Americans were to resist the temptation to strike back. They were instructed to turn the other cheek and to love their enemies. They were told to hate injustice but not the person who perpetuated it. They were taught that love would be the weapon by which opponents would be transformed (King 2010). The mixture of religious teaching and political action did not seem at all inconsistent to King's followers, for they were used to African American preachers also being political figures.

It is hard to imagine how the many rallies that King led could have remained nonviolent without the influence of religious teachings. Moreover, when people's homes and churches were being bombed and rallies were dispersed by police officers swinging billy clubs, religion served to shore up the courage and conviction of the people, for they were assured that God was on the side of justice and ultimate victory was certain. Some African American critics of nonviolence felt that King's religion was another form of opiate and that blacks should fight back. Nonetheless, there is little doubt that the civil rights movement of the 1950s and 1960s gained much of its impetus from a black Baptist preacher—Dr. Martin Luther King Jr. Clearly, the role of the minister has been a central one in the activism of the African American community.

The role of the pastor was not the only leadership role that the black church has afforded. In a

Photo by Dick DeMarsico, courtesy of Library of Congress, Prints & Photographs Division, NYWT&S Collection, reproduction number LC-USZ62-126559

Dr. Martin Luther King Jr. led civil rights marches throughout the United States. Black clergy have considerable social status and are often looked to for leadership on political and social justice issues within the larger community. This is another way in which a religious group—if it is an open system—can have "output" on the larger society.

society where African Americans have often held menial and low-status jobs, the roles of elder, deacon, Sunday school superintendent, or choir leader have provided leadership opportunities and respected positions in the community. Often these positions have been given exalted and lengthy titles. Such roles in exclusively black denominations enhance the self-esteem of individuals who have rather humble standing in the larger society (Baer 1984). This self-confidence and these leadership skills, again, are often used in the service of activism for change.

New Religious Movements in the African American Community

African American religion in the United States has also included many black sects and NRMs. There are a great variety of them, each emerging out of the common black experience of subjugation but each offering its own unique characteristics (Fauset 1944; Lincoln 1994; Washington 1964, 1972; Wilmore 1972). Two of the best-known African American NRMs were Father Divine's Peace Mission and the Lost/Found Nation of Islam (Black Muslims). The Father Divine movement started in 1932 when a man by the name of George Baker opened a mission in Harlem. He took the name of Major J. Divine and quickly gained notoriety by distributing alms among poor blacks. He taught that God is everywhere, everything, and everyone, and eventually his followers came to believe that Divine was God incarnate. Baker then came to be known as Father Divine. Under his direction, the mission developed into a communal living settlement and maintained extremely high standards of morality. Although the group was highly ascetic in character, the emphasis was not otherworldly. It was directed toward changing the socioeconomic system. The strategy of change focused primarily on benevolence for the poor rather than radical political changes. Because of its moderate stand on changing social structures, it did not incur the opposition of powerful conventional organizations. The movement spread across the country and was one of the larger African American NRMs in the United States.

The Lost/Found Nation of Islam was more radical in its outlook and its activism, and it has had considerable influence in many U.S. prisons—where much of the proselytization initially took place. The movement started in the summer of 1930 when an Arab peddler, known as Wali D. Fard, came to the African American neighborhoods of Detroit. He sold silks and other materials and preached that black people in Africa and the Middle East were Islamic, not Christian. Christianity was depicted as the religion of the white people with a white God and a white savior. Being a Christian was equated with worshiping white people and was described as the white society's way of duping blacks into subordinate roles.

Fard lectured on black civilization in Asia and Africa. He told inspiring (and often embellished) stories about black culture on other continents. All African Americans were depicted by Fard as Muslim in their origins and were referred to as the "Lost Tribe of Shabazz." Many African Americans were delighted with this stranger's stories of sophisticated and advanced black culture and his insistence on black superiority. It provided a basis for a sense of dignity and pride, which was often denied to poor ghetto blacks. Furthermore, the preacher's claim of Arab heritage lent credibility to his claims of firsthand knowledge of Africa and Arabia.

Fard developed a substantial following—estimated at 8,000 adherents. One of his devotees was a dynamic African American whom Fard renamed Elijah Muhammad. (Black Muslims refused to accept the names they received from slavery and were given a new name when they joined the Islamic temple.) When Fard mysteriously disappeared in 1934, Elijah Muhammad was named Minister of Islam. One of Muhammad's main disciples, in time, was Malcolm X.

The Black Muslims originally insisted that only black people could join. This political–religious group experienced its heyday in the 1960s. Malcolm X became the primary spokesperson and gained national attention as a militant civil rights leader, being among the first to stress "black pride" and "black is beautiful" as central themes. Propelled by his forceful and articulate speeches, the Black Muslim movement grew rapidly. Attention was also focused on the movement when such notable sports personalities as Muhammad Ali and Kareem Abdul-Jabbar converted to the Lost/Found Nation of Islam.

The Black Muslims have been a religious group that is as thoroughly political as it is religious. For them, the distinction between politics and religion is meaningless. They explicitly reject any otherworldly views, so the socioeconomic–political structures of this world are of central importance to their view of "salvation." In fact, the ultimate goal of the original Lost/ Found Nation of Islam was an autonomous and separate black nation in the United States.

The larger Islamic world did not recognize the legitimacy of the original Black Muslim theology. In terms of official Islamic orthodoxy, the teachings of the Lost/Found Nation of Islam were heretical. In short, the Lost/Found Nation of Islam was a folk religion, which had grown out of the experience of black America (Washington 1972). However, to call such a movement a folk religion is not to denigrate its importance as a religious movement. Scholar Eric Lincoln described the Black Muslims as one of the most important religious developments in the 20th-century United States. Because of the ascetic teachings, the emphasis on industry and hard work, and the extreme sacrifice and devotion to the cause, the Lost/Found Nation mobilized substantial financial and personal resources. Moreover, because of high levels of internal discipline, Muslim ministers have also been able to deliver a significant block of votes to politicians. By acting as a unified front, they were able to make their presence felt in the larger society (Lincoln 1994). They became a force for change.

Malcolm X formally broke with Muhammad in 1964 after a trip to Mecca. On that trip, he learned that the teachings of the Black Muslims were quite different from Orthodox Islam. He established the Muslim Mosque, Inc., that same year but was assassinated in 1965. Before he died, he repudiated the views of whites as intrinsically evil and introduced a movement toward a more orthodox Islamic faith. When Elijah Muhammad died in 1975, his son Warith (Wallace) Deen Muhammad became the new leader of the Lost/Found Nation of Islam. He modified doctrine to bring it more in line with Sunni Islam and changed the name of the group twice. It is now known as the American Society of Muslims. This mission was recognized in the Islamic world as a branch of orthodox Sunni Islam, and its North American membership has been estimated to be as high as 100,000. A splinter group continues to call itself the Nation of Islam and is led by Minister Louis Farrakhan, having a following of somewhere between 20,000 and 70,000. Farrahkan continues the black separatist teachings of Wali Fard and Elijah Muhammad (Lincoln 1994; Lincoln and Mamiya 1990).

In earlier chapters, we discussed the fact that sectarian movements are more common among socially and economically disfranchised groups. Because blacks in this country are disproportionately represented in this category, it is not surprising that African American religion is characterized by a large number of sectarian movements. Movements like the Black Muslims and Father Divine's Peace Mission actually comprise a relatively small percentage of the religiously affiliated African Americans in this country. Although 24% of Muslims in the United States today are black, only 1% of black Americans are Muslim (Pew Research Center Forum on Religion and Public Life 2007b). Nonetheless, they express an alternative mode of coping with the experience of being a subjugated minority.

African American Religion: Present Themes and Future Trends

James Cone (1969, 1970) and Gayraud Wilmore (1972) were among the first black theological scholars who stress the eschatological theme in Christianity and de-emphasize the otherworldly one. Cone and Wilmore are among a core of black theologians who have been articulating a "liberation theology," an emphasis on social and economic liberation at some future time in history. Otherworldliness is viewed by Cone, especially, as an opiate to black people. The true worldview of Christianity, according to these theologians, is eschatological. In fact, a Christianity that is not supportive of black power is viewed as not being Christianity at all. Liberation theologians insist that because Jesus advocated for the poor and the oppressed, so also must all true Christians. This has also led black theologians to seek common voice with peoples who are oppressed in other parts of the world. This sort of unified and liberation-oriented Christianity would certainly incline believers toward activism rather than passivity.

Even a brief look at African American faith communities is enough to demonstrate that the religion of any group is affected by the socioeconomic status of its members. Furthermore, the outlook any religion fosters may motivate people to seek change, or it may enhance acquiescence. If African American theologians who teach at major seminaries—scholars like Cone and Wilmore—are any indication of what the future will be, black ministers are likely to continue to be more politically involved than their European American counterparts. Moreover, if these theologians do set a course for the black church (and that is a big "if"), then the black church is likely to be increasingly an inspiration to social and economic militancy rather than an opiate. However, one empirical study indicates that while many African American pastors are interested in instilling ethnic pride and identity, the majority are not actively asserting liberation

theology, as such, in their preaching (Lincoln and Mamiya 1990). Indeed, as we saw in Chapter 9, the "prosperity gospel"—a theology that seems to legitimate the American status quo—is particularly strong in African American congregations, notably the megachurches of Creflo Dollar and T. D. Jakes.

Critical Thinking: Do you think that the black intelligentsia will ultimately have much influence on local black churches? Why or why not?

SUMMARY

In providing meaning in life, theology must address the real issues that face people. Because the problems of meaning in people's lives are different for the affluent and the poor, it is not surprising that theodicies are different. The theodicy of privilege tends to justify one's good fortune, whereas theodicies of despair tend to provide certain psychological compensations for and a sense of victory over one's adversities. Even the basic values and sense of morality tend to be different. Those in occupations where obeying rules is fundamental to success are more comfortable with religious systems that are precise and absolute about moral expectations. Those who are in fields where creativity and divergent thinking are the keys to occupational success are more comfortable with relativity, ambiguity, and open-endedness in systems of meaning.

Either religions of the oppressed and disfranchised can cause passivity and inaction in the face of social injustice, or they can inspire people to work for change. Theologies that are either otherworldly or apocalyptic (premillennial) tend to cause passivity, whereas postmillennial theologies tend to inspire activism.

African American religion provides an interesting example. Slave Christianity often inspired change and was used to transmit coded messages for escape, despite the efforts of slave owners to control slaves with religion. Further, the black church has often provided roles and leadership opportunities that enhanced self-esteem. African American pastors often became the central leaders in civil rights struggles and were the spokespersons for the African American community in the political arena. This opportunity for leadership by the black pastor made the role so attractive that a number of aspiring charismatic African Americans started their own sects and NRMs as channels to gain prestige and power within their own community.

Clearly, religion is correlated to socioeconomic status, and theology often serves as an ideology that is appropriate to one's economic circumstances.

PART VI

SOCIAL CHANGE
AND RELIGIOUS ADAPTATION

O ne of the realities of the modern world is social change. Some changes occur so rapidly that we can observe them over a few years. Others are long term and have been so gradual that individuals hardly see any change within their own lifetimes. Religion can be a source of stability and certainty in times of change, but some people also claim that if religion does not change with the times, it will become alien to the lives and experiences of the people. In these last three chapters, we explore ways in which religion has responded to shifts and modifications in the larger society.

In Chapter 13, we discuss the theory of secularization that has guided sociological research on religious change since the discipline's inception, as well as criticisms and revisions of that theory. In Chapter 14, we examine the various ways in which religion manifests itself "outside the (God) box." That is, we explore evidence of some alternative forms of religion that seem to be emerging in our rapidly changing society and that may be replacing traditional expressions of religion. In Chapter 15, we consider the religious implications of globalization—the trend toward the world becoming "one place."

13

SECULARIZATION

Religion in Decline or in Transformation?

HERE ARE SOME QUESTIONS TO PONDER AS YOU READ THIS CHAPTER

- What is *secularization*?
- Is secularization inevitable? Is it even happening?
- How is secularization linked to other social processes, such as pluralism?
- What is *civil religion*, and how does it function in a society? What are some different forms or styles it can take?
- What are some significant stages in the evolution of civil religion in the United States?
- Are the consequences of secularization destructive or beneficial to a democratic society?

In earlier chapters, we discussed the role of myth and explored the importance of world-view in religion and in the society at large. Until the 19th century, religion—in virtually every society—fundamentally shaped the worldview of the entire culture and profoundly influenced most other social institutions. In our contemporary world, other forces come into play, especially the advent of science as an institution, the greater sophistication of technology, and the higher levels of formal education in the general population. The scientific method and rational–legal analysis become the arbitrators of truth. Further, other institutions in the society appear to become less dependent on religious legitimation. The concept of secularization was developed originally by Max Weber and is closely tied to ideas of rationalization and bureaucratization that were part of his *Protestant Ethic and the Spirit of Capitalism* (Weber [1904–1905] 1958a; see also Chapter 9).

Industrialized societies tend to generate their own worldviews, independent of religious myths and symbols, and these secular worldviews may even begin to shape the traditional religious systems of belief. This may spell conflict not only between religious groups and the larger society, but also within religious groups themselves. Rationalization or *modernization* is a long-term process in the classical theories.

TRADITIONAL MODELS OF SECULARIZATION

Traditional views of secularization held that secularization is of considerable import, but various models emphasized different processes. One point of agreement is that traditional religious symbols are no longer a unifying force for industrialized society and religious ways of knowing are no longer given priority in all circumstances. The modern empirical scientific worldview has largely replaced the miraculous religious worldview, especially in institutions that are not explicitly religious. Truth and knowledge are gained through double-blind experimental studies rather than through nonrational visions or religious intuition. People look to science and technology to solve problems.

As a means of compensating, some clergy and philosophers have developed systematic theologies that are logical, coherent, and rational. Mythology has given way to empiricism, both in the secular world and within some religious groups. This change of worldview has been accompanied by structural changes in society, with institutions (family, government, economics, religion, education, science, health care, etc.) becoming separate and differentiated bodies. These institutions gain greater autonomy from religious authority.

We might, then, define secularization as transformation of a society involving (1) greater *institutional differentiation* and organizational autonomy from religious authority and (2) a more rational, utilitarian, and empiricist outlook on life and on decision making by individuals and groups. When the same sort of transformation occurs *within* a religion—either in the form of a theology that emphasizes logical reasoning and acceptance of scientific method and discoveries or as an organizational change using rational, utilitarian business practices in running the institution—it is sometimes called modernization.

That a process of change has taken place in the worldview and social organization of the Western world is unquestioned. How to understand and evaluate it is more difficult. A number of writers in the middle of the 20th century felt that this meant the decline of religion or even danger to the entire society. Others maintained that secularization is a healthy process that will strengthen the influence of religion. They acknowledge religious change but do not see this change as decline. To provide some sense of the traditional secularization debate, we will begin by exploring the issues as outlined by several key theorists who represent very different points of view.

Secularization as Religious Decline: Loss of Sacredness and Decline of Social Consensus

Peter Berger was very much alarmed by the process of secularization early in his career (Berger 1967, 1979). In the 1960s, he depicted this process as having many adverse effects on individuals and on the society as a whole. Berger defined secularization as "the process by which sectors of society and culture are removed from the domination of religious institutions and symbols" (Berger 1967:107).

In Berger's view, the function of religion in providing unifying symbols and a unifying worldview is extremely important. He insists that a society's *constructed world* (his term for worldview) is very fragile. It must be protected by being clothed in an aura of sacredness. The critically thinking empiricist allows that nothing is sacred; that is, nothing is beyond question and analysis. The world construction of the scientist is based on causality and logic. Because individual thinking is valued, the scientifically oriented society allows and even encourages a plurality of worldviews. In fact, Berger wrote that "the phenomenon called pluralism is a social-structural correlate of the secularization of consciousness" (Berger 1967:127). However, pluralism is not necessarily a good thing in his view. A multiplicity of worldviews may make all worldviews seem relative. None of them can be taken as absolute and above doubt, and this raises anxiety about life's meaning and purpose (Berger 1979). This lack of meaningfulness in life can be extremely disorienting to individuals, for critical thinking about one's worldview "was bought at the price of severe anomie and existential anxiety" (Berger 1967:125).

The dysfunctions of allowing pluralism of worldviews and of reducing the realm of the sacred are not limited to individuals. Pluralism may also pose threats to the stability of the entire society. As a functional theorist, Berger believes common beliefs, values, and symbols are the glue that holds a society together. Religion has

historically played this role. With the relativization of religion, individuals become aware of the plurality of possible religious views—each potentially legitimate—from which they must choose. The fact that one consciously selects a religious orientation (rather than being compelled by the conviction that there is only one possible view) makes the choice less than certain. Berger did not view this situation as one in which the individual is *free* to choose—an option now available to individuals. Rather, each person *must* choose; that is, one is coerced into doing so. Berger called this the "heretical imperative," because the Greek root of heresy (*herein*) means "to choose." The net effect, he believed, is a diminishing of the power of religion in the lives of people (Berger 1979). To use Clifford Geertz's phrase, it is the difference "between holding a belief and being held by one" (Geertz 1968:17).

Berger concluded that religion must accommodate, "play the game of religious free enterprise," and "modify its product in accordance with consumer demand," or it must entrench itself and maintain its worldview behind whatever socioreligious structures it can construct (Berger 1967:153). A religious group that takes the first course tends to become secularized from within and to lose its sense of transcendence or sacredness. It focuses on "marketing" the faith to a clientele that is no longer constrained to "buy." In the process, the faith may be severely compromised and changed. By contrast, if a religion fails to accommodate, the religion may end up being an "irrelevant" minority faith that does not respond to the needs of the society.

Berger described the effects of secularization as primarily destructive. The unifying power of religious symbols and the integrating function of a common religious worldview—a "sacred canopy"—are very important for social stability. The lack of a single worldview, couched in sacred symbols and an aura of absoluteness, is a fundamental concern for those approaching secularization from this point of view.

Finally, for Berger this secularization process was viewed as so powerful and sweeping that it was pretty much irresistible and inevitable in the Western world. Like it or not, secularization was the wave of the future.

This was his position in the 1960s, and it represented well the traditional view of secularization. In 1999, Berger reversed his position regarding the trend being religious decline, as we will see later. Still, his articulation of secularization was one of the more thorough statements of secularization theory for several decades.

Secularization as Religious Evolution and Development: Increased Complexity of Thought and Greater Religious Autonomy

Talcott Parsons and Robert Bellah have treated secularization as part of the increasing complexity and diversity of modern industrial society. Religion, both as institution and as individual belief system, has become increasingly differentiated from the rest of society. According to Parsons and Bellah, it has simultaneously become more of a private matter. However, they do not see this as a negative change (Bellah 1970c; Parsons 1964). The possibility of consciously choosing one's religious outlook, rather than being inculcated with a theology, may make religion more important to the individual.

Parsons insisted that Christianity might still have a great effect on Western society; after all, the institutions of the Western world were developed by people who were under the influence of the Judeo-Christian worldview. Moreover, private religiosity will continue to affect public behavior; ultimate values cannot help but affect an individual's "system of action." In this view, much of the influence of religion will be unconscious. Greeley put it this way: "Modern man, working in a large corporate structure that is infused somewhat by Christian ideas, with himself directed somewhat by the Christian ethic, may be behaving religiously a good deal of the time, though the fact that he is influenced by religion may not be immediately clear to him because the influence is both indirect and implicit" (Greeley 1972:134).

Bellah would agree with Berger that religious institutions exert less direct influence on secular institutions than in the past, but he explained this change as a process of religious evolution rather than decline. Bellah used a very inclusive definition of religion—"a set of symbolic forms and acts which relate [people] to the ultimate conditions of [their] existence" (Bellah 1970c:21). His focus on evolution involves an increase in the complexity of symbols over time, which is correlated with an increase in the complexity of social organization. Through this evolution, religion is able to do more than reaffirm the present social structure; it can challenge the current norms and values of the secular society and offer an alternative culture. Hence, the latter stages of evolution represent an increased autonomy of religion relative to its social environment. Bellah did not suggest that the evolutionary process is irreversible or unidirectional. He simply suggested a general trend of increasing differentiation of religion from the rest of the society. On the other hand, the trend is rooted in large-scale structural changes in the society, so one might reasonably predict that it will continue in democratic societies with high levels of educational attainment.

Bellah specified five stages of religious evolution: (1) primitive (e.g., Australian Aborigines), (2) archaic (e.g., Native American), (3) historic (e.g., Ancient Judaism, Confucianism, Buddhism, Islam, Early Palestinian Christianity), (4) early modern (e.g., Protestant Christianity), and (5) modern (religious individualism). He argued that beginning with the single cosmos of the undifferentiated primitive religious worldview in which life is a "one possibility thing," evolution in the religious sphere is toward the increasing differentiation and complexity of symbol systems. In the modern stage of religious evolution, the symbol system is "infinitely multiplex."

In the midst of this transformation, new forms of religiosity are emerging. These new forms are less dualistic (with the material world, which is evil, opposing spiritual existence, which is good) and involve more this-worldly spiritualities, which offer a symbol system that "relates people to the ultimate condition of their existence." Bellah wrote, "The analysis of modern [humanity] as secular, materialistic, dehumanized, and in the deepest sense areligious seems to me fundamentally misguided, for such a judgment is based on standards that cannot adequately gauge the modern temper" (Bellah 1970c:40). The attempts discussed in Chapter 1 to discover "invisible religions" or "lived religion" is in keeping with this emphasis on new forms of privatized religion (Ammerman 2014; Luckmann 1967; McGuire 2008; Wuthnow 1976b).

Religious evolution is seen by Bellah as an increase in the complexity of symbol systems and in the complexity of the organization of society. The later stages of the evolutionary process allow individuals to make choices about which worldview they will accept. Furthermore, individuals have more autonomy in being able to think for themselves and to create their own system of meaning. In this post-traditional situation, the individual confronts life as an "infinite possibility thing" (Bellah 1970c:40). Each person is "capable, within limits, of continual self-transformation and . . . of remaking the world, including the very symbolic forms . . . that [shape] his own existence" (Bellah 1970c:42).

This allows for greater freedom and in this sense may be viewed as an *advancement* for humankind. Several other researchers have pointed out that the idea of a "religious marketplace" can mean inexhaustible variety rather than watering down and marginalizing of religion (Finke and Stark 1992; Stark and Bainbridge 1985). As R. Stephen Warner put it, when it comes to religious commitment, achievement may be far superior to ascription (Warner 1993).

Parsons and Bellah each treated secularization as the process by which religion has become a private matter, and they believed that such secularization is taking place. Bellah and his colleagues would later give a prime example of religious privatization in *Habits of the Heart: Individualism and Commitment in American Life*

when discussing a young nurse they interviewed, Sheila Larson (a pseudonym), who told them the following:

> I believe in God. I'm not a religious fanatic. I can't remember the last time I went to church. My faith has carried me a long way. It's Sheilaism. Just my own little voice. (Bellah et al. 1985:221)

Noting that Sheilaism raises the possibility of over 200 million religions in the United States—an "infinite possibility thing" indeed—the authors conclude that "'Sheilaism' somehow seems a perfectly natural expression of current American religious life" (Bellah et al. 1985:221).

However, if secularization is referred to as a process by which religion decreases in importance and by which it has less influence on one's worldview and on social behavior, then Bellah and Parsons would deny that secularization is occurring. Differentiation of worldviews and pluralization of the culture are evaluated in positive terms. They represent progression of society rather than regression and dissolution.

Many theological liberals have de-emphasized the absoluteness of biblical authority (at least as literally understood) and emphasized that all life is to be understood in theological terms. Liberal theologies tend to reformulate the tradition so that it will be in harmony with the most recent scientific findings and other humanistic values in contemporary society. Scientific evidence may even be considered a legitimate starting point for "doing theology." Furthermore, a norm of logical consistency and coherence becomes a measuring stick for truth. Such theologies sometimes involve recasting biblical narratives so that they are consistent with the modern scientific worldview. For example, one strand of Methodist theology—developed by theologians Borden Parker Bowne, Albert Knudson, Edgar Brightman, and L. Harold DeWolf—maintains that because God is the creator of all of life and all that exists in this world, we must remain open to truth wherever it leads. Defending old dogma when new scientific methods prove the dogma wrong is irreligious, in this view. They insist that scientific methods are discovering what God created (Brightman 1940; Burrow 1999, 2006). This sort of interpretation, which invites rational and empirical outlooks into the heart of the faith, is referred to as theological modernism. Process theology also emerged in the 20th century, at a time in which social change seems to be the only certainty. One of the fundamental principles of process theology is that change is indisputable, inescapable, and eternal. Not even God is viewed as immutable and absolute; rather, He is viewed as changing and evolving.

Such theologies tend to be intentional in assimilating the religion to the values and perspectives of the larger society. Bellah and Parsons are more in tune with this more liberal strain of theology, and they are not inclined to think of it as less religious or as a sign of the decline of religion. Secularization and spirituality are *not* seen as opposites.

THE "NEW" PARADIGM

"Secularization" has been part and parcel of the sociological lexicon from the discipline's inception. Indeed, the assumed validity of the secularization perspective was so taken for granted for so many years that it became "part of the conventional sociological wisdom" (Lechner 1991b:1103). This conventional wisdom has been challenged in a series of insightful, if highly controversial, analyses by Rodney Stark, William Bainbridge, Roger Finke, and Stephen Warner, among others (Hadden 1987; Iannaccone 1995). Indeed, the idea that secularization is *not* inevitable now seems to have become a conventional position—a "new paradigm," as Warner (1993) has called it—at least in the United States. Even Berger claimed that "the assumption that we live in a secularized world is false. The world today, with some exceptions . . . is as furiously religious as it ever was, and in some places more so than ever" (Berger 1999:2). Indeed, Stark (2000b) claims that secularization theory is dead.

Although the "new paradigm" advocated by Warner (1993) cannot be reduced to a rational choice perspective, it is the case that the most severe critics of the "old" secularization paradigm have been rational choice theorists (Yamane 1997; Young 1997). Rational choice theorists begin with the observation that "humans seek what they perceive to be rewards and try to avoid what they perceive to be costs" (Stark and Bainbridge 1985:5). They add that some of the rewards are scarce and unequally distributed within society and some desired rewards (such as life after death) may not be available from the society at all. When humans do not have access to desired rewards, they seek compensators. "A compensator is a belief that a reward will be obtained in the distant future or in some other context which cannot be immediately verified" (Stark and Bainbridge 1985:6).

The affluent in society are able to satisfy most of their material wants and needs with empirically available methods. Those who are at the lower end of the socioeconomic hierarchy may desire compensation for their *inability* to meet their material needs, including everything from food and shelter to health care. Compensators who address needs that could be satisfied through empirical means but are denied because of scarcity or social competition are referred to as *specific compensators*. Supernaturalism that is geared exclusively to specific compensators is a form of "supernatural technology," a method of manipulating nonempirical forces in the service of this-worldly needs. (In Chapter 1, this orientation to the supernatural was called "magic" rather than religion.)

Stark and Bainbridge believe that religion, properly understood, deals only with *general compensators*. Yet they also point out that most religious organizations offer a mixture of general and specific compensators. Religious groups are being discredited, they believe, because empirical scientific methods are disproving many claims about specific compensators. This creates a problem of plausibility for many religious groups.

Doubts about the ability of supernatural methods to satisfy everyday empirical needs have caused skepticism about religious claims to satisfy general or nonempirical needs (e.g., hope for life after death). Stark and Bainbridge insist that science will ultimately drive out magic because modern science and technology prove more effective in addressing this-worldly needs. However, science can never replace religion, per se, because empirical methods are incapable of addressing nonempirical (spiritual) needs (Stark and Bainbridge 1985).

Critical Thinking: Is it true that religion and science address very different purposes and that one cannot ever fully replace the other? *Why do you think as you do?*

These "rational choice" theorists also maintain that the effectiveness of the scientific view of the world has created a problem for many traditional religious organizations. People in modern societies have come to depend increasingly on scientific empirical methods as sources of validation rather than on supernatural explanations. Many religious leaders have coped with the scientific revolution by lowering tension with the secular (this-worldly) culture: They adopt a more secular perspective (as discussed above). They develop a theology that is consistent with scientific empiricism, sometimes by shying away from supernaturalism altogether. In the 17th century, European scientists like Galileo were forced by the Christian Church to recant their findings, but "in this century it has been the religious intellectuals, not the scientists, who have done the recanting" (Stark and Bainbridge 1985:434). These rational choice theorists believe that when religious organizations abandon supernaturalism, they are only able to offer very weak general compensators (Finke and Stark 1992; Stark and Bainbridge 1985). The result of secularity even within religious systems is not a society of empirical secularists who eschew any sense of

supernaturalism, but a restoration of more otherworldly expressions of religion. These come in the form of renewals of traditional faiths (sects) or in the formation of entirely new religious movements (NRMs).

The movement away from supernaturalism and toward a purely secular outlook is not an inevitable process that spells a substantial and long-term decline of religion, as some secularization theorists have implied. Indeed, for Stark, it is not clear that supernaturalism has declined over the past few centuries at all. The inability of secularism to provide general compensators (a sense of meaning in life, the hope for an afterlife, and so forth) means that secularization is self-limiting. Secularization does not mean a decline of religion, the rational choice theorists tell us, but it may entail a reformation of traditional religions and the spawning of NRMs. In the region of the continent where traditional forms of religion are weakest (the Pacific Coast), NRMs are more abundant. They develop precisely to fill the vacuum of general (supernatural) compensators. Stark concluded that secularization is no longer a useful concept. Vigorous religious group identification, affirmation of beliefs in the supernatural by large numbers of people, and high weekly attendance rates are among his strongest evidence (Stark 2000b).

At the macro level, rational choice theorists advocate a "religious economies" approach. According to this model, a religious economy consists of all the religious activity going on in any society. Religious economies are like commercial economies in that they consist of a market of current and potential customers, a set of firms seeking to serve that market, and religious "product lines" offered by various firms (Stark and Bainbridge 1985, 1996). Also like commercial economies, religious economies thrive when they are allowed to operate without government interference. Finke summarized the logic of the model: Deregulation leads to pluralism, pluralism to competition, competition to specialization of product (catering to a market niche) and aggressive recruitment, specialization and recruitment to higher demand, and higher demand to greater participation (Finke 1990). Thus, as a "natural" consequence of the invisible hand operating unencumbered by state regulation, "over time the diversity of the religious market will reflect the very diversity of the population itself" (Finke 1990:622).

This basic model has been applied in several different studies, some of which take the unit of analysis for comparison to be the nation-state (Chaves and Cann 1992; Iannaccone 1992; Stark 1992) and some of which use subnational units of analysis such as cities (Finke and Stark 1988) or dioceses (Stark and McCann 1993). In the breakthrough article for the economics of religion, Finke and Stark tested perhaps the central hypothesis derived from the religious economies

model, namely that "religious pluralism" contributes to higher levels of religious participation (what they call "religious mobilization"). Using quantitative data from the 1906 Census of Religious Bodies, Finke and Stark studied the impact of "adherence" (their indicator of mobilization) on "pluralism" and found a positive relationship (Finke and Stark 1988).

While Finke and Stark and others provided empirical support for the religious economies perspective, the data on which the support is built do not give any evidence for a trend over time (Finke and Stark 1988). Thus, the empirical jewel in the religious economies crown is the award-winning book, *The Churching of America* (1992, 2005). Among other things, in this book Finke and Stark argue that between 1776 and 2000, religious "adherence" in the United States grew

Photo by Keith Roberts

The oldest Jewish synagogue in the United States is in Newport, Rhode Island, where separation of church and state and tolerance of other religious traditions was a founding principle. After George Washington was elected president of the new nation, he received a letter from that early Jewish congregation in Newport asking about his policies of pluralism. In response in 1790, Touro Synagogue received a handwritten letter signed by President Washington (prominently displayed in the synagogue) embracing an open and "liberal" policy to all American citizens, regardless of origins or religious affiliation. In this letter, George Washington affirmed a policy of religious pluralism from the very beginning of the country's existence as a nation.

from 17% to 62% and that this linear, upward slope is exactly the opposite of what is predicted by secularization theory (Finke and Stark 2005).

Thus, contrary to Peter Berger's thesis of the 1960s (see also Bruce 1999), rational choice theorists argue that pluralism in the society actually makes the religious market competitive, and therefore invigorates religious participation. They do not believe it undermines plausibility or commitment. Recent research, however, has questioned the positive connection between pluralism and participation in the

religious economies model (Norris and Inglehart 2011). This controversy is discussed in the "Doing Research on Religion" feature.

Critical Thinking: Some scholars maintain that ascription (birth into a religion where no options exist) makes for stronger religious commitment; others argue that achievement (choosing one's faith in a competitive marketplace) is best for religion. With which position do you agree? Why?

DOING RESEARCH ON RELIGION

The Controversy Over Secularization and Pluralism

One of the hotly contested points in the secularization debate is whether pluralism undermines religious commitment by making the faith position seem relative and less than certain—as Berger argued—or whether pluralism creates competition between religious groups—as rational choice theorists assert. The latter argue that religious pluralism creates more options for people so that they can choose from an array of religious products. Further, pluralism generates more vitality and energy among "religious entrepreneurs" as each tries to recruit members. The competition makes the entrepreneurs hungry and aggressive, thereby finding new niches in the market. Pluralism prevents religious leaders from becoming complacent. The latter happens where competition is missing. Pluralism, therefore, creates religious vigor according to rational choice theorists. In 1988, Roger Finke and Rodney Stark published a major article in support of the idea that pluralism and participation are positively related. They examined data from the 1906 U.S. Census of Religious Bodies on the 150 largest cities in the United States to test the following hypothesis: "The more pluralism, the greater the religious mobilization of the population—the more people there who will be committed to a faith" (Finke and Stark 1988:43). Their independent variable, pluralism, was measured using a religious diversity index that accounts for the number and size of different denominations. Using advanced statistical analyses (called multiple regression models), Finke and Stark found a strong, positive relationship between religious diversity and religious participation. From this they criticized the secularization thesis.

Kevin Breault responded to Finke and Stark's work using more recent data—the 1980 Glenmary data on churches and church membership—in which he found the exact opposite: "a highly significant, consistently negative relationship between religious pluralism and religious participation" (Breault 1989a:1049). In a comment on Breault's article, Finke and Stark rejected Breault's findings. They noted that they asked a colleague—fellow rational choice theorist Laurence Iannaccone—to replicate Breault's statistical models using the same Glenmary data and that Iannaccone found a highly significant *positive* relationship between pluralism and participation (correlation of 0.21) (Finke and Stark 1989). For his part, Breault replied with a defense of his methodology and conclusions. He, too, recalculated the pluralism index and religious adherence rates and again found a relationship of almost exactly the same magnitude as Iannaccone's, only *negative* (correlation of −0.22). The exchange ended at an impasse (Breault 1989b).

Almost a decade later, something very interesting happened. Another sociologist interested in the debate over pluralism and participation, Daniel Olson, tried to replicate the findings and found his results exactly in line with Breault's: a negative relationship (correlation of −0.22) between pluralism and participation (Olson 1998). How could Finke/Stark/Iannaccone and Breault/Olson come to the opposite conclusions using the same data and methods?

Olson explained that when he inspected the statistical analysis software program files that Iannaccone used—which were provided to Olson by Iannaccone in the spirit of scientific objectivity and empiricism that we discuss in Chapter 2—he discovered a simple mathematical error in the programming. The relationship between pluralism and participation in the 1980 Glenmary study was in fact negative.

Does the preponderance of the data support a positive or negative relationship between pluralism and participation? By extension, does the evidence support the secularization or new paradigm perspective on the effect of pluralism on religion more generally? Mark Chaves and Philip Gorski have done a secondary analysis of 193 empirical tests of the relationship. After careful critique of the methods of research in each study, they concluded that the large majority of studies indicate that pluralism in itself does *not* increase religious vigor or commitment in most social settings (Chaves and Gorski 2001). On the other hand, competition due to a plurality of religious groups does seem to increase religious commitment in *some* situations. More research is needed to understand the circumstances that create a growth situation and those that do not. Still, this review of an extensive body of empirical literature does indicate that no dependable *general law* can be supported that identifies pluralism as a consistent cause of religious vitality or of decline.

NEOSECULARIZATION THEORY

Although Rodney Stark has boldly declared secularization theory dead, many other scholars have attempted to breathe new life into the "old paradigm" of secularization theory. These scholars argue that individual-level data such as attendance at worship services and membership in religious communities are inadequate measures of a complex phenomenon of religious transformation that occurs at several levels. This new perspective is called "neosecularization" theory, *neo-* being a prefix meaning "new," from the Greek word for young (Yamane 1997).

Secularization at Various Levels of Social Analysis

Secularization, according to sociologist Mark Chaves (1993, 1994), is a process that can occur at the individual (micro) level, the organizational (meso) level, and the societal (macro) level. The extent of secularization varies at each level and in various social contexts. Indeed, in the United States, secularization may be occurring at the societal level but not at the individual level (Chaves and Gorski 2001). It is important to note that secularization here is conceived as the declining scope of religious authority; that is, the range of issues to which religious authority applies is narrowing as secularization occurs.

Thus, when individuals do not believe that their faith is relevant to everyday life—to their conduct on the job, in political choices, in regard to sexual behavior, in the science classroom, or in the attitudes toward race relations—secularization at the individual level has occurred. Within faith-based agencies (Baptist hospitals, Presbyterian colleges, Jewish social service foundations), if the decisions about how to deliver services or who will be hired or fired are based on systematic policies designed for organizational efficiency, then meso-level secularization is present within a religious organization (Chaves 1993). If decisions in the society at large are made without reference to religious ideas and ideals—for example, based on scientific or human rights arguments rather than on what is holy or sinful—then secularization at the societal level has occurred (Chaves 1993; Dobbelaere 1981, 2000; Yamane 1997).

Macro-Level Secularity

Although secularization theory views religion on three levels of analysis, the most important is the macro level (Tschannen 1991). The neosecularization paradigm emphasizes the centrality of institutional differentiation at the societal level. Institutional differentiation refers to the process by which "specialized institutions develop or arise to handle specific features or functions previously embodied in, or carried out by, one institution" (Wallis and Bruce 1991:4). As a consequence, in a highly differentiated society, the norms, values, and practices of the religious sphere have only an indirect influence on other spheres such as business, politics, leisure, and education (Wilson 1976). It is for this reason that we can point to differentiation as leading to a decline in the scope of religious authority: Specifically religious institutions have only a limited (or no) control over other institutional spheres.

Debates about prayer in schools, court decisions about "one nation under God" in the Pledge of Allegiance, and involvement of religious leaders in political issues suggest that societal-level secularization is a point of controversy in the United States. It is interesting, however, that the nature of various policy debates seems to be increasingly secular—based on rational consideration of social consequences and civic rights and responsibilities rather than on matters of sin or scriptural authority. As a Moral Majority lobbyist told researcher Allen Hertzke, "We can't afford to say, 'God settled it, that's it'" (Hertzke 1988:196). Televangelist Jerry Falwell also argued that in discussing abortion, the issue must be debated in terms of rights rather than theological imperatives: "We are reframing the debate. It is no longer a religious issue, but a civil rights issue" (quoted by Hertzke 1988:196). This framing of issues in terms of rational–legal authority rather than charismatic or traditional–religious authority suggests considerable secularization at the societal level (Yamane 2005).

The discourse following the terrorist attacks on 9/11 was also interesting, for media accounts often depicted governments that were not secular as being the most dangerous. Being "secular" was equated in the media with being democratic, rational, civil, and governed by law.

This can also be seen in the decline of "blue laws" in the United States. Blue laws are also called "Sunday statutes" or "Sunday closing laws," because they typically prescribe certain activities (especially the sale of alcohol) or require certain businesses to be closed (notably car dealerships) on Sundays. In their origins these prohibitions are government-enforced religious codes and so may be better called "Sabbath laws." The term *Sabbath* comes from the Hebrew word meaning rest (*shabbat*), and notably appears as the third of Ten Commandments in the Hebrew Scriptures: "Remember the Sabbath day, to keep it holy" (Exodus 20:8). In this religious tradition, God created the heavens, earth, and humankind in six days, and "on the seventh day he rested" (Genesis 2:2). In the Jewish tradition, the Sabbath is observed from sundown Friday through sundown Saturday. The dominance of Christianity in

Europe when these laws took on their current form dictated that they would apply to Sunday, the traditional Christian day of worship. In the New Haven Colony, the Sunday statutes were supposed to have been written on blue paper giving rise to the term *blue laws* (Laband and Heinbuch 1987).

Over time, many blue laws in the United States have been repealed, some only recently. For example, laws prohibiting department stores in Maine from opening on Sundays were overturned in 1990, and laws banning hunting on Sunday in Michigan were repealed in 2003. In most places today, commercial and recreational activity is governed by economic, not religious, norms. As we will explore further in the next chapter, sporting events that were once prohibited now dominate Sundays in many communities.

Sunday statutes still exist in a number of places. A few examples are Arkansas banning all alcohol sales, Illinois banning horse racing, Minnesota banning car sales, and North Carolina banning hunting. Bergen County, New Jersey, maintains a complete ban on sales of most retail products on Sundays, closing shopping malls entirely except for restaurants and movie theaters. Within that county, the town of Paramus prohibits all work on Sundays (Associated Press 2013). Even though residents of Paramus are as likely to give secular reasons for maintaining the laws as religious ones—for example, less traffic on the roads—the continued existence of these laws

Photo by Sandra Stroud Yamane

Along with Chick-fil-A, Hobby Lobby is the best-known national retail chain that is closed on Sunday. The store hours sign pictured here makes clear why. The company's motivation is further elaborated in its statement of purpose: "Honoring the Lord in all we do by operating the company in a manner consistent with Biblical principles." Hobby Lobby also professes to believe "that it is by God's grace and provision that Hobby Lobby has endured. He has been faithful in the past, and we trust Him for our future" (www.hobbylobby.com/our_company/purpose.cfm).

highlights the fact that the process of societal-level secularization is not uniform or inevitable. It is often the consequence of struggles between groups over how much religious versus secular authority should control the functioning of other social institutions (Smith 2003b). Today, any private business can *voluntarily choose* to be closed on Sunday, for religious or secular reasons. Most do not, but see the "Illustrating Sociological Concepts" box for a prominent exception.

ILLUSTRATING SOCIOLOGICAL CONCEPTS

Why Chick-fil-A Is Closed on Sundays (and Few Other Businesses Are)

S. Truett Cathy died in 2014 a rich man. The 93-year-old was a billionaire, in fact, but he could have been even richer had he opened his Georgia-based chain of nearly 2,000 Chick-fil-A restaurants on Sundays. The company had $5 billion in revenues in 2013 operating just 6 days a week.

According to the company's website (chick-fil-a.com), "Our founder, Truett Cathy, made the decision to close on Sundays in 1946 when he opened his first restaurant in Hapeville, Georgia. He has often shared that his decision was as much practical as spiritual." However, the company's official obituary emphasizes the religious origins of the company policy much more:

> Cathy was a devout Southern Baptist who taught Sunday school to 13-year-old boys for more than 50 years. As an extension of the founder's faith and the clearest example of incorporating biblical principles into the workplace, all Chick-fil-A restaurants—without exception—operate with a "Closed-on-Sunday" policy. Rare within the food service industry, this policy allows employees a day for family, worship, fellowship or rest, and also underscores Cathy's desire to put principles and people ahead of profits.

Chick-fil-A's claim to be exceptional in this respect is not just a public relations stunt. No other national food chain closes uniformly on Sundays. To the contrary, food service and other retail businesses are among the interests that have fought "blue laws" most vigorously.

The waning influence of governmentally enforced Sabbath restrictions is evidence of macro-level secularization. Business enterprises are free to operate according to their own institutional norms, which in a capitalist economy center on the pursuit of profit. Of course, the societal-level secularization represented by the institutional differentiation of religion from the economy does not mechanically lead to meso-level secularization. Organizations are free to choose whether to operate according to religious or secular principles, or some combination of the two.

Still, there is pressure for organizations to mimic other organizations in their institutional sphere (called "institutional isomorphism"). So, in the same way that religious colleges and hospitals have become more and more like secular colleges and hospitals, we might expect Chick-fil-A's religiously motivated business practices to decline now that its founder has passed. In the company's obituary for its founder, Chick-fil-A declared its restaurants "will remain privately held and closed on Sundays." Time will tell.

SOURCE: Chick-fil-A Press Room, "Truett Cathy, Chick-fil-A Founder and Chairman Emeritus, Dies at Age 93" (September 19, 2014). Retrieved from press.chick-fil-a.com/Pressroom/LatestNews/PressDetail/TruettCathyObituary

Critical thinking: Reflect on the ways in which "holy days" used for rest and worship have been transformed into busy shopping "holidays."

Meso-Level Secularity

Secularization at the meso level occurs when secular transformations take place within religious organizations. For this reason, Chaves also called this "internal secularization" (Chaves 1993). At this level of analysis, we see religious authority playing a diminished role in controlling the resources of religious organizations (including their core values and practical priorities), particularly the agency structures of religious organizations (e.g., religious boards, associations, lobbying arms, fund-raising units, schools, hospitals).

The secularization of higher education provides a good example of meso-level secularization. Most private universities in the United States began as religiously sponsored institutions. Prominent examples include such Ivy League schools as Harvard (Calvinist), Yale (Congregationalist), Princeton (Presbyterian), Brown (Baptist), and Dartmouth (Congregationalist), as well as other well-known universities like Chicago (Baptist), Duke (Methodist), Vanderbilt (Methodist), Boston (Methodist), and Wake Forest (Baptist). All of these institutions are now secularized in terms of their organizational structure and curriculum (Marsden 1994).

In the United States, some religiously related colleges, especially within fundamentalist or evangelical traditions, may make personnel decisions and curriculum decisions based on theological issues rather than on standard bureaucratic procedures and guidelines designed to determine functional competence. In so doing, they continue to assert religious authority in organizational

Photo by Sandra Stroud Yamane

Until the late 1960s, students at Wake Forest University had to attend weekly religious services at Wait Chapel on campus. Two decades after ending mandatory chapel for students, the university became formally independent of the Baptist State Convention of North Carolina, thereby completing the process of organizational secularization.

deliberations. This would indicate resistance to meso-level secularization. However, in a society that has experienced considerable institutional differentiation of religion from education, the resistance to internal secularization can come with a cost: diminished academic reputation (Burtchaell 1998). Of nationally prominent universities in the United States, few maintain a strong religious identity. Exceptions include Baylor (Baptist), Notre Dame (Catholic), Georgetown (Jesuit/Catholic), Brigham Young (Mormon), and Pepperdine (Churches of Christ), but the private institutions with the highest measures of academic reputation in the *U.S. News and World Report* ranking do not have strong religious identities (Mixon, Lyon, and Beatty 2004).

Similarly, many hospitals and social service agencies founded by religious bodies operate on the basis of management and administrative procedures used for any modern organization that has similar goals. Some religious agencies take pride in the fact that they are secularized in their operations—that they use conventional business practices and nonreligious organizational theories to operate. Some, like Catholic hospitals and hospital systems that grew tremendously in the 20th century, just do their best to negotiate between their religious values and the ever-present secular pressures to conform and survive (Wall 2011; White 2013).

Earlier in this chapter, we discussed the fact that liberal religious communities and theologians tend to adapt the faith system to accommodate science and other components of the modern world. In Chapter 8, we examined megachurches that focus on "marketing" the faith. An explicit marketing of religion was very much a part of 19th- and early 20th- century evangelism (Frankl 1987). Further, contemporary churches and televangelists who tend to employ marketing strategies for growth also tend to be rather conservative in their theologies, but they have adapted the principles of scientific management and the business world to the administration of their congregations and sometimes have adjusted the music

and theology based on what will "sell." This, in its own way, is a different form of secularization of religious organizations at the meso level—in this case done by conservative groups (Frankl 1987; Miller 1997; Sargeant 2000).

Micro-Level Secularity

At the individual level, what needs to be assessed in terms of secularization is the orientation people have to religious authority structures. A secularized society is one in which people will feel free to believe and act in ways that disregard, differ from, or even go against the prescribed views of religious authority structures. People's views and behaviors will be characterized by autonomy and choice. Echoing Sheila Larson from *Habits of the Heart*, supermodel Cindy Crawford has given a very succinct statement of modern religious autonomy, reminiscent of Sheilaism: "I'm religious but in my own personal way. I always say that I have a Cindy Crawford religion—it's my own" (quoted in Yamane 1997, p. 116).

Although we have an abundance of survey data on individuals' religious beliefs and practices, surveys rarely ask citizens whether and how religion affects their everyday decision making. One bit of longitudinal data that is useful comes from the "Middletown" studies. Stark and colleagues often cited evidence from Middletown as disconfirming secularization theory. For example, Finke and Stark pointed out that "in 1931 there was one 'house of worship' for every 763 residences of Muncie, Indiana (sociology's famous Middletown). By 1970, there was one church or temple for every 473 residents—a pattern of growth that applies across the nation" (Finke and Stark 1988:47). Stark and his colleagues failed to consider other findings from the Middletown studies, however. For example, Caplow, Bahr, and Chadwick show that individuals in Middletown were much less likely over time to believe that "Christianity is the one true religion" or that "it is wrong to attend movies on Sunday," and more likely to believe that "evolution is more accurate than [the Book of] Genesis." This indicates a decline in the scope of religious authority at the individual or micro level (Caplow et al. 1983).

Online Resources: Good-quality data are important to assessing the state of religion in contemporary society and, by extension, the accuracy of different theoretical approaches to it. Typically these data are created and disseminated by scholars working in universities. For example, the Center for Middletown Studies is housed at Ball State University (cms.bsu.edu/academics/center sandinstitutes/Middletown). Recently, a nonpartisan think tank in Washington, D.C., the Pew Research Center, has become an important source of factual information about demographics, public opinion, and social issues in the United States and globally (pewresearch.org). Throughout this textbook we have referred especially to data from its Religion and Public Life Project (pewforum .org), but also valuable are its Internet Project (pewinternet.org), Hispanic Trends Project (pewhispanic.org), Global Attitudes Project (pewglobal.org), and Social and Demographic Trends (pewsocialtrends.org). Each site allows you to access raw data, full reports, data summaries, and interactive data visualizations.

CONCLUDING REFLECTIONS ON SECULARIZATION

The primary assertion of the new secularization theorists is that some form of secularization is occurring at societal, organizational, and individual levels. However, there are several important caveats. First, neosecularization theorists do not necessarily think that religion is declining. They believe it is changing. Second, most such theorists concede that religion continues to be a

powerful force at the individual level and that it even has some influence in the larger culture (the macro level). Third, they maintain there is a trend toward secularization in most Western societies but that the trend is neither inevitable nor uniform in all societies and at all levels. This drift toward secularization may be counteracted by other social processes. Fourth, for most neosecularization theorists, secularization is *primarily* about reduction of influence of religion at the *macro* or societal level, not the individual level (Dobbelaere 2000; Lambert 2000; Martin 1978; Sommerville 2002; Wilson 1982; Yamane 1997). Dobbelaere wrote, "religiosity of individuals is not a valid indicator of societal secularization" (Dobbelaere 2000:36). Secularization, he said, is primarily about separation of the state, business, education, health care, science, and other realms of society from ecclesiastical and biblical authority.

On the other side of the argument, Rodney Stark, the most strident critic of secularization, has insisted that secularization is mostly about individual religious commitment. He grants that societal-level secularization—understood simply as the liberation of other institutions from the dominance of religious institutions—has indeed occurred (Stark 2000b). Of course, secularization at the *most* macro level—global—is just beginning to be analyzed (explored in the "Global Perspectives" feature on page 356).

One point raised by neosecularization theory is worth considering further: the claim that secularization may occur at the macro and meso levels while not really occurring at the micro level. Sommerville described this as "a secularization of things [structures and processes], but not of people" (Sommerville 2002:371). This may be true, but one would expect considerable strain and even overt conflict in society in such a situation. One wonders how long such tension may continue. The United States seems to have just such strain, expressed in the conflict between conservatives and liberals on public issues about prayer in schools, reference to God in the Pledge of Allegiance, prayer at the outset

GLOBAL PERSPECTIVES

Secularization and Global Perspective

The relatively recent emphasis on viewing social issues from a global perspective raises some interesting questions for those interested in secularization. Canadian sociologist Peter Beyer points out that the largest unit of social cooperation is not the nation, but the globe as an interactive human enterprise (Beyer 2000). Thus, we might ask whether religion has an influence on policy decisions and policy deliberation at the global level.

Clearly, if secularization is interpreted as meaning religion has no role and no influence outside the religious sphere, it is obvious that secularization has not occurred globally. The spread of Pentecostalism as a Christian movement to South America, Africa, and Asia in the last three decades has been phenomenal. Moreover, certain Islamic extremists have defined their faith as relevant to international relations, as the events of 9/11 made clear. Religion is hardly irrelevant across the globe.

Having said this, we must also conclude that at a global level, no particular theological authority has power to define reality or to determine policies unilaterally. The use of language to describe developed or disadvantaged societies is itself interesting. If a country has weak political or economic systems, poor educational attainment, poor health care institutions, and unsophisticated technologies, most people and global organizations would describe this country as "disadvantaged" or "underdeveloped." However, would the same happen if the *religious* organizations were weak or deteriorating? Beyer (2000) does not think so.

Further, when it comes to the deliberations of global agencies, international courts of justice, or the World Trade Organization, the guiding principles are based on utilitarian or functional rationality. For Weber, this was at the core of modernization. Thus, while the extent of secularization seems to be variable at national, organizational, and individual levels, Beyer concludes, "Religion . . . is *optional* at the level of global society" (Beyer 2000:90). This is another way of saying that at the most macro level of human interaction, religious authority structures are minimal, and secularization is well established.

Perhaps this is another reason why conservatives of nearly every religious stripe are leery of global processes and global organizations, like the United Nations. Our global organizations are governed by rational–legal authority. In a word, they are secularized.

---

of high school athletic events, and the presence of the Ten Commandments in courthouses and city buildings. How will this stress be resolved? The trend toward individualization of religion (for example, individuals saying they are "spiritual but not religious") may be one type of solution, since it involves separation of individual "spirituality" from "religious authority." In the view of neosecularization theorists, this is secularization at the individual level.

Critical Thinking: Would it, indeed, cause tensions or strains in the society if the society were secularized at the macro level but not at the micro level? Why or why not? If it would be expected to create tensions, how severe are those likely to be for the society? Why?

We might conclude with four observations about secularization: (1) Secularization at the macro level is clearly at work in all Western democratic societies; (2) secularization at the individual level is variable and is far from universal; (3) secularization is not inevitable or unstoppable; and (4) secularization is a useful concept for describing a social process, but its predictive power is limited.

In the end, religion is changing. Change in itself, however, is not the same as decline. Rather, adaptation is characteristic of all religion that survives over time. (Whether the adaptation is "good" or "bad" is a normative judgment rather than an analytical one.) Some sociologists have argued that one significant way religion has changed as society has become secularized at the institutional level is that it has become a generalized aspect of society itself, rather than a specific part of religious institutions and organizations. This is known as civil religion.

CIVIL RELIGION

Civil religion refers to the cultural beliefs, practices, and symbols that relate a nation to the ultimate conditions of its existence. The idea of civil religion can be traced to the French philosopher Jean-Jacques Rousseau's *On the Social Contract* ([1762] 1954). Writing in the wake of the Protestant–Catholic religious wars, Rousseau maintained the need for "social sentiments" outside of organized religion "without which a man cannot be a good citizen or faithful subject." The broader question motivating Rousseau concerned political legitimation without religious establishment.

Although he did not use the term, Émile Durkheim's work in *The Elementary Forms of the Religious Life* ([1912] 1995) was clearly influenced by his countryman's concern for shared symbols and the obligations they articulate. Recognizing that "the former gods are growing old or dying," Durkheim sought a more modern basis for the renewal of the collective sentiments societies need if they are to stay

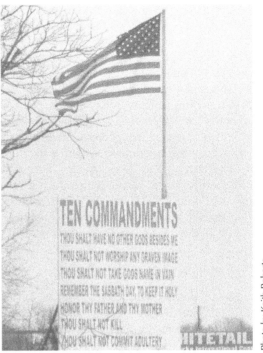

Photo by Keith Roberts

Public policy and the operation of institutions like the government are secularized—based on principles of rational deliberation, rather than doctrine, and scientific evidence, rather than scripture or dogma. Controversies arise over court challenges when religion does enter the public sphere. This sign was put up in Kentucky regarding whether the Ten Commandments could be posted in city hall or the courthouse. The courts ruled against it. This illustrates micro-level dissatisfaction with secularization occurring at the meso level.

together. He found that basis in the "hours of creative effervescence during which new ideals will once again spring forth and new formulas emerge to guide humanity for a time" (Durkheim [1912] 1995:429). Civil religious ideals arise from national civil religious rituals.

Robert Bellah's 1967 essay, "Civil Religion in America," brought the concept back into contemporary sociology. Like Rousseau and Durkheim, Bellah saw legitimation as a problem faced by every nation, and civil religion as one solution—under the right social conditions (Bellah [1967] 1970b). Following from his perspective on secularization in the course of religious evolution, Bellah argued that in premodern societies the solution consisted either in a fusion of the religious and political realms (in the archaic period) or in a differentiation but not separation (in the historic and early modern periods). Civil religion proper comes into existence only in the modern period when church and state are separated as well as structurally differentiated. In other words, a civil religion that is differentiated from both religion and the government is only possible in a modern, secularized society (Bellah 1970a, 1975).

Civil Religion in the United States

Bellah argued that civil religion exists alongside but distinct from formal organized religion. It is actually a religious "dimension" of society, characteristic of the American republic since its founding (Bellah 1970b). Civil religion is "an understanding of the American experience in the light of ultimate and universal reality" and can be found in presidential inaugural addresses from Washington to Obama, sacred texts (the Declaration of Independence) and places (Gettysburg), and community rituals (Memorial Day parades) (Bellah 1970b:186). It is especially evident in times of trial for the nation like the Revolution and the Civil War.

The mythology of American civil religion began early in the nation's history. In the speeches of some of the first presidents and in sermons of some colonial preachers, America was treated as the "Promised Land." In fact, in his second inaugural address, Thomas Jefferson explicitly compared the founding of the new nation to the founding of Israel, and Europe was defined as the contemporary Egypt—from which God's people had fled. This began a long process of myth development that has grown through the past 200 years. The belief in the American Dream, the

American Way of Life, and the fundamental goodness of America is expressed with reference to a supernatural blessing: "America, America, God shed His grace on thee, and crown thy good with brotherhood from sea to shining sea." Hymns such as these evoke a profound sense of reverence, for they express a deeply ingrained mythology. "God Bless America" serves much the same function.

Civil religion is also expressed through the rituals that take place on such "high holy days" as Memorial Day, the Fourth of July, and presidential inauguration days. The ceremonials on these days express central American values and inspire a feeling of unity and a sense of transcendence (greater purpose). The meaning of the nation is believed to transcend individual lives and is important in understanding the significance of contemporary events. The effort to stop Hitler and "make the world safe for democracy" provides one example. In the 1960s and 1970s, the space program and moon landings provided a sense of national accomplishment and collective identity. Currently the mission of the United States as a collective people seems to be focused on ridding the world of terrorists. Following the events of 9/11, freedom has become a uniting value that bonds people of many backgrounds and calls them to sacrifice and commitment for a shared purpose.

National ceremonies tend to emphasize the transcendent purpose of the nation. Most such celebrations occur around national shrines, which are themselves capable of eliciting a feeling of awe, for they symbolize both the ideals of the nation and the sacrifices made on the nation's behalf. Examples of national shrines are the Washington and Lincoln Memorials in Washington, D.C., the Capitol, the Tomb of the Unknown Soldier, war cemeteries, and the birthplaces or burial sites of American presidents. In an excellent analysis of the symbolism of a Memorial Day celebration in an American town, W. Lloyd Warner discussed the unifying quality of these rituals and symbols:

The cemetery and its graves become the objects of sacred rituals which permit opposing organizations, often in conflict, to subordinate their ordinary opposition and to cooperate in expressing jointly the larger unity of the total community through the use of common rites for their collective dead. (Warner 1953:24–25)

Because some sociologists view these ceremonials as the central expression of civil religion, content analyses of speeches and newspaper articles on Memorial Day and the Fourth of July and analyses of central themes in presidential inaugural addresses have become an important

Photo by Keith Roberts

Civil religion blends reverence for the nation with more traditional symbols of faith. Pictured is the chapel at Punchbowl, the Pacific cemetery for U.S. military personnel, located in Hawaii. Note that two U.S. flags are inside the altar area and are more prominent than two of the three religious symbols that also adorn the chancel: the Christian Cross, the Jewish Star of David, and the Buddhist Wheel of Dharma.

means of studying this phenomenon (Toolin 1983). There are also other national holidays, but they tend to be of somewhat lesser significance as expressions of civil religion: Thanksgiving (which George Washington first made a national holiday in 1789 so that citizens might thank God for the blessings of this land and this nation), Presidents' Day (birthday celebrations for admired presidents), and Labor Day (a time to celebrate the accomplishments of American labor and the upward social mobility provided for Americans through the labor movement).

The paramount sacred object in this religion is the American flag. The importance of this symbol can be seen not only in the prescribed handling of the flag (see the "Illustrating Sociological Concepts" feature in Chapter 4), but also in the intensity of the outrage when the stars and stripes are "desecrated"—treated inappropriately.

Daily recitation of the Pledge of Allegiance to the flag by schoolchildren became a major theme of George Bush Sr. in the 1988 presidential election. Particular national heroes, or saints, also serve as focal points for veneration and myth development. Washington and Lincoln are the most important and most widely recognized "saints," and are paid homage on Presidents' Day. For some people, Presidents Jefferson, Wilson, Franklin Roosevelt, and Kennedy are key figures. Sometimes folk heroes (like Betsy Ross, Daniel Boone, or Charles Lindbergh), business tycoons (who symbolize the rags-to-riches mythology), and military heroes (who symbolize courage and a willingness to sacrifice for the nation) are given honored status and held up to children as exemplary of the American Way. In many quarters, Martin Luther King Jr. has become a saint of the civil religion because of his efforts to apply the motto "freedom and justice for all" to all Americans. These national "saints" serve as inspirations and as behavioral models, much as Saint Francis, Mother Teresa, or Saint Teresa of Avila do in the Christian tradition.

Many observers of this American civil religion have been appalled by it, labeling it as idolatry of the nation or as "American Shinto" (Marty 1958).[1] Such scholars believe that, although many Americans attend weekly worship and have memberships in traditional religious groups, the central meaning system is Americanism. For these people, the flag is a more important symbol of their religion than is the Star of David or the Cross, and the Fourth of July is a more celebratory and meaningful holiday than Easter or Passover. This sort of analysis is by no means limited to social scientists, but it does suggest that civil religion sometimes replaces more traditional theological beliefs. Theologian H. Richard Niebuhr believed that nationalism was a greater threat to Christianity than atheism (Niebuhr 1960).

Although he has a more benign view of civil religion overall, Bellah partially agreed with Niebuhr when he insisted that "without an awareness that our nation stands under higher judgment, the tradition of the civil religion would be dangerous indeed" (Bellah 1970b:185). It would be dangerous because it would serve only to sanctify the status quo and the current social structures, regardless of whether they are just. He denied that the conservative function is the only role of civil religion in the United States. Its structural position relative to both church and state allows civil religion to act as a source not only of legitimation but also of prophetic judgment. That is, American civil religion proclaims judgment on the United States when the country fails to live up to its creed. The ideals of the nation provide a foundation for criticism and improvement.

For example, Martin Luther King Jr. criticized the nation while expressing his hopes for it in his "I Have a Dream" speech delivered at the March on Washington in 1963. It proved deeply moving to the American people because his dream was "deeply rooted in the American Dream":

> I have a dream . . . deeply rooted in the American dream . . . that one day this nation will rise up and live out the true meaning of its creed: "We hold these truths to be self-evident: that *all* men are created equal."
>
> I have a dream that my four . . . children will one day live in a nation where they will not be judged by the color of their skin . . . when all of God's children will be able to sing with new meaning "My country 'tis of thee, sweet land of liberty, of thee I sing. Land where my fathers died . . . from every mountainside, let freedom ring." (quoted in Lincoln 1968:65–66)

That speech became a major formulation of American civil religion. Although King was a Baptist preacher, he appealed not to values that are uniquely Christian but to ones that would be compelling to Americans of any religious stripe.

Over 40 years later, then presidential candidate Barack Obama addressed the issue of race in his 2008 "more perfect union" speech. His language, many observers immediately recognized, was civil religious:

> Two hundred and twenty one years ago, in a hall that still stands across the street, a group of men gathered and, with these simple words, launched America's improbable experiment in democracy. . . . The document they produced was eventually signed but ultimately unfinished. It was stained by this nation's original sin of slavery. . . . Of course, the answer to the slavery question was already embedded within our Constitution . . . a Constitution that promised its people liberty, and justice, and a union that could be and should be perfected over time. . . . Yet words on a parchment would not be enough. . . . What would be needed were Americans in successive generations who were willing to do their part . . . to narrow that gap between the promise of our ideals and the reality of their time. (quoted in Gorski 2010)

According to Bellah, at its best, civil religion guards against governments doing whatever they want to do and then sanctifying their actions;

---

[1]Shintoism is a Japanese religion (the state religion prior to 1945) that involves worship of ancestors and ancient heroes, a glorification of national accomplishments, and a deification of the emperor of Japan.

civil religion provides a standard of judgment for national policy. Unfortunately, civil religion is not always at its best. By 1975, Bellah declared in *The Broken Covenant: American Civil Religion in Time of Trial* that American civil religion was "an empty and broken shell" (Bellah 1975:142) because it had failed to inspire citizens and lost its critical edge.

In colonial days, said Bellah, a legal and economic system was devised that would protect the rights of the individual to pursue his or her own self-interests. However, a moral ethos counterbalanced narrow selfishness by proclaiming the obligation to act in the public interest. This moral climate was reinforced by two sources: the biblical concept of covenant with God and the secular republican political philosophy that called forth commitment to the common good. Bellah documented the self-sacrifice of many of the founders of the country, even while they defended the legal right of individuals to act in their own self-interest. Without this moral tone and sense of obligation, unfettered self-interest would destroy both the cohesion and the spirit of goodwill within the country. An endorsement of individualism, said Bellah, must be countered with some sense of obligation to the larger community. Bellah and his coauthors of *Habits of the Heart* believed that both the republican spirit and the sense of covenant have so deteriorated over the past two centuries that the nation now faces a national crisis (Bellah et al. 1985). A revival of civil religion is needed. The nature of that civil religion—the way we define the meaning of the nation and the core values that unite us—will be of critical importance in the development of the American character in the next century.

It is always difficult to tell for sure whether a major event will be a defining moment for a nation when one is very close to it. However, since the terrorist attacks on the United States on September 11, 2001, the mood and focus of the entire country have shifted dramatically. The sense of national identification and coherence was aroused, new heroes who sacrificed their lives for others became dominant, and stories/myths abounded about the courage and values of firefighters and other public servants. Common citizens, who forced the crashing of a plane they were on so that it would not crash into the White House or a highly populated area, became celebrated figures. Heroes and idols were no longer those who sought their own fortune, as was common in the 1980s, but those who sought a common good beyond their own self-interest. It appears that a new sense of national purpose may arise from the rubble of 9/11, but it is too early to analyze the character of this apparent new phase of American civil religion.

Regardless of one's personal evaluation of civil religion, the student of religion must keep in mind the key legitimating function it serves for societies characterized by differentiation of political and religious institutions. In these pluralistic, secular societies—societies in which no one religion can serve to sacralize the existing social arrangements and provide a common core of values—civil religion emerges to fill that void.

Critical Thinking: Robert Bellah said that the founders of the United States stressed individual freedom but counterbalanced that individualism with biblical and republican emphasis on community and the "common good." Bellah claimed that the counterbalance has faded, and Americans are now engrossed in a radical individualism that lacks the prophetic tradition of civil religion (calling people to a higher purpose and a greater generosity). Do you agree with Bellah? What is your rationale? What evidence supports your view?

Summary

Secularization has been viewed by sociologists as one of the most powerful forces in the modern world. Yet there are marked differences in what are considered the core characteristics of secularization and in the causes and effects of the process. Berger defined it as loss of sacredness, depicting secularization as causing a decline in religion. Parsons and Bellah viewed secularization as evolution, as an increased complexity in religious symbolism and religious structures. They understand secularization as involving change in religious worldviews but not necessarily as decline in religion.

Stark and Bainbridge agree with Berger that secularization is antithetical to religion, but they do not think that religion is therefore necessarily declining. They are convinced that secularization is "self-limiting" and is not an inevitable and overpowering force. They believe that magic, or supernatural solutions for this-worldly problems, will fade as secular scientific empiricism replaces it. Religion, properly understood, addresses general needs that cannot be solved by this-worldly methods.

Neosecularization theorists insist that secularization needs to be understood as the declining scope of religious authority at the macro, meso, and micro levels. At the societal (macro) level of analysis, secularization is characterized by institutional differentiation and increased autonomy of various aspects of life (business, politics, recreation, etc.) from religious authority. At the meso level, it involves organizations adopting a more "worldly," rational, utilitarian, and empirical/scientific approach to decision making. At the micro level, individuals do not orient their understandings of or actions in the world to the dictates of religious authority. This latter dimension typically involves a decrease in otherworldliness or supernaturalism.

Whether secularization entails a decline in religion or its transformation may depend in part on whether one uses a substantive or functional definition of religion, since not all scholars view supernaturalism as central to religion. Neosecularization theorists tend to argue that secularization is occurring in most Western societies at the macro and meso levels, but is more variable at the micro level. However, they no longer claim that it is an irresistible and inevitable force. As Bellah argued, under conditions of societal-level secularization, a meaning system that explores the ultimate significance of the nation can emerge: civil religion. Civil religion helps modern societies solve the problem of political legitimation that did not exist in societies not characterized by institutional differentiation of religion from political life. In that sense, it can be seen as a cultural response to secularization.

14

RELIGION OUTSIDE THE (GOD) BOX

Religion and the "Old" Media

Print Publishing

Radio

Televangelism

Religion and the "New Media"

Religion Online: Producing and Accessing Information

Online Religion: Practicing Faith on the Web

Religion and Sport

Muscular Christianity and the YMCA

Evangelical Protestant Sports Ministries

Religion and Spirituality at the Individual Level

Quasi-Religious Movements

Summary

HERE ARE SOME QUESTIONS TO PONDER AS YOU READ THIS CHAPTER

- What effect have technologies like the printing press and the radio had on faith and faith communities?
- Who is using television for religious purposes, and what impact might this have on religion in the future?
- How might the Internet affect religion as a communal/shared experience, and how might it influence individual faith systems?

(Continued)

(Continued)

- Is sport an avenue to enhance faith (and does a religious faith contribute to athletics)—or are they competing systems, each needing the time and energy of participants and social-izing participants in quite different values?
- What is the place of movements like astrology, scientology, and similar quasi-religious organizations in society?

Students are often told to think "outside the box"—to think broadly, critically, uncon-ventionally. Sociologists of religion are well served to do the same. Not all religion or religious-ness is to be found inside the "God Boxes" we think of as churches, synagogues, temples, and mosques. Thinking "outside the God Box" allows us to understand some important social changes that have taken place in modern society and the religious adaptations that have resulted.

Two of the most important aspects of contem-porary society are the media and sport. These arenas are often not taken seriously by students of religion, however, because they are "mass" or "popular" cultural phenomena. Religion is seen as serious and important while popular culture is silly and frivolous, yet the two commonly inter-sect. One cannot understand some very important developments in religion without understanding its relationship to the media and sport.

A number of social scientists maintain that religion is undergoing significant transformation as new forms of religion are emerging. Some of these new forms are nontheistic, and some even lack a supernatural dimension. For this reason, many sociologists prefer to call these processes "quasi-religious phenomena" or "functional alter-natives to religion." Regardless of what one calls them, these value perspectives provide many people with a sense of purpose in life and with a center of worth (which is the etymological basis for the word *worship*). When any ideology or value system becomes a meaning system—one that defines the meaning of life, death, suffering, and injustice—it usually takes on a sacred cast in the eyes of the adherents. By looking only inside the God Boxes, we overlook these alternative phenomena.

RELIGION AND THE "OLD" MEDIA

Although a study of radio/television and religion had already been published by the mid-1950s (Parker, Barry, and Smythe 1955), sociological study of media and religion really took off with the rise of modern "televangelism" in the 1970s and 1980s. Those who lived through those decades could not escape the sight (if not the influence) of "TV preachers" like Billy Graham, Oral Roberts, Rex Humbard, Robert Schuller, Pat Robertson, Jimmy Swaggart, and Jim and Tammy Faye Bakker. Even as those pioneers have passed from the earth or at least public con-sciousness, broader concerns about the relation-ship between religion and media have been addressed by sociologists.

As Stewart Hoover observed, "media are fundamentally technological in origin, and tech-nological change plays an important role in their development and evolution" (Hoover 2009:689). Our survey of the relationship between religion and the media, therefore, will look at the evolu-tion of media technologies from print and publishing to radio and television to "new media" like those developed for the Internet. Of course, technological developments cannot be understood independent of their economic, political, and social environments, so we pay some attention to those factors as well.

Print Publishing

The development of the mechanical (movable type) printing press by Johannes Gutenberg in 1440 was arguably the most important technological innovation of the second millennium. It had a monumental effect on all of the major institutions of society: education, medicine, politics, and, of course, religion. Indeed, the so-called Gutenberg Bible was the first major book printed using the press. It played a central role in ushering in the print revolution and also had a significant effect on the practice of religion itself (Man 2002).

Prior to the wide distribution of religious texts to people who were not ordained ministers, the hierarchies of Christendom controlled what was disseminated as Truth. The common (and typically illiterate) member of the local church did not have any basis for challenging the Pope or other ecclesiastical leaders. Those leaders were the authority. However, Martin Luther used the printed word in many powerful ways. He and other reformers claimed that the Bible alone was the ultimate source of Truth and religious authority. The church leaders were to be believed only insofar as they were faithful to the scriptures. Luther himself used the printed word to spread his version of Christian Truth, and he did so with a vengeance. He not only wrote more than other dissenters but he outpublished the entire legion of Vatican defenders (Brasher 2004). He published in the common languages of the people rather than in Latin, and the Protestant Reformation was launched. It is doubtful that this could have happened without the printing press. The printing press had similar revolutionary effects within Judaism (Brasher 2004).

Religious publishing today remains a vibrant cultural and economic phenomenon. According to the Association of American Publishers (2010), net sales of books in their "religious category" grew 2.4% from $557 million in 2002 to $658 million in 2009. Although this rate of growth was modest due to the challenging economic conditions of the time, it more than doubled the overall rate of growth in the book publishing industry over the same time period (1.1%). These sales are supported by organizations such as *Christian Retailing* magazine (which serves the $4.6 billion industry in "Christian products"), the Evangelical Christian Publishers Association, Religious Booksellers Trade Exhibit, and the Association for Christian Retail.

As in Gutenberg's day, Bibles lead the way. Indeed, nearly 28% of individuals surveyed by *Publishers Weekly* reported purchasing a Bible in the previous year (Elinsky 2005). Recently, religious fiction and self-help blockbusters have also contributed to this market segment. The "Left Behind" series of 16 novels, written by Tim LaHaye and Jerry Jenkins, have sold over 60 million copies. This is remarkable for a series of books that focus on the "end times" from a premillennial dispensationalist understanding of the Book of Revelation. Even more remarkable is that five of the books were *New York Times* best sellers, indicating their mass appeal. Another book that has dominated the best-seller list for years is megachurch pastor Rick Warren's *The Purpose Driven Life*. Published in 2002, it has sold over 30 million copies and is the best-selling hardback book in U.S. history. It has also been translated into 50 languages. Highlighting the articulation between different media platforms, megachurch pastor and televangelist Joel Osteen's book, *Your Best Life Now*, sold 700,000 copies in the first month after its publication in 2004 and was on the *New York Times* Best Sellers list for more than 200 weeks. It and his four subsequent books have all been number-one national best sellers.

Radio

The history of the development of radio technology is complex, but for our purposes we can note that in the 1920s commercial radio broadcasting began. Despite the fact that in 1930 the average cost of a radio receiver was $78 (equivalent to $1,019 in 2010 dollars), 40% of all U.S. households owned one. As the price dropped, that proportion more than doubled to 83% by 1940, and by 1950 nearly every household in the United States (96%) had a radio (Craig 2004).

Because broadcasting licenses issued by the Federal Communications Commission (FCC) required broadcasters to carry some programming that was directed to the public interest, from the start radio programming was often religious in nature, because religious programming was deemed to be for the public good. In the late 1920s, S. Parkes Cadman had a Sunday afternoon radio program on the NBC radio network. In the hour before Cadman, one could listen to the National Youth Conference of Dr. Daniel Poling, and Dr. Harry Fosdick's National Vespers service followed in the hour after. The Columbia Broadcasting System (CBS) also provided considerable religious programming. Together, they broadcast religious content from Protestants, Catholics ("Catholic Hour"), and Jews ("Jewish Art Program Sundays"). By 1931, *Time* magazine had taken note of the phenomenon, writing this:

> Enterprising evangelists and regularly employed clergymen snapped at radio's religious opportunities quickly after Westinghouse began broadcasting ten years ago. Three years ago first N.B.C., then Columbia systematized radio religion and offered time to Protestants, Catholics, and Jews. The three creeds took advantage of their opportunity. . . . Apart from such chain broadcasting are individual stations operated by churches, societies and evangelists. ("Religion: Air Worship" 1931)

By 1946, *Time* characterized "radio religion" as "a national institution," one that was "preached to an estimated congregation of ten million" ("Religion: Radio Religion" 1946).

Excluded from this national institution, however, were evangelical Protestants. Radio stations gave their free public interest time only to mainstream Protestant, Catholic, and Jewish groups. Unable to take advantage of the free airtime, entrepreneurial Protestants like Paul Rader, Aimee Semple McPherson, and Charles Fuller bought airtime for their programs and

thereby helped to transform the religious orientation of the American mass media in an evangelical direction (Hangen 2002). In less affluent parts of the world, like Latin America, radio remains the predominant vehicle for the dissemination of religious ideas. Even in the United States, one in five adults in 2014 said they had listened to religious talk radio in the previous week (Pew Research Center 2014b).

Televangelism

In 1950, 96% of American households owned radio receivers. In that same year, only 9% had television sets. The decade of the 1950s was the key period of transition from one technology to the other. As televisions became widely available in the 1950s, what was done previously by radio began to migrate to television. (Note that just as the advent of radio did not eliminate religious publishing, neither did the advent of television eliminate religious radio.)

By 1960, an important change in the regulation of the airwaves took place when the FCC ruled that television stations could count *paid* programming toward their "public interest" contribution. This effectively opened the door for those who carried on the entrepreneurial spirit several evangelists had brought to radio. The first three mass media evangelists to have a major television presence were Billy Graham, Oral Roberts, and Rex Humbard. They built not only on the radio evangelists who preceded them but also on the contributions of revivalists Charles Grandison Finney (1792–1875), Dwight L. Moody (1837–1899), and Billy Sunday (1862–1935).

Critical Thinking: The marketing perspective that drives much of the televangelism industry has its foundations in late 19th- and early 20th-century urban evangelism. At the website for this book (www.sage.com/rsp6e), an essay on "Evangelical Foundations of a Marketing Perspective on Conversion and Recruitment" examines this foundation. This essay may help you address the question of why evangelicals have been more inclined to a marketing perspective and more entrepreneurial as ministers of the Gospel. How does this historical perspective help you understand the contemporary patterns of television broadcasting?

Billy Graham (born in 1918) never established a weekly program, and his televised programming remained in the format of a worship service or a revival. Still, he was the first evangelistic fundamentalist to gain national recognition. Much of his early notoriety was because of an editorial directive from publisher William Randolph Hearst, who sent a simple memo to the editors of his nationwide chain of newspapers: "Puff Graham." Graham made the most of the subsequent publicity and became a role model for younger evangelists. More importantly, his career linked the evangelical tradition to the new media of television and radio. Eventually, he came to be a spiritual adviser to a number of U.S. presidents. Graham was the first evangelical to gain national credibility on television, and he was especially influential in challenging evangelicals to adopt the newest mass media technology to spread the faith.

Unlike Graham, Oral Roberts (1918–2009) was an innovative showman, introducing a variety of formats, using a wide range of entertainment forms, and showing the value of flexibility of material to meet changing markets. Most importantly, however, Roberts discovered that if a televangelist wants to raise money, the key is to build buildings, even if they seem outlandish. He discovered that people will contribute far more money to build a university (Oral Roberts University was founded in 1963) or a hospital (ORU School of Medicine operated from 1981 to 1989) than they will to buy airtime. In the 1980s, Roberts made an infamous plea to the viewers of his television ministry that if he did not raise $8 million by March 31, 1987, to help fund his medical center, God would "call him

home." His followers donated $9.1 million (Ostling 1987). The excess money brought in for building projects could then be used to support other projects such as broadcasting costs. With the oligarchical structure of the organization (with family members serving on the oversight board), Roberts and some other televangelists found they could make such transfers without challenge.

Rex Humbard (1919–2007) was the third of the original televangelists with nationwide programming. Humbard contributed two innovations. First, he created an intensely personal style, using a family format (telling stories to his gathered children and to the audience who became part of his family), sharing personal troubles, and airing feelings publicly. Humbard often cried on television and would bare his soul for his national audience. Whatever else this process did, it was highly profitable as people responded with their hearts to a person they had come to know intimately—more intimately than members of their own congregation. Later on, other televangelists also found that open displays of emotion build intense audience loyalty.

Second, Humbard built a cathedral especially designed and equipped for broadcasting. Graham and Roberts initially simply brought cameras into their existing services. By contrast, Humbard invested in the most sophisticated modern technology; he also established television effects as the highest priority in the architecture and decor of the cathedral.

Other televangelists have developed their own distinctive styles, theological orientations, and formats, yet each has built on these early foundations. Without these foundations, televangelism empires would probably not exist. Further, this legacy has encouraged religious leaders to be entrepreneurs. Interestingly, most of them would find that word—*entrepreneur*—to be a compliment. This is in sharp contrast to many mainline clergy who find this an insulting metaphor for the caregiving of clergy.

Critical Thinking: Has televangelism been an asset to the promotion of traditional orthodox Christianity, or does it threaten to undermine the faith through introduction of other motives and the aspirations of "entrepreneurs"?

The Televangelism Audience

The importance of televangelism as a resource to shape the larger culture depends in part on the nature of the audience: How large is the audience, and who is watching? Clearly, televangelists have the potential for an extensive audience, with some programs translated into other languages and broadcast into a dozen or more countries. Exact numbers on the size of the television church are, however, hard to come by. During the heyday of televangelism in the 1970s and early 1980s, televangelists tended to exaggerate the size of their audiences, as when Jerry Falwell claimed as many as 50 million viewers for his *Old-Time Gospel Hour.* Ratings company A. C. Nielsen recorded fewer than 2 million viewers for that program (Hadden 1987). At the same time, detractors tended to underestimate these audiences. For example, many were surprised when Nielsen reported in 1983 that 8 million cable subscribers watched Pat Robertson's *700 Club* (United Press International 1983).

More recently, the Pew Research Center asked a representative sample of U.S. adults if they had watched religious television in the previous week. Although affirmative responses to this question are not equivalent to being part of the televangelism audience, it is interesting to note that nearly one quarter (23%) said they had watched religious television in the previous week (Pew Research Center 2014b). Thus, despite the fact that obtaining complete figures is difficult, at best, viewership appears to be considerably higher and religious broadcasting more warmly accepted in the United States than elsewhere in the Global North, though growth is apparent in the Global South.

Among the controversial aspects of televangelism is the frequent requests made during broadcasts for viewers to send money. Oral Roberts's pleading for donations to save his life (noted above and in Chapter 9) is just the most infamous example of a common practice. Those viewers who send money to support the programming tend to increase their levels of commitment. By making an investment, they develop a sense of loyalty to the organization. The top televangelists of the 1970s and '80s brought in tens or even hundreds of millions of dollars each year to finance their programs and their projects (medical centers, universities, etc.). The television church had a committed core who provided a base of support for some truly enormous empires (Hadden and Shupe 1988; Peck 1993).

Another issue concerning the televangelism audience has to do with who regularly views and supports the televangelism. Studies of televangelism during its heyday found that viewers tended to already be evangelical in orientation. One rationale often given by televangelists for using television is to fulfill "the great commission" of Christ to spread the gospel. The idea is that television allows preachers to reach people who might otherwise never have heard of Christ. Yet empirical evidence suggested that televangelism has little persuasive impact in terms of converting nonbelievers; most viewers are already sympathetic to the basic philosophy (Gaddy 1984). This is not to say that religious broadcasting is insignificant. It simply highlights how televangelism serves as a reinforcer and a plausibility structure for those already committed.

Does Televangelism Undermine Commitment to Local Congregations?

Over the years, televangelism has come under heavy criticism for several reasons and from a number of quarters. Former evangelist Charles Templeton, who was himself involved in the production of religious television programming, assessed televangelism in this way:

Television Christianity is an undemanding faith; a media apostasy that tells listeners that to become a Christian all they have to do is "believe." . . . The offerings, [extracted] mostly from the poor, the elderly, and lonely women, amount to millions of dollars annually. Few of these dollars are used to give succor to the needy, to put food in empty bellies or to help the helpless and dispossessed. . . . There are, among the host of televangelists, exceptions to those I have described, but . . . on balance I think the contemporary television evangelist is deleterious to society. (cited in Bibby 1987:36)

No less a figure than Billy Graham spoke out against abuses, the most severe of which he believed was the constant harangue for money (Graham 1983). However, the most common complaint of critics has been that televised Christianity erodes support for local churches.

Yet research shows that the gratifications one receives from watching a televised worship service are different from those gained by attending local worship services. Among those who are regular viewers of television, experiencing solemnity and atmosphere, praying to God, experiencing God's presence, feeling forgiven for sins, demonstrating solidarity with Christian values, and getting a sense of distance from the worries of everyday life are all facilitated more by attending services in a local house of worship than by watching religious television (Petterson 1986). Indeed, viewers of religious television attend community worship services more frequently than nonviewers, and only a small proportion report watching services on television rather than supporting the neighborhood congregation. This is as true today as it was in the 1980s (Pew Research Center 2014b; Wuthnow 1987). Bibby found the same pattern in Canada, with religious television serving for most viewers as a supplement to attendance at worship rather than as a substitute (Bibby 1987). Only among the very elderly is religious television a substitute.

The second issue, of course, is whether financial contributions to television evangelists are replacing support to local faith communities. Most of the research indicates that money given to religious television programs is not in lieu of contributions to nearby congregations. They are donations made over and above the local church pledge and do not normally involve a decline in hometown contributions. The only category of viewers who seem to send money to televangelists that would otherwise be given to local churches comprises the very elderly or disabled persons who find it difficult to get out of the house to attend services (Gallup 1987; Petterson 1986).

The heyday of American televangelism was the late 1970s and early 1980s, and thus much of the scholarly research on televangelism is about that period. By the late 1980s, some serious scandals had undermined some of the cultural influence and social import of televangelism. In 1987, Jim Bakker stepped down as head of the PTL Television Network (which grew from his *PTL Club* program with wife Tammy Faye) just prior to news reports of his affair with Jessica Hahn and $279,000 in hush money paid to her. In 1989, Bakker was convicted in a federal court on 24 counts including fraud and conspiracy relating to money he embezzled from supporters. Jimmy Swaggart, whose television ministry was transmitted to thousands of stations every week, admitted in 1988 to transgressions with a prostitute and tearfully apologized on television in his well-known "I Have Sinned" speech (available on YouTube). The 2000s marked the passing of the founding generation of televangelists with the deaths of Rex Humbard and Oral Roberts and the gradual withdrawal from ministry of nonagenarian Billy Graham. Also, the ministry built by the late televangelist Robert Schuller—whose *Hour of Power* was broadcast from the Crystal Cathedral in Garden Grove, California, for three decades—was torn apart by debt and family division as he tried to transition out of the role of head minister.

Photo "CrystalCathedral" is licensed under CC BY-SA 3.0 via Wikimedia Commons

Robert Schuller (1926–2015) began his ministry in Garden Grove, California, in 1955 in space rented from a drive-in theater. He began broadcasting his weekly service as the *Hour of Power* in 1970. As his church grew, he commissioned the prominent architect Philip Johnson to build an enormous glass-walled church. The iconic $18 million Crystal Cathedral was dedicated in 1981. Schuller would continue to hold and broadcast weekly services from the Crystal Cathedral into the 21st century. The sagging economy, declining interest, and family infighting led Crystal Cathedral Ministries to file for bankruptcy in 2010. It subsequently sold the building to the Roman Catholic Church for $50 million in 2013.

Despite this, televangelism lives on, especially in the Global South (Leslie 2003; see also the next "Global Perspectives" feature). It also lives on in the United States, if in an altered form. According to Quentin Schultze, who specializes in the study of Christian media, "I don't see a scenario for maintaining a TV-based megachurch anymore. The days of doing that in the models of Schuller and Jimmy Swaggart and Oral Roberts are over" (Associated Press 2009). The new model of what we might call "mediated evangelism" may be seen in the work of African American ministers like T. D. Jakes and Creflo Dollar (Walton 2009), as well as white pastors like Joel Osteen and Rick Warren. As was noted in Chapter 8, each of these ministers leads one of

America's largest megachurches, and their ministries seem primarily oriented toward their local congregations. Still, they use all varieties of media, new and old (including television), to spread their messages. For example, Osteen's broadcasts from Lakewood Church are viewed by millions on local broadcast stations and cable networks (Discovery Channel, USA, Lifetime, ABC Family, Daystar, and Trinity Broadcasting Network) in the United States, as well as internationally in Australia, Canada, Egypt, India, and New Zealand, and on CNBC Europe. In a modernized version of an earlier technology, "Joel Osteen Radio" was launched in 2014, broadcasting 24/7 on SiriusXM. For his part, Rick Warren has purposely chosen not to broadcast regularly from his Saddleback Church, favoring attendance at live services instead. Nonetheless, he has a robust online presence and has also garnered a wide audience using a very old media technology (the book). In 2013 he also launched a radio program called "Daily Hope."

GLOBAL PERSPECTIVES

Televangelism Beyond the Borders of the United States

The globalization of religious broadcasting was itself a product of a global event: World War II. Broadcast stations and equipment were constructed and distributed around the world to conduct the war. Following the war, many of these stations were abandoned and appropriated by Christians with evangelical intents (Hadden 1990). There are now more than two dozen international radio broadcasting stations with evangelical Christian sponsorship, with the largest three producing 20,000 hours of programming weekly in 25 languages. This makes Christian stations the largest block of international radio broadcasters in the world (Hadden 1990). Televangelist Pat Robertson's Christian Broadcasting Network (CBN) is the largest of these, with offices in Africa, Asia, China, Europe, Indonesia, Latin America, the Middle East, Siam, and Singapore. An international edition of CBN's flagship program, *The 700 Club*, can be seen in more than 180 countries (Leslie 2003).

Support for televangelism is much stronger in the United States than in most other parts of the Global North. In 1958, 1 out of 10 Canadians were regular patrons of religious broadcasts, but within 30 years, the count had dropped to 1 in 25 (Bibby 1987). Even a report in 1998 on The Christian Channel in Canada (now Grace TV) indicated an audience of only 300,000 viewers nationwide (Gross and English 1998). This pattern seems to be consistent with the lack of growth of conservative evangelical Christianity generally in Canada.

Televangelism is also not widespread in Britain or elsewhere in Europe. William Kay noted that the United Kingdom's highly regulated broadcasting industry (dominated by the state-run British Broadcasting Corporation or BBC) severely curbed the rise of televangelism until recent years. While there are religious broadcasting efforts in the Netherlands and Germany, most broadcasting is Sunday morning services of mainline churches (Kay 2009). Viewers are primarily people who already attend church, and those numbers are very small in virtually every country in Europe (Davie 2000).

In Latin America, by contrast, where Pentecostalism is growing rapidly, locally owned and produced religious broadcasting began to take off in the late 1980s. Prior to that, American Pentecostal televangelists like Jimmy Swaggart and Jim Bakker were dominant. Given the comparative economic underdevelopment in much of Latin America, it is radio rather than television that continues to dominate in religious broadcasting, since even the poor can own radios. For example, the Catholic Church operates 181 radio stations in Brazil and 7 in Guatemala, and much of the programming on those stations is produced by those involved in the Catholic Charismatic Renewal—basically Catholic Pentecostalism (Chesnut 2010).

The Indian government's openness to satellite television makes it a fertile ground for televangelism. Looking just at networks that broadcast 24 hours a day, there are four Christian,

(Continued)

(Continued)

one Islamic, and one Hindu. A recent study of Christian Broadcasting Network India's programming finds a blending of American and Indian influences. The author cleverly calls this "masala McGospel" (James 2010). (In Chapter 15, we will examine the concept of "glocalization" to describe the blending of the global and local in the process of globalization.) If masala here represents the Indian culture and McGospel the homogenized, globalized ("McDonaldized") version of Christianity exported from the United States to India, the McGospel is trumping the masala.

Christian televangelism in some Islamic countries is highly controversial and perhaps even dangerous for the sponsors. Muslims want the Christian televangelism to end, viewing it as a foreign intrusion into their cultures. In Nigeria, there have been concerted efforts to stop these broadcasts ("Muslims Aim to End Televangelism" 1998). Some converts to Christianity have received death threats, and Christians at Nigerian television stations have been threatened, with assertions that they are fomenting religious crises in families and in the society at large. The hard sell evangelical approach has come to be viewed as a kind of religious colonialism (Hadden 1990).

Considering that over a third of evangelical Protestants (compared to just 10% of mainline Protestants) reported listening to religious talk radio in 2014, this embrace of an old media technology is a good way for Osteen and Warren to go back to the future (Pew Research Center 2014b).

RELIGION AND THE "NEW MEDIA"

If you are reading this textbook, chances are that you were "born digital"—that is, you are part of the first generation in human history to have been born into and come of age in a post–digital revolution social environment. Some have suggested that this will create a generation gap like never seen before between "digital natives" and their older kin (Palfrey and Gasser 2008). This raises the possibility of a religious gap based on orientation to "new media."

What exactly are "new media"? According to Bailey Socha and Barbara Eber-Schmid of the New Media Institute, "the definition of new media changes daily, and will continue to do so.

New media evolves and morphs continuously" (Socha and Eber-Schmid 2015). As a starting point, consider Wikipedia's definition:

New media refers to on-demand access to content anytime, anywhere, on any digital device, as well as interactive user feedback, and creative participation. Another aspect of new media is the real-time generation of new and unregulated content. Most technologies described as "new media" are digital, often having characteristics of being manipulated, networkable, dense, compressible, and interactive. Some examples may be the Internet, websites, computer multimedia, video games, augmented reality, CD-ROMS, and DVDs. New media does not include television programs (only analog broadcast), feature films, magazines, books, or paper-based publications—unless they contain technologies that enable digital interactivity. (Wikipedia 2015)

Although many faculty will warn their students of the dangers of using Wikipedia as an authoritative source in research, we use Wikipedia here because it is, in fact, an example of "new media" itself.

As the Wikipedia definition makes clear, new media are not reducible to information carried over the Internet, but the Internet is the most important aspect of new media. Internet usage has been skyrocketing. According to the Pew Research Center Internet and American Life Project (pewinternet.org), in 1995, 14% of U.S. adults used the Internet. That had grown by 2005 to 68% and by 2014 to 87%. Internet use by young adults is even higher, with 97% of 18- to 29-year-olds accessing the Internet. Among teens aged 12 to 17, Internet use surpassed 90% in 2005.

Expanding means of accessing the Internet have facilitated this widespread use and changed the nature of people's behavior online. High-speed (broadband, as opposed to dial-up) connections to the Internet allow people to spend more time and do more things online. This includes use of interactive applications on the web that have led some to speak of the second generation of the World Wide Web (WWW), or "Web 2.0." Unlike the first generation of the WWW, in which most users simply accessed (consumed) content created by others, Web 2.0 allows users to create content themselves, often in collaboration with others. Well-known examples are social networking sites (Facebook, Twitter, Instagram), blogs, wikis, and video-sharing sites like YouTube. Of adults on the Internet, 74% used social media in 2014. The situation is rendered still more dynamic by the fact that people access the Internet not only through computers but increasingly through personal digital media devices (58% by smartphones, 42% by tablet computers in 2014) (Pew Research Center Internet and American Life Project 2015).

Of course, our interest here is in how the technological changes represented by the new media affect the mass mediation of religion and in particular the new opportunities these media create for the practice of religion. As was the case with radio broadcasting, people have been using the Internet, and especially the WWW, for religious purposes from the beginning. Just 6 years after

Tim Berners-Lee *proposed the idea* of the web, *Time* magazine ran a story titled "Finding God on the Web." The story reported the following:

> Like schools, like businesses, like governments, like nearly everyone, it seems, religious groups are rushing online, setting up church home pages, broadcasting dogma and establishing theological newsgroups, bulletin boards and chat rooms. Almost overnight, the electronic community of the Internet has come to resemble a high-speed spiritual bazaar, where thousands of the faithful—and equal numbers of the faithless—meet and debate and swap ideas about things many of us had long since stopped discussing in public, like our faith and religious beliefs. (Ramo 1996)

Books titled *The Soul in Cyber-Space* (Groothius 1997) and *Cybergrace: The Search for God in the Digital World* (Cobb 1998) soon followed. If today's traditionally aged college students are "digital natives," a significant part of their native culture is religious. Gary Bunt, a sociologist who specializes in the study of religion on the Internet, recognizes that the Internet "holds transformative potential for religions," but he also cautioned that "there are dangers in over-emphasizing the transformative powers of the Internet in the area of religion" (Bunt 2009:705). In examining religion and the Internet from the perspective of both producers and consumers of content, we find that (so far, at least) much religion online is a natural extension of past media practices using new media technologies.

Religion Online: Producing and Accessing Information

Much of the total online activity around religion is what scholars call "religion online." Religion online is "information about religion that is accessed via computer-mediated networks" (Cowan 2007, following Helland 2000). From both the supply and demand sides, this is the bulk of the religious/spiritual activity that takes place online. Religious organizations put information online, and Internet users seek out that information. In this sense, the Internet stands in a continuous relationship with other media that came before it—a medium for the transmission of information to consumers.

Like all major organizations today, every major religious denomination has a web presence. Some, like the Church of Jesus Christ of Latter-day Saints, maintain multiple websites: lds.org, mormon.org, familysearch.org, mormonchannel.org, mormonnewsroom.org. This is not news. What is more noteworthy is the growth in new media use by congregations. Both the National Congregations Study (NCS; discussed in Chapter 8) and Faith Communities Today (FACT) provide solid data on this ongoing development. According to the NCS, from 1998 to 2006–2007 to 2012, the proportion of congregations with a website grew from 17% to 44% to 56%. As Mark Chaves and Shawna Anderson emphasized, this large change suggests that some 10,000 congregations per year are adding websites (Chaves and Anderson 2008). Because larger congregations are more likely to have websites, 83% of regular participants are in congregations with a web presence, up from 29% in 1998.

Even greater growth was found in the use of electronic mail to communicate with members. In 1998, 21% of congregations in the NCS used e-mail in this way, and by 2006–2007, the percentage had grown to 59%. Looked at from the individual perspective, the growth is even more dramatic: from 31% of attenders in congregations using e-mail in 1998 to 79% in 2006–2007. E-mail use was seen to be so universal in 2012 that the NCS dropped this question. FACT, a national study of thousands of U.S. congregations that has been conducted in 2000, 2005, 2008, and 2010, asked about e-mail use in 2010 and found that 90% of congregations reported using e-mail, up from 35% in 2000 (faithcommunitiestoday.org; Thumma 2012).

Instead of asking about e-mail use in 2012, the NCS added a question about whether the congregation has a Facebook page. Forty percent of congregations, involving 56% of all attendees, reported they did. FACT found a similar rate in 2010, which, as Scott Thumma notes, is quite remarkable since Facebook did not exist outside of .edu e-mail addresses until 2006 (Thumma 2012).

Because of their greater resources, their evangelistic orientations, and their embrace of what is current in the culture for marketing purposes, we would expect megachurches to be even more connected to the Internet than other congregations. This was true even in early 2000 when Thumma found that nearly every megachurch surveyed had an e-mail address, and 99% had a website (Thumma 2001). A 10-year follow up study in 2011 found that 88% of megachurch leaders use Facebook on a regular basis. It also found that "nearly three-fourths do podcasts, 56% blog and over a third use other Internet technologies such as streaming, Twitter, texting and online church services" (Bird and Thumma 2011:10). Unfortunately, we do not have such detailed data on these more interactive uses of the web by other congregations (but see Larsen 2000 for an early study).

As usual, leading the social media pack are megachurch superstar pastors like Rick Warren, Joel Osteen, and Andy Stanley of North Point Community Church in Georgia (the second largest U.S. megachurch) (Codone 2014). Looking at Twitter presence, for example, at the start of 2015, @AndyStanley had 434,000 followers, @RickWarren had 1.54 million followers, and @JoelOsteen topped them both with 3.12 million followers. It is worth noting that, at the same time, Islamic theologian @MohamadAlarefe had 10.6 million followers and His Holiness the 14th @DalaiLama had 10.1 million followers, placing them among the 100 most followed individuals and organizations on Twitter, according to twitaholic.com. Of course, another reality is that all of these religious figures combined cannot compare to @KatyPerry who had over 62 million followers at the same time.

Even while we marvel at the expansion of religion on the Internet, it is important to bear in mind what is called the "digital divide." This refers to the reality that many people are not able to fully participate in the digital revolution for economic or other social reasons. The divide can exist between different groups within a country. In the United States, there are digital divides by income, education, generation, race, and geographic region (see Pew Internet's "digital divide" page at www.pewinternet.org/topics/Digital-Divide.aspx). There is also a "global digital divide"—differences between entire countries and regions in access to digital communication technologies. For example, 78% of European households have Internet access, compared to just 11% of households in Africa and 36% in the Asia-Pacific region (International Telecommunications Union 2014).

In any case, official denominational and congregational websites, e-mail, and Facebook are just one way that religion goes online—and maybe not the most important. Stewart Hoover wrote of the media generally, "The social and institutional autonomy of the media sphere can thus be said to constitute a location for the making of religion that is in many ways independent from the religious doctrine, institution, and history" (Hoover 2009:694). Just as the advent of satellite broadcasting and cable democratized television, so too does computer technology and the Internet democratize the ability to produce and consume information. Even recognizing that a digital divide exists, the new media can lower barriers to entry for some groups—including religious ones—to have a public media presence. In this view, the WWW is the ultimate "spiritual marketplace." Over a decade ago, Brenda Brasher reported that there were more than a million religion websites, and they covered an extraordinarily wide range of religious beliefs and practices (Brasher 2004). The democratizing potential of the web may be seen most clearly in the robust web presence of new religious movements (NRMs) and nonmajority religions (Dawson and Cowan 2004).

Religion online is a mode of information dissemination called "one-to-many." There is one source and many recipients. The other side of the religion online equation, therefore, is how people access the information that is provided. One way to approach this issue is to look at how people use search engines to access religious information on the web. Using very new information science methods to examine over 5 million web searches from three search engines, Bernard Jansen and his colleagues found that most search terms employed in religious searches are associated with established, mainstream religions (Jansen, Tapia, and Spink 2010). Web search data do not support the idea of significant religious "seeking" online.

If not seeking, then there is nonetheless a great deal of religious sharing on the Internet. Nearly half (46%) of U.S. adults saw someone else share something about his or her religious faith on social networking sites or apps in 2014, and 20% of them had shared something about their own religious faith that way (Pew Research Center 2014b). In the end, the researchers conclude that most of the individuals are using the Internet to develop and express their personal religious and/or spiritual beliefs, but they are not true religious seekers. Instead, the cultivation of their personal faith online helps cement their preexisting beliefs and institutional attachments. The authors find this "interesting because many analysts have assumed that the Internet would make it more likely for people to leave churches in favor of more flexible online options for religious or spiritual activity. Faith-related activity online is a *supplement* to, rather than a *substitute* for offline religious life" (Hoover, Clark, and Rainie 2004:ii). It seems to function much the same way televangelism does. Those who attend religious services more often are more likely to share their religious faith online than infrequent attenders (Pew Research Center 2014b).

This is perfectly in sync with the way most religious groups are currently using the web: as online supplements to their "brick-and-mortar" operations. Although Gary Bunt noted that the "spiritual supermarket now has an online checkout" (Bunt

2009:706), most religious groups are not yet ready to give up the shop and move their entire operations online, nor must they do so in order to meet the market demands.

Critical Thinking: How often do you or people you know engage in faith-related online activity? In your experience, does it act as more of a *supplement* to or a *substitute* for offline religious life? How might religion online affect religious communities that exist in your own community?

Online Religion: Practicing Faith on the Web

In contrast to "religion online" is what scholars call "online religion." Douglas Cowan defined this as "the various ways in which religious faith is practiced over [computer-mediated] networks" (Cowan 2007:361). Early studies of religion on the Internet suggest some of the ways in which individuals engage more interactively while online. For example, Stewart Hoover and colleagues found some people send greeting cards related to religious holidays (35%) or make or respond to prayer requests (7%) (Hoover et al. 2004). Although these more interactive modes of online religion are not as common as the informational mode of religion online, they are interesting and suggestive of a possible future as the younger "digital generation" comes of age.

One of the most common forms of online religion is prayer sites. Many of these simply allow people to submit prayer requests, but one prayer site that has a strong interactive element is "Light a Candle." Entering this site (www.gratefulness.org/candles/enter.cfm?l=ENG), the visitor is told, "In many different traditions lighting candles is a sacred action. It expresses more than words can express. It has to do with gratefulness. From time immemorial, people have lit candles in sacred places. Why should cyberspace not be sacred?" Clicking Begin, the visitor is asked to

"take a deep breath and quiet your thoughts" and then continue on. The visitor is then taken to a page with 30 candles on it, some lit, others not. The virtual flames on the candle flicker slightly and the lit candles actually get smaller over time as they "burn." The visitor is able to light any additional candles by hovering the cursor over the wick and clicking on it. Before the candle is actually lit, however, the visitor is told on an intermediary screen, "Before continuing, reflect for a moment on your reason for lighting a candle."

On the subsequent screens, the visitor has the opportunity to add a dedication for the candle, enter initials to be able to find the candle again later, give a country of origin and state (for United States), and enter a name. On the final page, the unlit candle shows alongside the dedication. Clicking on the wick "lights" the candle. The visitor is then encouraged to "Stay here quietly, as long as you wish, before continuing." In addition to lighting his or her own candle, the visitor can also click on any of the "burning" candles to see the source and dedication. The day we visited in January 2015, 10,643 candles from 107 countries were lit, and it was possible to scroll through all 355 pages to look at them. Not all of the candles had a written dedication, but many did, including the following:

> *"Thinking of you and praying that you can find peace during this horrible time. My heart aches for you."—Anna from IL, United States*

> *"I pray that I can be a good father and that my divorce will not harm my children or my ex-wife."—BT from CA, United States*

> *"Ancient Gods and Goddesses, I invoke thee. Waters from the sky, Let it be." "I command thee now, to thee all. Listen to my desire, Rain fall!"— Mother Nature from Jeffersonville, IN, United States*

Although the candles on this site exist only virtually, the sentiments expressed in all of the candles we examined seem very real, and the process by which one proceeded to light the candle was thoughtful and deliberate—if the user brought that spirit with him or her to the action.

Another example of a website for prayer actually has a real-world dimension to it. The site virtualjerusalem.com has a 24-hour live "Kotel Cam," a streaming video webcam fixed on the Western Wall (Kotel) in the Old City of Jerusalem. The Kotel is the last remnant of the Second Temple and therefore seen by many as the most important site in the world for Jews. Millions visit the Kotel every year, but those who cannot visit can still partake of the tradition of writing prayers to be placed inside the cracks of the walls by filling in a "Send a Prayer" form online. As the site explains, the prayer "will be printed out in the Old City of Jerusalem where it will be placed in the Wall by a student of Aish HaTorah" (www.aish.com/w/note). According to Christopher Helland, the virtual world known as Second Life (secondlife.com) has an increasing religious presence within it. Virtual worlds are three-dimensional online spaces that people access in real time. In the case of Second Life, people create "avatars" (three-dimensional characters that represent themselves) who live "second" lives inside the virtual world (Helland 2007). They have houses and jobs, they shop and party, they have relationships, and sometimes they attend religious services. Because the content of Second Life is user-generated, these services take place in meeting places designed by other users who can purchase and build on land within the virtual world. Religious groups from all traditions have begun to explore the possibilities of having a presence in virtual reality. There are Buddhist and Hindu temples, LGBTQ (lesbian, gay, bisexual, transgender, and queer or questioning) friendly churches, Unitarian Universalist services, Wiccan covens, mosques, and synagogues (see Cohen 2012; Derrickson 2008; Grieve 2010; Radde-Antweiler 2008).

In its earliest days, the Internet was seen as a potentially "disruptive technology" because of its ability to allow users to be both creators and consumers (Oram 2001). It could allow people to circumvent established authorities—whether governments, corporations, or established religions—to collaborate with one another ("many-to-many" instead of "one-to-many") in the creation of innovative ideas and practices (Castells 2003). Second Life certainly holds out that possibility for people who want to express their religious creativity, to transform and adapt religious traditions, but just how revolutionary is religion in that virtual world? In 2011, Swedish sociologist of religion Stefan Gelfgren identified 114 Christian places in Second Life. He found that 7 in 10 places had a church with traditional architecture designed to be familiar to visitors, from which he concluded that "the degree of innovation and 'rule bending' are rather low" (Gelfgren 2014:52). Religion in Second Life, like other incarnations of digital religion, is an extension of, not a radical break from, religion in "first life" (Hutchings 2011). Of course, some Second Life religions are bigger than others. With an average attendance of 30,000 a week, LifeChurch.tv of Edmond, Oklahoma, was the third largest megachurch in the United States to start in 2015, according to the Hartford Institute for Religion Research's continually updated database (hirr.hartsem.edu/megachurch/database .html). LifeChurch.tv describes itself as a "multi-site" church with campuses in six states and one that meets exclusively via the Internet (called "Church Online" at live.lifechurch.tv). In addition, in the mid-2000s, LifeChurch.tv spent thousands of dollars developing a presence in Second Life. The same simulcast video that unites the church's physical campuses was streamed into the Second Life sanctuary on Experience Island and projected onto large screens at the front of the auditorium so that those in the virtual world could worship in sync with those in the real world. One story on this development reported 3,912 Second Life avatars visited the church in a single day (Simon 2007).

Not long after LifeChurch.tv was established, the Anglican Cathedral of Second Life opened it virtual doors. It offers seven services a week, including a Sunday Bible study, which people from 20 nations attend. In addition to its main cathedral, it also has a community center, peace garden, and labyrinth (Hutchings 2011). Those not involved in Second Life can take a video tour of Epiphany Island on the Anglican Church of Second Life's website (slangcath.wordpress.com). The website IslamOnline created a replica of the holy site of Mecca (Saudi Arabia) in Second Life so that individuals could learn about (and perhaps even perform) the Hajj, a pilgrimage that a Muslim is expected to undertake, according to the Five Pillars (duties) of Islam, at least once in a lifetime.

Online Resources: Not surprisingly, those interested in studying digital religion provide unique online resources to readers. The two primary scholarly journals in this area are *Online: The Heidelberg Journal of Religions on the Internet* (journals.ub.uni-heidelberg.de/index.php/religions/index) and the *Journal of Religion, Media, and Digital Culture* (jrmdc.com). Both adhere to "open access" policies—meaning their content is freely and immediately available to the public. All you need to do to read, download, copy, or print articles from these journals is to visit their websites.

These online religion developments are still relatively new, so not much research has been published examining how people experience this form of virtual faith and practice. Some questions do necessarily arise, though. First, are these practices likely to generate authentic religious experiences? Is there something about the incorporation of the whole body and all its senses in lighting a candle, for example, that makes deep experiences more likely? Second, are these religious practices and communities sustainable over time in the absence of face-to-face interactions? Can online religion exist separate from brick-and-mortar religion or only as an extension of it? Third, how will the economic costs and technological limits of the Internet affect the durability of these sorts of interactive websites? For example, in his scholarly analysis of virtual pilgrimages on the Internet, Mark MacWilliams discussed an Irish Holy Mountain virtual pilgrimage (the website no longer exists) (MacWilliams 2002). Also, it appears that LifeChurch.tv no longer has a formal presence in Second Life. These are among the most important questions about online religion that sociologists will be attempting to answer in the future.

Although this discussion has treated religion online and online religion as mutually exclusive categories, Douglas Cowan has argued that they are actually ends on a continuum (see Figure 14.1; Cowan 2007). Most religion on the Internet falls somewhere in the middle, providing some information and allowing for some interactivity. This is especially true as more and more religious groups use Web 2.0 social media like Facebook and Twitter to connect with the people, not to mention the emerging arena of mobile applications ("apps"). In 2009, a commercial for Apple's iPhone coined the (trademarked) phrase, "There's an app for that," referring to the handy software applications that were specifically designed to run on the company's smartphones. By 2010, the American Dialect Society had named *app* its word of the year. Today, there are untold thousands of religion apps available in Apple's App Store, Google's Play Store, and Amazon's Appstore for Android devices. Probably the most popular is the Bible app by YouVersion.com, which has been downloaded over 160 million times in hundreds of languages (Kuruvilla 2014). A more niche app is the "FlyRights" app developed by the Sikh Coalition to allow people to quickly and easily inform the Transportation Security Administration (TSA) and their government representatives of instances

Figure 14.1 Continuum of Types of Internet Religion

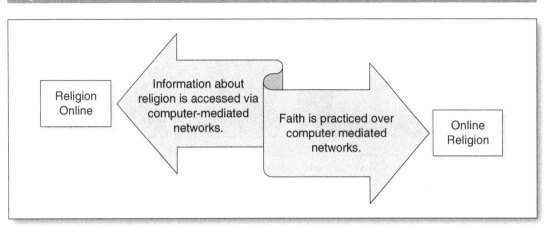

SOURCE: Cowan, Douglas. 2007. "Religion on the Internet." In *The Sage Handbook of the Sociology of Religion*. Edited by J. Beckford and N. J. Demerath III. Thousand Oaks, CA: Sage.

of unfair profiling by TSA representatives (as Sikhs are often confused with Muslims and discriminated against because of that) (Jansen 2013). There is no question that apps are not just the wave of the future, but are firmly entrenched in the *present* reality of digital religion.

Critical Thinking: "Apps" are technologies we take for granted today, but like all technologies, apps are developed to help people solve problems or address needs. Identify a religious problem or need that individuals today face. What app would you create to address that problem or need?

This blurring of the lines between "religion online" and "online religion" suggests we are entering a new phase in the understanding of digital religion, one that stresses how "the digital world has become woven into the fabric of our everyday lives and how the digital and physical are merging into a single, but mixed, hybrid state or a third space" (Gelfgren 2014:4). This third space does not exist wholly inside or wholly outside the historic God boxes.

RELIGION AND SPORT

Another "outside the box" arena of social life in which religion figures prominently is sport (Yamane, Mellies, and Blake 2010). Any casual observer surveying the world of sport cannot help but notice scenes like these: With a gold cross dangling from his ear, Barry Bonds hits another home run; when he touches home plate, he points to the sky. U.S. soccer star Landon Donovan makes the sign of the cross prior to taking penalty kicks, as do countless baseball players before stepping into the batter's box, U.S. football kickers prior to attempting field goals, and basketball players before shooting free throws. After leading the St. Louis Rams to a Super Bowl victory, quarterback Kurt Warner was asked by an interviewer on national television, "Kurt, first things first. Tell me about the final touchdown pass." Warner responded, "Well, first things first, I've got to thank my Lord and Savior up above. Thank you, Jesus!" After getting injured in the first game of the season, Wake Forest University quarterback Riley Skinner thanked God for the opportunity to play college football.

Photos by Sandra Stroud Yamane

Mobile computing technologies like tablets and smartphones create opportunities for those who can afford these technologies to access digital religion at any time and in (almost) any place. In the photo on the left the "Online Church" of LifeChurch.tv streams on an iPad. Viewers can click on the screen to indicate they are raising their hand to surrender their lives to Jesus. On the right of the screen, a live chat about the service takes place. In the photo on the right the free YouVersion Bible App is about to be downloaded from the Google Play Store. The app includes over 1,000 versions of the Christian Bible in nearly 800 languages (42 versions in English), along with dozens of reading plans tailored to different types of users.

Sociologists, however, are not casual observers of the social world. The vast amount of religious activity we see in and around sport today can obscure from view the long-term trend toward the secularization of sport. A comment by sports commentator Frank Deford made the point well: "Sport owns Sunday now, and religion is content to lease a few minutes before the big games" (Price 2005:198). In fact, secularism is a key characteristic that distinguishes modern sport from ancient athletics (Guttmann 1978). Secularism is particularly evident in the changing purpose of modern sport. From the beginning of human history, people aimed to please the gods through ceremonies, dance, and athletic activity. Originally, athletic competitions were fundamentally religious enterprises, meant to show special talents to the gods, express thanks to them, or implore them to take certain beneficent actions such as ensuring the earth's fertility (Guttmann 1978).

Examples abound. The Mayans and Aztecs erected stone ball courts next to their places of worship and often used stories of athletic competition to explain nature, believing, for example, that the sun and moon resulted from a game between the gods and a set of twin brothers. As a result of losing, the twin brothers lost their heads as a sacrifice. This tradition continued, with one player from every game being sacrificed. The secular Olympic Games we know today were created as an exercise of devotion to the Greek god Zeus. Athletes had to swear on the highest deity that they had been training for at least 10 months and would abide by the rules of competition. Violations of this oath led to fines that were used to construct statues of Zeus. The original Olympics lasted 5 days, of which only half of the time was used for competition; the entire first day was devoted to religious ceremonies. Native American tribes used sport to explain nature and to please the gods. Southwest Apaches used unwed males in relay races in honor of the masculine sun and the feminine moon (Baker 2007).

In the Western world, athletics began to be approached more secularly by the Romans, and their principal purpose became not religious expression but entertainment. Roman athletes focused on fighting, as in gladiator contests, and Roman sport often pitted the members of the lower classes against each other as entertainment for the elites. Victory usually allowed the competitor to survive, so winning was pretty important (Guttmann 1978)! Modern sports, though less extreme, have adopted this Roman value as part of their secularization. According to Lonnie Kliever, the secularization of sport parallels the general pattern of societal-level secularization (discussed in Chapter 13)—religion "has lost effective control over vast areas of cultural life that were once conducted under its watchful eye" (Kliever 2001:43). As with other institutional spheres—science and the arts, politics and economics, health care and social welfare—sport "operates under its own rules and pursues its own ends" (Kliever 2001:43).

This societal-level secularization changes the overall relationship between sport and religion as social institutions; it diminishes the religious significance of sport. At the same time, the institutional differentiation of religion from other social institutions facilitates the development of a free market for religion. This free market is a fertile soil in which organizations can freely compete for attention and adherents. Evangelical Christians in the United States in particular have been very adept at using sports organizations to advance religious ends—from the YMCA of yesterday to the sports ministries of today.

Muscular Christianity and the YMCA

The idea of "Muscular Christianity," a Christian commitment to health and "manliness," can be found in sections of the New Testament, but the term was not coined until the mid-1800s. Indeed, many Puritans were suspicious of sport for moral reasons. Like dancing, playing games was considered sinful—as an idle waste of time that could be better spent working or worshipping. Eventually, even these Protestant sects came to embrace sport, in part through the ideology of Muscular Christianity. Religious leaders who supported connecting religion and sport promoted the idea of the body as a temple.

This notion provided a framework in which both a sound mind and a sound body became essential in worship. The term *Muscular Christianity* was coined by the press to describe the work of authors Charles Kingsley and Thomas Hughes. Their "adventure novels replete with high principles and manly Christian heroes" sparked an interest in the social benefits of athleticism (Putney 2001:12–13). Muscular Christianity's main focus was to address the concerns of boys directly, not abstractly, so that they could apply religion to their lives. The idea did not catch on quickly in the United States, but over time it has become one of the most notable tools employed in Evangelical Protestant outreach ministries.

The Young Men's Christian Association (YMCA) was started in England with strict religious ideals. Appalled at city lifestyles, George Williams created the YMCA as a place where men could enjoy health fellowship with others. The YMCA's initial activities in England were Bible studies, Christian readings, and prayer; all amusements were prohibited. The YMCA was designed to educate and promote Christian responsibilities in a world of temptation and self-indulgence (Baker 2007). Card playing, billiards, secular reading, and physical activity were forbidden by early English leaders, only to become a vital part of the American YMCAs.

In 1851, under the leadership of Captain Thomas Sullivan and the Reverend Lyman Beecher, Boston became the first city in the United States to open a YMCA. The Boston association modeled its facilities after those of its English counterparts and emphasized the library and reading rooms where Bible classes could be held (Putney 2001). By 1856, there were over 50 YMCAs in the United States, from Georgia to California (Baker 2007). In time, American YMCAs began recruiting young men from all walks of life and employing a more secular approach than that of their English counterparts. Cards, secular novels, and athletic competition began to bring young men into the building, where leaders could preach the Word. Whereas English YMCAs acted as safe havens for Christian young men, American YMCAs used popular activities to recruit and convert non-Christians. In 1860, the annual convention of the American YMCA decided that gymnasiums should be built at all YMCA locations, and by 1890 more than half of the 400 YMCAs in the United States had on-site gyms, which were soon followed by bowling alleys, boxing rings, and swimming pools (Baker 2007). Through use of these facilities, as well as camping trips and baseball leagues, the YMCA used sport and teamwork to expose young men to Muscular Christianity and "lead men to Christ."

It is difficult to underestimate the contribution to modern sport made by individuals associated with the YMCA. The term *bodybuilding* was first used in 1881 by Robert Roberts, a devout Baptist and gymnasium superintendent at the Boston YMCA, and William Morgan invented volleyball while serving as an instructor at the Holyoke, Massachusetts, YMCA in 1895 ("The YMCA in the United States" 2010). However, the YMCA's greatest contribution to sport came from James Naismith, a Presbyterian seminary graduate who was in residence at the YMCA Training School in Springfield, Massachusetts, when he developed the modern game of basketball in 1891 (Baker 2007). The sport's popularity grew exponentially over the years, and it has become the most popular organized YMCA sport. It has also become one of the leading evangelical tools for other Christian organizations such as Athletes in Action (AIA).

Sport remains integral to YMCA programming today. The "Y" sponsors leagues for baseball, soccer, tennis, football, basketball, volleyball, and gymnastics. The prevalence of these secular activities marks a dramatic change in the means employed by YMCAs today as compared with those at the time of their founding, but what of the ends? Although the mission of the YMCA remains "to put

Christian principles into practice through programs that build healthy spirit, mind, and body for all," there is little organized effort at the Y to proselytize today. According to William Baker, "in 1888, most YMCA men agreed with Luther Gulick, who reminded them that the gymnasium should always be a means to the end 'of leading men to Christ'" (Baker 2007:55). More than 100 years later, that end has long been lost at the YMCA as the organization has internally secularized.

Evangelical Protestant Sports Ministries

As the YMCA decreased its emphasis on sport as a method of increasing the religious sensibilities of young men, other organizations arose to fill the void. Professional athletes began openly sharing their testimonies, a practice that opened the door for many prominent religious leaders to use famous athletes in their efforts to attract young people to meetings. Billy Sunday, the famous evangelist, had begun his career in professional sports in the early 20th century. The first of several evangelical sports organizations, Sports Ambassadors (SA), was established in 1952. SA accelerated the use of athletes as spokespersons for Christ by organizing exhibition games in order to draw large crowds; during halftime, players would share their personal testimonies (Ladd and Mathisen 1999).

As the popularity of sports grew on college campuses, so did the opportunity for ministry. The Fellowship of Christian Athletes (FCA) was created in 1954 as a student–athlete Christian ministry and grew into an organization of summer camps and retreats designed to promote Christian ideals among high school and collegiate athletes (Ladd and Mathisen 1999). Campus Crusade founder Bill Bright envisioned a more evangelical Christian ministry that he hoped would travel the world and preach the Gospel through sport. This approach became the focal point of its offshoot, AIA,

Although many players today do not know it, basketball was founded as a YMCA sport—part of an attempt to link Christian faith with sport through an idea of Muscular Christianity. Interestingly, this game is being played a few hundred yards from the first YMCA building ever built on a college campus in North America in 1883. The wood frame building is on the campus of Hanover College in Indiana, but it is now an Environmental Science Education Center—having become secularized like the YMCA itself. The sport spawned by the "Y" is alive and well on campus.

founded in 1966 and intentionally positioned to the theological "right" of FCA. Today, AIA has a presence on nearly 100 U.S. college campuses and 35 professional sports teams. It fields summer teams in baseball, basketball, soccer, tennis, volleyball, wrestling, track and field, power lifting, and sports medicine to promote the Christian message and personal testimonies of Christian athletes.

As Mathisen observed, the founding of SA meant that "an entirely new genre of religious organizational forms was created, with sport occupying an essential presence" (Mathisen 2006:299). SA, FCA, and AIA are the "Big 3"

Protestant sports ministries. Unlike in the formative years of the YMCA, which used religion to legitimize sport, the roles are now reversed: These organizations use sport to legitimize religion, which suggests the increasing social significance of sport and the relatively decreasing social significance of religion.

Religion and Spirituality at the Individual Level

In a secularized society, people can choose *whether* to be committed to a faith tradition and, if so, *how* they express that. They can choose to make religion part of their identity as an athlete or to make athletics part of their religious identity—or not. As the examples provided earlier suggest, many individuals do visibly choose to connect religion and sport. Still, for every Bob Cousy, who made the sign of the cross before shooting free throws, how many Catholic professional basketball players do not? Moreover, of all individuals who shoot free throws, how many make a religious sign prior to shooting? Unfortunately, efforts to measure this sport/faith relationship scientifically have lagged behind its media visibility.

Some smaller-scale studies suggest a link. For example, Eric A. Storch and his colleagues compared 57 intercollegiate athletes and 169 nonathlete undergraduates at the University of Florida and found that athletes had higher levels of conventional religious faith (Storch et al. 2004). There are good reasons to expect this finding. Sport shares many of the same values as certain religions, particularly evangelical Christianity (Mathisen 2006). Steven J. Overman highlighted the connection between sport and the Protestant ethic of success, self-discipline, and hard work (Overman 1997). The Protestant ethic—with its emphasis on delayed gratification—is especially conducive to participation in organized sporting competition rather than in free and expressive play (Coakley 2007).

How generalizable are the findings of Storch and his colleagues? That is a question taken up by David Yamane and Teresa Blake using representative data on college students collected by the Higher Education Research Institute at the University of California, Los Angeles (UCLA). Using multiple regression models that control for several other variables, Yamane and Blake found that college athletes are *less* religious than college students in general. It is possible that there is a value conflict between sport and religion (competitive aggression versus cooperation and compassion) that could lead to lower levels of religious commitment, but the authors believe that sport is better understood as a *secular competitor* to religion. Religion and sport, in this view, are part of a zero-sum game (only one can win), since both require investments of time and energy (Yamane and Blake 2008). Indeed, the most visible manifestations of religion in sport—wearing religious symbols or making religious gestures—require no real religious commitment by the individuals in question (think Barry Bonds). Generally, when push comes to shove for college athletes, sport wins out over religion.

Of course, in the contemporary United States, it is important to distinguish between religion and spirituality. Whereas religion is sometimes associated with inherited tradition and dogmatic beliefs, spirituality is seen as a quality of an individual, particularly as relates to his or her personal experience. Spirituality is sometimes seen as a more primary and pure relationship to the divine than is "religion." This distinction raises the possibility that college athletes are perhaps spiritual but not religious. If so, this might be accounted for in two ways. First, one can more easily be spiritual on one's own terms, making it easier for athletes to accommodate spirituality in their busy lives. Second, for some, athletics itself can be a form of spiritual practice, and their peak or flow experiences during performance may sensitize them to a spiritual dimension of life in general (Hoffman 1992; Jackson and Csikszentmihalyi 1999).

Yamane and Blake find no general support for this position. Their analyses of the UCLA data suggest that college athletes are actually *less* spiritual than students in general (Yamane and Blake 2008). Why would this be so? Perhaps, according to James Mathisen, because modern sport is the antithesis of play: "If play is free, sport is highly structured; if play is outside the ordinary, sport has become worklike; and, importantly, if play is intrinsic, sport is extrinsic" (Mathisen 2006:288). Therefore, as Mathisen noted, it may be precisely *outside* of formally organized sporting activity that we may see the true "signals of transcendence" that Peter Berger spoke of when examining *play* (Mathisen 2006). Lonnie Kliever also emphasized the notion that a modern ethic of work in sport trumps the ethic of play (Kliever 2001). Play, then, may be closer to spirituality than is sport.

Although college athletes appear generally to be less religious and spiritual than their fellow college students, one important exception emerges in Yamane and Blake's (2008) analyses. Evangelical Protestant athletes are *more* religious *and* spiritual than college students in general. This is not surprising given the history of "Muscular Christianity" in the United States, as well as the popularity of groups such as AIA and FCA on college campuses (Cherry, DeBerg, and Porterfield 2001). The theology of Muscular Christianity allows evangelical Protestants to sacralize sporting events and also provides a framework that allows athletes to negotiate conflicts between sport and their religious beliefs (Coakley 2007). This theology gets activated by AIA and FCA ministers and groups that provide strong systems of social support for belief and practice—"plausibility structures," as we called them in Chapter 8—that are key to sustaining religiosity (Berger 1967). These dynamics are not only evident in college sports, but as the "Illustrating Sociological Concepts" box makes clear, they can be seen in the world of professional sports also.

Of course, more systematic studies on more general populations are necessary in order to

ILLUSTRATING SOCIOLOGICAL CONCEPTS

Religion on the PGA Tour

When Webb Simpson won the 2012 U.S. Open—one of professional golf's four major championships—he joined an illustrious group of golfers who had played collegiately at Wake Forest University. However, unlike his fellow Wake Forest alumni and U.S. Open champions, Arnold Palmer and Curtis Strange, Simpson (born in 1985) is a "digital native." So it is not surprising that he maintains a regular presence on social media, including posting from his Twitter account @webbsimpson1.

Photo by Stuart Hemmingway

What may be surprising to some is that Simpson (a religion major in college) is well known for his Twitter posts of Bible verses, quotes from religious thinkers, and other faith-related content. A quick sampling of his Tweets reveals statements such as these:

- "Where sin runs deep, Grace is more."
- "#Christianity, if false, is of no importance, and if true, of infinite importance, the only thing it cannot be is moderately important" (C. S. Lewis).
- "Hebrews 4:14-16 is more than comforting to the Christian."

In a *Golf Digest* story, "The Soul of Pro Golf," writer Max Adler observes that Simpson is not alone in making his Christian faith very public. The story begins with Simpson telling interviewer Bob Costas how much he prayed during the final holes of the 2012 U.S. Open, but Adler goes on to discuss a dozen other professional golfers for whom faith is central to their identity.

As sociologist of religion Mark Chaves notes in the story, the visible religion in golf, as in American sport generally, is distinctively evangelical Protestant. Through their fellowship with one another and a strong theology rooted in "Muscular Christianity," evangelical Protestant golfers maintain a strong plausibility structure that supports them in their public expression of their faith.

(Continued)

(Continued)

Thus, Christianity on the various professional golf tours is not free-floating. It is supported by formal sport-based ministries like FCA Golf (fcagolf.org), the Ladies Professional Golf Association (LPGA) Tour Christian Fellowship, and the PGA Tour Players' Bible Study. Attendance at "PGA tour chaplain" Larry Moody's Wednesday night traveling fellowship ranges from a dozen to over 100, depending on the tournament.

Perhaps because it comes from a particular religious point of view, the public sharing of that faith is not embraced by all. A *Golf Digest* online survey of readers asking people their "reaction when you hear a tour pro in an interview thanking God after winning a tournament" found the following:

- 40.8%—Completely fine with it. Tells me who this player really is.
- 23.4%—OK, but move on.
- 18.1%—It's a little awkward.
- 17.7%—I'm offended by it. Doesn't belong in a sports contest.

Although not a scientific survey, these results show the very different perspectives people have on the issue of religion in sports.

Golfers like Bubba Watson, who thanked his "Lord and Savior, Jesus Christ" after winning the prestigious Masters Tournament, are sometimes ridiculed for thinking that God has nothing better to do than to get involved in a mere sporting event. However, the theology that animates many athletes, including professional golfers, is more subtle than that. "The Lord couldn't care less whether I win or lose," Adler quotes Watson as saying. "What matters to Him is how I play the game."

SOURCE: Adler, Max. 2012. "The Soul of Pro Golf." *Golf Digest* (November):102–108.

draw conclusions with certainty. For now, we would provisionally say that religion and sport in the lives of individuals are separate spheres of existence that connect at some times and for some people. However, as we would expect from the theory of secularization, there appears to be no inherent connection between them today.

Thus, to characterize the relationship between religion and sport in the modern United States as a "fusion" is an overstatement (Price 2005). At certain times and places, religion and sport do have a close relationship. Still, this is not the same as saying that sport has a constitutionally religious dimension, as in Mayan ball games or sumo wrestling under Shinto. The idea that sporting activity is fundamentally religious, or

that religious authorities can regulate sporting activity, is a thing of the past. The secularization of sport as a social institution is thus a reality. It is also a reality that sport instills values into young people that can have a pervasive and lifelong impact—rather *like* religion.

Critical Thinking: What comes to your mind when you see or hear athletes make public their religious beliefs and values? Would you say you are completely fine with it because it tells you who the player really is? Do you think, "OK, but move on"? Perhaps you find it a little awkward. Are you offended by it, or do you think it doesn't belong in a sports contest? Why?

QUASI-RELIGIOUS MOVEMENTS

As we saw in Chapter 7, loosely integrated societies, in which the intensity of commitment to cultural tradition is low, are more likely than tightly integrated ones to generate cults and other nontraditional social movements (Stark and Roberts 1982). So it is not surprising that in the United States—a pluralistic and rather loosely integrated society—there are many new religious and quasi-religious movements. Some of these movements hold rather esoteric beliefs; others are based on concepts from popular psychology literature and movements. Among the quasi-religious movements that we discuss in this section, none attracts a large following, and most do not attempt to articulate a comprehensive worldview that explains the meaning of death, suffering, and injustice. Nonetheless, they have collectively affected a significant segment of the North American population, especially in urban areas. Some of these kinds of movements elaborate their ideologies, develop theodicies, and evolve into full-blown NRMs.

One such quasi-religious orientation is astrology, a set of beliefs about impersonal forces in the universe that profoundly influence human life on earth. These forces can be "read" or predicted through an understanding of the stars. The zodiacal sign under which a person is born is thought to influence significantly (or even determine) one's personality structure and one's thinking processes. Astrology is not a new phenomenon, nor is it limited to any particular age group. It is not organized around a particular group of people (there is no "faith community"), there is no ordained clergy or other sanctioned leadership hierarchy, and there is no formal doctrine. Yet certain principles and beliefs, which are transmitted through books and word of mouth, are common to those who believe in astrology.

A surprisingly high number of Americans believe in astrology. According to the 2012 General Social Survey (GSS), 50% of U.S. adults read their horoscopes or personal astrology reports. Cohorts under 45 years of age are more likely to read their horoscopes than those over 45. Many who do not follow their horoscopes still know their zodiac sign and the characteristics of persons under that sign, and "half-believe" in the efficacy of astrology (i.e., they are not fully converts, but they remain open to astrology and believe that there is probably something valid about it). According to the 2005 Baylor Religion Survey (BRS), 15.1% of U.S. adults agreed or strongly agreed that astrology impacts one's life and personality (Bader, Mencken, and Baker 2010). Although those who attend religious services every week or more are less likely than average to read their horoscope (38%), those who attend religious services 1 to 3 times a month are more likely to do so (55%). The BRS found that interest in astrology was fairly consistent across religious traditions, ranging from a low of 13% (black Protestants) to a high of 18% (other religions) (Bader et al. 2010). So, astrology is sometimes integrated into the worldviews of persons who are members of mainline religious groups. Their religiosity is a synthesis or blend of a traditional religion and astrology. For others who are not active in traditional religious groups, astrology may play a more significant role in their overall worldview. One study in the 1970s found that astrology seems to serve as an alternative to conventional religion for some people—especially marginal or subjugated members of society: the poorly educated, nonwhites, females, the unemployed, the overweight, the unmarried, the ill, and the lonely (Wuthnow 1976a). Several decades later, Bader and his colleagues also found the strongest demographic characteristics of those interested in astrology were that they were lower income, younger, nonwhite, and female, and that they had low religious service attendance—all more marginalized characteristics (Bader et al. 2010).

Another form of quasi-religious movement has focused more on the development of untapped human capabilities. Transcendental Meditation (TM), Silva Mind Control, and Scientology are examples of this type of movement. Although TM and Silva Mind Control reached the peak of their popularity in the 1960s and 1970s, they continue to exist to this day, although they often play down the religious potential. The TM website (tm.org) boasts support from the Mayo Clinic, the Cleveland Clinic, and comedian Jerry Seinfeld, who on *Good Morning America* in 2013 said he had been practicing TM for 40 years. Silva International Inc.'s "Silva Method" website (silvamethod.com) notes that RCA Records, Green Mountain Coffee, and 1978 World Series MVP Bucky Dent endorse the "Silva Method."

TM is a meditation technique that bears some resemblance to yoga. Its advocates insist that it is not a new religion, and practitioners include both people who are active in traditional religious groups and those who are by traditional measures nonreligious. Some persons use this technique as a means of relaxation; others seek to tap the "cosmic consciousness" that is the ultimate source of energy in the universe.

TM was started in the late 1960s by a Hindu teacher, Maharishi Mahesh Yogi. It involves chanting a *mantra*—a word, phrase, or sound that is given to each recruit. A mantra is not to be shared with others, but chanting one and concentrating exclusively on it offers one a channel to inner bliss. TM masters maintain that such social problems as war, poverty, crime, and racism would disappear if everyone would engage in TM. They maintain that if everyone were in tune with the cosmic consciousness, most serious social problems would not exist. People would be more relaxed and more able to fulfill their cosmic purposes (Needleman 1970). TM claims it is not a religion but only a discipline of meditation. Still, the organization's webpage describes it in terms that have quasi-religious overtones:

> The Transcendental Meditation technique is based on the ancient Vedic tradition of enlightenment in India . . . handed down by Vedic masters from generation to generation for thousands of years. About 50 years ago, Maharishi—the representative in our age of the Vedic tradition—introduced Transcendental Meditation to the world, restoring the knowledge and experience of higher states of consciousness at this critical time for humanity. When we teach the Transcendental Meditation technique today, we maintain the same procedures used by teachers thousands of years ago for maximum effectiveness. (TM 2010)

While TM was founded by a Hindu leader, it is used by some Christians and by persons unaffiliated with any religious group. The organization claims 5 million practitioners worldwide (Bickerton 2003).

Scientology is a highly organized and fully institutionalized movement related to popular psychology and parapsychology (belief in clairvoyance, telepathic communication, and psychic healing) and uses an educational model. It offers to help people become "clear" and to maximize their human potential. The more courses one takes, the higher one moves in the stratification system of the group. This, of course, enhances instrumental commitment, for one makes a financial investment (the courses are not cheap) and begins to rise in the system of respectability and esteem within the group (Bainbridge and Stark 1980; Urban 2011; Wallis 1977).

The Silva Method is a similar training-based meditation movement that offers to help people develop their psychic powers (extrasensory perception) and move people to a new stage of human evolution (Silva Method 2010). Some observers view these movements as essentially business enterprises (the courses are substantial sources of income). For readers of this text, Scientology is probably best known for its association with high-profile celebrities like Tom Cruise and John Travolta, or for being ridiculed on an episode of *South Park* (Lewis 2009). However, Scientology is very explicit about its claim to being a serious religious movement, stressing that its philosophy is a synthesis of Western and Eastern spirituality with modern science (Scientology 2010). In fact, Scientology engaged in a long-term struggle with the U.S. government to be recognized as a tax-exempt religious organization, something it achieved in 1993 (Urban 2011).

Another form of quasi-religious movement is focused generally on science fiction and more specifically on the TV and film series *Star Trek*. *Star Trek* fan clubs have many characteristics that

Originally established in 1954, Scientology's largest North American church was rededicated in 2010 in a ceremony attended by thousands.

resemble religious bodies (Jindra 1994). Michael Jindra argued that "without its institutional and confessional forms, we often fail to recognize religion in our own society" (Jindra 1994:31), yet the *Star Trek* cult involves an origin myth, a set of beliefs, an organization to support and foster the beliefs, a network of fans who cultivate social bonds with one another, and rituals performed at collective gatherings. At one national *Star Trek* convention, a child was even playfully "baptized" into the pseudochurch. Even the television program's writer and director, Nicholas Meyer, has said that *Star Trek* "has evolved into a sort of secular parallel to the Catholic Mass" (quoted in Jindra 1994:32). The program is built on a positive view of the future and is based on rational decision making, egalitarian values, a universalism of all living beings in the universe, and belief in the ultimate progress of humanity. In one sense, the movement deeply expresses both an American and a modernist worldview. Much like many religious groups, the most profoundly committed fans also cope with stigma for their

beliefs. Yet many of these superfans suggest that *Star Trek* provides models and myths that influence them profoundly in everyday decisions and in making sense of the meaning of life.

The quasi-religious movements discussed here are only illustrative of a number of such movements that offer inner peace, ultimate fulfillment, spiritual expansion, or insights into the "truth" about human existence. Meher Baba, Spiritual Scientists, Association for Research and Enlightenment, Spiritual Frontiers Fellowship, and I Ching are only a few of the many other religious movements one might explore. Whether some of these are actually new religions may be debatable, but they do seem to represent a form of spirituality that might influence traditional religiosity or serve as an alternative mode of religion. For example, a person may use TM simply for stress reduction, to get into deeper touch with his or her inner self, or to tap a cosmic source of energy. Yet that person may not consider this activity "prayer" and may not respond positively to other traditional measures of religiosity (doctrinal orthodoxy, worship attendance, etc.). Likewise, a person who believes in astrology may not be religious in traditional ways, but he or she may use astrology as a worldview that offers to explain the meaning (or at least the cause) of events. Any empirical studies of religiosity that attempt to explain current trends and likely patterns for the future must take into account the possibility that religiosity is not declining but is changing in both form and substance.

Our own interpretation is that religion is not in a declining phase—but readers should remember that we use a broad definition of religion. Systems of meaning that offer to explain the meaning of human events through a worldview, an ethos, and a system of symbols are not likely to disappear. However, certain traditional views and certain established religious institutions may well decline in their influence. Whether the reader views this change of religiosity as a decline in religion will be determined largely by his or her operational definition of religion.

Critical Thinking: In our society, there is a wide range of quasi-religious movements affecting Americans. These movements' core values often come from conflicting sources: traditional Judeo-Christian theology, or patriotism, or pop psychology, or playboy philosophy, or consumerism, or astrology. What are the consequences of this for religion? Why?

Summary

In this chapter, we highlighted the benefits of "thinking outside the (God) box" for understanding religion in modern society. Looking only at religious organizations proper—churches, temples, sects, denominations, and congregations—we get

a different view than if we look at the many ways that religion has changed its relationship with our social institutions and taken on a more fluid form in our culture.

Our first focus here was on religion and the media. These two institutions have long had a close relationship, with religious leaders and groups using the media to reach far beyond the walls of their congregations. The new media based on computer technology and the Internet at first blush would seem to pose revolutionary new possibilities for religion, but thus far, on both the production and consumption sides, action has been fairly traditional. New thinking in this area opens up the possibility of digital religion as a third space integrating religion offline and religion online.

A second focus was on religion and sport. As the historical connection between religion and sport was broken in modern society, action moved to the organizational level, with parachurch groups like the YMCA taking center stage and negotiating the secular environment. At the individual level, there is no integral connection between religion and sport; as in other matters of faith in modern society, athletes can choose to integrate these two identities or not.

Our third and final consideration was quasi-religious movements. Astrology, TM, Silva Mind Control, and Scientology are among these. They each attempt to explore supernatural forces and/or philosophies of life that can bring greater fulfillment.

Some scholars believe that these alternative forms of religion mean that religion is not so much declining in North America as changing in significant ways. New forms are emerging, and old forms are taking on modified form. Religion in North America clearly does adjust and adapt to the larger society of which it is a part. As we will see in the next chapter, religion is also affecting and being affected by globalization.

15

RELIGION AND GLOBALIZATION

HERE ARE SOME QUESTIONS TO PONDER AS YOU READ THIS CHAPTER

- What is *globalization*, and why is it relevant to the study of religion?
- How might religion influence global events?
- How does the process of globalization influence religion?
- How might the existence of a religious transnational organization influence the power or legitimacy of a religious community within a nation?
- How do transnational migration patterns influence religion?
- How might a religious group contribute to conflict and warfare, even though the meaning system stresses a commitment to peace?

A consistent theme throughout this text has been that religion is a complex system that is involved in complex inter-relationships with other structures and processes of the society. The meaning system, for example, is composed of an interplay of rituals, myths, and symbols, all of which reinforce a worldview and a sacred set of moods and motivations. That meaning system, in turn, is only one subsystem of the larger system we call religion. This larger system is made up of meaning, belonging, and structural (institutional) systems, all of which are interrelated in complex and sometimes contradictory ways. We found, for example, that the vested interests of officials in the institutional system may cause them to behave in ways that run counter to the meaning system—as occurs when denominations refuse to promote clergywomen to large and successful churches or when clergy are not promoted when they speak out against racism or other forms of inequity and bigotry.

Religion, in turn, is part of a larger system, the nation, and is in interaction with economic,

Photo courtesy of the artist

"Hero, Leader, God" by Alexander Kosolapov (www.sotsart.com) in "Post Pop: East Meets West," an exhibition at the Saatchi Gallery in London, November 2014–February 2015. The reality of globalization and the complex relationships between political, economic, and religious systems is captured by this sculpture of Vladimir Lenin, Mickey Mouse, and Jesus of Nazareth walking hand-in-hand. Although one might think the artist is depicting Lenin as the "hero," Mickey Mouse as the "leader," and Jesus as the "god," it is also possible to see each figure embodying all three characteristics, suggesting parallels between three important global forces: Soviet communism, American consumer capitalism, and the Christian religion.

health care, political, and educational institutions. Sometimes these interactions are mutually supportive and integrative, and sometimes they are conflictual.

The nation as a macro system, in turn, relates to yet a larger system: the world system of interdependent nations, involving transnational division of labor and mutual dependence for needed resources and products (see Figure 3.5 on page 75). In this web of networks, subsystems can impact larger systems in important ways: For example, economic collapse in a country can affect not only that nation but the interaction of that nation with other nations. The processes in a more macro system can also shape processes in smaller systems: A multinational trade treaty or decisions made by the United Nations (UN) may profoundly affect the

internal workings of a country's economy and therefore the economic circumstances of a family.

This chapter will briefly explore the role of religion in the largest of networks, as the entire world increasingly takes on the characteristics of a social system. We will find that even at this level, what religions *say* may differ in important ways from what they actually *do*. We will find that religion can affect global processes, but it is also often affected by them.

This brings us back to the open systems model and challenges us to recognize that some of the inputs that impact religion are from global forces—not just ones within national borders (see Figure 15.1). Further, as we shall see later in this chapter, religion may have *outputs* that impact international relations and global processes.

Figure 15.1 Open Systems in a Global Social Environment

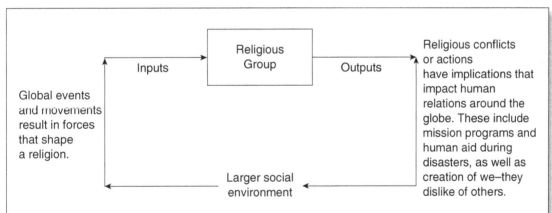

The idea that religious groups might impact international events suddenly became more real to many Americans on 9/11, when the World Trade Center was attacked in New York City. Religion had emboldened 19 men in an extremist Islamic movement to believe that their suicide would ensure a place in the afterlife. That religious outlook had also been used to create an intense sense of "us" versus "them." The result was catastrophic for the United States, for its citizens' sense of security and safety, and for international relations. It resulted in reallocation of financial priorities for a number of countries and a number of businesses (such as airline companies). Whole new security industries and technologies have been developed in response. The world is a different place, and religion played a role in the transformation.

Critical Thinking: What are some ways in which various nations, industries, and international relationships have been affected by the attacks on the World Trade Center and the Pentagon on 9/11? How was religion involved in *initiating* these changes? How have faith communities been *affected* by this event?

THE GLOBALIZATION PROCESS

During the past century and a half, and more especially during the past 50 years, societies around the world have been undergoing a radical transformation; each society and nation has become less an isolated and autonomous unit. The process, called globalization, has involved the entire world becoming "a single sociocultural place" (Robertson 1989). This change involves several interdependent processes: (1) a structural interdependence of nation-states; (2) a synthesis and cross-fertilization of cultures as societies borrow ideas, technologies, artistic concepts, mass media procedures, and definitions of human rights from one another; (3) a change in socialization to a broader inclusiveness of others as being "like us" and to a sense of participation in a global culture; and (4) an increase in individualism, accompanied by a decrease in traditional mechanisms of control, such as strong clan and family ties (Robertson 1989).

One scholar points out that the change of the millennium (January 1, 2000) was perhaps the first time that people around the globe all celebrated the same event. Because of mass media, the change to the third millennium on the Western calendar was acknowledged with celebrations in each of the 24 time zones, with those in other time zones watching. This, said Jose Casanova, is surely the first collective celebratory event of a virtual gathering community around the entire planet (Casanova 2001). This might be considered evidence of our becoming a single sociocultural place.

There are several theories of global interdependence and transformation. One of the most widely discussed perspectives in the 1980s and 1990s has been "world systems theory," developed in large part by Immanuel Wallerstein (1974, 1979, 1984). This perspective, sometimes also referred to as "dependency theory," is based on a Marxian or conflict model. Affluent industrial societies based on a capitalistic economy are referred to as the *core* of the world economy. Interestingly, the most powerful countries in the world have formed a policy and consultation group—calling themselves the Group of 7 (or the G7—the United States, Japan, Germany, Canada, France, Great Britain, and Italy). When Russia was added in 1998, the group became known as the G8, though in 2014 Russia was indefinitely suspended for its annexation of Crimea and hostility against Ukraine.

The G7 uses its collective power to regulate global economic policies to ensure stability (and thereby ensure that members' interests are secure). The G7 has the power to control world markets through the World Trade Organization, the World Bank, and the International Monetary Fund (Brecher, Costello, and Smith 2006; Stein 2006; Weidenbaum 2006; Weller and Hersh 2006).

Poor, nonindustrialized societies are viewed as part of the *periphery*. These peripheral countries typically have narrow, export-oriented economies, based largely on providing raw materials to the industrialized countries. They import manufactured products and in the process develop enormous debts to the richer nations. As a result, they become highly dependent on the developed countries. They remain poor not because of lack of resources or hard work but because they are exploited by the "haves" who control capital and technology (Shannon 1989). These nations responded to the creation of the G7 with an organization of their own that they called the G77. They are attempting to create collective unity so they will have some power to determine their own destinies (Brecher et al. 2006; Hayden 2006). Figure 15.2 shows where the G7 and G77 nations are located. As you can see, the G7 nations are all located above the 15th degree of north latitude, so the current terms used for the most powerful and less affluent countries are the Global North and the Global South.

Although Wallerstein's world systems theory says little directly about religion, it assumes that secularization is an unstoppable force and that religion is a relic destined for decline. Thus, religion does not receive much attention by these theorists (Robertson 1992; Simpson 1991). The prime movers of social behavior are thought to be economic. Like most neo-Marxian theories, when religion *is* discussed, it is often viewed simply as a mechanism by which the affluent preserve their power and keep the poor in their place. Ironically, as we shall see,

some religious movements—especially within the Roman Catholic Church—use world systems theory to explain poverty in poor countries, despite the theory's indifference to religious variables.

An alternative view of globalization is set forth by Roland Robertson, whose perspective takes cultural values and norms more seriously as determinants of social processes. Robertson is convinced that religion is an important player in the global transformation process. Since he gave more consideration to the role of religion, we will explore his sociocultural theory in more depth in this chapter. However, those interested in global inequality issues should continue to be aware of the insights offered by Wallerstein relative to how power is used to serve the self-interests of the "haves" of the world.

Figure 15.2 Countries of the Group of 7, Major Emerging Economies, and Countries of the Group of 77

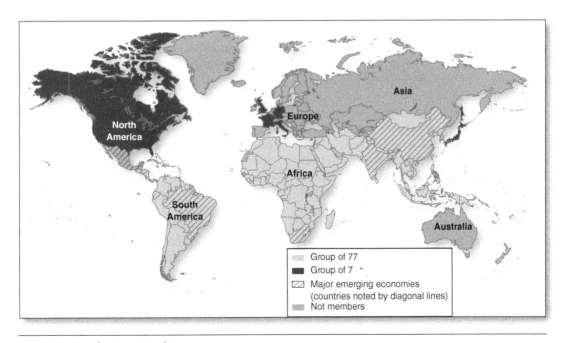

SOURCE: Map by Anna Versluis.

According to Robertson, globalization has been influenced by religion and has impacted religion in important ways; it has been both a dependent and independent variable relative to religion. The topic of globalization is itself a complex issue, and as with other issues in this book, we can only illustrate some of the issues and demonstrate how sociological perspectives can be applied to the globalization process. Our discussion here will explore the emergence of global theologies, the impact of globalization on traditional religions, and the role of religions in international politics.

Critical Thinking: Provide examples—from economics, socialization, or other dimensions of life—of the impact of globalization on your own life.

WORLD RELIGIONS AND THE EMERGENCE OF GLOBAL THEOLOGIES

Robert Wuthnow insisted that the Christian tradition has always been cross-national in character. Certainly Judaism and Islam have long histories of spanning cultures and regions before any "nation," in the modern sense, even existed (Wuthnow 2009). Along with these three traditions, Hinduism and Buddhism are typically counted as the five major world religions. Just as the U.S. Census does not include a question about religious affiliation, so too is there no global religious census. Still, some good estimates suggest there are roughly 2.3 billion Christians, 1.6 billion Muslims, 967 million Hindus, 505 million Buddhists, and 15 million Jews. In addition, there are 685 million people who belong to ethnic folk religions and over 800 million who are religiously unaffiliated or atheist. The religious diversity and composition of the world are set forth in Table 15.1.

Online Resources: The Pew-Templeton Global Religious Futures Project (global-religiousfutures.org) makes freely available data on a variety of aspects of religion around the world. This includes information on religious affiliations and beliefs/practices, social and political attitudes, government regulations and social conflict, and more. An interesting interactive component of the website is the "Data Explorer," which allows the user to create custom data visualizations as pie charts, bar charts, or geographic maps. These visualizations and the underlying data can be downloaded and shared with the click of a button. The data come from the Pew Research Center's (pewresearch.org) various projects.

Religious groups are probably the first transcultural or transnational institutions and religious individuals among the first migrants (Levitt 2003). Still, one interesting religious development during the past 120 years is the increase of global perspectives in the theologies and ethical systems of major world religions. Contemporary religious groups often stress the idea that the world is a single place and that all humans are children of the same God. Rather than stressing differences based on ethnicity or race, contemporary world religions often combat bigotry with affirmations of the fundamental similarity of people everywhere.

Religions often construct images of the oneness of the world in their myths (Simpson 1991). The modern imagery of the "global village," for example, was advanced by the World Council of Churches. The image itself creates a view of a closed, close-knit, interdependent, communal society (Turner 1991a). Perhaps it is because of unifying images that religion often serves as a basis for unity and integration, even when language differences might separate. Roman

Table 15.1 Religious Membership Around the Globe

Religion	Membership (in millions)	Percentage of World Population
Christian (Total)	2,319.8	33.1
Roman Catholic	1,200.9	17.0
Protestant	430.6	6.0
Independent	356.7	5.0
Orthodox	277.6	3.8
Unaffiliated	110.1	1.6
Muslim	1,609.2	22.9
Hindu	967.2	13.8
Nonreligious	679.0	9.7
Buddhist	504.8	7.2
Chinese Folk Religions	437.1	6.2
Other Ethnoreligions	247.5	3.5
Atheist	136.3	1.9
Sikh	24.8	0.4
Jewish	15.0	0.2
Spiritist	13.7	0.2
Taoist	8.5	0.1
Confucianist	8.2	0.1
Baha'i	7.5	0.1
Jain	5.5	0.1
Shintoist	2.8	a
Zoroastrian	.2	a

SOURCE: Adapted from "World Adherents of Religions by Continental Area 2012," p. 701 in *The World Almanac and Book of Facts*. Copyright © 2014 by Infobase Learning.

NOTE: Numbers add up to more than the total world population because many people identify themselves with more than one religious tradition. Thus, the percentages will also add up to more than 100%. Percentages are rounded.

a = Less than 0.05%.

Catholics speaking different languages and hailing from different parts of the globe may feel unified by their commonly held Catholic symbols. Members of the same religious tradition often feel a bond and are inclined to cooperate with others perceived as "like us" when the two might just as easily have adopted a posture of animosity. Religion serves as a master status in this situation rather than nationality being primary. George Thomas points out that theorists can no longer assume, as they did only a few decades ago, that the nation was the defining reference group for all people in virtually all circumstances (Thomas 2001). Globalization has changed that, and religion can now play a different role, at least in some cases.

Some social scientists believe this change in the direction of accommodation and tolerance of other religious traditions is itself a result of increased global interdependence (Lee 1992; Meyer 1988; Thomas 1991). As we are forced to trade and interact with people in other parts of the world who control resources we need, it soon becomes clear that judgmental attitudes implying their inferiority—and an accompanying self-righteous posture regarding our own moral and spiritual values—are dysfunctional. Thus, since about 1875, many Christian theologians and ecclesiastical leaders have offered conciliatory attitudes toward other Christian churches and toward other religions.

Liberal theologies sometimes suggest that God may speak to people through other religious traditions, though Christianity may be depicted in these theologies as the fullest and most complete expression of God's Truth. More recent liberal formulations even hesitate to assert that Christianity is the fullest and most complete expression, for that implies a superiority/inferiority posture that continues to offend members of other traditions. Many theologians and church leaders now simply assert that Christ is the way they personally came to know God, either affirming or remaining mute on the matter of whether other faiths are equally valid paths to God.

Indeed, Thomas pointed out that in a world cultural context, proselytizing (aggressively trying to convert others) "is viewed as a type of cultural supremacy and even as an act of aggression against an ethno-cultural group" (Thomas 2001:527). Forcing one's own religion into another culture comes to be viewed as a form of cultural colonialism.

It is noteworthy that these very liberal or "tolerant" religions are usually strongest in precisely those areas characterized by cultural diversity and most involved in international transactions. Urban areas, coastal trade centers, and other "crossroads" of cultures and people are more likely to generate such outlooks than rural areas where the people rarely encounter much heterogeneity.

This shift in theology seems to be a result of globalization, but it has also resulted in counter-theologies and reactions that will be discussed later. Still, the trend toward greater tolerance on the part of the mainstream denominations was clear. The change in the position of the Roman Catholic Church during the 20th century was dramatic. In 1910, Pope Pius X required all Roman Catholic clergy and teachers to sign an "antimodernist oath." By the 1950s, Pope Pius XII acknowledged truth and goodness outside of Christianity, and in an encyclical, *Evangelii Praecones*, asserted that rather than attacking other religions as evil when evangelizing, the Gospel should be assimilated into whatever is "good and honorable and beautiful" in existing religions.

The Second Vatican Council (1962–1965) opened the door even farther to viewing other religions as "colleagues with similar problems" rather than as enemies (Sheard 1987). It is in this new context that the indigenous religion among Pueblo Indians in the Southwest of the United States—once brutally suppressed with acts of terrorism and torture and rituals strictly forbidden by church and state—is now becoming officially blended into Roman Catholic Christianity. Developments in Zuni Pueblo, the largest of the 19 New Mexican Indian pueblos, are a case in point.

Catholicism first encountered the Zuni in 1540 in the form of Spanish explorer Francisco Vázquez de Coronado and his 2,000-person expedition in search of the Seven Cities of Gold (Flint 2008). When Coronado, representing the Spanish crown and the Catholic Church that legitimated it, arrived at Zuni pueblo, he read aloud and had translated a legal summons called the *Requerimiento*:

> We ask and require . . . that you acknowledge the Church as the ruler and superior of the whole world, and the high priest called Pope, and in his name the King and Queen [of Spain] . . . our lords, in his place, as superiors and lords and kinds of these islands and this mainland. . . . If, [however,] you do not do [what I ask] or you maliciously delay it, I assure you that, with the help of God, I will attack you mightily. I will make war [against] you everywhere and in every way I can. And I will subject you to the yoke and obedience of the Church and His Majesty. I will take your wives and children, and I will make them slaves . . . I will take your property. I will do all the harm and damage to you that I can. (quoted in Flint 2008:70, 109)

Although the Zuni responded by firing arrows at Coronado's party, they were eventually subdued. Thus, near the center of the pueblo stands the old Catholic mission church, Our Lady of Guadalupe, which was built in 1629 using slave labor. Catholic missionaries fled after the pueblo revolts of 1680 but periodically returned, including in 1923 when Franciscan missionaries built a new church in Zuni pueblo. Over the years, the old mission church near the traditional dance plaza fell into disrepair.

After Vatican II, the Zuni tribe entered into an agreement with the Catholic Church (and the National Park Service) to excavate and restore Our Lady of Guadalupe. During the restoration, a Zuni Catholic artist, Alex Seowtewa, learned from his father and other pueblo elders that earlier in the church's history it had kachina paintings on its walls. Kachinas are spirit-beings that are integral to the traditional religions of the pueblo Indians and they believe are critical to rainfall. In 1970, Seowtewa (and his son Ken) received permission from the Catholic parish priest to paint murals of kachina dancers on the upper walls of the church. The murals represent the seasonal cycles of Zuni ceremonial observances (Kennedy and Simplicio 2009). For his work, Seowtewa is sometimes called the Zuni Michelangelo, after the famed painter of the ceiling of the Sistine Chapel. As with Michelangelo, this work was done with the blessing and cooperation of the Catholic officials who are now much more open to the inculturation (adaptation to local religions and cultures) of the Catholic faith (Francis 2000). Actually, it is mostly leaders of Zuni Kivas who feel that their religion is being compromised and that a sacrilege is being perpetrated by its official incorporation into the Roman Catholic Church (Haederle 1991; Keith 1999). Kivas are religious fraternal societies that meet in wholly or partially underground ceremonial structures and that host kachina dancers. A few of the panels from the beautiful paintings on the walls of the Roman Catholic mission church can be seen at www.hanksville.org/voyage/misc/Zmission.html.

Critical Thinking: What might be some consequences of a synthesis of religions—as represented in the blending of Zuni kachinas alongside paintings of Jesus inside a Christian sanctuary? What do you make of concerns expressed by Zuni Kiva leaders and kachina dancers who believe their religion is being compromised by its incorporation into the Roman Catholic Church? What are the positive and negative results of this expansion of religion?

Sometimes the impulse to modify the group's theology or system of ethics can come from internal dynamics within a religion. As the membership composition of a religious group changes, with a marked increase in membership in one region, there may be theological ramifications.

The Roman Catholic Church, an international organization whose historic development and population base was European, is now undergoing transition from a Global North (industrialized, largely capitalistic, and powerful countries) to a Global South (poor, nonindustrialized nations) entity. Catholicism is experiencing growth in South America and Africa, causing the population makeup of the membership of this transnational church to shift (Budde 1992; Della Cava 2001). In 2013, Jorge Mario Bergoglio of Argentina became the first Pope from the Southern Hemisphere, the first from the Americas, and the first non-European since Gregory III in 741. Two Africans, Cardinal Peter Turkson of Ghana and Cardinal Francis Arinze of Nigeria, were among the frontrunners in the conclave, which ultimately elected Bergoglio, now Pope Francis.

As its membership majority has shifted from the Northern to the Southern Hemisphere, many Catholic theologians and priests have supported one or another version of liberation theology. Liberation theology tends to be highly critical of capitalistic economic systems and to view the world through the lens of conflict theory, championing the cause of those exploited by the capitalistic world system. The major cause of poverty in the Global South is identified not as slow adoption of industrialization but as neocolonial *exploitation* by the affluent nations of the world. Such direct attacks on capitalism as a system, attribution of sinister motives to the policy makers of G7 countries, and legitimation of movements antagonistic to the interests of affluent capitalists are bound to create tensions between the church and Western leaders.

This has created an interesting dilemma for the Roman Catholic Church; it is placed in a position of choosing between defending the self-interests of the poor—the new and very sizable constituency of the church—or sacralizing the interests of the affluent capitalistic countries that have been its historic constituency. Even within a single country, like Brazil, the church has

found that liberation theology resulted in an expansion of Catholicism's constituency among the poor, but an alienation of middle-class members who offer leadership skills and financial resources (Della Cava 2001). Further, the "we" within the transnational Roman Catholic organization now includes people from a vast array of cultures, races, and regions of the globe. The church is itself increasingly multicultural. While Roman Catholicism is the most vivid example of these internal transformations, other Christian denominations are also experiencing substantial ethnic diversity (Della Cava 2001).

The trend toward interreligious accommodation, the inclination to define other religious groups as fellow travelers, the desire for "dialogue" and discovery of common ground with other religions, and internal cultural diversity all compel established religious groups to accept pluralism as a positive value. Indeed, whether within the church, temple, or mosque or beyond its walls, embracing pluralism appears to be a critical first step toward accommodation of diverse peoples and alternative social systems. Those who believe that globalization is an unstoppable trend would interpret increased religious tolerance as the inevitable wave of the future.

On the other hand, a few evangelical Christian groups have tried to develop their own version of globalized theology, and these models do not emphasize pluralism and diversity. In a study of the conservative faith movement in Sweden and the United States, Coleman found that specialization of roles by various national groups was emphasized. Interdependence was recognized, but there was no particular expectation of equity, unification, and homogenization of peoples and cultures. The point that this study makes is that "globalization cannot be regarded as an internally homogeneous, inexorable phenomenon" (Coleman 1993:371).

We have already discussed the fact that the Roman Catholic Church is an international body that must be sympathetic to the circumstances of people in many nations. It cannot align itself with the economic and political interests of one nation or set of nations without risking the alienation of tens of millions of members in another part of the world. There are other ways in which multinational religious organizations can be involved in social and economic policies of a nation, as well.

In Poland, during the 1970s and 1980s, the citizenry often felt colonized by a foreign power—the Soviet Union. The Communist government in Poland was extremely unpopular and the people had no real way to make the government more responsive to their needs. In a survey conducted in 1983, only 3% of the respondents felt that the government and the Communist Party represented the interests of the Polish people. By contrast, 60% identified the Catholic Church and the Pope as protecting Polish interests (Tamney 1992). Given the strong presence of the Catholic Church in the Philippines, Catholic priests may well be able to play a similar role there as some justice struggles play out.

Joseph Tamney reported that the Catholic Church became a real power broker in negotiations between unions and the government. Indeed, bishops in Poland sometimes took on a role akin to a union leader and in so doing became major players in the political future of the country (Tamney 1992). Since those bishops were ultimately responsible to the Pope and had a source of support external to the nation, they experienced a good deal of independence. Clergy who were supported by a state church, one financed with tax dollars, would not likely have the same freedom to challenge the government. The global nature of the Catholic Church influenced the role bishops could play in the Polish situation.

The locus of control of a religious hierarchy is an important issue. On the one hand, a religious structure may involve an organization that is external to any one nation and includes representation from many countries. Alternatively, a religious body may be *autocephalous*—that is,

they are not *organizationally* linked to congregations in other countries; the religious hierarchy and membership is contained within a single nation. Transnationalism can influence the power of religious officials in our complex global environment. On the other hand, in an autocephalous religious community, the vitality of the community may be connected more closely to its functions in the mobilization of political power of a particular state or for affirming ethnic identity (Turner 1991b). Poland is an especially intriguing case in that a single religion tended to be identified with national pride and culture, but that religion was global in its power base. That combination provided an exceptionally strong base for challenging governmental policies (Tamney 1992).

Globalization will no doubt take many forms and result in a wide array of efforts to define its meaning and delineate the appropriate form of its evolution. Religious groups will likely make many attempts to define what global interdependence should look like. The one generalization that seems fairly certain is that religions can no longer ignore global interdependence and the fact that the world is to some extent becoming "a single sociocultural place." Theologies of the major world religions will likely be permanently affected by the expansion of vision to include the entire world.

Interestingly, Catalina Romero raised the opposite problem. Denominations typically establish policies in an effort to address specific problems. The problems are specific to a particular place and time, so the religious officials are necessarily thinking locally (Romero 2001). However, what happens when the solution is broadcast globally? What are the consequences? The Roman Catholic Church has faced unexpected results when the Pope has said something in Rome or in Poland, but the circumstances were very different in South America or in Africa. Pope John Paul II's strong language espousing liberation and justice in Eastern Europe was interpreted in Peru as support for a movement calling for rich countries to forgive the debt of poor countries. Sometimes decisions and polices in one locale can have unanticipated interpretations and impacts elsewhere, especially if ecclesiastical leaders do not think globally before they speak (Romero 2001).

IMPACT OF GLOBALIZATION ON RELIGION

The interdependence of the world has long been a factor in shaping religious movements. Robert Wuthnow argued that much religious change, including even the Protestant Reformation, has been caused by international processes (Wuthnow 1980). We do not have space for a long-term overview here, so we will limit the discussion to the modern world. Globalization in the past century has affected religion in a number of ways. In this section we will explore two processes that illustrate how religion is a *dependent* variable (a consequence): (1) modernization and secularization of social structures and cultures and (2) demographic migration patterns.

Diffusion of Modernization and Religious Response

The ability of a society to function effectively in the interdependent world system seems to require "modernization." As societies modernize (which typically means becoming more Westernized), religious institutions are often relegated to a less encompassing role in social life. As we saw in Chapter 13, this process of institutional differentiation is definitive of societal-level secularization. It also has organizational- and individual-level correlates: Religious organizations begin to provide services that are perceived not as mandatory but as "optional" (Turner 1991b). Joseph Tamney described this as "selective religiosity." Official religious pronouncements compete with efforts by the state to define acceptable social behavior, and the individual is free to select which pronouncements to follow (Tamney 1992).

© istockphoto.com/Richard Stamper

This Buddhist monk, in traditional monastic dress, works on the most modern symbol of technology—a laptop computer in Wat Arun, Bangkok, Thailand. The reach of modernization—including into religious groups—has been extensive.

As governments become more concerned about "quality of life" issues and expand the scope of their concerns, they begin to encroach on the traditional realm of religion (Shupe and Hadden 1989; Thomas 1991). Religious groups traditionally had monopolistic control over education, stability of marriage ties, grief adjustment following death, and the provision of charities to help the destitute. However, in the modern world, those services are increasingly provided by "helping" or "service" professionals certified by governments (Turner 1991b). Indeed, Wuthnow claimed that around the globe, as government spending to enhance the life quality, health, and education of the citizenry increases, religious affiliation usually decreases (Wuthnow 1991). Moreover, governments increasingly become embroiled in disputes over issues of morality, justice, and meaning as they promulgate norms governing a very wide range of behaviors (Shupe and Hadden 1989). National governments have displaced many of the social contributions of religious communities.

In addition, as the world globalizes, international nongovernmental organizations (INGOs) begin to expand to fulfill some of these same functions. The Economic and Social Council (ECOSOC) of the United Nations (UN), in fact, grants consultative status to nearly 4,000 INGOs, which allows them to participate in ECOSOC meetings alongside UN member nations (csonet .org). Beginning with the first INGO—Anti-Slavery International, established in 1839—this sector of global civil society has grown dramatically (Keck and Sikkink 1998). In 1854, there were only six INGOs, but by 1945, there were over a thousand. As John Boli and George Thomas argued, these INGOs play a key role in "constructing world culture." They addressed issues of poverty, education, peace, women's rights, reproductive health, and other areas of traditional interest to religious organizations (Boli and Thomas 1999). Not surprisingly, then, many INGOs are religiously affiliated—around 10% of those with consultative status with ECOSOC (Petersen 2010), and over 3,000 of the more than 60,000 INGOs listed by the Union of International Associations (Boli and Brewington 2007). Still, that 90% or more of INGOs are secular in mission.

There is also an emerging field of (secular) international law that defines boundaries of acceptable behavior in everything from commerce to human rights (Berman 1991; Lechner 1991a). The Hague, Netherlands–based International Court of Justice, founded in 1946 and known as the World Court, is the judicial branch of the United Nations. It both bases its decisions on secular international law and in the process helps to develop that law (Tams 2014). A regional

example is the European Court of Human Rights, permanently established in 1998, with one judge from each of the 47 member states of the Council of Europe. Individuals who believe their rights have been violated by a member state can bring a case before the court. In a recent case, a 24-year-old French woman challenged a ban in France on wearing any clothing in public that covered the face. This included, and in fact was targeted at, the wearing of the Muslim full-face veil called a *niqab*. In this legal contest between religious rights and secular law, secular law prevailed, as it had in previous cases concerning the wearing of headscarves (*hijab*) by Muslims in Turkey and Germany (Elver 2012).

Moreover, the utilitarian and rational pursuit of self-interest in the political and economic realms has divorced them from religious norms. Turner pointed out that distribution of resources is no longer tied directly to honor, loyalty, and obedience to traditional authority, as it once was. The result is that adultery, divorce, adolescent disobedience of parents, premarital sexual activity, and other traditionally forbidden religio-moral behaviors are not accompanied by economic sanctions. Religious norms lose their clout, and the realm of religious influence becomes more narrowly focused (Turner 1991b).

Another way to conceptualize this is to think of rational-utilitarian ties between people, ones stressing mutual self-interests and negotiation of resources in the interaction, as "contractual" relations. This is in contrast to "covenantal" relations: emotive-expressive ties based on bonding, shared values, and sense of commitment to specific other persons. The latter represent familial and religious relationships, while the former are more characteristic of bureaucratic, governmental, and economic affiliations. David Bromley and Bruce Busching (1988) and Bryan Turner (1991b) argue that the covenantal realm is shrinking in the face of expanding contractual ties. This is a global trend, and it provides a profound threat to most traditional religions. Benjamin Barber reduced this tension between the forces of tribalism and globalism to a simple equation: *Jihad vs. McWorld* (Barber 1995).

When threatened, religious groups often respond the way any human group that is threatened does: They circle the wagons or strike back against the threat. This religious response frequently takes the form of fundamentalist movements.

Religious Fundamentalism

A number of scholars point out that the rise of religious fundamentalism and other legalistic, literalistic, and rigid revitalization movements in the 20th century is not a process unique to a single religious tradition or society. Therefore, it cannot be interpreted simply in light of local or national events, or in terms of characteristics of a given religion. Its cause, they assert, is global (Antoun 2008; Marty 2001; Robertson 1989; Thomas 1991; Turner 1991a; Wuthnow 1980). Whether the fundamentalism is Boko Haram in Nigeria or the Wahhabi Islamic movement in Saudi Arabia, the Hasidic or *Haredi* groups within Judaism, the 969 Movement among Buddhists in Burma, extremist fundamentalist groups within Christianity like Christian Reconstructionism in the United States and Joseph Kony's Lord's Resistance Army in central Africa, or the Malaysian Dukway sect, the cause appears to be *reaction against* global modernization (Chua 2006; Davidman 1990; Ingersoll 2015; Marty and Appleby 1992, 1994; Shupe and Hadden 1989).

About these revitalization movements around the world, religious historian Martin Marty wrote:

> Members of fundamentalist movements almost everywhere think they are old-time religion. But they're not. Fundamentalism comes after the Enlightenment in the West. It comes after the worldwide spread of technology and industry and along with the earliest stages of global economies. It is late-modern, and some people would say it is postmodern. Fundamentalism is a movement to fight back, and modernity is the enemy. (Marty 2001:44)

To the extent that globalization is experienced as Westernization, it is interpreted not as a benign force for global improvement but as "Coca-Colonization" or "Westoxification" (Turner 2010).

These revivalist or fundamentalist movements, regardless of the religious tradition, have certain prevailing characteristics (Antoun 2008; Heilman 1992; Marty 2001).

1. *Radicalism*—efforts to revitalize an idealized culture depicted in the past, a golden age or a golden place. That age is often frozen on paper in the form of scripture and usually depicts the ideas and social arrangements set forth by the founder of the group.

2. *Scripturalism*—absolutist interpretations of *selective* sections of scripture (many passages being ignored or *not* interpreted literally) and the belief that God speaks solely and decisively through the scriptures. The scriptures can be cited for "proof" in almost any kind of argument—moral, supernatural, literary, or scientific.

3. *Traditionism*—the need to demonstrate that there is nothing in the archaic and holy past that does not have direct application to the way we live today (Antoun 2008).

4. *Oppositionism*—extreme hostility to secularization or modernization. This may well be the defining characteristic of these movements, but this opposition is also selective. Aspects of technology—such as computers, the Internet, and cell phones—may be adopted and utilized to further the religious tradition.

5. *Totalism*—a posture that identifies religious issues as all-or-nothing conflicts where no compromise is tolerated. Often the most extreme hatred is directed toward others of the same tradition who fail to define the key issues the same way or fail to recognize that a win–lose war is at stake.

6. *Puritanism*—the quest for purity in an impure world. While many other kinds of religious movements also have this passion for purity, the drive for internal purity and for militant opposition to the "unclean" is a feature of fundamentalist movements. Of course, various

traditions have different ideas about the core elements of spiritual and moral purity.

Scholars believe that the formation of such movements in diverse traditions and places around the world is rooted in several features of the globalization process.

First, the pluralism and relativity of a diverse world is threatening to traditions that always protected the absoluteness of norms and values (Robertson 1989; Thomas 1991). Bryan Turner pointed out that the whole idea that alternative lifestyles might be tolerable is offensive to those who are very certain that they alone know the Truth (Turner 1991b).

Second, fear of economic dependence on other peoples—some of whom are very different and are viewed as undependable—stimulates a desire to reassert autonomy and, at least symbolically, to proclaim one's uniqueness (Robertson 1989). Fundamentalism or rigid revivalism is in large part an attempt to reestablish independence from the world system.

Third, fundamentalism represents a reaction against the institutional differentiation that is a characteristic of modernization and secularization. Ironically, the blending of Islamic fundamentalism with governmental functions is much more a 20th-century phenomenon than a historic one (Turner 1991a, 1991b). It represents a desire to merge institutions in reaction to the Western pattern of differentiating institutions. Muslim fundamentalists do not want religion removed from other spheres of life, and they react by forging an even closer marriage between religion and other societal functions. In essence, these are nativistic movements reacting against changes that they identify as part of neocolonialism. They are convinced—with some cause—that the acceptance of globalism involves *ethnocide*, the death of their traditional culture. Fundamentalism is an attempt to defend their culture.

Fourth, fundamentalisms are sometimes counteractions against religious reforms themselves (Moaddel 2005). As Iran underwent modernization in the mid-20th century, official Islam in that country underwent reformulation, becoming liberated from folk versions and emphasizing a universalistic monotheism. It also embraced aspects of secularization, including changing roles for women and economic reform that eventually left Iran highly dependent on the United States and other Western nations. Yet modernization of the country also resulted in some economic dislocations and a degree of "cultural wobble." As conservatives rejected modernism in favor of traditionalism, they also rejected the new interpretation of Islam. Rather than returning to polytheistic folk versions of the faith, conservatives forged a literalistic and uncompromising interpretation of Islam (Turner 1991a, 1991b). Official Islam as it was taught by the elites was seen as having sold out to Westernization; it was depicted as a traitor religion that abandoned traditional roots. This perspective is sometimes called "Islamism," though many Muslims object to this term since it applies one interpretation of Islam to all believers.

Some have argued that the most extreme incarnations of Islamism—such as the Taliban in Afghanistan and Osama bin Laden's Al Qaeda network—are evidence of the political *failure* of these groups to establish a truly Islamic state in which *Shari'a* (Islamic) law would govern (Kepel 2002; Turner 2010). Whether the recent attempt of Sunni Muslims to establish an Islamic state in Iraq and Syria will prove this interpretation wrong remains to be seen (see the "Illustrating Sociological Concepts" feature on the religious fundamentalism of ISIS on page 406). While the examples used here have been mostly of Islamic fundamentalism, as noted earlier these movements are occurring across religious traditions. In every case, they represent reclaiming of authority over a sacred tradition that "is to be reinstated as an antidote for a society [astray] from its cultural moorings" (Shupe and Hadden 1989:111). The ultimate cause of the straying is the process of globalization.

ILLUSTRATING SOCIOLOGICAL CONCEPTS

The Religious Fundamentalism of ISIS

The Islamic State in Iraq and Syria (ISIS) took many people by surprise in 2014. It began the year as an insurgent movement battling Shiite Muslim authorities and other factional groups in Iraq and Syria. By the end of the year its brutal fighting had gained it control over a large portion of northern Iraq and eastern Syria, including the second largest city in Iraq and the largest oil field in Syria. Along the way, ISIS gained international attention for the videotaped beheadings of two journalists and two humanitarian aid workers. It is now in the process of establishing a government based on Islamic law.

Although the origins of ISIS are complex, and are tied up with intrareligious conflicts between Sunnis and Shiites within Islam, the goals of ISIS are distinctively antimodern. Instead of having political and legal institutions that are differentiated from the dominant religion, ISIS has announced the creation of a *caliphate* or Islamic state that knows no national borders.

A *caliphate* is led by a *caliph*—someone who is the religious and political successor to the Muslim Prophet Muhammad and therefore has authority over all the world's Muslims. (Note, however, that just because someone declares a caliphate or himself a caliph does not make it so.) In the case of ISIS, its *caliph* is Abu Bakr al-Baghdadi, who has publicly implored Muslims to fulfill their religious obligation to wage a global *jihad* (holy war) against enemies of *Allah* (God). Al-Baghdadi has called on all believers from around the world to join the fight for the Islamic state. Many have done so, especially young, disaffected men. An estimated 16,000 individuals from as many as 90 countries have joined ISIS since 2012. This includes significant numbers from Western countries like Sweden, Belgium, and the United States. The ISIS supporter who was shown on video decapitating Western hostages was determined by voice analysis to be British.

In areas under its control, ISIS governs by its absolutist interpretation of *Shari'a* law. This Islamic law is based on the sacred scriptures of Islam, the *Qur'an* and *Hadith*. Among the *Shari'a* laws and punishments promoted by ISIS are stoning women to death for adultery, execution for homosexuality, amputation of hands for theft, and public lashings of women for inappropriate dress and men for pornography. The Islamic state has also begun to establish a government structure including a *Shura* council responsible for interpreting and enforcing Islamic law.

The future of ISIS and its *caliphate* is uncertain. Beyond its enemies in the Shiite Muslim world, parts of the same global community against which ISIS is reacting are rising up against it. The U.S. State Department considers Abu Bakr al-Baghdadi a terrorist and has offered a reward of $10 million for information leading to his capture or death. In August 2014, the United Nations Security Council has issued a resolution condemning ISIS's terrorism, violence, human rights abuses, and "violations of international humanitarian law." A UN commission subsequently concluded that ISIS had committed crimes against humanity and its leaders should be brought to justice before the International Criminal Court.

We must add that worldwide revivalistic movements are not the only type of religious reaction attributed to global modernism. An alternative response to institutional differentiation and the narrowing scope of religious influence is privatization of religion (Robertson 1989; Turner 1991a, 1991b). Since religions with a universal message are not linked closely to a specific ethnic group or geographic region, and since religious institutions have been moved to the periphery of social life, individuals are freer to formulate their own theology, their own meaning system. This privatization of religion works well with consumer capitalism on a global scale. According to Turner,

> perhaps the real effect of globalization is the triumph of heterodox, commercial, hybrid popular religion over orthodox, authoritative professional versions of the spiritual life. . . . [The] global commodification of religion . . . renders much of belief and practice compatible with secular capitalism. The tensions between religion and the secular begin to disappear as a consequence of the incorporation of religion into modern consumerism. (Turner 2010:662–663)

Global trends toward diversity and institutional autonomy may be linked to the rise in individualization of religion, as well as to the formation of fundamentalist movements. In the face of global interdependence, liberals may tend toward privatization of religion, while conservatives tend to institute movements proclaiming absolute and infallible answers to questions of meaning and morality.

Critical Thinking: Why is pluralism so threatening to so many religions around the world? Why is pluralism central to globalization? Is acceptance of pluralism important to world peace? Why or why not?

World Population Patterns and Religious Consequences

Another way in which global trends may influence religion is through demographic changes, especially the massive human geographic mobility that has taken place since the 19th century. Of course, migration and its relationship to religion is nothing new. As Peggy Levitt put it, "You know, Abraham was really the first immigrant" (Levitt 2003:847). Protestant and Catholic Christians fled England to found colonies in North America in which they could freely practice their faith; French Huguenots migrated to Switzerland and Holland for more tolerance. More recently, changes in U.S. immigration laws in 1965 allowed for increased immigration into North America. Much of this immigration was from non-European regions of the world, especially Asia. With these new immigrants came many new religious traditions. Gordon Melton, a specialist on new religious movements (NRMs), insists that part of the increase in the number of NRMs in North America is simply a function of high global immigration rates (Melton 1993).

Improved communication technologies have brought new awareness of other parts of the world, and advanced transportation technologies have allowed more people to move to new locations than at any time in human history (Wuthnow and Offutt 2008). According to the United Nations Population Division (2013), the United States is home to one fifth of all the immigrants in the world, and the percentage of the U.S. population that is foreign-born has grown from 9.1% in 1990 to 14.3% in 2013. Other G7 nations with large immigrant populations are Britain (12.4% of total population), Germany (11.9%), and France (11.6%).

Some less populous countries have even higher proportions of immigrants. Eighty-four percent of those living in the United Arab Emirates, 74% in Qatar, 60% in Kuwait, and

55% in Bahrain are immigrants. Many of the migrants to these Gulf states are treated more like temporary workers than permanent immigrants. We analyze the religious consequences of this migration by looking at two broad categories of phenomena: (1) glocalization and (2) transnational religious connections.

Glocalization

The term *glocalization* was brought into the sociology of religion by globalization theorist Roland Robertson (1992, 1995). It derives from a Japanese concept, *dochakuka*, which roughly translates as "global localization," that was used to characterize the marketing process of tailoring global products to local tastes (Robertson 1992). Applied to the sociology of religion, glocalization focuses our attention on the reality that the standardizing processes of globalization do not simply wipe out particular local cultures, nor do global migrants simply abandon their cultures of origin. Globalization and glocalization go hand in hand producing both homogenization (McDonald's in India!) and hetereogeneity (they serve a Maharaja Mac, a Big Mac with lamb or chicken, and the McAloo Tikki, a vegetarian burger, because most Indians do not eat beef). Thus, "globalization is

Photo by Manoj Pariyadath

Adapting to the local, religiously influenced food culture of India with a chicken and vegetarian menu has helped McDonald's to succeed there, as in this restraint in Kochi. In 2014, Burger King opened its first restaurant in New Delhi, and is following suit with a beef- and pork-free menu. Its signature "burger" there is the Chicken, Veg, or Mutton (lamb) Whopper.

always also *glocalization*, the global expressed in the local and the local as the particularization of the global" (Beyer 2007:98).

Glocalization occurs because, when religious individuals migrate, they bring their religions with them into a new sociocultural setting. Giulianotti and Robertson identified four different glocalization strategies that are developed by these individuals relative to those new sociocultural environments:

- *Relativization:* The social actors seek to preserve their prior cultural institutions, practices, and meanings within the new environment—maintaining differentiation from the host culture.
- *Accommodation:* The social actors absorb pragmatically the practices, institutions, and meanings associated with other societies, in order to maintain key elements of the local culture.
- *Hybridization:* The social actors synthesize local and other cultural phenomena to produce distinctive, hybrid cultural practices, institutions, and meanings.
- *Transformation:* The social actors come to favor the practices, institutions, or meanings associated with other cultures. Transformation may produce fresh cultural forms or, more extremely, the abandonment of the local culture in favor of alternative and/or hegemonic cultural forms. (Giulianotti and Robertson 2007:135)

Relativization involves migrants preserving their local cultural practices and maintaining some separation from the host culture. In her work on religious transnationalism, Peggy Levitt described the re-creation of the Devotional Associates of Yogeshwar or the Swadhyaya movement, in Lowell, Massachusetts, by immigrants from Gujarat, India. She explained that Swadhyaya members have maintained the founder's teachings, albeit in a new sociocultural setting (Levitt 2004).

For example, all followers are supposed to "devote time to God" by participating in Yogeshwar Krishi. In India, these are cooperative farms or fishing enterprises, created by the movement. Members donate their labor each month and then distribute their earnings to the poor. To do Yogeshwar Krishi in Chicago, Swadhayees formed a small company that made ink refills for pens where they work in addition to their full-time jobs. In Massachusetts, groups of families get together to assemble circuit boards on contract from computer companies.

The Gujarati migrants maintained their local religious practices as a way of insulating themselves from "what they perceived as inferior Western values," and in general "they wanted to remain socially apart." (Levitt 2004:13)

Accommodation is similar to relativization, in terms of the maintenance of prior local culture, but differs in the level of engagement with the host culture. Accommodating glocalization involves some absorption of the host culture. In a study of Tamil Hindus from Sri Lanka living in Germany, Martin Baumann and Kurt Salentin found that the immigrant experience "favors as well as demands the adoption of organizational patterns found in the host society" (Baumann and Salentin 2006:309). Thus, although Hindu religiousness in South Asia is largely noncongregational, in Germany it is much more centered on the congregation as a communal place of worship. The same congregational pattern has been found among immigrant religions in Houston, Texas, and, as was discussed at length in Chapter 8, elsewhere in the United States, reflecting the de facto congregationalism of American religion (Yang and Ebaugh 2001). An opposite process of accommodation takes place among Muslims in France, according to Caitlin Killian (2007). Based on interviews with immigrant African Muslim women in France, Killian argued that they have accommodated to the secularized culture of France by transforming Islam from a publicly celebrated community of believers to a privately practiced religion of the heart.

Hybridization as a glocalizing strategy involves a synthesis of the local and host cultures into a (relatively) new set of cultural forms. Various religious syncretisms fall under this umbrella, including ones like voodoo and Santeria in the Caribbean that result from forced migration (the export of African religions via slavery) or the distinctively African forms of Christianity that result from missionary activity on that continent (importation of Christianity into Africa). Anthropologist Karen Richman has written about the fascinating dynamics that take place within Haitian Catholicism: "a complex, syncretic blend of European and African-Creole religious ideologies and practices, centered around the material reality of spiritual affliction, sorcery, and magic" (Richman 2005:165). It came about due to the combination of African religions carried by slaves and the Catholicism of the French colonialists. Historically the Haitians who have immigrated to the United States have continued to practice their creolized Catholicism (McAlister 1998), but Richman found that many more recent immigrants to Palm Beach County in South Florida have been converting to evangelical Protestantism, creating yet another new mix: a "modern, ascetic cloak worn by the new converts" underneath which "spiritual healing, sorcery, and magic remain at the heart of their syncretic practices" (Richman 2005:165).

Transformational glocalization occurs when migrants favor the religious practices of the receiving culture over their local culture. Fenggang Yang's study of Chinese converts to Christianity in the United States provides a good example of this modality. Yang found that the environment of far-reaching change in China and the subsequent "chain migration"—running from one strange place to another—fundamentally altered the religious needs and outlooks of the population. These changes, he found, meant that the message of evangelical Christianity is more compatible with their needs and perspectives than had been the case with previous cohorts of Chinese people (Yang 1998). As a consequence, they have been more willing to abandon their traditional religions and embrace Protestant Christianity.

Just as globalization is a multifaceted phenomenon, so too is glocalization. In fact, it is probably more accurate to refer to glocalizations (plural), in light of this discussion of four different approaches to glocalization by which the global becomes local. Our discussion so far has focused on the various glocalization projects that are undertaken by migrants to negotiate the relationship between their local cultures of origin and their new host cultures. However, migrants do not simply move and leave behind the world from which they came. The growing field of transnationalism highlights the ongoing connections people have with their communities of origin and how those origins continue to influence religious development in the new locale.

Transnational Religious Connections

A second consequence of increasing migration for religion is what Robert Wuthnow and Stephen Offutt called "transnational religious connections." The idea recognizes that people who migrate often continue to have ties to the home community, communicating with, remitting money, visiting, and even retiring to the home country (Wuthnow and Offutt 2008). Some have called them "transmigrants" rather than "immigrants" for this reason (Basch, Schiller, and Blanc 1994). Moreover, some flows of people across national borders are intentionally short term, such as missionaries, short-term volunteers, and even tourists. As these people flow back and forth in their transnational religious connections, several changes may take place.

Since family members may no longer be united by common nationality or territorial bond, religion may become a more important element of belonging and connectedness. Heidi Larson found this among Hindu, Muslim, and Sikh immigrants living in England. Most of these immigrants come from countries with higher levels of religiosity than the receiving country, so maintaining their ethnic community is intimately tied to maintaining their religious

Photo by Keith Roberts

This is a Christian festival in Peru, but mixed in with the Virgin Mary are celebrations of various other heroes and figures from a local religion, all escorted by a military band. The synthesis is part of the glocalization that occurs as a world religion blends with local customs and beliefs.

commitment (Larson 2000). The second generation, children of immigrants, sometimes attempt to practice a version of their religion that is stripped of the ethnic cultural elements (Voas and Fleischmann 2012).

Further, the religious practices, rituals, and beliefs of a home country may be influenced as people back home hear of the experiences and religious celebrations of their geographically mobile kin. Peggy Levitt found that with the Dominican Republic located in geographical proximity to the United States, there is a fairly high level of migration and visitation back and forth (Levitt 1998). Dominican family members now living in Boston not only return occasionally

for visits, but "adopt-a-parish" ties have encouraged communication and visits by priests and others. The clergy in the Dominican Republic have begun to adopt ideas of ministry (a more "professional" relationship to the congregation) and more rationalized (bureaucratic) procedures of running the church as an organization. Rituals have sometimes been affected, too, as immigrants have communicated ideas and practices back to the home Dominican village.

The result has been local-level globalization— expanded perspectives and practices even in an isolated island village. At the same time, family members now in Boston maintain connections to the home community, and this prevents complete assimilation and cultural absorption of the immigrants into the mainstream of the larger American society. Both churches are influenced by the transnational migration (Levitt 1998).

Not all transnational movements of people are intended to be permanent or semipermanent. Some are short term by design, and yet they can have important religious implications. Barak Kalir, for example, studied religious conversion among Chinese temporary workers in Israel brought in mostly from the villages of Fujian to do construction work. The visas for these workers in Israel are limited to 5 years. Despite the fact that they knew they would return to their homeland in due time, many still converted to evangelical Protestantism during their stays. Actually, as Kalir explained, it is not *despite* the fact that they would be returning to China that these migrant workers converted; it is *because* they would be returning. "Finding Jesus in the Holy Land" allows temporary migrant workers to be involved in a religious tradition that they associate with modernity and progress (and hence high status) and a religious organization that affords them opportunities to cultivate practical skills and network connections (Kalir 2009).

Thus, conversion to Christianity for these migrant workers increases their cultural capital (knowledge, skills, education), symbolic capital (honor, prestige, recognition), and social capital (connections to social networks), which can be deployed to their advantage when they return to their rural, uneducated, lower-class origins. Kalir's insight into this transnational religious connection is only possible because he shifted his "analytical gaze from the host country [to] consider more pertinently the effects that a conversion to Christianity carries for Chinese migrants when they return back home" (Kalir 2009:143).

Professional religious workers—aka missionaries—continue to be a significant transnational connection in the religious field. According to Wuthnow and Offutt, in 2001 there were 42,787 American missionaries working full-time in other countries, an increase of 16% over the previous decade (Wuthnow and Offutt 2008). The International Mission Board of the Southern Baptist Convention, for example, had a budget of nearly $300 million in 2005 and a staff of 500 full-time employees (Wuthnow and Offut 2008). Missionary activities do not exist only at the denominational level; they are connected to local congregations as well. Of church members in the United States, 74% report that their congregation supported a foreign missionary in the previous year, 40% said their congregation has a committee with an international focus, and 20% have a full-time staff member in their congregation responsible for global ministries and missions (Wuthnow and Offutt 2008). Thus, the average member of a congregation in the United States has considerable exposure to transnational connections through his or her local congregation.

Last, even people who go abroad for short periods of time can find themselves affected religiously. In the U.S. context, these are known as "short-term mission trips." Wuthnow and Offutt estimated that 1.6 American church members participate in such trips annually, with a median length of 8 days (Wuthnow and Offutt 2008). Although this does not necessarily yield permanent transnational connections, the individuals who take them can have transformative religious experiences. Using longitudinal survey data from the National Study of Youth and Religion, scholars found that adolescents who had reported not participating in a "mission trip or religious service project" in 2002 but who had participated by 2005 (17% of the adolescents surveyed) had also increased religious involvement and solidified religious beliefs over that time span (Trinitapoli and Vaisey 2009). The mission trip, it seems, had a significant effect on the adolescents' religiosity, at least in the short term.

Related to short-term missions are pilgrimages. A pilgrimage can be defined as "a journey undertaken for religious purposes that culminates in a visit to a place considered to be the site or manifestation of the supernatural" (Tomasi 2002). As with mission trips, these can be domestic or transnational, but the best-known pilgrimage sites entail transnational travel for most pilgrims. Millions of people every year engage in this transnational religious practice, including some 2.5 million Muslims making the annual *Hajj* to Mecca, 1.8 million individuals (Christians and Jews) visiting the Holy Land of Israel, and well over 100,000 pilgrims traveling annually to Kashmir to see the Amarnath cave shrine and worship Lord Shiva (Wuthnow and Offutt 2008).

As with mission trips, we can ask what the religious effect is of these pilgrimages. Sociologist Matthew Loveland has investigated this for American Catholics. Owing to its sacramental imagination, Catholicism has a host of pilgrimage sites, among the best known being the Vatican (Italy) and the various shrines to Marian apparitions in Fatima, Portugal (4 million visitors annually), in Lourdes, France (5 million), and in Mexico City (10 million). Using data from a national survey of U.S. Catholics, Loveland found that those Catholics who had undertaken a pilgrimage (15%) were transformed by the experience, resulting in more orthodox religious beliefs. They were significantly more likely than the Catholics who had not been on a religious pilgrimage to support the church hierarchy's teachings against the use of contraception and for a celibate priesthood (Loveland 2008).

Religion, then, can be influenced in important ways by global trends. The emergence of global theologies and the global diffusion of modernization, the concurrent secularization of social structures and cultures, and demographic migration patterns have all impinged on religion. All three subsystems of religion can be affected: (1) the institutional structure and its tie to other institutions in the society, (2) the sense of religious belonging as a source of personal identity, and (3) the meaning system, which tries to make sense of people's experiences and establish norms of behavior. Before we conclude this look at religion in a global context, however, we need to understand that religion is not always just a

dependent variable in (or reactionary force against) globalization processes. Sometimes religion plays a more *causal* or proactive role in global affairs.

Critical Thinking: Based on your reading of this section, what are the most important ways that you think religion has been *affected by* globalization? *Why* are these the primary influences on religion?

THE ROLE OF RELIGION IN GLOBAL AFFAIRS

From Geertz's definition of religion, we hold that religion establishes "powerful, pervasive, and long lasting moods and motivations" in people. We observe on any given day around the world instances in which these moods and motivations lead people to work toward peace and greater cooperation and instances in which they drive people toward violence and conflict. Belief in the same God can lead one group of people to run hospice programs for people dying of AIDS and another group to slaughter their neighbors. R. Scott Appleby calls both of these groups "religious militants," because of the intensity of their belief (especially in self-sacrifice). That intensity derives from the same sacred source, but leads to different outcomes because of the "ambivalence of the sacred" and the internal pluralism of religious traditions (Appleby 2000).

In this last section, we consider these two different ways religion manifests itself in global affairs—through nationalism and violence and through humanitarianism and peace—and conclude by raising the question of whether a global civil religion is possible.

Nationalism and Violence

Although there is a great deal of religious diversity in the world (as seen in Table 15.1), most countries are not religiously diverse. Looking at 232 countries and territories, the Pew Research Center concluded that only 12 were highly diverse religiously (with Singapore at the top), and no countries in Europe, North America, or the Middle East–North Africa were highly diverse. In fact, almost 60% of countries examined fell into the low religious diversity category, many with 80% or more of their population coming from one religious group. Incredibly, 99.8% of Somalis identify as Muslim, 99.5% of Romanians as Christian, 96.9% of Cambodians as Buddhist, 80.7% of Nepalese as Hindu, and 75.6% of Israelis as Jewish (Pew Research Center 2014c).

When one religious tradition dominates a country's population, the lines demarcating national identity, ethnic identity, and religious identity can become blurred. The patriotic sentiment that arises around the blurring of national and ethnic identities is called *ethnonationalism.* Not all ethnonationalism has a religious dimension. In fact, scholars of nationalism for many years thought of it as a distinctively secular phenomenon (Gorski and Türkmen-Dervişoğlu 2013). The more recent discovery of the religious dimension highlights how violence against religio-ethnic minorities can result when nationalism becomes religiously motivated or legitimated.

As noted in our discussion of fundamentalist religious movements earlier in this chapter, this ethnonationalism is not limited to particular religious traditions. For example, the Eastern Orthodox Serbs in Bosnia-Herzegovina sought to ethnically cleanse the territory of all Roman Catholic Croats and Muslim Bosniaks (see Chapter 10). Orthodox nationalist movements are also growing in Russia, some of which see Moscow as the "New Rome" (Gorski and Türkmen-Dervişoğlu 2013). Islamic nationalism is evident in Algeria, Iran, Pakistan, Saudi Arabia, and Syria, to name but a few (Moaddel 2005).

Hindu nationalist movements include Rashtriya Swayamsevak Sangh and the Vishwa Hindu Parishad in India, both of which promote the Hindutva ideology that advocates defining Indian culture as Hindu culture. In recent decades, they have been responsible for the destruction of mosques and churches in India. The political arm of this movement is the Bharatiya Janata Party (BJP), which is one of the two major political parties in India (Ghassem-Fachandi 2012; van der Veer 1994).

Although only 3 in 10 Buddhists live in countries where they are the majority, it is precisely in those countries where we see what Michael Jerryson has called "Buddhist fury" most clearly. The population of Thailand, for example, is 93.2% Buddhist, which leads to a religious nationalism holding that to be Thai is to be Buddhist (Jerryson 2011). In this context, Thai monks are not simply religious figures, but are "walking embodiments of Thai nationalism" (Jerryson 2011:50). This can lead to violent victimhood for the 5.5% of the Thai population that are Muslim, who are seen as religio-political outsiders and subject to a Buddhist "holy war."

A similar dynamic is at play in Myanmar (formerly called Burma), which is 80% Buddhist. Despite the small number of Muslims in the country (only 4% of the population), some Buddhists fear or resent their presence in what they see as a Buddhist nation. This Buddhist nationalism and Islamophobia are embodied in the 969 Movement led by Buddhist monk Ashin Wirathu. In 2013, *Time* magazine put a picture of the orange-robed, bald-headed monk on its cover with a caption: "The Face of Buddhist Terror." Wirathu has been quoted as saying, "You can be full of kindness and love, but you cannot sleep next to a mad dog," and "If we are weak our land will become Muslim." Such sentiments have led to anti-Muslim violence, including hundreds of dead and tens of thousands displaced (Fuller 2013).

Religious groups often are faced with a dilemma (Robertson 1989). Church officials may choose to embrace the emerging global culture, acknowledge and celebrate global economic interdependence, and foster greater tolerance and open-mindedness toward those who are "different." The alternative course would be to intensify the solidarity between the religion and the national or ethnic group and to stress the differences between "us" and "them." The latter course is likely to buoy the numbers of adherents. Although virtually all religions give lip service to a desire for world peace, and although world peace requires greater tolerance and understanding between people, an institution is actually rewarded with increased numbers and additional resources if it takes the path of identifying with ethnic pride. Having a pledge of allegiance to the flag during a worship service, for example, may be popular with the congregation and result in numerical and financial growth, but it fosters loyalty to something other than the deity and may contribute to more intense we–they sentiments regarding nationalism. The institutional reward system (growth of the congregation) may actually work *against* openness to diversity. Despite meaning system proclamations in support of peace and tolerance of others, the drive for institutional survival may entice religious leaders to follow a path leading to popularity and membership growth. Those religions that do not choose this path may dwindle in numbers and risk their continued viability.

The consequences of religiously inspired ethnonationalism are not only for the unfortunate out-groups that are on the receiving end of its hostility. Political scientist Ted Jelen pointed out that there is great danger to the dominant religious tradition itself if it sacralizes the nation and its political structures. In theological terms, this can easily become idolatry. The nation or the land or the political entity becomes sacred in itself and begins to be the primary sense of worth for the citizenry (Jelen 1995). (See the "Illustrating Sociological Concepts" feature online at www.SAGE.com/rsp6e for an extended discussion of this issue in Wales.)

It is worth noting that some violence that appears to be religiously motivated at first blush is actually driven by other concerns that are then clothed in sacred symbols. For R. Scott Appleby,

the conflicts between Catholics and Protestants in Northern Ireland are an example (Appleby 2000). This has led some, like religion scholar Karen Armstrong, to argue that religious violence itself is a misconception—at least as concerns the major wars in human history. The most extensive acts of violence in the past century have been committed by secular states: Stalin's Russia, Nazi Germany, Mao's China (Armstrong 2014).

On a smaller scale than warfare, terrorist violence has often had a religious connection and, in recent history, a connection to Islam. Addressing this connection, sociologist Charles Kurzman turns the analysis on its head. Instead of asking why Islam is associated with terrorism, he wonders why there are so *few* Muslim terrorists (Kurzman 2011). As observed in Table 15.1, there are 1.6 billion Muslims in the world. Yet Islamic fundamentalists have recruited very few of them to their cause. These are what Kurzman calls "the missing martyrs." In the January 2015 Islamic terrorist attack on the French satirical magazine *Charlie Hebdo*, one of the victims was Ahmed Merabet. Merabet was a French police officer and Muslim—one of nearly 5 million Muslims in France, in fact. According to Kurzman, Muslims throughout the world find Islamic terrorism abhorrent; all the more so, in fact, as the violence is committed in the name of their religion (Kurzman 2011).

In *The Better Angels of Our Nature* (2011), Steven Pinker observes that more Americans die from "lightening, deer, peanut allergies, bee stings, and 'ignition or melting of nightware'" than by terrorist attacks" (p. 345). He puts this curious lack of religious violence in a broader (world-historical) perspective. Although religiously motivated nationalism and religiously justified violence is evident throughout the world, Pinker argues that the world today is less violent than at any point in human history. The mechanisms driving this pacification of humanity are complex, but include a humanitarian revolution (concern for other people as human beings) and its contemporary correlate, a rights revolution (for ethnic minorities, women, children, sexual minorities, and even animals). These, too, have a religious connection (Pinker 2011).

Humanitarianism and Peace

If Ashin Wirathu is the face of Buddhist violence, then Tenzin Gyatso is the face of Buddhist peace, and a much more recognizable one at that, especially under his official title: His Holiness the 14th Dalai Lama of Tibet. The stark contrast between the two exemplifies Appleby's idea of the ambivalence of the sacred and how that can lead to both religiously militant violence and religiously militant peace (Appleby 2000). With respect to the latter, some of the most recognizable humanitarians in the past century have been religious leaders. Like Tenzin Gyatso, other notable religious figures who have won the Nobel Peace Prize are Swedish Archbishop Nathan Söderblom, World Student Christian Federation leader John Raleigh Mott, theologian and medical missionary Albert Schweitzer, Dominican priest Fr. Georges Pire of Belgium, Rev. Dr. Martin Luther King Jr., Mother Teresa of Calcutta, Episcopal Bishop Desmond Tutu of South Africa, and Catholic Bishop Carlos Filipe Ximenes Belo of East Timor. The great Indian pacifist Mohandas Gandhi never won despite being nominated 5 times, though in the year following his death no award was given since the Nobel rules prohibited a posthumous award. In addition, the British Friends Service Council and the American Friends Service Committee—the peace and social justice arms of the Religious Society of Friends (Quakers)—shared the prize as organizations (Nordlinger 2012).

Many other winners of the Nobel Prize have been strongly motivated by their religious beliefs. Former U.S. president and Southern Baptist Jimmy Carter is one example. Another is the youngest winner of the prize, 17-year-old Malala Yousafzai, a Pakistani Muslim. She won the award in 2014 for her activism on behalf of education for girls in the Swat Valley, which the

Taliban had banned. Yousafzai, who was shot in the head by a Taliban gunman, contrasted her understanding of Islam to that of the Taliban in a speech before the United Nations: "They think that God is a tiny, little conservative being who would point guns at people's heads just for going to school. These terrorists are misusing the name of Islam for their own personal benefit. . . . Islam is a religion of peace, humanity and brotherhood" (Yousafzai 2013).

Yousafzai is one of five Muslims to have won the Nobel Peace Prize since 2000 (Jenkins 2014). As with nationalism and violence, efforts at humanitarianism and peace can be found in many religious traditions. Protestant and Catholic Christianity, Islam, Buddhism, Hinduism, and Judaism are all well represented among Nobel Peace Prize winners, as well as the less recognized masses of individuals doing humanitarian and peace work around the globe. Organizations also play a key role in these processes.

For the thousand years prior to the 18th century, remarkably few efforts had been made to reach out to persons in other cultures except in the name of conquest (Hunter 1983; Lee 1992). Then in the 18th and 19th centuries, outreach programs were focused mostly on proselytizing and conversions, though they did provide humanitarian aid also (Ferris 2005). In the 20th century, some religious missions became more focused on helping rather than converting the other. The World Council of Churches, Caritas Internationalis, Church World Service, World Vision, and many others have all sponsored a variety of programs aimed at health care, poverty relief, and amelioration of suffering caused by natural disasters. These major organizations have signed onto a code of conduct developed by the International Federation of Red Cross and Red Crescent Societies for humanitarian agencies, which includes among its 10 principles that aid "is given regardless of the race, creed, or nationality of the recipients" and "will not be used to further a particular political or religious standpoint" (Walker 2005).

The amount of humanitarian aid provided by these faith-based organizations (FBOs) is substantial. It has been estimated that 90% of all relief to refugees after World War II was provided by religious agencies. Today, the value of the aid provided by the World Council of Churches and Caritas Internationalis alone is estimated at over $1 billion each annually. As much as half of all health and education services in sub-Saharan Africa may be provided by FBOs, and one third of all AIDS patients in the world are cared for in Catholic institutions (Ferris 2005).

The dilemma, of course, is that these very programs tend to assume and enhance Westernization of the cultures. In the process, indigenous ways of life are often undermined. Humanitarian missionaries respond that ethnocide—the destruction of the cultures of another people, especially indigenous or minority people—has already occurred. The only question is whether organizations in the more developed countries are going to help poor countries to cope with the new global environment. Moreover, there is evidence that at least some missionaries have helped to revitalize and to preserve aspects of indigenous cultures. The role of missionaries has been complex (Sanneh 1991).

Still, there is a concern that goes beyond that of Christian mission programs undermining traditional culture and beliefs. Graham Howes documented the fact that the mission programs to Latin America sponsored by U.S. churches have often been aligned with U.S. international interests and may have done more for the United States than for the target country (Howes 1991). Clearly the U.S. government has intentionally tried to use (even manipulate) religiously sponsored mission programs to achieve objectives that primarily served capitalism, business interests, and U.S. national security. Whether the programs helped the people in the target countries was of secondary interest (Howes 1991). In any case, concern about the ethics of changing other cultures and of being intrusive with North American culture has caused mainline denominations to cut back on evangelistic orientations to missions.

Of course, religious groups from Global North countries are also frequently involved in benevolence programs directed toward impoverished areas of the world. These programs have the potential to enhance goodwill between countries, but occasionally the manner in which assistance is provided can be demeaning to the recipient nation or people. If the latter occurs, the net result could be hostile feelings rather than ones of mutual respect and appreciation. In any case, whether the concern is international bigotry, prospects for economic cooperation and trade, a struggle for human rights and justice, or a desire for world peace, religious groups and individuals are likely to be important players in the outcome.

Critical Thinking: Do you see the "ambivalence of the sacred" leading to both violence and peace in your social world as the authors suggest, or do you see one happening more than the other? Think about these processes both on the global scale and in your everyday life.

Toward a Global Civil Religion?

In Chapters 3 and 13, we discussed Émile Durkheim's idea, elaborated in recent years by Robert Bellah, that societies—especially pluralistic ones—need a common core of sacred symbols, values, and beliefs to enhance social integration and to provide an overarching system of meaning. In his essay on civil religion, Bellah expressed his expectation that a global civil religion would eventually emerge, alluding to the possibility of "American civil religion becoming simply one part of a new civil religion of the world" (Bellah 1970b:186). The world has no such universal system, no myths, rituals, and symbols that powerfully unite the people of the globe, though some allow that a global civilization could give rise to a global civil religion, whose "pantheon of saints" might include Mohandas Gandhi, Mother Teresa, and the Dalai Lama (Juergensmeyer 2006).

More realistically, the spread of human rights and international law gives some prospect that a global civil society united under some common core beliefs could be a possible future (Casanova 2001; Cristi and Dawson 2007), although we observed earlier the secularist understandings sometimes adopted by international courts are off-putting to some religious groups. George Thomas pointed out that even the UN's Universal Declaration of Human Rights has language that is offensive to some religious people. The UN document, drafted after World War II and the horrors of the Nazi Holocaust against Jews, Gypsies, and homosexuals, recognizes the human right to choose one's religion (Thomas 2001). The very notion that one chooses one's religion is itself a form of modernization, for it stresses both individualism and freedom of choice (Thomas 2001). Choice relativizes religion—one has a right to choose Religion A or Religion B. Indeed, relativization of cultural values is central to the globalization process and is an aspect of contemporary life that fundamentalists vehemently reject in the religious sphere (Campbell 2005).

Not only does the globe lack a comprehensive and unifying meaning system, but the planet is actually populated by religions that have historically each claimed exclusive access to divine truth. Bryan Turner wrote, "It is difficult to imagine how one can have several universalistic, global, evangelistic religions within the same world political space. How can one have mutually exclusive households within the world cultural system?" (Turner 1991a:179). In fact, concern about the uncivil nature of some forms of religion dates back at least to Jean-Jacques Rousseau, who stated in *The Social Contract* that some religions are contrary to order and peace within a nation: "It is impossible to live at peace with those we regard as damned. . . . [T]he man who makes bold to say 'outside the church is no

salvation' should be driven from the state" (Rousseau [1762] 1954:221, 223).

It is not just social coherence that is at stake. In the midst of a pluralistic world, with extraordinarily powerful self-interests inclining nations and societies to conflict, world organizations such as the World Court and the United Nations lack the legitimated authority that civil religion can provide (Berman 1991; Meyer 1980; Robertson 1989, 1991; Simpson 1991). Without some sacralization of their authority, such bodies find it very difficult to make their policies binding.

Of course, many other sociologists insist that the primary "glue" that unites most modern societies is not common beliefs and values anyway. Economic interdependence, technological linkages between social units, and bureaucratic processes provide the primary coherence, they argue (Turner 1991b; Wallerstein 1974, 1984). For these scholars, a global civil religion is unnecessary.

Critical Thinking: Is a core set of common values and beliefs important to an integrated and well-functioning society? Does *global* harmony and genuine cooperation require some global religion? If so, how will this affect existing world religions? If not, what does the lack of importance of global religion say about the role and the vitality of religion in the future?

SUMMARY

Religion is not only itself a complex social system, with internal processes that are sometimes integrative and sometimes contradictory and conflictive, but it is one part of the larger national and global macro systems. Religion can both affect and be affected by globalization processes.

Globalization involves several interdependent processes: structural interdependence of nation-states, synthesis and cross-fertilization of cultures as a modern secularized global culture emerges, a change in socialization to a broader inclusiveness of others as being "like us," and an increase in individualism and reduction of traditional mechanisms of social control.

Theologies of world religions have been influenced by this globalization trend. As people have traded and become increasingly interdependent, liberal theologies have emerged that view other religions as colleagues with similar problems and allow the possibility that other traditions may also offer insights into divine truth. Further, shifts in the membership composition of religious organizations with global constituencies can cause a shift in theological views and ethics, as occurs with the anticapitalist liberation theology of Roman Catholics in Global South countries. The Catholic Church finds itself in a dilemma as to whether it should sacralize the social system of its traditional constituency, the affluent Western world, or support its rapidly growing population in the Southern Hemisphere. In any case, global perspectives seem to be emerging in the theologies of many groups, as diverse groups try to make sense of this new and compelling social reality.

Globalization impacts religion in a number of ways. The emerging global culture is a highly secularized one stressing a rational-utilitarian outlook on the world and calling for institutional differentiation of religion from other spheres. This means that "covenantal relations," characterized by love, commitment, and sacrifice on behalf of others, are waning as the self-interested utilitarian "contractual relations" of government and economics expand. In reaction to this and to the compromises to modernism made by liberal theologies, a pattern of rigid and uncompromising revivalistic movements has developed in religions around the world. These revivalistic or "fundamentalist" religions attempt to reclaim sacred authority over a society and culture, combatting ethnocide of their culture by the press of global homogeneity. This means that fundamentalist movements are a result of worldwide trends, not just local factors.

The movement of people around the globe has increased. It both is affected by and affects religion. Sociologists studying transnational migration have used the term *glocalization* to describe the need for migrant communities to negotiate the relationship between the global and the local and have described various strategies of glocalization employed by migrants (relativization, accommodation, hybridization, and transformation). Transnational religious connections are formed by "transmigrants"—immigrants, temporary migrants, missionaries, and pilgrims—and their effect on religious communities and individuals.

Because the sacred is fundamentally ambivalent and religious traditions are internally diverse, religiously motivated action can be directed toward nationalism and violence or humanitarianism and peace.

Many scholars believe that social systems need either a unifying religious system or a "civil religion." The entire world has no single set of sacred symbols, beliefs, and values that unify all people and that legitimate the growing number of global institutions designed to reduce conflicts and meet human needs. These scholars feel that the lack of any legitimating and solidifying sacred system is a problem in the prospect for world peace.

Religion is, indeed, a complex phenomenon. It is composed of many parts and is itself one component of yet larger systems. It may contribute to integration or to schism, it may give voice to one set of values yet undermine those values in other ways, it may elicit the most noble and caring qualities of persons, or it may foster the most hateful and narrow-minded forms of bigotry. Whatever else one may conclude about religion, it is a multifaceted, dynamic, and always interesting part of our social system and of our most intimate personal lives. Its role in the emerging world system is no less intriguing and important.

EPILOGUE

The Sociological Perspective on Religion: A Concluding Comment

Sociology seeks to understand the social processes of religion. Because the discipline is limited to empirical investigation, it does not address the truth or falsity of a religious system. The researcher adopts a posture of at least temporary agnosticism. Nonetheless, explanations of cause and effect are offered with only empirically identifiable causes being noted. Hence, the effect is apparently to explain away any supernatural causes. Sociology offers only one lens or one vantage point for understanding religious processes, and it tends to operate within the confines of that vantage point. Other disciplines and other vantage points can offer other insights.

Furthermore, the interpretations of causality that are presented in this book represent the current understandings of sociologists, and the social sciences remain ever open to new data and new perspectives. Social scientists must always be willing to accept a new interpretation if it seems more plausible and if the data support it. The discipline will continue to develop, and new data may support or disprove theories about religious behavior that now seem plausible. Methods of data collection and data interpretation are constantly being challenged and reassessed. The social scientist must always remain open to new data and fresh insights. That is the nature of science as a mode of inquiry.

Regardless, the meaning of a transcendent dimension of life for individuals can never be fully grasped through objective, scientific study. Margaret Poloma insisted that scientific empiricism is itself a worldview and that the determinism of the social sciences can dull one's sensitivity to the mystical, intuitive, symbolic–imagistic side of life (Poloma 1982b). Milton Yinger stated the case eloquently:

> No one would claim that the analysis of paint, painter, and patron exhausts the meaning of art; we are becoming cautious about making equivalent claims for the analysis of religion. The scientist must realize that propositions derived from objective study do not exhaust the meaning of things. (Yinger 1970:2)

Social psychologist James Vander Zanden pointed out that our five senses are limited to certain sensations. We know that there are wavelengths of light that we cannot see and frequencies of sound we cannot hear. Yet we do not deny that they exist (Vander Zanden 1987). Scientists have now demonstrated that some creatures have sensory capabilities not even available to humans. Some birds, for example, are sensitive to changes in barometric pressures and to the earth's magnetic fields; in fact, some arctic species have magnetite in their heads, which some scientists think is how these birds know the location of the earth's poles. Most birds can see ultraviolet rays, and some sharks find their prey through sensitivity to magnetic fields given off by fish buried in the sand. Many snakes can *see* infrared rays that we only experience as heat. Vander Zanden concluded that we must never forget the limitations of our own empirical senses: Scientists must approach all forms of human knowledge with a healthy dose of humility.

Indeed, Canadian sociologist of religion Reginald Bibby pointed to the myopic view that a strictly empiricist assumption can entail:

> The old analogy still applies: limiting religion's potential fullness to science's eyes is like searching for a lost key only under a light because the lighting is better there, or like searching for handwritten material on a computer because it's easier than going through the endless number of file cabinet drawers. (Bibby 2002:228)

With Milton Yinger, Thomas O'Dea, Reginald Bibby, and others, we remain convinced that neither theism nor atheism is inherently unsophisticated (Bibby 2002; O'Dea 1966; Yinger 1970). Both are assumptions about the nature of the world that are of interest to sociologists.

The purpose of this text has been neither to destroy the faith of believers nor to make believers out of skeptics. The purpose has been to help readers gain insight into the complexity of religion and the relationship between religion and society. In the process, the views of readers (including their worldviews) may have been changed or modified. Sometimes the insights of social scientists are unsettling, for they challenge our assumptions about reality. That is the nature of the search for truth; the seeker must be willing to follow the data wherever they lead.

Certainly, sociology does not offer the *whole* truth about religion or about any aspect of human life, but sociological investigation can *contribute* to a *holistic* understanding of human experience—including religious experience. As we suggested in Chapter 2, sociological study of religion cannot be proven to be directly beneficial to religious faith, but surely ignorance is more harmful in the long run than is disquieting knowledge. Likewise for nonbelievers, ignorance of this phenomenon—which is so important to many people—leaves a gap that prevents a holistic understanding of the human experience.

Future contributions to the understanding of religion require two characteristics: (1) uncompromising academic rigor and (2) an honest recognition of the limitations of our current knowledge. Certainly, there is much that we do not know about religion and about religious behavior. We only hope that our own fascination with the sociology of religion has been contagious to the readers and that this brief introduction will serve only as the beginning of a continuing inquiry.

BIBLIOGRAPHY

Alba, Richard, Albert J. Raboteau, and Josh DeWind, eds. 2008. *Immigration and Religion in America: Comparative and Historical Perspectives*. New York: New York University Press.

Allport, Gordon W. 1966. "The Religious Context of Prejudice." *Journal for the Scientific Study of Religion* (Fall):447–457.

Altman, Dennis. 1982. *The Homosexualization of America*. New York: St. Martin's Press.

Ammerman, Nancy. 1987. *Bible Believers: Fundamentalists in the Modern World*. New Brunswick, NJ: Rutgers University Press.

Ammerman, Nancy. 1990. *Baptist Battles: Social Change and Religious Conflict in the Southern Baptist Convention*. New Brunswick, NJ: Rutgers University Press.

Ammerman, Nancy. 1997. *Congregation and Community*. New Brunswick, NJ: Rutgers University Press.

Ammerman, Nancy. 2003. "Religious Identities and Religious Institutions." Pp. 207–224 in *Handbook of the Sociology of Religion*. Edited by M. Dillon. Cambridge: Cambridge University Press.

Ammerman, Nancy. 2005. *Pillars of Faith: American Congregations and Their Partners*. Berkeley: University of California Press.

Ammerman, Nancy. 2006. "Denominationalism/ Congregationalism." Pp. 353–372 in *Handbook of Religion and Social Institutions*. Edited by H. R. Ebaugh. New York: Springer.

Ammerman, Nancy. 2009. "Congregations: Local, Social, and Religious." Pp. 562–580 in *The Oxford Handbook of the Sociology of Religion*. Edited by P. Clarke. New York: Oxford University Press.

Ammerman, Nancy. 2014. *Sacred Stories, Spiritual Tribes: Finding Religion in Everyday Life*. New York: Oxford University Press.

Ammerman, Nancy, Jackson Carroll, Carl Dudley, and William McKinney. 1998. *Studying Congregations: A Handbook*. Nashville, TN: Abingdon Press.

Anderson, Charles. 1970. *White Protestant Americans*. Englewood Cliffs, NJ: Prentice Hall.

Anglican Church in North America. 2015. *About*. Retrieved from Anglicanchurch.net/?/main/page/about-acna

Anthony, Francis-Vincent, Chris A. M. Hermans, and Carl Sterkens. 2010. "A Comparative Study of Mystical Experience Among Christian, Muslim, and Hindu Students in Tamil Nadu, India." *Journal for the Scientific Study of Religion* 49:264–277.

Anti-Defamation League. 2014a. *ADL Global 100*. Retrieved from global100.adl.org

Anti-Defamation League. 2014b. *ADL Audit: Anti-Semitic Incidents Declined 19 Percent Across the United States in 2013*. Retrieved from www.adl .org/press-center/press-releases/anti-semitism-usa/adl-audit-anti-semitic-incidents-2013.html

Antoun, Richard T. 2008. *Understanding Fundamentalism: Christian, Islamic, and Jewish Movements*. 2nd ed. Lanham, MD: Rowman & Littlefield.

Appleby, R. Scott. 2000. *The Ambivalence of the Sacred: Religion, Violence, and Reconciliation*. Lanham, MD: Rowman & Littlefield.

Armstrong, Karen. 2014. *Fields of Blood: Religion and the History of Violence*. New York: Knopf.

Arnett, Jeffrey J. 2004. *Emerging Adulthood: The Winding Road From the Late Teens Through the Twenties*. New York: Oxford University Press.

Arweck, Elizabeth and Martin D. Stringer. 2002. *Theorizing Faith: The Insider/Outsider Problem in the Study of Ritual.* Birmingham, AL: University of Birmingham.

Aslan, Reza. 2011. *No god but God: The Origins, Evolution, and Future of Islam.* New York: Random House.

Assimeng, Max. 1987. *Saints and Social Structures.* Jema, Ghana: Ghana Publishing Co.

Associated Press. 2009. *Family Spat Divides Televangelism Empire* (January 31). Retrieved from www.nbcnews.com/id/28953451/ns/us_news-faith/t/family-spat-divides-televangelism-empire

Associated Press. 2013. *Battle Over Bergen County Blue Laws Set to Resume* (February 3). Retrieved from www.nj.com/bergen/index.ssf/2013/02/battle_over_bergen_county_blue_laws_set_to_resume.html

Association of American Publishers. 2010. *Industry Statistics 2009* (April 7). Retrieved from publishers.org/main/IndustryStats/indStats_02.htm

Austin, Allen D., ed. 1997. *African Muslims in Antebellum America.* Rev. ed. New York: Routledge.

Bader, Christopher D., F. Carson Mencken, and Joseph O. Baker. 2010. *Paranormal America: Ghost Encounters, UFO Sightings, Bigfoot Hunts, and Other Curiosities in Religion and Culture.* New York: New York University Press.

Baer, Hans A. 1984. *The Black Spiritual Movement: A Religious Response to Racism.* Knoxville: University of Tennessee Press.

Bagby, Ihsan. 2003. "Imams and Mosque Organization in the United States: A Study of Mosque Leadership and Organizational Structure in American Mosques." Pp. 113–134 in *Muslims in the United States.* Edited by P. Strum and D. Tarantolo. Washington, DC: Woodrow Wilson International Center for Scholars.

Baggett, Jerome. 2009. *Sense of the Faithful: How American Catholics Live Their Faith.* New York: Oxford University Press.

Bainbridge, William Sims. 1978. *Satan's Power: Ethnography of a Deviant Psychotherapy Cult.* Berkeley: University of California Press.

Bainbridge, William Sims and Rodney Stark. 1979. "Cult Formation: Three Compatible Models." *Sociological Analysis* (Winter):283–295.

Bainbridge, William Sims and Rodney Stark. 1980. "Scientology: To Be Perfectly Clear." *Sociological Analysis* (Summer):128–316.

Bainbridge, William Sims and Rodney Stark. 1981. "The Consciousness Reformation Reconsidered." *Journal for the Scientific Study of Religion* (March):1–15.

Bainton, Roland. 1960. *Christian Attitudes Toward War and Peace: A Historical Survey and Critical Re-evaluation.* New York: Abingdon Press.

Bakalian, Anny and Medhi Bozorgmehr. 2009. *Backlash 9/11: Middle Eastern and Muslim Americans Respond.* Berkeley: University of California Press.

Baker, Joseph. 2008. "An Investigation of the Sociological Patterns of Prayer Frequency and Content." *Sociology of Religion* 69:169–185.

Baker, Joseph and Buster Smith. 2009. "The Nones: Social Characteristics of the Religiously Unaffiliated." *Social Forces* 87:1251–1263.

Baker, William. 2007. *Playing With God: Religion and Modern Sport.* Cambridge, MA: Harvard University Press.

Balch, Robert W. 1980. "Looking Behind the Scenes in a Religious Cult: Implications for the Study of Conversion." *Sociological Analysis* (Summer):137–143.

Balch, Robert W. and David Taylor. 1976. "Salvation in a UFO." *Psychology Today* (October):58–66, 106.

Balch, Robert W. and David Taylor. 1977. "Seekers and Saucers." *American Behavioral Scientist* (July/August):839–860.

Balch, Robert W. and David Taylor. 2002. "Making Sense of the Heaven's Gate Suicides." Pp. 209–228 in *Cults, Religion, and Violence.* Edited by D. G. Bromley and J. G. Melton. New York: Cambridge University Press.

Ballantine, Jeanne and Floyd Hammack. 2008. *The Sociology of Education: A Systematic Analysis.* 6th ed. Upper Saddle River, NJ: Prentice Hall.

Ballantine, Jeanne, Keith A. Roberts, and Kathleen Odell Korgen. 2016. *Our Social World.* 5th ed. Thousand Oaks, CA: Sage.

Baltzell, E. Digby. 1964. *The Protestant Establishment.* New York: Random House.

Bandura, Albert. 1977. *Social Learning Theory.* New York: General Learning Press.

Bang, Esther, M. E. L. Hall, T. L. Anderson, and M. M. Willingham. 2005. "Ethnicity, Acculturation, and Religiosity as Predictors of Female College Students' Role Expectations." *Sex Roles* 53:231–237.

Banks, Adelle M. 2012. "Methodists Reach Across Historic Racial Boundaries With Communion

Pact." *Christianity Today* (May 7). Retrieved from www.christianitytoday.com/gleanings/2012/may/methodists-reach-across-historic-racial-boundaries-with.html

Bankston, Carl and Min Zhou. 2000. "De Facto Congregationalism and Social Mobility in Laotian and Vietnamese Immigrant Communities: A Study of Religious Institutions and Economic Change." *Review of Religious Research* 41:453–470.

Bao, Wan-Ning, Les Whitbeck, Danny Hoyt, and Rand Conger. 1999. "Perceived Parental Acceptance as a Moderator of Religious Transmission Among Adolescent Boys and Girls." *Journal of Marriage and Family* 61:362–374.

Barber, Benjamin. 1995. *Jihad vs. McWorld: How Globalism and Tribalism Are Reshaping the World.* New York: Random House.

Barker, Eileen. 1984. *The Making of a Moonie: Brainwashing or Choice?* New York: Basil Blackwell.

Barker, Eileen. 2007. "Charting the Information Field: Cult-Watching Groups and the Construction of Images of New Religious Movements." Pp. 309–330 in *Teaching New Religious Movements.* Edited by D. Bromley. New York: Oxford University Press.

Barlow, Philip L. 1991. *Mormons and the Bible: The Place of the Latter-day Saints in American Religion.* New York: Oxford University Press.

Barnouw, Victor. 1982. *An Introduction to Anthropology: Ethnology.* 4th ed. Homewood, IL: Dorsey Press.

Baroja, Julio Caro. 1964. *The World of the Witches.* Chicago: University of Chicago Press.

Barrett, David, George Kurian, and Todd Johnson, eds. 2001. *World Christian Encyclopedia.* 2 vols. New York: Oxford University Press.

Barro, Robert, Jason Hwang, and Rachel McCleary. 2010. "Religious Conversion in 40 Countries." *Journal for the Scientific Study of Religion* 49(1):15–36.

Bartkowski, John P. 2001. *Remaking the Godly Marriage: Gender Negotiation in Evangelical Families.* New Brunswick, NJ: Rutgers University Press.

Bartkowski, John P. and Jen'nan Ghazal Read. 2003. "Veiled Submission: Gender, Power, and Identity Among Evangelical and Muslim Women in the United States." *Qualitative Sociology* 26:71–92.

Basch, Linda, Nina Glick Schiller, and Cristina Szanton Blanc. 1994. *Nations Unbound: Transnational Projects, Postcolonial Predicaments, and Deterritorialized Nation-States.* London: Gordon and Breach.

Batson, C. Daniel. 1977. "Experimentation in Psychology of Religion: An Impossible Dream." *Journal for the Scientific Study of Religion* (December):413–418.

Batson, C. Daniel, Patricia Schoenrade, and W. Larry Ventis. 1993. *Religion and the Individual: A Social-Psychological Perspective.* New York: Oxford University Press.

Baumann, Martin and Kurt Salentin. 2006. "Migrant Religiousness and Social Incorporation: Tamil Hindus From Sri Lanka in Germany." *Journal of Contemporary Religion* 21:297–323.

Bayer, Alan E. 1975. "Sexist Students in American Colleges: A Descriptive Note." *Journal of Marriage and the Family* (May):391–396.

Beck, Marc. 1978. "Pluralist Theory and Church Policy Positions on Racial and Sexual Equality." *Sociological Analysis* (Winter):338–350.

Becker, Howard. 1932. *Systematic Sociology.* New York: Wiley.

Beckford, James A. 1985. *Cult Controversies: The Societal Response to the New Religious Movements.* London: Tavistock.

Bell, Daniel. 1976. *The Cultural Contradictions of Capitalism.* New York: Basic Books.

Bellah, Robert N. 1967. "Civil Religion in America." *Dædalus* 96(1):1–21.

Bellah, Robert N. 1970a. "Christianity and Symbolic Realism." *Journal for the Scientific Study of Religion* (Summer):89–96.

Bellah, Robert N. [1967] 1970b. "Civil Religion in America." Pp. 168–215 in *Beyond Belief: Essays on Religion in a Post-Traditional World.* New York: Harper & Row.

Bellah, R. N. 1970c. "Religious Evolution." Pp. 20–50 in *Beyond Belief: Essays on Religion in a Post-Traditional World.* New York: Harper & Row.

Bellah, Robert N. 1975. *The Broken Covenant: American Civil Religion in Time of Trial.* New York: Seabury Press.

Bellah, Robert N., Richard Madsen, William M. Sullivan, Ann Swidler, and Steven M. Tipton. 1985. *Habits of the Heart: Individualism and Commitment in American Life.* Berkeley: University of California Press.

Bender, Courtney. 2010. *The New Metaphysicals: Spirituality and the American Religious Imagination.* Chicago: University of Chicago Press.

Bengtson, Vern, Casey Copen, Norella Putney, and Merril Silverstein. 2009. "A Longitudinal Study of the Intergenerational Transmission of Religion." *International Sociology* 24:325–345.

Benokraitis, Nijole V. 2010. *Marriages and Families: Changes, Choices, and Constraints.* 12th ed. Englewood Cliffs, NJ: Prentice Hall.

Benz, Ernest. 1964. "On Understanding Non-Christian Religions." Pp. 3–9 in *Religion, Culture, and Society*, edited by L. Schneider. New York: Wiley.

Berger, Helen A. 1999. *A Community of Witches: Contemporary Neo-paganism and Witchcraft in the United States.* Columbia: University of South Carolina Press.

Berger, Peter L. 1967. *The Sacred Canopy.* Garden City, NY: Doubleday.

Berger, Peter L. 1974. "Some Second Thoughts on Substantive Versus Functional Definitions of Religion." *Journal for the Scientific Study of Religion* (June):125–133.

Berger, Peter L. 1979. *The Heretical Imperative.* Garden City, NY: Anchor Press.

Berger, Peter L. 1981. "The Class Struggle in American Religion." *The Christian Century* (February): 194–200.

Berger, Peter L. 2008. "'You Can Do It!' Two Cheers for the Prosperity Gospel." *Books & Culture* (September–October). Retrieved from www.book sandculture.com/articles/2008/sepoct/10.14.html

Berger, Peter L. and Thomas Luckmann. 1966. *The Social Construction of Reality.* Garden City, NY: Doubleday.

Berman, Harold J. 1991. "Law and Religion in the Development of a World Order." *Sociological Analysis* (Spring):27–36.

Berry, Brewton and Henry L. Tischler. 1978. *Race and Ethnic Relations.* 4th ed. Boston: Houghton Mifflin.

Besecke, Kelly. 2013. *You Can't Put God in a Box: Thoughtful Spirituality in a Rational Age.* New York: Oxford University Press.

Beyer, Peter. 2000. "Secularization From the Perspective of Globalization." Pp. 81–93 in *The Secularization Debate.* Edited by W. H. Swatos Jr. and D. V. A. Olson. Lanham, MD: Rowman & Littlefield.

Beyer, Peter. 2007. "Globalization and Glocalization." Pp. 88–117 in *Sage Handbook of the Sociology of Religion.* Edited by J. Beckford and N. J. Demerath III. Los Angeles: Sage.

Beyerlein, Kraig. 2004. "Specifying the Impact of Conservative Protestantism on Educational Attainment." *Journal for the Scientific Study of Religion* 42:505–518.

Beyerlein, Kraig and Mark Chaves. 2003. "The Political Activities of Religious Congregations in the United States." *Journal for the Scientific Study of Religion* 42:229–246.

Bibby, Reginald W. 1978. "Why Conservative Churches Really Are Growing: Kelley Revisited." *Journal for the Scientific Study of Religion* (June):129–138.

Bibby, Reginald W. 1979. "Religion and Modernity: The Canadian Case." *Journal for the Scientific Study of Religion* (March):1–17.

Bibby, Reginald W. 1987. *Fragmented Gods: The Poverty and Potential of Religion in Canada.* Toronto: Irwin.

Bibby, Reginald W. 2002. *Restless Gods: The Renaissance of Religion in Canada.* Toronto: Stoddard.

Bibby, Reginald W. and Merlin B. Brinkerhoff. 1973. "The Circulation of the Saints: A Study of People Who Join Conservative Churches." *Journal for the Scientific Study of Religion* (September):273–283.

Bibby, Reginald W. and Merlin B. Brinkerhoff. 1983. "The Circulation of the Saints Revisited." *Journal for the Scientific Study of Religion* (September):253–262.

Bibby, Reginald W. and Merlin B. Brinkerhoff. 1992. "On the Circulatory Problems of Saints: A Response to Perrin and Mauss." *Review of Religious Research* (December):170–175.

Bibby, Reginald W. and Merlin B. Brinkerhoff. 1994. "Circulation of the Saints, 1966–1990: New Data, New Reflections." *Journal for the Scientific Study of Religion* (September):273–280.

Bickerton, Ian. 2003. "Bank Makes an Issue of Mystic's Mint." *Financial Times* (February 8):9.

Billig, Michael. 1995. *Banal Nationalism.* Thousand Oaks, CA: Sage.

Bird, Phyllis. 1974. "Images of Women in the Old Testament." Pp. 41–88 in *Religion and Sexism.* Edited by R. R. Ruether. New York: Simon & Schuster.

Bird, Warren. 2014. *Leadership Network/Generis Multisite Church Scorecard: Faster Growth, More New Believers and Greater Lay Participation.* Dallas: Leadership Network. Retrieved from leadnet.org

Bird, Warren and Scott Thumma. 2011. *A New Decade of Megachurches: 2011 Profile of Large Attendance Churches in the United States.* Retrieved from hirr.hartsem.edu/megachurch/ New-Decade-of-Megachurches-2011Profile.pdf

Blanchard, Dallas A. and Terry J. Prewitt. 1993. *Religious Violence and Abortion: The Gideon Project.* Gainesville: University Press of Florida.

Bloch, Jon P. 2001. "The New and Improved Clint Eastwood: Change and Persistence in Promise Keepers Self-Help Literature." Pp. 11–31 in *Promise Keepers and the New Masculinity: Private Lives and Public Morality.* Edited by R. H. Williams. Lanham, MD: Lexington Books.

Bogan, Jesse. 2009. *America's Biggest Megachurches* (June 26). Retrieved from www.forbes .com/2009/06/26/americas-biggest-mega-churches-business-megachurches.html

Boli, John and David Brewington. 2007. "Religious Organizations." Pp. 203–232 in *Religion, Globalization, and Culture.* Edited by P. Beyer and L. Beaman. Leiden: Brill.

Boli, John and George Thomas. 1999. *Constructing World Culture: International Nongovernmental Organizations Since 1875.* Stanford, CA: Stanford University Press.

Bonifacio, Glenda Tibe and Vivienne S. M. Angeles. 2010. *Gender, Religion, and Migration: Pathways of Integration.* Lanham, MD: Lexington Books.

Bonilla-Silva, Eduardo. 2009. *Racism Without Racists: Color-Blind Racism and the Persistence of Racial Inequality in the United States.* New York: Rowman & Littlefield.

Borg, Marcus. 2001. *Reading the Bible Again for the First Time.* San Francisco: HarperCollins.

Borg, Marcus J. 2011. *Speaking Christian.* New York: HarperCollins.

Bowler, Kate. 2013. *Blessed: A History of the American Prosperity Gospel.* New York: Oxford University Press.

Bowles, Samuel and Herbert Gintis. 1976. *Schooling in Capitalist America.* New York: Basic Books.

Brasher, Brenda. 1998. *Godly Women: Fundamentalism and Female Power.* New Brunswick, NJ: Rutgers University Press.

Brasher, Brenda. 2004. *Gimme That Online Religion.* New Brunswick, NJ: Rutgers University Press.

Breault, Kevin. 1989a. "New Evidence on Religious Pluralism, Urbanism, and Religious Participation." *American Sociological Review* 54:1048–1053.

Breault, Kevin. 1989b. "A Reexamination of the Relationship Between Religious Diversity and Religious Adherents." *American Sociological Review* 54:1056–1059.

Brecher, Jeremy, Tim Costello, and Brendan Smith. 2006. "Globalization and Social Movements." Pp. 330–347 in *Globalization: The Transformation of Social Worlds.* Edited by D. S. Eitzen and M. B. Zinn. Belmont, CA: Wadsworth.

Brightman, Edgar Sheffield. 1940. *A Philosophy of Religion.* New York: Greenwood Press.

Bromley, David G. 1991. "Satanism: The New Cult Scare." Pp. 49–72 in *The Satanism Scare.* Edited by J. T. Richardson, J. Best, and D. G. Bromley. New York: Aldine de Gruyter.

Bromley, David G. 1997. "Remembering the Future: A Sociological Narrative of Crisis Episodes, Collective Action, Culture Workers, and Countermovements." *Sociology of Religion* (Summer):105–140.

Bromley, David G. 2007. "Methodological Issues in the Study of New Religious Movements." Pp. 65–90 in *Teaching New Religious Movements.* Edited by D. Bromley. New York: Oxford University Press.

Bromley, David G. 2009. "New Religions as a Specialist Field of Study." Pp. 723–741 in *The Oxford Handbook of the Sociology of Religion.* Edited by P. Clarke. New York: Oxford University Press.

Bromley, D. G. and Bruce C. Busching. 1988. "Understanding the Structure of Contractual and Covenantal Social Relations: Implications for the Sociology of Religion." *Sociological Analysis* (December), 15S–32S.

Bromley, David G. and J. Gordon Melton, eds. 2002. *Cults, Religion, and Violence.* New York: Cambridge University Press.

Bromley, David G. and Anson D. Shupe Jr. 1979. *Moonies in America: Cult, Church, and Crusade.* Beverly Hills, CA: Sage.

Bromley, David G. and Anson D. Shupe Jr. 1981. *Strange Gods: The Great American Cult Scare.* Boston: Beacon Press.

Brooke, Grant. 2011. "The Case for the Prosperity Gospel." *Huffington Post*, May 25. Retrieved from www.huffingtonpost.com/grant-brooke-mdiv/the-doubters-case-for-the_b_746062.html

Bruce, Steve. 1995. "The Truth About Religion in Britain." *Journal for the Scientific Study of Religion* (December):417–430.

Bruce, Steve. 1999. *Choice and Religion: A Critique of Rational Choice Theory.* Oxford: Oxford University Press.

Bruce, Steve. 2002. *God Is Dead: Secularization in the West.* Oxford: Blackwell.

Bruce, Tricia Colleen. 2011. *Faithful Revolution: How Voice of the Faithful Is Changing the Church.* New York: Oxford University Press.

Budde, Michael L. 1992. *The Two Churches: Catholicism and Capitalism in the World System.* Durham, NC: Duke University Press.

Bullough, Vern L. 1973. *The Subordinate Sex: A History of Attitudes Toward Women.* Urbana: University of Illinois Press.

Bunt, Gary. 2009. "Religion and the Internet." Pp. 705–720 in *The Oxford Handbook of the Sociology of Religion.* Edited by P. Clarke. Oxford: Oxford University Press.

Burawoy, Michael. 1987. "The Limits of Wright's Analytical Marxism and an Alternative." *Berkeley Journal of Sociology* 32:51–72.

Burgess, Ernest W. 1916. *The Function of Socialization in Social Evolution.* Chicago: University of Chicago Press.

Burke, Kenneth. 1935. *Permanence and Change.* New York: New Republic.

Burrow, Rufus, Jr. 1999. *Personalism: A Critical Introduction.* St. Louis, MO: Chalice Press.

Burrow, Rufus, Jr. 2006. *God and Human Dignity: The Personalism, Theology, and Ethics of Martin Luther King, Jr.* Notre Dame, IN: Notre Dame University Press.

Burstein, Paul. 2007. "Jewish Educational and Economic Success in the United States: A Search for Explanations." *Sociological Perspectives* 50:209–228.

Burtchaell, James. 1998. *The Dying of the Light: The Disengagement of Colleges and Universities From Their Christian Churches.* Grand Rapids, MI: Eerdmans.

Byrne, Donn and Carl McGraw. 1964. "Interpersonal Attraction Toward Negroes." *Human Relations* (August):201–213.

Byrne, Donn and Terry J. Wong. 1962. "Racial Prejudice, Interpersonal Attraction, and Assumed Dissimilarity of Attitudes." *Journal of Abnormal and Social Psychology* (October): 246–253.

Cadge, Wendy and Elaine Howard Ecklund. "Immigration and Religion." *Annual Review of Sociology* 33:359–379.

Cainkar, Louise A. 2009. *Homeland Insecurity: The Arab American and Muslim American Experience After 9/11.* New York: Russell Sage Foundation.

Campbell, Colin. 1983. "Romanticism and the Consumer Ethic: Intimations of a Weber-Style Thesis." *Sociological Analysis* 44:279–296.

Campbell, Ernest Q. and Thomas F. Pettigrew. 1959. *Christians in Racial Crisis.* Washington, DC: Public Affairs Press.

Campbell, George V. P. 2005. *Everything You Know Seems Wrong: Globalization and the Relativization of Tradition.* Lanham, MD: University Press of America.

Campbell, Heidi, ed. 2013. *Digital Religion: Understanding Religious Practice in New Media Worlds.* Routledge, London.

Cantrell, Randolph, James Krile, and George Donohue. 1983. "Parish Autonomy: Measuring Denominational Differences." *Journal for the Scientific Study of Religion* 22:276–287.

Caplow, Theodore, Howard Bahr, and Bruce Chadwick. 1983. *All Faithful People: Change and Continuity in Middletown's Religion.* Minneapolis: University of Minnesota Press.

Carden, Maren Lockwood. 1969. *Oneida.* New York: Harper & Row.

Carl, Noah and Francesco C. Billari. 2014. "Generalized Trust and Intelligence in the United States." *PLoS ONE* 9(3):e91786. doi:10.1371/journal.pone.0091786

Carpenter, Dale. 2012. *Flagrant Conduct: The Story of Lawrence v. Texas: How a Bedroom Arrest Decriminalized Gay Americans.* New York: Norton.

Carus, Carl G. [1853] 1925. In *Symbolik der Menschlichen Gestalt.* Edited by T. Lessing. Celle: N. Kampmann.

Casanova, Jose. 2001. "Religion, the New Millennium, and Globalization." *Sociology of Religion* (Winter):415–441.

Castells, Manuel. 2003. *The Internet Galaxy: Reflections on the Internet, Business, and Society.* New York: Oxford University Press.

Cauthen, Kenneth. 1962. *The Impact of American Religious Liberalism.* New York: Harper & Row.

Chang, Patricia M. Y. 1997. "Female Clergy in the Contemporary Protestant Church: A Current Assessment." *Journal for the Scientific Study of Religion* (December):565–573.

Chaves, Mark. 1993. "Denominations as Dual Structures: An Organizational Analysis." *Sociology of Religion* (Summer):147–169.

Chaves, Mark. 1994. "Secularization as Declining Religious Authority." *Social Forces* (March): 749–774.

Chaves, Mark. 1997. *Ordaining Women: Culture and Conflict in Religious Organizations*. Cambridge, MA: Harvard University Press.

Chaves, Mark. 2004. *Congregations in America.* Cambridge, MA: Harvard University Press.

Chaves, Mark. 2011. *American Religion: Contemporary Trends*. Princeton, NJ: Princeton University Press.

Chaves, Mark and Shawna Anderson. 2008. "Continuity and Change in American Congregations: Introducing the Second Wave of the National Congregations Study." *Sociology of Religion* 69(Winter):415–440.

Chaves, Mark and Shawna L. Anderson. 2014. "Changing American Congregations: Findings From the Third Wave of the National Congregations Study." *Journal for the Scientific Study of Religion* 53 (December):676–686.

Chaves, Mark and David Cann. 1992. "Regulation, Pluralism, and Religious Market Structure: Explaining Religion's Vitality." *Rationality and Society* 4:272–290.

Chaves, Mark and James Cavendish. 1997. "Recent Changes in Ordination Conflicts: The Effect of a Social Movement on Interorganizational Controversy." *Journal for the Scientific Study of Religion* (December):574–584.

Chaves, Mark and Phillip S. Gorski. 2001. "Religious Pluralism and Religious Participation." *Annual Review of Sociology* 27:261–281.

Chaves, Mark, Mary Ellen Konieczny, Kraig Beyerlein, and Emily Barman. 1999. "The National Congregations Study: Background, Methods, and Selected Results." *Journal for the Scientific Study of Religion* 38(4):458–476.

Chaves, Mark and John Sutton. 2004. "Organizational Consolidation in American Protestant Denominations, 1890–1990." *Journal for the Scientific Study of Religion* 43:51–66.

Chaves, Mark and William Tsitsos. 2001. "Congregations and Social Services: What They Do, How They Do It, and With Whom." *Nonprofit and Voluntary Sector Quarterly* 30:660–683.

Cherlin, Andrew. 2013. *Public and Private Families: An Introduction*. 7th ed. New York: McGraw-Hill.

Cherry, Conrad, Betty DeBerg, and Amanda Porterfield. 2001. *Religion on Campus*. Chapel Hill: University of North Carolina Press.

Chesnut, R. Andrew. 2010. "Conservative Christian Competitors: Pentecostals and Charismatic Catholics in Latin America's New Religious Economy." *SAIS Review* 30:91–103.

Christerson, Brad, Korie L. Edwards, and Michael O. Emerson. 2005. *Against All Odds: The Struggle for Racial Integration in Religious Organizations.* New York: NYU Press.

Chua, Amy. 2006. "Globalizing Hate." Pp. 234–238 in *Globalization: The Transformation of Social Worlds.* Edited by S. D. Eitzen and M. B. Zinn. Belmont, CA: Wadsworth.

Cimino, Richard and Don Lattin. 2002. *Shopping for Faith: American Religion in the New Millennium.* San Francisco: Jossey-Bass.

Clinebell, Howard J. 1965. *Mental Health Through Christian Community.* Nashville, TN: Abingdon Press.

Coakley, Jay. 2007. *Sports in Society: Issues and Controversies.* Boston: McGraw-Hill.

Cobb, Jennifer. 1998. *Cybergrace: The Search for God in the Digital World.* New York: Random House.

Codone, Susan. 2014. "Megachurch Pastor Twitter Activity: An Analysis of Rick Warren and Andy Stanley, Two of America's Social Pastors." *Journal of Religion, Media, & Digital Culture* 3 (August):1–32. Retrieved from jrmdc.com/wp-content/uploads/2014/09/Codone-Megachurch-Pastors.pdf

Cohen, Jere. 2002. *Protestantism and Capitalism: The Mechanisms of Influence.* New York: Aldine de Gruyter.

Cohen, Steven M. 1983. *American Modernity and Jewish Identity.* New York: Tavistock.

Cohen, Yoel. 2012. *God, Jews and the Media: Religion and Israel's Media.* New York: Routledge.

Cohn, Norman. 1964. "Medieval Millenarism: Its Bearing on the Comparative Study of Millenarian Movements." Pp. 168–181 in *Religion, Culture, and Society.* Edited by L. Schneider. New York: Wiley.

Coleman, James S. 1988. "Social Capital in the Creation of Human Capital." *American Journal of Sociology* 94(Supplement):S95–S120."

Coleman, Simon. 1993. "Conservative Protestantism and the World Order: The Faith Movement in the United States and Sweden." *Sociology of Religion* (Winter):353–373.

Coleman, Simon. 2000. *The Globalisation of Charismatic Christianity: Spreading the Gospel of Prosperity.* Cambridge: Cambridge University Press.

Collett, Jessica and Omar Lizardo. 2009. "A Power-Control Theory of Gender and Religiosity." *Journal for the Scientific Study of Religion* 48:213–231.

Collins, Randall. 1980. "Weber's Last Theory of Capitalism: A Systematization." *American Sociological Review* 45(December):925–942.

Commission for Religious Relations With the Jews. 1988. *We Remember: A Reflection on the Shoah.* Retrieved from http://www.vatican.va/roman_curia/pontifical_councils/chrstuni/documents/rc_pc_chrstuni_doc_16031998_shoah_en.html

Condran, John G. and Joseph B. Tamney. 1985. Religious "Nones": 1957 to 1982. *Sociological Analysis* (Winter):415–424.

Cone, James H. 1969. *Black Theology and Black Power.* New York: Seabury Press.

Cone, James H. 1970. *Liberation.* Philadelphia: Lippincott.

Cone, James H. 1972. *The Spirituals and the Blues.* Westport, CT: Greenwood Press.

Cornwall, Marie. 1987. "The Social Bases of Religion: A Study of Factors Influencing Religious Belief and Commitment." *Review of Religious Research* (September):44–56.

Cornwell, John. 1999. *Hitler's Pope: The Secret History of Pius XII.* New York: Viking.

Coser, Lewis A. 1954. *The Functions of Social Conflict.* New York: Free Press.

Coser, Lewis A. 1967. *Continuities in the Study of Social Conflict.* New York: Free Press.

Council on American–Islamic Relations. 2014. *Vision, Mission, Core Principles.* Retrieved from www.cair.com/about-us/vision-mission-core-principles.html

Cowan, Douglas. 2007. "Religion on the Internet." In *Sage Handbook of the Sociology of Religion.* Edited by J. Beckford and N. J. Demerath III. Thousand Oaks, CA: Sage.

Cox, Edwin. 1967. *Sixth Form Religion.* London: SCM Press.

Cox, Harvey. 1964. *On Not Leaving It to the Snake.* New York: Macmillan.

Cox, Harvey. 2009. *The Future of Faith.* New York: HarperCollins.

Craig, Steve. 2004. "How America Adopted Radio: Demographic Differences in Set Ownership Reported in the 1930–1950 U.S. Censuses." *Journal of Broadcasting & Electronic Media* 48:179–195.

Cristi, Marcela and Lorne L. Dawson. 2007. "Civil Religion in America and in Global Context." Pp. 251–276 in *Handbook of Sociology of Religion.* Edited by J. Beckford and N. J. Demerath III. London: Sage.

Daly, Mary. 1970. "Women and the Catholic Church." Pp. 124–138 in *Sisterhood Is Powerful.* Edited by R. Morgan. New York: Vintage Books.

D'Antonio, William V., Michele Dillon, and Mary L. Gautier. 2013. *American Catholics in Transition.* Lanham, MD: Rowman & Littlefield.

Darley, J. M. and C. Daniel Batson. 1973. "From Jerusalem to Jericho: A Study of Situational and Dispositional Variables in Helping Behavior." *Journal of Personality and Social Psychology* (July):100–108.

Darnell, Alfred and Darren Sherkat. 1997. "The Impact of Protestant Fundamentalism on Educational Attainment." *American Sociological Review* 62:306–316.

Davidman, Lynn. 1990. "Accommodation and Resistance to Modernity: A Comparison of Two Contemporary Orthodox Jewish Groups." *Sociological Analysis* (Spring):35–51.

Davidman, Lynn. 1991. *Tradition in a Rootless World: Women Turn to Orthodox Judaism.* Berkeley: University of California Press.

Davidson, James D. 1977. "Socio-economic Status and Ten Dimensions of Religious Commitment." *Sociology and Social Research* (July):462–485.

Davidson, James D. and Ralph E. Pyle. 2011. *Ranking Faiths: Religious Stratification in America.* Lanham, MD: Rowman & Littlefield.

Davie, Grace. 1994. *Religion in Britain Since 1945: Believing Without Belonging.* Oxford: Blackwell.

Davie, Grace. 2000. *Religion in Modern Europe: A Memory Mutates.* Oxford: Oxford University Press.

Davies, John. 1993. *A History of Wales.* London: Penguin Books.

Davies, Thomas Richard. 2008. *The Rise and Fall of Transnational Civil Society: The Evolution of International Non-governmental Organizations Since 1839.* (Working Paper CUTP/003) (April). City University London, Centre for International Politics.

Davis, James A., Tom W. Smith, and Peter V. Marsden. 2003. *General Social Surveys, 1972–2002* [cumulativefile]. 2nd ICPSR version. Chicago, IL: National Opinion Research Center; Storrs, CT: Roper Center for Public Opinion Research, University of Connecticut; Ann Arbor, MI: Interuniversity Consortium for Political and Social Research.

Davis, Kingsley. 1949. *The Human Society*. New York: Macmillan.

Davis, Shannon N. and Theodore N. Greenstein. 2009. "Gender Ideology: Components, Predictors, and Consequences." *Annual Review of Sociology* 35:87–105.

Dawson, Lorne. 1990. "Self-affirmation, Freedom, and Rationality: Theoretically Elaborating 'active' Conversions." *Journal for the Scientific Study of Religion* (June):141–163.

Dawson, Lorne. 2009. "Church-Sect-Cult: Constructing Typologies of Religious Groups." Pp. 525–544 in *The Oxford Handbook of the Sociology of Religion*. Edited by P. Clarke. New York: Oxford University Press.

Dawson, Lorne and Douglas Cowan. 2004. *Religion Online: Finding Faith on the Internet*. New York: Routledge.

deGobineau, C. A. [1855] 1970. "Essay on the Inequality of the Human Races." In *Gobineau: Selected Political Writings*. Edited by M. Biddiss. London: Jonathon Cape.

Delhey, Jan and Kenneth Newton. 2005. "Predicting Cross-National Levels of Social Trust: Global Pattern or Nordic Exceptionalism?" *European Sociological Review* 21 (September):311–327.

Della Cava, Ralph. 2001. "Transnational Religions: The Roman Catholic Church in Brazil and the Orthodox Church in Russia." *Sociology of Religion* (Winter):535–550.

Demerath, N. J., III. 1965. *Social Class in American Protestantism*. Chicago: Rand McNally.

Demerath, N. J., III. 2000. "The Varieties of the Sacred Experience: Finding the Sacred in a Secular Grove." *Journal for the Scientific Study of Religion* (March):2–11.

Dempewolff, Judith Ann. 1974. "Some Correlates of Feminism." *Psychological Reports* (April): 671–676.

Denton, Melinda L. 2004. "Gender and Marital Decision Making: Negotiating Religious Ideology and Practice." *Social Forces* 82:1151–1180.

Denton, Melinda L. 2012. "Family Structure, Family Disruption, and Profiles of Adolescent Religiosity." *Journal for the Scientific Study of Religion* 51(1):42–64.

Denton, Melinda, Lisa Pearce, and Christian Smith. 2008. *Religion and Spirituality on the Path Through Adolescence, Research Report Number 8*. National Study of Youth and Religion, University of North Carolina at Chapel Hill.

Denzin, Norman K. 2009. *The Research Act: A Theoretical Introduction to Sociological Methods*. Chicago: Aldine Transaction.

Derrickson, Krystina. 2008. "Second Life and the Sacred: Islamic Space in a Virtual World." *Digital Islam*. Retrieved from http://www.digitalislam.eu/article.do?articleId=1877.

Deutscher, Irwin. 1966. "Words and Deeds: Social Science and Social Policy." *Social Problems* (Winter):235–254.

Deutscher, Irwin. 1973. *What We Say, What We Do*. Glenview, IL: Scott, Foresman.

DeYoung, Curtiss, Michael O. Emerson, George Yancey, and Karen Chai Kim. 2003. *United by Faith: The Multiracial Congregation as an Answer to the Problem of Race*. New York: Oxford University Press.

Dillon, Michele. 1996. "Cultural Differences in Abortion Discourse of the Catholic Church: Evidence From Four Countries." *Sociology of Religion* (January):25–36.

Dillon, Michele. 1999. *Catholic Identity: Balancing Reason, Faith, and Power*. Cambridge, UK: Cambridge University Press.

Dillon, Michele. 2007. "Age, Generation, and Cohort in American Religion and Spirituality." Pp. 526–548 in *The Sage Handbook of the Sociology of Religion*. Edited by J. Beckford and N. J. Demerath III. Thousand Oaks, CA: Sage.

Dillon, Michele and Paul Wink. 2007. *In the Course of a Lifetime: Tracing Religious Belief, Practice, and Change*. Berkeley: University of California Press.

DiMaggio, Paul and Walter Powell. 1983. "The Iron Cage Revisited: Institutional Isomorphism and Collective Rationality in Organizational Fields." *American Sociological Review* 48:147–160.

Djamba, Yanyi K., and Sitawa R. Kimuna. 2014. "Are Americans Really in Favor of Interracial Marriage? A Closer Look at When They Are Asked About Black-White Marriage for Their Relatives." *Journal of Black Studies* 45(6):528–544.

Dobbelaere, Karel. 1981. *Secularization: A Multidimensional Concept*. Beverly Hills, CA: Sage.

Dobbelaere, Karel. 2000. "Toward an Integrated Perspective of the Processes Related to the Descriptive Concept of Secularization." Pp. 21–39 in *The Secularization Debate*. Edited by W. H. Swatos Jr. and D. V. A. Olson. Lanham, MD: Rowman & Littlefield.

Domhoff, G. William. 2013. *Who Rules America? The Triumph of the Corporate Rich.* Columbus, OH: McGraw-Hill.

Dougherty, Kevin D., and Kimberly R. Huyser. 2008. "Racially Diverse Congregations: Organizational Identity and the Accommodation of Differences." *Journal for the Scientific Study of Religion* 47(1):23–43.

Douglas, Mary. 1966. *Purity and Danger.* London: Routledge and Kegan Paul.

Douglas, Mary. 1968. "Pollution." Pp. 336–341 in *International Encyclopedia of the Social Sciences.* Vol. XII, edited by D. Sills. New York: Macmillan and Free Press.

Douglass, Jane Dempsey. 1974. "Women and the Continental Reformation." Pp. 292–318 in *Religion and Sexism.* Edited by R. R. Ruether. New York: Simon & Schuster.

Downton, James V., Jr. 1979. *Sacred Journeys: The Conversion of Young Americans to Divine Light Mission.* New York: Columbia University Press.

Downton, James V., Jr. 1980. "An Evolutionary Theory of Spiritual Conversion and Commitment: The Case of Divine Light Mission." *Journal for the Scientific Study of Religion* (December): 381–396.

Du Bois, W. E. B. 1903. *The Souls of Black Folks.* Chicago: A. C. McClurg.

Durkheim, Émile. [1912] 1995. *The Elementary Forms of the Religious Life.* Translated by K. E. Fields. New York: Free Press.

Dynes, Russell R. 1955. "Church-Sect Typology and Socioeconomic Status." *American Sociological Review* (October):555–560.

Edgell, Penny, Joseph Gerteis, and Douglas Hartmann. 2006. Atheists as "Other": Moral Boundaries and Cultural Membership in American Society." *American Sociological Review* 71 (April):211–234.

Edwards, Jonathan. [1741] 1966. "Sinners in the Hands of an Angry God." Pp. 156–160 in *Jonathan Edwards: Basic Writings,* edited by O. E. Winslow. New York: New American Library.

Edwards, Korie L. 2008. *The Elusive Dream: The Power of Race in Multiracial Churches.* New York: Oxford University Press.

Edwards, Korie L., Brad Christerson, and Michael O. Emerson. 2013. "Race, Religious Organizations, and Integration." *Annual Review of Sociology* 39:211–228.

Eichler, Margrit. 1972. *Charismatic and Ideological Leadership in Secular and Religious Millenarian Movements: A Sociological Study.* PhD dissertation, Duke University. Ann Arbor, MI.

Eirich, Gregory M. 2012. "Parental Religiosity and Children's Educational Attainment in the United States." Pp. 183–203 in *Religion, Work and Inequality.* Edited by L. A. Keister, J. McCarthy, and R. Finke. Bingley, UK: Emerald.

Eisinga, Rob, Albert Felling, and Jan Peters. 1990. "Religious Belief, Church Involvement, and Ethnocentrism in the Netherlands." *Journal for the Scientific Study of Religion* 29(1): 54–75.

Eitzen, D. Stanley and Maxine Baca Zinn. 2006. *Globalization: The Transformation of Social Worlds.* Belmont, CA: Wadsworth.

Ekici, Tufan and Deniz Yucel. 2014. "What Determines Religious and Racial Prejudice in Europe? The Effects of Religiosity and Trust." *Social Indicators Research,* 1–29. DOI:10.1007/s11205-014-0674-y

Eliade, Mircea. 1959. *The Sacred and the Profane: The Nature of Religion.* Translated by W. R. Trask. New York: Harcourt, Brace World.

Elinsky, Rachel. 2005. "Religious Publishing for the Red State Consumers and Beyond." *Publishing Research Quarterly* 21:11–29.

Elver, Hilal. 2012. *The Headscarf Controversy: Secularism and Freedom of Religion.* New York: Oxford University Press.

Emerson, Michael O. (with Rodney Woo). 2006. *People of the Dream: Multiracial Congregations in the United States.* Princeton, NJ: Princeton University Press.

Emerson, Michael O. and Laura J. Essenburg. *What Is Marriage? Americans Dividing* (June 24). Retrieved from kinder.rice.edu/uploadedFiles/Kinder_Institute_for_Urban_Research/Publications/White_Papers/Marriage%20Definition%20White%20Paper.pdf

Emerson, Michael O., and Karen Chai Kim. 2003. "Multiracial Congregations: A Typology and Analysis of Their Development." *Journal for the Scientific Study of Religion* 42:217–227.

Emerson, Michael O., William Mirola, and Susanne Monahan. 2011. *Religion Matters: What Sociology Teaches Us About Religion in Our World.* Boston: Allyn & Bacon.

Emerson, Michael O. and Christian Smith. 2000. *Divided by Faith: Evangelical Religion and the Problem of Race in America.* New York: Oxford University Press.

Emerson, Robert M., Rachel I. Fretz, and Linda L. Shaw. 1995. *Writing Ethnographic Field Notes.* Chicago: University of Chicago Press.

Erickson, Joseph A. 1992. "Adolescent Religious Development and Commitment: A Structural Equation Model of the Role of Family, Peer Group, and Educational Influences." *Journal for the Scientific Study of Religion* 31:131–152.

Erikson, Kai. 1966. *Wayward Puritans.* New York: Wiley.

Erzen, Tanya. 2006. *Straight to Jesus: Sexual and Christian Conversions in the Ex-Gay Movement.* Berkeley: University of California Press.

Estus, Charles and Michael A. Overington. 1970. "The Meaning and End of Religiosity." *American Journal of Sociology* (March):760–778.

Fabian, Stephen Michael. 1992. *Space-Time of the Bororo of Brazil.* Gainesville: University Press of Florida.

Faith and Leadership. 2010. *Clergy Women Make Connections.* Durham, NC: Duke Divinity School. Retrieved from www.faithandleadership.com/features/articles/clergy-women-make-connections?page=full&print=true

Fallding, Harold. 1980. "An Overview of Mainline Protestantism in Canada and the United States of America." Pp. 249–257 in *Yearbook of American and Canadian Churches, 1980.* Edited by C. H. Jacquet, Jr. Nashville, TN: Abingdon Press.

Fanfani, Amintore. 1936. *Catholicism, Protestantism, and Capitalism.* New York: Sheed and Ward.

Farber, I. E., Harry F. Harlow, and Louis Jolyon West. 1951. "Brainwashing, Conditioning, and D. D. D. (Debility, Dependency, and Dread)." *Sociometry* (December):271–283.

Farley, John E. 2010. *Majority-Minority Relations.* 6th ed. Upper Saddle River, NJ: Prentice Hall.

Fauset, Arthur H. 1944. *Black Gods of the Metropolis.* Philadelphia: University of Pennsylvania Press.

Federal Bureau of Investigation. 2014. *2013 Hate Crime Statistics.* Retrieved from www.fbi.gov/about-us/cjis/ucr/hate-crime/2013

Ferguson, Marilyn. 1987. *The Aquarian Conspiracy.* Los Angeles: J. P. Tarcher.

Ferraro, Kenneth and Jessica Kelley-Moore. 2002. "Religious Consolation Among Men and Women: Do Health Problems Spur Seeking?" *Journal for the Scientific Study of Religion* 39:220–244.

Ferris, Elizabeth. 2005. *Faith-Based and Secular Humanitarian Organizations. International Review of the Red Cross* 87 (June):311–325.

Festinger, Leon, Henry W. Riecken, and Stanley Schachter. 1956. *When Prophecy Fails.* New York: Harper & Row.

Fialka, John. 2003. *Sisters: Catholic Nuns and the Making of America.* New York: St. Martin's Press.

Finke, Roger. 1990. "Religious Deregulation: Origins and Consequences." *Journal of Church and State* 32:609–626.

Finke, Roger. 1997. "The Consequences of Religious Competition: Supply-Side Explanations for Religious Change." Pp. 45–64 in *Rational Choice Theory and Religion: Summary and Assessment.* Edited by L. A. Young. New York: Routledge.

Finke, Roger and Rodney Stark. 1988. "Religious Economies and Sacred Canopies: Religious Mobilization in American Cities, 1906." *American Sociological Review* (February):41–49.

Finke, Roger and Rodney Stark. 1989. "Evaluating the Evidence: Religious Economies and Sacred Canopies." *American Sociological Review* 54:1054–1056.

Finke, Roger and Rodney Stark. 1992. *The Churching of America, 1776–1990: Winners and Losers in Our Religious Economy.* New Brunswick, NJ: Rutgers University Press.

Finke, Roger and Rodney Stark. 1998. "Religious Choice and Competition." *American Sociological Review* 63:761–766.

Finke, Roger and Rodney Stark. 2001. "The New Holiness Clubs: Testing Church-to-Sect Propositions." *Sociology of Religion* (Summer):175–189.

Finke, Roger and Rodney Stark. 2005. *The Churching of America, 1776–2005: Winners and Losers in Our Religious Economy.* 2nd ed. New Brunswick, NJ: Rutgers University Press.

Fitzgerald, Scott T. and Jennifer L. Glass. 2012. "Conservative Protestants, Early Transitions to Adulthood, and the Intergenerational Transmission of Class." Pp. 49–72 in *Religion, Work and Inequality.* Edited by L. A. Keister, J. McCarthy, and R. Finke. Bingley, UK: Emerald.

Fitzgerald, Scott T., and Jennifer L. Glass. 2014. "Conservative Protestants, Normative Pathways, and Adult Attainment." Pp. 97–118 in *Religion and Inequality: Research and Theory on Religion's Role in Stratification.* Edited by L. A. Keister and D. E. Sherkat. Cambridge: Cambridge University Press, p. 100.

Flint, Richard. 2008. *No Settlement, No Conquest: A History of the Coronado Entrada.* Albuquerque: University of New Mexico Press.

Flory, Richard and Donald Miller. 2008. *Finding Faith: The Spiritual Quest of the Post-Boomer Generation.* New Brunswick, NJ: Rutgers University Press.

Form, William. 2000. "Italian Protestants: Religion, Ethnicity, and Assimilation." *Journal for the Scientific Study of Religion* (September):307–320.

Francis, Mark. 2000. *Shape a Circle Ever Wider: Liturgical Inculturation in the United States.* Chicago: Liturgy Training.

Frank, Mark G. and Thomas Gilovich. 1988. "The Dark Side of Self- and Social Perception: Black Uniforms and Aggression in Professional Sports" *Journal of Personality and Social Psychology* 54(1):74–85.

Frankl, Razelle. 1987. *Televangelism: The Marketing of Popular Religion.* Carbondale: Southern Illinois University Press.

Frankl, Victor. 1963. *Man's Search for Meaning.* New York: Washington Square Press.

Frazier, E. Franklin. 1957. *Negroes in the United States.* Rev. ed. New York: Macmillan.

Frazier, E. Franklin. 1963. *The Negro Church in America.* New York: Schocken Books.

Fredman, Ruth Gruber. 1981. *The Passover Seder.* Philadelphia: University of Pennsylvania Press.

Freese, Jeremy. 2004. "Risk Preferences and Gender Differences in Religiousness: Evidence From the World Values Survey." *Review of Religious Research* 46:88–91.

Freston, Paul. 2007. "Evangelicalism and Fundamentalism: The Politics of Global Popular Protestantism." Pp. 205–226 in *The Sage Handbook of the Sociology of Religion.* Edited by J. Beckford and N. J. Demerath III. Thousand Oaks, CA: Sage.

Froese, Paul and Christopher D. Bader. 2010. *America's Four Gods: What We Say About God and What That Says About Us.* New York: Oxford University Press.

Fukuyama, Yoshio. 1961. "The Major Dimensions of Church Membership." *Review of Religious Research* (Spring):154–161.

Fuller, Thomas. 2013. "Extremism Rises Among Myanmar Buddhists." *New York Times* (June 20). Retrieved from www.nytimes.com/2013/06/21/world/asia/extremism-rises-among-myanmar-buddhists-wary-of-muslim-minority.html

Fulton, Aubyn S., Richard L. Gorsuch, and Elizabeth A. Manard. 1999. "Religious Orientation, Antihomosexual Sentiment, and Fundamentalism Among Christians." *Journal for the Scientific Study of Religion* (March):14–22.

Gaddy, Gary. 1984. "The Power of the Religious Media: Religious Broadcast Use and the Role of Religious Organizations in Public Affairs." *Review of Religious Research* (June):289–302.

Gaertner, Samuel L. and John F. Dovidio. 1986. "The Aversive Form of Racism." Pp. 61–89 in *Prejudice, Discrimination, and Racism: Theory and Research.* Edited by J. F. Dovidio and S. L. Gaertner. San Diego, CA: Academic Press.

Gallagher, Sally K. 2003. *Evangelical Identity and Gendered Family Life.* New Brunswick, NJ: Rutgers University Press.

Gallagher, Sally K. and Christian Smith. 1999. "Symbolic Traditionalism and Pragmatic Egalitarianism: Contemporary Evangelicals, Family, and Gender." *Gender and Society* 13:211–233.

Gallup. 1987. *The Gallup Report: Religion in America.* Princeton, NJ: Author.

Gallup. 2000. *Gallup Poll Topics: A–Z.* Retrieved from www.gallup.com/poll/indicators/indreligion.asp

Gallup. 2009. *Muslim Americans: A National Portrait. The Muslim West Facts Project.* Retrieved from www.gallup.com/strategicconsulting/153572/REPORT-Muslim-Americans-National-Portrait.aspx

Gallup. 2013. *Islamophobia: Understanding Anti-Muslim Sentiment in the West.* Retrieved from www.gallup.com/poll/157082/islamophobia-understanding-anti-muslim-sentiment-west.aspx

Gallup, George, Jr. and D. Michael Lindsay. 1999. *Surveying the Religious Landscape: Trends in U.S. Beliefs.* Harrisburg, PA: Morehouse.

Gay, David A., Christopher G. Ellison, and Daniel A. Powers. 1996. "In Search of Denominational Subcultures: Religious Affiliation and 'pro-family' Issues Revisited." *Review of Religious Research* 38:3–17.

Geertz, Clifford. 1957. "Ritual and Social Change: A Javanese Example." *American Anthropologist* (February):32–54.

Geertz, Clifford. 1958. "Ethos, World View and the Analysis of Sacred Symbols." *The Antioch Review* (Winter):421–437.

Geertz, Clifford. 1966. "Religion as a Cultural System." Pp. 1–46 in *Anthropological Approaches to the Study of Religion*. Edited by M. Banton. London: Tavistock.

Geertz, Clifford. 1968. *Islam Observed: Religious Development in Morocco and Indonesia*. Chicago: University of Chicago Press.

Geertz, Clifford. 1973. "Thick Description: Toward an Interpretive Theory of Culture." Pp. 3–30 in *The Interpretation of Cultures: Selected Essays*. New York: Basic Books.

Gelfgren, Stefan. 2014. "Virtual Christian Places: Between Innovation and Tradition." *Online: Heidelberg Journal of Religions on the Internet* 6:42–65.

Gerbner, George, Larry Gross, Stewart Hoover, Michael Morgan, Nancy Signorilli, Harry Cotugno et al. 1984. *Religion and Television*. Philadelphia: University of Pennsylvania and The Gallup Organization.

Ghassem-Fachandi, Parvis. 2012. *Pogrom in Gujarat: Hindu Nationalism and Anti-Muslim Violence in India*. Princeton, NJ: Princeton University Press.

Gill, Sam D. 1982. *Native American Religions*. Belmont, CA: Wadsworth.

Gill, Sam D. 2004. *Native American Religions*. 2nd ed. Belmont, CA: Wadsworth.

Gillis, Chester. 1999. *Roman Catholicism in America*. New York: Columbia University Press.

Giulianotti, Richard and Roland Robertson. 2007. "Forms of Glocalization." *Sociology* 41:133–152.

Glock, Charles Y. and Rodney Stark. 1966. *Christian Beliefs and Anti-Semitism*. New York: Harper & Row.

Gmelch, George J. 1971. "Baseball Magic." *Transaction* (June):39–41, 54.

Goode, Erich. 1967. "Some Critical Observations on the Church-Sect Typology." *Journal for the Scientific Study of Religion* (April):69–77.

Goodstein, Laurie. 2010. "Lutherans Offer Warm Welcome to Gay Pastors." *New York Times* (July 25). Retrieved from www.nytimes.com/2010/07/26/us/26lutheran.html

Goodstein, Laurie and Dalia Sussman. 2010. "Catholics Criticize Pope on Abuse Scandal, but See Some Hope." *New York Times* (May 4). Retrieved from www.nytimes.com/2010/05/05/us/05poll.html

Gorski, Philip S. 2000. "Historicizing the Secularization Debate: Church, State, and Society in Late Medieval and Early Modern Europe, CA 1300 to 1700." *Social Forces* (February):138–167.

Gorski, Philip S. 2003. *The Disciplinary Revolution: Calvinism and the Rise of the State in Early Modern Europe*. Chicago: University of Chicago Press.

Gorski, Philip S. 2010. *A Neo-Weberian Theory of American Civil Religion* (January 8). Retrieved from blogs.ssrc.org/tif/2010/01/08/a-neo-weberian-theory-of-american-civil-religion/

Gorski, Philip S. and Gülay Türkmen-Dervişoğlu. 2013. "Religion, Nationalism, and Violence: An Integrated Approach." *Annual Review of Sociology* 39:193–210.

Gorsuch, Richard L. and Daniel Aleshire. 1974. "Christian Faith and Ethnic Prejudice: A Review and Interpretation of Research." *Journal for the Scientific Study of Religion* (September):281–307.

Graham, Billy. 1983. "The Future of T.V. Evangelism." *TV Guide* (March):4–11.

Gray, Mark, Mary Gautier, and Thomas Gaunt. 2014. "Cultural Diversity in the Catholic Church in the United States." Washington, DC: CARA. Retrieved from www.usccb.org/issues-and-action/cultural-diversity/upload/cultural-diversity-cara-report-phase-1.pdf

Greeley, Andrew M. 1970. "Religious Intermarriage in a Denominational Society." *American Journal of Sociology* 75: 949–952.

Greeley, Andrew M. 1972. *The Denominational Society*. Glenview, IL: Scott, Foresman.

Greeley, Andrew M. 1974. *Ethnicity in the United States*. New York: Wiley.

Greeley, Andrew M. 1995. *Religion as Poetry*. New Brunswick, NJ: Transaction Publishers.

Greeley, Andrew M. 2000. *The Catholic Imagination*. Berkeley: University of California Press.

Green, Robert W., ed. 1959. *Protestantism and Capitalism: The Weber Thesis and Its Critics*. Boston: Heath.

Gregg, Stephen E. 2014. "Fieldwork." Pp. 25–28 in *The Bloomsbury Companion to New Religious Movements*. Edited by G. D. Chryssides and B. E. Zeller. London: Bloomsbury.

Greil, Arthur L. and David R. Rudy. 1984. "What Have We Learned From Process Models of Conversion? An Examination of Ten Case Studies." *Sociological Focus* (October):305–323.

Gremillion, Joseph and Jim Castelli. 1987. *The Emerging Parish: The Notre Dame Study of Catholic Life Since Vatican II*. San Francisco: Harper & Row.

Grieve, Gregory. 2010. "Virtually Embodying the Field: Silent Online Buddhist Meditation, Immersion, and the Cardean Ethnographic Method." *Online: Heidelberg Journal of Religions on the Internet* 4:35–62.

Griffin, Glenn A., Richard L. Gorsuch, and Andrea Lee Davis. 1987. "A Cross-Cultural Investigation of Religious Orientation, Social Norms, and Prejudice." *Journal for the Scientific Study of Religion* (September):358–365.

Griffith, R. Marie. 2000. *God's Daughters: Evangelical Women and the Power of Submission.* Berkeley: University of California Press.

Groothius, Douglas. 1997. *The Soul in Cyber-Space.* Grand Rapids, MI: Baker Books.

Gross, Thomas K. and Carey W. English. 1998. "Bible Thumping Hits TV." *U.S. News and World Report* (January 26):47.

Guest, Matthew. 2009. "The Reproduction and Transmission of Religion." Pp. 652–670 in *The Oxford Handbook of the Sociology of Religion.* Edited by P. Clarke. New York: Oxford University Press.

Gunnoe, M. J. and K. A. Moore. 2002. "Predictors of Religiosity Among Youth Aged 17–22: A Longitudinal Study of the National Survey of Children." *Journal for the Scientific Study of Religion* 17:359–379.

Gusfield, J. R. 1963. *Symbolic Crusade: Status Politics and the American Temperance Movement.* Chicago: University of Chicago Press.

Guttmann, Allen. 1978. *From Ritual to Record: The Nature of Modern Sports.* New York: Columbia University Press.

Hadaway, Christopher Kirk, Penny L. Marler, and Mark Chaves. 1993. "What the Polls Don't Show: A Closer Look at U.S. Church Attendance." *American Sociological Review* (December):741–752.

Hadden, Jeffrey K. 1969. *The Gathering Storm in the Churches.* Garden City, NY: Doubleday.

Hadden, Jeffrey K. 1987. "Religious Broadcasting and the New Christian Right." *Journal for the Scientific Study of Religion* (March):1–24.

Hadden, Jeffrey K. 1990. "The Globalization of American Televangelism." *International Journal of Frontier Missions* (January):1–10.

Hadden, Jeffrey K. 1991. "The Globalization of American Televangelism." Pp. 221–244 in *Religion and Global Order.* Edited by R. Robertson and W. R. Garrett. New York: Paragon.

Hadden, Jeffrey K. and Anson D. Shupe Jr. 1988. *Televangelism: Power and Politics on God's Frontier.* New York: Holt.

Haederle, Michael. 1991. "Indian Artist Blends Catholic and Zuni Traditions in Murals." *Los Angeles Times* (December 25).

Halaby, Charles. 2004. "Panel Models in Sociological Research: Theory Into Practice." *Annual Review of Sociology* 30:507–544.

Hall, John R. 2002. "Mass Suicide and the Branch Davidians." Pp. 149–169 in *Cults, Religion, and Violence.* Edited by D. G. Bromley and J. G. Melton. New York: Cambridge University Press.

Hall, Mitchell. 1990. *Because of Their Faith: CALCAV and Religious Opposition to the Vietnam War.* New York: Columbia University Press.

Hamberg, Eva. 2009. "Unchurched Spirituality." Pp. 742–757 in *Oxford Handbook of the Sociology of Teligion,* edited by P. Clarke. Oxford: Oxford University Press.

Hamilton, Malcolm. 2009. "Rational Choice Theory: A Critique." Pp. 116–133 in *The Oxford Handbook of the Sociology of Religion.* Edited by P. Clark. New York: Oxford University Press.

Hammond, Phillip. 1992. *Religion and Personal Autonomy: The Third Disestablishment in America.* Columbia: University of South Carolina Press.

Hangen, Tona. 2002. *Redeeming the Dial: Radio, Religion, and Popular Culture in America.* Chapel Hill: University of North Carolina Press.

Hannan, Michael and Nancy Tuma. 1979. "Methods of Temporal Analysis." *Annual Review of Sociology* 5:303–328.

Hardie, Jessica Halliday, Lisa D. Pearce, and Melinda Lundquist Denton. 2013. "The Dynamics and Correlates of Religious Service Attendance in Adolescence." *Youth & Society.* DOI:0044118X13483777.

Hargrove, Barbara. 1979. *The Sociology of Religion.* Arlington Heights, IL: AHM.

Harper, Douglas. 2012. *Visual Sociology.* New York: Routledge.

Harrison, Milmon. 2005. *Righteous Riches: The Word of Faith Movement in Contemporary African American Religion.* New York: Oxford University Press.

Harrison, Rebecca. 2007. "African Anglicans to Snub Pro-Gay Rights U.S. Bishop." *Reuters.* Retrieved from www.reuters.com/article/idUSL0885356520070111

Hartley, Eugene L. 1946. *Problems in Prejudice.* New York: King's Crown Press.

Hawley, John Stratton. 1986. "Images of Gender in the Poetry of Krishna." Pp. 231–256 in *Gender and Religion.* Edited by C. W. Bynum, S. Harrell, and P. Richman. Boston: Beacon Press.

Hayden, Tom. 2006. "Seeking a New Capitalism in Chiapas." Pp. 328–354 in *Globalization: The Transformation of Social Worlds.* Edited by D. S. Eitzen and M. B. Zinn. Belmont, CA: Wadsworth.

Hayes, Bernadette C. 1995. "The Impact of Religious Identification on Political Attitudes." *Sociology of Religion* (Summer):177–194.

Heilman, Samuel. 1992. *Defenders of the Faith: Inside Ultra-Orthodox Jewry.* New York: Schocken Books.

Helland, Christopher. 2000. "Online-Religion/Religion-Online and Virtual Communities." Pp. 205–223 in *Religion on the Internet: Research Prospects and Promises.* Edited by J. K. Hadden and D. E. Cowan. London: JAIPress/Elsevier Science.

Helland, Christopher. 2007. *Turning Cyberspace Into Sacred Space: Examining the Religious Revolution Occurring on the World Wide Web.* Retrieved from video.google.com/videoplay?docid=-6186132236261787419&q=type%3Agoogle+engEDU

Henley, Nancy M. and Fred Pincus. 1978. "Interrelationship of Sexist, Racist and Homosexual Attitudes." *Psychological Reports* (February):83–90.

Herberg, Will. 1955. *Protestant-Catholic-Jew.* Garden City, NY: Doubleday.

Herbrechtsmeier, William. 1993. "Buddhism and the Definition of Religion: One More Time." *Journal for the Scientific Study of Religion* (March):1–18.

Herskovits, Melville. 1958. *The Myth of the Negro Past.* Boston: Beacon Press.

Hertel, Bradley R. and Michael Hughes. 1987. "Religious Affiliation, Attendance and Support for Profamily Issues in the United States." *Social Forces* 65:858–882.

Hertzke, Allen D. 1988. *Representing God in Washington: The Role of Religious Lobbies in the American Polity.* Knoxville: University of Tennessee Press.

Hesselbart, Susan. 1976. "A Comparison of Attitudes Toward Women and Attitudes Toward Blacks in a Southern City." *Sociological Symposium* (Fall):45–68.

Hesser, Gary and Andrew J. Weigert. 1980. "Comparative Dimensions of Liturgy: A Conceptual Framework and Feasibility Application." *Sociological Analysis* (Fall):215–229.

Hochschild, Arlie Russell. 2001. *The Time Bind: When Work Becomes Home and Home Becomes Work.* New York: Holt.

Hodson, Randy and Teresa A. Sullivan. 2012. *The Social Organization of Work.* 5th ed. Belmont, CA: Wadsworth.

Hoffmann, John P. and John P. Bartkowski. 2008. "Gender, Religious Tradition and Biblical Literalism." *Social Forces* 86:1245–1272.

Hoffman, Shirl. 1992. "Evangelicalism and the Revitalization of Religious Ritual in Sport." Pp. 111–125 in *Sport and Religion.* Edited by S. J. Hoffman. Champaign, IL: Human Kinetics.

Hoge, Dean R. and Jackson W. Carroll. 1978. "Determinants of Commitment and Participation in Suburban Protestant Churches." *Journal for the Scientific Study of Religion* (June):107–128.

Hoge, Dean R. and David A. Roozen. 1979. *Understanding Church Growth and Decline, 1950–1978.* New York: Pilgrim Press.

Homans, George C. 1941. "Anxiety and Ritual: The Theories of Malinowski and Radcliffe-Brown." *American Anthropologist* (April):164–172.

Hood, Ralph W., Jr., R. J. Morris, and P. J. Watson. 1989. "The Differential Report of Prayer Experience and Religious Orientation." *Review of Religious Research* 31:39–45.

Hoover, Stewart. 2009. "Religion and the Media." Pp. 688–704 in *The Oxford Handbook of the Sociology of Religion.* Edited by P. Clarke. Oxford: Oxford University Press.

Hoover, Stewart, L. S. Clark, and L. Rainie. 2004. *Faith Online.* Washington, DC: Pew Internet and American Life Project.

Hostetler, John A. 1993. *Amish Society.* 4th ed. Baltimore: Johns Hopkins University Press.

Hout, Michael and Claude Fischer. 2002. "Why More Americans Have No Religious Preference: Politics and Generations." *American Sociological Review* 67:165–190.

Hout, Michael and Claude Fischer. 2009. *The Politics of Religious Identity in the United States, 1974–2008* (August 9). Paper presented at the annual meeting of the American Sociological Association, San Francisco, CA.

Hout, Michael, Andrew Greeley, and Melissa Wilde. 2001. "The Demographic Imperative in Religious

Change in the United States." *American Journal of Sociology* 107:468–500.

Howe, Neil and William Strauss. 1993. *13th Gen: Abort, Retry, Ignore, Fail?* New York: Vintage Books.

Howe, Neil and William Strauss. 2000. *Millennials Rising: The Next Great Generation.* New York: Vintage Books.

Howes, Graham. 1991. "'God Damn Yanquis'— American Hegemony and Contemporary Latin American Christianity." Pp. 83–97 in *World Order and Religion.* Edited by W. C. Roof. Albany: State University of New York Press.

Hudson, Winthrop S. 1949. "Puritanism and the Spirit of Capitalism." *Church History* (March):3–17.

Human Rights Campaign. 2003. *Answers to Questions About Marriage Equality.* Washington, DC: Human Rights Campaign, Family Net Project.

Hummer, Robert, Richard Rogers, Charles Nam, and Christopher Ellison. 1999. "Religious Involvement and U.S. Adult Mortality." *Demography* 36:273–285.

Hunt, Larry L. and Janet G. Hunt. 1977. "Black Religion as Both Opiate and Inspiration of Civil Rights Militance: Putting Marx's Data to the Test." *Social Forces* (September):1–14.

Hunt, Stephen. 2007. "Religion as a Factor in Life and Death Through the Life-Course." Pp. 608–629 in *The Sage Handbook of the Sociology of Religion.* Edited by J. Beckford and N. J. Demerath III. Thousand Oaks, CA: Sage.

Hunter, James Davidson. 1983. *American Evangelicalism.* New Brunswick, NJ: Rutgers University Press.

Hutchings, Tim. 2011. "Contemporary Religious Community and the Online Community." *Information, Communication & Society* 14(8):1118–1135.

Iannaccone, Laurence R. 1982. "Let the Women Be Silent." *Sunstone* (May/June):38–45.

Iannaccone, Laurence R. 1990. "Religious Practice: A Human Capital Approach." *Journal for the Scientific Study of Religion* 29(3):297–314.

Iannaccone, Laurence R. 1992. "Religious Markets and the Economics of Religion." *Social Compass* 39:123–131.

Iannaccone, Laurence R. 1994. "Why Strict Churches Are Strong." *American Journal of Sociology* (March):1180–1211.

Iannaccone, Laurence R. 1995. "Voodoo Economics? Reviewing the Rational Choice Approach to Religion." *Journal for the Scientific Study of Religion* (March):76–88.

Iannaccone, Laurence R. 1997. "Rational Choice: Framework for the Scientific Study of Religion." Pp. 25–42 in *Rational Choice Theory and Religion: Summary and Assessment.* Edited by L. A. Young. New York: Routledge.

"Illinois Diocese Votes to Split From Church." 2008. *New York Times* (July 26). Retrieved from www.nytimes.com/2008/11/09/us/09quincy.html?ref=v_gene_robinson

Ingersoll, Julie J. 2015. *Building God's Kingdom: Inside the World of Christian Reconstruction.* New York: Oxford University Press.

Inglehart, Ronald and Pippa Norris. 2003. *Rising Ride: Gender Equality and Cultural Change Around the World.* Cambridge, UK: Cambridge University Press.

International Telecommunications Union. 2014. *The World in 2014: ICT Facts and Figures.* Geneva: International Telecommunications Union. Retrieved from www.itu.int/en/ITU-D/Statistics/Documents/facts/ICTFactsFigures2014-e.pdf

Investigative Staff of the Boston Globe. 2002. *Betrayal: The Crisis in the Catholic Church.* Boston: Little, Brown.

Jackson, Lynne M. and Bruce Hunsberger. 1999. "An Intergroup Perspective on Religion and Prejudice." *Journal for the Scientific Study of Religion* (December):509–523.

Jackson, Susan and Mihaly Csikszentmihalyi. 1999. *Flow in Sports: The Keys to Optimal Experiences and Performances.* Champaign, IL: Human Kinetics.

Jacobs, Janet. 1987. "Deconversion From Religious Movements." *Journal for the Scientific Study of Religion* (September):294–308.

James, Jonathan. 2010. *McDonaldization, Masala McGospel and Om Economics: Televangelism in Contemporary India.* New Delhi: Sage Publications India.

James, William. [1902] 1958. *Varieties of Religious Experience.* New York: New American Library.

Jansen, Bart. 2013. "'FlyRights' App by Sikh Coalition Allows Quick Reporting of Unfair TSA Profiling." *USA Today* (November 27). Retrieved from www.huffingtonpost.com/2013/11/27/fly-rights-app-sikh-coalition_n_4345101.html

Jansen, Bernard J., Andrea Tapia, and Amanda Spink. 2010. "Searching for Salvation: An Analysis of US Religious Searching on the World Wide Web." *Religion* 40:39–52.

Jelen, Ted G. 1995. "Religion and the American Political Culture: Alternative Models of Citizenship and Discipleship." *Sociology of Religion* (Fall):271–284.

Jenkins, J. Craig. 1977. "Radical Transformation of Organizational Goals." *Administrative Science Quarterly* (December):568–586.

Jenkins, Jack. 2014. "Yes Bill Maher, Muslims Win Nobel Peace Prizes Too." *Think Progress* (October 11). Retrieved from thinkprogress.org/world/2014/10/10/3578515/malala-nobel-peace-prize-muslim

Jenkins, Philip. 2000. *Mystics and Messiahs: Cults and New Religions in American History.* New York: Oxford University Press.

Jenkins, Philip. 2002. *The Next Christendom: The Coming of Global Christianity.* New York: Oxford University Press.

Jerryson, Michael K. 2011. *Buddhist Fury: Religion and Violence in Southern Thailand.* New York: Oxford University Press.

Jindra, Michael. 1994. "Star Trek Fandom as a Religious Phenomenon." *Sociology of Religion* (Spring):27–51.

Johnson, Benton. 1963. "On Church and Sect." *American Sociological Review* (August):539–549.

Johnson, Martin and Phil Mullins. 1992. "Mormonism: Catholic, Protestant, Different?" *Review of Religious Research* (September):51–62.

Johnson, Paul E. 1959. *Psychology of Religion.* Rev. ed. Nashville, TN: Abingdon Press.

Johnson, Stephen D. 2006. "Religion and Anti-Islamic Attitudes." *Review of Religious Research* 48(September):5–16.

Johnstone, Ronald L. 2007. *Religion in Society: A Sociology of Religion.* 7th ed. Upper Saddle River, NJ: Pearson Prentice Hall.

Jordan, Winthrop D. 1968. *White Over Black.* Baltimore: Penguin.

Judah, J. Stillson. 1974. *Hare Krishna and the Counterculture.* New York: Wiley.

Juergensmeyer, Mark. 2006. "Thinking Globally About Religion." Pp. 3–13 in *The Oxford Handbook of Global Religions.* Edited by M. Juergensmeyer. New York: Oxford University Press.

Kahoe, Richard D. 1974. "The Psychology and Theology of Sexism." *Journal of Psychology and Theology* (Fall):284–290.

Kalir, Barak. 2009. "Finding Jesus in the Holy Land and Taking Him to China: Chinese Temporary Migrant Workers in Israel Converting to Evangelical Christianity." *Sociology of Religion* 70:130–156.

Kalton, Graham. 1983. *Introduction to Survey Sampling.* Beverly Hills, CA: Sage.

Kanter, Rosabeth Moss. 1972. *Commitment and Community.* Cambridge, MA: Harvard University Press.

Karabel, Jerome. 2005. *The Chosen: The Hidden History of Admission and Exclusion at Harvard, Yale, and Princeton.* New York: Houghton Mifflin.

Kay, William K. 2009. "Pentecostalism and Religious Broadcasting." *Journal of Beliefs and Values* 30(3):245–254.

Keck, Margaret and Kathryn Sikkink. 1998. *Activists Beyond Borders: Advocacy Networks in International Politics.* Ithaca, NY: Cornell University Press.

Keister, Lisa A. 2003. "Religion and Wealth: The Role of Religious Affiliation and Participation in Early Adult Asset Accumulation." *Social Forces* 82:173–205.

Keister, Lisa A. 2005. *Getting Rich: America's New Rich and How They Got That Way.* Cambridge: Cambridge University Press.

Keister, Lisa A. 2007. "Upward Wealth Mobility: Exploring the Roman Catholic Advantage." *Social Forces* 85:1195–1226.

Keister, Lisa A. 2008. "Conservative Protestants and Wealth: How Religion Perpetuates Asset Poverty." *American Journal of Sociology* 113:1237–1271.

Keister, Lisa A. 2011. *Faith and Money: How Religion Contributes to Wealth and Poverty.* New York: Cambridge University Press.

Keister, Lisa A. 2012. "Religion and Wealth Across Generations." Pp. 131–150 in *Religion, Work and Inequality.* Edited by L. A. Keister, J. McCarthy, and R. Finke. Bingley, UK: Emerald.

Keith, Katherine Drouin. 1999. "Zuni Murals Connect Two Cultures." *National Catholic Reporter* (March 26).

Kelley, Dean M. 1972. *Why Conservative Churches Are Growing.* New York: Harper & Row.

Kelley, Dean M. 1978. "Comment: Why Conservative Churches Are Still Growing." *Journal for the Scientific Study of Religion* (June):165–172.

Kelsey, George D. 1965. *Racism and the Christian Understanding of Man.* New York: Scribner.

Kennedy, Tom and Dan Simplicio. 2009. "First Contact at Hawikku (Zuni): The Day the World Stopped." Pp. 61–72 in *Telling New Mexico: A*

History. Edited by M. Weigle. Santa Fe: Museum of New Mexico Press.

Kepel, Giles. 2002. *Jihad: The Trail of Political Islam*. London: I. B. Taurus.

Kephart, William M. and William W. Zellner. 1998. *Extraordinary Groups: An Examination of Unconventional Life-styles*. 6th ed. New York: St. Martin's Press.

Kilbourne, Brook and James T. Richardson. 1989. "Paradigm Conflict, Types of Conversion, and Conversion Theories." *Sociological Analysis* (Spring):1–21.

Killian, Caitlin. 2007. "From a Community of Believers to an Islam of the Heart: 'Conspicuous' Symbols, Muslim Practices, and the Privatization of Religion in France." *Sociology of Religion* 68:305–320.

Kinder, Donald R. and D. O. Sears. 1981. "Symbolic Racism Versus Racial Threats to the Good Life." *Journal of Personality and Social Psychology* 40:414–431.

King, Martin Luther, Jr. 2010. *Stride Toward Freedom: The Montgomery Story*. Boston: Beacon Press.

King, Pamela E., James L. Furrow, and Natalie Roth. 2002. "The Influence of Families and Peers on Adolescent Religiousness." *The Journal for Psychology and Christianity* 2:109–120.

Kirkpatrick, L. A. 1993. "Fundamentalism, Christian Orthodoxy, and Intrinsic Religious Orientation as Predictors of Discriminatory Attitudes." *Journal for the Scientific Study of Religion* (March):256–268.

Kliever, Lonnie. 2001. "God and Games in Modern Culture." Pp. 39–48 in *From Season to Season: Sports as American Religion*. Edited by J. L. Price. Macon, GA: Mercer University Press.

Kluckhohn, Clyde. 1972. "Myths and Rituals: A General Theory." Pp. 93–105 in *Reader in Comparative Religion: An Anthropological Approach*. 3rd ed., edited by W. A. Lessa and E. Z. Vogt. New York: Harper & Row.

Knickmeyer, Ellen. 2008. "Turkey's Gul Signs Head Scarf Measure." *The Washington Post* (February 23). Retrieved from www.washingtonpost.com/wp-dyn/content/article/2008/02/22/AR2008022202988.html

Knox, Robert. 1850. *Races of Men*. Philadelphia: Lea and Blanchard.

Knudsen, Dean D., John R. Earle, and Donald W. Schriver Jr. 1978. "The Conception of Sectarian Religion: An Effort at Clarification." *Review of Religious Research* (Fall):44–60.

Koch, Bradley. 2014. "Who Are the Prosperity Gospel Adherents?" *Journal of Ideology* 36:1–46.

Koch, Jerome R. and Evans W. Curry. 2000. "Social Context and the Presbyterian Gay/Lesbian Debate: Testing Open Systems Theory." *Review of Religious Research* (December):206–214.

Kohn, Melvin L. 1989. *Class and Conformity: A Study in Values*. Midway Reprint Edition. Chicago: University of Chicago Press.

Kosmin, Barry A. and Ariela Keysar. 2006. *Religion in a Free Market: Religious and Non-religious Americans*. Ithaca, NY: Paramount Market.

Kosmin, Barry A. and Ariela Keysar. 2009. *Summary Report: American Religious Identification Survey (2008)* (March). Hartford, CT: Trinity College. Retrieved from www.americanreligionsurvey-aris.org/

Kosmin, Barry A. and Seymour P. Lachman. 1993. *One Nation Under God: Religion in Contemporary American Society*. New York: Harmony.

Kovel, Joel. 1970. *White Racism: A Psychohistory*. New York: Pantheon Books.

Kox, William, Wim Meeus, and Hart Harm't. 1991. "Religious Conversion of Adolescents: Testing the Lofland and Stark Model of Religious Conversion." *Sociological Analysis* (Fall):227–240.

Krause, Neal. 2001. "Social Support." Pp. 272–294 in *The Handbook of Aging and the Social Sciences*. Edited by R. H. Binstock and L. K. George. New York: Academic Press.

Krause, Neal. 2006. "Aging." Pp. 139–160 in *The Handbook of Religion and Social Institutions*. Edited by H. R. Ebaugh. New York: Springer.

Kraybill, Donald B. 2001. *The Riddle of Amish Culture*. Rev. ed. Baltimore: John Hopkins University Press.

Krippendorff, Klaus. 2013. *Content Analysis: An Introduction to Its Methodology*. 3rd ed. Thousand Oaks, CA: Sage.

Kurien, Prema. 1998. "Becoming American by Becoming Hindu: Indian Americans Take Their Place at the Multicultural Table." Pp. 37–70 in *Gatherings in Diaspora: Religious Communities and the New Immigration*. Edited by R. S. Warner and J. Wittner. Philadelphia: Temple University Press.

Kuruvilla, Carol. 2014. "The Bible App Reveals Its Most Popular Verses of 2014." *The Huffington Post* (December 29). Retrieved from www.huffingtonpost.com/2014/12/29/most-popular-bible-verse-2014_n_6350212.html

Kurzman, Charles. 2011. *The Missing Martyrs: Why There Are So Few Muslim Terrorists.* New York: Oxford University Press.

Laband, David N. and Deborah Hendry Heinbuch. 1987. *Blue Laws: The History, Economics, and Politics of Sunday-Closing Laws.* Lanham, MD: Lexington Books.

LaBarre, Weston. 1972. *The Ghost Dance.* New York: Dell.

Ladd, Thomas and James Mathisen. 1999. *Muscular Christianity: Evangelical Protestants and the Development of American Sport.* Grand Rapids, MI: Baker Books.

Lambert, Yves. 2000. "Religion in Modernity as a New Axial Age: Secularization or New Religious Forms?" Pp. 95–125 in *The Secularization Debate.* Edited by W. H. Swatos Jr. and D. V. A. Olson. Lanham, MD: Rowman & Littlefield.

Larsen, Elena. 2000. *Wired Churches, Wired Temples: Taking Congregations and Missions Into Cyberspace.* Washington, DC: Pew Internet & American Life Project.

Larson, Heidi. 2000. "'We Don't Celebrate Christmas, We Just Give Gifts': Adaptions to Migration and Social Change Among Hindu, Muslim, and Sikh Children in England." Pp. 283–302 in *Family, Religion, and Social Change in Diverse Societies.* Edited by S. K. Houseknecht and J. G. Pankhurst. New York: Oxford University Press.

Lawson, Ronald. 1995. "Broadening the Boundaries of Church-Sect Theory." *Journal for the Scientific Study of Religion* (December):652–672.

Lawson, Ronald. 1996. "Onward Christian Soldiers: Seventh-day Adventists and the Issue of Military Service." *Review of Religious Research* (March):193–218.

Lawson, Ronald. 1998. "Sect-State Relations: Accounting for the Differing Trajectories of Seventh-day Adventists and Witnesses." *Sociology of Religion* (Winter):351–377.

Lawton, Leora and Regina Bures. 2001. "Parental Divorce and the 'Switching' of Religious Identity." *Journal for the Scientific Study of Religion* 40:99–111.

Laythe, Brian, Deborah Finkel, and Lee Kirkpatrick. 2001. "Predicting Prejudice From Religious Fundamentalism and Right Wing Authoritarianism." *Journal for the Scientific Study of Religion* 40(March):1–10.

Lazerwitz, Bernard, J. Alan Winter, Arnold Dashefsky, and Ephraim Tabory. 1998. *Jewish Choices:* *American Jewish Denominationalism.* Albany: SUNY Press.

Leach, Edmund R. 1972. "Ritualization in Man in Relation to Conceptual and Social Development." Pp. 333–337 in *Reader in Comparative Religion.* 3rd ed., edited by W. A. Lessa and E. Z. Vogt. New York: Harper & Row.

Lechner, Frank L. 1991a. "Religion, Law, and Global Order." Pp. 263–280 in *Religion and Global Order.* Edited by R. Robertson and W. R. Garrett. New York: Paragon.

Lechner, Frank L. 1991b. "The Case Against Secularization: A Rebuttal." *Social Forces* 69:1103–1119.

Lechner, Frank L. 2003. "Defining Religion: A Pluralistic Approach for the Global Age." Pp. 67–83 in *Defining Religion: Investigating the Boundaries Between the Sacred and the Secular,* edited by A. Greil and D. Bromley. Oxford: Elsevier.

Lechner, Frank L. 2007. "Rational Choice and Religious Economies." Pp. 81–97 in *The Sage Handbook of the Sociology of Religion.* Edited by J. Beckford and N. J. Demerath III. Thousand Oaks, CA: Sage.

Lee, Richard Wayne. 1992. "Christianity and the Other Religions: Interreligious Relations in a Shrinking World." *Sociological Analysis* (Summer):125–139.

Lehman, David. 2010. "Rational Choice and the Sociology of Religion." Pp. 181–200 in *The New Blackwell Companion to the Sociology of Religion.* Edited by B. Turner. Malden, MA: Blackwell.

Lehman, Edward C., Jr. 1980. "Patterns of Lay Resistance to Women in Ministry." *Sociological Analysis* (Winter):317–338.

Lehman, Edward C., Jr. 1981. "Organizational Resistance to Women in Ministry." *Sociological Analysis* (Summer):101–118.

Lehman, Edward C., Jr. 1985. *Women Clergy: Breaking Through Gender Barriers.* New Brunswick, NJ: Transaction Books.

Lehman, Edward C., Jr. 1987a. "Sexism, Organizational Maintenance, and Localism: A Research Note." *Sociological Analysis* (Fall):274–282.

Lehman, Edward C., Jr. 1987b. "Research on Lay Members' Attitudes Toward Women in Ministry: An Assessment." *Review of Religious Research* (June):319–329.

Lehne, Gregory K. 1995. "Homophobia Among Men: Supporting and Defining the Male Role."

Pp. 325–336 in *Men's Lives*. 3rd ed. Edited by M. Kimmel and M. Messner. Boston: Allyn & Bacon.

Lenski, Gerhard. 1963. *The Religious Factor*. Rev. ed. Garden City, NY: Doubleday.

Leslie, Michael. 2003. *International Televangelism/ American Ideology: The Case of the 700 Club* (May 2–4). Paper presented at the International Conference on Television in Transition, MIT, Boston.

Levine, Saul V. 1984. *Radical Departures: Desperate Detours to Growing Up*. San Diego: Harcourt Brace Jovanovich.

Levitt, Mairi. 1995. "Sexual Identity and Religious Socialization." *British Journal of Sociology* 46:529–536.

Levitt, Peggy. 1998. "Local Level Global Religion: The Case of the U.S.-Dominican Migration." *Journal for the Scientific Study of Religion* (March):74–89.

Levitt, Peggy. 2003. "You Know, Abraham Was Really the First Immigrant: Religion and Transnational Migration." *International Migration Review* 37:847–873.

Levitt, Peggy. 2004. "Redefining the Boundaries of Belonging: The Institutional Character of Transnational Religious Life." *Sociology of Religion* 65:1–18.

Lewis, Amanda. 2003. *Race in the Schoolyard*. New Brunswick, NJ: Rutgers University Press.

Lewis, James R., ed. 2009. *Scientology*. New York: Oxford University Press.

Lidwell, William. 2013. *"Black and White": How Color Affects You, What Science Reveals*. Chantilly, VA: The Great Courses.

Lieberson, Stanley. 2000. *A Matter of Taste: How Names, Fashions, and Culture Change*. New Haven, CT: Yale University Press.

Lifton, Robert J. 1954. "Home by Ship: Reaction Patterns of American Prisoners of War Repatriated From North Korea." *American Journal of Psychiatry* 110(10):732–739.

Lightfoot, Neil R. 2003. *How We Got the Bible*. Grand Rapids, MI: Baker Books.

Lincoln, C. Eric. 1968. *Is Anybody Listening to Black America?* New York: Seabury Press.

Lincoln, C. Eric. 1994. *The Black Muslims in America*. 3rd ed. Grand Rapids, MI: Eerdmans.

Lincoln, C. Eric and Lawrence H. Mamiya. 1990. *The Black Church in the African American Experience*. Durham, NC: Duke University Press.

Lindner, Eileen W., ed. 2000. *Yearbook of American and Canadian Churches*. Nashville, TN: Abingdon Press.

Lindner, Eileen W., ed. 2010. *Yearbook of American and Canadian Churches*. Nashville, TN: Abingdon Press.

Lipman-Blumen, Jean. 1972. "How Ideology Shapes Women's Lives." *Scientific American* (January):33–42.

Lipset, Seymour. 1960. *Political Man*. Garden City, NY: Doubleday.

Lockhart, William H. 2001. "'We Are All One Life,' but Not of One Gender Ideology: Unity, Ambiguity, and the Promise Keepers." Pp. 73–92 in *Promise Keepers and the New Masculinity: Private Lives and Public Morality*. Edited by R. H. Williams. Lanham, MD: Lexington Books.

Lofland, John. 1977. *Doomsday Cult*. Enlarged ed. New York: Irvington.

Lofland, John and Norman Skonovd. 1981. "Conversion Motifs." *Journal for the Scientific Study of Religion* (December):373–385.

Lofland, John and Rodney Stark. 1965. "Becoming a World Saver: A Theory of Conversion to a Deviant Perspective." *American Sociological Review* 30(6):863–874.

Loftus, Jeni. 2001. "America's Liberalization in Attitudes Toward Homosexuality, 1973–1998." *American Sociological Review* 66:762–782.

Longerich, Peter. 2010. *Holocaust: The Nazi Persecution and Murder of the Jews*. New York: Oxford University Press.

"Los Angeles Diocese Elects Second Gay Episcopal Bishop, Highlighting an Anglican Split." 2009. *New York Times* (December 6). Retrieved from www.nytimes.com/2009/12/07/us/07episcopal .html?_r=1&ref=v_gene_robinson

Loveland, Matthew. 2003. "Religious Switching: Preference Development, Maintenance, and Change." *Journal for the Scientific Study of Religion* 42:147–157.

Loveland, Matthew. 2008. "Pilgrimage, Religious Institutions, and the Construction of Orthodoxy." *Sociology of Religion* 69:317–334.

Luckmann, Thomas. 1967. *The Invisible Religion*. New York: Macmillan.

Luker, Kristin. 2008. *Salsa Dancing Into the Social Sciences: Research in an Age of Info-Glut*. Cambridge, MA: Harvard University Press.

Machalek, Richard and Michael Martin. 1976. "Invisible Religions: Some Preliminary Evidence."

Journal for the Scientific Study of Religion (December):311–322.

MacLeod, Jay. 2008. *Ain't No Makin' It: Aspirations and Attainment in a Low-Income Neighborhood.* 3rd ed. Boulder, CO: Westview.

MacWilliams, Mark. 2002. "Virtual Pilgrimages on the Internet." *Religion* 32:315–335.

Maguire, Brendan and Georgie Ann Weatherby. 1998. "The Secularization of Religion and Television Commercials." *Sociology of Religion* 59:171–178.

Mahler, Jonathan. 2005. "The Soul of the New Exurb." *New York Times Magazine*, March 27. Retrieved from www.nytimes.com/2005/03/27/magazine/327MEGACHURCH.html

Malinowski, Bronisław. 1931. "Culture." Pp. 621–645 in *Encyclopaedia of the Social Sciences.* Vol. IV, edited by E. R. A. Seligman and A. Johnson. New York: Macmillan.

Malinowski, Bronisław. 1944. *A Scientific Theory of Culture and Other Essays.* Chapel Hill: University of North Carolina Press.

Malinowski, Bronisław. 1948. *Magic, Science, and Religion and Other Essays.* New York: Free Press.

Man, John. 2002. *Gutenberg: How One Man Remade the World With Words.* New York: John Wiley.

Mannheim, Karl. 1927. "The Problem of Generations." Pp. 98–110 in *Essays in the Sociology of Knowledge.* London: RKP.

Manning, Christel. 1999. *God Gave Us the Right: Conservative Catholic, Evangelical Protestant, and Orthodox Jewish Women Grapple With Feminism.* New Brunswick, NJ: Rutgers University Press.

Marett, Robert R. 1914. *The Threshold of Religion.* London: Methuen.

Mark, Melvin M. and Charles S. Reichardt. 2009. "Quasi-experimentation." Pp. 182–213 in *Sage Handbook of Applied Social Research Methods.* 2nd ed., edited by L. Bickman and Debra Rog. Thousand Oaks, CA: Sage.

Marler, Penny Long and C. Kirk Hadaway. 2002. "'Being Religious' or 'Being Spiritual' in America: A Zero-Sum Proposition?" *Journal for the Scientific Study of Religion* 41(2):289–300.

Marsden, George. 1991. *Understanding Fundamentalism and Evangelicalism.* Grand Rapids, MI: Eerdmans.

Marsden, George. 1994. *The Soul of the American University: From Protestant Establishment to Established Nonbelief.* New York: Oxford University Press.

Marti, Gerardo. 2008. *Hollywood Faith: Holiness, Prosperity, and Ambition in a Los Angeles Church.* New Brunswick, NJ: Rutgers University Press.

Marti, Gerardo. 2009. "Affinity, Identity, and Transcendence: The Experience of Religious Racial Integration in Diverse Congregations." *Journal for the Scientific Study of Religion* 48:54–69.

Marti, Gerardo. 2012. *Worship Across the Racial Divide: Religious Music and the Multiracial Congregation.* New York: Oxford University Press.

Martin, David A. 1969. *The Religious and the Secular: Studies in Secularization.* London: Routledge & Kegan Paul.

Martin, David A. 1978. *A General Theory of Secularization.* Oxford, England: Basil Blackwell.

Martin, David A. 1993. *Tongues of Fire: The Explosion of Protestantism in Latin America.* New York: Blackwell.

Martin, Patricia Yancey, Marie Withers Osmond, Susan Hesselbart, and Meredith Wood. 1980. "The Significance of Gender as a Social and Demographic Correlate of Sex Role Attitudes." *Sociological Focus* (October):338–396.

Martin, Todd F., James M. White, and Daniel Perlman. 2003. "Religious Socialization: A Test of the Channeling Hypothesis of Parental Influence on Adolescent Faith Maturity." *Journal of Adolescent Research* 18:169–187.

Martin, William. 1972. *Christians in Conflict.* Chicago: Center for the Scientific Study of Religion, University of Chicago.

Martins, Stuart and Arthur Magida. 2003. *How to Be a Perfect Stranger: The Essential Religious Etiquette Handbook.* Woodstock, VT: Skylight Paths.

Marty, Martin. 1958. *The New Shape of American Religion.* New York: Free Press.

Marty, Martin E. 1972. "Ethnicity: The Skeleton of Religion in America." *Church History* (March):5–21.

Marty, Martin E. 2001. "The Logic of Fundamentalism." *Boston College Magazine* (Fall):44–46.

Marty, Martin and R. Scott Appleby, eds. 1992. *The Glory and the Power: The Fundamentalist Challenge to the Modern Age.* Boston: Beacon Press.

Marty, Martin and R. Scott Appleby, eds. 1994. *Accounting for Fundamentalism: The Dynamic Character of Movements.* Chicago: University of Chicago Press.

Marx, Gary. 1967. *Protest and Prejudice.* New York: Harper & Row.

Marx, Karl. [1844] 1977. *A Contribution to the Critique of Hegel's "Philosophy of Right."* Edited by J. O'Malley. Cambridge: Cambridge University Press.

Marx, Karl. [1852] 2008. *The 18th Brumaire of Louis Bonaparte.* LaVergne, TN: Wildside Press.

Maslow, Abraham. 1964. *Religions, Values, and Peak Experiences.* Columbus: Ohio State University Press.

Mason, Karen and Larry L. Bumpass. 1975. "U.S. Women's Sex Role Ideology, 1970." *American Journal of Sociology* (March):1212–1219.

Mathisen, James A. 1987. "Thomas O'Dea's Dilemmas of Institutionalization: A Case Study and Reevaluation After Twenty-Five Years." *Sociological Analysis* (Winter):302–318.

Mathisen, James A. 2006. "Sport." Pp. 285–303 in *Handbook of Religion and Social Institutions.* Edited by H. R. Ebaugh. New York: Springer.

Mauss, Armand L. and Philip L. Barlow. 1991. "Church, Sect, and Scripture: The Protestant Bible and Mormon Sectarian Retrenchment." *Sociological Analysis* (Winter):397–414.

McAlister, Elizabeth. 1998. "The Madonna of 115th Street Revisited: Vodou and Haitian Catholicism in the Age of Transnationalism." Pp. 123–160 in *Gatherings in Diaspora: Religious Communities and the New Immigration.* Edited by R. S. Warner and J. Wittner. Philadelphia: Temple University Press.

McCallion, Michael, David Maines, and Susan Wolfel. 1996. "Policy as Practice: First Holy Communion as a Contested Situation." *Journal of Contemporary Ethnography* 25:300–326.

McCloud, Sean. 2007. "Liminal Subjectivities and Religious Change: Circumscribing Giddens for the Study of Contemporary American Religion." *Journal of Contemporary Religion* 22(October):295–303, 309.

McCutcheon, Alan L. 1988. "Denominations and Religious Intermarriage: Trends Among White Americans in the Twentieth Century." *Review of Religious Research* (March):213–227.

McGaw, Douglas B. 1979. "Commitment and Religious Community: A Comparison of a Charismatic and a Mainline Congregation." *Journal for the Scientific Study of Religion* (June):146–163.

McGuire, Meredith B. 2002. *Religion: The Social Context.* 5th ed. Belmont, CA: Wadsworth.

McGuire, Meredith B. 2008. *Lived Religion: Faith and Practice in Everyday Life.* New York: Oxford University Press.

McLaughlin, Elenor Commo. 1974. "Equality of Souls, Inequality of Sexes: Women in Medieval Theology." Pp. 213–266 in *Religion and Sexism.* Edited by R. R. Ruether. New York: Simon & Schuster.

McMurry, Mary. 1978. "Religion and Women's Sex-Role Traditionalism." *Sociological Focus* (April):81–95.

McPherson, Miller, Lynn Smith-Lovin, and James Cook. 2001. "Birds of a Feather: Homophily in Social Networks." *Annual Review of Sociology* 27:415–444.

McRoberts, Omar M. 2003. *Streets of Glory: Church and Community in a Black Urban Neighborhood.* Chicago: University of Chicago Press.

Mead, Frank, Samuel Hill, and Craig Atwood, eds. 2005. *Handbook of Denominations in the United States.* 12th ed. Nashville, TN: Abingdon Press.

Meier, Harold C. 1972. "Mother Centeredness and College Youths' Attitudes Towards Social Equality for Women: Some Empirical Findings." *Journal of Marriage and the Family* (February):115–121.

Melton, J. Gordon. 1993. "Another Look at New Religions." *Annals of the American Academy of Political and Social Science* (May):97–112.

Menschung, Gustav. 1964. "The Masses, Folk Belief, and Universal Religion." Pp. 269–272 in *Religion, Culture, and Society.* Edited by L. Schneider. New York: Wiley.

Merton, Robert K. 1949. "Discrimination and the American Creed." Pp. 99–126 in *Discrimination and National Welfare.* Edited by R. M. MacIver. New York: Institute for Religious Studies.

Merton, Robert K. 1968. *Social Theory and Social Structure.* New York: Free Press.

Metropolitan Community Church. 2010. *History of MCC.* Retrieved from http://ufmcc.com/over view/history-of-mcc/

Meyer, John W. 1980. "The World Polity and the Authority of the National-State." Pp. 109–137 in *Studies of the modern world-system.* Edited by A. Bergson. New York: Academic Press.

Meyer, John W. 1988. *The Evolution of a World Religious System: Some Research Design Ideas.* Paper presented at the annual meeting of the Association for the Sociology of Religion, Atlanta, GA.

Miller, Alan and John Hoffman. 1995. "Risk and Religion: An Explanation of Gender Differences in Religiosity." *Journal for the Scientific Study of Religion* 34:63–75.

Miller, Alan and Rodney Stark. 2002. "Gender and Religiousness: Can Socialization Explanations Be Saved?" *American Journal of Sociology* 107:1399–1423.

Miller, Donald E. 1997. *Reinventing American Protestantism.* Berkeley: University of California Press.

Mitchell, Barbara. 2006. *The Boomerang Age: Transitions to Adulthood in Families.* New Brunswick, NJ: Transaction.

Mixon, Stephanie Litizzette, Larry Lyon, and Michael Beatty. 2004. "Secularization and National Universities: The Effect of Religious Identity on Academic Reputation." *Journal of Higher Education* 75:400–419.

Moaddel, Mansoor. 2005. *Islamic Modernism, Nationalism, and Fundamentalism: Episode and Discourse.* Chicago: University of Chicago Press.

Moberg, David. 1980. "Prison Camp of the Mind." Pp. 318–330 in *Society as It Is.* Edited by G. Gaviglio and D. E. Raye. New York: Macmillan.

Moberg, David. 1984. *The Church as a Social Institution.* 2nd ed. Grand Rapids, MI: Baker Book House.

Mooney, Margarita. 2009. *Faith Makes Us Live: Surviving and Thriving in the Haitian Diaspora.* Berkeley: University of California Press.

Morin, Stephen F. and Ellen M. Garfinkle. 1978. "Male Homophobia." *Journal of Social Issues* 34(1):29–47.

Morris, Aldon. 1986. *The Origins of the Civil Rights Movement: Black Communities Organizing for Change.* New York: Free Press.

Mosse, George L. 1985. *Toward the Final Solution: A History of European Racism.* Madison: University of Wisconsin Press.

Mullen, Mike. 1994. "Religious Polities as Institutions." *Social Forces* 73:709–728.

Murvar, Vatro. 1975. "Toward a Sociological Theory of Religious Movements." *Journal for the Scientific Study of Religion* (September):229–256.

Musick, March and John Wilson. 1995. "Religious Switching for Marriage Reasons." *Sociology of Religion* (Fall):257–270.

"Muslims Aim to End Televangelism." 1998. *Christianity Today* 42(3):78.

Myers, Scott M. 1996. "An Interactive Model of Religiosity Inheritance: The Importance of Family Context". *American Sociological Review* 61:858–866.

Myrdal, Gunnar. 1944. *An American Dilemma.* New York: Harper & Row.

National Conference of State Legislatures. 2011. *Common-Law Marriage.* Retrieved from www.ncsl.org/default.aspx?tabid=4265

National Science Foundation. 2000. *Frequency of Reading Astrology Reports, by Selected Characteristics, 1985–1999.* Washington, DC: Congressional Information Service.

Neal, Derek. 1997. "The Effects of Catholic Secondary Schooling on Educational Achievement." *Journal of Labor Economics* 15(1):98–123.

Neal, Lynn S. 2011. "'They're Freaks!' The Cult Stereotype in Fictional Television Shows, 1958–2008." *Novo Religio* 3:81–107.

Needleman, Jacob. 1970. *The New Religions.* Garden City, NY: Doubleday.

Neihardt, John G. 1961. *Black Elk Speaks.* Lincoln: University of Nebraska Press.

Neitz, Mary Jo. 1990. "Steps Toward a Sociology of Religious Experience: The Theories of Mihaly Csikszentmihalyi and Alfred Schutz." *Sociological Analysis* (Spring):15–33.

Neitz, Mary Jo. 2000. "Queering the Dragonfest: Changing Sexualities in a Post-Patriarchal Religion." *Sociology of Religion* (Winter):369–391.

Nelsen, Hart M., Robert F. Everett, Paul Douglas Mader, and Warren C. Hamby. 1976. "A Test of Yinger's Measure of Nondoctrinal Religion: Implications for Invisible Religion as a Belief System." *Journal for the Scientific Study of Religion* (September):263–268.

Nelsen, Hart M., Thomas W. Madron, and Raytha L. Yokley. 1975. "Black Religion's Promethean Motif: Orthodoxy and Militancy." *American Journal of Sociology* (July):139–146.

Nelsen, Hart M. and Anne Kuesener Nelsen. 1975. *Black Church in the Sixties.* Lexington: University Press of Kentucky.

Nelsen, Hart M. and William E. Snizek. 1976. "Musical Pews: Rural and Urban Models of Occupational and Religious Mobility." *Sociology and Social Research* (April):279–289.

Nelsen, Hart M., Raytha Yokley, and Anne Nelsen, eds. 1971. *The Black Church in America.* Lexington: University Press of Kentucky.

Nelson, Geoffrey. 1968. "The Concept of Cult." *Sociological Review* (November):351–363.

Nelson, Mary. 1975. "Why Witches Were Women." Pp. 335–350 in *Women: A Feminist Perspective*. Edited by Jo Freeman. Palo Alto, CA: Mayfield.

Nelson, Timothy. 2005. *Every Time I Feel the Spirit: Religious Experience and Ritual in an African American Church*. New York: New York University Press.

Nelson, Timothy J. 2009. "At Ease With Our Own Kind: Worship Practices and Class Segregation in American Religion." Pp. 45–68 in *Religion and Class in America: Culture, History, and Politics*. Leiden, Netherlands: Brill.

Nesbitt, Paula D. 1997. "Clergy Feminization: Controlled Labor or Transformative Change?" *Journal for the Scientific Study of Religion* (December):585–598.

Newcomb, Theodore and George Svehla. 1937. "Intrafamily Relationships in Attitude." *Sociometry* 1:180–205.

Newport, Frank. 1979. "The Religious Switcher in the United States." *American Sociological Review* (August):528–552.

Newport, Frank. 2013. "In U.S., 87% Approve of Black-White Marriage, vs. 4% in 1958." Retrieved from www.gallup.com/poll/163697/approve-marriage-blackswhites.aspx

Niebuhr, H. Richard. [1929] 1957. *The Social Sources of Denominationalism*. New York: Meridian Books.

Niebuhr, H. Richard. 1960. "Faith in God and in Gods." Pp. 114–126 in *Radical Monotheism and Western Culture*. New York: Harper & Row.

Noel, Donald L. 1968. "A Theory of the Origins of Ethnic Stratification." *Social Problems* (Fall):157–172.

Nordlinger, Jay. 2012. *Peace, They Say: A History of the Nobel Peace Prize, the Most Famous and Controversial Prize in the world*. New York: Encounter Books.

Norris, Pippa and Ronald Inglehart. 2011. *Sacred and Secular: Religion and Politics Worldwide*. 2nd ed. Cambridge, UK: Cambridge University Press.

Nossiter, Adam. 2014. "Nigeria Tries to 'Sanitize' Itself of Gays." *New York Times* (February 8). Retrieved from www.nytimes.com/2014/02/09/world/africa/nigeria-uses-law-and-whip-to-sanitize-gays.html?ref=world&_r=1

Nottingham, Elizabeth K. 1971. *Religion: A Sociological View*. New York: Random House.

Oberlin, Kathleen C. 2014. *Mobilizing Epistemic Conflict: The Creation Museum and the Creationist Social Movement*. PhD dissertation, Department of Sociology, Indiana University, Bloomington.

O'Dea, Thomas F. 1957. *The Mormons*. Chicago: University of Chicago Press.

O'Dea, Thomas F. 1961. "Five Dilemmas in the Institutionalization of Religion." *Journal for the Scientific Study of Religion* (October):30–39.

O'Dea, Thomas F. 1966. *The Sociology of Religion*. Englewood Cliffs, NJ: Prentice Hall.

O'Dea, Thomas F. 1968. "Sects and Cults." Pp. 130–136 in *International Encyclopedia of the Social Sciences*. Vol. 14. New York: Macmillan.

Olsen, Marvin. 1978. *The Process of Social Organization: Power in Social Systems*. 2nd ed. New York: Holt, Rinehart & Winston.

Olson, Daniel V. A. 1998. "Religious Pluralism in Contemporary U.S. Counties." *American Sociological Review* 63:759–761.

Olson, Laura, Wendy Cadge, and James Harrison. 2006. "Religion and Public Opinion About Same-Sex Marriage." *Social Science Quarterly* 87:340–360.

Oram, Andy, ed. 2001. *Peer-to-Peer: Harnessing the Power of Disruptive Technologies*. Sebastopol, CA: O'Reilly & Associates.

Orru, Marco and Amy Wang. 1992. "Durkheim, Religion, and Buddhism." *Journal for the Scientific Study of Religion* (March):47–61.

Ostling, Richard. 1987. "Raising Eyebrows and the Dead." *Time* (July 13).

Oswald, Ramona Faith. 2000. "A Member of the Wedding? Heterosexism and Family Ritual." *Journal of Social and Personal Relationships* (June):349–368.

Oswald, Ramona Faith. 2001. "Religion, Family, and Ritual: The Production of Gay, Lesbian, and Transgendered Outsiders-Within." *Review of Religious Research* (December):39–50.

Otto, Rudolf. 1923. *The Idea of the Holy*. London: Oxford University Press.

Overman, Steven J. 1997. *The Influence of the Protestant Ethic on Sports and Recreation*. Aldershot, UK: Averbury.

Ozorak, Elizabeth W. 1989. "Social and Cognitive Influences on the Development of Religious Beliefs and Commitment in Adolescence." *Journal for the Scientific Study of Religion* 28:448–463.

Pagels, Elaine. 1979. *The Gnostic Gospels.* New York: Vintage Books.

Palfrey, John and Urs Gasser. 2008. *Born Digital: Understanding the First Generation of Digital Natives.* New York: Basic Books.

Park, Jerry Z. and Samuel H. Reimer. 2002. "Revisiting the Social Sources of American Christianity 1972–1998." *Journal for the Scientific Study of Religion* 41(4):733–746.

Parker, Everett, David Barry, and Dallas Smythe. 1955. *The Television-Radio Audience and Religion.* New York: Harper.

Parker, Robert Allerton. 1935. *A Yankee Saint: John Humphrey Noyes and the Oneida Community.* New York: Putnam.

Parsons, Talcott. 1964. "Christianity in Modern Industrial Society." Pp. 233–270 in *Sociological Theory, Values, and Sociocultural Change.* Edited by E. Tiryakian. Glencoe, IL: Free Press.

Parvey, Constance F. 1974. "The Theology and Leadership of Women in the New Testament." Pp. 117–149 in *Religion and Sexism.* Edited by R. R. Ruether. New York: Simon & Schuster.

Peck, Janice. 1993. *The Gods of Televangelism: The Crisis of Meaning and the Appeal of Religious Television.* Crosskill, NJ: Hampton.

Peek, Lori. 2005. "Becoming Muslim: The Development of a Religious Identity." *Sociology of Religion* 66:215–242.

Peek, Lori. 2011. *Behind the Backlash: Muslim Americans After 9/11.* Philadelphia: Temple University Press.

Pelikan, Jaroslav. 2003. *Credo: Historical and Theological Guide to Creeds and Confessions of Faith in the Christian Tradition.* New Haven, CT: Yale University Press.

Pennings, Ray. 2011. *Cardus Education Survey.* Hamilton, Ontario: Cardus. Retrieved from www.tpcs.org/about-us/Cardus-Cardus_Education_Survey_Phase_I_Report.pdf

Perkins, H. Wesley. 1983. "Organized Religion as Opiate or Prophetic Stimulant: A Study of American and English Assessments of Social Justice in Two Urban Settings." *Review of Religious Research* (March):206–224.

Perkins, H. Wesley. 1985. "A Research Note on Religiosity as Opiate or Prophetic Stimulant Among Students in England and the United States." *Review of Religious Research* (March):269–280.

Perrin, Robin D. 1989. "American Religion in the Post-Aquarian Age: Values and Demographic Factors in Church Growth and Decline." *Journal for the Scientific Study of Religion* (March):75–89.

Perrin, Robin D., Paul Kennedy, and Donald E. Miller. 1997. "Examining the Sources of Conservative Church Growth." *Journal for the Scientific Study of Religion* (March):71–80.

Perrin, Robin D. and Armand L. Mauss. 1991. "Saints and Seekers: Sources of Recruitment to the Vineyard Christian Fellowship." *Review of Religious Research* (December):97–111.

Perry, Troy D. 2010. *The Lord Is My Shepherd, and He Knows I'm Gay (Excerpts).* Retrieved from ufmcc.com/overview/history-of-mcc/

Petersen, Larry R. and Gregory V. Donnenwerth. 1998. "Religion and Declining Support for Religious Beliefs About Gender Roles and Homosexual Rights." *Sociology of Religion* (Winter):353–371.

Petersen, Marie Juul. 2010. "International Religious NGOs at the United Nations: A Study of a Group of Religious Organizations." *Journal of Humanitarian Assistance* (November 17). Retrieved from sites.tufts.edu/jha/archives/847

Petterson, Thorlief. 1986. "The American Uses and Gratifications of T.V. Worship Services." *Journal for the Scientific Study of Religion* (December):391–409.

Petts, Richard and Chris Knoester. 2007. "Parents' Religious Heterogamy and Children's Well Being." *Journal for the Scientific Study of Religion* 48:373–389.

Pew Hispanic Center. 2011. *The Mexican-American boom: Births Overtake Immigration* (July 14). Retrieved from http://www.pewhispanic.org/files/reports/144.pdf

Pew Research Center. 2013. *A Survey of LGBT Americans: Attitudes, Experiences and Values in Changing Times* (June 13). Retrieved from www.pewsocialtrends.org/files/2013/06/SDT_LGBT-Americans_06-2013.pdf

Pew Research Center. 2014a. *Public Sees Religion's Influence Waning* (September 22). Retrieved from www.pewforum.org/2014/09/22/public-sees-religions-influence-waning-2

Pew Research Center. 2014b. *Religion and Electronic Media: One-in-Five Americans Share Their Faith Online* (November 6). Retrieved from www.pewforum.org/files/2014/11/Religion-and-Electronic-media-11-06-full.pdf

Pew Research Center. 2014c. *Global Religious Diversity: Half of the Most Religious Diverse*

Countries Are in Asia-Pacific Region (April 4). Retrieved from www.pewforum.org/2014/04/04/global-religious-diversity/

Pew Research Center for the People and the Press. 2009. *Majority Continues to Support Civil Unions.* Retrieved from http://people-press.org/reports/

Pew Research Center Forum on Religion and Public Life. 2005. *Myths of the Modern Megachurch* (May 23). Retrieved from http://pewforum.org/Christian/Evangelical-Protestant-Churches/Myths-of-the-Modern-Megachurch.aspx

Pew Research Center Forum on Religion and Public Life. 2006. *Overview: Pentecostalism in Latin America.* Retrieved from http://pewforum.org/Christian/Evangelical-Protestant-Churches/Overview-Pentecostalism-in-Latin-America.aspx

Pew Research Center Forum on Religion and Public Life. 2007a. *Changing Faiths: Latinos and the Transformation of American Religion* (April 25). Retrieved from www.pewforum.org/Changing-Faiths-Latinos-and-the-Transformation-of-American-Religion.aspx

Pew Research Center Forum on Religion and Public Life. 2007b. *Muslim Americans: Middle Class and Mostly Mainstream* (May 22). Retrieved from www.pewresearch.org/pubs/483/muslim-americans

Pew Research Center Forum on Religion and Public Life. 2008a. *A Portrait of American Catholics on the Eve of Pope Benedict's Visit to the U.S.* (March 27). Retrieved from www.pewforum.org

Pew Research Center Forum on Religion and Public Life. 2008b. *U.S. Religious Landscape Survey.* Retrieved from religions.pewforum.org

Pew Research Center Forum on Religion and Public Life. 2009. *A Religious Portrait of African Americans* (January 30). Retrieved from pewforum.org/A-Religious-Portrait-of-African-Americans.aspx

Pew Research Center Forum on Religion and Public Life. 2010. *Religion Among the Millennials* (February). Retrieved from www.pewforum.org/files/2010/02/millennials-report.pdf

Pew Research Center Forum on Religion and Public Life. 2012a. *"Nones" on the Rise: One-in-Five Adults Have No Religious Affiliation.* Retrieved from http://www.pewforum.org/files/2012/10/NonesOnTheRise-full.pdf

Pew Research Center Forum on Religion and Public Life. 2012b. *The Global Religious Landscape.* Retrieved from http://www.pewforum.org/files/2014/01/global-religion-full.pdf

Pew Research Center Forum on Religion and Public Life. 2013. *The World's Muslims: Religion, Politics and Society* (April 30). Retrieved from www.pewforum.org/2013/04/30/the-worlds-muslims-religion-politics-society-morality/

Pew Research Center Forum on Religion and Public Life. 2014. *Millennials in Adulthood: Detached From Institutions, Networked With Friends* (March 7). Retrieved from www.pewsocialtrends.org/2014/03/07/millennials-in-adulthood/

Pew Research Center Global Attitudes Project. 2013. *The Global Divide on Homosexuality* (June 4). Retrieved from www.pewglobal.org/2013/06/04/the-global-divide-on-homosexuality

Pew Research Center Global Attitudes Project. 2014. *Global Views on Morality* (April 15). Retrieved from www.pewglobal.org/2014/04/15/global-morality

Pew Research Center Internet and American Life Project. 2015. *Three Technology Revolutions.* Retrieved from www.pewinternet.org/three-technology-revolutions/

Pew Research Center Religion and Public Life Project. 2015. *Gay Marriage Around the World* (January 6). Retrieved from www.pewforum.org/2013/12/19/gay-marriage-around-the-world-2013/

Pharr, Suzanne. 1997. *Homophobia: A Weapon of Sexism.* Berkeley, CA: Chardon Press.

Pinker, Steven. 2011. *The Better Angels of Our Nature: Why Violence Has Declined.* New York: Viking.

Poloma, Margaret M. 1982a. *The Charismatic Movement: Is There a New Pentecost?* Boston: Twayne.

Poloma, Margaret M. 1982b. "Toward a Christian sociological perspective: religious values, theory and methodology." *Sociological analysis* (summer): 95–108.

Poloma, Margaret M. 1989. *The Assemblies of God at the Crossroads: Charisma and Institutional Dilemmas.* Knoxville: University of Tennessee Press.

Poloma, Margaret M. 2005. "Charisma and Structure in the Assemblies of God: Revisiting O'Dea's Five Dilemmas." Pp. 45–96 in *Church, Identity, and Change: Theology and Denominational Structures in Unsettled Times.* Edited by D. A. Roozen and J. R. Nieman. Grand Rapids, MI: Eerdmans.

Pope, Liston. 1942. *Millhands and Preachers.* New Haven, CT: Yale University Press.

Pope, Liston. 1957. *Kingdom Beyond Caste.* New York: Friendship.

Popenoe, David. 1993. "American Family Decline, 1960–1990: A Review and Appraisal." *Journal of Marriage and the Family* 55:527–555.

Postmes, T. and N. R. Branscombe, eds. 2010. *Rediscovering Social Identity.* London: Psychology Press.

Pratt, James Bissett. 1964. "Objective and Subjective Worship." Pp. 143–156 in *Religion, Culture, and Society.* Edited by L. Schneider. New York: Wiley.

Price, Jammie and Michael G. Dalecki. 1998. "The Social Basis of Homophobia: An Empirical Illustration." *Sociological Spectrum* (April–June):143–159.

Price, Joseph L. 2005. "An American Apotheosis: Sports as Popular Religion." Pp. 195–212 in *Religion and Popular Culture in America.* Rev. ed. Edited by B. D. Forbes and J. H. Mahan. Berkeley: University of California Press.

Priest, Robert J. and Alvaro L. Nieves, eds. 2007. *This Side of Heaven: Race, Ethnicity, and Christian Faith.* New York: Oxford University Press.

Purvis, Sally. 1995. *The Stained-Glass Ceiling: Churches and Their Women Pastors.* Louisville, KY: Westminster/John Knox.

Putnam, Robert D. 2000. *Bowling Alone: The Collapse and Revival of American Community.* New York: Simon & Schuster.

Putnam, Robert D. and David E. Campbell. 2010. *American Grace: How Religion Divides and Unites Us.* New York: Simon & Schuster.

Putney, Clifford. 2001. *Muscular Christianity: Manhood and Sports in Protestant America 1880–1920.* Cambridge, MA: Harvard University Press.

Pyle, Ralph. 2006. "Trends in Religious Stratification: Have Religious Group Socioeconomic Distinctions Declined in Recent Decades?" *Sociology of Religion* 67:61–79.

Quinley, Harold E. 1974. *The Prophetic Clergy: Social Activism Among Protestant Ministers.* New York: Wiley.

Radcliffe-Brown, A. R. 1939. *Taboo.* Cambridge, MA: Harvard University Press.

Radde-Antweiler, Kerstin. 2008. "'Virtual Religion': An Approach to a Religious and Ritual Topography of Second Life." *Online: Heidelberg Journal of Religions on the Internet* 3(1):174–211.

Ramo, Joshua Cooper. 1996. "Finding God on the Web." *Time* (December 16). Retrieved from www

.time.com/time/magazine/article/0,9171, 985700,00.html

Read, Jen'nan Ghazal. 2003. "The Sources of Gender Role Attitudes Among Christian and Muslim Arab-American Women." *Sociology of Religion* 64(2):207–222.

Read, Jen'nan Ghazal and John Bartkowski. 2000. "To Veil or Not to Veil? A Case Study of Identity Negotiation Among Muslim Women in Austin, Texas." *Gender and Society* 14:395–417.

ReconcilingWorks. 2015. "Reconciling in Christ." Retrieved www.reconcilingworks.org/

Redekop, Calvin. 1974. "A New Look at Sect Development." *Journal for the Scientific Study of Religion* (September):345–352.

Regnerus, Mark, Christian Smith, and Brad Smith. 2004. "Social Context in the Development of Adolescent Religiosity." *Applied Developmental Science* 8:27–38.

Regnerus, Mark and Jeremy Uecker. 2006. "Finding Faith, Losing Faith: The Prevalence and Context of Religious Transformations During Adolescence." *Review of Religious Research* 47:217–237.

Regnerus, Mark and Jeremy Uecker. 2007. "Religious Influences on Sensitive Self-Reported Behaviors: The Product of Social Desirability, Deceit, or Embarrassment?" *Sociology of Religion* 68:145–163.

"Religion: Air Worship." 1931. *Time* (February 9). Retrieved from www.time.com/time/magazine/article/0,9171,741032-1,00.html

"Religion: Radio Religion." 1946. *Time* (January 21). Retrieved from www.time.com/time/magazine/article/0,9171,934406,00.html

Richardson, James T. 1985. "Paradigm Conflict in Conversion Research." *Journal for the Scientific Study of Religion* (June):163–719.

Richardson, James T., Joel Best, and David G. Bromley, eds. 1991. *The Satanism Scare.* New York: Aldine de Gruyter.

Richman, Karen. 2005. "The Protestant Ethic and the Dis-spirit of Vodou." Pp. 165–187 in *Immigrant Faiths: Transforming Religious Life in America.* Edited by K. Leonard, A. Stepick, M. Vasquez, & J. Holdaway. Lanham, MD: AltaMira Press.

Robbins, Thomas and Dick Anthony. 1978. "New Religions, Families, and Brainwashing." *Society* (May/June):77–83.

Robbins, Thomas and Phillip Charles Lucas. 2007. "From 'Cults' to New Religious Movements: Coherence, Definition, and Conceptual Framing in the Study of New Religious Movements." Pp. 227–247 in *The Sage Handbook of the Sociology of Religion*. Edited by J. Beckford and N. J. Demerath III. Thousand Oaks, CA: Sage.

Roberts, Keith A. 1992. "Ritual and the Transmission of a Cultural Tradition: An Ethnographic Perspective." Pp. 74–98 in *Beyond Establishment: Protestant Identity in a Post Protestant Age*. Edited by J. Carroll and W. C. Roof. Louisville, KY: Westminster/John Knox.

Robertson, H. M. [1933] 1959. *Aspects of the Rise of Economic Individualism: A Criticism of Max Weber and His School*. New York: Kelley & Millman.

Robertson, Roland. 1989. "Globalization, Politics, and Religion." Pp. 1–9 in *The Changing Face of Religion*. Edited by J. A. Beckford and T. Luckmann. London: Sage.

Robertson, Roland. 1991. "Globalization, Modernization, and Postmodernization: The Ambiguous Position of Religion." Pp. 281–291 in *Religion and Global Order*. Edited by R. Robertson and W. R. Garrett. New York: Paragon.

Robertson, Roland. 1992. *Globalization: Social Theory and Global Culture*. London: Sage.

Robertson, Roland. 1995. "Glocalization: Time-Space and Homogeneity-Heterogeneity." Pp. 25–44 in *Global Modernities*. Edited by M. Featherstone, S. Lash, and R. Robertson. London: Sage.

Rodriguez, Eric M. and Suzanne C. Ouellette. 2000. "Gay and Lesbian Christians: Homosexual and Religious Identity Integration in the Members and Participants of a Gay-Positive Church." *Journal for the Scientific Study of Religion* 39(3):333–347.

Rokeach, Milton, ed. 1968. "The Nature of Attitudes." In *Beliefs, Attitudes, and Values*. San Francisco: Jossey-Bass.

Rokeach, Milton, Patricia W. Smith, and Richard I. Evans. 1960. "Two Kinds of Prejudice or One?" Pp. 132–168 in *The Open and Closed Mind*. Edited by M. Rokeach. New York: Basic Books.

Romero, Catalina. 2001. "Globalization, Civil Society and Religion From a Latin American Perspective." *Sociology of Religion* (Winter):475–490.

Roof, Wade Clark. 1978. *Commitment and Community*. New York: Elsevier.

Roof, Wade Clark. 1993. *A Generation of Seekers: The Spiritual Journeys of the Baby Boom Generation*. San Francisco: Harper.

Roof, Wade Clark. 1999. *Spiritual Marketplace: Baby Boomers and the Remaking of American Religion*. Princeton, NJ: Princeton University Press.

Roof, Wade Clark. 2009. "Generations and Religion." Pp. 616–634 in *The Oxford Handbook of the Sociology of Religion*. Edited by P. Clarke. Oxford: Oxford University Press.

Roof, Wade Clark and William McKinney. 1987. *American Mainline Religion: Its Changing Shape and Future*. New Brunswick, NJ: Rutgers University Press.

Rosenfeld, Michael J. 2008. "Racial, Educational, and Religious Endogamy in the United States: A Comparative Historical Perspective." *Social Forces* 87(September):1–32.

Rosewicz, Barbara. 1985. "At Jerusalem Church, People Often Ignore Tenth Commandment." *Wall Street Journal* (April 5):1, 5.

Rothenberg, Paula S. 2012. *White Privilege*. 4th ed. New York: Worth.

Rousseau, Jean-Jacques. [1762] 1954. *The Social Contract*. Translated by W. Kendall. Chicago: Henry Regnery Company.

Ruether, Rosemary Radford. 1974a. "Misogynism and Virginal Feminism in the Fathers of the Church." Pp. 150–183 in *Religion and Sexism*. Edited by R. R. Ruether. New York: Simon & Schuster.

Ruether, Rosemary Radford. 1974b. "The Persecution of Witches." *Christianity and Crises* (December 23):291–295.

Ruether, Rosemary Radford. 1975. *New Woman, New Earth*. New York: Seabury Press.

Ryder, Norman B. 1965. "The Cohort as a Concept in the Study of Social Change." *American Sociological Review* 30:843–861.

Saad, Lydia. 2012. *U.S. Acceptance of Gay/Lesbian Relations in the New Normal* (May 14). Retrieved from www.gallup.com/poll/154634/acceptance-gay-lesbian-relations-new-normal.aspx

Samuelsson, Kurt. [1957] 1961. *Religion and Economic Action*. Translated by E. G. French. New York: Basic Books.

Sanneh, Lamin. 1991. "The Yogi and the Commissar: Christian Missions and the New World Order in Africa." Pp. 173–192 in *World Order and Religion*. Edited by W. C. Roof. Albany: State University of New York Press.

Sargeant, Kimon Howland. 2000. *Seeker Churches: Promoting Traditional Religion in a Nontraditional Way*. New Brunswick, NJ: Rutgers University Press.

Scaff, Lawrence A. 2011. *Max Weber in America*. Princeton, NJ: Princeton University Press.

Scheepers, Peer, Merove Gijsberts, and Evelyn Hello. 2002. "Religion and Prejudice Against Ethnic Minorities in Europe: Cross-National Tests on a Controversial Relationship." *Review of Religious Research* (March):242–265.

Schensul, Jean J. and Margaret D. LeCompte, eds. 2013. *The Ethnographer's Toolkit*. 2nd ed. (7 vols.). Lanham, MD: AltaMira Press.

Schieman, Scott and Jong Hyun Jung. 2012. "'Practical Divine Influence': Socioeconomic Status and Belief in the Prosperity Gospel." *Journal for the Scientific Study of Religion* 51(4):738–756.

Schneider, Louis. 1970. *Sociological Approach to Religion*. New York: Wiley.

Schoenherr, Richard. 2002. In *Goodbye Father: The Celibate Male Priesthood and the Future of the Catholic Church*. Edited by D. Yamane. New York: Oxford University Press.

Schuenemeyer, Michael D. 2015. Personal communication with Keith Roberts, January 26.

Schwadel, Philip. 2008. "Poor Reenagers' Religion." *Sociology of Religion* 69(2):125–149.

Schwadel, Philip. 2010. "Period and Cohort Effects on Religious Nonaffiliation and Religious Disaffiliation: A Research Note." *Journal for the Scientific Study of Religion* 49:311–319.

Scientology. 2010. *Scientology Is a Religion*. Retrieved from www.scientology.org

Sewell, William and Robert Hauser. 1975. *Education, Occupation, and Earnings: Achievement in the Early Career*. New York: Academic Press.

Shannon, Thomas Richard. 1989. *An Introduction to the World-System Perspective*. Boulder, CO: Westview Press.

Shannon, William. 1963. *The American Irish*. New York: Macmillan.

Sharot, Stephen. 1991. "Judaism and the Secularization Debate." *Sociological Analysis* (Fall):255–275.

Shaw, Susan M. and Janet Lee. 2005. *Women's Voices, Feminist Visions: Classic and Contemporary Readings*. 3rd ed. Boston: McGraw-Hill.

Sheard, Robert B. 1987. *Interreligious Dialogue in the Catholic Church Since Vatican II*. Lewiston, NY: Mellon.

Sherkat, Darren E. 1997. "Embedding Religious Choices: Integrating Preferences and Social Choices Into Rational Choice Theories of Religious Behavior." Pp. 65–85 in *Rational Choice Theory and Religion: Summary and Assessment*. Edited by L. A. Young. New York: Routledge.

Sherkat, Darren E. 2003. "Religious Socialization: Sources of Influence and Influences of Agency." Pp. 151–178 in *Handbook of the Sociology of Religion*. Edited by M. Dillon. New York: Cambridge University Press.

Sherkat, Darren E. 2010. "Religion and Verbal Ability." *Social Science Research* 39:2–13.

Sherkat, Darren E. 2011. "Religion and Scientific Literacy in the United States." *Social Science Quarterly* 92(5):1134–1150.

Sherkat, Darren E. 2012. "Religion and the American Occupational Structure." Pp. 75–102 in *Religion, Work and Inequality*. Edited by L. A. Keister, J. McCarthy, and R. Finke. Bingley, UK: Emerald.

Sherkat, Darren E. 2014. *Changing Faith: The Dynamics and Consequences of Americans' Shifting Religious Identities*. New York: New York University Press.

Sherkat, Darren E. and Christopher G. Ellison. 2001. "Recent Developments and Current Controversies in the Sociology of Religion." *Annual Review of Sociology* 27:363–386.

Sherkat, Darren E. and John Wilson. 1995. "Preferences, Constraints, and Choices in Religious Markets: An Examination of Religious Switching and Apostasy." *Social Forces* (March):993–1026.

Shields, David L. 1986. *Growing Beyond Prejudices: Overcoming Hierarchical Dualism*. Mystic, CT: Twenty-Third.

Shipps, Jan. 1985. *Mormonism: The Story of a New Religious Tradition*. Urbana: University of Illinois Press.

Shupe, Anson D., Jr. 1995. *In the Name of All That's Holy: A Theory of Clergy Malfeasance*. New York: Praeger.

Shupe, Anson D., Jr. 1998. *Wolves Within the Fold: Religious Leadership and Abuses of Power*. New Brunswick, NJ: Rutgers University Press.

Shupe, Anson D., Jr., and David G. Bromley. 1978. "Witches, Moonies, and Evil." *Society* (May/June):75–76.

Shupe, Anson and Susan E. Darnell. 2006. *Agents of Discord: Deprogramming, Pseudo-science, and the American Anticult Movement*. New Brunswick, NJ: Transaction.

Shupe, Anson, D., Jr., and Jeffrey K. Hadden. 1989. "Is There Such a Thing as Global Fundamentalism?" Pp. 109–122 in *Secularization and Fundamentalism Reconsidered*. Edited by J. K. Hadden and A. Shupe. New York: Paragon.

Shupe, Anson D., Jr., William A. Stacey, and Susan Darnell. 2000. *Bad Pastors: Clergy Misconduct in Modern America*. New York: New York University Press.

Siegel, Karolynn and Eric W. Shrimshaw. 2002. "The Perceived Benefits of Religious and Spiritual Coping Among Older Adults Living With HIV/AIDS." *Journal for the Scientific Study of Religion* 41:87–101.

Sikkink, David. 1999. "The Social Sources of Alienation From Public Schools." *Social Forces* 78:51–86.

Sikkink, David and Jonathan Hill. 2006. "Education." Pp. 41–66 in *The Handbook of Religion and Social Institutions*. Edited by H. R. Ebaugh. New York: Springer.

Silva Method. 2010. *The Silva Method*. Retrieved from www.silvamethod.com

Simon, Stephanie. 2007. "It's Easter; Shall We Gather at the Desktops?" *Los Angeles Times* (April 8). Retrieved from articles.latimes.com/2007/apr/08/nation/na-virtual8

Simpson, John H. 1991. "Globalization and Religion: Themes and Perspectives." Pp. 1–18 in *Religion and Global Order*. Edited by R. Robertson and W. R. Garrett. New York: Paragon.

Simpson, John H. 1996. "'The Great Reversal': Selves, Communities, and the Global System." *Sociology of Religion* (Summer):115–125.

Sito-Sucic, Daria and Matt Robinson. 2013. "After Years of Toil, Book Names Bosnian War Dead." *Reuters* (February 15). Retrieved from www.reuters.com/article/2013/02/15/us-bosnia-dead-idUSBRE91E0J220130215

Skeggs, Beverly. 2004. *Class, Self, Culture*. London: Routledge.

Sklare, Marshall and Joseph Greenblum. 1979. *Jewish Identity on the Suburban Frontier*. 2nd ed. Chicago: University of Chicago Press.

Smelser, Neil J. 1962. *Theory of Collective Behavior*. New York: Free Press.

Smith, Carole R., Lev Williams, and Richard H. Willis. 1967. "Race, Sex, and Belief as Determinants of Friendship Acceptance." *Journal of Personality and Social Psychology* (February):127–137.

Smith, Christian. 1996a. *Disruptive Religion: The Force of Faith in Social Movement Activism*. New Brunswick, NJ: Rutgers University Press.

Smith, Christian. 1996b. *Resisting Reagan: The U.S. Central America Peace Movement*. Chicago: University of Chicago Press.

Smith, Christian. 1998. *American Evangelicalism: Embattled and Thriving*. Chicago: University of Chicago Press.

Smith, Christian. 2003a. *Moral, Believing Animals: Human Personhood and Culture*. New York: Oxford University Press.

Smith, Christian. 2003b. *The Secular Revolution: Power, Interests, and Conflict in the Secularization of American Public Life*. Berkeley: University of California Press.

Smith, Christian (with Melinda Lundquist Denton). 2005. *Soul Searching: The Religious and Spiritual Lives of American Teenagers*. New York: Oxford University Press.

Smith, Christian (with Snell, P.). 2009. *Souls in Transition: The Religious and Spiritual Lives of Emerging Adults*. New York: Oxford University Press.

Smith, Christian and Robert Faris. 2005. "Socioeconomic Inequality in the American Religious System: An Update and Assessment" *Journal for the Scientific Study of Religion* 44:95–104.

Smith, Jesse. 2010. "Becoming an Atheist in America: Constructing Identity and Meaning From the Rejection of Theism." *Sociology of Religion* 72(1):1–23.

Smith, Tom W. 1992. "Are Conservative Churches Growing?" *Review of Religious Research* (June):305–329.

Smith, Tom W. and Jaesok Son. 2013. *Trends in Public Attitudes About Sexual Morality* (April). Chicago: National Opinion Research Center. Retrieved from www.norc.org/PDFs/sexmoral-final_06-21_FINAL.PDF

Snell, Patricia. 2009. "What Difference Does Youth Group Make? A Longitudinal Analysis of Religious Youth Group Participation Outcomes." *Journal for the Scientific Study of Religion* 48(3):572–587.

Snow, David A. and Cynthia L. Phillips. 1980. "The Lofland-Stark Conversion Model: A Critical Reassessment." *Social Problems* (April):430–447.

Socha, Bailey and Barbara Eber-Schmid. 2015. *What Is New Media?* New York: New Media Institute. Retrieved from www.newmedia.org/what-is-new-media.html

Sommerville, C. John. 2002. "Stark's Age of Faith Argument and the Secularization of Things: A Commentary." *Review of Religious Research* (Fall):361–372.

Southwold, Martin. 1982. "True Buddhism and Village Buddhism in Sri Lanka." Pp. 137–152 in *Religious Organization and Religious Experience.* Edited by J. Davis. London: Academic Press.

Spickard, James V. 1998. "Rethinking Religious Social Action: What Is 'Rational' About Rational Choice Theory?" *Sociology of Religion* (Summer):99–115.

Spickard, James V. 2005. "Ritual, Symbol, and Experience: Understanding Catholic Worker House Masses." *Sociology of Religion* 66 (December):337–357.

Spinoza, Baruch. [1670] 2009. *A Theologico-Political Treatise.* Gloucestershire, UK: Dodo Press.

Spiro, Melford. 1966. "Religion: Problems of Definition and Explanation." Pp. 85–126 in *Anthropological Approaches to the Study of Religion,* edited by M. Banton. London: Tavistock.

Spiro, Melford. 1978. *Burmese Supernaturalism.* Philadelphia: Institute for the Study of Human Issues.

Spitz, Bob. 1992. "Mrs. Gere Goes to Hollywood." *Redbook* 179(5):110–116.

Staples, Clifford L. and Armand L. Mauss. 1987. "Conversion or Commitment: A Reassessment of the Snow and Machalek Approach to the Study of Conversion." *Journal for the Scientific Study of Religion* (June):133–147.

Starhawk. 1989. *Spiral Dance: A Rebirth of the Ancient Religion of the Great Goddess.* San Francisco: HarperSanFrancisco.

Stark, Rodney. 1972. "The Economics of Piety: Religious Commitment and Social Class." Pp. 483–503 in *Issues in Social Inequality.* Edited by G. W. Thielbar and S. D. Feldman. Boston: Little, Brown.

Stark, Rodney. 1984. "The Rise of a New World Faith." *Review of Religious Research* (September):18–27.

Stark, Rodney. 1986. "The Class Basis of Early Christianity: Inferences From a Sociological Model." *Sociological Analysis* (Fall):216–225.

Stark, Rodney. 1992. "Do Catholic Societies Really Exist?" *Rationality and Society* 4:261–271.

Stark, Rodney. 1995. "Reconstructing the Rise of Christianity: The Role of Women." *Sociology of Religion* (Fall):229–244.

Stark, Rodney. 2000a. "Religious Effects: In Praise of 'Idealistic Humbug.'" *Review of Religious Research* (March):289–310.

Stark, Rodney. 2000b. "Secularization, R.I.P." Pp. 41–66 in *The Secularization Debate.* Edited by W. H. Swatos, Jr., and D. V. A. Olson. Lanham, MD: Rowman & Littlefield.

Stark, Rodney and William Sims Bainbridge. 1979. "Of Churches, Sects, and Cults: Preliminary Concepts for a Theory of Religious Movements." *Journal for the Scientific Study of Religion* (June):119–121.

Stark, Rodney and William Sims Bainbridge. 1985. *The Future of Religion: Secularization, Renewal, and Cult Formation.* Berkeley: University of California Press.

Stark, Rodney and William Sims Bainbridge. 1996. *A Theory of Religion.* New Brunswick, NJ: Rutgers University Press.

Stark, Rodney and Roger Finke. 1988. "American Religion in 1776: A Statistical Portrait." *Sociological Analysis* (Spring):39–51.

Stark, Rodney and Roger Finke. 2000. *Acts of Faith: Explaining the Human Side of Religion.* Berkeley: University of California Press.

Stark, Rodney, Roger Finke, and Laurence R. Iannaccone. 1995. "Pluralism and Piety: England and Wales, 1951." *Journal for the Scientific Study of Religion* (December):431–444.

Stark, Rodney and Charles Y. Glock. 1968. *American Piety: The Nature of Religious Commitment.* Berkeley: University of California Press.

Stark, Rodney and Charles Y. Glock. 1969. "Prejudice and the Churches. Pp. 70–95 in *Prejudice U.S.A.* Edited by C. Y. Glock and E. Siegelman. New York: Praeger.

Stark, Rodney and Laurence R. Iannaccone. 1994. "A Supply-Side Reinterpretation of the 'Secularization' of Europe." *Journal for the Scientific Study of Religion* (September):230–252.

Stark, Rodney and James McCann. 1993. "Market Forces and Catholic Commitment: Exploring the New Paradigm." *Journal for the Scientific Study of Religion* 32:111–124.

Stark, Rodney and Lynne Roberts. 1982. "The Arithmetic of Social Movements: Theoretical Implications." *Sociological Analysis* (Spring): 53–67.

Stark, Werner. 1967. *Sectarian Religion. Vol. 2, The Sociology of religion: A Study of Christendom.* New York: Fordham University Press.

Stein, Nicholas. 2006. "No Way Out." Pp. 293–299 in *Globalization: The Transformation of Social Worlds*. Edited by D. S. Eitzen and M. B. Zinn. Belmont, CA: Wadsworth.

Steinberg, Stephen. 1965. "Reform Judaism: The Origin and Evolution of a 'Church Movement.'" *Journal for the Scientific Study of Religion* (October):117–129.

Stevens, Mitchell. 2003. *Kingdom of Children: Culture and Controversy in the Homeschooling Movement*. Princeton, NJ: Princeton University Press.

Stoll, David. 1990. *Is Latin America Turning Protestant? The Politics of Evangelical Growth*. Berkeley: University of California Press.

Stolzenberg, Ross, Mary Blair-Loy, and Linda Waite. 1995. "Age and Family Life Cycle Effects on Church Membership." *American Sociological Review* 60:84–103.

Storch, Eric A., Jonathan W.. Roberti, Erica A. Bravata, and Jason B. Storch. 2004. "Strength of Religious Faith: A Comparison of Intercollegiate Athletes and Non-athletes." *Pastoral Psychology* 52:485–492.

Straus, Roger. 1976. "Changing Oneself: Seekers and the Creative Transformation of Life Experience." Pp. 252–273 in *Doing Social Life*. Edited by J. Lofland. New York: Wiley Interscience.

Straus, Roger. 1979. "Religious Conversion as a Personal and Collective Accomplishment." *Sociological Analysis* (Summer):158–165.

Suchman, Mark C. 1992. "Analyzing the Determinants of Everyday Conversion." *Sociological Analysis*:S15–33.

Sullins, D. Paul. 2000. "The Stained Glass Ceiling: Career Attainment for Women Clergy." *Sociology of Religion* (Fall):243–266.

Sullins, D. Paul. 2006. "Gender and Religion: Deconstructing Universality, Constructing Complexity." *American Journal of Sociology* 112 (November):838–880.

Surratt, Geoff, Greg Ligon, and Warren Bird. 2009. *The Multisite Church Revolution*. Grand Rapids, MI: Zondervan.

Swatos, William H., Jr. 1998. "Denomination/ Denominationalism." Pp. 134–136 in *Encyclopedia of Religion and Society*. Edited by W. H. Swatos. Walnut Creek, CA: AltaMira.

Takayama, K. Peter. 1975. "Formal Polity and Change of Structure: Denominational Assemblies." *Sociological Analysis* 36:17–28.

Takayama, K. Peter and Lynn Weber Cannon. 1979. "Formal Polity and Power Distribution in American Protestant Denominations." *Sociological Quarterly* 20:321–332.

Talmon, Yonina. 1965. "The Pursuit of the Millennium: The Relation Between Religion and Social Change." Pp. 522–537 in *Reader in Comparative Religion*. 2nd ed., edited by W. A. Lessa and E. Z. Vogt. New York: Harper & Row.

Tamadonfar, Mehren. 2001. "Islam, Law, and Political Control in Contemporary Iran." *Journal for the Scientific Study of Religion* (June):205–219.

Tamney, Joseph B. 1992. *The Resilience of Christianity in the Modern World*. Albany: State University of New York Press.

Tamney, Joseph B. and Steven D. Johnson. 1985. "Consequential Religiosity in Modern Society." *Review of Religious Research* (June):360–378.

Tamney, Joseph B. and Steven D. Johnson. 1998. "The Popularity of Strict Churches." *Review of Religious Research* (March):209–223.

Tams, Christian J. 2014. *The World Court's Role in the International Law-Making Process* (March 8). Retrieved from dx.doi.org/10.2139/ssrn.2406311

Tawney, R. H. [1924] 1954. *Religion and Capitalism*. New York: New American Library.

Taylor, Kevin M. 2008. *Facebookismanity, St. Tupac Shakur, and Lucid Dreaming: What College Students Want From Religion*. Paper presented at the annual meeting of the Association for the Sociology of Religion, Boston, August.

Tedlin, Kent. 1978. "Religious Preference and Pro/Anti Activism on the Equal Rights Amendment Issue." *Pacific Sociological Review* (January):55–66.

Theissen, Gerd. 1978. *Sociology of Early Palestinian Christianity*. Philadelphia: Fortress.

Theodorou, Angelina. 2014. *64 Countries Have Religious Symbols on Their National Flags*. FactTank, Pew Research Center, November 25. Retrieved from www.pewresearch.org/fact-tank/2014/11/25/64-countries-have-religious-symbols-on-their-national-flags

Thomas, Charles B., Jr. 1985. "Clergy in Racial Controversy: A Replication of the Campbell and Pettigrew Study." *Review of Religious Research* (June):379–390.

Thomas, George M. 1991. "A World Polity Interpretation of U.S. Religious Trends Since World War II." Pp. 217–247 in *World Order and Religion*. Edited by W. C. Roof. Albany: State University of New York Press.

Thomas, George M. 2001. "Religions in Global Civil Society." *Sociology of Religion* (Winter):515–533.

Thompson, Edward H., Jr. 1991. "Beneath the Status Characteristic: Gender Variations in Religiousness." *Journal for the Scientific Study of Religion* (December):381–394.

Thornton, Arland and Deborah Freedman. 1979. "Changes in the Sex Role Attitudes of Women, 1962–1977: Evidence From a Panel Study." *American Sociological Review* (October):831–842.

Thumma, Scott. 2001. *Megachurches Today 2000.* Hartford, CT: Hartford Institute for Religion Research. Retrieved from hirr.hartsem.edu/mega-church/faith_megachurches_FACTsummary.html

Thumma, Scott. 2012. *Virtually Religious: Technology and Internet Use in American Congregations.* Hartford, CT: Hartford Institute for Religion Research. Retrieved from faithcommunitiestoday .org/report-congregations-and-their-use-internet-technologies

Thumma, Scott and Warren Bird. 2008. "Changes in American Megachurches: Tracing Eight Years of Growth and Innovation in the Nation's Largest-Attendance Congregations (September)." Retrieved from hirr.hartsem.edu/megachurch/ megachurches_research.html

Thumma, Scott, Dave Travis, and Warren Bird. 2005. *Megachurches Today 2005: Summary of Research Findings.* Retrieved from hirr.hartsem.edu/mega-church/megachurches_research.html

Tillich, Paul. 1957. *Dynamics of Faith.* New York: Harper & Row.

Titiev, Mischa. 1972. "A Fresh Approach to the Problem of Magic and Religion." Pp. 430–433 in *Reader in Comparative Religion: An Anthropological Approach.* 3rd ed., edited by W. A. Lessa and E. Z. Vogt. New York: Harper & Row.

Toal, Gerard and Carl T. Dahlman. 2011. *Bosnia Remade: Ethnic Cleansing and Its Reversal.* New York: Oxford University Press.

Tomasi, Luigi. 2002. "Homo Viator: From Pilgrimage to Religious Tourism Via the Journey." Pp. 1–24 in *From Medieval Pilgrimage to Religious Tourism.* Edited by W. Swatos and L. Tomasi. Westport, CT: Praeger.

Toolin, Cynthia. 1983. "American Civil Religion From 1789 to 1981: A Content Analysis of Presidential Inaugural Addresses." *Review of Religious Research* (September):39–48.

Transcendental Meditation. 2010. *The TM Technique.* Retrieved from www.tm.org

Trevor-Roper, Hugh. 1967. "Witches and Witchcraft." *Encounter* (June):13–34.

Trible, Phyllis. 1979. "Eve and Adam: Genesis 2–3 Reread." Pp. 74–83 in *Womanspirit Rising.* Edited by C. P. Christ and J. Plaskow. New York: Harper & Row.

Trinitapoli, Jenny. 2005. "Congregation-Based Services for Elders: An Examination of Patterns and Correlates." *Research on Aging* 27:241–264.

Trinitapoli, Jenny and Stephen Vaisey. 2009. "The Transformative Role of Religious Experience: The Case of Short-Term Missions." *Social Forces* 88:121–146.

Tschannen, Olivier. 1991. "The Secularization Paradigm: A Systematization." *Journal for the Scientific Study of Religion* (December):395–415.

Turner, Bryan S. 1991a. "Politics and Culture in Islamic Fundamentalism." Pp. 161–181 in *Religion and global order.* Edited by R. Robertson and W. R. Garrett. New York: Paragon.

Turner, Bryan S. 1991b. *Religion and Social Theory.* London: Sage.

Turner, Bryan S. 2010. "Religion in a Post-secular Society." Pp. 648-67 in *The New Blackwell Companion to the Sociology of Religion.* Edited by B. S. Turner. Malden, MA: Wiley-Blackwell.

Turner, Jonathan H. and Alexandra Maryanski. 1979. *Functionalism.* Menlo Park, CA: Benjamin/ Cummings.

Tylor, Edward B. [1873] 1958. *Primitive Culture,* Vol. II. New York: Harper & Row.

Uecker, Jeremy E. and Jonathan P. Hill. 2014. "Religious Schools, Home Schools, and the Timing of First Marriage and First Birth." *Review of Religious Research* 56(June):189–218.

United Nations Population Division. 2013. *Trends in International Migrant Stock: The 2013 Revision.* United Nations database, POP/DB/MIG/Stock/ Rev.2013. Retrieved from www.un.org/en/devel-opment/desa/population/migration/publications/ migrationreport/migreport.shtml

United Press International. 1983. *"Televangelists" Reach the Multitudes* (November 22). Retrieved from news.google.com

Urban, Hugh B. 2011. *The Church of Scientology: A History of a New Religion.* Princeton, NJ: Princeton University Press.

U.S. Bureau of Labor Statistics. 2006. *Women in the Professions.* Retrieved from www.bls.gov/opub/ ted/2006/dec/wk1/art02.htm

U.S. Bureau of Labor Statistics. 2009. *Labor Force Statistics From the Current Population Survey: Women in the Labor Force.* Retrieved from www .bls.gov/cps/wlf-intro-2009.htm

U.S. Census Bureau. 2012. *Statistical Abstract of the United States.* Retrieved from www.census.gov/ compendia/statab.

U.S. Census Bureau. 2013. *Current Population Survey, 2013 Annual Social and Economic Supplement.* Retrieved from www.census.gov/hhes/socdemo/ education/data/cps/2013/tables.html.

U.S. Flag Code. 2007. *U.S. Flag Code* (Federal Flag Code Amendment Act of 2007). Retrieved from www.suvcw.org/flag.htm

Vaisey, Stephen. 2009. "Motivation and Justification: A Dual-Process Model of Culture in Action." *American Journal of Sociology* 114(May):1675–1715.

Van Ausdale, Debra and Joe R. Feagin. 1996. "Using Racial and Ethnic Concepts: The Critical Case of Very Young Children." *American Sociological Review* (October):779–793.

van Biema, David and Jeff Chu. 2006. "Does God Want You to Be Rich?" *Time* (September 18). Retrieved from http://content.time.com/time/ magazine/article/0,9171,1533448,00.html

Van der Leeuw, Gerardus. 1963. *Religion in Essence and Manifestation.* Vol. I. New York: Harper Torchbooks.

Van der Veer, Peter. 1994. *Religious Nationalism: Hindus and Muslims in India.* Berkeley: University of California Press.

Vander Zanden, James W. 1983. *American Minority Relations.* 4th ed. New York: Knopf.

Vander Zanden, James W. 1987. *Social Psychology.* 4th ed. New York: Random House.

Vernon, Glenn M. 1968. "The Religious 'Nones': A Neglected Category." *Journal for the Scientific Study of Religion* 7(Autumn):219–229.

Vidler, Alec R. 1961. *The Church in an Age of Revolution, 1989 to the Present Day.* London: Hodder & Stoughton.

Voas, David and Fenella Fleischmann. 2012. "Islam Moves West: Religious Change in the First and Second Generations." *Annual Review of Sociology* 38:525–545.

Vogt, Evon Z. 1952. "Water Witching: An Interpretation of a Ritual Pattern in a Rural American Community." *Scientific Monthly* (September):175–186.

Voicu, Malina. 2009. "Religion and Gender Across Europe." *Social Compass* 56(2):144–162.

Vrame, Anton. 2008. "Four Types of 'Orthopraxy' Among Orthodox Christians in America.'" Pp. 279–308 in *Thinking Through Faith: New Perspectives From Orthodox Christian Scholars.* Edited by A. Papanikolaou and E. H. Prodromou. Crestwood, NY: St. Vladimir's Seminary Press.

Walker, Peter. 2005. "Cracking the Code: The Genesis, Use and Future of the Code of Conduct." *Disasters* 29(4):323–336.

Wall, Barbra. 2011. *American Catholic Hospitals: A Century of Changing Markets and Missions.* New Brunswick, NJ: Rutgers University Press.

Wallace, Anthony F. C. 1972. "Revitalization Movements." Pp. 503–512 in *Reader in Comparative Religion: An Anthropological Approach.* 3rd ed., edited by W. A. Lessa & E. Z. Vogt. New York: Harper & Row.

Wallace, Ruth A. 1992. *They Call Her Pastor: A New Role for Catholic Women.* Albany: State University of New York Press.

Wallerstein, Immanuel. 1974. *The Modern World System.* New York: Academic Press.

Wallerstein, Immanuel. 1979. *The Capitalist World Economy.* New York: Cambridge University Press.

Wallerstein, Immanuel. 1984. *The Politics of the World Economy.* New York: Cambridge University Press.

Wallis, Roy. 1977. *The Road to Total Freedom: A Sociological Analysis of Scientology.* New York: Columbia University Press.

Wallis, Roy and Steve Bruce. 1991. "Secularization: Trends, Data, and Theory." *Research in the Social Scientific Study of Religion* 3:1–31.

Walls, A. F. 1991. "World Christianity, the Missionary Movement, and the Ugly American." Pp. 147–172 in *World Order and Religion.* Edited by W. C. Roof. Albany: State University of New York Press.

Walton, Jonathan L. 2009. *Watch This! The Ethics and Aesthetics of Black Televangelism.* New York: New York University Press.

Wang, Wendy. 2012. *The Rise of Intermarriage.* Washington, DC: Pew Research Center. Retrieved from www.pewsocialtrends.org/2012/02/16/the- rise-of-intermarriage

Ward, Martha C. and Monica Edelstein. 2006. *A World Full of Women.* 4th ed. Boston: Pearson Education.

Warner, R. Stephen. 1993. "Work in Progress Toward a New Paradigm for the Sociological Study of Religion in the United States." *American Journal of Sociology* (March):1044–1093.

Warner, R. Stephen. 2005. *A Church of Our Own: Disestablishment and Diversity in American Religion.* New Brunswick, NJ: Rutgers University Press.

Warner, R. Stephen and Judith G. Wittner, eds. *Gatherings in the Diaspora: Religious Communities and the New Immigration.* Philadelphia: Temple University Press.

Warner, W. Lloyd. 1953. *American Life: Dream and Reality.* Chicago: University of Chicago Press.

Washington, Joseph R., Jr. 1964. *Black Religion.* Boston: Beacon Press.

Washington, Joseph R., Jr. 1972. *Black Sects and Cults.* Garden City, NY: Doubleday.

Watt, William Montgomery. 1996. *A Short History of Islam.* Oxford: Oneworld.

Waugh, Earle. 1994. "Reducing the Distance: A Muslim Congregation in the Canadian North." Pp. 572–611 in *American Congregations: Portraits of Twelve Religious Communities.* Edited by J. Wind & J. Lewis. Chicago: University of Chicago Press.

Weaver, Horace R. 1975. *Getting Straight About the Bible.* Nashville, TN: Abingdon Press.

Weber, Max. 1946. *From Max Weber: Essays in Sociology.* Edited and translated by H. H. Gerth and C. W. Mills. New York: Oxford University Press.

Weber, Max. 1947. *The Theory of Social and Economic Organization.* Edited and translated by A. M. Henderson and T. Parsons. New York: Oxford University Press.

Weber, Max. 1949. *The Methodology of the Social Sciences.* New York: Free Press.

Weber, Max. [1920–1921] 1951. *The Religion of China.* Translated by H. H. Gerth. New York: Free Press.

Weber, Max. [1920–1921] 1952. *Ancient Judaism.* Edited and translated by H. H. Gerth and D. Martindale. New York: Free Press.

Weber, Max. [1904–1905] 1958a. *The Protestant Ethic and the Spirit of Capitalism.* Translated by T. Parsons. New York: Scribner.

Weber, Max. [1920–1921] 1958b. *The Religion of India.* Edited and translated by H. H. Gerth and D. Martindale. New York: Free Press.

Weber, Max. [1923] 1961. *General Economic History.* Translated by F. H. Knight. New York: Collier Books.

Weber, Max. [1922] 1963. *The Sociology of Religion.* Translated by E. Fischoff. Boston: Beacon Press.

Weidenbaum, Murray. 2006. "Globalization: Wonderland or Waste Land?" Pp. 53–60 in *Globalization: The Transformation of Social Worlds.* Edited by D. S. Eitzen and M. B. Zinn. Belmont, CA: Wadsworth.

Weinberg, George. 1973. *Society and the Healthy Homosexual.* Garden City, NY: Doubleday.

Welch, Susan. 1975. "Support Among Women for the Issues of the Women's Movement." *Sociological Quarterly* (Spring):216–227.

Weller, Christian E. and Adam Hersh. 2006. "Free Markets and Poverty." Pp. 69–73 in *Globalization: The Transformation of Social Worlds.* Edited by D. S. Eitzen and M. B. Zinn. Belmont, CA: Wadsworth.

Wellington, Elizabeth. 2014. *Digital Disciples.* Faith & Leadership, Duke University Divinity School. Retrieved from www.faithandleadership.com/features/articles/digital-disciples

Welter, Barbara. 1976. "The Feminization of American Religion, 1800–1860." *Dimity Convictions.* Athens: Ohio University Press.

Western Jurisdictional Conference. 2012. *Western Jurisdiction: Gay Issue Stand Wrong.* Retrieved from www.umc.org/news-and-media/western-jurisdiction-gay-issue-stand-wrong

White, Kenneth R. 2013. "When Institutions Collide: The Competing Forces of Hospitals Sponsored by the Roman Catholic Church. *Religions* 4:14–29. DOI:10.3390/rel4010014.

Whitehead, Andrew L. 2010. "Sacred Rites and Civil Rights: Religion's Effect on Attitudes Toward Same-Sex Unions and the Perceived Cause of Homosexuality." *Social Science Quarterly* 91:63–79.

Whitehead, Andrew L. 2012. "Gender Ideology and Religion: Does a Masculine Image of God Matter?" *Review of Religious Research* 54:139–156.

Whitehead, Andrew L. 2013. "Gendered Organizations and Inequality Regimes: Gender, Homosexuality, and Inequality Within Religious Congregations." *Journal for the Scientific Study of Religion* 52(3):476–493.

Wikipedia. 2015. *New Media.* Retrieved from en.wikipedia.org/wiki/New_media

Wilcox, Melissa M. 2003. *Coming Out in Christianity: Religion, Identity, and Community.* Bloomington: Indiana University Press.

Wilcox, Melissa M. 2013. *Religion in Today's World: Global Issues, Sociological Perspectives.* New York: Routledge.

Wilcox, W. Bradford. 2006. "Family." Pp. 97–120 in *The Handbook of Religion and Social Institutions.* Edited by H. R. Ebaugh. New York: Springer.

Williams, Gwyneth I. 2001. "Masculinity in Context: An Epilogue." Pp. 105–114 in *Promise Keepers and the New Masculinity: Private Lives and Public Morality.* Edited by R. H. Williams. Lanham, MD: Lexington Books.

Williams, Michael A. 1986. "Uses of Gender Imagery in Ancient Gnostic Texts." Pp. 196–227 in *Gender and Religion.* Edited by C. W. Bynum, S. Harrell, and P. Richman. Boston: Beacon Press.

Williams, Peter W. 1980. *Popular Religion in America: Symbolic Change and the Modernization Process in Historical Perspective.* Englewood Cliffs, NJ: Prentice Hall.

Williams, Rhys and Gira Vashi. 2007. "*Hijab* and American Muslim Women: Creating the Space for Autonomous Selves." *Sociology of Religion* 68(3):269–287.

Williams, Roman R. 2010. "Space for God: Lived Religion at Work, Home, and Play." *Sociology of Religion* 71(3):257–279.

Wilmore, Gayraud S. 1972. *Black Religion and Black Radicalism.* Garden City, NY: Doubleday.

Wilson, Bryan R. 1959. "An Analysis of Sect Development." *American Sociological Review* (February):3–15.

Wilson, Bryan R. 1970. *Religious Sects.* New York: McGraw-Hill.

Wilson, Bryan R. 1976. *Contemporary Transformations of Religion.* Oxford: Clarendon Press.

Wilson, Bryan R. 1982. *Religion in Sociological Perspective.* New York: Oxford University Press.

Wilson, Gerald L., Joann Keyton, David Johnson, Cheryl Geiger, and Johanna C. Clark. 1993. "Church Growth Through Member Identification and Commitment: A Congregational Case Study." *Review of Religious Research* (March):259–272.

Wimberley, Ronald C., Thomas C. Hood, C. M. Lipsey, Donald Clelland, and Marguerite Hay. 1975. "Conversion in a Billy Graham Crusade: Spontaneous Event or Ritual Action?" *The Sociological Quarterly* (Spring):162–170.

Winter, J. Alan. 1977. *Continuities in the Sociology of Religion.* New York: Harper & Row.

Witten, Marsha. 1995. *All Is Forgiven: The Secular Message in American Protestantism.* Princeton, NJ: Princeton University Press.

Wolfe, Alan. 2003. *The Transformation of American Religion: How We Actually Live Our Faith.* New York: Free Press.

Wolkomir, Michelle. 2006. *Be Not Deceived: The Sacred and Sexual Struggles of Gay and Ex-Gay Christian Men.* New Brunswick, NJ: Rutgers University Press.

Wood, James R. 1970. "Authority and Controversial Policy: The Churches and Civil Rights." *American Sociological Review* (December):1057–1069.

Wood, James R. 1981. *Leadership in Voluntary Organizations: The Controversy Over Social Action in Protestant Churches.* New Brunswick, NJ: Rutgers University Press.

Wood, James R. and Jon P. Bloch. 1995. "The Role of Church Assemblies in Building a Civil Society: The Case of the United Methodist General Conference's Debate on Homosexuality." *Sociology of Religion* (Summer):121–136.

World Almanac. 2014. "World Adherents of Religions by Continental Area 2012." New York: World Almanac Books.

Wright, Derek and Edwin Cox. 1967. "A Study of the Relationship Between Moral Judgment and religious Belief in a Sample of English Adolescents." *Journal of Social Psychology* (June):135–144.

Wrong, Dennis H. 1961. "The Oversocialized Conception of Man in Modern Sociology." *American Sociological Review* 26(2):183–193.

Wuthnow, Robert. 1973. "New Forms of Religion in the Seminary." Pp. 187–203 in *Religion in Sociological Perspective.* Edited by C. Y. Glock. Belmont, CA: Wadsworth.

Wuthnow, Robert. 1976a. "Astrology and Marginality." *Journal for the Scientific Study of Religion* (June):157–168.

Wuthnow, Robert. 1976b. *The Consciousness Reformation.* Berkeley: University of California Press.

Wuthnow, Robert. 1980. "World Order and Religious Movements." Pp. 57–75 in *Studies of the modern world-system.* Edited by A. Bergson. New York: Academic Press.

Wuthnow, Robert. 1981. "Two Traditions of Religious Studies." *Journal for the Scientific Study of Religion* (March):16–32.

Wuthnow, Robert. 1987. "The Social Significance of Religious Television." *Review of Religious Research* (December):125–134.

Wuthnow, Robert. 1988. *The restructuring of American religion: Society and faith since World War II.* Princeton, NJ: Princeton University Press.

Wuthnow, Robert. 1991. "International Realities: Bringing the Global Picture Into Focus." Pp. 19–37 in *World Order and Religion.* Edited by W. C. Roof. Albany: State University of New York Press.

Wuthnow, Robert. 1994a. *God and Mammon in America.* New York: Free Press.

Wuthnow, Robert, ed. 1994b. *I Come Away Stronger: How Small Groups Are Shaping American Religion.* Grand Rapids, MI: Eerdmans.

Wuthnow, Robert. 1996. *Poor Richard's Principle.* Princeton, NJ: Princeton University Press.

Wuthnow, Robert. 1998. *After Heaven: Spirituality in America Since the 1950s.* Berkeley: University of California Press.

Wuthnow, Robert. 1999. *Growing Up Religious: Christians and Jews and Their Journeys of Faith.* Boston: Beacon Press.

Wuthnow, Robert. 2009. *Boundless Faith: The Global Outreach of American Churches.* Berkeley: University of California Press.

Wuthnow, Robert and John Evans, eds. 2002. *The Quiet Hand of God: Faith-Based Activism and the Public Role of Mainline Protestantism.* Berkeley: University of California Press.

Wuthnow, Robert and Stephen Offutt. 2008. "Transnational Religious Connections." *Sociology of Religion* 69:209–232.

Yamane, David. 1997. "Secularization on Trial: In Defense of a Neosecularization Paradigm." *Journal for the Scientific Study of Religion* (March):109–122.

Yamane, David. 1998. "Spirituality." In *Encyclopedia of Religion and Society.* Edited by W. H. Swatos. Walnut Creek, CA: AltaMira.

Yamane, David. 2000. "Naked Public Square or Crumbling Wall of Separation? Evidence From Legislative Hearings in Wisconsin." *Review of Religious Research* 42 (December):175–192.

Yamane, David. 2005. *The Catholic Church in State Politics: Negotiating Prophetic Demands and Political Realities.* Lanham, MD: Rowman & Littlefield.

Yamane, David. 2014. *Becoming Catholic: Finding Rome in the American Religious Landscape.* New York: Oxford University Press.

Yamane, David and Teresa Blake. 2008. *Sport and Sacred Umbrellas on Campus: The Religiosity and Spirituality of College Athletes.* Unpublished manuscript, Department of Sociology, Wake Forest University, Winston-Salem, NC.

Yamane, David and Sarah MacMillen. 2006. *Real Stories of Christian Initiation: Lessons For and From the RCIA.* Collegeville, MN: Liturgical Press.

Yamane, David, Charles Mellies, and Teresa Blake. 2010. "Playing for Whom? Sport, Religion, and the Double Movement of Secularization in America." Pp. 81–94 in *Sociology of Sport and Social Theory.* Edited by E. Smith. Champaign, IL: Human Kinetics.

Yamane, David and Megan Polzer. 1994. "Ways of Seeing Ecstasy in Modern Society: Experiential-Expressive and Cultural-Linguistic Views." *Sociology of Religion* 55:1–25.

Yancey, George. 1999. "An Examination of the Effects of Residential and Church Integration on Racial Attitudes of Whites." *Sociological Perspectives* 42:279–304.

Yang, Fenggang. 1998. "Chinese Conversion to Evangelical Christianity: The Importance of Social and Cultural Contexts." *Sociology of Religion* (Fall):273–257.

Yang, Fenggang. 1999. *Chinese Christians in America: Conversion, Assimilation, and Adhesive Identities.* College Station, PA: PSU Press.

Yang, Fenggang and Helen Rose Ebaugh. 2001. "Transformations in New Immigrant Religions and their Global Implications." *American Sociological Review* 66:269–288.

Yinger, J. Milton. 1961. "Comment." *Journal for the Scientific Study of Religion* (October):40–44.

Yinger, J. Milton. 1969. "A Structural Examination of Religion." *Journal for the Scientific Study of Religion* (Spring):88–100.

Yinger, J. Milton. 1970. *The Scientific Study of Religion.* New York: Macmillan.

Yinger, J. Milton. 1977. "A Comparative Study of the Substructure of Religion." *Journal for the Scientific Study of Religion* (March):67–86.

"The YMCA in the United States." 2010. *YMCA of the USA.* Retrieved from http://www.ymca.net/history/

Young, Lawrence. 1997. *Rational Choice Theory and Religion: Summary and Assessment.* New York: Routledge.

Yousafzai, Malala. 2013. "Making a Wish for Action on Global Education." *Address before the United Nations Youth Assembly* (July 12). Retrieved from webtv.un.org/watch/malala-yousafzai-addresses-united-nations-youth-assembly/2542094251001/

Yu, Eui-Young. 1988. "The Growth of Korean Buddhism in the United States, With Special Reference to Southern California." *The Pacific World: Journal of the Institute of Buddhist Studies* (n.s.) 4:82–93.

Yukich, Grace. 2013. *One Family Under God: Immigration Politics and Progressive Religion in America.* New York: Oxford University Press.

Zablocki, Benjamin. 1971. *The Joyful Community: An Account of the Bruderhof.* Baltimore: Penguin Books.

Zaechner, R. C., ed. 1967. *The Concise Encyclopedia of Living Faith.* Boston: Beacon Press.

Zaimov, Stoyan. 2013. "African Anglicans Say Gay Bishops Affirmation 'Shatters Hopes of Reconciliation.'" *Christian Post.* www.christian post.com/news/african-anglicans-say-gay-bishops-affirmation-shatters-hopes-of-reconciliation-88038.

Zhai, J. E., Christopher G. Ellison, N. Glenn, and E. Marquardt. 2007. "Parental Divorce and Religious Involvement Among Young Adults." *Sociology of Religion* 68(2):125–144.

Zubrzycki, Geneviève. 2010. "Religion and Nationalism: A Critical Re-examiniation." Pp. 606–625 in *The New Blackwell Companion to the Sociology of Religion.* Edited by B. S. Turner. Malden, MA: Wiley-Blackwell.

Zuckerman, Phil. 2003. *Invitation to the Sociology of Religion.* New York: Routledge.

Zuckerman, Phil. 2008. *Society Without God: What the Least Religious Nations Can Tell Us About Contentment.* New York: New York University Press.

Zuckerman, Phil. 2012. *Faith No More: Why People Reject Religion.* New York: Oxford University Press.

NAME INDEX

Adler, Max, 385–386
Alba, Richard, 56
Aleshire, Daniel, 258
Allport, Gordon W., 258
Altman, Dennis, 422
Ammerman, Nancy, 16, 17, 36, 37, 39, 42, 104, 189,
    196, 197, 199, 201, 344
Anderson, Charles, 66
Anderson, Shawna L., 195 (figure), 199,
    202 (table), 203, 254, 254 (figure),
    302, 303 (figure), 374
Anderson, T. L.
    see Bang, Esther
Angeles, Vivienne S. M., 56
Anglican Church in North America, 304
Anthony, Dick, 134
Anthony, Francis-Vincent, 84
Anti-Defamation League (ADL), 62–63
Antoun, Richard T., 404
Appleby, R. Scott, 404, 413, 415, 416
Armstrong, Karen, 415
Arnett, Jeffrey J., 110
Arweck, Elizabeth, 181
Aslan, Reza, 3, 89
Assimeng, Max, 164, 177
Associated Press (AP), 351, 370
Association of American Publishers, 365
Atwood, Craig, 190
Austin, Allen D., 423

Bader, Christopher D., 292, 387
Baer, Hans A., 320, 328, 334
Bagby, Ihsan, 198
Baggett, Jerome, 291, 298

Bahr, Howard, 354–355
    see also Caplow, Theodore
Bainbridge, William Sims, 8, 133, 134, 138,
    140, 177, 180, 183, 186, 344, 345–346,
    362, 388
Bainton, Roland, 423
Bakalian, Anny, 64
Baker, Joseph O., 130, 244, 245 (figure), 387
    see also Bader, Christopher D.
Baker, William, 282, 380, 381
Balch, Robert W., 134, 138, 139, 163, 181
Ballantine, Jeanne, 72, 85, 235, 264
Baltzell, E. Digby, 241
Bandura, Albert, 104
Bang, Esther, 291, 292
Banks, Adelle M., 192
Bankston, Carl, 198
Bao, Wan-Ning, 105
Barber, Benjamin, 404
Barker, Eileen, 134, 181
Barlow, Philip L., 173, 182
Barman, Emily, 33
Barnouw, Victor, 83, 88
Baroja, Julio Caro, 134
Barrett, David, 424
Barro, Robert, 141
Barry, David, 364
Bartkowski, John P., 291, 292, 295
Basch, Linda, 410
Batson, C. Daniel, 46, 93, 316, 317
Baumann, Martin, 409
Bayer, Alan E., 424
Beatty, Michael, 354
Becker, Howard, 424

Subject Index

New York, 305
New York Times Best Sellers, 365
New Zealand, 141, 296
Niebuhr, H. Richard, 170–173, 188
Nietzsche, Friedrich, 55
Nigeria, 74, 296, 372, 404
9/11 terrorist attacks, 64–65, 68, 264, 266–267, 350, 361
969 Movement, 404, 414
Niqab, 403
Nobel Peace Prize, 416
Nonaffiliated populations, 125 (table), 128–131
Noncelibate clergy, 304
Non-Christian Asian immigrants, 198
Nonconformist thinking, 317
Nondenominational Christians
    apostasy, 151–152, 155
    denominational decline, 195 (figure)
    denominational growth and decline, 150
    household wealth, 239
    nondenominationalism, 195
    religious self-identification, 124, 125 (table)
    religious switching, 145 (table),
        146 (table), 151
    retention rates, 150
    socioeconomic status, 237 (table)
Nondenominationalism, 195 (figure), 195–196
    see also Evangelical churches
Non-empirical force, 81
"Nones"
    African Americans, 252–253
    apostasy, 151–152, 155
    basic concepts, 128–131
    gender composition, 278, 278 (table)
    global perspectives, 128–129
    household wealth, 240, 240 (table)
    LGBTQ (lesbian, gay, bisexual, transgender, and
        queer or questioning) community, 301 (table),
        301–302
    membership comparisons, 397 (table)
    occupational position, 238 (table)
    race and ethnicity, 251 (table), 252 (table)
    religious self-identification, 124, 125 (table)
    religious switching, 151
    retention rates, 150
    socioeconomic status, 237 (table)
Nonindustrialized countries, 394
Nonrational experiences, 80–84, 86, 98 (figure), 138
Nontraditional families, 107
"No One Understands Like Jesus" (hymn), 313

No religious preference
    African Americans, 252–253
    apostasy, 151–152, 155
    basic concepts, 128–131
    denominational decline, 195 (figure)
    gender composition, 278, 278 (table)
    global perspectives, 128–129
    household wealth, 240, 240 (table)
    LGBTQ (lesbian, gay, bisexual, transgender, and
        queer or questioning) community, 301 (table),
        301–302
    membership comparisons, 397 (table)
    nondenominationalism, 195
    occupational position, 238 (table)
    race and ethnicity, 251 (table), 252 (table)
    religious self-identification, 124, 125 (table)
    religious switching, 145 (table), 146 (table), 151
    retention rates, 150
    socioeconomic status, 237 (table)
North American Lutheran Church, 192, 304
North Carolina, 351
Northern Ireland conflict, 274
North Point Community Church (Georgia),
    205, 206, 374
Norway, 289, 297, 305
"Nothing but the Blood" (hymn), 313
Notre Dame University, 354
Nuclear family, 103–104, 107

Obama, Barack, 191, 360
Obama, Michelle, 191
Objectification versus alienation dilemma, 164–165
Objectivation, 79
Objectivity, 28–29, 48
"O Brother Man, Fold to Thy Heart" (hymn), 314
Occupational position, 238 (table), 238–239,
    241 (figure)
Ofshe, Richard, 134
Oglala Sioux, 96–97
Old Testament, 282–283
Olympic Games, 380
Oneida Community, 162
Online religion, 376–379, 379 (figure), 380
Open and Affirming, 302
Open-ended surveys, 35–38
Open-mindedness, 122
Open systems model
    basic concepts, 71–76, 73 (figure)
    church–sect typology, 174 (figure), 174–175

CPSIA information can be obtained
at www.ICGtesting.com
Printed in the USA
FSHW012237270120
66487FS

9 781452 275826